Inside
MAPI

Irving De la Cruz
Les Thaler

Microsoft Press

PUBLISHED BY
Microsoft Press
A Division of Microsoft Corporation
One Microsoft Way
Redmond, Washington 98052-6399

Copyright © 1996 by Irving De la Cruz and Les Thaler

Library of Congress Cataloging-in-Publication Data
De la Cruz, Irving. 1973-
    Inside MAPI / Irving De la Cruz, Les Thaler.
      p.   cm.
    Includes index.
    ISBN 1-57231-312-9
    1. Application software--Development.   2. Client/server computing.
    3. Telecommunication. I. Thaler, Les. 1956-   . II. Title.
    QA76.76.A65D4   1996
    005.7' 13--dc20   96-33177
                                            CIP

Printed and bound in the United States of America.

1 2 3 4 5 6 7 8 9 MLML 1 0 9 8 7 6

Distributed to the book trade in Canada by Macmillan of Canada, a division of Canada Publishing Corporation.

A CIP catalogue record for this book is available from the British Library.

Microsoft Press books are available through booksellers and distributors worldwide. For further information about international editions, contact your local Microsoft Corporation office. Or contact Microsoft Press International directly at fax (206) 936-7329.

Acquisitions Editor: Eric Stroo
Project Editor: Victoria Thulman
Technical Editor: Marc Young

To my wife, Emma, for her support and understanding
To my parents, Julio and Marina De la Cruz,
for encouraging my curiosity

To my parents, Ruth C. and R.M. Thaler

CONTENTS SUMMARY

Foreword xv
Acknowledgments xvii
Introduction xix

PART I: THE MAPI COMPONENTS

CHAPTER ONE
The MAPI Architecture   **3**

CHAPTER TWO
MAPI Properties   **27**

CHAPTER THREE
MAPI Containers   **67**

CHAPTER FOUR
MAPI Tables and Notifications   **81**

CHAPTER FIVE
MAPI Client Applications   **113**

PART II: WINDS CASE STUDY
AND IMPLEMENTATIONS

CHAPTER SIX
MAPI Service Providers   **197**

CHAPTER SEVEN
Implementing Service Providers: A Case Study   **233**

CHAPTER EIGHT
Message Transport Providers   **245**

CHAPTER NINE

Developing Address Book Providers **335**

CHAPTER TEN

Developing Message Store Providers **475**

PART III: APPENDIXES

APPENDIX A

Named Properties **563**

APPENDIX B

Multivalue Properties **569**

Index 571

TABLE OF CONTENTS

Foreword xv
Acknowledgments xvii
Introduction xix

PART I: THE MAPI COMPONENTS

CHAPTER ONE

The MAPI Architecture   **3**

What Is MAPI? 3
Email and Electronic Messaging—
   The Historical Motivation for MAPI 5
Messaging Applications Today 6
Architectural Overview 10
   Benefits of the MAPI Architecture 12
MAPI Components 13
   The Layered Model 14

CHAPTER TWO

MAPI Properties   **27**

MAPI and COM 27
IMAPIProp 28
   Transacted and Nontransacted Objects 31
A Closer Look at MAPI Properties 34
   Standard Properties vs. Custom Properties 37
   Object Identification: Entry Identifiers 39
   Miscellaneous Identity Properties 41
Manipulating the Object Properties: *IMAPIProp* Details 42
   How MAPI Returns Errors.. 42
   The *GetLastError* Method 44
   The MAPI Memory Management Model 46
   Properties Available in an Object 49

Requesting Properties from an Object 50

Setting Properties on an Object 55

Deleting Properties in an Object 59

Copying the Contents of an Object 61

Saving the Object Changes Permanently 64

A Look Ahead 66

CHAPTER THREE

MAPI Containers   **67**

The Standard Container Interface 69

Data Tables of Containers 70

Opening Objects in a Container 74

Access Level 75

Search Containers 76

CHAPTER FOUR

MAPI Tables and Notifications   **81**

The Rationale for MAPI Tables 81

MAPI Table Basics 83

SRowSet and *SRow* 84

Abstract Table Operations 86

Views and Queries 88

Defining Queries 88

Selecting: *SetColumns* 89

Filtering: *Restrict* 90

Sorting: *SortTable* 99

Querying: *QueryRows*, *HrQueryAllRows* 100

Positioning: *SeekRow*, *FindRow* 101

Miscellaneous Table Methods 105

Notifications 106

The MAPI Notification Engine 107

A Look Ahead 111

CHAPTER FIVE

MAPI Client Applications   **113**

What Is a Client? 113

Common Client Attributes 116

Client Access to the Messaging System 116

The MAPI Session 117

Basic Client Operations 118

Client Interaction with Providers 120

Important Client-Side Properties Accessed in HelloMAPI 129

HelloMAPI: A Minimal MAPI Mail Client 135

    Program Description 135

    Classes and Data Structures 136

    User Interface 137

    HelloMAPI.CPP: Implementation Details 144

PART II: WINDS CASE STUDY
AND IMPLEMENTATIONS

CHAPTER SIX

MAPI Service Providers   **197**

What to Consider When Designing a Specific Provider 198

How Service Providers Are Implemented 200

    How MAPI Interfaces Are Implemented 203

    General Guidelines for Implementation 205

    How Providers Are Installed, Registered, and Configured 213

The MAPI Spooler 225

Message Paths During Sending and Receiving 226

    Message Submission (Outbound) 227

    Message Reception (Inbound) 229

A Look Ahead 231

CHAPTER SEVEN

Implementing Service Providers: A Case Study   **233**

The WINDS Mail System 233

    The WINDS Server 234

    The WINDS Administrator 235

    The WINDS Message Service 237

MSLMS: A Personal Message Store Provider 241

    CDataBase 242

ABPAB: A Personal Address Book Provider 243

CHAPTER EIGHT

Message Transport Providers   **245**

How Transports Interact with the MAPI Subsystem 246

    Outbound Logic 247

    Inbound Logic 248

How Transports Interact with Message

   Store Providers and Address Book Providers 249

General Requirements for All Message Transports 249

Using TNEF for Message Data Encapsulation 254

Client Access to Message Transports 255

Developing a Message Transport:

   The WINDS Transport (XPWDS) 256

    Implementing Stub Interfaces 257

    Editing the MAPISVC.INF File 258

    Implementing *ServiceEntry* 259

    Implementing *XPProviderInit* 268

    Implementing *IXPProvider* 269

    Implementing *IXPLogon* 278

    Implementing *IMAPIStatus* 311

   Remote Transports 314

    General Requirements 315

   Our Remote Transport Implementation: XPWDSR 316

    Implementing *IMAPIFolder* 322

    Implementing *IMAPIStatus* on Remote Transports 327

CHAPTER NINE

Developing Address Book Providers   **335**

General Requirements 336

    Address Book Provider Interfaces 337

    The Provider-to-Database Interface 338

    Writable Address Book Providers 340

    Entry IDs 341

Case Study of Two Implementations: ABPAB and ABWDS 343

    Common Design Features 344

Logging On to an Address Book Provider 345

    Service Configuration 346

    Provider Logon 350

Editing the MAPISVC.INF File 354
Address Book Provider Properties 355
Returning the Root Hierarchy 359
Database Primitives 360
Returning Recipient Entries 370
Implementing *IMAPIProp* 370
Derived Classes 381
IABLogon::OpenEntry, Revisited 383
Viewing an Entry 391
Display Tables 391
Resolving Names 398
PR_ANR 404
IABLogon::PrepareRecips 405
One-offs and the Session One-off Table 408
Writable Address Book Providers 415
IABContainer::CreateEntry 416
Notifications 429
DeleteEntries 433
SaveChanges 437
CopyEntries 440
Server-Based Address Book Providers 442
The Design of ABWDS 442

CHAPTER TEN

Developing Message Store Providers   **475**

What Is a Message Store Provider? 475
How Message Store Providers
Interact with the MAPI Subsystem 476
Logging On to a Message Store Provider 477
How Message Store Providers Interact with Address Book
Providers and Message Transport Providers 478
Client Access to Message Store Providers 478
Requirements of All Message Store Providers 479
Store Providers Must Support Opening a Root Folder and
Getting a Hierarchy and Contents Table on It 479
Store Providers Must Register at Least One UID 479

Store Providers Must Support the Interfaces Required to
    Interact with Client Applications and the MAPI Subsystem 480
Store Providers Must Support the Opening of Their Objects
    Through *IMsgStore::OpenEntry* and *IMSLogon::OpenEntry* ... 481
All Store Provider Interfaces Must Be Thread-Safe 481
Store Providers Must Expose Their
    Capabilities in PR_STORE_SUPPORT_MASK 482
Support for Notifications 485
Store Providers with Unique Requirements 485
Default Message Store Providers 485
Public Folder Store Providers 488
Read-Only Store Providers 488
Developing a Message Store Provider 490
Implementing Stub Interfaces 490
Adding the Entries of Your Store Provider to MAPISVC.INF 491
Implementing *ServiceEntry* 492
Implementing *MSProviderInit* 496
Debugging Message Store Providers 497
Implementing MSLMS and MSWDS 497
Common Design Features 498
Implementing *IMSProvider* 508
Implementing *IMsgStore* 515
IMsgStore::SaveChanges 518
IMsgStore::SetProps 518
Unsupported Methods 519
Opening Objects in the Store Provider 519
Support for Setting the Receive Folder 524
The Message Store Provider Outgoing Queue Table 524
Methods Called Only by the MAPI Spooler 525
Aborting Submitted Messages 526
Logging Off from a Store Provider 526
Implementing *IMSLogon* 527
Implementing *IMAPIFolder* 528
Folder Tables 532
Opening Objects in a Folder 532
Managing Folder Messages 532
CMAPIFolder::CopyMessages 535

CMAPIFolder::DeleteMessages 535

CMAPIFolder::SetReadFlags 535

CMAPIFolder::Get/SetMessageStatus 535

Managing Subfolders 536

Unsupported Methods in Our *IMAPIFolder* Implementation 541

Implementing *IMessage* 541

Getting Properties 544

Setting Properties 544

Opening Interfaces on Properties 545

Deleting Properties 546

Copying the Object and Its Properties 546

Named Property Support 546

Managing Recipients.. 546

Managing Attachments 548

Submitting Messages 550

Modifying the Message Read State 555

Saving Changes on a Message 556

Implementing *IAttach* 556

Opening Interfaces on Properties 558

Committing Changes in Attachments 559

Conclusion 560

PART III: APPENDIXES

APPENDIX A

Named Properties   **563**

Getting the List of Named Properties in an Object 564

Setting Named Properties 566

Some Idiosyncrasies of *IMAPIProp::GetIDsFromNames* 568

APPENDIX B

Multivalue Properties   **569**

Index 571

FOREWORD

Every day we are relying more on electronics to handle our most basic communication needs. Electronic mail, for example, is becoming commonplace in both businesses and homes. To ensure that this transition to increasingly complex electronic systems continues efficiently, we must determine how to integrate the myriad systems available to the consumer. Consumers will demand compatibility among their desktop applications and the electronic communication infrastructure. Multimedia messaging—involving not only text-based messages but pictures and sounds—is right around the corner.

The future looks bright, but how does a developer reach nirvana while faced with the confusing and inconsistent standards and APIs that each independent messaging system has created? SMTP and POP are becoming the default protocols for messaging systems, but how does a creator of an application ensure that his product will work smoothly with these different messaging systems and continue to work into the future given the changing protocols, features, etc.? How can you protect your development investment?

The answer is by using the Messaging API (MAPI). Though MAPI is a bit complex, it is a powerful tool for developers. MAPI's client/server architecture is insurance against the unpredictability of the future.

Extended MAPI gives developers the power and flexibility to create a whole new generation of messaging and workflow applications. But with that power comes a certain amount of complexity. The authors of this book have done an outstanding job of managing this complexity and have succeeded in organizing their material in a way that makes MAPI accessible. If you have any interest in electronic messaging, email, or workflow applications, you will find the architectural discussions worthwhile.

Inside MAPI is the best single source of information on how to write MAPI clients and service providers. De la Cruz and Thaler have given MAPI developers what they really need to design and implement MAPI components: a clear and well-written description of *what* each MAPI component is, *why* it behaves as it does, and *how* it should be implemented. Developers will find the sample code and the hands-on approach of this book invaluable in designing and implementing Extended MAPI components. This book definitely belongs on the shelf of every serious MAPI developer.

Dan Fay
Messaging Technical Evangelist
Microsoft Corporation
danf@microsoft.com

ACKNOWLEDGMENTS

A book of this scope is the effort of many people, most of whom don't appear on the byline. We'd like to acknowledge their contributions—without them this project wouldn't have been possible.

Dana Birkby spent innumerable hours reviewing the technical content of this book, reading our source code, and, in general, keeping us honest to the spirit and letter of the MAPI specification. Without his prodigious technical knowledge, tireless efforts, and enduring patience, this book wouldn't have been an *Inside* book. Joel Soderberg contributed greatly to our understanding of transport providers and the MAPI spooler. Thanks also to Al Henriquez for reviewing our manuscript and providing valuable feedback on its form and content, and to Nishad Mulye for reviewing the sample finder and remote mail viewer applications on the companion CD-ROM.

We'd like to acknowledge Kraig Brockschmidt's assistance in getting this project off the ground and his timely advice on how to write a book. We also thank Eric Stroo, the Microsoft Press acquisitions editor who, in addition to having great taste in music, had the perspicacity to encourage us to write this book. The folks at Microsoft Press were invaluable in making this project a smooth one, especially Victoria Thulman and Marc Young. Thanks also go to Press staff Richard Carey, Travis Beaven, Barb Runyan, Linda Robinson, and Paul Vautier.

Special thanks to Cindy Kasin for making this project possible and to Mike Harris for help designing our Web page.

INTRODUCTION

In little more than 25 years, computer networks have evolved from exotic experimental systems to ubiquitous and indispensable parts of everyday life. No single invention has had a more dramatic impact on the form and function of computer technology or a greater effect on ordinary people's lives. Networks span continents, bridge oceans, and reach out into the heavens to such extent that there is no place on the planet so remote as to be inaccessible by telephone, email, or fax. Engineers teleconference from offices in Glasgow, Tel Aviv, and Amsterdam. A schoolgirl visits a Web site in England from her bedroom in Nova Scotia. Funds are transferred from a bank in New York to one in Berlin in order to consummate a deal in Brazil. International boundaries are increasingly arbitrary, time is foreshortened, and what was impossible yesterday is mundane today. The global village is *now,* and in the words of an old cliché, You ain't seen nothin' yet.

Networks have become such an integral part of business that we are seldom aware of their existence and rarely stop to consider how their use has changed the nature of ordinary commercial transactions. When we withdraw money from an automated teller machine, purchase gasoline from a card-reading pump, or book an airline reservation, we are setting in motion a complex sequence of events involving hardware and software of every description. And while network technology has embedded itself almost unnoticed in the ordinary instruments of commerce, the imminent prospect of individuals harnessing this power to communicate with one another has unleashed a tidal wave of public interest.

It's paradoxical that networking technology, which has so completely and profoundly transformed our business institutions, has had so little impact on our cultural institutions. Only now that the tantalizing prospect of giving private citizens access to global networks is a reality is this technology captivating the public imagination and imprinting itself on our cultural icons. The revolution has been more than 20 years in the making, but the news is only now reaching the home front. Suddenly, it seems, everyone is talking "netspeak," and while opinions about the technology range from the technically astute to the absurd, and with the forums from the hallowed halls of Congress to the corner drugstore, there can be no denying it: We are experiencing a phenomenon.

Even the Internet, whose social status was hitherto relegated to the obscurity of academics and pencil-headed geeks, seems to be enjoying newfound celebrity as a media darling, Hollywood film star, and vice-presidential pet.

Messaging, the subject of this book, is a natural consequence of this technological growth. With the proliferation of wide and local area networks and the availability of cheap computing power, many applications that were fantasies only a decade ago are now feasible. Software vendors, eager to capitalize on the growing demand for products that exploit this technology, are creating a generation of end-user applications that let users access network resources in new and imaginative ways. These messaging and workflow applications are becoming widespread in business and industry, and are consequently one of the fastest growing segments of the commercial software market.

So where does MAPI (Messaging Application Programming Interface) fit into this milieu of technological change? MAPI is a specification for messaging, a standard way of doing things, and a hedge against the uncertainties of the future. While messaging applications aren't new, the idea of explicitly specifying the components of an application and codifying the interfaces between them is. This is what MAPI is all about: a specification of what the pieces are, what they do, and how they fit together. It is a contract between high-level end-user applications and low-level messaging system components that promises a high degree of interoperability for MAPI-compliant software. The application writer benefits because his product enjoys greater connectivity to multiple messaging systems and independence from a particular system or protocol. Implementers of the low-level messaging system components also benefit because they have a (potentially) larger installed base of applications that can use their services. Total interoperability is realized, however, only when each component fully complies with the MAPI specification. To understand how to implement MAPI-compliant applications, you must first understand MAPI's architecture, its design goals, and its purpose.

The architecture of MAPI is designed to be resilient in the face of changing technical requirements. Existing network protocols are well understood and documented. New ones will evolve and succeed or fail on their technical merits and the vagaries of the marketplace. MAPI insulates applications from these dynamics by specifying a high-level system architecture without regard to low-level implementation details. Because the components of a MAPI system are modular and their interfaces explicit, they can be easily replaced as dictated by changes in the underlying technology.

Microsoft's contribution to MAPI is twofold. First, Microsoft has taken a leadership position in promulgating the MAPI standard and in encouraging the independent software vendor (ISV) community to develop MAPI products.

Secondly, Microsoft has made Windows a universal messaging platform by integrating the MAPI subsystem into the core components of the Windows 95 and Windows NT operating systems (a Win16 version is also available for backward compatibility with Windows 3.*x*). These components, which we call *the MAPI run time,* are in the form of system dynamic-link libraries (DLLs) that must be resident in order to load and run MAPI applications. Whereas these key components are proprietary, the vast majority of MAPI is in the public domain. Any software developer can write MAPI components and distribute them freely without license or royalty. This strategy is in keeping with Microsoft's policy of owning the operating system while at the same time actively encouraging applications development.

This book is for the following three categories of readers:

- Readers who have a general interest in understanding MAPI and its capabilities

- Readers who desire a deeper understanding of MAPI's architecture

- Readers who plan to implement MAPI-compliant messaging systems or components

Chapter 1 is a high-level overview of the MAPI architecture and where it fits in the messaging and workflow application picture, and is hence targeted at this first category of reader.

Chapters 2–6 discuss the components, objects, interfaces, and data structures that comprise MAPI systems. The material in these chapters is more technical in nature than the material in Chapter 1 and presumes some familiarity with C++. If you are contemplating a MAPI project and want to know what's involved, you should read Chapters 2–6 at the very least.

Chapters 7–10 are devoted to the nitty-gritty implementation details of developing service providers. In them we present a case study of the WINDS messaging system, which consists of a post-office server application as well as message store providers, transport providers, and address book providers. The WINDS messaging system addresses most of the important technical considerations relevant to developing MAPI-compliant components. We provide the source code in its entirety on the companion CD-ROM, so it is only excerpted in the text to clarify specific examples. We target *only* Win32 platforms, so if you're developing Win16 components, you'll have to modify the code provided.

If you are new to MAPI, expect to feel a little overwhelmed at first. Not only is MAPI big and complicated, but it borrows heavily from other big, complicated technologies as well. You will need to know a little about the OLE

Component Object Model (COM), a little about client-server programming and distributed computing, and a little about the Windows API. (We highly recommend that you read Chapters 1–4 of Kraig Brockschmidt's *Inside OLE*.) You might need to do some database programming, and more than likely you'll be using C++. You'll learn about objects, interfaces, and properties, GUIDs, MUIDs, and IIDs. And the MAPI header files contain hundreds of tortuously nested data structures and macro definitions.

So be forewarned: The learning curve is steep. But be encouraged, too. Although MAPI can sometimes appear to be a many-headed Hydra, it is, in fact, a powerful and well-crafted specification for implementing messaging applications. MAPI was created to make their development faster and easier, and to enable total interoperability between different vendors' products. MAPI will help you make sense out of messaging; this book will help you make sense out of MAPI.

THE MAPI
COMPONENTS

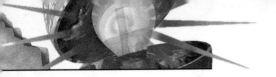

The first part of this book is devoted to the fundamentals of MAPI programming. Chapter 1 provides a broad overview of the MAPI architecture, the MAPI subsystem, and the role of MAPI clients and service providers. The information in this chapter is high-level and is targeted not only at MAPI developers but at anyone who needs to understand the "big picture."

Chapters 2–5 are more for developers who must understand the programming issues inherent in writing MAPI components. If you plan to write a MAPI client or service provider, you must follow certain programming conventions so that your code interacts properly with other components and the MAPI subsystem. These conventions include how to manipulate MAPI Component Object Model (COM) interfaces, manage memory, and access data in the form of MAPI properties and tables. Chapter 2 covers MAPI properties, Chapter 3 covers common MAPI interfaces, and Chapter 4 explains how to use MAPI tables and notifications.

In Chapter 5, we bring all the pieces together in a simple client application that demonstrates how to use most of the tools discussed in the preceding chapters. Even if your interest in MAPI lies only in implementing service providers, we suggest you read Chapters 1–5 anyway—not only because MAPI service providers also make use of properties, tables, notifications, and interfaces, but because understanding how a service provider works is easier if you understand how its interfaces are used by a MAPI client side.

CHAPTER ONE

The MAPI Architecture

The Messaging Application Programming Interface, or MAPI, employs a layered architecture designed to fulfill three principle requirements: interoperability between components, extensibility, and modularity. In this chapter we give an overview of what MAPI is and explain how its architecture was designed to address these requirements. We also examine some of the historical reasons for the creation of MAPI and summarize some of its most important features.

What Is MAPI?

One of the greatest challenges we faced in writing this book was figuring out how to explain the high-level concepts without overwhelming the reader with details. It's difficult to discuss MAPI's architecture without first defining its low-level components, but then it's also hard to explain the components without first discussing the context in which they function. We call this dilemma the "chicken-and-egg syndrome" because it's like trying to explain where chickens come from without ever describing what an egg is. We also tried to address some common misconceptions about what MAPI is and how it's used. This confusion stems partly from the fact that MAPI, like messaging, is relatively new, and partly because MAPI, while similar to other APIs in some superficial respects, is fundamentally different from them in most of the ways that count. A big part of why MAPI is so misunderstood is that it's complicated. It's complicated because messaging is complicated, and messaging is complicated because the underlying technologies are difficult and the demands we place on them are high.

Although MAPI calls itself an application programming interface, it's really not an API in the traditional sense. The APIs that Windows programmers know and love are essentially libraries of related functions that can be called from a Windows application. It seems that if a programming task is sufficiently complex, sooner or later Microsoft is sure to write an API that wraps up all the troublesome complexities into a simple, easy-to-use interface.

That's not quite how it works with MAPI, however. MAPI isn't just a library of functions. In fact, MAPI isn't an implementation at all, but a specification for an entire messaging subsystem and all the components that interact with it. The MAPI specification defines the architecture of this subsystem, what the external components are and how they behave, and the interfaces between the subsystem and the components. So, in the first place, MAPI is an architectural specification—not a library.

In the second place, MAPI isn't really written by Microsoft; only the messaging subsystem is owned and implemented exclusively by Microsoft. The external components are created and marketed by independent software vendors (ISVs) wanting to add a certain functionality to the messaging system, or to provide compatibility with existing systems. (Microsoft has, of course, implemented its own version of some of these components, but none of these are required to run the MAPI messaging subsystem.)

Finally, the interfaces between MAPI components aren't defined as functions that an application can simply call. Instead, each component exposes one or more Component Object Model (COM) interfaces. MAPI applications almost never call APIs. Instead they obtain COM interfaces and call methods on those interfaces.

Simple MAPI: MAPI "Version 0"

Another source of confusion surrounding MAPI is that Microsoft *did* implement a library of 12 functions that was *also* called MAPI. This API was essentially a public version of the functions used by the Microsoft Mail client to communicate with Microsoft Mail post offices. Extended MAPI version 1, the subject of this book, completely supersedes this older version. The old MAPI API is now called *Simple MAPI*. The MAPI version 1 SDK includes a rewritten version of the Simple MAPI API for backwards compatibility, although internally it uses Extended MAPI and bears little resemblance to its predecessor.

Following is a summary of what MAPI is and is not:

- MAPI is not a library—it's an architectural specification that defines a messaging subsystem.

- The specification includes definitions of various external components, what they do, and the interfaces they expose.

■ These components can be implemented by any vendor, not just by Microsoft.

■ The interfaces between components aren't APIs, but COM interfaces.

Email and Electronic Messaging— The Historical Motivation for MAPI

MAPI was developed to provide a standardized application-level interface that lets messaging components talk to widely incompatible messaging systems. Microsoft likes to point out that the MAPI specification was written in collaboration with over 100 software vendors, and hence represents a true industrywide consensus of what features the next generation of messaging systems should provide. The uncharacteristic spirit of cooperation this effort engendered was inspired by the commonsense realization that economies of scale also apply to software, and that having many competing messaging standards in the marketplace doesn't serve the consumer's *or* the vendor's interests.

In a way, the PC world has been both blessed and cursed by a lack of standards. On the one hand, it's possible that the intense competition in this market and the *absence* of industry standards contributed more to advancing the state of the art than premature adoption of standards would have. This may be true, but it's also clear that as messaging systems have become more complex, the lack of standards has actually started to impede application development.

The problem boils down to the fact that existing PC messaging systems were based on proprietary interfaces. Not long after the messaging systems of the current generation were introduced, it became apparent that the services they provided could also be used to advantage by other applications. Third-party vendors mused, "Wouldn't it be nice if my word processor could send a document by calling the email system code?" But, invariably, the messaging code for sending and receiving documents was proprietary. So, an enterprising vendor had to license it from each messaging-system vendor that she wanted her application to play with. This provided a *financial* disincentive for developing messaging applications.

The key players first addressed this dilemma by creating APIs that exported some of their messaging systems' internal functions. For example, Microsoft came up with Simple MAPI (not to be confused with MAPI version 1, which is the subject of this book), and Lotus published its own API: VIM. These efforts fell a bit short of the mark, first because they weren't based on any industry consensus about what features to provide, and then because they didn't provide enough features anyway. MAPI version 1 was created to fill the void.

5

The requirements for the new standard dictated that it should do the following:

- Support the features demanded by the next generation of messaging applications

- Be based on broad, industrywide consensus

- Be nonproprietary

- Allow conforming systems to talk to any email protocol

- Allow backward compatibility with existing messaging systems

Messaging Applications Today

As messaging technology has evolved, the notion of what a messaging application is has also changed. Messaging today is more than just email, and messaging applications are often qualitatively different from conventional email readers. The simplest of these are ordinary stand-alone programs that let users send documents to an email address without the bother of starting a separate email program. A user creates a document and sends it from the same application, either as an attachment to an ordinary email message or as a message in some application-specific format.

More complex applications provide additional functionality and are better able to pass data, or interoperate, with other applications. They require the services of the underlying messaging system for message and recipient storage and retrieval, addressing, and message transport; and they can also support advanced features, such as electronic forms, advanced search capabilities, and public folders.

Forms and Public Folders

Forms

A *form* is a special type of an electronic message in exactly the same way that a paper form is a special type of a written message. Forms are useful when the message is in boilerplate format or when the information content is easily standardized. Some examples include the following:

- *A time card.* The data consists of employee name, social security number, and dates and hours worked.

- *An order form.* The user enters the merchandise's catalog numbers, his or her address, and credit card number.

- *A survey.* The data is entered by "filling in the blanks" or by selecting one of multiple choices.

Forms have specialized viewing and editing needs that are provided by a window called a *form viewer* that is activated whenever the user opens the form. Every message has an attribute called a *message class* that identifies which viewer should be used to display the form. A *form server* is an application that implements a form viewer associated with a particular message class. A client can display any form if the requisite form server is installed on the user's machine. The form server can be downloaded and installed automatically on the user's machine when the form using it is first opened.

Public Folders

Public folders are message containers that are accessible by more than one user simultaneously. Here are some examples of useful public folders:

- *A bulletin board.* This folder contains messages advertising items to buy and sell, job opportunities, and so on. Users are granted read/write access to browse the folder or post messages.

- *A suggestion box.* Employees post messages that are periodically reviewed by the company's management. Users have write-only access.

- *A news service.* Messages containing newsworthy items are posted daily by the folder administrator. Users have read-only access.

Public folders often have a form associated with them that is activated whenever a message is read or composed in the folder. For example, an employer might set up a public folder to survey employee job satisfaction and associate a form with it that offers several choices: Satisfied, Very Satisfied, and Ecstatic.

We mentioned earlier that use of proprietary interfaces made it difficult and costly for ISVs to develop messaging applications because of the licensing requirements. Making the interfaces standard, open, and public also makes communication between different vendors' products *technically* feasible. Consider a non-MAPI messaging system that maintains a database of messages. Suppose a developer wanted to write an application that captured certain types of messages and saved them to an SQL database. Such a task would be difficult or impossible if the interfaces for accessing the message database were private.

Another drawback to using private or proprietary interfaces is that an end user can't freely mix and match different vendors' offerings to suit her requirements. In our previous example, she wouldn't be able to replace the default message database with another vendor's product.

These limitations made it difficult for third-party vendors to develop and market software that extended or interoperated with existing messaging applications. MAPI removes these barriers by specifying the architecture of the messaging system and making the interfaces public. The goal was to make MAPI open, modular, and extensible so that the specification would be able to grow and adapt to new requirements as technology and demands changed.

MAPI is an open specification in the sense that MAPI-compliant systems can freely communicate with other messaging systems. Internally, MAPI components talk to each other through a set of carefully specified interfaces that define only how the various components interact, not how they are implemented. Because the internals are hidden, MAPI-compliant components are highly interoperable, allowing end users and administrators to easily configure a user's workstation with various combinations of components from one or more vendors. Figure 1-1 on the facing page illustrates this flexibility.

This degree of independence, of course, demands that the function of each component be well defined, the implementations highly modular, and the external interfaces completely specified. Beyond that, however, designers of MAPI components are pretty much free to do what they please. For example, the MAPI specification defines one component, called a *transport provider,* whose job is to transport messages between the user's machine and the back-end messaging system. A transport provider's external interfaces are totally explicit, but there is absolutely no mention in the specification about how the provider actually transmits the message. The messaging system's delivery medium could be TCP/IP (Transmission Control Protocol/Internet Protocol), modem, wireless, postal mail, or carrier pigeon.

Even though the external interfaces are explicit, the functional requirements of each component are sufficiently general so that they can be extended as novel applications or technologies emerge. As cellular telephone service

8

becomes cheaper and more widely available, more and more wireless transport providers will be created to take advantage of this accessibility. Changes in our socioeconomic conditions will also suggest new applications that an extensible MAPI specification should be able to accommodate. Perhaps telecommuting will become popular, and housebound workers will create a demand for MAPI clients that let them pay bills electronically from their home computers.

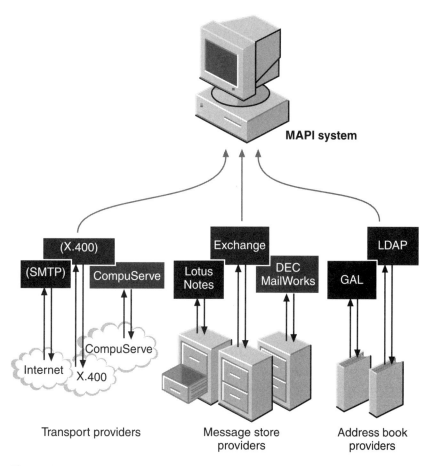

Figure 1-1.
MAPI lets the end user "mix and match" components from different vendors.

Architectural Overview

The MAPI architecture differentiates between consumers of messaging services and producers of messaging-system services. On the consumer side are the *client* applications that send and receive messages. On the producer side are one or more back-end systems: the post offices, mailboxes, message databases, recipients, networks, gateways, administration programs, and so on that constitute the underlying messaging system. Producers provide access to the messaging system's functionality through one or more *service provider* dynamic-link libraries (DLLs) that can be installed on the client-side machine. The MAPI subsystem is a layer between the consumer and the producer that acts as a broker between the various components by routing client requests to the correct service provider, and that enables the parts to communicate in a predictable way. Figure 1-2 on the facing page illustrates the overall structure of MAPI.

The idea behind MAPI is to push the idiosyncrasies of the underlying messaging systems down to the producer level and hide them from the consumer level behind a standardized API. This API specifies the functionality available to consumers and gives them an open, nonproprietary interface to talk to. Anything that is unique or proprietary to a specific messaging back end (hardware, network protocols, file formats, and so on) is isolated at the producer level. The client always sees a consistent interface regardless of which messaging back end it's connected to. The idea behind MAPI is basically this: "You can use any messaging system underneath, but on top we all agree to talk MAPI."

Clients communicate with the back-end system through the client interface of the MAPI subsystem. The client interface forms a kind of contract between a client application and the messaging subsystem that guarantees that a consistent set of interfaces will always be available to the client regardless of which back end it's connected to. The Extended MAPI client interface returns OLE COM objects to the client, which the client then uses to request services from the MAPI subsystem.[1] The names and semantics of these interfaces are completely defined by the MAPI specification.

The MAPI subsystem is the middle layer between the client requesting services and the messaging system providing them and can therefore be visualized as being sandwiched between the client interface on top and the service provider interface on the bottom. MAPI is based on a client-server architecture where the client application plays the role of the client and the

---

1. Microsoft also provides other client interfaces that use different paradigms (OLE messaging, for example, which is based on OLE Automation objects) or that emulate older API sets (such as Simple MAPI or CMC). These interfaces are weaker than Extended MAPI, and we don't cover them in this book.

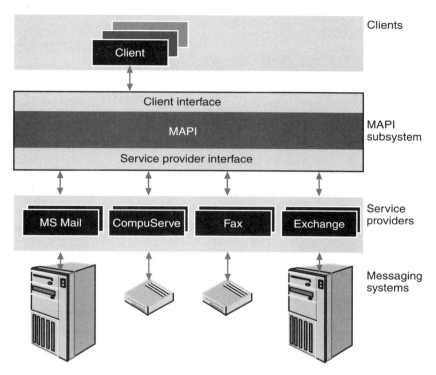

Figure 1-2.
The MAPI architecture consists of three separate layers: the client applications, the MAPI subsystem, and the service providers that communicate with specific messaging systems.

remote messaging system plays the role of the server. All client requests must pass through the MAPI subsystem before being handled by the server. Interfaces such as the MAPI subsystem are sometimes referred to as *middleware* in client-server terminology because the client doesn't connect directly to the server process but does go through this intermediate layer of software.

The service providers are replaceable modules that communicate with the messaging-system back end. A client requests services from the MAPI subsystem via the client interface; the MAPI subsystem routes the request to the correct service provider; the service provider connects to the back end, obtains the requested data, and returns the data to the MAPI subsystem, which then passes it back to the client. Figure 1-3 on the following page illustrates this.

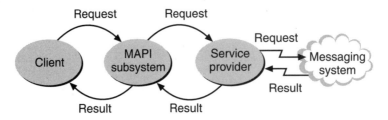

Figure 1-3.
Clients request services from the MAPI subsystem.

The service providers communicate with the MAPI subsystem through the service provider interface, which provides the same type of uniform access to providers as the client interface does to clients. The service provider interface is a set of interfaces exposed by COM objects that are implemented within the service provider module. Because a service provider's behavior and interfaces are specified by MAPI, anyone who knows how to communicate with a specific messaging system can write a service provider that lets a MAPI client connect to that back end. For proprietary systems, the messaging-system vendor will usually supply the service providers needed to connect to it, but for published standards such as X.400 or SMTP any interested developer can write fully compliant service providers. All that's required for a service provider to work correctly in a MAPI system is conformance to the MAPI service provider interface and the ability to access the back end.

Benefits of the MAPI Architecture

So why is any of this important? The answer is that these two sets of interfaces, the client–to–MAPI interfaces and the MAPI–to–service provider interfaces, provide a homogenous way for clients to access heterogeneous messaging systems. End users can now connect to any back end by simply installing and configuring sets of service providers. Suppose an end user wanted to use his MAPI client to send and receive messages to an existing Microsoft Mail post office. All he'd have to do to make this happen is install and configure the Microsoft Mail service providers. Suppose he also wanted to send and receive CompuServe mail, faxes, and voicemail from the same client. Solution? Install and configure the CompuServe, fax, and voicemail providers. Three months later his company decides to upgrade its mail system to Microsoft Exchange Server. He simply installs and configures Microsoft's Exchange providers.

This example, although slightly contrived, illustrates an important motivation for MAPI: the concept of the *universal inbox*, which is a single application or area on the desktop wherein the user views and manipulates all electronic correspondence, be it email, fax, voicemail, scheduling information, documents, and so on. The universal inbox depends on a user being able to install any kind and number of service providers and having the service providers run concurrently so that the client can connect to different messaging systems simultaneously.

The situation is analogous to how a Windows application attains device-independence from various printers: The drivers that access each printer are installed and managed by the system, and all an application has to do to print is make the correct API calls and the system invokes the appropriate driver to do the work. MAPI service providers give clients the same kind of independence—the client application calls a standard interface method, and the system loads the appropriate service provider and executes the correct code.

The preceding scenario is one example of how the MAPI architecture makes total interoperability possible—it's the ability to pass data seamlessly between different vendors' products. Since the MAPI interfaces are standardized, a client needs only to be MAPI-compliant to communicate with any number of MAPI service providers. Not only can MAPI clients operate seamlessly with multiple service providers, but data can be copied from one provider to another. MAPI accomplishes this feat by specifying a uniform way to access and represent data that is passed to and from the MAPI subsystem. This uniform data representation is managed by a MAPI interface that is required on all MAPI objects that store data.

MAPI also makes messaging systems easily extensible. New behavior can be added to a MAPI-compliant system by adding or replacing a service provider module instead of upgrading, rewriting, or (even worse) replacing the entire system. Extensibility allows systems to be easily maintained and upgraded at minimal expense. End users also experience less disruption from an upgrade or full-scale migration to a new system because the changes can be accomplished in stages: first by installing the clients, then the service providers, and then by replacing the back-end components.

Finally, developing MAPI clients also entails less risk for the vendor because MAPI clients don't have to be ported to multiple messaging systems—the middleware layer of MAPI hides the idiosyncrasies of each back end. Vendors producing MAPI service providers and messaging systems benefit because they don't have to worry about compatibility problems between their products and the clients that use them.

MAPI Components

MAPI implementations must adhere to a prescribed programming model: the OLE COM. All MAPI components use or implement MAPI objects, and all MAPI objects are COM objects. The client–to–MAPI and MAPI–to–service provider interfaces are both sets of COM interfaces. The MAPI specification defines the form and function of these objects, and COM specifies the mechanism for object creation and destruction.

The MAPI specification also provides a standard model of data abstraction and encapsulation over and above the use of COM. MAPI defines a set of named attributes, or properties, that have specific uses and predefined data types. An object's properties are analogous to the private data in a C++ class: They can be accessed only by calling public methods on the object's property interface.

The Layered Model

Figure 1-4 on the facing page shows the layered model we discussed earlier in slightly more detail. Because clients are consumers of messaging services, they are highest in the message-service food chain and hence occupy the top level of the MAPI architecture. Clients are the components that end users are most likely to see and interact with because they often provide some kind of user interface (UI) for creating and displaying a message's contents. While providing a UI is commonplace, it is by no means required by the MAPI spec. Examples of different client applications are provided in Chapter 5.

The MAPI subsystem consists of the MAPI run-time component and the message spooler. The MAPI run time is a DLL that contains a set of MAPI base-objects and APIs used by the other components. These objects and APIs include interfaces or functions for initializing the MAPI subsystem, starting a MAPI session, managing memory, administering profiles, displaying a standardized user interface, and so on. What these objects and APIs are and how to use them is addressed in subsequent chapters.

The spooler is an independent process that manages the flow of messages in and out of the system. It sets the delivery order of both inbound and outbound messages and routes them to the appropriate components.

The bottom layer is occupied by the service providers that communicate with the underlying messaging system. In MAPI (as in life), those at the bottom do most of the work for those at the top. A service provider is a DLL that returns interfaces to both MAPI and the spooler via the service provider interface. The MAPI subsystem can call these interfaces directly or pass them to the client through the client–to–MAPI interface. Either way, clients request services by calling methods on these interfaces, and the provider tries to satisfy these requests by directly manipulating the messaging system.

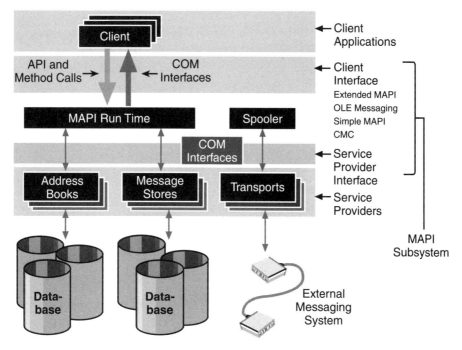

Figure 1-4.
The MAPI architecture, in detail, showing individual components.

MAPI defines three principal service providers: a *message store provider* for creating, submitting, and storing messages; an *address book provider* for looking up recipients' email addresses; and a *transport provider* for handling the physical transmission of messages over some medium. (There are a few others, but they are outside the scope of this book.)

Clients

A client is a process that requests services of the MAPI subsystem in order to manipulate messages. A client is typically, though not always, an end-user application for creating, sending, and "viewing" messages of one kind or another. (Of course, a message doesn't always provide a visual representation. How do you "view" voicemail, for example?) To this end, clients often provide a user interface through which the user can make requests and issue commands. Figure 1-5 illustrates some common requests that a client might make and which provider is invoked to service the request.

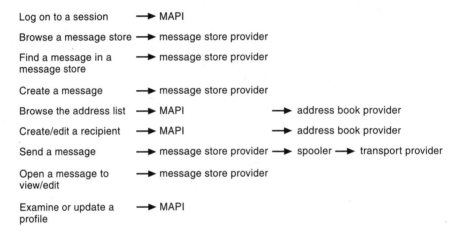

Figure 1-5.
The left side represents client requests. The components that are involved in servicing the request are shown to the right.

A client must *log on* to a MAPI session before it can request services. Logging on causes an instance of each store provider and/or address book provider to be loaded and mapped into the client's address space. MAPI knows which providers to load by looking in the profile specified in the logon operation. Essentially, the profile is a list that the user creates that names which providers should be available in the current session. Providers can be grouped into *message services*, which means that a set of one or more providers is designed to be installed and configured as a unit instead of piecemeal. Logging on also starts the spooler, which loads and initializes the required transport providers. Note that whereas address book providers and message store providers run in the client's context, a transport provider runs exclusively in the spooler's context. This division of labor has some important implications, as we will see later.

Profiles and Sessions

Profiles

A *profile* is a named list of message services and configuration data created by the user. A *message service* is a group of one or more service providers that share common configuration code. Profiles are created and configured using a configuration utility such as the Control Panel's Mail and Fax applet. This utility lets the user select which message services to include in the profile. The selected message services are then configured, which means that data needed by the providers in each message service is gathered from the user or the system. Providers almost always need some configuration data from the user (the name of a remote server or the path to a local database file, for example) to function properly; they obtain this data by executing the configuration code. A profile can specify any number of message services, and a user can have as many profiles as she finds convenient. For example, she may have two profiles on her laptop: one that contains configuration information for server-based providers used in the office, and another that contains information for modem- or wireless-based providers used for home or travel.

Sessions

A *session* is a period of fixed duration during which work is done. In the context of MAPI, "work" refers to a series of client requests to MAPI that are serviced by one or more providers. A session starts when a client logs on to the MAPI subsystem and ends when the client logs off. A profile name is specified in the logon process to tell MAPI which providers it should load to service the client's requests.

MAPI Run-time Component

The *MAPI run-time component* acts as a broker between clients and service providers and is integrated into the Windows operating system as part of the messaging subsystem. This component directly manages the client and service provider interfaces.

The MAPI run-time component also implements its own interfaces for creating and administering profiles, managing a session, and accessing multiple address book providers. In addition, MAPI provides a suite of APIs for allocating and freeing memory, handling MAPI data structures, and performing sundry other "housekeeping" chores. Some of these APIs must be used (service providers must use the MAPI memory management APIs, for example), whereas others are provided purely for convenience. We'll point out which ones are mandatory as we examine the details of coding MAPI components.

Message Store Providers

A *message store provider* is a DLL that manipulates a database of messages. A message store provider is organized as a hierarchy of folders and messages. (See Figure 1-6.) Folders are objects that can contain other folders and messages. A client can create any number of folders in a message store provider and use them as it sees fit. For example, certain types (or classes) of messages can be routed directly to a specific folder for special processing.

Although the store provider DLL runs in the client's context and is therefore local to the user's machine, the database accessed by the provider can be local or server-based. Server-based store providers are particularly interesting because they allow multiuser access to the same set of messages, which allows store providers to implement public folders whose contents can be viewed by groups of users. It's important to note that the store provider is more than a static repository of messages. Inbound messages are received by the store provider; outbound messages are also created and submitted for delivery there. Because the store provider runs in the client's context, and the client has no direct interface with the transport provider that delivers the message, you might wonder how a message is passed from the store provider to the transport provider, and vice versa.

The answer is twofold: Either the spooler also loads an instance of the message store provider and can therefore access messages or, in the case of a *tightly-coupled store,* the message store provider handles the message transmission itself and bypasses the spooler and transport provider entirely. See Chapters 6, 8, and 10 for more information about this subject and its design implications.

One final note about store providers: There is no restriction on the number or types of store providers that can be run in a given session. MAPI allows messages and folders to be freely moved and copied between store providers, subject to the write permissions of the individual provider. In fact, a user will frequently include at least two store providers in his profile—a local "personal" store provider and a server-based store provider.

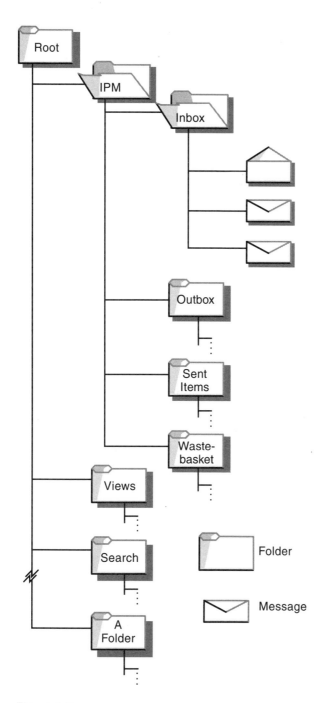

Figure 1-6.
Message store providers implement a hierarchical database of folders and messages.

Address Book Providers

An *address book provider* is a layer on top of a database of message recipients. This database is queried to find addressing information for a recipient when a message is addressed. An address book provider is organized hierarchically like a store provider, but the address book provider objects are called containers and recipients rather than folders and messages.

An *address book provider container* is an object that can contain subcontainers, distribution lists, and recipients. Address book provider entries are created in a container in much the same way that messages are created in a folder. Database queries are performed on an individual container, not on the database at large.

The number of containers in an address book provider isn't limited by MAPI, and a container may have any number of subcontainers and recipients. Address book providers that implement multiple containers typically do so for grouping recipient records that share a common property. An address book provider that contains records from recipients on multiple messaging systems might segregate the recipients into different containers based on the address format (or address type); for example, all X.400 recipients would be stored in one container, SMTP users in another, and so forth. Other possibilities include having separate containers based on routing information (for example, the user's subnet), physical site (locality), or departmental or other bureaucratic grouping.

A *distribution list* is a special kind of container that lets a group of recipients be addressed as a single recipient. A copy of the message is sent to each member of the distribution list when the list is expanded. The leaf nodes of the address book provider container hierarchy are individual recipients, or mail users. Mail users are objects that are addressable; that is, they have email addresses to which messages can be sent and from whence messages can originate.

Like message store providers, address book providers can be local or server-based. Server-based address book providers typically contain global or enterprisewide address lists, whereas local address book providers are usually personal address books, or *PABs*, that are composed of user-created entries. Like message store providers, any number of address book providers can be present in a given session, and entries can be copied between providers, subject to the write permissions and methods supported by the containers involved. (Figure 1-7 on the facing page illustrates the address book provider structure.)

Transport Providers

The physical delivery of a MAPI message to and from the underlying messaging system is handled by a *transport provider*. The transport provider's job

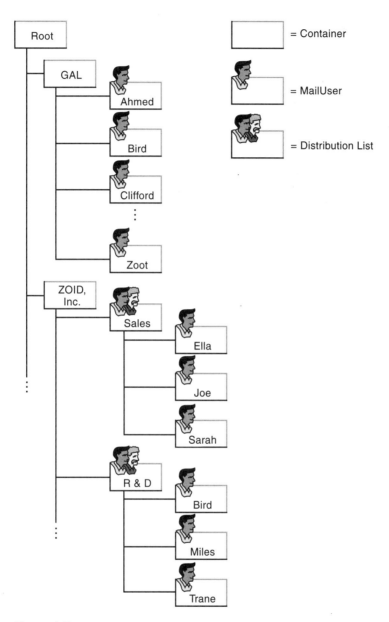

Figure 1-7.

Individual address book providers implement hierarchical databases of containers, distribution lists, and recipients. MAPI merges each provider's root container so that a client application can treat multiple address book providers as if they were a single address book provider.

is to accept an outbound message, translate it into a stream of bytes that the underlying system understands, and then transmit the byte stream via the messaging system. Inbound messages come to a transport provider from the messaging system, are encoded into a MAPI message, and then handed to the spooler for delivery to the message store provider.

The underlying messaging system to which the transport provider connects dictates which protocol the transport provider uses to establish and maintain the connection. Some protocols are proprietary, such as the protocol used by Microsoft Mail post offices, and some are de facto, or prescribed, standards, such as SMTP or X.400. In any case, only the transport provider knows or cares about transmission details like the protocol; these details are always hidden within the transport provider layer and are completely transparent to the layers above it. Transport providers run in the spooler's context and consequently have no direct interaction with MAPI clients. Instead, messages are passed to and from the transport provider via the MAPI spooler, which manages the various transport providers running in the current session.

When an outbound message is created by the client, it is first submitted to the message store provider, which in turn hands it to the spooler. The spooler selects one of the installed transport providers and passes it a copy of the message or generates a nondelivery report if no suitable transport provider can be found. The selection criteria are based on what type of messaging system the recipient resides on.

Inbound messages come to the transport provider by whatever mechanism is used by the underlying messaging system. A transport provider notifies the spooler when new mail has arrived so the spooler can start the inbound processing logic. Sometime after the spooler receives the new mail notification, it will call into the transport provider, passing it a "blank" message object. The transport provider decodes the inbound stream onto the message object by setting properties on the message object, and the spooler then places the message object in the message store provider's receive folder.

The MAPI Spooler

The spooler is a separate process that is part of the messaging subsystem. Because transport providers run solely in the spooler's context, clients can't directly access transport providers to request delivery services from the external messaging system. Instead, communication with the external system must pass through the spooler. But the spooler and client are both separate processes, so how is this communication effected? The answer is *through the message store provider*, an instance of which is loaded in the client's *and* the spooler's contexts. As noted earlier, outbound messages are composed in the client and submitted to the message store provider for delivery. A request to deliver an outgoing message causes the message object to be handed to the spooler, which selects one or more transport providers (based on the address type) to deliver the message. The spooler also prepares messages for delivery by making sure that each recipient has complete addressing information before passing it to the waiting transport provider. Figure 1-8 on the following page illustrates the flow of outbound messages.

It's important to note that the message store provider provides the link between the spooler and the client application. Transport providers notify the spooler of new mail through a method call or by being polled, and the spooler responds by creating a message object in the message store provider's receive folder. The spooler then calls a method on the message store provider that tells the client-side instance of the message store provider that new mail has arrived. Message store providers must use some form of interprocess communication, such as shared memory, pipes, or remote procedure calls, to communicate this information between the two contexts. The client-side context generates a new mail notification, for which clients typically register so that they can update their user interfaces or alert the user that new mail has been received. Figure 1-9 on page 25 shows the flow of inbound messages.

A single instance of the spooler runs regardless of the number of active sessions. For example, if session A is started using the services of messaging system A′ and session B is running concurrently using messaging system B′, then the spooler must coordinate the flow of messages from two independent processes and two sets of service providers. To help manage multiple message sources and destinations, the spooler maintains an internal queue of outbound messages that it constructs by merging each message store provider's outgoing message queue. It is the spooler's responsibility to sort the entries in the outbound queue so that messages submitted to a given message store provider are passed to the transport providers in the same *order* in which they were submitted by the client.[2]

---

2. Actually, the requirement is only that messages submitted in a given store provider must be sent in the order submitted, not that all messages submitted in all store providers get sent in strict chronological order.

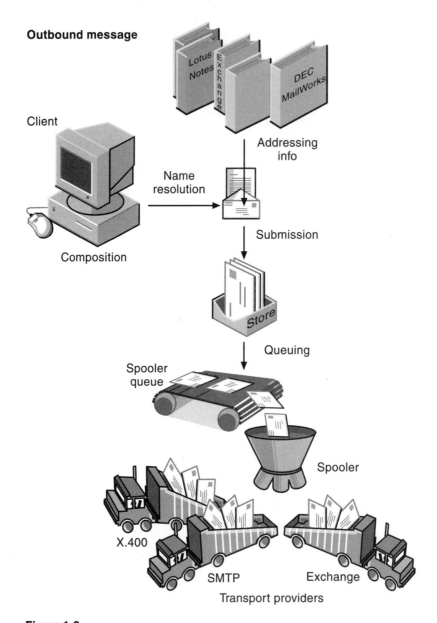

Outbound message

Client

Composition

Name resolution

Addressing info

Submission

Store

Queuing

Spooler queue

Spooler

X.400

SMTP

Exchange

Transport providers

Figure 1-8.
An outbound message is created in a message store provider folder. The recipient's address, obtained from the address book provider, is added to the message envelope before it is submitted in the message store provider. Submission places the message in the spooler's outbound queue. The spooler dequeues the message, examines the recipients, and passes it to one or more transport providers for delivery.

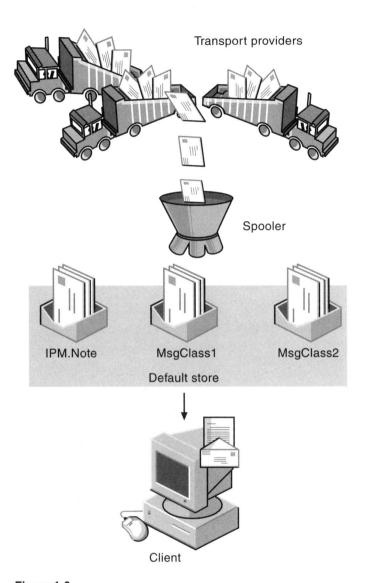

Figure 1-9.
A message arrives from the foreign system via a transport provider, which notifies the spooler. The spooler creates a message object in the message store provider and passes it to the transport provider, which translates the message's foreign attributes into MAPI properties. The spooler passes the newly formed message to the message store provider and notifies the message store provider that new mail has arrived.

MAPI Properties

MAPi is the messaging and workflow component of the Windows Open Systems Architecture (WOSA) standard created by Microsoft and its partners to make the Windows family of operating systems a complete and robust platform for general and vertical applications. The foundation of the MAPI architecture is the Component Object Model (COM), which provides a straightforward and powerful model for implementing sophisticated API sets. This chapter provides a brief overview of COM as it relates to MAPI interfaces. We take an in-depth look at one interface, *IMAPIProp*, and explain how clients use it to manipulate an object's data in the form of MAPI properties. We also examine MAPI's memory management APIs.

MAPI and COM

APIs that follow the COM architecture are specified by defining interfaces. An interface is simply an abstract base class[1] that contains a set of related functions (called methods). MAPI specifies each interface's name, its numeric interface identifier (or IID), the class definition (in a header file), the semantics of each method, the provider that implements it, the meaning of the methods' parameters, possible return values, and the "direction" of each parameter.

An interface definition does not include data or implementation code. This is one of the most attractive and elegant concepts of the COM architecture. Because of this, a vendor can design an API for a given architecture and publish its interfaces. Any interested developer wanting to use the published interface can do so by implementing the interface's methods. The designer of the interface doesn't have to write a single line of code and can instead concentrate on refining the interface design and specification.

---

1. Abstract base classes, being part of the object-oriented paradigm, are supported syntactically by the C++ language. C programmers can still derive from an abstract base class by defining the derived class as a structure whose first member is a pointer to a table of function pointers (the vtbl) containing the class's methods. See the MAPI documentation for details.

Once an interface is published under a given name with a unique ID, its name, ID, and methods are basically cast in stone to assure compatibility with applications that use them. If the interface is altered because the methods in it are changed or because the parameter list is modified, the altered interface is considered a new interface and a new name and interface ID must be given to it.

Typically, interfaces are implemented in C++ because of the language's native efficiency; ease of programming; and support for object-oriented features such as classes, inheritance, data encapsulation, strict typing, and compile-time error checking, which helps catch common mistakes in the definition and use of class instances. The decision to use one language over another should be based on what the programmer is most comfortable with. We chose C++ for the sample code developed in this book and highly recommend it, but COM interfaces can also be implemented in C, although the coding details are more tedious and error prone.

Since all MAPI interfaces are COM-based, they are derived from the *IUnknown* base class. *IUnknown* comprises the *AddRef, Release,* and *QueryInterface* methods. *QueryInterface* lets you obtain a different interface from an object if the target object's IID is known and the parent interface can return the requested interface. But how do you get that first MAPI interface? The answer is by calling a MAPI API. Once you have the first interface pointer, you can obtain new interfaces through *QueryInterface* or through other methods on the interface. A MAPI client application, for example, must always first obtain the session interface *IMAPISession* by calling the *MAPILogonEx* API. From that first interface, the client can request other interfaces by calling methods such as *IMAPISession::OpenEntry* on the session object.

IMAPIProp

MAPI objects are entities that represent and contain data. The interfaces an object exposes are designed to manipulate, store, and retrieve the data contained in the object. An interface's methods are always public, but the object's data is always private, meaning that it is accessible only through the interface's published methods.

MAPI objects are black boxes when it comes to manipulating data: The data source, its method of storage and retrieval, and any internal data structures are known only to the implementation of the particular interface. The location of the data (locality) as well as its structure are completely transparent to the interface user. (See Figure 2-1 on the facing page.)

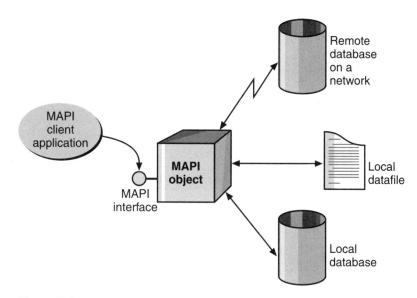

Figure 2-1.
The data storage mechanism is known only to the provider implementing the object. How the data is represented internally and where it resides are hidden from the client.

This design offers a tremendous advantage both to users of MAPI objects and to implementers of those objects. To interface users, the code that retrieves and displays data is completely decoupled from the underlying data storage and retrieval mechanisms. This means that the back-end data source can be changed, upgraded, revised, or even completely replaced without affecting the consumer of the interface.

Because all data is private, MAPI specifies an interface that provides a standard way to manipulate an object's data. This interface is *IMAPIProp*. *IMAPIProp* is the most fundamental interface in MAPI and the base class from which all MAPI containers are derived. It is used to read, write, save, delete, and modify an object's data. The abstract base class definition of this interface is as follows:

```
// Abstract definition of IMAPIProp
class IMAPIProp : public IUnknown
{
public :
    virtual HRESULT GetLastError
                        (HRESULT                 hResult,
                         ULONG                   ulFlags,
                         LPMAPIERROR *           ppMAPIError) = 0;
```

(continued)

29

```
virtual HRESULT SaveChanges
                (ULONG                      ulFlags) = 0;
virtual HRESULT GetProps
                (LPSPropTagArray            pPropTagArray,
                 ULONG                      ulFlags,
                 ULONG *                    pcValues,
                 LPSPropValue *             ppPropArray) = 0;
virtual HRESULT GetPropList
                (ULONG                      ulFlags,
                 LPSPropTagArray *          ppPropTagArray) = 0;
virtual HRESULT OpenProperty
                (ULONG                      ulPropTag,
                 LPCIID                     piid,
                 ULONG                      ulInterfaceOptions,
                 ULONG                      ulFlags,
                 LPUNKNOWN *                ppUnk) = 0;
virtual HRESULT SetProps
                (ULONG                      cValues,
                 LPSPropValue               pPropArray,
                 LPSPropProblemArray *      ppProblems) = 0;
virtual HRESULT DeleteProps
                (LPSPropTagArray            pPropTagArray,
                 LPSPropProblemArray *      ppProblems) = 0;
virtual HRESULT CopyTo
                (ULONG                      ciidExclude,
                 LPCIID                     rgiidExclude,
                 LPSPropTagArray            pExcludeProps,
                 ULONG                      ulUIParam,
                 LPMAPIPROGRESS             pProgress,
                 LPCIID                     pInterface,
                 LPVOID                     pDestObj,
                 ULONG                      ulFlags,
                 LPSPropProblemArray *      ppProblems) = 0;
virtual HRESULT CopyProps
                (LPSPropTagArray            pIncludeProps,
                 ULONG                      ulUIParam,
                 LPMAPIPROGRESS             pProgress,
                 LPCIID                     pInterface,
                 LPVOID                     pDestObj,
                 ULONG                      ulFlags,
                 LPSPropProblemArray *      ppProblems) = 0;
virtual HRESULT GetNamesFromIDs
                (LPSPropTagArray *          ppPropTags,
                 LPGUID                     pPropSetGuid,
                 ULONG                      ulFlags,
                 ULONG *                    pcPropNames,
                 LPMAPINAMEID **            pppPropNames) = 0;
```

```
virtual HRESULT GetIDsFromNames
                (ULONG                    cPropNames,
                 LPMAPINAMEID *           ppPropNames,
                 ULONG                    ulFlags,
                 LPSPropTagArray *        ppPropTags) = 0;
};
```

As you can see by the names of the *IMAPIProp* methods, this interface supports most of the operations you'll use to manipulate an object's data. Not all methods are equally useful to all objects, but some methods of *IMAPIProp* are required in order to achieve minimal functionality. If you are developing a service provider that implements objects derived from *IMAPIProp*, the methods you don't support can simply be stub functions that return an error (i.e., MAPI_E_NO_SUPPORT) to the user of the interface. The only methods you are required to implement are *IMAPIProp::GetProps*, *IMAPIProp::GetPropList*, *IMAPIProp::SetProps*, and *IMAPIProp::SaveChanges*. (For service providers that expose read-only objects, *IMAPIProp::SetProps* still needs to be implemented but should return MAPI_E_NO_ACCESS for all properties clients attempt to set.) The rest of the methods are considered optional, though support for *IMAPIProp::CopyProps*, *IMAPIProp::CopyTo*, *IMAPIProp::DeleteProps*, and *IMAPI-Prop::GetLastError* is highly recommended if these methods apply to the particular object in question. Callers of *IMAPIProp* methods must always be prepared to handle the MAPI_E_NO_SUPPORT error before proceeding to the next executable statement. The same principle of partial interface implementation applies to all MAPI interfaces: Consumers of MAPI objects must be prepared to handle method calls that, for one reason or another, aren't implemented by the provider.

Transacted and Nontransacted Objects

Modifications to a MAPI object's data can be *transacted*, meaning that changes to the data won't occur until they are explicitly committed. Some MAPI objects use the transacted model, and others don't: Those that do are called s*napshot* objects, and those that don't are called *multiview* objects.

Snapshot Objects

Snapshot objects contain unique copies of the entire data set they view or represent. (See Figure 2-2 on the following page.) If two objects, *A* and *B*, are looking at the same data, changes made by *A* are not immediately visible to *B*. *A*'s changes must be saved, or committed, before they are visible to *B*. Changes made to a snapshot object's data aren't permanent until the changes are committed. If multiple objects are modifying the same data concurrently, the last object to save wins. We'll examine this in some detail later.

An example of a snapshot object is a message (the *IMessage* interface), which represents a mail message in a store provider. Two message objects opened on the same physical data act independently of each other. Changes in one don't appear in the other, and modifications to the object's data are not permanent until the user of the message object commits its changes by calling the *SaveChanges* method. Other examples of transacted objects are message attachments (the *IAttach* interface) and address book provider entries (the *IMailUser* and *IDistList* interfaces).

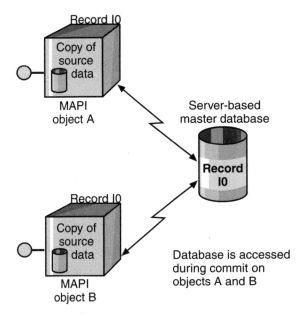

Figure 2-2.
Snapshot objects hold an entire copy of the data they represent. Changes to one of the data objects are independent of the other.

Multiview Objects

Multiview objects present a view of the same data regardless of the number of objects viewing that data. Unlike snapshot objects, which contain unique copies of a data set, multiview objects share a single copy of the data they represent, so if objects *A* and *B* are opened, changes to *A* are immediately reflected in *B*. (See Figure 2-3 on the facing page.) This implies that changes to multiview objects are not transacted, and hence any modification to the data is immediately and permanently saved to the object's storage medium. In this nontransaction model, consumers of multiview objects must be careful about how they modify the object's data—there are no rollback mechanisms once a change is made.

MAPI specifies that some objects be multiview to facilitate implementation of the *IMAPIProp* interface for existing data sources that aren't transacted. Some data sources can potentially grow very large, making it almost impossible to implement an efficient transaction model on top of an existing database system. An example of this kind of object is a folder (the *IMAPIFolder* interface), which is a store provider object containing messages and other folders. A complete folder hierarchy tree, including all children, grandchildren, and so on, can grow to be very large. If the folder object were transacted, changing a leaf node of the tree would require a transaction on its parent folder, which would cause a transaction on the grandparent, and so on, making the implementation an unwieldy mess. Other objects that fit this model include the message store provider object (the *IMsgStore* interface), the address book objects (the *IAddrBook* and *IABContainer* interfaces), the providers, and the system status object (the *IMAPIStatus* interface).

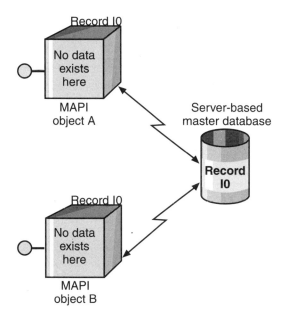

Figure 2-3.
Multiview objects are simply a reflection (or view) of the data they represent. The database is accessed every time something is requested on A or B so that changes to one of the objects are reflected immediately in the other.

A Closer Look at MAPI Properties

So far we have presented MAPI objects as entities that contain data and implement standard methods to manipulate that data. But how is this data presented to the consumer? MAPI specifies a uniform way for encapsulating data that is read or written to an object. Data in a MAPI object is viewed by the outside world (i.e., outside the implementation's internal representation) as *properties*. A property is simply a data structure that holds the raw bytes of data and some information about how to interpret those bytes. The data can be of any data type: either an intrinsic data type such as int or float or a user-defined type such as a string, metafile, or wave file. The property data structure defined by MAPI is *SPropValue* and has the following definition:

```
typedef union _PV
{
    short int           i;
    LONG                l;
    ULONG               ul;
    float               flt;
    double              dbl;
    unsigned short int  b;
    CURRENCY            cur;
    double              at;
    FILETIME            ft;
    LPSTR               lpszA;
    SBinary             bin;
    LPWSTR              lpszW;
    LPGUID              lpguid;
    LARGE_INTEGER       li;
    SShortArray         MVi;
    SLongArray          MVl;
    SRealArray          MVflt;
    SDoubleArray        MVdbl;
    SCurrencyArray      MVcur;
    SAppTimeArray       MVat;
    SDateTimeArray      MVft;
    SBinaryArray        MVbin;
    SLPSTRArray         MVszA;
    SWStringArray       MVszW;
    SGuidArray          MVguid;
    SLargeIntegerArray  MVli;
    SCODE               err;
    LONG                x;
} __UPV;

typedef struct _SPropValue
{
    ULONG        ulPropTag;
```

```
    ULONG        dwAlignPad;
    union _PV    Value;
} SPropValue, *LPSPropValue;
```

The data represented by the property is stored in the *Value* member. This member is a union of the different types of data or data structures that a property can hold. The *ulPropTag* member identifies the data type and is used to discriminate which member of the union holds the data.

The *ulPropTag* member contains a 32-bit unsigned integer called a *property tag*. The lower 16 bits of a property tag is the *property type*, which indicates the data type. The available property types and their corresponding members in the *Value* union are listed in the table in Figure 2-4 on the following page.

The upper 16 bits of a property tag comprise the *property ID*. The property ID is a number from 0 through 0xFFFF that allows us to distinguish properties from one another. The property ID space is split into logical property ID *ranges* according to which object or MAPI component is associated with the given property. In Figure 2-4 on the following page, we show how the different data types map to the members in the *SPropValue.Value* union. Notice that the PT_MV_XXX property types and their corresponding members are conspicuously absent from the table. These missing members are used to store what MAPI calls *multivalue* properties, which simply means that a single property tag holds several values. For example, a multivalue version of the property tag PR_OFFICE_TELEPHONE_NUMBER would hold several phone numbers. (Multivalue properties are discussed in more detail in Appendix B.)

Most property tags are defined by MAPI. These predefined tags include the usual properties for messages, folders, address book entries, system attributes, and so on. The predefined properties are defined with the prefix PR_ to indicate that they are properties. For example, MAPI defines the property PR_CREATION_TIME, which has a property tag of 0x30070040. The property ID is 0x3007, and the type is 0x0040 (PT_SYSTIME). From the table in Figure 2-4, we know that PT_SYSTIME properties store their data in the *ft* member of the *Value* union. You would access the data for *SPropValue* containing the PR_CREATION_TIME property like this:

```
LPSPropValue pProp;
// Code to get the data from the object
  ⋮
if (PR_CREATION_TIME == pProp -> ulPropTag)
{
    FILETIME ft = pProp -> Value.ft;
    // Code to use ft
      ⋮
}
  ⋮
```

35

Note that before using the property's data, you must make sure that *IMAPIProp* did indeed return the property you requested—you can't blindly assume that the property value is there. In the case of nonpointer property types such as PT_LONG and PT_BOOLEAN, using the property value without first checking whether the requested property was returned would cause the code to behave erratically. In the case of pointer property types such as PT_BINARY and PT_STRING8, using an invalid pointer indiscriminately could cause access violations or crashes.

Property Type	Description	Data Member in Value Union
PT_UNSPECIFIED	Reserved for interface use	*x*
PT_NULL	Null property value	*x*
PT_I2, PT_SHORT	Signed 16-bit value	*i*
PT_I4, PT_LONG	Signed or unsigned 32-bit value	*l, ul*
PT_R4, PT_FLOAT	34-bit floating point	*flt*
PT_R8, PT_DOUBLE	Floating point double	*dbl*
PT_CURRENCY	Signed 64-bit integer	*cur*
PT_APPTIME	Application time	*at*
PT_ERROR	32-bit error value	*err*
PT_BOOLEAN	16-bit Boolean (nonzero true)	*b*
PT_OBJECT	Embedded object in a property	*x*
PT_I8, PT_LONGLONG	64-bit signed integer	*li*
PT_STRING8	Null-terminated 8-bit character string	*lpszA*
PT_UNICODE	Null-terminated Unicode string	*lpszW*
PT_SYSTIME	FILETIME 64-bit integer with number of 100 nanosecond periods since Jan 1, 1601	*ft*
PT_CLSID	OLE GUID	*lpguid*
PT_BINARY	Counted byte array; binary large object (blob)	*bin*

Figure 2-4.
Types of property data and their corresponding SPropValue data members.

36

Standard Properties vs. Custom Properties

MAPI defines property tags for most common or generic attributes of messaging objects. For example, MAPI defines property tags for attributes such as a message's subject, its size, the number of messages in a folder, and so on. More specialized attributes associated with specific objects are not completely specified, however.

Some properties, such as PR_DISPLAY_NAME and PR_ENTRYID, are common to most MAPI objects. Others are specific to providers or to particular objects. PR_EMAIL_ADDRESS, for example, is a message recipient property; it has no meaning when applied to an attachment object. At an even more detailed level, some properties can be associated with specific message classes. A *message class* is a string property that identifies a particular type of message. Generic email messages that arrive in the user's Inbox are of class IPM.Note. Each class has a set of specialized properties associated with it, and messages of the class are expected to support at least some of the class's properties. IPM.Note messages typically have a PR_BODY property containing a clear text version of the message content, but PR_BODY probably wouldn't apply to a class whose messages consist of wave files.

Message classes let vendors whose applications send or receive specialized MAPI messages publish custom property tags specific to their applications. An application handling messages of that class knows in which properties the message object stores required data. MAPI reserves the 0x6800 through 0x7FFF property ID range for message class properties.

Providers can also define custom properties not associated with a message class using the standard property types (PT_XXX) but with property IDs from a different range. MAPI defines property ID ranges for the providers' use and also for transmittable and nontransmittable properties of messages. A client or provider can also ask the *IMAPIProp* interface to generate an ID on the fly, given a well-known name string. This last type of custom property is called a *named property,* and it is used to extend the set of MAPI-defined properties. (We discuss this property tag type in detail in Appendix A.)

The table in Figure 2-5 on the following page shows the ranges that MAPI has established for defining custom properties. Each range has particular attributes and rules associated with it that must be followed by anyone defining custom properties. If you need to define your own property tag, make sure that you pick an ID from the range that suits your needs. All the ranges are inclusive, meaning that the range includes the boundary values as valid IDs.

Property ID Range	Description
0x4000 through 0x57FF	Used by transports to define custom message envelope properties. Properties defined in this range are transmitted.
0x5800 through 0x5FFF	Used by transports to define custom properties associated with each recipient. Properties defined in this range are not transmitted.
0x6000 through 0x65FF	Custom properties defined by anyone. Properties defined in this range can be set on any object, but they will not be transmitted by a transport when set on message objects.
0x6600 through 0x67FF	Used by any MAPI service provider for anything it needs—for example, to define configuration properties. Properties in this range are not transmitted by a transport.
0x6800 through 0x7BFF	Used by anyone defining a message class other than IPM.Note. The properties in this range *are* transmitted when the message is sent out.
0x7C00 through 0x7FFF	Used by anyone defining a message class other than IPM.Note. The properties in this range *are not* transmitted by a transport.
0x8000 through 0xFFFE	Used by the MAPI object implementation to assign IDs on named properties. When set on messages, the property ID of the custom property tag is not transmitted, but the name is.

Figure 2-5.
Defined ranges for property IDs.

To illustrate the use of the property ranges in Figure 2-5, consider the following example. A developer is writing a transport provider for dial-up connections. One of the properties that is unique to this type of transport is the phone number of the server to which it connects. The developer of the service provider might want to store this configuration information with MAPI to facilitate automatic logon. To do so, the developer defines a custom property by combining a property ID from the range 0x6600 through 0x67FF—for example, 0x6610—with the property type PT_STRING8:

```
#define PR_MY_XP_SERVER_PHONE    PROP_TAG(PT_STRING8, 0x6610)
```

The *PROP_TAG* macro is defined by MAPI in the MAPIDEFS.H header file and does the bit-shifting of the property tag and the property ID. This same technique is used if you are defining custom properties for a particular message class, except that the property ID is taken from the 0x6800 through 0x7BFF or 0x7C00 through 0x7FFF range.

Object Identification: Entry Identifiers

There are all kinds of objects in the MAPI architecture. Some MAPI objects are containers of potentially thousands of objects. For example, a store provider can contain hundreds of folders and thousands of messages. How do you tell MAPI you want to access a specific object, and how does MAPI tell the objects apart? Each of these objects always has an intrinsic property, a binary token, that gives it a unique identity in the collection in which it resides. This property is called the *entry identifier* (entry ID), and its property tag is PR_ENTRYID. Its uniqueness is guaranteed by the service provider such that no two existing objects it supplies can ever have the same entry ID.

Entry IDs are partially meaningful to MAPI and client applications but are fully interpreted only by the provider that implements the corresponding object. An exception to this rule is the following: An attachment object (the *IAttach* interface) does not have an entry ID because it's considered to be an extended property of a message object and therefore does not have its own identity but rather one derived from the parent message.

Components of an Entry Identifier

The entry ID of an object is a data structure defined by MAPI as follows:

```
typedef struct
{
    BYTE    abFlags[4];
    BYTE    ab[1];
} ENTRYID, *LPENTRYID;
```

The *abFlags* and *ab* members contain data that MAPI and clients can interpret. The *abFlags* member holds a bitmap of flags that identify certain attributes of the entry ID. Clients and MAPI use this value to determine how long the information that the entry ID supplies is valid. The *ab* member is the beginning of a GUID that identifies the provider that supplies this object. MAPI uses this GUID to route and forward client requests to the provider that is supplying the object.

After the *ab* member, service providers are free to append any members needed to identify the object within its own storage. Following is an example of how a message store provider could define its entry ID structure:

```
typedef struct _PRIVATE_ENTRYID
{
    // MAPI-required fields
    BYTE          abFlags[4];
    MAPIUID       uidGlobal;          // This maps to the ab member.
    // Provider-defined fields
    BYTE          bVersion;           // Version of the schema
    BYTE          bObject;            // Object type
    BYTE          bPad[2];            // Alignment pad
    DWORD         dwRecordID;         // Object ID in database
} PRIVATE_ENTRYID;
```

Entry IDs are created by service providers. Clients do not compose an entry ID structure; they must obtain it from the object or from the list of a container's child objects. The service provider can put anything it wants after the MAPI-defined members: The data is interpreted only by the provider. When an entry ID is retrieved, it comes back in a blob of binary data—for example, *SPropValue.Value.bin.lpb*. The blob is typecast to the *ENTRYID* type, which imposes the *ENTRYID* structure on the data.

Types of Entry Identifiers

The entry IDs returned to a client by a service provider can be of several types, depending on how the client obtains that entry ID. The type of entry ID is marked in the *abFlags[0]* member of the *ENTRYID* structure. The possible bits for this member are the following:

- MAPI_SHORTTERM
- MAPI_NOTRECIP
- MAPI_THISSESSION
- MAPI_NOW
- MAPI_NOTRESERVED

Of these possible bits, two of the most important characteristics that can be obtained are the entry ID longevity across time and the entry ID validity across MAPI sessions. With respect to longevity, entry IDs can be of two kinds: long-term entry IDs (if the MAPI_SHORTTERM bit is not present in *abFlags[0]*) and short-term entry IDs (if the MAPI_SHORTTERM bit is present in *abFlags[0]*).

Long-term entry IDs are valid for as long as the object exists in the service provider that holds it. They must be valid across MAPI sessions, so, for example, a client can save the long-term entry ID of an open folder to permanent storage and then later retrieve it to get the same folder and restore the client's display state. When an object is deleted, its entry ID becomes invalid. Providers are encouraged, though not required, to avoid reusing a long-term entry ID after the object has been deleted and to keep the long-term entry ID when an object is moved from one container to another.

Short- and long-term entry IDs give developers flexibility in implementing service providers. Supplying a short-term entry ID is efficient because it is faster to compute, saves memory consumption, and reduces network traffic. The provider computes and returns a long-term entry ID only if specifically requested.

Miscellaneous Identity Properties

In addition to entry IDs, MAPI defines a few other properties to help identify MAPI objects and their data.

PR_SEARCH_KEY

This property is a special binary token that most objects have. For message store providers, the search key is used to identify the data item to which an object refers. For example, suppose you have an object that holds a data set *A*. Another object is created and the contents of the first object are copied onto the new object. The second object will also hold the same data set *A*, so the PR_SEARCH_KEY property on both objects would be the same. A message store service provider typically assigns a GUID to this property's value to ensure its uniqueness. On address book provider objects (i.e., *IMailUser* and *IDistList* interfaces), the value for PR_SEARCH_KEY is computed by the provider using a special rule. We will discuss this later.

PR_RECORD_KEY

This property is also a special binary token that is present on most message store provider objects. It is used to uniquely identify an object within the entire store provider database. By looking at the definition of this property, you wouldn't necessarily see the difference between it and the entry ID. The difference is that the record key is a *binary-comparable* property that clients can use to distinguish two objects (e.g., by using *memcmp*). The entry IDs cannot be directly compared by a client to distinguish two objects because a given object might have different entry IDs. A client must ask the service provider or MAPI to do the comparison. An object's long-term and short-term entry IDs do not have the same binary value even though they refer to the same object.

A store provider guarantees that no two existing objects can ever have the same record key. We must point out that the uniqueness of the record key only applies to the original message in the same store provider. Two objects from two different store provider instances might have the same record key.

PR_STORE_RECORD_KEY

This property is similar to PR_RECORD_KEY except that it is used to distinguish two different message store providers, and it offers a binary-comparable property to clients. This property is available in all objects supplied by a store provider to identify the store provider that created the original object.

Manipulating the Object Properties: *IMAPIProp* Details

We've talked about objects, data, and properties as separate things and mentioned the *IMAPIProp* interface and given its abstract definition. Now you need an explanation of each method in that interface and a demonstration of how to apply the concepts covered so far. First, though, it's important to discuss issues that affect how we interact with every MAPI interface.

How MAPI Returns Errors

In an ideal world, things never fail—computers have limitless memory, hard drives never fill up, networks never go down, and programs never have bugs. In the real world, things fail all the time, and good programs should be robust enough to handle failures gracefully. For this reason, all MAPI methods return an error status to indicate success or failure. When a failure occurs, a MAPI interface can tell the client exactly what happened. The client can then attempt to recover or display additional information to the user or, even better, work around the error if possible.

MAPI uses and extends the COM error-handling framework where the return value of an interface method is always a type LONG value known as an HRESULT. The HRESULT information returned by a service provider is broken up into groups of bits that convey information about the call's success or failure and an interface-specific error code. (Since we target Win32 programmers as the main audience of this book, we won't discuss the Win16 counterpart, SCODEs. In Win32, SCODEs and HRESULTs are interchangeable and equivalent.)

COM methods can be completely successful or partially successful, or they can fail altogether. Complete failure is indicated when the high order (or severity bit) of an HRESULT is set. If the severity bit is clear but the rest of the bits are nonzero, then the call was partially successful. Only when the entire return value is 0 (S_OK is the constant used) does the client know that the method was completely successful. To test return values from interface methods returning HRESULTs, COM defines the following macros:

- *FAILED.* Returns *TRUE* to indicate that the severity bit field is 1, meaning that the method call failed. If the method call is at least partially successful, the macro returns *FALSE.*

- *SUCCEEDED.* Returns *TRUE* if the severity bit field is 0, meaning that the method call was partially or completely successful.

In cases where a client expects complete success, the return code should be tested against S_OK, not using the macros.

Deferring Errors

MAPI object implementations can defer returning error codes when the processing done by a method is asynchronous. This technique allows them to return success (S_OK) without actually finishing the task, but also allows the implementation to buffer the request or complete it in the background and return any errors about it in a later method call.

The implementation must not defer errors unless the client application allows it to do so. The client gives the object the opportunity to defer errors by passing the flag MAPI_DEFERRED_ERRORS in methods that take flags as parameters.

When a method is called with deferred errors, if the method arguments are correct and there are enough resources to buffer the request, the method returns S_OK. If the method fails after the call is returned to the client, the next method called on that object returns the error of the previous call. This complicates the error recovery logic of the client.

Client applications are encouraged to allow the service provider to handle deferred error processing because doing so can improve performance. If the service provider used does not support deferred error processing, it will simply ignore the flag and return the error right after the method call. For server-based MAPI service providers (e.g., Exchange Server), using deferred errors improves the scalability of the server by reducing the RPCs to the server, which in turn improves the performance of all applications using the server.

The MAPI-defined errors returned by MAPI interface methods are named MAPI_E_XXX. Partial success is indicated by returning a warning (MAPI_W_XXX). These constants are defined in the file MAPICODE.H.

The *GetLastError* Method

A client application that provides a user interface must obtain all the information it can from the object when an error occurs so that the user can take appropriate actions. MAPI applications that run unattended are also likely to want to obtain detailed information on error conditions so anomalies can be logged or forwarded as appropriate. MAPI defines a set of standard error codes for use by MAPI interfaces, and an interface method should return the error code that most closely describes the cause of the error. But because the predefined error codes are general, it can be difficult to determine why an error occurred by only examining the return value. Sometimes more information is needed, especially when displaying UI to the user.

The *IMAPIProp* interface (and some other MAPI interfaces) defines the *GetLastError* method for precisely this reason. This method is used by a client to obtain a textual description and context information about an error that has just occurred in a service provider. The semantics of this method are similar to the Win32 API *GetLastError*, except that in the case of MAPI, the error returned is from a given MAPI object without regard to what thread, client, or application is using it.

To use this method, a client must receive the error code from a method on the object in use. For example, if two similar objects, *A* and *B*, exist and an error occurs in object *A*, only object *A* would return the correct information in its *GetLastError* call. Calling object *B*'s *GetLastError* with the error code of object *A* could not return the correct information because the objects are not aware of each other's error conditions.

A client passes the error code returned from a method to *GetLastError*, which returns the error description. Following is a client-side code fragment to show how this is done:

```
LPMESSAGE pMsgObj;
// Code to get an IMessage object
:
HRESULT hResult = pMsgObj -> GetProps(…);    // Discussed later
if (FAILED(hResult))
{
    LPMAPIERROR pErr;
    if (S_OK == pMsgObj -> GetLastError(hResult, 0, &pErr))
```

```
    {
        // Use and/or display the information in
        // the MAPIERROR structure.
        ⋮
    }
}
⋮
```

As you can see in the previous code, the call to *GetLastError* returns a pointer to a *MAPIERROR* structure, which holds the information about the error that just occurred. This structure is defined by MAPI as follows:

```
typedef struct _MAPIERROR
{
    ULONG   ulVersion;
    LPTSTR  lpszError;
    LPTSTR  lpszComponent;
    ULONG   ulLowLevelError;
    ULONG   ulContext;
} MAPIERROR, *LPMAPIERROR;
```

The textual description of the cause or nature of the error is returned in the *lpszError* member, which could be used by client applications to display a message box to the user. The other members contain information specific to the object implementation. The primary purpose of these members is to enhance the troubleshooting process and product support by associating errors seen by the user with specific locations and situations in the code. Service providers usually define specific contexts for common error codes. The better the error context is defined, the easier it is to pinpoint the error location and determine the cause of the error.

Error Codes on Interfaces

Each method of a MAPI interface has a set of MAPI-defined error codes that can be returned for certain conditions and for which the caller might want to take specific action. Outside of those conditions, implementations can return any error that makes sense for a given situation, including custom HRESULTs (which are defined by following the specified rules for creating new HRESULTs).

MAPI defines all success codes (including warnings) for any method in its interfaces. COM interface rules dictate that the set of success codes for an interface is fixed; implementations cannot add new success codes, although they can add new failure codes.

The MAPI Memory Management Model

Memory management is one of the most important issues in the design of an API. This is especially true for MAPI because memory is often allocated by a service provider and passed to a client that is then responsible for freeing the allocation. MAPI enforces some rules that make clear who owns a block of memory, how that memory is allocated, and how and when the memory can be freed.

The MAPI memory management scheme simplifies allocating and freeing memory and addresses the needs of both client applications and service providers. It involves only three functions: *MAPIAllocateBuffer*, *MAPIAllocateMore*, and *MAPIFreeBuffer*. These are used as follows: Any memory allocated with either of the first two functions can be deallocated by using the third without regard to whether a client or provider originally allocated it. This facilitates transfers of blocks of memory between providers and clients. For example, if a client requests properties from an object, the object allocates the necessary block of memory using the MAPI memory management APIs and returns the block to the client. From then on, the object implementation is no longer responsible for that block; the responsibility of freeing the memory rests on the client application.

Allocating Linked Memory Blocks

Allocating and freeing properties can be tedious and error prone. Using the MAPI memory management APIs makes this task a little less onerous. For example, suppose a client application requests a message object (the *IMessage* interface) to return the PR_DISPLAY_TO, PR_SENDER_NAME, and PR_SUBJECT properties. Each of these properties is of type PT_STRING8 (or PT_UNICODE if the client supports Unicode), meaning that the actual data bytes are stored in arrays of characters. (See Figure 2-6 on the facing page.)

The message object returning these properties allocates an array of three *SPropValue* structures and arrays of characters for the data in each property structure. After this is done and the data is copied, all the allocated blocks of memory are returned to the client application.

The problem comes when the client is ready to free these separate memory blocks, because it must walk the entire array of properties, check the type in the property tag member to determine whether the data value is a pointer to another memory block, and free the block if it is. In addition, the client has to remember how many properties were in a given *SPropValue* array so it can iterate through the array's contents. *And,* it must carry this information around as long as it holds the *SPropValue* array.

Array of properties

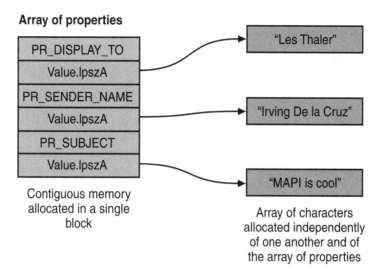

Figure 2-6.
The memory arrangement of a property array, with the data requested of a MAPI object by a MAPI client.

For this reason, MAPI devised the concept of linked memory blocks. A linked memory block is a chunk of memory allocated with the *MAPIAllocate-More* function. It is linked to an existing chunk of memory that was allocated with *MAPIAllocateBuffer.* Any number of memory blocks can be linked together, but all of them can have only one parent memory block, as shown in Figure 2-7.

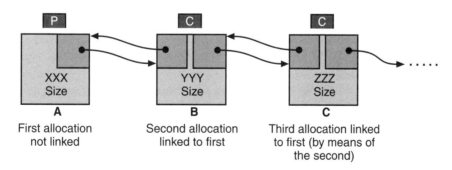

Figure 2-7.
A graphical representation of the chain created by using MAPI memory management functions. The links and MAPI information about each block are managed by MAPI and are totally transparent to the user.

Releasing this chain of memory allocations is accomplished by a single call. When the memory blocks are no longer needed, only the parent allocation needs to be released with *MAPIFreeBuffer*—internally, MAPI frees all the blocks that were chained to the parent allocation. Note that nodes in the chain cannot be deleted by themselves, nor can they be resized. Once a block of memory is allocated and linked, it will remain in the chain until the parent link is released. Releasing a node in a chain causes *MAPIFreeBuffer* to return an error, and nothing is freed.

Rule for Allocating a Memory Block

In a chain of MAPI-allocated memory blocks, the parent link node must be allocated with the *MAPIAllocateBuffer* function. Any other blocks linked to the chain must be allocated with the *MAPIAllocateMore* function. Each node cannot be resized, and each child link node cannot be released until the entire chain is released, which is accomplished by releasing the parent link node.

NOTE: If you are writing a client application, the memory management functions are used just like standard API functions and are imported from MAPI32.LIB when the application is linked. In the case of service providers, MAPI will pass function pointers to each of these APIs during the initialization of the provider. The provider implementation must save them for later use. Service providers cannot use the API functions directly, as clients do.

Now let's see how the client application example mentioned earlier can be coded to use the MAPI memory management functions. The following is a code fragment in an *IMAPIProp::GetProps* implementation on a service provider that assumes PR_DISPLAY_TO, PR_SENDER_NAME, and PR_SUBJECT were requested:

```
// For simplicity, we have not included the code to check for
// possible failures in the memory allocations.
// The m_szDisplayTo, m_szSender, and m_szSubject variables are
// the object data members that hold the strings that we'll return to
// the client.
// m_pfnMAPIAllocateBuffer, m_pfnMAPIAllocateMore, and
// m_pfnMAPIFreeBuffer are function pointers to the MAPI memory
// management APIs, which are passed to the provider during
// initialization.
⋮
```

```
LPSPropValue pProps;
ULONG ulSize = sizeof(SPropValue) * 3;
// Allocate an array of 3 SPropValue structures.
// This is the parent node of the allocation chain.
m_pfnMAPIAllocateBuffer(ulSize, (LPVOID *)&pProps);
pProps[0].ulPropTag = PR_DISPLAY_TO;
pProps[1].ulPropTag = PR_SENDER_NAME;
pProps[2].ulPropTag = PR_SUBJECT;

LPSTR pStr;
ulSize = sizeof(char) * (lstrlen(m_szDisplayTo) + 1);
// Allocate a child node for the string in the first
// property structure. This is linked to the parent.
m_pfnMAPIAllocateMore(ulSize, pProps, (LPVOID *)&pStr);
lstrcpy(pStr, m_szDisplayTo);
pProps[0].Value.lpszA = pStr;

ulSize = sizeof(char) * (lstrlen(m_szSender) + 1);
// Ditto for the second node
m_pfnMAPIAllocateMore(ulSize, pProps, (LPVOID *)&pStr);
lstrcpy(pStr, m_szSender);
pProps[1].Value.lpszA = pStr;

ulSize = sizeof(char) * (lstrlen(m_szSubject) + 1);
// Ditto for the third node
m_pfnMAPIAllocateMore(ulSize, pProps, (LPVOID *)&pStr);
lstrcpy(pStr, m_szSubject);
pProps[2].Value.lpszA = pStr;
    ⋮
```

When the client is finished using the returned properties, it simply calls *MAPIFreeBuffer* on the returned *pProps* pointer. This single call takes care of releasing the memory blocks for the strings in each of the data members of the individual properties.

There are also other benefits to using the MAPI memory management APIs. For example, the MAPI memory management functions provide leak detection and memory overrun detection using a virtual memory pool, which greatly simplify the task of tracking heap-corruption and overrun problems. Some of these topics are covered in later chapters.

Properties Available in an Object

A MAPI object is defined as an entity that holds data. This data is stored in the form of properties. A client application can obtain a MAPI object that holds some properties, but how does the client know what properties are available on an object? This is the purpose of *IMAPIProp::GetPropList*, which returns a list of property tags corresponding to the properties set on an object. The information is returned in the form of a *property tag array* (an *SPropTagArray*). MAPI defines this data structure as follows:

```
typedef struct _SPropTagArray
{
    ULONG    cValues;
    ULONG    aulPropTag[1];
} SPropTagArray, *LPSPropTagArray;
```

The structure and the *aulPropTag* member array are allocated by the object implementation and returned to the client. The client uses the information returned and releases the property tag array (using *MAPIFreeBuffer*) when finished. The client-side code looks like the following:

```
LPMESSAGE pMsgObj;
// Code to get an IMessage object
⋮
LPSPropTagArray pTags;
HRESULT hResult = pMsgObj -> GetPropList(0, &pTags);
if (S_OK == hResult)
{
    // Use pTags here.
    ⋮
    MAPIFreeBuffer(pTags);
}
else
{
    // Call pMsgObj -> GetLastError(…);
}
⋮
```

Service providers that implement this method must return the property tags for all properties in its current data set. Note that the call to *GetPropList* should never return a warning (i.e., partial success), so testing the return value against S_OK is a valid assumption.

Requesting Properties from an Object

Now that we have the list of properties, how do we ask the object to return the data for the properties in which we are interested? There are two methods for requesting properties stored in MAPI objects: *IMAPIProp::GetProps* and *IMAPIProp::OpenProperty*.

The *IMAPIProp::GetProps* method is used to obtain one or more properties in a single call. A client application passes an array of property tags (an *SPropTagArray*), and the object then returns an array of *SPropValue* structures containing the requested properties. A client passing an array of property tags in a given order should expect the property values to return in the same order. The MAPI object implementation is responsible for maintaining this order. If a property requested by a client is not currently available or for some reason could not be returned, the MAPI object should return the error information in that property's slot in the array. An error code describing why the property requested was not returned is set in the *err* member of the *Value* union of the *SPropValue* structure. To indicate that a property was not returned, the provider implementing a MAPI object changes the property tag type in the corresponding *SPropValue* structure to the type PT_ERROR. If some, but not all, properties are not returned, the *IMAPIProp::GetProps* method returns the warning error code MAPI_W_ERRORS_RETURNED to indicate partial success. The following code fragment shows how a provider sets the *ulPropTag* and *Value.err* members for a property that can't be returned in a call to *GetProps*:

```
// Code fragment in a service provider that cannot return
// PR_DISPLAY_NAME because it does not exist
LPSPropValue pProps;
HRESULT hResult;
⋮
enum
{
    ENTRYID,
    NAME,
    SIZE
};
// PR_DISPLAY_NAME is the 2nd property returned.
if (…)
{
    // Failed to get PR_DISPLAY_NAME
    pProps[NAME].ulPropTag = PROP_TAG(PT_ERROR, PROP_ID(PR_DISPLAY_NAME));
    pProps[NAME].Value.err = MAPI_E_NOT_FOUND;
    hResult = MAPI_W_ERRORS_RETURNED;
}
return hResult;
```

The memory for the property data is linked to the property array, so when a client is finished using the property data, everything is released with a call to *MAPIFreeBuffer.* Here is a code fragment that a client could use to retrieve properties from a MAPI object:

```
LPMAPIFOLDER pFldObj;
// Code to get an IMAPIFolder object
  :
enum
{
    COUNT,
    UNREAD,
    SIZE,
    NUM_PROPS
};
const static SizedSPropTagArray(NUM_PROPS, sptFolderPropTags) =
{
    NUM_PROPS,
    {
        PR_CONTENT_COUNT,
        PR_CONTENT_UNREAD,
        PR_DISPLAY_NAME
    }
};
LPSPropValue pProps;
ULONG ulCount;
HRESULT hResult = pFldObj -> GetProps
                    ((LPSPropTagArray)&sptFolderPropTags,
                     0,
                     &ulCount,
                     &pProps);
if (SUCCEEDED(hResult))
{
    // Before using the property, make sure it was returned by the
    // provider. A quick check of the property tag should suffice.
    if (PR_CONTENT_COUNT == pProps[COUNT].ulPropTag)
    {
        // Use the property value here.
    }
    if (PR_CONTENT_UNREAD == pProps[UNREAD].ulPropTag)
    {
        // Use the property value here.
    }
    if (PR_DISPLAY_NAME == pProps[READ].ulPropTag)
    {
        // Use the property value here.
    }
    MAPIFreeBuffer(pProps);
}
```

```
else
{
    // Call pFldObj -> GetLastError(…);
}
⋮
```

In the code above, we used the macro *SizedSPropTagArray*, which is defined by MAPI to help clients or providers define arrays of property tags that will be used in *IMAPIProp::GetProps*. Always use the *FAILED* or *SUCCEEDED* macros to test the return code. Nothing is allocated if *GetProps* fails; a client is responsible for freeing the property array if *GetProps* returns a warning or S_OK.

ANSI and Unicode Strings and *IMAPIProp::GetProps*

All the property tags for string properties have been defined for both ANSI and Unicode character sets. MAPI defines the properties in three forms: character set neutral, ANSI, and Unicode. If character set neutral property tags are used in a project, they default to ANSI or Unicode depending on whether the project is compiled for ANSI or Unicode. When a client application wants to specifically retrieve the Unicode version of a string property, it does so by using the Unicode version of the property tag. The Unicode property tags are of the form PR_XXX_W, where XXX is the name of the property. For example, the Unicode version of the display name property tag is PR_DISPLAY-_NAME_W. Likewise, the ANSI property tag is defined in the form PR_XXX_A, so to retrieve the ANSI version of PR_DISPLAY_NAME, for example, you would specify PR_DISPLAY_NAME_A. If the provider cannot supply the property string value in the required character set specified by the client, it will return the error MAPI_E_BAD_CHAR-WIDTH for each failed string property in the *Value.err* member of the property structure.

Retrieving Large Data Properties

Sometimes an object holds a property that contains a very large data value, or the property is the representation of another object embedded in the first. Consider, for example, the message body property PR_BODY. Potentially, this property data can grow to be several kilobytes or megabytes (depending on the sender), thus making a call to *GetProps* ineffective at getting and returning it in a single memory block. For efficiency and performance reasons, the provider shouldn't allocate valuable memory, copy the entire data of the property, and return it to the client. Instead, the client can request that a different interface be used to manipulate the data of the property in small pieces. This is why the *IMAPIProp::OpenProperty* method exists. This method gives the client the opportunity to *open* a property and examine the data using a more suitable interface. Service providers that implement the *IMAPIProp* interface can limit the amount of data they return in a property during a call to *GetProps*. Typically, this threshold is anywhere between 4 KB and 16 KB. When a property contains data that is larger than the threshold of the provider, the provider should return the E_OUTOFMEMORY error code in the property value list for that particular property to inform the client application that it should use an alternate method to retrieve the information. (E_OUTOFMEMORY is identical to MAPI_E-_NOT_ENOUGH_MEMORY. See MAPICODE.H for more information.)

OLE defines the *IStream* interface, which is ideal for manipulating large amounts of data available in the properties of MAPI objects. (Refer to the OLE Programmer's Reference in the Win32 SDK documentation for information about this interface.) A client application would then use *IMAPIProp-::OpenProperty* and request an *IStream* interface be opened on the desired property. The client would then use the *IStream::Read, IStream::Seek,* and *IStream::Stat* methods to retrieve the data stored in the property. (The *Stat* method is not always implemented, so be on the lookout for this condition.) A typical situation in which a client needs to use *OpenProperty* instead of *GetProps* is in the retrieval of PR_BODY (PR_RTF_COMPRESSED for RTF-aware clients), which holds the message body text. (RTF means Rich Text Format. Refer to the MSDN for more information on the specification of this format.) The following code fragment shows how this is done by a client:

```
LPMESSAGE pMsgObj;
// Code to get an IMessage object
⋮
LPSTREAM pStream;
HRESULT hResult = pMsgObj -> OpenProperty
                            (PR_BODY,
                             &IID_IStream,
                             STGM_READ | STGM_DIRECT,
                             MAPI_DEFERRED_ERRORS,
                             (LPUNKNOWN *)&pStream);
if (S_OK == hResult) // No warnings are returned in this call.
{
    hResult = pStream -> Read(…); // Read the data and use it.
    pStream -> Release();
}
```

```
else
{
    // Call pMsgObj -> GetLastError(…);
}
⋮
```

If an implementation cannot open the specified property with the requested interface, it will return the error E_NOINTERFACE. (E_NOINTERFACE is identical to MAPI_E_INTERFACE_NOT_SUPPORTED.) *OpenProperty* is not valid for all property types. Multivalue properties or properties of type PT_LONG, for example, cannot have interfaces opened on them, and a service provider implementation will return E_NOINTERFACE if a client calls *OpenProperty* on them. This method can be used only on properties of type PT_OBJECT, PT_STRING8, PT_UNICODE, or PT_BINARY—any other property type will return E_NOINTERFACE.

Setting Properties on an Object

To set properties on a MAPI object, a client application uses the *IMAPIProp-::SetProps* method, which takes an array of *SPropValue* structures initialized by a client with the appropriate data. The implementation of the object copies the data to its internal storage, making the new properties available for future client requests. The client-side code to execute this action looks like the following fragment:

```
LPATTACH pAttObj;
char szFile[MAX_PATH];
// Code to get an IAttach interface
⋮
LPSPropProblemArray pProblems = NULL;
SPropValue spvProps[3] = { 0 };
spvProps[0].ulPropTag = PR_DISPLAY_NAME;
spvProps[0].Value.lpszA = "Attached File";
spvProps[1].ulPropTag = PR_ATTACH_FILENAME;
spvProps[1].Value.lpszA = szFile;
spvProps[2].ulPropTag = PR_ATTACH_METHOD;
spvProps[2].Value.l = ATTACH_BY_REFERENCE;
HRESULT hResult = pAttObj -> SetProps
                            (3,
                             spvProps,
                             &pProblems);
```

(continued)

55

```
if (S_OK == hResult) // No warnings returned in this call
{
    if (pProblems)
    {
        // Find out which properties failed.
        ⋮
        MAPIFreeBuffer(pProblems);
    }
}
else
{
    // Call pAttObj -> GetLastError(…);
}
⋮
```

A request to set properties on an object can be partially honored by an implementation, depending on what properties are being stored. Some implementations allow only certain properties to be set; others allow only MAPI-defined properties to be set. But most implementations allow a client application to set any arbitrary property that is not computed internally by the object. We must also point out that *IMAPIProp::SetProps* has the same rules as *GetProps* for setting properties that are too large (i.e., larger than the provider's threshold). When large properties cannot be set with *SetProps*, the provider returns the specific error code in the problem array returned to the client.

Computed Properties

Some properties represent intrinsic attributes of MAPI objects and should be present at all times. They are called computed properties, and PR_ENTRYID and PR_RECORD_KEY are two examples. The term *computed* is used because the service provider implementing the interface is the only one that can set, modify, and alter the properties' values. For example, it would not make sense for a client application to be allowed to arbitrarily change the value of an object's entry ID, since the provider would then be unable to identify the indicated object.

When a call to *SetProps* fails to set one or more properties on a MAPI object, the service provider returns an array of structures (an *SPropProblemArray*) that describe the reason for the failure(s). The *SPropProblemArray* is a counted array of data structures (called *SPropProblems*) in which the actual error codes for each failure are returned. These structures are defined as follows:

```
typedef struct _SPropProblem
{
    ULONG    ulIndex;
    ULONG    ulPropTag;
    SCODE    scode;
} SPropProblem, *LPSPropProblem;

typedef struct _SPropProblemArray
{
    ULONG         cProblem;
    SPropProblem  aProblem[1];
} SPropProblemArray, *LPSPropProblemArray;
```

If one or more of the properties cannot be set (e.g., the property is computed), the service provider implementing *IMAPIProp::SetProps* allocates an *SPropProblemArray* large enough to hold one problem per failure. In each entry the provider stores the error code (in the *scode* member), the failed property's property tag, and the index into the *SPropValue* array of the errant property.

A client calling *IMAPIProp::SetProps* is not required to pass a pointer to accommodate the *SPropProblemArray* and should pass NULL if the information is not needed. If the client passes a valid pointer to an *SPropProblemArray* and the returned pointer is non-NULL, the client must release the allocated memory using *MAPIFreeBuffer*. Applications using the returned problem array can do so if and only if the *SetProps* call returns S_OK. If the function fails, the client application should not use the problem array and should assume the service provider did not allocate one.

It is important to note that the *SPropValue* array holding the properties to be set in the object does not need to be allocated with the MAPI memory management functions. In fact, it does not need to be allocated dynamically at all. As demonstrated earlier, the array can be declared on the stack. The same applies to the data to be set on each of the properties. The *SetProps* implementation is required to make a copy of any data passed to it, so the client need only guarantee that the data structures stay in scope for the duration of the method call.

Setting Large Properties

Just as it is not efficient for *IMAPIProp* implementations to return large data properties in the *GetProps* call, it is cumbersome, tedious, and inefficient for both service providers and clients to set very large properties using *IMAPIProp::SetProps*. For this reason, when a client application needs to store a property containing a large data value, it should use the *IMAPIProp::OpenProperty* method.

Clients should first open an appropriate interface on the desired property (using *OpenProperty*) and then use the new interface to store the data in the object. This same method should be used when a client needs to embed another object as the data of a property—for example, an embedded OLE object as the attachment in a message.

When setting large properties on a new object, the client must specify two extra flags in the *OpenProperty* call: MAPI_MODIFY and MAPI_CREATE. These indicate that the client needs read/write access to the interface returned, and if the object implementation can't find the property, it should create a new one. Here is a code fragment that makes the client-side call to open an attachment property on an object and store data in it:

```
// In the code below, m_pSrcStorage holds an IStorage interface on a
// file that will be added to the attachment in a message.
LPATTACH pAttObj;
// Code to get an IAttach interface
⋮
LPSTORAGE pStorage;
HRESULT hResult = pAttObj -> OpenProperty
                            (PR_ATTACH_DATA_OBJ,
                             &IID_IStorage,
                             STGM_READWRITE | STGM_DIRECT,
                             MAPI_DEFERRED_ERRORS |
                             MAPI_CREATE |
                             MAPI_MODIFY,
                             (LPUNKNOWN *)&pStorage);
if (S_OK == hResult) // No warnings are returned in this call.
{
    m_pSrcStorage -> CopyTo(pStorage);
    pStorage -> Commit(STGC_DEFAULT);
    pStorage -> Release();
}
else
{
    // Call pAttObj -> GetLastError(…);
}
⋮
```

Finally, MAPI objects allow client applications to set properties only if the application opened the object with write access. Read-only objects return the error E_ACCESSDENIED. (E_ACCESSDENIED is identical to MAPI_E_NO-_ACCESS.) The desired access level is requested when the application opens a given object. (We will discuss this in more detail later.) Clients determine the access level of an object dynamically by requesting the PR_ACCESS_LEVEL property. If the value stored is 0, the object is read-only. If the value is equal to the constant MAPI_MODIFY, then the object will allow setting new properties. Alternatively, clients can request PR_ACCESS. The return value is a bitmap of flags indicating multiple attributes of the object. If the returned value has the MAPI_ACCESS_MODIFY bit set, the object allows setting properties. These two properties, PR_ACCESS and PR_ACCESS_LEVEL, are part of the intrinsic attributes of most MAPI objects. Clients cannot set their values to change the access level dynamically, as this attribute is determined by the service provider.

IStream and *IStorage* on Opened Properties

Microsoft has implemented a version of the *IStream* and *IStorage* interfaces known as *compound files*. This is the implementation returned by the OLE APIs *StgCreateDocfile* and *StgOpenStorage*. In this implementation of *IStream* and *IStorage*, the *IStream* interface isn't transacted and, therefore, calls to *IStream::Commit* are unnecessary. *IStorage* can be opened using the transaction model for changes, requiring applications to save modifications to the object by calling *IStorage::Commit*.

MAPI service providers supplying implementations of *IMAPIProp* return private *IStream* and *IStorage* implementations that might differ from the OLE compound files implementation. In other words, both *IStream* and *IStorage* may be transacted, depending on the implementations. For this reason, clients should always call the *Commit* method on *IStream* and *IStorage* interfaces returned in an *IMAPIProp::Open-Property* call if the property data is modified.

Deleting Properties in an Object

Client applications can also delete an object's properties by calling the *IMAPIProp::DeleteProps* method. The caller creates an array of property tags (an *SPropTagArray*) listing the properties to be deleted. If the requested properties are not among the computed ones, they are deleted. If one or more properties cannot be deleted, the implementation returns an array of problems (an *SPropProblemArray*) following the same rules as for *IMAPIProp::SetProps*. Even if none of the properties can be deleted, the call to *DeleteProps* returns S_OK, but with all of the requested properties specified in the problem array. The client-side code to delete properties looks like this:

```
LPMESSAGE pMsgObj;
// Code to get an IMessage object
⋮
const static SizedSPropTagArray(3, sptSenderPropTags) =
{
    3,
    {
        PR_SENDER_NAME,
        PR_SENDER_EMAIL_ADDRESS,
        PR_SENDER_ENTRYID
    }
};
LPSPropProblemArray pProblems = NULL;
HRESULT hResult = pMsgObj -> DeleteProps
                              ((LPSPropTagArray)&sptSenderPropTags,
                               &pProblems);
if (S_OK == hResult) // No warnings returned in this call
{
    if (pProblems)
    {
        // Find out which properties could not be deleted.
        ⋮
        MAPIFreeBuffer(pProblems);
    }
}
else
{
    // Call pMsgObj -> GetLastError(…);
}
⋮
```

The problem array is handled exactly the same way in *DeleteProps* as it is in *SetProps*: If NULL is passed in the *pProblems* parameter, the provider doesn't return any error information and the caller won't know which properties were not deleted.

MAPI objects can contain properties that represent other objects or properties. If a delete request on one of these properties fails to delete *all* the things represented, the property, along with the error code, is returned in the problem array even though the deletion might have been partially successful. PR_MESSAGE_RECIPIENTS and PR_MESSAGE_ATTACHMENTS are examples of this type of property. The former represents the message's recipients, and the latter represents the message's attachments (the *IAttach* interface). Suppose, for example, that a client calls *DeleteProps* to delete PR_MESSAGE-_ATTACHMENTS, but for some reason the provider can't delete one or more of the message attachments. In this case, the implementation should return an error code and PR_MESSAGE_ATTACHMENTS in the *SPropProblemArray* argument. This is the expected behavior when a client request to delete a PT_OBJECT property fails.

Copying the Contents of an Object

Consider an object that contains properties in which we are interested. We need to get the object's data and copy it to a second object in a distinct location. How can we accomplish this? One possible solution would be to call *GetProps* on the first object, retrieve the data, and then call *SetProps* on the second object. This approach is partially correct, but it is also tedious and error prone, not to mention inefficient. We say it is partially correct because there might be properties that cannot be returned in a single *GetProps* call (e.g., large properties), which means that a manual copy must do a series of *OpenProperty* calls. Other properties on an object might be of type PT_OBJECT, and these can be accessed only by means of opening an interface on the object and then copying the interface into a similar one on the destination object.

IMAPIProp provides a method that hides these complexities within the implementation. *IMAPIProp::CopyProps* takes a list of properties to copy from the source object and sets them onto the destination object. The implementation handles the details of opening additional interfaces when necessary. If the source and destination objects are implemented by the same service provider, chances are good that the implementation can optimize the copy process and improve the efficiency and speed of the operation. Manually copying the object with *GetProps* and *SetProps* is unlikely to be as efficient because the caller knows nothing of the object's low-level implementation. The implementation of *CopyProps* also takes care of copying named properties from the source object to the destination object. Following is a client-side code fragment that demonstrates how *CopyProps* is used:

```
LPMESSAGE pSrcObj, pDstObj;
// Code to get the two IMessage objects
⋮
const static SizedSPropTagArray(3, sptPropTags) =
{
    3,
    {
        PR_BODY,
        PR_MESSAGE_ATTACHMENTS,
        PR_MESSAGE_CLASS
    }
};
```

(continued)

```
LPSPropProblemArray pProblems = NULL;
HRESULT hResult = pSrcObj -> CopyProps
                                ((LPSPropTagArray)&sptPropTags,
                                 0,
                                 NULL,
                                 &IID_IMessage,
                                 (LPVOID)pDstObj,
                                 0,
                                 &pProblems);
if (S_OK == hResult) // No warnings returned in this call
{
    if (pProblems)
    {
        // Find out which properties could not be deleted.
        ⋮
        MAPIFreeBuffer(pProblems);
    }
}
else
{
    // Call pSrcObj -> GetLastError(…);
}
⋮
```

As with other methods in the *IMAPIProp* interface, *CopyProps* returns an *SPropProblemArray* when it fails to copy one or more properties. A client can use this array if the function returns S_OK and the returned pointer to the problem array is non-NULL.

Copying Computed Properties

CopyProps will work with any properties except computed properties. It is the responsibility of the destination object to enforce this rule and not allow a source object to set any of its intrinsic attributes. If a call to *CopyProps* includes computed properties, MAPI_E_COMPUTED is returned in the problem array for each computed property.

Properties that can't be copied with *CopyProps* include PR_ENTRY-ID, PR_RECORD_KEY, PR_MAPPING_SIGNATURE, PR_PARENT_ENTRYID, PR_MESSAGE_SIZE, and PR_STORE_SUPPORT_MASK. Many implementations don't allow PR_LAST_MODIFICATION_TIME and PR_CREATION_TIME in a *CopyProps* call because they are also computed.

Sometimes we don't want to just copy data from one object to another, but rather *move* data from the source object to the destination object such that the moved properties are deleted from the source object. This can be done by calling *IMAPIProp::CopyProps* and passing the MAPI_MOVE flag.

Copying Entire Objects

The *CopyProps* method is not appropriate if the caller wants to copy *all* of the source object's properties to another object. Ideally, you should use a single method for this task: *IMAPIProp::CopyTo. CopyTo* is used to dump the contents of one object onto another and provides two sets of parameters for specifying items that can be excluded from the copy.

The first set is a counted array of interface identifiers (the *ciidExclude* and *rgiidExclude* parameters), which are interfaces common to the source and destination objects themselves. The most common example of excluding an interface is when you "dumb down" the copy to *IMAPIProp*. If you wanted only to copy folder properties to another folder or message properties to another message without the special logic for contained objects, you would exclude IID_IMAPIFolder and IID_IMessage, respectively, and the operation would be like a call to *CopyProps*. This feature is most useful when both objects support interfaces unknown to MAPI that embody their own special copy semantics over and above the MAPI semantics; you would exclude such interfaces to "dumb down" the copy to MAPI semantics. Excluding interfaces is not a very common practice, and not all implementations support this because the logic is complex.

The second set of parameters is an *SPropTagArray* of property tags that specifies properties that should not be copied from the source onto the destination. This array can be used to exclude properties and contained objects during the copy operation. An admittedly contrived example of excluding objects in *CopyTo* would be when a folder with 100 messages is to be copied to an empty one but none of the source folder's messages are to be copied. In this case, the caller would pass a property tag array with the property PR_CONTAINER_CONTENTS. It is the destination object's responsibility to adjust any properties that might be dependent on the excluded ones. In this example, the destination folder's PR_CONTENT_COUNT, which gives the number of messages in a folder, would not be altered. Implementations must always honor this property tag list and exclude the indicated properties. Implementations that can't support this functionality should delegate the *CopyTo* call to MAPI's *CopyTo* implementation in the support object (*IMAPISupport::CopyTo*).

Following is a client-side code fragment that demonstrates how *CopyTo* is used:

```
LPMESSAGE pSrcObj, pDstObj;
// Code to get the two IMessage objects
⋮
LPSPropProblemArray pProblems = NULL;
HRESULT hResult = pSrcObj -> CopyTo
                            (0,
                             NULL,
                             NULL,
                             0,
                             NULL,
                             &IID_IMessage,
                             (LPVOID)pDstObj,
                             0,
                             &pProblems);
if (S_OK == hResult) // No warnings returned in this call
{
    if (pProblems)
    {
        // Find out which properties could not be deleted.
        // Ignore any property tag whose error is MAPI_E_COMPUTED.
        ⋮
        MAPIFreeBuffer(pProblems);
    }
}
else
{
    // Call pSrcObj -> GetLastError(…);
}
⋮
```

This method also returns an *SPropProblemArray* when it fails to copy one or more properties. The source object cannot know a priori what the destination object's computed properties are, and neither can the caller. The caller should exclude properties known to be computed and ignore any MAPI_E-_COMPUTED errors that result from the properties copied.

Saving the Object Changes Permanently

When a client modifies a transacted object, the changes are cached within the object and the underlying data storage is not altered until the changes are committed by the client. This improves the performance and responsiveness of objects where data access is expensive, e.g., a network server. Committing the changes is accomplished by calling the *SaveChanges* method, which causes any modifications made to the cached data via *DeleteProps, SetProps, Open-Property, CopyProps,* or *CopyTo* to be written to the underlying storage medium. Here is a client-side code fragment showing how this method is used:

```
LPMESSAGE pMsgObj;
// Code to get and modify the IMessage object
  ⋮
HRESULT hResult = pMsgObj -> SaveChanges(0);
if (S_OK != hResult) // No warnings returned in this call
{
    // Call pMsgObj -> GetLastError(…);
}
  ⋮
```

SaveChanges takes a single flag argument that indicates the state in which the object will be left when the call is completed. If no flags are specified (i.e., 0 is passed), the default behavior is to prepare the object for release, which makes all methods except *Release* and *AddRef* inaccessible. After a call to *SaveChanges* with 0, every method on the object's interfaces should return E_ACCESSDENIED. If the caller needs access to the object after committing changes, it should specify KEEP_OPEN_READONLY or KEEP_OPEN_READ-WRITE in *ulFlags*, depending on the access level it needs afterwards.

The first *SaveChanges* call on an object by a client may have special semantics. Some implementations compute object attributes on the first committing call (e.g., PR_ENTRYID and PR_CREATION_TIME), so that if one of these intrinsic properties is not found during a call to *GetProps*, it is possible that the object hasn't been committed and the property hasn't yet been computed.

As mentioned earlier, transacted objects are a snapshot of the data source. When multiple objects view the same data source, they might compete with one another for access. For example, if two attachment objects make changes to the same data, the first object to call *SaveChanges* will succeed (assuming no errors). If the second object then attempts *SaveChanges,* the method might return MAPI_E_OBJECT_CHANGED, indicating that another object has already committed its data. The caller can override this error by passing the FORCE_SAVE flag in *SaveChanges.* In this case, the last one committing its data wins: The first object's modifications are overwritten by the second transaction.

Another situation peculiar to transacted objects occurs if a transacted object is deleted while another caller has it open. When *SaveChanges* is called, the MAPI_E_OBJECT_DELETED error code is returned. If the caller persists in storing the information, even if after the object has been deleted, then it must create a new object of the same type and call *CopyTo* to store the original information and then call *SaveChanges* on the newly created object.

A Look Ahead

Understanding how to manipulate MAPI properties is fundamental to writing MAPI clients and providers. All MAPI programs use properties, for properties encapsulate the basic units of data that each MAPI component processes. It should be clear how encapsulating data in MAPI properties makes it easier for various components to exchange data—properties standardize the format of the data, and *IMAPIProp* supplies the mechanism for accessing it. Standardizing properties advances the cause of interoperability.

In the next two chapters, we'll take a look at some other fundamental MAPI objects: MAPI containers and MAPI tables. Don't be surprised if what you read in Chapter 3 doesn't immediately make complete sense to you. In many respects, containers and tables are complementary subjects, so you need to be exposed to both before you can fully appreciate either. As you become more familiar with these objects, their use will strangely start to make sense to you, and you will achieve that state of inner peace and tranquility that we prop-tops like to call *Mapiness*.

CHAPTER THREE

MAPI Containers

As we have seen so far, MAPI defines several objects that are used to manipulate collections of other objects. Some of these objects represent items in a collection of similar types of data elements. For example, a folder is an object that is used to manipulate a collection of message objects and/or folders. MAPI calls this type of object a *container*, and its sole purpose is to manage collections of similar objects. Containers are named as such because they *contain* other objects, creating a parent-child relationship between the container and the contained objects.

MAPI formalizes this parent-child relationship by defining a new interface, *IMAPIContainer*, for objects that allow the storage and creation of child objects within them. The nesting of containers within containers can be arbitrarily deep, creating hierarchies of MAPI objects, as shown in Figure 3-1 on the following page. There is one exception to this: messages with attachments. The *IMessage* interface does not implement the *IMAPIContainer* interface, and it is typically not thought of as a container. Messages do not have a hierarchical relationship with their attachments. (See the sidebar beginning on page 78 for an overview of common MAPI objects.)

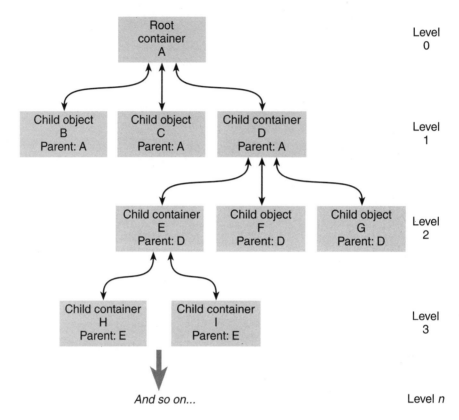

Figure 3-1.
Logical relationship between MAPI containers and objects.

Address book providers and message store providers implement contain-ers to store sets of objects that share common properties. Although the rela-tionship between a container and its children is hierarchical, the set of a container's children is actually represented by one or more tables, where each row is a child object and each column is a property of the item in a given row. As you might expect, MAPI defines a generalized interface, *IMAPITable*, for viewing tabular data, and one of this interface's most important uses is to pro-vide a uniform way of accessing the contents of MAPI containers. Figure 3-2, on the facing page, shows how a container's children might be represented by tables. (We examine *IMAPITable* in detail in Chapter 4.)

Container Contents Table

Instance Key	Name	Entry ID	Object Type
1	"Irving"	412421	6
2	"Les"	314781	6
3	"Emma"	915340	6
And so on...			
n	"Joe"	786341	6

Container Hierarchy Table

Instance Key	Name	Entry ID	Object Type	Depth
1	"Friends"	124765	8	1
2	"Team"	357124	8	1
3	"Managers"	666716	8	1
And so on...				
n	"All"	999888	8	1

Figure 3-2.
The children of a MAPI container are represented by rows in a table or tables.

The Standard Container Interface

MAPI defines a set of operations that are used to view a container's objects. These operations are abstract in the sense that they expose common functionality without regard to the type of object stored in the container. For example, a distribution list in an address book provider and a folder in a store provider are both MAPI containers. Even though the objects stored in a folder are very different from those in a distribution list, viewing either container's contents is accomplished through the same sequence of method calls on the parent container. This functional "lowest common denominator" is embodied in the *IMAPIContainer* interface, whose methods follow:

```
// Abstract definition of IMAPIContainer
class IMAPIContainer : public IMAPIProp
{
public :
    virtual HRESULT GetContentsTable
                    (ULONG            ulFlags,
                     LPMAPITABLE *    ppTable) = 0;
```

(continued)

```
virtual HRESULT GetHierarchyTable
                    (ULONG                  ulFlags,
                     LPMAPITABLE *          ppTable) = 0;
virtual HRESULT OpenEntry
                    (ULONG                  cbEntryID,
                     LPENTRYID              pEntryID,
                     LPCIID                 pInterface,
                     ULONG                  ulFlags,
                     ULONG *                pulObjType,
                     LPUNKNOWN *            ppUnk) = 0;
virtual HRESULT SetSearchCriteria
                    (LPSRestriction         pRestriction,
                     LPENTRYLIST            pContainerList,
                     ULONG                  ulSearchFlags) = 0;
virtual HRESULT GetSearchCriteria
                    (ULONG                  ulFlags,
                     LPSRestriction *       ppRestriction,
                     LPENTRYLIST *          ppContainerList,
                     ULONG *                pulSearchState) = 0;
};
```

The *IMAPIContainer* interface is derived from *IMAPIProp*, so all container objects must also implement *IMAPIProp*'s methods. You can think of the *IMAPIContainer* interface as an extension of *IMAPIProp* that adds the capability to have and view child objects. *IMAPIContainer* is never directly implemented, but used only as a base class for further derivation. Distribution lists, folders, and address book containers are examples of MAPI container objects that derive indirectly first from *IMAPIContainer*, then directly from another abstract base class such as *IDistList*, *IMAPIFolder*, or *IABContainer*. Each of these subsequent derivations adds the methods specific to the type of object stored within the container. For this reason, methods for creating, deleting, copying, and moving child objects aren't part of the *IMAPIContainer* interface but are instead part of the interfaces derived from *IMAPIContainer*. For *IDistList* and *IABContainer*, for example, the object creation method is called *CreateEntry*, whereas for *IMAPIFolder*, the method is either *CreateMessage* or *CreateFolder*.

Data Tables of Containers

The parent-child relationship of containers to the objects they contain suggests a tree, or hierarchy, of containers and objects. Each internal node of the tree is another container, and leaf nodes are messages or recipients, depending on whether the root is a folder or an address book container. *IMAPIContainer* provides methods for traversing this tree of containers: *GetHierarchyTable* and *GetContentsTable*. *GetHierarchyTable* returns a *hierarchy table* containing only subcontainers, or non–leaf nodes—not the property objects, or leaf nodes. A client typically uses *GetHierarchyTable* to populate a control, such as a tree view, of the folders in a message store provider or the containers in an address book provider.

By default, the hierarchy table includes only the immediate children of the container whence the call was made, but a client can also request the entire tree be returned in a single call. The provider is free to honor such requests or not. For example, consider the following code fragment:

```
LPMAPIFOLDER pFldObj;
⋮
// Code to get an IMAPIFolder interface
⋮
LPMAPITABLE pTable;
HRESULT hResult = pFldObj -> GetHierarchyTable
                            (MAPI_DEFERRED_ERRORS,
                             &pTable);
if (S_OK == hResult) // No warnings returned in this call
{
    // Use the returned table.
    ⋮
    pTable -> Release();
}
```

This code requests a hierarchy table containing *pFldObj*'s immediate subfolders. We could have asked to retrieve all the subfolders that are children, grandchildren, and great-grandchildren of the *pFldObj* folder by specifying CONVENIENT_DEPTH in the *ulFlags* parameter. Each row in the returned table has a column that tells which level the row's occupant occupies with respect to the container where the *GetHierarchyTable* call was made. Had we requested CONVENIENT_DEPTH in the example above, this property, PR_DEPTH, would have been set to 0 for *pFldObj*, 1 for *pFldObj*'s children, 2 for its grandchildren, and so on. PR_DEPTH is available only as a column in the hierarchy table because it has no intrinsic meaning for the child object; it only makes sense relative to a parent container.

We must point out that the CONVENIENT_DEPTH flag is not particularly useful and thus little used—it doesn't mean "return the entire hierarchy" but "return as much of the hierarchy as is convenient." Most containers return only a single level, so applications must code for descending the hierarchy that way anyway; the additional efficiency gained by using CONVENIENT_DEPTH isn't usually worth the extra code. Most commercial service providers don't support this flag because it can be very expensive in terms of performance to compute the entire hierarchy of folders, and because the same effect can be achieved with a combination of method calls. Clients should therefore be prepared to traverse the hierarchy of containers by repeatedly calling the *GetHierarchyTable* method on the different levels.

You obtain the table of leaf-node objects in a container by calling the *IMAPIContainer::GetContentsTable* method. Whereas the hierarchy table contains only subcontainers, the contents table lists only objects that are not subcontainers of the parent object. So don't expect to get subcontainers in the contents table or property objects in the hierarchy table. (The exception to this rule is a distribution list, which is a special case of an *IABContainer* object: The *IDistList* interface is identical to *IABContainer* and contains no unique methods. The only difference is that a distribution list can't have subcontainers, although it can have child distribution lists, which appear in its contents table.) The code to obtain a contents table looks like the following fragment:

```
LPDISTLIST pDLObj;
    ⋮
// Code to get an IDistList interface
    ⋮
LPMAPITABLE pTable;
HRESULT hResult = pDLObj -> GetContentsTable
                            (MAPI_DEFERRED_ERRORS,
                             &pTable);
if (S_OK == hResult) // No warnings returned in this call
{
    // Use the returned table.
    ⋮
    pTable -> Release();
}
```

The information returned in the contents table is often used by a client to populate user interface controls: A folder's contents table might be retrieved, for example, to populate a list box or tree view with the titles of messages residing in that folder.

An application might also need to create objects in a folder that are hidden from the view but that should also be accessible through a table. For this reason, a folder has the following two sets of objects in its contents table:

- *Regular.* These are normally displayed by clients in their user interface. The regular objects are listed in a normal contents table.

- *Associated.* These are objects created for custom purposes by client applications. The container returns the list of associated items in a folder container by returning an associated contents table.

By default, the *GetContentsTable* method returns a table consisting only of regular objects. A client obtains the associated contents table by passing the

MAPI_ASSOCIATED flag to *GetContentsTable*. Figure 3-3 shows the three types of tables supported by MAPI containers.

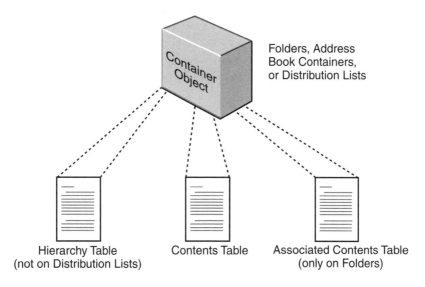

Folders, Address
Book Containers,
or Distribution Lists

Hierarchy Table   Contents Table   Associated Contents Table
(not on Distribution Lists)   (only on Folders)

Figure 3-3.
Tables available in a MAPI container.

Associated Contents Table Support by Message Store Providers

Although not required by the MAPI 1.0 specification, message store providers are highly encouraged to support the creation of associated messages and to return the associated contents table when requested. Client applications use such items to store information about the view settings of a folder. The forms library provider also uses associated messages in folders to store per-folder form information. Public folder message store providers are strongly recommended to support the associated contents table because public-folder–based applications typically create hidden messages for their operational needs.

All default message store providers are expected to support the creation of associated messages and the related contents table.

A good client, however, should not rely on the message store provider supporting associated messages and should have a contingency plan ready in case there is no such support in the profile's default store provider.

Associated objects are only applicable to message store providers and the *IMAPIFolder* interface. No other interface derived from *IMAPIContainer* (i.e., *IABContainer* and *IDistList*) supports associated messages. A client should not attempt to obtain an associated contents table from any container in an address book provider.

Opening Objects in a Container

We know that child objects are represented by rows in a container's contents or hierarchy table. The client can view rows in these tables to obtain information about the container's children but otherwise has no direct access. So how does a client modify the data of a container's child object? The client opens the object, which returns an interface that allows it to access the object.

The Entry ID in Tables

Depending on the service provider implementation, the entry IDs returned in contents and hierarchy tables can be short-term or long-term. A short-term entry ID can be used in any method that requires an entry ID, but is valid only for the duration of the current MAPI session. Client applications should *not* store a short-term entry ID with the expectation that it will be valid in a different session. If a client needs to save an object's entry ID, it must obtain a long-term entry ID by opening the object and calling its *GetProps* method, requesting PR_ENTRYID.

GetProps is guaranteed to always return a long-term entry ID whereas the entry ID found in tables isn't required to be long-term. To find out whether the entry IDs in the container tables are short-term or long-term, you must examine the *abFlags* member of the ENTRYID structure.

The Microsoft Exchange Server is an example of a service provider implementation that uses short-term entry IDs in its container tables. Short-term entry IDs may be used because they can be generated quickly and might save memory in large contents or hierarchy tables.

The following code fragment demonstrates how to use *OpenEntry* to open a message object. The fourth parameter, *ulFlags*, specifies the level of access that the caller is requesting on the opened object (i.e., read-only, read/write, etc.).

```
LPMDB pMDB; // IMsgStore interface pointer
⋮
// Code to get an IMsgStore interface
⋮
ULONG ulObjType;
LPMAPIFOLDER pFolder;
HRESULT hResult = pMDB -> OpenEntry
                          (0,
                           NULL,
                           &IID_IMAPIFolder,
                           MAPI_DEFERRED_ERRORS,
                           &ulObjType,
                           (LPUNKNOWN *)&pFolder);
if (S_OK != hResult) // No warnings expected
{
    // Something failed. Clean up and return.
}
LPENTRYID  pEID;
ULONG      cbEID;
⋮
// Code to get the entry ID from a table in a folder
⋮
LPMESSAGE pMsgObj;
hResult = pFolder -> OpenEntry
                      (cbEID,
                       pEID,
                       &IID_IMessage,
                       MAPI_MODIFY | MAPI_DEFERRED_ERRORS,
                       &ulObjType,
                       (LPUNKNOWN *)&pMsgObj);
if (S_OK != hResult) // No warnings expected
{
    // Something failed. Clean up and return.
    ⋮
}
```

In the first *OpenEntry* call, we pass 0 and NULL as the first two arguments for the *cbEntryID* and *lpEntryID* parameters. This so-called *null entry ID* is used by convention to represent the topmost container available from a service provider. In the case of a store provider, the null entry ID corresponds to its root folder; for an address book provider, it returns the root container.

Access Level

A client can open an object for read/write access by setting or clearing the MAPI_MODIFY bit in the *ulFlags* parameter. (By default, an object opens with read-only access.) The implementation of *OpenEntry* returns an object with the requested access rights or fails the call if the object doesn't support the minimum requested access or the caller has insufficient permission to access the object as requested. Implementations of *OpenEntry* usually allow the caller to open an object with a permission level that is equal to the container in which the object was opened but not higher. For example, a client application can request to open a read/write instance of a message from a read/write folder, but it cannot open a read/write instance of a message from a read-only instance of a folder.

The access level of an object cannot be promoted dynamically: The caller must open the object with the highest access level required. If the caller opens the object with a lower access level and then subsequently decides it needs higher access, it should release the object and reopen it with the higher access level. Note that the access level is a per-instance attribute of the object: A given access level applies only to the interface pointer just obtained. Opening another instance of the object at a higher access level doesn't retroactively promote the access level of other open instances of the same object.

While you can't promote an object's access level, you can demote an object opened with read/write access to read-only access by calling the *IMAPIProp::SaveChanges* method and specifying the flag KEEP_OPEN_READONLY. Most implementations will demote the access level of an object when clients call this method with this flag.

Search Containers

Search containers are special container objects implemented by message store and address book providers. These objects allow a client to specify criteria for searching for an item (or items) among objects contained within a message store provider or address book provider. Search containers exist only to hold the results of the search. Their contents or hierarchy tables list the objects that match the search criteria. A client sets the search criteria and triggers the container to start searching. Each hit is added to the contents or hierarchy table of the search container as the search progresses. The items in these tables are not really stored in the search container; instead what is shown in its tables are *links* to items in other containers. The search criteria are specified using a series of *restrictions*. (Restrictions are covered in detail in the next chapter.)

The caller sets up a restriction to use as the search criteria and passes it in a call to *IMAPIContainer::SetSearchCritieria*, which starts the search. The client can also control the priority of the search and a list of containers to search by passing combinations of flags in *ulFlags* and a list of containers in *lpContainerList*. Once the search is started, it can be aborted and restarted by calling the same method with different combinations of flags.

Following is a sample code fragment that sets the search criteria and starts a search. This example, while contrived, shows the sequence of calls a client must make when searching a container. (We discuss how a client performs a search in more detail in Appendix A.)

```
LPMAPIFOLDER    pSearchFolder;
LPSRestriction pSearchCriteria;
  ⋮
// Create search-container folder object (IMAPIFolder)
HRESULT hResult = pParentFolder ->
                        CreateFolder(FOLDER_SEARCH,…, &pSearchFolder);
  ⋮
// Code to build a restriction array. We will show this later.
  ⋮
ENTRYLIST eidList;
  ⋮
// Code to build a list of subcontainers where the search will
// take place. This list of subcontainers represents the
// "domain of the search."
  ⋮
hResult = pSearchFolder -> SetSearchCriteria(pSearchCriteria,
                              &eidList,
                              BACKGROUND_SEARCH ¦  // Priority
                              SHALLOW_SEARCH ¦     // Nonrecursive
                              RESTART_SEARCH);     // Start now
if (S_OK != hResult) // No warnings expected
{
// Something failed. Clean up and return.
  ⋮
}
// When the search is completed, the clients receive a
// "notification" of search completion. We will
// discuss this later.
  ⋮
```

After a client sets the search criteria, the criteria is stored and maintained on the search container object for as long as it exists in memory or in permanent storage. If a client needs to clear the restriction on the object, it passes a NULL pointer to an array of restrictions, thus removing the previously stored conditions.

A client can obtain the current search criteria and the status of an ongoing search by calling *IMAPIContainer::GetSearchCriteria.* This call returns the restriction defining the current search criteria, the list of entry IDs of containers that are being or will be searched, and the state of the search at the time of the call. The code fragment on the next page shows how this method is used.

```
LPMAPIFOLDER pSearchFolder;
    ⋮
// Code to get a search-container folder object (IMAPIFolder)
    ⋮
LPSRestriction pSearchCriteria = NULL;
LPENTRYLIST pEIDList = NULL;
ULONG ulSearchState;
HRESULT hResult = pSearchFolder -> GetSearchCriteria
                                   (0,
                                    &pSearchCriteria,
                                    &pEIDList,
                                    &ulSearchState);
if (S_OK != hResult) // No warnings expected
{
    // Something failed. Clean up and return.
        ⋮
}
// Use the information returned in the above call.
    ⋮
// Cleanup
MAPIFreeBuffer(pEIDList);
MAPIFreeBuffer(pSearchCriteria);
pSearchFolder -> Release();
```

Overview of Common MAPI Objects

Here is a brief description of the objects exposed in hierarchy and contents tables by the different MAPI containers. (In this list, we include attachments for the sake of completeness, even though these are not listed in the containers' tables.)

Folders

A folder is an object that implements the *IUnknown*, *IMAPIProp*, *IMAPIContainer*, and *IMAPIFolder* interfaces. A folder container is implemented by the message store provider and holds many objects including messages and other folders. Store providers can implement a special type of folder called a *search results* folder. This folder implements the search method (e.g., *SetSearchCriteria*, *GetSearchCriteria*) of the *IMAPIContainer* interface. Another type of folder is the *public folder*, which is simply a folder that might be accessed by more than one user simultaneously. A public folder is useful for storing documents and/or files and provides a central location for management, access, and maintenance of shared information.

Messages

A message—the basic entity in a message store provider—is the object that implements the *IUnknown*, *IMAPIProp*, and *IMessage* interfaces. It's most often used to store the data of an email message but can also be used for any data storage purposes. For example, in public-folder–based applications, a message can store sales information, procedural documents, job listings, and so on.

Attachments

An attachment is a data object, embedded in a message, that implements the *IUnknown*, *IMAPIProp*, and *IAttach* interfaces. (MAPI 1.0 does not define any specific methods for the *IAttach* interface.) An attachment is used by clients to store large data files or other types of binary information that will be delivered with a message but is not part of the message's content. The most typical use of an attachment is in an email message where the attachment is a binary file that is sent along with the rest of the email text. An attachment object doesn't have an entry ID, so many operations (e.g., notifications) aren't applicable to it.

Distribution Lists

A distribution list implements the *IUnknown*, *IMAPIProp*, *IMAPIContainer*, and *IDistList* interfaces. It is like a recipient in that a client can name it as a recipient of a message, allowing the client to send a message to multiple recipients without having to list each one individually. A distribution list typically contains mail users but might also include other distribution lists. A distinctive characteristic of a distribution list is that even though it is a container that can have children, the distribution list doesn't appear in an address book provider's hierarchy table—rather, it is listed like an ordinary mail user in the container's contents table. The rationale for this behavior is that a distribution list is used most often to address messages and should therefore be visible along with the rest of the container's addressable objects.

Mail Users

These objects implement the *IUnknown*, *IMAPIProp*, and *IMailUser* interfaces. (MAPI 1.0 does not define any specific methods for the *IMailUser* interface.) A mail user object is the simplest object in an address book provider. It stores the data properties associated with each addressable recipient of a messaging system and contains all the necessary information, such as email address, email address type, and delivery options, needed to deliver a message to a particular recipient.

MAPI Tables and Notifications

Tables are an integral part of the MAPI programming paradigm, so understanding how to manipulate them is essential to effective MAPI programming. All sorts of data are stored in tables. Clients use tables to see the contents of folders and address book containers. Providers implement them for the clients' use and use them internally as well. Even dialog boxes are described by MAPI tables.

Clients and providers can ask to be notified when objects they're holding change. Providers generate these notifications when they detect changes in the objects they provide. The message store provider, for example, generates a notification on receipt of new mail, and table implementations generate notifications when rows are added, deleted, or modified. This chapter examines how MAPI tables and notifications are used.

The Rationale for MAPI Tables

The definition of a table depends on whom you're talking to. To the computer scientist, a table is an abstract data type that represents a set of things whose members have common characteristics. Each member of the set occupies a row in the table, and each column contains a different attribute of the member occupying that row. In relational database terminology, a table is a subset of records from one or more databases, where each row represents a record and the columns are record fields. To a programmer writing an application, a table might be a data structure such as a two-dimensional array.

MAPI tables share many of these characteristics, but none of these definitions fit MAPI tables precisely. A MAPI table isn't an abstraction but rather an interface, *IMAPITable*, that allows its user to manipulate sets of data. A MAPI table also isn't a data structure, although you can obtain data structures by calling methods on the *IMAPITable* interface. And finally, MAPI tables aren't used just to represent database records but are designed to be general-purpose interfaces that can be used to access almost any type of data.

Specific examples of "sets of things" that MAPI represents in tabular form are the set of service providers in a profile, a set of recipients in an address book provider, a set of messages in a folder, and a set of recipients of a message. Note that the objects represented by the rows are somewhat homogeneous: It doesn't make sense to have a table where one row represents a provider, another a folder, and a third a recipient. The columns in each case are properties of the object represented by a given row.

MAPI tables are used to construct *views* of a set of data. A view is a set of rows and columns that reflects some user-defined arrangement of the underlying data. We use the term "view" in an abstract sense to denote the way the data is arranged, rather than to mean a physical data structure that you can access in a program. The table user defines a view by creating a query that specifies which subset of the underlying data is to be retrieved and then *executes the query* to obtain a data structure called a *row set* that contains the actual data. Only the data that meets the conditions specified by the query is returned in the row set.

Relational database technology is also based on a tabular view of data sets, and since address book providers and store providers are database interfaces, they return MAPI tables that represent sets of database records. So in this case, MAPI tables are somewhat (but not fully) analogous to relational database tables. If the underlying database implementation is relational, as is often the case, creating a view might be equivalent to formulating a query in the underlying database's data manipulation language (e.g., SQL). If the underlying database implementation is not relational, then it's up to the provider to map the record set onto an *IMAPITable* interface.

Although MAPI tables provide some quasi-relational functionality, it would be a mistake to carry the analogy too far. In the first place, MAPI represents the underlying databases (e.g., message store provider and address book provider) as hierarchies of containers, not tables. A MAPI table provides a tabular view of a single container, and there's no way to join tables from different containers. Secondly, MAPI tables are designed to work the same way regardless of the type of data source backing them. They can be layered on top of many different database back ends, and their semantics remain the same. The common interface hides the underlying implementation details and allows providers using different database models to interoperate with MAPI clients and other providers. Thirdly, whereas relational systems often provide a formal data representation language, MAPI tables make use of a handful of general-purpose data structures. And finally, the query capabilities of MAPI tables are much weaker than most commercial relational database management systems.

But most of all, *IMAPITable* is intended to provide a single, uniform interface that can be used to represent data from almost any source—not just databases. Its power, as well as its shortcomings, stems from the fact that it is designed to do most things well at the expense of some specialized capabilities.

MAPI Table Basics

We have already mentioned that MAPI tables are not data structures, but they are also qualitatively different from other MAPI objects, particularly those derived from *IMAPIProp*. An instance of an *IMAPITable* has no data of its own, but is instead an interface used solely for viewing other objects' data. *IMAPITable*'s neuter status also means that it doesn't have an entry ID to uniquely identify it, as other MAPI objects do.

In a MAPI table, columns are represented by properties (PR_XXX) and each row consists of a subset of properties of the object occupying that row. Notice that a row doesn't contain the object itself, but only a representation of the object, i.e., its properties.

The preceding statement is best clarified with an example. An address book container comprises a set of recipient objects, each object having a common set of properties, such as the recipient's name (PR_DISPLAY_NAME), email address (PR_EMAIL_ADDRESS), and address type (PR_ADDRTYPE). The database file backing the container might consist of a homogeneous set of records, one per recipient, with distinct fields for name, email address, address type, and so on. Let's suppose the database has 100 records and that, consequently, the address book container has 100 recipients. We would like to create a view of only those recipients whose names are "Irving De la Cruz" or "Les Thaler," and we would like the view to contain the following three columns: PR_DISPLAY_NAME, PR_ADDRTYPE, and PR_EMAIL_ADDRESS. Figure 4-1 on the following page illustrates conceptually what such a view would look like.

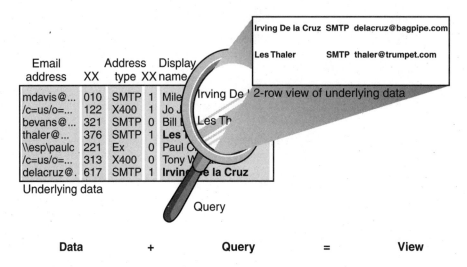

Figure 4-1.
Although the container's underlying database has 100 records and many fields, we create a three-column view of only two records.

SRowSet and SRow

If we retrieve the physical rows by executing a query, the net result is a row set with two rows: one for recipient Irving De la Cruz and one for Les Thaler. The definition of the row set data structure is as follows:

```
typedef struct _SRowSet
{
    ULONG cRows;              // Number of rows in aRow[]
    SRow  aRow[MAPI_DIM];     // Array of rows
} SRowSet, *LPSRowSet;
```

Each row is contained in an *SRow* data structure, as shown in this code:

```
typedef struct _SRow
{
    ULONG ulAdrEntryPad;    // For alignment
    ULONG cValues;          // Number of columns in lpProps
    LPSPropValue lpProps;   // Properties in each column
} SRow, *LPSRow;
```

So our two heroes would be returned in **pRows*, a pointer to an *SRowSet* structure, looking something like this:

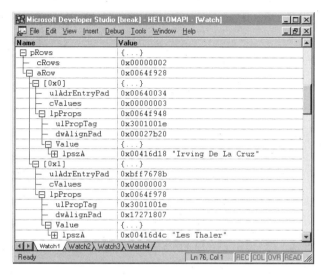

A couple of things are worth mentioning regarding *SRowSets* and *SRows*. First, note that the typedef of *SRowSet* declares the *aRow* member to be an array of one (MAPI_DIM) element. You will rarely, if ever, declare a variable of type *SRowSet*. Instead, you will call an *IMAPITable* method such as *QueryRows* that will allocate a row set and return it in an *LPSRowSet* pointer you pass to the call. The allocation of the row set will be a contiguous block of memory large enough to contain *cRows* number of *SRows* starting at *&aRow[0]*.

If you need to declare an *SRowSet* variable, use the *SizedSRowSet* macro or allocate the variable dynamically using *MAPIAllocateBuffer* and *MAPIAllocate-More*, as shown in the following code:

```
// Allocate an SRowSet with 2 rows containing
// space for 3 string columns given by szGlobal.
LPTSTR    szGlobal[2][3] =
            {"Irving De la Cruz", "delacruz@bagpipe.com", "SMTP",
             "Les Thaler",        "thaler@trumpet.com",  "SMTP"};
HRESULT   hRes  = S_OK;
ULONG     cRows = 2;
LPSRowSet pRows = NULL;

hRes = MAPIAllocateBuffer(CbNewSRowSet(cRows), (LPVOID *)&pRows);

for (ULONG i = 0; i < cRows; i++)
```

(continued)

```
{
    hRes = MAPIAllocateBuffer(sizeof(SPropValue)*3,
                              (LPVOID *)&pRows -> aRow[i].lpProps);
    for (ULONG j = 0; j < 3; j++)
    {
        // All property values are strings in this example.
        ULONG cbData = lstrlen(szGlobal[i][j]) + 1; // Extra is for NULL
        hRes = MAPIAllocateMore(cbData,
                                pRows -> aRow[i].lpProps,
                                (LPVOID *)&pRows ->
                                    aRow[i].lpProps[j].Value.lpszA);
    }
}
```

The *SRowSet* structure and each *lpProps* array are allocated separately using *MAPIAllocateBuffer*, but any additional memory for individual property values (such as PT_STRING8s or PT_BINARYs) is allocated by *MAPIAllocateMore*. This allows the entire row set to be freed by a single call to the *FreeProws* API, which walks the row set and frees each row's nested properties. If you request a row set through an *IMAPITable* method, it's your responsibility to free it when you're finished using it; you should use *FreeProws* for this purpose.

Abstract Table Operations

In the previous examples, we hinted at *IMAPITable*'s query capabilities without defining what they are. The table in Figure 4-2 formally enumerates exactly which operations are available from the *IMAPITable* interface. We define these operations in terms of a set of database "primitives" that is used to construct views of the underlying data. Figure 4-2 lists the primitives, what they do, and the corresponding *IMAPITable* methods. Figure 4-3, on the facing page, illustrates how a view is constructed on the data by applying some of these operations.

Primitive	Purpose	*IMAPITable* Method
Selecting	Specifies which columns to include in the view	*SetColumns*

Figure 4-2. *(continued)*

IMAPITable *methods map to a set of database primitives and are used to construct views of the underlying data, retrieve rows from a view, or position the table cursor.*

Primitive	Purpose	*IMAPITable* Method
Filtering	Specifies that only rows satisfying a certain condition should be included in the view	*Restrict*
Sorting	Specifies how rows will be ordered in the view	*SortTable*
Querying	Returns rows in the current view	*QueryRows, HrQueryAllRows*
Positioning	Moves the table cursor to a given row	*SeekRow, SeekRowApprox, CreateBookmark, FindRow*

Even though MAPI tables support some familiar database operations, they aren't fully equivalent to tables found in the relational model. MAPI tables are read-only, so there is no *Update* primitive. The implementation generates notifications when the underlying data changes, but there is no mechanism in *IMAPITable* for adding, deleting, or otherwise modifying the underlying data set.

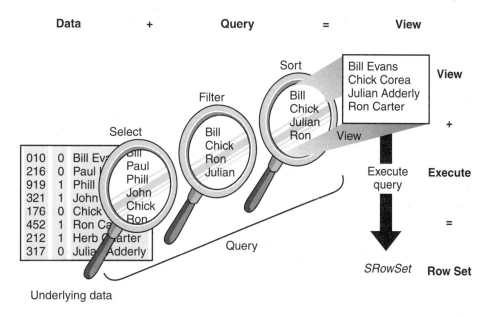

Figure 4-3.
In this example, a view is defined by applying a column set, a filter, and a sort to the underlying data.

Views and Queries

Most operations are applied to MAPI tables to obtain a row set. Whereas a view is an abstraction, a row set is something concrete that you can use in your application. Using MAPI tables is usually a three-step process: First you obtain an *IMAPITable* interface; then you define a query that specifies the view (i.e., the conditions for membership in the row set); and finally, you execute the query to obtain the result—an *SRowSet*. In other words:

Obtain *IMAPITable*
IMAPITable + Query = View
View + Execute = *SRowSet*

There are three ways a table user obtains an *IMAPITable* interface:

- By calling a MAPI API such as *BuildDisplayTable*

- By obtaining one from another interface in a method call, such as *IMAPIContainer::GetContentsTable*

- By calling *IMAPIProp::OpenProperty* on a PT_OBJECT property that returns a table interface

Defining Queries

IMAPITable implementations are required to provide a default view that specifies which rows are returned in the absence of a user-defined query. The default view usually comprises whatever columns the implementation can produce easily and as many rows as the implementation can conveniently return. Often a default sort order is also imposed.

The default view is sometimes adequate, but you will usually want to define your own view by setting up a query. This is because you will—at the very least—want to be assured that the data you're seeking is included in the table's column set! Beyond that, you will often want to apply sorting or filtering primitives to find specific rows rather than manually searching a large row set for the target data. The selection, filtering, and sorting primitives are used to define queries. If you plan on defining a query that involves sorting, you should apply the column selection and filtering primitives first, and then sort the table. Sorting is typically the most expensive operation because it involves data movement, so for most implementations it pays to winnow away any rows that won't be part of the final view before you sort.

Selecting: *SetColumns*

Selection is accomplished by the *SetColumns* method. This method is completely straightforward: You pass in an array of property tags that specifies the table columns you want in the final view. When the query is executed, the rows returned will contain only those properties (*SPropValues*) requested, and they will be in the same order as requested in the property tag array. If you select columns that aren't available in the underlying data, executing the query will return an *SPropValue* for that column whose property type is set to PT_ERROR and whose *SPropValue.Value.err* member contains an error code such as MAPI_E_NOT_FOUND. The semantics are the same as in *GetProps*.

Some table implementations support "lazy evaluation" of the *SetColumns* call. Lazy evaluation means that the operation isn't actually performed until the results are needed. The caller requests lazy evaluation of the column set by passing TBL_BATCH in the *ulFlags* parameter. If the implementation can honor the request, it will defer changing the view's column set until the query is executed. If it cannot, the flag is ignored.

Asynchronous calls to *SetColumns* can also be requested by passing TBL_ASYNC in *ulFlags*. This causes *SetColumns* to start the operation and return immediately without waiting for it to complete. You determine when the operation is complete by polling the table's status with periodic calls to *IMAPITable::GetStatus*—which returns TBLSTAT_SETTING_COLS while the operation is in progress and TBLSTAT_COMPLETE on completion—or by registering for fnevTableModified event notifications via *IMAPITable::Advise*. Look at the code in Figure 4-4, in which *SetColumns* selects columns into a view:

```
// Demonstrates IMAPITable::SetColumns
LPMAPITABLE pTbl = NULL;
HRESULT      hRes;
SizedSPropTagArray(4, sptCols) = {4, {PR_DISPLAY_NAME,
                                      PR_EMAIL_ADDRESS,
                                      PR_ADDRTYPE,
                                      PR_ENTRYID}};
hRes = pContainer -> GetContentsTable(0, &pTbl);
if (SUCCEEDED(hRes))
{
    hRes = pTbl -> SetColumns((LPSPropTagArray)&sptCols, 0);
    :
    pTbl -> Release();
}
:
```

Figure 4-4.
SetColumns *selects columns into a view.*

The code in Figure 4-4 selects four columns into the view of a container's contents, which is obtained from the *GetContentsTable* method on the container. The desired columns are given in the *SPropTagArray sptCols*, which is declared on the stack using the *SizedSPropTagArray* macro and initialized with the property tags we're requesting. Later, when a query is executed, the values returned in the property array of each row will contain (in order) PR_DISPLAY_NAME, PR_EMAIL_ADDRESS, PR_ADDRTYPE, and PR_ENTRYID, or an error code if the column can't be set to the requested property. Notice that the address of the *SPropTagArray* must be cast to *LPSPropTagArray* because the *SizedSPropTagArray* macro places a tag in the structure definition that isn't in the typedef of *LPSPropTagArray*.

You can determine a view's column set by calling *IMAPITable::QueryColumns*, passing either 0 or TBL_ALL_COLUMNS in the *ulFlags* parameter. The method returns an *SPropTagArray* structure containing either the property tags of the current column set or all possible column tags, respectively.

Filtering: *Restrict*

The *Restrict* method specifies a condition for membership in the view. Any row meeting the criteria given in *Restrict* will be returned in an *SRowSet* when the query is executed. *Restrict* takes two parameters: a pointer to an *SRestriction* data structure containing the condition and a ULONG bitmap of flags. The table flags TBL_BATCH and TBL_ASYNC can be passed, and their effect is the same as for *SetColumns*.

The *SRestriction* data structure lets you construct arbitrarily complex Boolean expressions that can contain any number of nested expressions. Each expression is a condition against which the object embodied in each row is tested when the query is executed. The expression is evaluated according to the usual rules, and if found to be true for the object in that row, the row is included in the view; otherwise, it's excluded.

The standard Boolean operators (AND, OR, NOT), an existence operator, comparison operators (<, <=, >, >=, !=, ==), the bitwise AND (&) operator, a size comparison operator, and a few others are provided by *SRestrictions*. Suppose you want to find all messages in a folder whose subject is "Book." Of those, you want to view only those messages that have a body longer than 100 bytes or those messages that haven't been read and have file attachments. A Boolean expression, such as the following, eliminates the ambiguity:

(Subject == "Book") && (Body > 100 ¦¦ (HasAttach && !Read))

You construct an *SRestriction* that represents a parse tree of the expression. Figure 4-5 shows the parse tree, and the code in Figure 4-6 shows the resulting *SRestriction* data structures and call to *Restrict*.

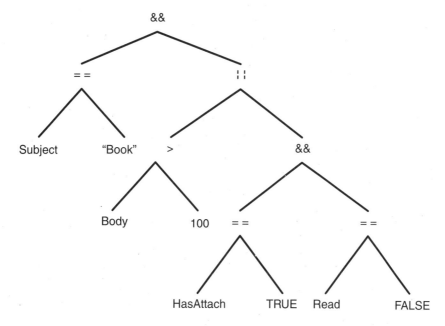

Figure 4-5.
The parse tree of the Boolean expression (Subject == "Book") && (Body > 100 ¦¦
(HasAttach && !Read)).

Because the data structures are unwieldy and tedious to initialize, it pays to shorten the tree as much as possible by rearranging even moderately complex expressions. This minimizes the amount of code you have to write! If you inadvertently constructed an expression such as

$A + AB + AC$

you could save yourself some coding by simplifying it to *A*. (By the distributive law of Boolean algebra, $A + AB + AC = A(1 + B + C) = A$. *B* and *C* are "don't care" terms since their input doesn't affect the result.)

```
//:::::::::::::::::::::::::::::::::::::::::::::::::::::::::::::::
//
// Demonstrates how to restrict a folder's contents table
// for messages that match the following condition:
```

Figure 4-6.   *(continued)*
An SRestriction *and* Restrict *call.*

Figure 4-6. *continued*

```
//
// (Subject == "Book") && (Body > 100 || (HasAttach && !Read))
//
LPSRowSet  pRows = NULL;
SizedSPropTagArray(2, spt) = {2, PR_SUBJECT, PR_MESSAGE_SIZE};
SRestriction srRoot,
             srLevel1[2],
             srLevel2[2],
             srLevel3[2];

SPropValue  spvSubj, spvAttach;

spvSubj.ulPropTag = PR_SUBJECT;
spvSubj.Value.lpszA = "Book";

spvAttach.ulPropTag = PR_HASATTACH;
spvAttach.Value.b = TRUE;

// Root &&
srRoot.rt = RES_AND;
srRoot.res.resAnd.cRes = 2;
srRoot.res.resAnd.lpRes = srLevel1;

// Subject == "Book"?
srLevel1[0].rt = RES_PROPERTY;
srLevel1[0].res.resProperty.relop = RELOP_EQ;
srLevel1[0].res.resProperty.ulPropTag = PR_SUBJECT;
srLevel1[0].res.resProperty.lpProp = &spvSubj;

// ||
srLevel1[1].rt = RES_OR;
srLevel1[1].res.resOr.cRes = 2;
srLevel1[1].res.resOr.lpRes = srLevel2;

// Body > 100?
srLevel2[0].rt = RES_SIZE;
srLevel2[0].res.resSize.relop = RELOP_GT;
srLevel2[0].res.resSize.ulPropTag = PR_BODY;
srLevel2[0].res.resSize.cb = 100;

// &&
srLevel2[1].rt = RES_AND;
srLevel2[1].res.resAnd.cRes = 2;
srLevel2[1].res.resAnd.lpRes = srLevel3;
```

```
// HasAttach == TRUE?
srLevel3[0].rt = RES_PROPERTY;
srLevel3[0].res.resProperty.relop = RELOP_EQ;
srLevel3[0].res.resProperty.ulPropTag = PR_HASATTACH;
srLevel3[0].res.resProperty.lpProp = &spvAttach;

// Is the MSGFLAG_READ bit clear?
srLevel3[1].rt = RES_BITMASK;
srLevel3[1].res.resBitMask.relBMR = BMR_EQZ;
srLevel3[1].res.resBitMask.ulPropTag = PR_MESSAGE_FLAGS;
srLevel3[1].res.resBitMask.ulMask = MSGFLAG_READ;

// Select only PR_SUBJECT.
hRes = pCTbl -> SetColumns((LPSPropTagArray)&spt, TBL_BATCH);

// Filter on our expression.
hRes = pCTbl -> Restrict(&srRoot, TBL_BATCH);

// Execute the query, returning up to 100 rows.
hRes = pCTbl -> QueryRows(100, 0, &pRows);
{
    // Do something with the rows.
    ⋮
}
FreeProws(pRows);
pCTbl -> Release();
⋮
```

You can debug your restrictions by passing each subtree in turn to *Restrict*, starting from the bottommost subtree and working upward to the root. In this example, you might want to try *Restrict* with *srLevel3[1]*, then with *srLevel3[0]*. Next you'd try *srLevel2[1]* and then *srLevel2[0]*, and so on until you finally arrived at *srRoot*.

Note that the call to *SetColumns* preceding *Restrict* selects only PR_SUBJECT and PR_MESSAGE_SIZE, yet we are restricting on two other properties. The properties tested in the restriction must be in the underlying data's column set, but for most implementations, they needn't be selected into the current view. For implementations that restrict on the selected column set, the order of these calls can be significant.

A restriction stays in effect until it is removed or a new restriction is applied by a fresh call to *Restrict*. Calls to *Restrict* don't accumulate—two successive calls both work on the same underlying data such that the second call doesn't restrict the results of the first. Passing NULL in the *lpRestriction* parameter removes the current restriction. MAPI provides a fairly comprehensive set of operators you can use with *Restrict*. The table in Figure 4-7 lists them and explains their functions.

MAPI Restriction Types

Operator	Data Structure	Comments
RES_AND	```typedef struct { ULONG cRes; LPSRestriction lpRes; } SAndRestriction;```	The logical AND of *lpRes[0]*, *lpRes[1]*,...,*lpRes[n]*.
RES_BITMASK	```typedef struct { ULONG relBMR; ULONG ulPropTag; ULONG ulMask; } SBitMaskRestriction;```	Evaluates to TRUE if a bitwise AND (&) of the property value in the column given by *ulPropTag* with *ulMask* is zero or non-zero, depending on whether BMR_EQZ or BMR_NEZ is set in *relBMR*. Use only with PT_LONG properties.
RES_COMMENT	```typedef struct { ULONG cValues; LPSRestriction lpRes; LPSPropValue lpProp; } SCommentRestriction;```	Contains data that is stored with the restriction but not evaluated.
RES_COMPAREPROPS	```typedef struct { ULONG relop; ULONG ulPropTag1; ULONG ulPropTag2; } SComparePropsRestriction;```	Compares the values in two columns of the same table. The comparison is evaluated using the operator in *relop*. The columns to compare are given by *ulPropTag1* and *ulPropTag2*; they must have the same property type.

Figure 4-7.

(continued)

The comprehensive set of operators you can use with Restrict.

Figure 4-7. *continued*

Operator	Data Structure	Comments

RES_CONTENT	```typedef struct```
	 ```{```
	     ```ULONG ulFuzzyLevel;```
	     ```ULONG ulPropTag;```
	     ```LPSPropValue lpProp;```
	 ```} SContentRestriction;```
		Similar to a property restriction but allows searching of binary or string properties for a match based on a substring, a prefix string, an exact match, a "loose" match, or a case-(in)sensitive match. Most operations are available only to PT_STRING8 properties. How the match is determined is specified by *ulFuzzyLevel* (e.g., FL_SUBSTRING).

RES_EXIST	```typedef struct```
	 ```}```
	     ```ULONG ulReserved1;```
	     ```ULONG ulPropTag;```
	     ```ULONG ulReserved2;```
	 ```} SExistRestriction;```
		Tests for a property's existence.

RES_NOT	```typedef struct```
	 ```{```
	     ```ULONG ulReserved;```
	     ```LPSRestriction lpRes;```
	 ```} SNotRestriction;```
		The logical negation of *lpRes*.

RES_OR	```typedef struct```
	 ```{```
	     ```ULONG cRes;```
	     ```LPSRestriction lpRes;```
	 ```} SOrRestriction;```
		The logical OR of *lpRes[0]*, *lpRes[1],...,lpRes[n]*.

(continued)

Figure 4-7. *continued*

Operator	Data Structure	Comments
| RES_PROPERTY | ```
typedef struct
{
    ULONG relop;
    ULONG ulPropTag;
    LPSPropValue lpProp;
}SPropertyRestriction;
``` | Specifies a table column to search and a value to compare against that column. The comparison operator is *relop*. (For example, RELOP_GT is equivalent to >.) The column property tag is *ulPropTag*, and *lpProp* contains a property value used to compare against the corresponding row's column value. |
| RES_SIZE | ```
typedef struct
{
    ULONG relop;
    ULONG ulPropTag;
    ULONG cb;
}SSizeRestriction;
``` | Compares the size of the value in column *ulPropTag* against *cb* using the relational operator given in *relop*. |
| RES_SUBRESTRICTION | ```
typedef struct
{
    ULONG ulSubObject;
    LPSRestriction lpRes;
} SSubRestriction;
``` | Allows subrestrictions (i.e., restrictions on a table within a table) on PT_OBJECT values that support a table interface, e.g., PR_MESSAGE_RECIPIENTS. For each row, the implementation opens the table interface on *ulSubObject* and applies the restriction given in *lpRes* to the newly opened table. |

MAPI tables also let you restrict on columns containing PR_MESSAGE_ATTACHMENTS or PR_MESSAGE_RECIPIENTS. Recall that PR_MESSAGE_ATTACHMENTS and PR_MESSAGE_RECIPIENTS are PT_OBJECT
```

properties, so the property's data isn't available from its column in the table. Instead, you access a PT_OBJECT property's data by calling *OpenProperty* on the parent object, which returns an interface (*IMAPITable*, in this case) that you use to access the data.

As an example, consider a store provider's receive folder that contains 100 messages. We have a pointer to the folder's contents table and would like to create a view of all messages in the folder with recipients named "lest." Each recipient's name, along with some other information, is embodied in the recipient table of each message, not in the folder's contents table. So how do we find only messages sent to "lest"? There are two ways to do this. The hard way follows (in pseudocode):

```
// Wrong!!
Get the contents table rows
For each row
    Retrieve the entry ID column
    Call OpenEntry on the entry ID to get an IMessage object
    Call IMessage::OpenProperty(…PR_MESSAGE_RECIPIENTS…) getting back
                    an IMAPITable interface on the recipient table
    Call IMAPITable::Restrict (or FindRow) on PR_DISPLAY_NAME == "lest"
    If ("lest" is found in the restricted table)
        Remember the entry ID of the message
    Release stuff
    Free stuff
    Go to the next row
Create an OR restriction on each remembered entry ID
Restrict the contents table using the restriction
```

A couple of things are wrong with this approach, not the least of which is the programming effort involved in coding it! Another problem is that you must keep track of the "hits" somehow—by saving them in a list, for example. If your ultimate goal is to obtain a contents table containing only the hits, you'll have to form a restriction based on each hit's entry ID and then restrict the contents table. This solution might work if you only have a couple of hits, but *Restrict* is likely to yield MAPI_E_TOO_COMPLEX for any significant number of hits—not to mention the hassle of setting up such a large restriction. (An equally cheesy alternative is to obtain an *ITableData* interface, add each hit's data as a row using *ITableData::HrModifyRow*, then return an *IMAPITable* interface via *ITableData::HrGetView*. But the table you return is a completely separate object, not the original contents table. If all you want is a row set with the hits, you could call *GetProps* on each hit and add the properties to an *SRowSet*, but then you have to worry about allocating memory for the *SRowSet*, resizing it, etc. Yuk!)

An easier, faster, and less error-prone way (a way that actually works) to accomplish what we're trying to do is to construct a subrestriction on PR_MESSAGE_RECIPIENTS and let the implementation do the work. Subrestrictions use the RES_SUBRESTRICTION operator to do restrictions where the target data is contained in a "table within a table," such as searching messages' recipient or attachment tables from the contents table of a folder. The code in Figure 4-8 demonstrates how this is done and also shows how to use RES_CONTENT restrictions. Notice that we only have to access the folder's contents table, not the individual messages:

```
//::::::::::::::::::::::::::::::::::::::::::::::::::::::::::::::::::::
// Demonstrates a subrestriction on PR_MESSAGE_RECIPIENTS
// on the message recipients' PR_DISPLAY_NAME

SRestriction srRoot,
             srSub;
SPropValue   spvName;

spvName.ulPropTag = PR_DISPLAY_NAME;
spvName.Value.lpszA = "lest";

srSub.rt = RES_CONTENT;
srSub.res.resContent.ulFuzzyLevel = FL_FULLSTRING | FL_IGNORECASE;
srSub.res.resContent.ulPropTag = PR_DISPLAY_NAME;
srSub.res.resContent.lpProp = &spvName;

srRoot.rt = RES_SUBRESTRICTION;
srRoot.res.resSub.ulSubObject = PR_MESSAGE_RECIPIENTS;
srRoot.res.resSub.lpRes = &srSub;

hRes = pCTbl -> SetColumns((LPSPropTagArray)&spt, TBL_BATCH);
hRes = pCTbl -> Restrict(&srRoot, 0);
hRes = pCTbl -> QueryRows(100, 0, &pRows);
{
    // Do something with the rows.
    ⋮
}
FreeProws(pRows);
pCTbl -> Release();
⋮
```

Figure 4-8.
Using a content restriction and subrestriction to restrict on a nested table.

Sorting: *SortTable*

You can specify a sort in your query by using the *IMAPITable::SortTable* method. *SortTable* takes the same TBL_XXX flags as *SetColumns* and *Restrict*, and the semantics are the same. *SortTable* also takes a pointer to an *SSortOrderSet* data structure, which specifies the keys used in the sort. The definition of *SSort-OrderSet* is as follows:

```
typedef struct _SSortOrderSet
{
    ULONG cSorts;
    ULONG cCategories;
    ULONG cExpanded;
    SSortOrder aSort[MAPI_DIM];
} SSortOrderSet, *LPSSortOrderSet;
```

The *cCategories* and *cExpanded* members are used with categorized tables, which we don't deal with here. The *cSorts* member indicates the number of keys given in *aSort*, which is an array of *cSorts* keys with *aSort[0]* being the primary key, *aSort[1]* the secondary key, and so on. Each key is an *SSortOrder* structure,

```
typedef struct _SSortOrder
{
    ULONG ulPropTag;
    ULONG ulOrder;
} SSortOrder, *LPSSortOrder;
```

where *ulPropTag* gives the key's property tag and *ulOrder* specifies whether the sort is to be ascending or descending (TABLE_SORT_ASCEND or TABLE-_SORT_DESCEND). Whether the results of a sort depend on the keys being selected in the current view is implementation-dependent, but all keys are required to exist in the underlying data. If the key properties don't exist, or if the implementation requires the key to be a column in the current view and it isn't, *SortTable* returns MAPI_E_TOO_COMPLEX. If the requested sort, though legal, is too expensive or difficult for the implementation to compute—or for sundry other reasons—MAPI_E_TOO_COMPLEX can be returned.

The *SortTable* method should be called after any *Restrict* call because the implementation can optimize the operation by not sorting rows that have been excluded from the view. Keep in mind that implementations aren't required to support *SortTable* at all and can return MAPI_E_NO_SUPPORT from this method. The code in Figure 4-9, on the following page, demonstrates how to use *SortTable*.

```
//:::::::::::::::::::::::::::::::::::::::::::::::::::::::
// Demonstrates SortTable.
//
LPSRowSet   pRows = NULL;
SizedSPropTagArray(2, spt) = {2, PR_NORMALIZED_SUBJECT,
                                  PR_MESSAGE_SIZE};
SizedSSortOrderSet(2, sso) = {2, 0, 0,
                              {PR_NORMALIZED_SUBJECT, TABLE_SORT_ASCEND,
                               PR_MESSAGE_SIZE, TABLE_SORT_DESCEND}};

// Select columns first.
hRes = pCTbl -> SetColumns((LPSPropTagArray)&spt, 0);

// Sort DOES depend on result of Restrict
// so remove any previous restriction and sort
// unrestricted table.
hRes = pCTbl -> Restrict(NULL, 0);

// Sort.
hRes = pCTbl -> SortTable((LPSSortOrderSet)&sso, 0);
// Execute query.
hRes = pCTbl -> QueryRows(100, 0, &pRows);
{
    // Do something with the rows.
    ⋮
}
FreeProws(pRows);
pCTbl -> Release();
⋮
```

Figure 4-9.
SortTable. *The primary key is PR_SUBJECT, ascending. The secondary key is PR_MESSAGE_SIZE, descending.*

The example in Figure 4-9 shows how to set up the *SSortOrderSet* data structure. You can use the *SizedSSortOrderSet* macro to declare a sort order on the stack and initialize it statically as shown. Note that the primary key specifies an ascending order, whereas the secondary key requests descending order. This causes rows with the same subject value to appear in descending order of message size.

Querying: *QueryRows, HrQueryAllRows*

By now you've probably figured out that *IMAPITable::QueryRows* executes a query constructed with *SetColumns, Restrict,* and *SortTable* and returns the view in an *SRowSet*. The *QueryRows* method doesn't accept TBL_XXX in the *ulFlags* parameter, so you can assume the operation will complete before the call returns. The *lRowCount* parameter specifies the maximum number of rows this method should return to you. (You can attempt to determine the total number of rows in the current view by calling *GetRowCount*, but this method doesn't guarantee more than an approximation.) Typically, you will pass the maximum number of rows that you, the caller, are prepared to handle; or you can use *HrQueryAllRows* and request the entire row set. The number of rows actually returned is stored in the *SRowSet::cRows* member.

When the query is executed, the table cursor is moved past the last row returned in the view, unless TBL_NOADVANCE is passed in the *ulFlags* parameter, in which case the cursor doesn't move at all. The default behavior leaves the table cursor pointing at the next unread row, while TBL_NO-ADVANCE puts the burden of adjusting the cursor on the caller. Note that the cursor's position is with respect to the current view, not the record's position in the underlying data. (Remember that the view is a table regardless of the underlying data's implementation. The concept of a row might or might not apply to the underlying data.) You request the next *lRowCount* rows by passing a positive value in *lRowCount* or request the previous *lRowCount* rows by passing a negative value. The *SRowSet::cRows* value might differ from *abs(lRowCount)* if the last row in the view is reached before the requested number of rows are found. In this case, the cursor position doesn't "wrap around" but stays at the first or last row of the view. Attempting to read past the beginning or end of the current view returns 0 rows and leaves the cursor position unchanged.

MAPI provides a wrapper API that combines the *SetColumns*, *Restrict*, *Sort-Table*, and *QueryRows* methods into a single call: *HrQueryAllRows*. You can use this API for most situations. Figures 4-6, 4-8, and 4-9 show how *QueryRows* can be called. In each of those examples, a single call to *HrQueryAllRows* passing the *SPropTagArray* (in *SetColumns*), the *SRestriction* (in *Restrict*), and the *SSortOrder* (from *SortTable*) replaces the three calls to *SetColumns*, *Restrict*, and *SortTable*.

Positioning: *SeekRow, FindRow*

The positioning methods always work on a view, not on the underlying data set. The view can be the default view—defined by the implementation—or defined explicitly by *SetColumns*, *Restrict*, and *SortTable*. If you position the cursor, or table row pointer, on a given row in the view, the cursor might or might not point to the same row if the view changes. Applying a new restriction or sort order, for example, always returns the cursor to the first row.

A cursor position can be remembered by creating a bookmark so that the cursor can be moved and returned to an earlier row. Bookmarks are created by calling the *CreateBookmark* method, which allocates and returns a BOOK-MARK data structure that represents the current cursor position. The bookmark must be freed by *FreeBookmark* when you're finished using it. Changing the view through *Restrict* or *SortTable* invalidates all outstanding bookmarks, so you should free them before calling either method. There are three predefined bookmarks you can pass to any table method requiring a bookmark:

- BOOKMARK_CURRENT, which specifies the current position of the cursor

- BOOKMARK_BEGINNING, which marks the first row in the view

- BOOKMARK_END, which specifies the last row

The simplest positioning method is *SeekRow*, which simply moves the cursor forward or backward a certain number of rows. The cursor origin from which the offset is calculated is specified by the bookmark passed in *bkOrigin*; the cursor is positioned *lRowCount* rows before or after this row. Normally, *SeekRow* positions the cursor on the requested row, but it can also be set immediately after the last row if the requested position is past the end of the view, or immediately preceding the first row if the new position would be before the first row. The number of rows searched is passed back in *lplRowsSought*.

SeekRowApprox is a close cousin to *SeekRow*, but instead of specifying an exact location, it positions the cursor at an approximate position in the view. The target row is given as a fraction of the rows in the view with respect to the first row. For example, if you want to move to the row located at the approximate halfway point in the view, you could pass 300 and 600 (or 50 and 100) in *ulNumerator* and *ulDenominator*. The actual numeric values aren't important—the ratio of *ulNumerator* to *ulDenominator* is what counts. The *SeekRowApprox* method is used to correlate a scrolling list box's thumb position with the cursor position of the table from which the list box is populated. If the number of records in the data set is large, you will want to retrieve only as many rows as can be viewed in the list box at one time. When the user scrolls past the last visible row, you call *SeekRowApprox* to reposition the cursor based on the thumb position and then call *QueryRows* for a new row set to load in the list box.

The *FindRow* method moves the cursor to the next row that matches a content restriction. It is often used to facilitate scrolling a list box via a MAPI table. A substring is entered by the user, translated into a restriction, and then passed to *FindRow*, which positions the cursor on the first row that matches the substring. As the user enters more characters (e.g., in the combo box), the substring grows and is passed to *FindRow* and the cursor is repositioned. This process continues until the substring can no longer be matched, whereupon *FindRow* returns MAPI_E_NOT_FOUND. See the table in Figure 4-10.

Substring as Input by User	Cursor Position

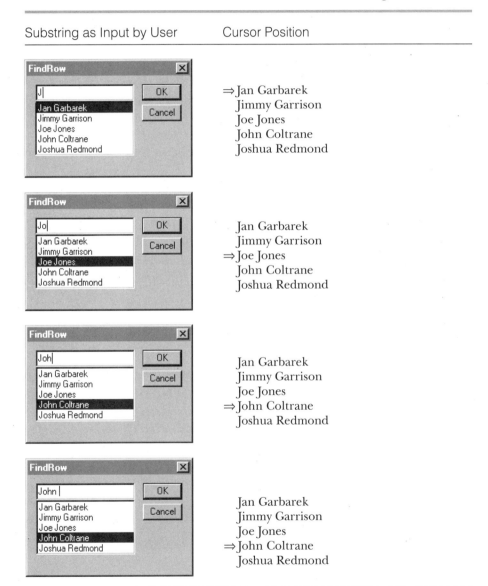

⇒Jan Garbarek
Jimmy Garrison
Joe Jones
John Coltrane
Joshua Redmond

Jan Garbarek
Jimmy Garrison
⇒Joe Jones
John Coltrane
Joshua Redmond

Jan Garbarek
Jimmy Garrison
Joe Jones
⇒John Coltrane
Joshua Redmond

Jan Garbarek
Jimmy Garrison
Joe Jones
⇒John Coltrane
Joshua Redmond

Figure 4-10. *(continued)*
Each successive call to FindRow *used with a content restriction moves the cursor to the next row that matches successively longer prefixes, until no match is found.*

Figure 4-10. *continued*

Substring as Input by User	Cursor Position

Jan Garbarek
Jimmy Garrison
Joe Jones
John Coltrane
⇒ Joshua Redmond

MAPI_E_NOT_FOUND

The *FindRow* method takes three parameters: the restriction criterion, a bookmark giving the row from which to start the search, and a flag specifying the search direction. Although this example uses a restriction based on a string property, *FindRow* will position the cursor on the first row that matches any arbitrary criterion. Notice that *FindRow* only works as expected if the view is sorted and the search direction matches the sort order. Figure 4-11 demonstrates how to use *FindRow*.

```
//:::::::::::::::::::::::::::::::::::::::::::::::::::::::::::
//
// Demonstrates using FindRow to do substring matches
//
//
BOOKMARK      BookMark    = BOOKMARK_BEGINNING;
HRESULT       hRes        = S_OK;
LPSRowSet     pRow        = NULL;
LPSTR         szSubStr[6] = {"J", //Simulates user input
                             "Jo",
                             "Joh",
                             "John",
                             "John ",
                             "John M"};
SPropValue    spv;
SRestriction srName;
SizedSPropTagArray(1, sptCols) = {1, PR_DISPLAY_NAME};
SizedSSortOrderSet(1, sso) = {1, 0, 0, {PR_DISPLAY_NAME,
                                    TABLE_SORT_ASCEND}};

// Select columns first.
hRes = pCTbl -> SetColumns((LPSPropTagArray)&sptCols, TBL_BATCH);
```

Figure 4-11.   *(continued)*
FindRow, *using a content restriction, searches for substring matches.*

Figure 4-11. *continued*

```
// Sort ascending.
hRes = pCTbl -> SortTable((LPSSortOrderSet)&sso, 0);

srName.rt = RES_CONTENT;
srName.res.resContent.ulPropTag = PR_DISPLAY_NAME;
srName.res.resContent.ulFuzzyLevel = FL_SUBSTRING | FL_IGNORECASE;
srName.res.resContent.lpProp = &spv;
spv.ulPropTag  = PR_DISPLAY_NAME;

for (int i = 0; i < 6; i++, BookMark = BOOKMARK_CURRENT)
{
    spv.Value.lpszA = szSubStr[i];
    hRes = pCTbl -> FindRow(&srName, BookMark, 0);

    if (FAILED(hRes))
        break;
}
if (SUCCEEDED(hRes))
{
    // Get the match.
    hRes = pCTbl -> QueryRows(1, 0, &pRow);
    {
        // Found a match; do something with row.
        FreeProws(pRow);
    }
}
    :
pCTbl -> Release();
```

Miscellaneous Table Methods

IMAPITable includes several other utility methods that don't implement any of the primitives discussed in this chapter but are useful nevertheless. Their use is, for the most part, straightforward. These utility methods include the following:

- *QueryColumns*, which returns the column set selected in the current view, the column set in the default view, or the set of available columns in the underlying data.

- *QueryPosition*, which returns the current cursor position as an integer. The first row in the view is designated as row 0. The numerator and denominator of a fraction, representing the approximate cursor position, are also returned.

■ *QuerySortOrder*, which returns the current sort order.

■ *GetStatus*, which returns a value indicating whether an operation is in progress, has completed, or has produced an error. Applications can poll the table's status to determine when an asynchronous operation has completed.

■ *Abort*, which terminates an asynchronous operation.

■ *GetRowCount*, which returns the approximate number of rows in the view.

Notifications

Messaging systems are dynamic. Changes occur in MAPI objects as a result of a client's actions or external events. MAPI provides a way for users of MAPI objects to retrieve information about changes to an object's internal state or underlying data. The mechanism by which this is accomplished is called a *notification.*

Notifications are used to signal the occurrence of one or more events, such as new mail arriving in the user's Inbox. Tables also generate notifications when data is modified, added, or deleted from the underlying data set. Handling event notifications is important to applications that must update user interfaces, as in the case of a tree-view control that gets redrawn when a folder is created or deleted.

MAPI clients and providers register their interest in receiving notifications for certain events, and the object generates the notification when the event of interest occurs. The object user registers with the object by calling its *Advise* method, and the object generates the notification by invoking a callback function implemented by the object user. The callback function is actually a method called *OnNotify* on the *IMAPIAdviseSink* interface. A pointer to an *IMAPIAdviseSink* interface, along with a bitmap of events of interest to the object user, is passed in the call to *Advise.*

An object user implements the *IMAPIAdviseSink* interface and receives notifications on the *OnNotify* method. The object user specifies the events in which it's interested by passing a bitmap of flags to the *Advise* method. MAPI defines several fnevXXX constants that can be combined to represent the events of interest. The provider implementing the notifying object saves the *IMAPIAdviseSink* interface and event mask so that if and when a registered event occurs, it can easily locate the subscriber's *IMAPIAdviseSink* and call the *OnNotify* method. The provider passes back a connection number in *Advise*'s *lpulConnection* parameter, which it uses to locate each requester's *IMAPIAdviseSink* object. The meaning of **lpulConnection* is opaque to the object user—it could be an index into a provider-implemented table of advise sinks, for example—and would only be used by the subscriber to cancel the registration in the call to the object's *Unadvise* method.

The signature of the *Advise* method depends on the interface: For high-level interfaces such as *IMAPISession*, *IMsgStore*, or *IAddrBook*, the signature includes an entry ID that identifies an object accessible from or managed by the high-level interface. Folders and messages, for example, don't expose *Advise*. You must register for notifications on these objects by first obtaining their entry IDs and passing them to *IMsgStore::Advise*. When the identity of the object generating the notification is unambiguous (a MAPI table, for example), the *Advise* method doesn't take an entry ID. (Tables don't have entry IDs. Note that we again relax our definition of object to include tables.)

Notifications are made asynchronously and can even occur on a thread different from the one calling *Advise*. A provider could spawn a separate thread to handle the notification and inadvertently turn a single-threaded application into a multithreaded one. This could cause synchronization problems for applications that aren't thread-safe, as the *OnNotify* call could then occur at any time and cause contention for shared resources. If the client isn't thread-safe, or requires the *OnNotify* call to occur on a specific thread, it should call the *HrThisThreadAdviseSink* API to wrap the advise sink object. The wrapped advise sink object is passed to *Advise* and functions exactly as described with one important proviso: The call to *OnNotify* is guaranteed to occur on the same thread from which *HrThisThreadAdviseSink* was called. Note that the thread making the call to *HrThisThreadAdviseSink* must have a message loop.

MAPI notifications are sent across process boundaries. Suppose, for example, that client A has registered for notifications on the message store provider and is viewing a folder. If client B deletes a message from the same folder, the store provider must broadcast a notification of the deletion that can be received by client A so that A can update its UI.

The MAPI Notification Engine

MAPI provides a *notification engine* that implements cross-process notifications. Developers writing service providers can save themselves a lot of work by using MAPI's implementation instead of writing their own. This is how the notification engine works: A provider calls *IMAPISupport::Subscribe* to register a notification request in much the same way as a client calls *Advise* on a specific interface. The *Subscribe* method takes a unique binary key that identifies the object, an event mask that specifies the events of interest, and a pointer to an advise sink object; it returns a unique connection number. The key can be an entry ID, but since the key is not interpreted by MAPI, it can also be any unique

107

number. When the provider determines that a change has occurred to the object associated with the key, it calls *IMAPISupport::Notify*. MAPI keeps the advise sink objects and their registered event masks in a table or list in which every node is identified by the connection number returned by *Subscribe*.

The MAPI notification engine creates a hidden window for processing the *Notify* call. When the provider calls *Notify*, it passes the key, which MAPI posts in a message to this hidden window. The window procedure searches the list for the key and calls the advise sink object's *OnNotify* if the key and event match those stored in the list node. MAPI will create a separate thread and message loop for this window if the client passes MAPI_MULTITHREAD_NOTI-FICATIONS to *MAPIInitialize*; otherwise, it uses the calling application's message loop. The consequence of all of this is that the *OnNotify* call can be made on a thread different from the application's main thread. Consequently, blocking calls such as *WaitForSingleObject*, or *Read* and *Write*, will hang the message loop and cause all other notifications to come grinding to a halt until the thread is rescheduled. In short, applications need to be careful when it comes to notifications! The rules are as follows:

- If your client is single-threaded, call *MAPIInitialize* without MAPI-_MULTITHREAD_NOTIFICATIONS or wrap your advise sink objects using *HrThisThreadAdviseSink*.

- If your client is multithreaded, pass MAPI_MULTITHREAD_NOTI-FICATIONS to *MAPIInitialize*. If you want the notification to occur on a specific thread, wrap your advise sink object with *HrThisThread-AdviseSink*.

OnNotify contains the logic that handles the event notification. A typical use of *OnNotify* is to send a window message to a dialog procedure or a window procedure to update a control in the window. Figure 4-12 demonstrates how to implement *IMAPIAdviseSink::OnNotify* and how to register for notifications.

```
/////////////////////////////////////////////////////////////////////
// Implementation of IMAPIAdviseSink::OnNotify
STDMETHODIMP_(ULONG)
CAdviseSink::OnNotify(ULONG           cNotif,
                      LPNOTIFICATION  pNotifications)
{
```

Figure 4-12. *(continued)*

Stub implementation of IMAPIAdviseSink::OnNotify. *Any number of notification structures can be passed in* lpNotifications. *The call to* Advise *is passed the entry ID of the message store provider.*

Figure 4-12. *continued*

```
for (ULONG i = 0; i < cNotif; i++)
{
    switch (pNotifications[i].ulEventType)
    {
        case fnevObjectCreated :
            // An object was created in container
            // pNotifications[i].info.obj.lpParentID.
            break;
        case fnevObjectDeleted :
            // An object was deleted from container
            // pNotifications[i].info.obj.lpParentID.
            break;
        case fnevObjectModified :
            // Object pNotifications[i].info.obj.lpEntryID
            // was modified.
            break;
        case fnevObjectMoved :
            // Object was moved from container
            // pNotifications[i].info.obj.lpOldParentID
            // to container
            // pNotifications[i].info.obj.lpParentID.
            break;
        case fnevNewMail :
            // New mail arrived in folder
            // pNotifications[i].info.newmail.lpParentID.
            break;
        case fnevCriticalError :
            // Error was caused by object
            // pNotifications[i].info.err.lpEntryID;
            // SCODE is in pNotifications[i].info.err.scode;
            // more info is in the error struct
            // pNotifications[i].info.err.lpMAPIError.
            break;
        case fnevSearchComplete :
            break;
        case fnevStatusObjectModified :
            break;
        case fnevExtended :
            // Provider defined blob of data is in
            // pNotifications[i].info.ext.pbEventParameters.
            break;
    }
}
return S_OK;
```

(continued)

Figure 4-12. *continued*

```
}

/////////////////////////////////////////////////////////////////////

ULONG cbFolderEID;
LPENTRYID pFolderEID;
⋮
// Code to get a folder entry ID
⋮
#define EVENT_MASK (fnevObjectDeleted  !\
                    fnevObjectCreated   !\
                    fnevObjectModified !\
                    fnevObjectCopied)
ULONG     ulCnxNum;
CAdviseSink * pAdviseSink = new CAdviseSink();
hRes = pMsgStore -> Advise(cbFolderEID,
                           pFolderEID,
                           EVENT_MASK,
                           pAdviseSink,
                           &ulCnxNum);

⋮
pMsgStore -> Unadvise(ulCnxNum);
pAdviseSink -> Release();
⋮
```

Since *IMAPIAdviseSink* is directly derived from *IUnknown* and contains only the single *OnNotify* method, we've omitted showing the *IUnknown* methods. The code in Figure 4-12 shows how a client would register for the events given by EVENT_MASK with the message store provider. You pass the entry ID of the object of interest as well as a bitmap of fnevXXX constants in the call to *Advise*, and a connection number is returned. The connection number is used to cancel the registration in a later call to *Unadvise*. Objects that contain child objects will let you advise on their children if you know the child's entry ID. You should use prudence when registering with top level objects. For example, if you were to register for all notifications on a message store provider, a change to a single message would cause a notification on the message, the parent folder, and the message store provider. It's possible to inadvertently get inundated with notifications.

When the event occurs, the *OnNotify* method is called and the event or events are passed in an array of *NOTIFICATION* structures. We've included a case for every possible event in *OnNotify*'s switch statement, although in practice you might handle some and not others, or handle different events in different advise sinks. The *NOTIFICATION* array in *pNotifications* describes each event and gives the entry ID of the object or objects involved. How you interpret the entry ID depends on the type of event. For fnevObjectCreated or fnevObject-Deleted events, *pNotifications[i].info.obj.lpParentID* gives the entry ID of the container in which the object was created or deleted.

If the notification type is fnevObjectMoved, *pNotifications[i].info.obj.lp-ParentID* will contain the destination container and *pNotifications[i].info.obj-.lpOldParentID* the source. The fnevNewMail event contains the receive folder's entry ID in *pNotifications[i].info.newmail.lpParentID,* and so on. Notice that *IMAPITable::Advise* doesn't take an entry ID as a parameter (tables don't have entry IDs, right?). Table notifications are generated on changes to the view or the underlying data.

MAPI tables must specify an index column that is unique for each row in the view. PR_INSTANCE_KEY is the usual choice, since this property must be unique in each instance (or view) of the table object. The *lpNotifications-[i].info.tab.propIndex* gives the index value of the row added, deleted, or modified, except when a TABLE_CHANGED or TABLE_RELOAD event occurs, when it points to NULL. The *lpNotifications[i].info.tab.propPrior* gives the index value of the row immediately preceding the row that was added, deleted, or modified. In the case of TABLE_ROW_DELETED, TABLE_RELOAD, and TABLE_CHANGED notifications, *lpNotifications[i].info.tab.propPrior* points to NULL. The prior row's index will also be NULL if the row affected by the operation is the first row in the table. The *lpNotifications[i].info.tab.row* gives the row's new columns, subject to the prevailing column set, and also points to NULL for TABLE_CHANGED events.

A Look Ahead

We've seen how MAPI tables provide a uniform, easy-to-use interface for manipulating sets of data and how the *IMAPITable* interface was designed to be a general-purpose mechanism for providing this access. When you consider the vastly different ways that MAPI tables are used, you begin to appreciate the power and elegance of this interface.

We've also pointed out some of *IMAPITable*'s limitations, but keep in mind that our treatment of MAPI tables in this chapter has focused on how tables are used, not how they're implemented. Some providers—store providers and address book providers in particular—are both users and implementors of MAPI tables. Remote transports must also implement *IMAPITable*. In fact, any provider that implements an interface derived from *IMAPIContainer* will probably have to supply one or more *IMAPITable* implementations, and a provider is free to implement *IMAPITable* in whatever manner is optimal for its particular needs. We'll discuss some possible alternatives when we cover the WINDS service providers later in this book.

Clients and providers also use MAPI notifications, although only providers (not clients) implement notifications. We'll also discuss how notifications are implemented by the provider when we examine the WINDS case study.

MAPI Client Applications

This chapter deals with the upper layer of the MAPI architecture—the client to MAPI interface—and shows how clients navigate around the messaging system by calling MAPI APIs and interface methods. We describe some of the common operations MAPI clients are likely to perform and present a minimal implementation, HelloMAPI, that demonstrates these operations.

What Is a Client?

A MAPI client is a program that requests services of a messaging system to do some work. The term *client* describes the program's relationship with the underlying messaging system rather than the work it's designed to do and corresponds loosely to its accepted meaning in client-server computing. In the client-server model, the server is an autonomous process that waits for clients to connect to it, handles their requests, and returns the results. The connection is explicit, and the client-to-server relationship is many-to-one.

The situation is similar in MAPI except that the identity and possibly the existence of the server process is hidden behind the middle layer of MAPI through which client service requests pass. For this reason, interfaces such as MAPI are sometimes referred to as "middleware" because they interpose a layer of software between the process requesting services and the process or processes providing them. The MAPI architecture doesn't even require the existence of a server process: MAPI transport providers, for example, can make peer-to-peer connections that are essentially client-to-client transactions. To the client, these details are hidden, however. It operates in its own world, blissfully ignorant of how the various minion providers actually do the work. (See Figure 5-1 on the following page.)

MAPI clients are consumers of services. They can be almost any type of application that needs the services of a MAPI messaging system. Traditional email clients for composing, viewing, addressing, sending, and receiving email

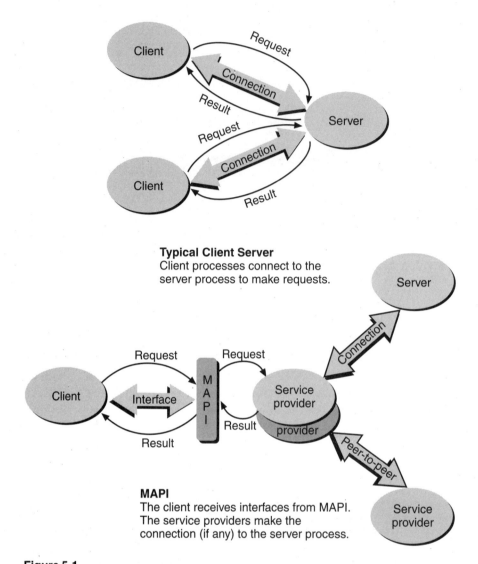

Typical Client Server
Client processes connect to the
server process to make requests.

MAPI
The client receives interfaces from MAPI.
The service providers make the
connection (if any) to the server process.

Figure 5-1.
*A client process in the client-server model connects to a server process to request services.
MAPI clients might or might not communicate with a server process. The middle layer of
MAPI hides these details.*

messages are probably the most familiar examples, but many new and interesting client applications will continue to be developed as MAPI's rich feature set
becomes better known. At one end of the spectrum are those applications for
which the ability to send and receive messages is an ancillary capability that is
related to, though not strictly essential to, the program's main purpose. A word

processor or spreadsheet program that can send documents in a MAPI message would be an example of such an application. Microsoft likes to call these types of applications *mail-aware* because they have some limited messaging capacity without fully exploiting the underlying messaging system.

At the other end of the spectrum are those clients for which the ability to send and receive messages is a primary requirement, and are therefore dependent on the underlying system for basic functionality. Applications of this type are called *messaging-based* because they make extensive use of messaging system services and are more likely to fully exploit MAPI's advanced features. For example, messaging-based clients might use some of the following:

- *Private message classes.* Applications that need to send and receive messages with specialized data content can set a custom value in PR_MESSAGE_CLASS to distinguish their special-case messages from others. Private message classes are most often used with forms but can also be defined by any application that uses MAPI messages to pass data. Schedule+ is an example: A user's free and busy times, as well as meeting requests and responses, are sent in MAPI messages. The message class is also used to specify in which receive folder inbound messages should be placed.

- *Forms.* These are messages that have special display requirements. Some examples include an employee time card, a help-desk order form, and a customer satisfaction survey. Form messages are rendered by an application known as a form server, which is invoked by the client when one of these special-purpose messages is opened or created. The message class identifies which form server should be invoked to render a particular form.

- *Public folders.* Clients can post and retrieve messages in folders that are accessible by groups of users. For example, a client can create a classified-ad public folder in which users post messages offering items for sale or purchase. A form is often associated with the public folder for browsing its contents or posting new messages.

- *Automated mailbox agents.* These are special-purpose clients that monitor a mailbox and automatically process incoming or outgoing messages. Examples include an out-of-office assistant that automatically replies to a vacationing user's incoming messages, a service that automatically forwards inbound mail to another mailbox, or a list server that manages membership in a mailing list and handles distributing messages to its members.

115

Common Client Attributes

MAPI clients can come in so many varieties that it's difficult to generalize about what they do. Clients are processes that are consumers of services provided by the back-end messaging system. They can be background processes that run unattended and require little or no user intervention; programs that occasionally require user input—for configuration or administrative purposes, for example; or programs that are totally interactive.

Clients often provide some kind of user interface, although this is by no means a requirement. They typically allow the creation, "viewing," delivery, and reception of MAPI messages and often provide an interface to one or more messaging system components, such as a message store provider or address book provider, through which users can manipulate folders and messages or recipient information.

Clients always run in the context of a MAPI session and must obtain an *IMAPISession* object before requesting services. The act of acquiring a session object, or *logging on,* is what "connects" a client to the MAPI subsystem and, by implication, to the underlying messaging services. Once this connection exists, the client can do useful work.

Client Access to the Messaging System

Clients should access the back-end messaging system only through an interface provided by MAPI. Direct access to a provider's code or data is discouraged by the MAPI specification because it violates the requirement for interoperability between components. A client that bypasses MAPI and directly accesses a provider's code or data is making an assumption about which providers will be running in a given session. It's an assumption that becomes invalid as soon as the user adds new providers to the profile. Recall that the MAPI architecture uses a three-layered model. (See Figure 1-2 on page 11.)

The MAPI-to-client interface provides the mechanism for passing client requests to the back-end messaging system and for retrieving results. MAPI clients, as object consumers, make service requests by calling MAPI APIs to obtain interfaces. Through an interface method, a client can request that work be done or it can obtain another interface. MAPI provides the interfaces to the client, and MAPI and the service providers provide the code that implements the interfaces. The service providers talk to the underlying messaging system, and everyone is happy.

It's slightly dogmatic to say that clients only access the messaging system through the MAPI layer. In practice, the interface pointer that MAPI passes back to the client often references code that lives in the provider, so the client is actually calling into a DLL loaded in its own address space. The point is this: *Where* the code is actually running is intentionally hidden from the calling application—it can be implemented in a DLL loaded in the client process, running in a different process, or even running on another machine and accessed through remote procedure calls.

All the client knows for sure is that it requests an interface and is returned a pointer through which it can make method calls. MAPI handles loading the providers, checking versions, and marshalling remote interfaces on behalf of the caller. In version 1 of MAPI, interface pointers almost always point to provider code in a local DLL, to MAPI code, or to MAPI code that wraps provider code. But this could change in the future, and from the client's perspective, it won't matter if it does.

The MAPI Session

Clients always run in a MAPI session. For our present purposes, we can define a session to be a period of time during which a client uses the messaging system to do some work. Note that a session is dynamic and temporal, as opposed to a profile, which is passive and static. A MAPI session has a beginning, a middle, and an end. The beginning occurs when a client logs on to the messaging system; the end comes when it logs off. In between, the client will obtain interfaces, make method calls, and maybe interact with the user, all with the expectation of doing some useful work. Figure 5-2 illustrates a MAPI session.

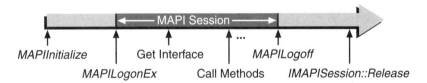

Figure 5-2.
This timeline depicts a MAPI session. MAPI sessions begin when the client logs on. Work is done by calling interface methods; then the client logs off.

Programmatically, logging on is accomplished by a call to *MAPIInitialize* followed by *MAPILogonEx*. This sequence of calls does the following:

- Initializes the MAPI subsystem.

- Specifies which profile to use.

■ Loads and initializes the service providers listed in the user's profile.[1]

■ Logs on to each provider and checks its configuration. Providers can display UI or obtain the user's security credentials from the operating system at this time.

■ Starts the spooler or hooks a running instance and increments its reference count if it's already running.

Logging on establishes the user's identity and security credentials, either by an explicit password or by querying the operating system. This is important for providers that talk to secure systems and must validate a user's identity and permissions before granting access. Providers can get the user's credentials directly from the operating system or can force the user to supply additional credentials as they see fit. Microsoft Exchange, for example, lets a user access an Exchange Server mailbox based on the credentials used to log on to the operating system. MAPI maintains an internal database known as the *profile section* of the current session in which providers can store logon information from session to session.

A call to *MAPILogonEx* can pass the name of a profile explicitly, display a dialog box that lets the user choose a profile, use the profile of an existing shared session, or use a default. The profile contains a list of message services—or sets of service providers—that will be used to access the underlying messaging system. Because the user can choose the profile, he can have multiple profiles configured with different sets of providers for connecting to different messaging systems. A mobile user might have two profiles on his laptop: one with providers for accessing the messaging system via modem or wireless, and one with LAN-based providers for the office. The user can log on to multiple, concurrent sessions with any profile and create separate, independent sessions; or he can log on to a shared session that uses the same profile.

Basic Client Operations

If the logon operation succeeds, MAPI returns a pointer to an *IMAPISession* interface to the client. The client can use the pointer to call methods on *IMAPISession*, open other interfaces, and do useful work. The following list identifies some tasks a client might want to perform:

■ Open one or more message store providers

■ Open the MAPI address book provider

---

1. Some providers are loaded only when called.

- Enumerate a store provider's folder hierarchy or a folder's contents

- Compose a message

- Save or retrieve a message in a store provider

- Attach a file to a message

- Add addressing information to a message

- Copy or move a message between folders

- Delete a message in a folder

- Reply to an inbound message or forward it to another user

- Browse the MAPI address book provider for recipients

- Force immediate delivery of a pending message

We'll informally consider this list to be our requirements for HelloMAPI, the minimal MAPI mail client example we develop in the rest of the chapter. This list is by no means exhaustive; in fact, it is deliberately limited to those operations that we will demonstrate in the HelloMAPI sample client. While the sample we present here is a far cry from a commercial application, it's certainly not a toy either—it's a fully functioning mail client capable of interacting with the most complex and sophisticated messaging systems on the market today. This is the power of MAPI—the ability to interoperate with other vendors' components by means of standard interfaces.

It's also worthwhile to point out which features are missing from HelloMAPI that might be found in a commercial application. Specifically, we don't support the following:

- Message service or profile configuration

- Formatted text (also known as *rich text format,* or RTF)

- Embedded messages or OLE objects

- Fancy UI, such as tree-views, toolbars, cool icons, and so on

- Direct address book provider interaction

- Forms

- Opening an *IStream* interface on the message body

- Conversation threading

- Notifications

- Per-message or per-recipient options

Client Interactions with Providers

Clients interact extensively with message store providers and address book providers but have almost no interaction with the spooler or transport providers. This makes sense if you consider the MAPI architecture: Messages and recipients are objects that are directly manipulated by the end user, whereas the transports and spooler represent the delivery mechanism of the underlying system and are therefore hidden.

Messages live within folders, folders are arranged hierarchically within a store provider, and any number of store providers can be present in a session. Often a client must traverse the hierarchy of folders of one or more store providers to find a particular message so it can obtain its entry ID and open the message. Opening the message returns an *IMessage* interface, which the client can then use to access properties of the message. The same is true for folder objects: You must obtain the folder's entry ID and open an *IMAPIFolder* interface before you can manipulate the folder or its contents.

There are several ways to traverse this hierarchy, depending on which tree of folders you want to access. The most general method is to call *IMAPISession::GetMsgStoresTable*, search for the store provider of interest, open the store provider and obtain its hierarchy table, search for the target folder, obtain *its* contents table, search for the target message, obtain its entry ID, then use the entry ID to open the message. You can see the pattern here: open object, get table, search table, open object, get table, search table, and so on. Figure 5-3 on page 122 shows how to traverse the store provider hierarchy to open a message.

So to access an existing message, for example, the client must perform the following sequence of actions:

1. Call *IMAPISession::GetMsgStoresTable*, to obtain a table of the store providers in the current session.

2. Search the table for a particular store provider. Its entry ID is a column in the target's row.

3. Call *IMAPISession::OpenMsgStore*, passing the entry ID. An *IMsgStore* interface is returned.

4. Call *IMsgStore::OpenEntry*, passing NULL in *lpEntryID* to open the root folder. The call passes back an *IMAPIFolder* interface.

5. Call *IMAPIFolder::GetHierarchyTable*, to obtain a table of subfolders. If the implementation supports the CONVENIENT_DEPTH flag, the entire hierarchy of folders is returned in a single table.[2] If not, the client must repeatedly open subfolders and get their hierarchy tables.

6. Search the table for a particular folder, obtaining its entry ID.

7. Call *IMsgStore::OpenEntry* for the target folder using the entry ID from the previous step. An *IMAPIFolder* interface is returned.

8. Call *IMAPIFolder::GetContentsTable*, which returns a table containing the target message's entry ID.

9. Call *IMsgStore::OpenEntry*, passing the message's entry ID, which returns an *IMessage* interface.

10. Call *IMessage* methods: *GetProps, SetProps, SaveChanges, SubmitMessage,* and so on.

MAPI provides some shortcuts if you want to access a particular store provider (the default store, for example) or a particular parent folder (the IPM subtree, for example), or a specific subfolder (the receive folder, for example). Notice that whereas *IMAPISession::OpenEntry* can also return the same interfaces as the special-purpose *OpenXXX* calls, a call to *IMAPISession::OpenEntry* will be less efficient since it must do the extra work of examining the entry ID and routing the call to the correct provider. If you are holding only the entry ID and don't know exactly which object you need, *IMAPISession::OpenEntry* is useful. The same is true for the *IAddrBook* methods that open specific address book objects.

Message creation is essentially the same process: Call *OpenXXX* until you get to the desired folder, and then call *IMAPIFolder::CreateMessage* instead of *OpenEntry*. A message is always created and submitted in a folder, usually the Outbox. Submission causes the store provider to place the message in its outgoing queue where it gets picked up by the spooler and handed to one or more transport providers for delivery. Which transport is selected for a given recipient is based on the recipient's address type and the address types for which the transport can handle delivery.

---

2. Actually, CONVENIENT_DEPTH requests the implementation to return as much of the hierarchy as it can. The implementation decides how many levels are returned, which makes CONVENIENT_DEPTH practically useless since the caller must handle implementations that return fewer levels or don't support this flag at all.

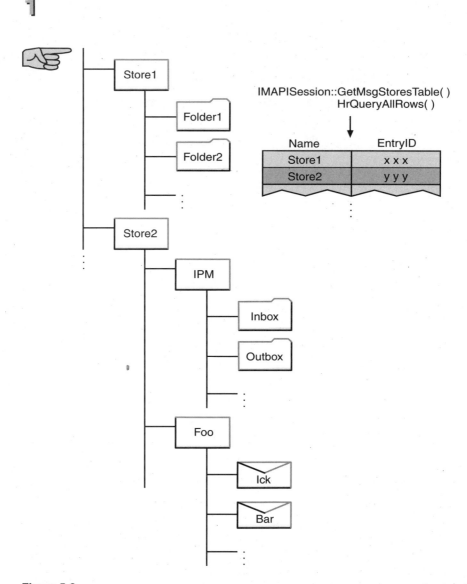

Figure 5-3. *(continued)*
This figure consists of four illustrations and continues on pages 123 and 124. It depicts the most general way to access a particular message, which is through a series of
OpenXXX *and* GetXXXTable *calls. This example shows the hierarchy and sequence of calls used to access message* Bar.

Figure 5-3. *continued*

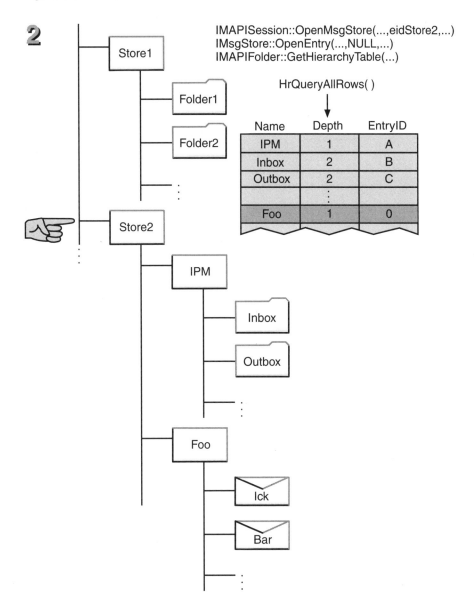

(continued)

PART I: THE MAPI COMPONENTS

Figure 5-3. *continued*

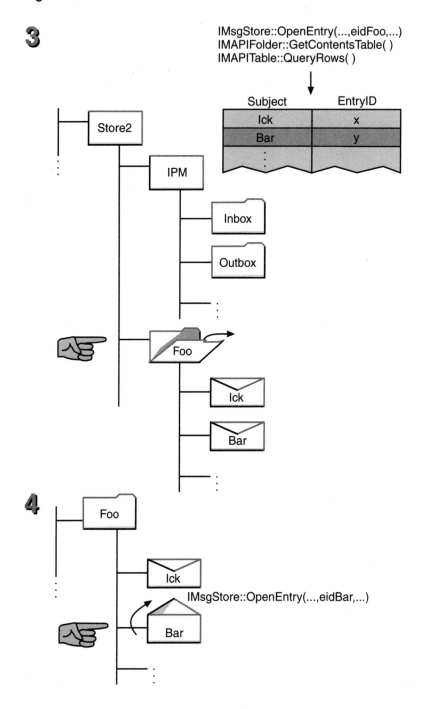

124

Because a message can have multiple recipients of different address types, the spooler might submit a message to more than one transport. The address type, along with other recipient information, is kept in a table that is a PT_OBJECT property of the message—PR_MESSAGE_RECIPIENTS. Notice that there is a qualitative difference between a message's recipients and its contents. Properties such as PR_MESSAGE_RECIPIENTS, PR_SENDER-_XXX, PR_DELIVER_TIME, and others are called *envelope properties* because they provide message delivery information rather than message content information. This distinction is important because the envelope will be pretty much the same regardless of the content, which can vary widely depending on the message class.

Recipient information usually comes from one or more address book providers and is set into the recipient table by a client's call to *IMessage-::ModifyRecipients*. Clients can get recipient information directly from individual address book providers—the hard way—or by high-level calls to the *IAddrBook* interface. *IAddrBook* is an interface implemented by MAPI that constructs a *supercontainer* composed of each address book provider's root container. When the session is started, *IAddrBook* logs on to each address book provider in the profile and obtains its root container. These containers become subcontainers of the *IAddrBook* supercontainer. The idea is to give the client an easy way to access entries in multiple address book providers while maintaining the appearance of a single address book provider.

To accomplish this illusion, *IAddrBook* supplies methods for browsing the supercontainer (i.e., the individual address book containers, albeit transparently); obtaining *resolved* address book provider entries if only a friendly name is known; viewing an entry's properties, or *details page*; and adding or deleting entries within a modifiable container. *IAddrBook* supplies dialog boxes that make it less obvious that the data might be coming from different providers. Each entry's details page, for example, has a consistent look, even though the data used to populate two different pages might belong to completely different messaging systems.

Resolved Names

A name is considered fully resolved when it maps to a single recipient's entry ID. Resolving a name is the process of searching the address book providers for a display name and returning the corresponding entry ID. Ambiguities can exist when the display name isn't unique within the installed address book providers or when the entry has a slightly different spelling (for example, Miles Davis vs. Miles D. Davis) than the name supplied by the user.

Although the entry ID alone identifies the recipient, a client needs to provide the PR_DISPLAY_NAME, PR_ADDRTYPE, PR_ENTRY-ID, and PR_RECIPIENT_TYPE properties to successfully submit the message. Submitting a message with fewer than these minimum properties can cause a run-time error or a nondelivery report to be generated. The address type lets the spooler know which transport should handle delivery to the recipient; the entry ID lets the transport open the entry and obtain necessary addressing information; and the other two properties are required columns in the message's recipient table.

If the client knows all of these properties for a given recipient, it can add the recipient directly to the message by calling *ModifyRecipients*. Often, the client has only a display name entered by the user. In this case, calling *IAddrBook::ResolveName* will return the other properties if an unambiguous match can be found in an address book container. *ResolveName* can display a dialog box to let the user choose the desired recipient if no unique match is found.

Clients pass an *ADRLIST* structure to *ResolveName* containing one or more *ADRENTRY*s representing the unresolved names. Each *ADRENTRY* might be missing one or more required properties that *ResolveName* must fill in to fully resolve the name. If, for example, the client passes an *ADRLIST* with a recipient (an *ADRENTRY*) for which only the PR_DISPLAY_NAME and PR_RECIPIENT_TYPE properties are known, *ResolveName* will return the *ADRLIST* with the *ADRENTRY* modified to contain *at least* two additional properties—the entry ID and address type. This means that *ResolveName* must allocate a larger *rgPropVals* array, copy the existing properties and new properties to the new array, and then free the old one. Clients must be careful how they allocate *ADRLISTs* and *ADRENTRYs* so that this reallocation and freeing can work. The rules follow:

- Allocate the *ADRLIST* with *MAPIAllocateBuffer*.

- Allocate each *ADRENTRY*'s *rgPropVals* array separately, using *MAPIAllocateBuffer*. Note that the entire *rgPropVals* allocation must be a contiguous (single) allocation; it's an array, after all.

- If an *SPropValue* in the *rgPropVals* array has blobs of memory hanging off of it—that is, binary or string property values that are referenced through pointers such as *SPropValue.Value.bin.lpb* or *SPropValue.Value.lpszA*—these property values should be allocated with *MAPIAllocateMore*, passing the *rgPropVals* array as the parent block.

- Free each member of the *rgPropVals* array with a single call to *MAPIFreeBuffer* and free the *ADRLIST* with *MAPIFreeBuffer*. Or, better yet, free everything with a single call to *FreePadrlist*.

These rules are simple and straightforward if you consider what's going on behind the *ResolveName* call, but to make it even clearer, consider the diagram in Figure 5-4 on the following page.

(continued)

continued

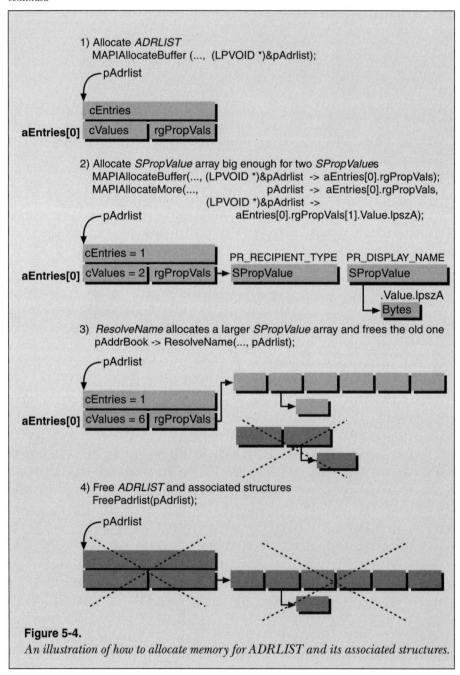

1) Allocate *ADRLIST*
   MAPIAllocateBuffer (..., (LPVOID *)&pAdrlist);

pAdrlist

cEntries

aEntries[0] cValues   rgPropVals

2) Allocate *SPropValue* array big enough for two *SPropValues*
   MAPIAllocateBuffer(..., (LPVOID *)&pAdrlist -> aEntries[0].rgPropVals);
   MAPIAllocateMore(...,   pAdrlist -> aEntries[0].rgPropVals,
                 (LPVOID *)&pAdrlist ->
                        aEntries[0].rgPropVals[1].Value.lpszA);

pAdrlist

cEntries = 1   PR_RECIPIENT_TYPE   PR_DISPLAY_NAME

aEntries[0] cValues = 2 rgPropVals   SPropValue   SPropValue

                                              .Value.lpszA
                                              Bytes

3) *ResolveName* allocates a larger *SPropValue* array and frees the old one
   pAddrBook -> ResolveName(..., pAdrlist);

pAdrlist

cEntries = 1

aEntries[0] cValues = 6 rgPropVals

4) Free *ADRLIST* and associated structures
   FreePadrlist(pAdrlist);

pAdrlist

Figure 5-4.
An illustration of how to allocate memory for ADRLIST and its associated structures.

A client has almost no direct interaction with the spooler or individual transports. Despite this restriction, a client can command a particular transport to deliver messages previously queued for deferred delivery, or request the spooler to force delivery of all pending messages by calling *IMAPIStatus::FlushQueues* (which is covered later).

Important Client-Side Properties Accessed in HelloMAPI

Before diving into the specific coding details of HelloMAPI, you should be acquainted with some of the properties accessed in the HelloMAPI sample. Although many of these properties are important for most MAPI clients, this list should not be considered exhaustive. Each application has different requirements and might make use of additional or different properties.

Most properties that a client manipulates fall into one of four categories: message properties, store provider properties, attachment properties, or recipient properties. The following table summarizes how these properties are used in the HelloMAPI sample:

Properties Used in the HelloMAPI Sample

Property Tag	Description
Store Provider Properties	
PR_DEFAULT_STORE	One store provider in the session is designated as the default. The only special requirements imposed on the default store provider are that it must support creation, modification, and submission of messages. MAPI creates the IPM subtree in the default store provider if it doesn't already exist. This property is a column in the session message store table; its value is *TRUE* if a store provider is the default.

(continued)

129

Properties Used in the HelloMAPI Sample *continued*

Property Tag	Description
PR_IPM_SUBTREE_ENTRYID	*HrValidateIPMSubtree* returns the PR_IPM_XXX_ENTRYID properties. This property is the entry ID of the IPM subtree's root folder, returned by *HrValidateIPMSubtree*.
PR_IPM_OUTBOX_ENTRYID	The entry ID of the IPM subtree's Outbox, returned by *HrValidateIPMSubtree*.
PR_IPM_SENTMAIL_ENTRYID	The entry ID of the IPM subtree's Sent Items folder, returned by *HrValidateIPMSubtree*.
PR_IPM_WASTEBASKET_ENTRYID	The entry ID of the IPM subtree's Deleted Items folder.
PR_VALID_FOLDER_MASK	This property is also returned by *HrValidateIPMSubtree* and contains a bitmap of flags where each bit represents a folder in the IPM subtree. A folder's bit is set if the folder was successfully opened or created in the call to *HrValidateIPMSubtree*. If a folder's bit is clear, the corresponding entry ID property is invalid.
PR_STORE_SUPPORT_MASK	Contains a bitmap of flags describing supported operations in the store provider. Most everything we need to do is specifically supported by the default store provider, so this property only tells us if we can add attachments. Other capabilities we can query on this property are notifications, searching, rich text format (RTF) support, sorting, support for OLE objects, attachments, and message submission.

Property Tag	Description
Message Properties	
PR_MESSAGE_CLASS	Messages have a class attribute that determines which receive folder they should be routed to and which form should be activated to view the message. We handle only regular email, or IPM.Note messages. If we don't explicitly set the message class on outgoing messages, the message class defaults to IPM. We call *Get-ReceiveFolder* to return the entry ID of the IPM.Note Inbox.
PR_SUBJECT	The message subject.
PR_NORMALIZED_SUBJECT	The message subject without the "RE:" or "FW:" prefix.
PR_BODY	The message's text. We treat it like a string, but you can also open an *IStream* interface on this property by calling *OpenProperty*. PR_BODY is a plaintext version of the message body; if an RTF version exists, it is kept in a separate property. We support only plaintext messages.
PR_MESSAGE_FLAGS	A bitmap of flags that describes the message's state. Defined bits reveal whether the message has attachments and whether it's been read, submitted but not yet delivered, sent, and so on. We use this property to tell whether the message has been sent.
PR_MESSAGE_ATTACHMENTS	Represents the attachment table in calls to *OpenProperty*.
PR_MESSAGE_RECIPIENTS	Represents the recipient table in calls to *OpenProperty*.

(continued)

131

Properties Used in the HelloMAPI Sample *continued*

Property Tag	Description
PR_HASATTACH	*TRUE* if the message has attachments.
PR_MESSAGE_DELIVERY_TIME	The UTC (coordinated universal time) when the message was delivered. This is set by the transport; we only read it.
PR_SENDER_NAME	The display name of the user that actually sent the message.
PR_SENT_REPRESENTING_ENTRYID	This property gives the entry ID of the person on whose behalf the message was sent: the principal. The PR_SENDER_XXX properties identify who actually sent the message, whereas the PR_SENT_REPRESENTING_XXX properties identify who it's from. Most of the time, these properties represent the same person, but MAPI allows a message to be sent by a delegate on another's behalf. A secretary might send messages on the boss's behalf, for example. In that case, PR_SENDER_XXX would point to the secretary, and PR_SENT_REPRESENTING_XXX would point to the boss. We use the PR_SENT_REPRESENTING_XXX properties to construct a resolved name for the principal on an inbound message so that we can reply to the message without looking up the name in the address book provider and because we want the reply to go to the principal, not to the delegate.
PR_SENT_REPRESENTING_NAME	The principal sender's display name.
PR_SENT_REPRESENTING_ADDRTYPE	The principal sender's address type.
PR_SENT_REPRESENTING_EMAIL-_ADDRESS	The principal sender's email address. This isn't a required property on a resolved name, but it's good to have it.

Property Tag	Description
PR_SENT_REPRESENTING-_SEARCH_KEY	A concatenation of the address type and email address. Tells whether the sender is the current user.
PR_RECEIVED_BY_SEARCH_KEY	This is set by the transport to the user's search key when an inbound message is received. Used to filter out the user from the reply recipients in the recipient table.

Recipient Properties

Property Tag	Description
PR_DISPLAY_NAME	This property and the next three properties are required for a recipient to be considered resolved. No message can be submitted to an unresolved recipient. The display name is the recipient's friendly name.
PR_ENTRYID	The recipient's entry ID. Comes from an entry in an address book provider or from a "one-off" entry that MAPI creates if the recipient isn't in an address book provider. Required for a recipient to be considered resolved.
PR_ADDRTYPE	The recipient's address type specifies the type of messaging system through which the recipient receives mail—for example, SMTP or X.400. MAPI uses the address type to determine which transport should handle delivery to this recipient. Required for a recipient to be considered resolved.
PR_RECIPIENT_TYPE	The recipient's type: To, Cc, or Bcc. The primary addressees are To recipients. Recipients that receive copies and are visible to all other recipients are Cc (carbon copy). Recipients that receive copies but aren't visible to other recipients are Bcc (blind carbon copy). Required for a recipient to be considered resolved.

(continued)

133

Properties Used in the HelloMAPI Sample *continued*

Property Tag	Description
PR_SEARCH_KEY	A concatenation of the address type and email address. Used to filter the user out of the recipient table on reply messages.
PR_EMAIL_ADDRESS	The email address is interpreted by the transport that handles delivery. Not required for resolved names.
Attachment Properties	
PR_ATTACH_FILENAME	The attachment's filename, excluding the path.
PR_ATTACH_NUM	Each attachment is assigned a unique number, which is used to identify the attachment in the attachment table. (We store this property for illustration purposes only.)
PR_ATTACH_DATA_BIN	Indicates the attachment's data is a blob of bytes written to the message, as opposed to an OLE object.
PR_ATTACH_METHOD	Identifies the attachment type. Attachments can have their data written to the message object (ATTACH_BY_VALUE); or they can be embedded OLE objects (ATTACH_OLE), embedded messages (ATTACH_EMBEDDED_MSG), or a shared file (ATTACH_BY_REFERENCE). We support only ATTACH_BY_VALUE.
PR_RENDERING_POSITION	Gives the character offset within the message body where the attachment will be rendered. A value of −1 (0xFFFFFFFF) indicates no rendering.
Miscellaneous Property	
PR_SENT_REPRESENTING_RECIP-_TYPE	This is an invented property defined as PR_NULL. We use it because there is no equivalent property for senders as PR_RECIPIENT _TYPE is for recipients. Passing PR_NULL in a call to *GetProps* reserves a space in the returned property array into which we plug the recipient type when we reply.

HelloMAPI: A Minimal MAPI Mail Client

The size and complexity of a MAPI client application is mostly a function of how many features it supports and how sophisticated the user interface is. Our primary requirements for HelloMAPI were to demonstrate the tasks a client might want to perform (see pages 118-119) without getting bogged down in the UI code. We hope that by focusing on MAPI you will understand the programming techniques so well that writing your own "killer" client will be easy. At the very least, HelloMAPI can serve as a point of departure for more ambitious projects.

So we've kept the user interface to the absolute minimum—a main application window, two dialog boxes, and a single dialog procedure—in the interest of covering as much material as possible in a limited amount of space. We've also taken a few shortcuts (also in the interest of saving space) that you should probably consider carefully before grafting them to a commercial application. Most of these are benign, but some bear mentioning as a kind of disclaimer. The chief offender in the "do as I say, not as I do" category is the use of *HrQueryAllRows* to query the Inbox contents table. As we pointed out in Chapter 4, *HrQueryAllRows* should be used only if the number of rows returned is relatively small and it makes sense to have the entire row set in memory at once. Folder contents tables can be potentially huge, so you should not, in general, use *HrQueryAllRows* for loading them.

We've also gone kind of light on error handling. A production version should be liberally sprinkled with calls to *GetLastError*. A commercial product should also expect to open an *IStream* interface on PR_BODY or PR_RTF-_COMPRESSED if the text exceeds a certain commonsense size, such as 8 KB. We always treat the body of a message like a string, but your client should be a little smarter. Other things not supported include emptying the Deleted Items folder (or Wastebasket), viewing folders other than the Inbox, deleting attachments, and handling notifications. (The most visible consequence of this last omission is that there's no way to inform the user when new mail arrives; for example, the Inbox viewer isn't automatically updated.)

Program Description

Program initialization occurs automatically on startup in the WM_CREATE handler of the main window procedure. If initialization fails, we display an error dialog box and let the user break into a debugger or exit; otherwise, we enter our message loop and process user commands. The flow of the program is as shown on the following page, in pseudocode:

```
Create main application window
Initialize MAPI
Log on
Instantiate handy HelloMAPI objects
Open the default store provider
Open top-level address book provider
Open IPM folders
Do
    Process user commands
Until quit
Log off
Exit
```

Classes and Data Structures

We declare two classes that are used throughout the program. The first, *CSession*, encapsulates all the objects we'll obtain from the session, provides a convenient place to cache data, and includes some helper methods for doing some routine housekeeping chores. When the session object, top-level address book provider, and message store provider are opened, the pointers to these interfaces are cached in public data members for later use. Pointers to the open IPM folders are also saved, as are the folders' entry IDs.

Most of the main window's message-handling logic is provided by methods on the *CSession* object that simply wrap the appropriate MAPI interface calls with error handling and user-interface logic. The way that each method works is explained in detail later.

CContext is used to pass data into a dialog procedure; it has no methods, just data members. We keep track of where we are in the user interface by creating a *CContext* object and saving our state in the *m_ulContext* member. This member can have one of the following values:

- CTX_COMPOSE. We are composing a brand new message (as opposed to submitting one or saving one in the Inbox). In this context, we are manipulating a message that doesn't have an entry in the store provider yet, so the dialog box will be populated by user input, not by the act of opening a message and getting its properties.

- CTX_SAVED. The message exists in the Inbox. It must be opened and its properties retrieved to populate the dialog box, but the message hasn't been submitted yet, so one or more required properties might be missing—in particular, the message might not have a recipient table yet.

136

- CTX_READNOTE. The message has already been submitted; it has a sender and a recipient table—in other words, the message has enough information for us to create a reply.

- CTX_REPLY, CTX_REPLY_ALL, CTX_FORWARD. An open message object (the original message) is being held, and a new reply message is about to be created. Some of the original message's properties will be copied to the reply message, and the reply will be submitted to the original message's sender (CTX_REPLY), to all recipients (CTX_REPLY_ALL), or to a different recipient altogether (CTX_FORWARD). The *m_pMsg* member contains a pointer to the message to which we're replying.

User Interface

The HelloMAPI main window has four menu items: Inbox, New Message, Exit, and About. Inbox displays the contents of the user's Inbox folder, where incoming messages are received and outgoing messages are composed and saved. (See Figure 5-5.)

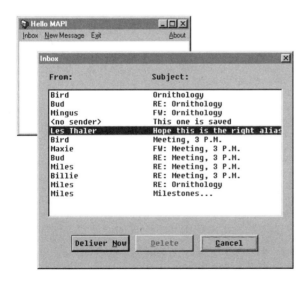

Figure 5-5.
The HelloMAPI Inbox dialog box.

The list box in the Inbox dialog box is loaded from the folder's contents table. Each message's PR_SENT_REPRESENTING_NAME and PR_SUBJECT properties are concatenated, and the formatted string is stuffed in the list box. The dialog template uses a fixed pitch font to make aligning the fields in columns easier. If the message hasn't been submitted yet, the PR_SENT-_REPRESENTING_NAME property won't be found in the table row, so a placeholder "<no sender>" string is inserted in its place. A placeholder is also inserted for a message that has no PR_SUBJECT property, except that the tag is "<no subject>". This prevents blank entries from being added to the list box for messages that have no sender and no subject.

The entry ID and PR_MESSAGE_FLAGS property is copied into a structure, and a pointer is saved to it in the list box entry's item data. When the user double-clicks a message for viewing, the entry ID and flags from the item data are retrieved and passed to the *ComposeNote* dialog procedure in a *CContext* object. The flags are examined to determine which dialog box to use when the message is viewed or displayed (i.e., which context we will be in when we display the message).

The Inbox dialog box also has a Delete button that is enabled when the list box receives focus. The highlighted message is moved to the Deleted Items folder (or Wastebasket). MAPI clients shouldn't delete IPM messages outright but should move them to the Wastebasket and destroy them only when the user explicitly empties the Wastebasket. A single call to *IMAPIFolder::EmptyFolder* will permanently delete all the messages in a folder, but because HelloMAPI doesn't provide a way to view the Wastebasket before irrevocably destroying its contents, it is safer to leave them there.

Note that HelloMAPI doesn't support notifications, so new mail arriving in the receive folder won't automatically update the Inbox viewer. The dialog box must be dismissed and then reopened for changes in its contents to be seen. A full-featured client would call *Advise* on the store provider for new mail notifications *and* on a specific folder's contents table whenever it displayed the UI for that folder. New mail notifications are triggered for all incoming messages, regardless of message class or destination folder. A client can respond to new mail notifications by "beeping" or by changing the look of an icon. Notifications on a folder's contents are relevant only when the user is doing something with the folder (viewing its contents, for example) and are only received when the client is holding the table's *IMAPITable* interface, has called *Advise* through it, and a row is subsequently added, deleted, or modified in the table's underlying data.

The New Message menu item brings up a dialog box in which the user can compose a new message and submit or save it. The IDD_COMPOSE dialog box is displayed in the CTX_COMPOSE context. This means that the message doesn't exist yet and that the user must create it rather than open an existing entry. All controls in the dialog box are initially blank.

Data that the user enters in the various controls will become properties of the message if the Save or Send button is clicked. The user can attach files to the message by clicking the Attach File button. The attached files are displayed in the Attachments list box. Clicking Cancel releases the message object without committing any of the data.

Choosing the Exit menu item starts the termination logic. The *CSession* object is deleted, which frees all the cached data and releases the object interfaces. The main window is destroyed, and a call to *PostQuitMessage* is made to terminate the message loop. This is also the code path for unhandled errors in *WndMain*, the main window procedure.

And finally, choosing the About menu item displays a copyright and version dialog box.

Dialog Boxes and Dialog Processing

Double-clicking a message in the Inbox viewer causes either the IDD_COMPOSE or the IDD_READNOTE dialog box to be displayed. IDD_READNOTE is used if the message has been submitted; otherwise, IDD_COMPOSE is used. These dialog boxes are similar in many ways: Both use the *ComposeNote* dialog procedure and have virtually identical controls. The differences are chiefly in how each dialog box is populated and how the dialog box's data is processed (see Figure 5-6 on the following page).

For example, both dialog boxes have recipient edit controls, but for the CTX_COMPOSE or CTX_FORWARD contexts, the recipient information comes from the address book provider when the user clicks the To button. The recipients' properties are added directly to the message's recipient table. In the CTX_READNOTE and CTX_REPLY_XXX contexts, the message has already been submitted, so it has a recipient table and sender properties. The edit control is populated from the PR_SENT_REPRESENTING_XXX properties of the message, and the To button is replaced by a From button that lets the user display the sender's details page. The recipient table is used later to set the To recipients in a reply message.

Both dialog boxes have an edit control for the message body, which is populated from user input in the CTX_COMPOSE context or from the existing message's PR_BODY property in all other contexts. We access this property as a string and copy it in one gulp, although for large message bodies you're better off opening an *IStream* interface on PR_BODY and using the *IStream::Read* and *IStream::Write* methods.

For reply or forwarded messages (CTX_REPLY_XXX or CTX_FORWARD), a dotted line ("- - - -") is added to the message body as a prefix to separate the sender's message from the reply text. When the message is submitted or saved, the contents of the edit control are dumped into PR_BODY, which will then contain the text of the message being replied to, the "- - - -" separator prefix, and any text entered by the user.

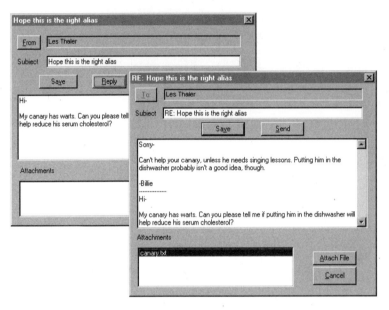

Figure 5-6.
The IDD_READNOTE dialog box (background) is displayed for an existing message, IDD_COMPOSE (foreground) for a new one. In this case, a reply to an existing message is being composed.

Both dialog boxes have list boxes that show the names of attached files. In the CTX_READNOTE context, the list box is read-only; you can add attachments only to a new message (including a reply) or to a saved message. The attachments' filenames are columns in the message's attachment table and are either retrieved from there to populate the list box or saved there when a file is attached.

Both dialog boxes also have a Save button that saves any message changes to disk. Neither dialog box is dismissed after clicking Save. Note that a submitted message can be opened, modified, and saved; in this case, the message is opened in the CTX_READNOTE context. Why? Because it has sender information and a recipient table.

Finally, both dialog boxes have a Subject edit control. In the CTX_COMPOSE context, this control is populated from user input; in all other contexts, the data comes from the message's PR_SUBJECT property. If the message is a reply (CTX_REPLY_XXX), the "RE:" prefix is added. For the CTX_FORWARD context, the subject is prefixed with "FW:".

The main difference between the two dialog boxes is that IDD_COMPOSE has a Send button, whereas IDD_READNOTE has Reply, Reply All, and Forward buttons. For the CTX_COMPOSE and CTX_SAVED contexts, the Send button is enabled only after recipient information has been added to the message. Since IDD_READNOTE is displayed only in the CTX_READNOTE context (the message already has a recipient table and PR_SENT-_REPRESENTING_XXX properties), the Reply, Reply All, and Forward buttons are always enabled.

ComposeNote dialog procedure The *ComposeNote* dialog procedure's logic depends on the context in which it's called. Some window messages are received in only one context; others are handled differently depending on the context at the time of the call. The following text explains the logic.

WM_INITDIALOG This message is handled in all contexts. The context is passed in *lParam*, and a *CContext* object is created and initialized. A new message is created in *pNewMsg*, and the dialog box controls are populated as described in the following list:

- CTX_COMPOSE. The *pNewMsg* variable points to a brand new message obtained from *CreateMessage*. The message doesn't have any properties set yet, so the controls are all blank. The *pOrigMsg* variable is initialized to NULL.

- CTX_SAVED, CTX_READNOTE. The *pNewMsg* variable points to an existing message obtained from *OpenEntry*. The entry ID passed in the *CContext* object is used, and *GetProps* is called to populate the controls from the entry's property set. The *pOrigMsg* variable is initialized to NULL.

- CTX_REPLY_XXX, CTX_FORWARD. *ComposeNote* is being called from within the dialog procedure to reply to or forward an open message. Using the same dialog procedure for all contexts means pointers have to be maintained for two message objects: the Inbox message we just opened and are replying to (or forwarding), and the newly created reply message.

Because the dialog procedure is called from the dialog's message loop (first in the READNOTE context, then in the REPLY_XXX context), an automatic variable can't be used to maintain the Inbox message pointer. Instead, the Inbox message pointer is copied to *pOrigMsg* before the reply message is created and is restored after the reply is sent. The process is as follows:

- The original message pointer is passed in the *CContext* object. Save it in *pOrigMsg*.

- The reply message is created in *pNewMsg*. Then, depending on one of the following contexts, a series of actions occurs:

  ❑ CTX_REPLY. The original sender becomes the reply message's recipient. The body, subject, and flags are copied from the original message to the reply message. Note that attachments aren't copied. The subject is prefixed with "RE:" and the body with "- - - -".

  ❑ CTX_REPLY_ALL. All the original message's recipients, excluding the user, become the reply message's recipients. The body, subject, and flags are copied from the original message to the reply message, and the body and subject prefixes are added. Attachments are not copied.

  ❑ CTX_FORWARD. The entire original message is copied to the new forwarded message. Message attachments are included, but the sender's name and message recipients are excluded. The subject is prefixed with "FW:" and the body with "- - - -". The To button is enabled so that the user can select the new recipient from the address book provider.

WM_COMMAND (case IDC_SEND)   This window message is sent in the CTX_COMPOSE or CTX_SAVED contexts. We submit the message pointed to by *pNewMsg* and release it. Then we restore the original message, *pOrigMsg*, to *pNewMsg*. If we are called from the IDD_READNOTE dialog box, the reply or forward message is submitted and the original message is restored to *pNewMsg*. Otherwise, *pOrigMsg* will be NULL and *pNewMsg* is restored to NULL. We end the dialog and return.

WM_COMMAND (case IDC_ATTACH_FILE)   For the CTX_REPLY_XXX and CTX_COMPOSE contexts, we use *GetOpenFileName* to let the user select a file and attach it to the message. Note that reply messages shouldn't contain any attachments from the original message—the sender and other recipients already have them—but they *should* contain any new attachments the user chooses to attach. New attachments are added to the message's attachment table via the *IMessage::CreateAttach* method.

In the CTX_FORWARD and CTX_SAVED contexts, the attachments are rows in the message's attachment table, but the user can add more. The attachment table is queried to obtain the attached files' names, which are then added to the Attachments list box. New attachments are added in the same way as for the CTX_SAVED context. Note that the attachment table is a *property* of the message; it doesn't have a life of its own. This means that changes to the attachment table aren't committed until the message is saved or submitted, although changes to the table will be visible immediately after a call to an *IAttach* method.

WM_COMMAND (case IDC_TO) The To button is disabled if the context is CTX_REPLY_XXX. For all other contexts, this message is handled by calling *IAddrBook::Address*, which displays a dialog box that lets the user browse the installed address book provider for recipients to add to the message's To line. We don't support adding Cc (carbon copy) or Bcc (blind carbon copy) recipients, although we handle them in replies if they are found on an inbound message.

Browsing the address book provider is the only way the user can add recipients to a message; we don't let him type them in manually. This is a simplifying restriction to our implementation that shouldn't exist in a commercial product—it saves us from having to parse the To string and resolve ambiguous names. *IAddrBook::Address* passes back fully resolved names we can add "as is" to the recipient table. (A commercial application should support direct entry of recipients, not only for the user's convenience but because this is the only way to address a recipient whose email address is known but for whom there isn't an entry in the address book provider, i.e., a one-off recipient).

WM_COMMAND (case IDC_ERROR_EXIT) The same logic is used to handle IDOK and IDCANCEL messages; for example, after the Send operation completes or the user clicks the Cancel button. The *OnError* macro checks the error code of a function call and displays a message box if an error is detected. When the user dismisses the message box, we post ourselves an IDC_ERROR_EXIT message, release the object pointed to by *pNewMsg*, restore *pOrigMsg*, and end the dialog.

WM_COMMAND (cases IDC_REPLY_XXX, IDC_FORWARD) These messages are sent only in the CTX_READNOTE context when the user clicks the Reply, Reply All, or Forward buttons. We create a *CContext* object initialized with the appropriate context and a pointer to the original message and its entry ID, then call the *ComposeNote* dialog procedure with the IDD_COMPOSE resource. We get called at *ComposeNote* in this new context, and processing starts at the WM_INITDIALOG case.

WM_COMMAND (case IDC_FROM) This message is sent only in the CTX_READNOTE context when the user clicks the From button. This displays the sender's *details page,* a dialog box provided by the *IAddrBook* interface that shows a recipient's addressing information.

HelloMAPI.CPP: Implementation Details

We have divided the HelloMAPI program source code (which is shown in Figure 5-7) into two files: HelloMAPI.CPP, which contains the majority of the program logic and any MAPI-specific code; and MAIN.CPP, which contains *WinMain,* other Windows user-interface code, and some miscellaneous helper functions. The class declaration and data structures are in HelloMAPI.H. Only HelloMAPI.CPP is reproduced here; the other files can be found on the companion CD-ROM. What follows is a blow-by-blow explanation of how we use the MAPI methods to implement the HelloMAPI client. We present these in a depth-first order as they appear in *WndProc* and *ComposeNote.*

```
//////////////////////////////////////////////////////////////////////
// HelloMAPI.CPP
// This module contains all the MAPI code for a minimal extended MAPI
// mail client.
//
// Author:    Les Thaler
// Copyright (c) 1996 Irving De la Cruz and Les Thaler
//
#include <windows.h>

#define USES_IID_IMAPITable
#define USES_IID_IMessage
#define USES_IID_IMAPIStatus
#define INITGUID

#include <initguid.h>
#include <mapiguid.h>
#include <mapix.h>
#include <mapiutil.h>
#include <mapitags.h>
#include "hellomapi.h"
SizedSPropTagArray(NUM_MSG_PROPS, g_sptMsgProps) = {NUM_MSG_PROPS,
                                                    PR_SUBJECT,
                                                    PR_BODY,
```

Figure 5-7. *(continued)*
HelloMAPI source code.

Figure 5-7. *continued*

```
                                                     PR_MESSAGE_FLAGS,
                                                     PR_SENDER_NAME,
                                                     PR_HASATTACH};

SizedSPropTagArray(NUM_RECIP_PROPS, g_sptRecips) = {NUM_RECIP_PROPS,
                                                     PR_DISPLAY_NAME,
                                                     PR_ENTRYID,
                                                     PR_ADDRTYPE,
                                                     PR_RECIPIENT_TYPE,
                                                     PR_EMAIL_ADDRESS,
                                                     PR_SEARCH_KEY};

SizedSPropTagArray(NUM_RECIP_PROPS, g_sptSender) =
                            {NUM_RECIP_PROPS,
                             PR_SENT_REPRESENTING_NAME,
                             PR_SENT_REPRESENTING_ENTRYID,
                             PR_SENT_REPRESENTING_ADDRTYPE,
                             PR_SENT_REPRESENTING_RECIP_TYPE,
                             PR_SENT_REPRESENTING_EMAIL_ADDRESS,
                             PR_SENT_REPRESENTING_SEARCH_KEY};

/////////////////////////////////////////////////////////////////////////
//  Main Window procedure
//
LRESULT CALLBACK WndProc(HWND hWnd, UINT message, WPARAM wParam,
                                                 LPARAM lParam)
{
    static  PCSession pCSess;
            HINSTANCE hInst   =
                        (HINSTANCE)GetWindowLong(hWnd, GWL_HINSTANCE);
            WORD      wmId    = LOWORD(wParam),
                      wmEvent = HIWORD(wParam);

    if (!hInst)
        return 0;

    switch (message)
    {
      case WM_CREATE:
          OnError(hWnd, InitSession(hWnd, hInst, &pCSess));
          break;
      case WM_COMMAND:
          switch (wmId)
          {
```

(continued)

Figure 5-7. *continued*

```
        case IDM_INBOX:
            OnError(hWnd,
                    pCSess -> ShowDialog(hWnd,
                    CTX_INBOX,
                    pCSess -> m_psbFolderEID[IPM_ROOT].cb,
                    (LPENTRYID)pCSess ->
                    m_psbFolderEID[IPM_ROOT].lpb,"Inbox"));
            break;

        case IDM_SEND:
            OnError(hWnd, pCSess ->
                    ShowDialog(hWnd, CTX_COMPOSE, 0, NULL,
                            "New Message"));
            break;

        case IDM_ABOUT:
            DialogBox(hInst, "AboutBox", hWnd, (DLGPROC)About);
            break;

        case ID_ERROR_EXIT:
        case IDM_EXIT:
            if (pCSess)
                delete pCSess;

            DestroyWindow(hWnd);
            break;

        default:
            return (DefWindowProc(hWnd, message, wParam, lParam));
        }
        break;

    case WM_DESTROY:
        PostQuitMessage(0);
        break;
    case WM_SYSCOMMAND:
        if (SC_CLOSE == wParam)
            if (pCSess)
                delete pCSess;
        // Fall through
    default:

        return (DefWindowProc(hWnd, message, wParam, lParam));
```

```
    }
    return (0);
}

///////////////////////////////////////////////////////////////////////////
// Initializes MAPI, logs on, creates and initializes the CSession
// object
STDMETHODIMP InitSession(HWND hWnd, HINSTANCE hInst, PCSession * ppCSess)
{
    LPMAPISESSION pSession = NULL;
    PCSession     pCSess   = NULL;
    HRESULT       hRes;

    if (FAILED(hRes = MAPIInitialize(NULL)))
        return hRes;

    if (FAILED(hRes = MAPILogonEx((ULONG)hWnd,
                                  NULL,
                                  NULL,
                                  LOGON_FLAGS,
                                  &pSession)))
        goto Quit;

    pCSess = new CSession(pSession, hInst);

    if (!pCSess)
    {
        hRes = MAPI_E_NOT_ENOUGH_MEMORY;
        goto Quit;
    }

    // Initialize CSession object.
    if (FAILED(hRes = pCSess -> Init()))
        goto Quit;


    // Open default message store provider.
    if (FAILED(hRes = pCSess -> OpenDefStore(hWnd)))
        goto Quit;
```

(continued)

Figure 5-7. *continued*

```
    // Open top-level address book provider.
    if (FAILED(hRes = pSession -> OpenAddressBook((ULONG)hWnd,
                                                   NULL,
                                                   0,
                                                   &pCSess -> m_pAddrBook)))
{
        ShowLastError(hRes, hWnd, pSession);
        goto Quit;
    }

    // Get IPM folder entry IDs.
    if (FAILED(hRes = pCSess -> OpenIPMSubtree(hWnd)))
        goto Quit;

    hRes = pCSess -> GetSpoolerStatus();
Quit:
    if (FAILED(hRes))
    {
        // Destructor releases session and uninitializes.
        if (pCSess)
            delete pCSess;
        else
        {
            if (pSession)
                pSession -> Release();

            MAPIUninitialize();
        }
        return hRes;
    }

    *ppCSess = pCSess;
    return hRes;
}


///////////////////////////////////////////////////////////////////////////
// Create an array of entry IDs for the IPM subtree folders.
//
STDMETHODIMP CSession::Init()
{
    HRESULT hRes;

    if (FAILED(hRes = MAPIAllocateBuffer(NUM_FOLDERS * sizeof(SBinary),
                                         (LPVOID *)&m_psbFolderEID)))
        goto Quit;
```

```
        ZeroMemory((LPVOID)m_psbFolderEID, NUM_FOLDERS * sizeof(SBinary));

Quit:
    return hRes;
}


////////////////////////////////////////////////////////////////////////
// Open the default store provider for this session.
//
STDMETHODIMP CSession::OpenDefStore(HWND hWnd)
{
    LPMAPITABLE         pStoresTbl = NULL;
    LPSRowSet           pRow       = NULL;
    SBinary             sbEID      = {0, NULL};
    static SRestriction sres;
    SPropValue          spv;
    HRESULT             hRes;

    static SizedSPropTagArray(2, sptCols) = {2, PR_ENTRYID,
                                                PR_DEFAULT_STORE};

    if (FAILED(hRes = m_pSess -> GetMsgStoresTable(0, &pStoresTbl)))
    {
        ShowLastError(hRes, hWnd, m_pSess);
        goto Quit;
    }

    sres.rt = RES_PROPERTY;
    sres.res.resProperty.relop = RELOP_EQ;
    sres.res.resProperty.ulPropTag = PR_DEFAULT_STORE;
    sres.res.resProperty.lpProp = &spv;

    spv.ulPropTag = PR_DEFAULT_STORE;
    spv.Value.b   = TRUE;
    if (FAILED(hRes = HrQueryAllRows(pStoresTbl,
                          (LPSPropTagArray)&sptCols,
                          &sres,
                          NULL,
                          0,
                          &pRow)))
        goto Quit;
```

(continued)

149

Figure 5-7. *continued*

```
    if (pRow                  &&
        pRow -> cRows           &&
        pRow -> aRow[0].cValues &&
        PR_ENTRYID == pRow -> aRow[0].lpProps[0].ulPropTag)
    {
        sbEID  = pRow -> aRow[0].lpProps[0].Value.bin;
    }
    else
    {
        hRes = MAPI_E_NOT_FOUND;
        goto Quit;
    }


    if (FAILED(hRes = m_pSess -> OpenMsgStore((ULONG)hWnd,
                                              sbEID.cb,
                                              (LPENTRYID)sbEID.lpb,
                                              NULL,
                                              MDB_WRITE,
                                              &m_pMDB)))
    {
        ShowLastError(hRes, hWnd, m_pSess);
        goto Quit;
    }

Quit:
    FreeProws(pRow);

    if (pStoresTbl)
        pStoresTbl -> Release();

    return hRes;
}


//////////////////////////////////////////////////////////////////////////
//
// Open each folder, and save a pointer to open interfaces.
//
STDMETHODIMP CSession::OpenIPMSubtree(HWND hWnd)
{
    LPSPropValue  pProps = NULL;
    HRESULT       hRes;
    ULONG         cProps,
                  ulObjType;
```

```
SBinary       sbInboxEID;
int           i;
static SizedSPropTagArray(NUM_FOLDERS, sptFldrs) =
                          {NUM_FOLDERS,PR_NULL,
                           PR_IPM_OUTBOX_ENTRYID,
                           PR_IPM_WASTEBASKET_ENTRYID,
                           PR_IPM_SENTMAIL_ENTRYID,
                           PR_IPM_SUBTREE_ENTRYID};


if (FAILED(hRes = m_pMDB -> GetProps((LPSPropTagArray)&sptFldrs,
                                      0,
                                      &cProps,
                                      &pProps)))
    goto Quit;


// Get Inbox folder's entry ID.
if (FAILED(hRes = m_pMDB -> GetReceiveFolder("IPM.Note",
                                             0,
                                             &sbInboxEID.cb,
                                             (LPENTRYID *)&sbInboxEID.lpb,
                                             NULL)))
{
    ShowLastError(hRes, hWnd, m_pMDB);
    goto Quit;
}


pProps[INBOX].Value.bin = sbInboxEID;


for (i = INBOX; i < NUM_FOLDERS; i++)
{
    if (pProps[i].ulPropTag != sptFldrs.aulPropTag[i])
    {
        hRes = MAPI_E_NOT_FOUND;
        goto Quit;
    }
    // Copy the folder's entry ID to class member.
    if (FAILED(hRes = CopySBinary(&m_psbFolderEID[i],
                                  &pProps[i].Value.bin,
                                  (LPVOID)m_psbFolderEID)))
            goto Quit;
}
```

(continued)

Figure 5-7. *continued*

```
    for (i = INBOX; i <= WASTE; i++)
    {
        if (FAILED(hRes = m_pSess ->
                            OpenEntry(m_psbFolderEID[i].cb,
                                (LPENTRYID)m_psbFolderEID[i].lpb,
                                NULL,
                                MAPI_MODIFY,
                                &ulObjType,
                                (LPUNKNOWN *)&m_pFolders[i])))
        {
            ShowLastError(hRes, hWnd, m_pSess);
            goto Quit;
        }

        if (MAPI_FOLDER != ulObjType)
        {
            hRes = MAPI_E_INVALID_OBJECT;
            goto Quit;
        }
    }

Quit:
    MAPIFreeBuffer((LPVOID)pProps);
    MAPIFreeBuffer(sbInboxEID.lpb);
    return hRes;
}


///////////////////////////////////////////////////////////////////////////
// Gets the spooler's status object from the session status table
//
STDMETHODIMP CSession::GetSpoolerStatus()
{
    LPMAPITABLE     pTbl  = NULL;
    LPMAPISTATUS    pStat = NULL;
    LPSRowSet       pRow  = NULL;
    HRESULT         hRes;
    SRestriction    sres;
    SPropValue      spv;
    ULONG           ulObjType;

    const static SizedSPropTagArray(2, sptCols) =
                {2, PR_RESOURCE_TYPE, PR_ENTRYID};

    if (FAILED(hRes = m_pSess -> GetStatusTable(0, &pTbl)))
        goto Quit;
```

```
    sres.rt = RES_PROPERTY;
    sres.res.resProperty.relop     = RELOP_EQ;
    sres.res.resProperty.ulPropTag = PR_RESOURCE_TYPE;
    sres.res.resProperty.lpProp    = &spv;

    spv.ulPropTag = PR_RESOURCE_TYPE;
    spv.Value.l   = MAPI_SPOOLER;

    if (FAILED(hRes = HrQueryAllRows(pTbl,
                                (LPSPropTagArray)&sptCols,
                                &sres,
                                NULL,
                                0,
                                &pRow)))
        goto Quit;

    if (!pRow -> cRows ||
        PR_ENTRYID != pRow -> aRow[0].lpProps[1].ulPropTag)
    {
        hRes = MAPI_E_NOT_FOUND;
        goto Quit;
    }

    hRes = m_pSess -> OpenEntry(pRow -> aRow[0].lpProps[1].Value.bin.cb,
                            (LPENTRYID)pRow ->
                                    aRow[0].lpProps[1].Value.bin.lpb,
                            &IID_IMAPIStatus,
                            MAPI_BEST_ACCESS,
                            &ulObjType,
                            (LPUNKNOWN *)&pStat);

    if (FAILED(hRes) || MAPI_STATUS != ulObjType)
    {
        hRes = hRes ? hRes : MAPI_E_INVALID_OBJECT;
        goto Quit;
    }
    m_pSpoolerStat = pStat;

Quit:
    if (pTbl)
        pTbl -> Release();

    FreeProws(pRow);
    return hRes;
}
```

(continued)

Figure 5-7. *continued*

```
/////////////////////////////////////////////////////////////////////////////
//  Brings up the correct dialog for the context
//·
STDMETHODIMP CSession::ShowDialog(HWND       hWnd,
                                  ULONG      ulCtx,
                                  ULONG      cbEID,
                                  LPENTRYID  pEID,
                                  LPSTR      szTitle,
                                  LPMESSAGE  pMsg)
{
    PContext pCtx = new CContext(ulCtx, cbEID, pEID, this, szTitle, pMsg);

    if (!pCtx)
        return MAPI_E_NOT_ENOUGH_MEMORY;

    DialogBoxParam(m_hInst,
                MAKEINTRESOURCE(CTX_INBOX ==
                                    ulCtx ? IDD_INBOX : CTX_READNOTE ==
                                    ulCtx ? IDD_READNOTE : IDD_COMPOSE),
                hWnd,
                (DLGPROC)(CTX_INBOX ==
                    ulCtx ? ViewInbox : ComposeNote),
                (LPARAM)pCtx);
    delete pCtx;
    return S_OK;
}


/////////////////////////////////////////////////////////////////////////////
//  Inbox viewer's dialog procedure
//
LRESULT CALLBACK ViewInbox(HWND hDlg, UINT message, WPARAM wParam,
                                                    LPARAM lParam)
{
    static PContext    pCtx;
    static PCSession   pCSess;
        HRESULT        hRes = S_OK;

    switch (message)
    {
        case WM_INITDIALOG:
            InitDialog(hDlg, lParam, pCtx);
            pCSess = pCtx -> m_pSess;
            hRes = LoadListBox(hDlg, lParam, IDC_CTBL_LIST);
            OnError(hDlg, hRes);
```

```
        ShowWindow(hDlg, SW_HIDE);
        return TRUE;

case WM_COMMAND:
    WORD    wNotif = HIWORD(wParam),
            wCtlID = LOWORD(wParam);

    switch (wCtlID)
    {
        case IDC_FLUSH:
            OnError(hDlg, pCSess -> FlushQs(hDlg));
            break;

        case IDC_DELETE:
            OnError(hDlg, pCSess -> DeleteMsg(hDlg));
            return TRUE;

        case IDC_CTBL_LIST:
            switch (wNotif)
            {
                case LBN_SELCHANGE:          // An item is
                                            // highlighted.
                    EnableWindow(GetDlgItem(hDlg, IDC_DELETE),
                            TRUE);
                    return TRUE;

                case LBN_DBLCLK:            // Open selected message.
                {
                    PSMsgID  pMsgID = NULL;
                    ULONG    ulCtx;
                    if (LB_ERR == GetLBSelection
                                    (hDlg,
                                     wCtlID,
                                     (LPVOID *)&pMsgID))
                        OnError(hDlg, MAPI_E_CALL_FAILED);

                    ulCtx = ((!pMsgID -> ulFlags) ||
                            (pMsgID -> ulFlags & MSGFLAG_UNSENT) ?
                                CTX_SAVED : CTX_READNOTE);
                    OnError(hDlg,
                            pCSess -> ShowDialog(hDlg,
                                        ulCtx,
                                        pMsgID -> sbEID.cb,
```

(continued)

155

Figure 5-7. *continued*

```
                                             (LPENTRYID)pMsgID -> sbEID.lpb));
                          return TRUE;
                    }
                    default:
                          return FALSE;
              }
              break;

          case IDOK:
          case IDCANCEL:
          case ID_ERROR_EXIT:
              EmptyListBox(hDlg, IDC_CTBL_LIST);
              EndDialog(hDlg, TRUE);
              return (TRUE);
          default:
              return FALSE;
        }
        break;
    }
    return FALSE;
}


///////////////////////////////////////////////////////////////////////////
//  Loads the ViewInbox list box from the Inbox contents table
//
STDMETHODIMP LoadListBox(HWND hDlgParent, LPARAM lParam, ULONG ulCtlID)
{
    LPMAPITABLE  pCTbl = NULL;
    LPSRowSet    pRows = NULL;
    TCHAR        szSndr[MAX_SNDR],
                 szSubj[MAX_SUBJ],
                 szBuf[MAX_SUBJ + MAX_SNDR + 4];
    HRESULT      hRes;
    PCSession    pCSess;
    PContext     pCtx;
    ULONG        i;
    enum {NAME, SUBJ, EID, FLAGS, NUM_COLS};
    static SizedSPropTagArray(NUM_COLS, sptCols) =
              {NUM_COLS,
               PR_SENT_REPRESENTING_NAME,
               PR_SUBJECT,
               PR_ENTRYID,
```

```
                PR_MESSAGE_FLAGS};
pCtx = (PContext)lParam;
pCSess = pCtx -> m_pSess;
if (FAILED(hRes = pCSess -> m_pFolders[INBOX] ->
    GetContentsTable(0, &pCTbl)))
    goto Quit;

// You should use QueryRows, SeekRowApprox since ContentsTable can be
// huge!
if (FAILED(hRes = HrQueryAllRows(pCTbl,
                                 (LPSPropTagArray) &sptCols,
                                 NULL,
                                 NULL,
                                 0,
                                 &pRows)))
    goto Quit;

for (i = 0; i < pRows -> cRows; i++)
{
    HRESULT hr;
    ULONG   ulIdx;
    PSMsgID pMsgID = NULL;

    if (PR_ENTRYID == pRows -> aRow[i].lpProps[EID].ulPropTag)
    {
        LPSBinary pMsgEID = NULL;

        if (SUCCEEDED(hr = MAPIAllocateBuffer(sizeof(SMsgID),
                                              (LPVOID *)&pMsgID)))
        {
            if (SUCCEEDED(hr =
                CopySBinary(&pMsgID -> sbEID,
                            &pRows -> aRow[i].lpProps[EID].Value.bin,
                            pMsgID)))
            {
                if (PR_MESSAGE_FLAGS ==
                    pRows -> aRow[i].lpProps[FLAGS].ulPropTag)
                    pMsgID -> ulFlags =
                        pRows -> aRow[i].lpProps[FLAGS].Value.l;
                else
                    pMsgID -> ulFlags = 0;

                if (PR_SENT_REPRESENTING_NAME ==
```

(continued)

157

Figure 5-7. *continued*

```
                                pRows -> aRow[i].lpProps[NAME].ulPropTag)
                                lstrcpyn(szSndr,
                                        pRows -> aRow[i].lpProps[NAME].Value.lpszA,
                                        MAX_SNDR);
                        else
                                lstrcpy(szSndr,"<no sender>");

                        if (PR_SUBJECT ==
                                pRows -> aRow[i].lpProps[SUBJ].ulPropTag)
                                lstrcpyn(szSubj,
                                        pRows -> aRow[i].lpProps[SUBJ].Value.lpszA,
                                        MAX_SUBJ);
                        else
                                lstrcpy(szSubj,"<no subject>");

                        // lstrcpyn doesn't terminate n length strings.
                        szSubj[MAX_SUBJ - 1] = szSndr[MAX_SNDR - 1] = '\0';
                        wsprintf(szBuf, SZ_FRMT, szSndr, szSubj);
                        ulIdx = SendDlgItemMessage(hDlgParent,
                                                ulCtlID,
                                                LB_ADDSTRING,
                                                0,
                                                (LPARAM)szBuf);
                        if (LB_ERR != ulIdx)
                                ulIdx = SendDlgItemMessage(hDlgParent,
                                                        ulCtlID,
                                                        LB_SETITEMDATA,
                                                        ulIdx,
                                                        (LPARAM)pMsgID);
                }
                if (S_OK != hr || LB_ERR == ulIdx)
                {
                        MAPIFreeBuffer((LPVOID)pMsgEID);
                        hRes = MAPI_W_ERRORS_RETURNED;
                }
            }
        }
    }

Quit:
    FreeProws(pRows);

    if (pCTbl)
        pCTbl -> Release();
    return hRes;
```

```
}

/////////////////////////////////////////////////////////////////////////
//  Forces spooler to flush inbound and outbound queues (ALL transports)
//
STDMETHODIMP CSession::FlushQs(HWND hWnd)
{
    return m_pSpoolerStat -> FlushQueues((ULONG)hWnd,0,NULL,FLUSH_FLAGS);
}


/////////////////////////////////////////////////////////////////////////
//
//  Gets the current selection's item data from the list box. Extracts the
//  message's entry ID and uses it to move message to Deleted Items folder.
//
STDMETHODIMP CSession::DeleteMsg(HWND hDlg)
{
    HRESULT       hRes   = S_OK;
    PSMsgID       pMsgID = NULL;
    LONG          lIdx   =
                      GetLBSelection(hDlg,IDC_CTBL_LIST,(LPVOID*)&pMsgID),
                  lCnt;
    SBinaryArray sbaEID;

    if (LB_ERR == lIdx)
        return MAPI_E_CALL_FAILED;
    sbaEID.cValues = 1;
    sbaEID.lpbin = &(pMsgID -> sbEID);

    // Move the selected message to the delete folder.
    hRes = m_pFolders[INBOX] -> CopyMessages(&sbaEID,
                                             NULL,
                                             m_pFolders[WASTE],
                                             (ULONG)hDlg,
                                             NULL,
                                             MESSAGE_MOVE !
                                             MESSAGE_DIALOG);

    if (FAILED(hRes))
        goto Quit;

    MAPIFreeBuffer((LPVOID)pMsgID);
```

(continued)

Figure 5-7. *continued*

```
    lCnt = SendDlgItemMessage(hDlg,
                              IDC_CTBL_LIST,
                              LB_DELETESTRING,
                              lIdx,
                              0);
    if (LB_ERR == lCnt)
    {
        hRes = MAPI_E_CALL_FAILED;
        goto Quit;
    }

    if (lCnt)                // If more, move highlight to next entry.
        SendDlgItemMessage(hDlg,
                           IDC_CTBL_LIST,
                           LB_SETCURSEL,
                           (lIdx >= lCnt ? lCnt - 1: lIdx),
                           0);
    else                     // No more, disable delete button.
        EnableWindow(GetDlgItem(hDlg, IDC_DELETE), FALSE);

Quit:
    return hRes;
}


//////////////////////////////////////////////////////////////////////////////
//   ComposeNote and ReadNote dialog procedure
//
LRESULT CALLBACK ComposeNote(HWND hDlg, UINT message, WPARAM wParam,
                                                      LPARAM lParam)
{
    static  LPMESSAGE pNewMsg;
    static  LPMESSAGE pOrigMsg;
    static  PContext  pCtx;
    static  PCSession pCSess;
            HRESULT   hRes    = S_OK;


    switch (message)
    {
        case WM_INITDIALOG:
            InitDialog(hDlg,lParam,pCtx);
            pCSess = pCtx -> m_pSess;
            pOrigMsg = pCtx -> m_pMsg;  // NULL except in
                                        // CTX_REPLY_XX/FORWARD
```

```
      pNewMsg = NULL;

      switch(pCtx -> m_lContext)
      {
          case CTX_COMPOSE:           // New message, from 'New Message'
                                      // menu item
              OnError(hDlg,
                      pCSess -> m_pFolders[INBOX] ->
                          CreateMessage(NULL, 0, &pNewMsg));
              EnableWindow(GetDlgItem(hDlg, IDC_SEND), FALSE);
              break;

          case CTX_SAVED:             // Opening existing message in the
                                      // Inbox
          case CTX_READNOTE:
              OnError(hDlg,
                      pCSess -> PopulateReadNote(hDlg, pCtx, &pNewMsg));
              break;

          case CTX_REPLY:             // We already have an Inbox message
                                      // open;
          case CTX_REPLY_ALL:         // we want to forward it or reply.
          case CTX_FORWARD:
              OnError(hDlg,
                      pCSess -> CreateReplyNote(hDlg, pCtx, &pNewMsg));
              break;
      }
      ShowWindow (hDlg, SW_HIDE);
      return (TRUE);

  case WM_COMMAND:
      WORD    wNotif = HIWORD(wParam),
              wCtlID = LOWORD(wParam);

      switch(wCtlID)
      {
          case IDC_TO:                // Enabled only for new message or
                                      // forward
              // Browse address book.
              hRes = pCtx -> m_pSess -> AddRecips(hDlg,
                                                  pCtx -> m_szTitle,
                                                  pCSess,
                                                  pNewMsg);
```

(continued)

161

Figure 5-7. *continued*

```
                    if (MAPI_E_USER_CANCEL == hRes)
                        return FALSE;

                    OnError(hDlg, hRes);
                    EnableWindow(GetDlgItem(hDlg, IDC_SEND), TRUE);
                    break;
                case IDC_FROM:
                    // View sender details.
                    OnError(hDlg, pCSess -> SenderDetails(&hDlg, pNewMsg));
                    break;
                case IDC_SAVE:
                    OnError(hDlg, pCSess -> Save(hDlg, pNewMsg));
                    break;
                case IDC_ATTACH_FILE:
                    OnError(hDlg, pCSess -> AttachFile(hDlg, pNewMsg));
                    break;
                case IDC_SEND:
                    // Submit message.
                    OnError(hDlg, pCSess -> SendNote(hDlg, pNewMsg));

                    // SendNote releases pNewMsg.
                    pNewMsg = pOrigMsg; // Restore message we "replied to."
                    EndDialog(hDlg, TRUE);
                    return (TRUE);
                case IDC_REPLY:         // Reply to/forward a message in our
                case IDC_REPLY_ALL:     // Inbox.
                case IDC_FORWARD:
                {
                    ULONG ulCtx =
                        (IDC_REPLY     == wCtlID ? CTX_REPLY :
                         IDC_REPLY_ALL == wCtlID ? CTX_REPLY_ALL :
                         IDC_FORWARD   == wCtlID ? CTX_FORWARD :
                         (hRes = MAPI_E_CALL_FAILED));

                    OnError(hDlg, hRes);

                    hRes = pCSess -> ShowDialog(hDlg,
                                                ulCtx,
                                                pCtx -> m_cbEID,
                                                pCtx -> m_pParentEID,
                                                "",
                                                pNewMsg);
```

```
                    if (pNewMsg)
                        pNewMsg -> Release();

                    pNewMsg = pOrigMsg;     // Restore any replied-to message.
                    OnError(hDlg, hRes);
                    EndDialog(hDlg, TRUE);
                    return TRUE;
                }

                case IDC_BODY:              // Move caret to beginning.
                    if (EN_SETFOCUS == wNotif)
                        SendMessage((HWND)lParam, EM_SETSEL, 0, 0);
                    break;
                case IDOK:
                case IDCANCEL:
                case ID_ERROR_EXIT:
                    // Release message object.
                    if (pNewMsg)
                        pNewMsg -> Release();

                    pNewMsg = pOrigMsg;     // Restore any replied-to message.
                    EndDialog(hDlg, TRUE);
                    return (TRUE);
                default:
                    return FALSE;
            }
            break;
    }
    return FALSE;
}


//////////////////////////////////////////////////////////////////////////////
// Populates read-note dialog box controls from message properties
//
STDMETHODIMP CSession::PopulateReadNote(HWND hDlg, PContext pCtx,
                                        LPMESSAGE * ppMsg)
{
    HRESULT        hRes    = S_OK;
    LPMESSAGE      pMsg    = NULL;
    LPMAPITABLE    pTbl    = NULL;
    LPSRowSet      pRows   = NULL;
    LPSTR          szToLine = NULL;
    ULONG          ulObjType;

    *ppMsg = NULL;
```

(continued)

Figure 5-7. *continued*

```
    if (FAILED(hRes = m_pMDB -> OpenEntry(pCtx -> m_cbEID,
                                          pCtx -> m_pParentEID,
                                          NULL,
                                          MAPI_BEST_ACCESS,
                                          &ulObjType,
                                          (LPUNKNOWN *)&pMsg)))
        return hRes;

    if (MAPI_MESSAGE != ulObjType)
    {
        hRes = MAPI_E_INVALID_OBJECT;
        goto Quit;
    }

    if (FAILED(hRes = PopulateNote(hDlg, pMsg)))
        goto Quit;

    if (FAILED(hRes = pMsg -> GetRecipientTable(0, &pTbl)))
        return hRes;

    if (FAILED(hRes = HrQueryAllRows(pTbl,
                                     (LPSPropTagArray)&g_sptRecips,
                                     NULL,
                                     NULL,
                                     0,
                                     &pRows)))
        goto Quit;

    if (pRows -> cRows)
    {
        szToLine = ConcatRecips((LPADRLIST)pRows);
        SetDlgItemText(hDlg, IDC_RECIP, szToLine);
        EnableWindow(GetDlgItem(hDlg, IDC_SEND), TRUE);
    }
    else
        EnableWindow(GetDlgItem(hDlg, IDC_SEND), FALSE);

Quit:
    if (FAILED(hRes))
        if (pMsg)
            pMsg -> Release();

    if (pTbl)
        pTbl -> Release();
```

```
    MAPIFreeBuffer((LPVOID)szToLine);
    FreeProws(pRows);
    *ppMsg = pMsg;

    return hRes;
}


///////////////////////////////////////////////////////////////////////////////
//  Populates dialog controls with properties from the message
//
STDMETHODIMP PopulateNote(HWND hDlg, LPMESSAGE pMsg)
{
    LPSPropValue    pProps = NULL;
    HRESULT         hRes;
    ULONG           cVals,
                    i;

    if (FAILED(hRes = pMsg -> GetProps((LPSPropTagArray)&g_sptMsgProps,
                                        0,
                                        &cVals,
                                        &pProps)))
        goto Quit;
    else
        hRes = S_OK;

    if (PR_SUBJECT == pProps[SUBJ].ulPropTag)
        {
            SetDlgItemText(hDlg, IDC_SUBJECT, pProps[SUBJ].Value.LPSZ);
            SetWindowText(hDlg, pProps[SUBJ].Value.LPSZ);
        }

    if (PR_BODY == pProps[BODY].ulPropTag)
        SetDlgItemText(hDlg, IDC_BODY, pProps[BODY].Value.LPSZ);

    if (PR_SENDER_NAME == pProps[SNDR].ulPropTag)
        SetDlgItemText(hDlg, IDC_SENDER, pProps[SNDR].Value.LPSZ);

    if (PR_HASATTACH == pProps[ATT].ulPropTag && pProps[ATT].Value.b)
        {
```

(continued)

Figure 5-7. *continued*

```
LPMAPITABLE pAttTbl = NULL;
LPSRowSet   pows    = NULL;
static SizedSPropTagArray(2, sptCols) = {2, PR_ATTACH_FILENAME,
                                            PR_ATTACH_NUM};


if (SUCCEEDED(hRes = pMsg -> OpenProperty(PR_MESSAGE_ATTACHMENTS,
                                          &IID_IMAPITable,
                                          0,
                                          0,
                                          (LPUNKNOWN *)&pAttTbl)))

    if (SUCCEEDED(hRes = pAttTbl -> SetColumns
                                    ((LPSPropTagArray)&sptCols,
                                    TBL_BATCH)))

        if (SUCCEEDED(hRes = HrQueryAllRows(pAttTbl,
                                            (LPSPropTagArray)&sptCols,
                                            NULL,
                                            NULL,
                                            0,
                                            &pRows)))

            for (i = 0; i < pRows -> cRows; i++)
            {
                ULONG ulIdx;

                if (PR_ATTACH_FILENAME ==
                    pRows -> aRow[i].lpProps[0].ulPropTag)
                    ulIdx =
                        SendDlgItemMessage(hDlg,
                                IDC_ATTACHMENTS,
                                LB_ADDSTRING,
                                0,
                                (LPARAM)pRows ->
                                    Row[i].lpProps[0].Value.LPSZ);

                if (PR_ATTACH_NUM ==
                    pRows -> aRow[i].lpProps[1].ulPropTag)
                    SendDlgItemMessage(hDlg,
                                IDC_ATTACHMENTS,
                                LB_SETITEMDATA,
                                ulIdx,
                                (LPARAM)pRows ->
                                    aRow[i].lpProps[1].Value.1);
```

```
                        }

        FreeProws(pRows);

        if (pAttTbl)
            pAttTbl -> Release();
    }
Quit:
    MAPIFreeBuffer((LPVOID)pProps);
    return hRes;
}


//////////////////////////////////////////////////////////////////////////////
// Calls IAddrBook::Address to add recipients to message and populate TO
// control
//
STDMETHODIMP CSession::AddRecips(HWND       hDlg,
                                 LPSTR      szTitle,
                                 PCSession pSess,
                                 LPMESSAGE pMsg)
{
    LPADRLIST   pAdrList = NULL;
    LPSTR       szRecips = NULL;
    HRESULT     hRes;
    ADRPARM     AdrParm;
    // Let user select recipients only from address book.
    ZeroMemory((LPVOID)&AdrParm, sizeof(ADRPARM));

    // Set up the ADRPARM struct for Address.
    AdrParm.ulFlags              = DIALOG_MODAL | AB_RESOLVE;
    AdrParm.cDestFields          = 1;
    AdrParm.nDestFieldFocus      = 0;
    AdrParm.lpszNewEntryTitle    = szTitle;
    AdrParm.lpszDestWellsTitle   = "";
    AdrParm.lpszCaption          = "Browse Address Book";

    if (FAILED(hRes = m_pAddrBook -> Address((ULONG *)&hDlg,
                                        &AdrParm,
                                        &pAdrList)))

        goto Quit;

    // E.g., user cancelled
    if (!pAdrList || !pAdrList -> cEntries)
    {
```

(continued)

167

Figure 5-7. *continued*

```
        hRes = MAPI_E_USER_CANCEL;
        goto Quit;
    }

    // Passing 0 replaces the entire table with pAdrList.
    if (FAILED(hRes = pMsg -> ModifyRecipients(0, pAdrList)))
        goto Quit;

    szRecips = ConcatRecips(pAdrList);

    if (!szRecips)
    {
        hRes = MAPI_E_CALL_FAILED;
        goto Quit;
    }

    SetDlgItemText(hDlg, IDC_RECIP, szRecips);
    MAPIFreeBuffer((LPVOID)szRecips);

Quit:
    FreePadrlist(pAdrList);
    return hRes;
}

/////////////////////////////////////////////////////////////////////////
//  Displays the sender's details page, e.g., when the From button is
//  clicked.
//
STDMETHODIMP CSession::SenderDetails(HWND * phDlg, LPMESSAGE pMsg)
{
    LPSPropValue    pspv = NULL;
    HRESULT         hRes;

    if (FAILED(hRes =
        HrGetOneProp(pMsg, PR_SENT_REPRESENTING_ENTRYID, &pspv)))
        return hRes;

    hRes = m_pAddrBook -> Details((ULONG *)phDlg,
                                  NULL,
                                  NULL,
                                  pspv -> Value.bin.cb,
                                  (LPENTRYID)pspv -> Value.bin.lpb,
```

```
                                NULL,
                                NULL,
                                NULL,
                                DIALOG_MODAL);
    MAPIFreeBuffer((LPVOID)pspv);
    return MAPI_E_USER_CANCEL == hRes ? S_OK : hRes;
}


//////////////////////////////////////////////////////////////////////////
// Commits changes on the message object, e.g., when user clicks Save
//
STDMETHODIMP CSession::Save(HWND hDlg, LPMESSAGE pMsg)
{
    LPSPropValue  pspvSaved = NULL,
                  pspvEID   = NULL;
    HRESULT       hRes;

    if (FAILED(hRes = MAPIAllocateBuffer(sizeof(SPropValue) * 3,
                                    (LPVOID *)&pspvSaved)))
        return hRes;

    pspvSaved[SUBJ].ulPropTag = PR_SUBJECT;
    pspvSaved[BODY].ulPropTag = PR_BODY;
    pspvSaved[FLAG].ulPropTag = PR_MESSAGE_FLAGS;

    if (FAILED(hRes = GetUIData(hDlg, pspvSaved)))
        goto Quit;

    pspvSaved[FLAG].Value.l = MSGFLAG_UNSENT | MSGFLAG_READ;

    if (FAILED(hRes = pMsg -> SetProps(3, pspvSaved, NULL)))
        goto Quit;

    pMsg -> SaveChanges(KEEP_OPEN_READWRITE);

Quit:
    MAPIFreeBuffer((LPVOID)pspvSaved);
    return hRes;
}


//////////////////////////////////////////////////////////////////////////
// Display dialog for choosing a file, then attach it to message.
//
```

(continued)

Figure 5-7. *continued*

```
STDMETHODIMP CSession::AttachFile(HWND hWnd, LPMESSAGE pMsg)
{
    LPSTREAM      pStrmSrc  = NULL,
                  pStrmDest = NULL;
    LPATTACH      pAtt      = NULL;
    ULONG         ulAttNum,
                  ulIdx;
    HRESULT       hRes;
    OPENFILENAME  ofn;
    TCHAR         szFile[MAX_PATH];
    STATSTG       StatInfo;

    enum {FILENAME, METHOD, RENDERING, NUM_ATT_PROPS};
    SPropValue    spvAttach[NUM_ATT_PROPS];

    ZeroMemory((LPVOID)&ofn, sizeof(ofn));

    lstrcpy(szFile, "*.*");
    ofn.lStructSize = sizeof(ofn);
    ofn.hwndOwner   = hWnd;
    ofn.lpstrFilter = "All files\0*.*\0";
    ofn.lpstrFile   = szFile;
    ofn.nMaxFile    = MAX_PATH;
    ofn.lpstrTitle  = "Attach File";
    ofn.Flags       = OFN_NONETWORKBUTTON | OFN_FILEMUSTEXIST |
                      OFN_NOCHANGEDIR     | OFN_PATHMUSTEXIST;

    if (GetOpenFileName(&ofn))
    {
        if (FAILED(hRes = OpenStreamOnFile(MAPIAllocateBuffer,
                                           MAPIFreeBuffer,
                                           STGM_READ,
                                           ofn.lpstrFile,
                                           NULL,
                                           &pStrmSrc)))
            goto Quit;

        if (FAILED(hRes = pMsg -> CreateAttach(NULL, 0, &ulAttNum, &pAtt)))
            goto Quit;

        if (FAILED(hRes = pAtt -> OpenProperty(PR_ATTACH_DATA_BIN,
                                               (LPIID)&IID_IStream,
                                               0,
```

170

```
                                           MAPI_MODIFY | MAPI_CREATE,
                                           (LPUNKNOWN *)&pStrmDest)))
        goto Quit;

    pStrmSrc -> Stat(&StatInfo, STATFLAG_NONAME);

    if (FAILED(hRes = pStrmSrc -> CopyTo(pStrmDest,
                                         StatInfo.cbSize,
                                         NULL,
                                         NULL)))
        goto Quit;

    spvAttach[FILENAME].ulPropTag = PR_ATTACH_FILENAME;
    spvAttach[FILENAME].Value.lpszA = &ofn.lpstrFile[ofn.nFileOffset];

    spvAttach[METHOD].ulPropTag = PR_ATTACH_METHOD;
    spvAttach[METHOD].Value.l = ATTACH_BY_VALUE;

    spvAttach[RENDERING].ulPropTag = PR_RENDERING_POSITION;
    spvAttach[RENDERING].Value.l = -1;

    if (FAILED(hRes = pAtt -> SetProps(NUM_ATT_PROPS,
                                       (LPSPropValue)&spvAttach,
                                       NULL)))
        goto Quit;

    pAtt -> SaveChanges(0);
    ulIdx = SendDlgItemMessage(hWnd,
                               IDC_ATTACHMENTS,
                               LB_ADDSTRING,
                               0,
                               (LPARAM)&ofn.lpstrFile[ofn.nFileOffset]);
    if (LB_ERR != ulIdx)
        ulIdx = SendDlgItemMessage(hWnd,
                                   IDC_ATTACHMENTS,
                                   LB_SETITEMDATA,
                                   ulIdx,
                                   (LPARAM)ulAttNum);
}

Quit:
    if (pStrmDest)
        pStrmDest -> Release();
```

(continued)

Figure 5-7. *continued*

```
    if (pStrmSrc)
        pStrmSrc -> Release();

    if (pAtt)
        pAtt -> Release();

    return hRes;
}


/////////////////////////////////////////////////////////////////////////////
// Gets properties from dialog, sets them in message; moves message
// to the Outbox, and submits it
//
STDMETHODIMP CSession::SendNote(HWND hDlg, LPMESSAGE pMsg)
{
    LPSPropValue  pspvEID    = NULL,
                  pspvOut    = NULL;
    LPMESSAGE     pSubmitMsg = NULL;
    ENTRYLIST     eidMsg;
    HRESULT       hRes;

    if (FAILED(hRes =
        MAPIAllocateBuffer(sizeof(SPropValue) * NUM_OUTBOUND_PROPS,
                           (LPVOID *)&pspvOut)))
        return hRes;

    if (FAILED(hRes = GetUIData(hDlg, pspvOut)))
        goto Quit;

    if (FAILED(hRes = SetOutgoingProps(pMsg, pspvOut)))
        goto Quit;

    if (FAILED(hRes = m_pFolders[OUTBOX] -> CreateMessage(NULL,
                                                          0,
                                                          &pSubmitMsg)))

        goto Quit;

    if (FAILED(hRes = pMsg -> CopyTo(0,
                                     NULL,
                                     NULL,
                                     (ULONG)hDlg,
                                     NULL,
                                     &IID_IMessage,
                                     pSubmitMsg,
```

```
                                      0,
                                      NULL)))
            goto Quit;

    if (FAILED(hRes = pSubmitMsg -> SubmitMessage(0)))
        goto Quit;

    if (FAILED(hRes = HrGetOneProp(pMsg, PR_ENTRYID, &pspvEID)))
        goto Quit;

    eidMsg.cValues = 1;
    eidMsg.lpbin   = &pspvEID[0].Value.bin;

    pMsg -> Release();  // Can't delete an open message

    if (FAILED(hRes = m_pFolders[INBOX] -> DeleteMessages(&eidMsg,
                                            (ULONG)hDlg,
                                            NULL,
                                            MESSAGE_DIALOG)))
        goto Quit;

Quit:
    if (pSubmitMsg)
        pSubmitMsg -> Release();
    MAPIFreeBuffer(pspvEID);
    MAPIFreeBuffer(pspvOut);

    return hRes;
}

//////////////////////////////////////////////////////////////////////////
// Sets mandatory outgoing message properties
//
STDMETHODIMP    CSession::SetOutgoingProps(LPMESSAGE pMsg,
                                        LPSPropValue pspvOut)
{
    LPSPropValue  pspv = NULL;
    HRESULT       hRes;

    pspvOut[OBFLAG].ulPropTag = PR_MESSAGE_FLAGS;
    pspvOut[OBSUBJ].ulPropTag = PR_SUBJECT;
    pspvOut[OBBODY].ulPropTag = PR_BODY;
    pspvOut[OBSENT].ulPropTag = PR_SENTMAIL_ENTRYID;
```

(continued)

173

Figure 5-7. *continued*

```
    if (FAILED(hRes = CopySBinary(&pspvOut[OBSENT].Value.bin,
                                  &m_psbFolderEID[SENT],
                                  pspvOut)))
        goto Quit;

    pspvOut[OBFLAG].Value.l = MSGFLAG_SUBMIT | MSGFLAG_READ;

    if (SUCCEEDED(hRes = HrGetOneProp(pMsg, PR_HASATTACH,&pspv)))
        pspvOut[OBFLAG].Value.l != (pspv -> Value.b ? MSGFLAG_HASATTACH : 0);

    if (FAILED(hRes = pMsg -> SetProps(NUM_OUTBOUND_PROPS, pspvOut, NULL)))
        goto Quit;

    hRes = pMsg -> SaveChanges(KEEP_OPEN_READWRITE);

Quit:
    MAPIFreeBuffer(pspv);
    return hRes;
}


////////////////////////////////////////////////////////////////////////////
// Creates a reply message, copies/sets appropriate properties, enables
// dialog box controls
//
STDMETHODIMP CSession::CreateReplyNote(HWND          hDlg,
                                       PContext      pCtx,
                                       LPMESSAGE * ppReplyMsg)
{
    LPSTR       szToLine = NULL;
    LPMESSAGE   pNewMsg  = NULL;
    SPropValue  spvNew[3];
    HRESULT     hRes;

    static const SizedSPropTagArray(13, sptExclude) =
                              {13,
                               PR_SENDER_NAME,
                               PR_SENDER_ADDRTYPE,
                               PR_SENDER_EMAIL_ADDRESS,
                               PR_SENDER_ENTRYID,
                               PR_SENDER_SEARCH_KEY,
                               PR_SENT_REPRESENTING_NAME,
                               PR_SENT_REPRESENTING_ADDRTYPE,
```

```
                                    PR_SENT_REPRESENTING_EMAIL_ADDRESS,
                                    PR_SENT_REPRESENTING_ENTRYID,
                                    PR_SENT_REPRESENTING_SEARCH_KEY,
                                    PR_MESSAGE_RECIPIENTS,
                                    PR_BODY,
                                    PR_SUBJECT};

spvNew[FLAG].ulPropTag = PR_MESSAGE_FLAGS;
spvNew[SUBJ].ulPropTag = PR_SUBJECT;
spvNew[BODY].ulPropTag = PR_BODY;
spvNew[SUBJ].Value.lpszA = NULL;
spvNew[BODY].Value.lpszA = NULL;
spvNew[FLAG].Value.l = MSGFLAG_SUBMIT | MSGFLAG_UNSENT | MSGFLAG_READ;

if (FAILED(hRes = m_pFolders[INBOX] -> CreateMessage(NULL,
                                                     0,
                                                     &pNewMsg)))
    goto Quit;

if (CTX_FORWARD == pCtx -> m_lContext)
{   // Copy everything (e.g., attachments) except recips, subject, body.
    hRes = (pCtx -> m_pMsg) -> CopyTo(0,
                                      NULL,
                                      (LPSPropTagArray)&sptExclude,
                                      (ULONG)hDlg,
                                      NULL,
                                      &IID_IMessage,
                                      pNewMsg,
                                      0,
                                      NULL);
    if (FAILED(hRes))
        goto Quit;
}
else    // Replies have only what we set explicitly.
    if (FAILED(hRes = SetReplyRecips(pNewMsg,
                                     pCtx -> m_pMsg,
                                     pCtx -> m_lContext,
                                     &szToLine)))
        goto Quit;

// Add "RE:" or "FW:" prefix to subject.
if (FAILED(hRes = PrefixSzProp(pCtx -> m_pMsg,
                               PR_NORMALIZED_SUBJECT,
```

(continued)

Figure 5-7. *continued*

```
                                    CTX_FORWARD == pCtx -> m_lContext ?
                                        FW_PREFIX : RE_PREFIX,
                                    &spvNew[SUBJ].Value.lpszA)))
        goto Quit;

    // Add "----\n" to body.
    if (FAILED(hRes = PrefixSzProp(pCtx -> m_pMsg,
                            PR_BODY,
                            REPLY_BODY_PREFIX,
                            &spvNew[BODY].Value.lpszA)))
        goto Quit;

    if (FAILED(hRes = pNewMsg -> SetProps(3, spvNew, NULL)))
        goto Quit;

    SetDlgItemText(hDlg, IDC_RECIP, szToLine);
    EnableWindow(GetDlgItem(hDlg, IDC_TO),
                pCtx -> m_lContext == CTX_FORWARD);
    EnableWindow(GetDlgItem(hDlg, IDC_SEND),
                pCtx -> m_lContext != CTX_FORWARD);

    if (CTX_FORWARD == pCtx -> m_lContext)
    {
        EnableWindow(GetDlgItem(hDlg, IDC_REPLY), FALSE);
        EnableWindow(GetDlgItem(hDlg, IDC_REPLY_ALL), FALSE);
    }

    if (SUCCEEDED(hRes = PopulateNote(hDlg, pNewMsg)))
        *ppReplyMsg = pNewMsg;

Quit:
    if (FAILED(hRes))
        if (pNewMsg)
            pNewMsg -> Release();

    MAPIFreeBuffer((LPVOID)szToLine);
    MAPIFreeBuffer((LPVOID)spvNew[SUBJ].Value.lpszA);
    MAPIFreeBuffer((LPVOID)spvNew[BODY].Value.lpszA);

    return hRes;
}
```

```
////////////////////////////////////////////////////////////////////////
//  Gets message sender or recipients and makes them the recipients of the
//  new reply message. The user is excluded on replies.
//
STDMETHODIMP CSession::SetReplyRecips(LPMESSAGE pReplyMsg,
                                       const LPMESSAGE pOrigMsg,
                                       ULONG ulTo,
                                       LPSTR * pszToLine)
{
    HRESULT       hRes       = S_OK;
    LPMAPITABLE   pTbl        = NULL;
    LPSPropValue  pspvSndr    = NULL,
                  pspvRecdBy  = NULL;
    LPADRLIST     palTbl      = NULL,
                  palTo       = NULL;
    BOOL          fAddSndr    = TRUE;
    ULONG         ulCnt,
                  cRecips;
    int           i, j;

    // Get all sender properties we need for a resolved name.
    if (HR_FAILED(pOrigMsg -> GetProps((LPSPropTagArray)&g_sptSender,
                                        0,
                                        &ulCnt,
                                        &pspvSndr)))
    {
        hRes = MAPI_E_NOT_FOUND;
        goto Quit;
    }

    // Convert the PR_SENT_REPRESENTING_XXX tags to PR_XXX tags.
    for (i = 0; i < (int)ulCnt; i++)
    {
        if (pspvSndr[i].ulPropTag != g_sptSender.aulPropTag[i])
        {
            hRes = MAPI_E_NOT_FOUND;
            goto Quit;
        }
        pspvSndr[i].ulPropTag = g_sptRecips.aulPropTag[i];
    }

    pspvSndr[RECIP].Value.l = MAPI_TO;
```

(continued)

177

Figure 5-7. *continued*

```
if (FAILED(hRes = HrGetOneProp(pOrigMsg,
                               PR_RECEIVED_BY_SEARCH_KEY,
                               &pspvRecdBy)))
    goto Quit;

if (CTX_REPLY == ulTo)
    cRecips = 1;                // Always reply to sender, even if us.
else
{
    // Turn inbound recips to reply recips. Can't restrict for this.
    if (FAILED(hRes = pOrigMsg -> GetRecipientTable(0, &pTbl)))
        goto Quit;

    // Use rows we got from table as ADRLIST. They're same structs.
    if (FAILED(hRes = HrQueryAllRows(pTbl,
                                     (LPSPropTagArray)&g_sptRecips,
                                     NULL,
                                     NULL,
                                     0,
                                     (LPSRowSet *)&palTbl)))
        goto Quit;

    cRecips = palTbl -> cEntries;

    for (i = 0; i < (int)palTbl -> cEntries; i++)
        if (MAPI_BCC == palTbl -> aEntries[i].rgPropVals[RECIP].Value.l ||
            palTbl -> aEntries[i].rgPropVals[SKEY].Value.bin ==
                pspvSndr[SKEY].Value.bin ||
            palTbl -> aEntries[i].rgPropVals[SKEY].Value.bin ==
                pspvRecdBy[0].Value.bin)
        {
            cRecips--;
            palTbl -> aEntries[i].cValues = 0;
            MAPIFreeBuffer((LPVOID)palTbl -> aEntries[i].rgPropVals);
            palTbl -> aEntries[i].rgPropVals = NULL;
        }

    if (cRecips)
        fAddSndr = FALSE;
    else
        cRecips = 1;
}
```

```
    // Create merged ADRLIST of filtered table entries + (possibly) sender.
    if (FAILED(hRes = MAPIAllocateBuffer(CbNewSRowSet(cRecips),
                                 (LPVOID*)&palTo)))
        goto Quit;

    palTo -> cEntries = 0;

    if (fAddSndr)
    {
        palTo -> aEntries[0].cValues = ulCnt;        // Add to ADRLIST.
        palTo -> aEntries[0].rgPropVals = pspvSndr;
        pspvSndr = NULL;          // So we don't have to check when freeing
        palTo -> cEntries++;
        cRecips--;
    }

    // If there are any more from the table, add them.
    if (cRecips)
        for (i = 0, j = palTbl -> cEntries; i < j; i++)
        {
            if (palTbl -> aEntries[i].cValues)    // Hasn't been filtered out
                palTo -> aEntries[palTo -> cEntries++] =
                    palTbl -> aEntries[i];

            palTbl -> cEntries--;                // When done, it should be empty.
        }
    // Keep CC recips as MAPI_CC, but display them all on our TO line.
    *pszToLine = ConcatRecips((LPADRLIST)palTo);
    hRes = pReplyMsg -> ModifyRecipients(0, palTo);

Quit:
    FreePadrlist(palTo);
    FreePadrlist(palTbl);
    MAPIFreeBuffer((LPVOID)pspvSndr);
    MAPIFreeBuffer((LPVOID)pspvRecdBy);

    if (pTbl)
        pTbl -> Release();

    return hRes;
}
```

(continued)

Figure 5-7. *continued*

```
/////////////////////////////////////////////////////////////////////////
//  Extracts display names from an ADRLIST and concats with ';' between
//  each
//
LPSTR WINAPI ConcatRecips(LPADRLIST pAdrList)
{
    ULONG   cBytes   = 0;
    int     cRecips  = 0;
    LPSTR   szRecips = NULL,
          * szNameArray;

    if (0 == pAdrList -> cEntries)
        return NULL;

    szNameArray = new LPSTR[pAdrList -> cEntries];

    if (!szNameArray)
        return NULL;

    for (int i = 0; i < (int)pAdrList -> cEntries; i++)
    {
        LPSPropValue pProp =
            PpropFindProp(pAdrList -> aEntries[i].rgPropVals,
                          pAdrList -> aEntries[i].cValues,
                          PR_DISPLAY_NAME);

         if (pProp)
         {
            szNameArray[cRecips] = pProp -> Value.lpszA;
            cBytes += lstrlen(szNameArray[cRecips++]);
         }
    }

    cBytes += cRecips; // For the ';' delimiters and NULL

    if (FAILED(MAPIAllocateBuffer(sizeof(TCHAR) * (cBytes + 1),
                                  (LPVOID *)&szRecips)))
        return NULL;

    szRecips[0] = '\0';

    for (i = 0; i < cRecips; i++)
```

```
        {
            lstrcat(szRecips, szNameArray[i]);
            lstrcat(szRecips, ";");
        }

        szRecips[cBytes - 1] = '\0';    // Overwrites trailing ";" if
                                        // only 1 recip
        delete [] szNameArray;
        return szRecips;
}


/////////////////////////////////////////////////////////////////////////
// Adds a prefix (e.g., "FW: ") to a string property and returns
// new string
//
STDMETHODIMP CSession::PrefixSzProp(LPMESSAGE    pMsg,
                                    ULONG        ulPropTag,
                                    LPTSTR       szPrefix,
                                    LPTSTR *     pszProp)
{
    HRESULT         hRes  = S_OK;
    LPSTR           szTemp = NULL;
    LPSPropValue    pspv  = NULL;
    ULONG           cb    = lstrlen(szPrefix);

    *pszProp = NULL;

    // Get string to prefix.
    if (FAILED(hRes = HrGetOneProp(pMsg, ulPropTag, &pspv)))
    {
        // That property not set, return prefix.
        hRes = MAPIAllocateBuffer(sizeof(TCHAR) * (cb + 1),
                                  (LPVOID *) pszProp);

        if (FAILED(hRes))
            return hRes;
        lstrcpy(*pszProp, szPrefix);
        return hRes;
    }

    cb = lstrlen(szPrefix) + lstrlen(pspv -> Value.lpszA) + 1;
    hRes = MAPIAllocateBuffer(sizeof(TCHAR) * cb, (LPVOID *)&szTemp);
```

(continued)

181

Figure 5-7. *continued*

```
    if (FAILED(hRes))
        goto Quit;

    wsprintf(szTemp, "%s%s", szPrefix, pspv -> Value.lpszA);

Quit:
    MAPIFreeBuffer((LPVOID)pspv);
    *pszProp = szTemp;
    return hRes;
}
```

The first thing to note is the inclusion of the following files and the USES_XXX symbols:

```
#include <windows.h>
#define USES_IID_IMAPITable
#define USES_IID_IMessage
#define USES_IID_IMAPIStatus
#define INITGUID
#include <initguid.h>
#include <mapiguid.h>
```

These statements are needed because we pass the addresses of IID_IMAPITable, IID_IMessage, and IID_IMAPIStatus in subsequent method calls. Each OLE COM interface has a *globally unique identifier,* or *GUID,* associated with it. The GUID is a 128-bit number that serves as a unique name for the interface; no two interfaces will have the same GUID even if the abstract base classes bear the same name. When a new interface is created, a new GUID is also created using the GUIDGEN.EXE utility, and a constant with that number is defined in a header file. MAPI interface GUIDs are defined in MAPIGUID.H by macros that expand to either an initialized data structure or an external reference to one, depending on whether the INITGUID symbol is defined.

To use the MAPI-defined interface IDs (IIDs), you must define INIT-GUID and the appropriate USES_IID_XXX symbols in exactly one source module in the project. You also have to include OBJBASE.H, INITGUID.H and MAPIGUID.H. (OBJBASE.H is included by WINDOWS.H, so we don't explicitly include it.) Note that the order is significant because MAPIGUID.H depends on INITGUID.H, and INITGUID.H depends on INITGUID and OBJBASE.H. The USES_IID_XXX symbols have to come before you include MAPIGUID.H. If you do this wrong, you'll get linker errors complaining of unresolved externals.

We use the *SizedSPropTagArray* macro to declare and initialize the global property tag arrays *g_sptMsgProps*, *g_sptRecips*, and *g_sptSender*. The first array is the standard set of message properties that we will always need. The second array holds recipient properties that are columns in the recipient table, and the third array stores properties derived from the PR_SENT_REPRESENT-ING_XXX properties.

InitSession

The program is initialized in *WndProc* by the *InitSession* function, which first makes a call to *MAPIInitialize* and *MAPILogonEx* to start a MAPI session. The *MAPIInitialize* function initializes the MAPI subsystem's internal data structures and calls *CoInitialize*, which initializes the OLE COM library. (If your application makes MAPI calls from multiple threads, each thread must also call *CoInitialize*.) The *MAPIInitialize* function must be called before any other MAPI API.

The call to *MAPILogonEx* logs the user on to a MAPI session and returns a pointer to an *IMAPISession* interface. The LOGON_FLAGS symbol passed to *MAPILogonEx* is defined in HelloMAPI.H to be a bitwise OR of the MAPI_EXPLICIT_PROFILE, MAPI_LOGON_UI, MAPI_ALLOW_OTHERS, and MAPI_NEW_SESSION flags. Passing the MAPI_EXPLICIT_PROFILE and MAPI_LOGON_UI flags to *MAPILogonEx* tells MAPI to display a logon dialog box and let the user choose the profile he wants to use for the session. The MAPI_ALLOW_OTHERS flag tells MAPI to let other clients "piggyback" on this session, while MAPI_NEW_SESSION indicates that this client will always start a new session instead of piggybacking on an existing one. A client piggy-backing on an existing session will not invoke the logon dialog box and will share the same profile used by the existing session. The *MAPILogonEx* function also loads the service provider DLLs listed in the profile and starts the spooler if it isn't already running.

Next, *InitSession* creates and initializes a *CSession* object and calls *Open-DefStore*. This function gets the message store table from the session object and restricts it to the row containing the default store provider, i.e., the row whose PR_DEFAULT_STORE column evaluates to *TRUE*. The message store table contains a row for each store provider in the current session. There can be any number of store providers in a session, but only one can be designated the default. Only the default store provider can receive messages from the MAPI spooler, so the default store provider must contain at least the IPM subtree.

We obtain the default store provider's entry ID from the table and use it in *IMAPISession::OpenMsgStore* to obtain a pointer to the default store provider's *IMsgStore* interface. Notice the chain of events: We make a call to MAPI

(*MAPILogonEx*) to obtain the *IMAPISession* interface, then call two methods on the interface, *GetMsgStoresTable* and *OpenMsgStore*, through which we obtain the desired interface—*IMsgStore*.

We pause here to illustrate a point raised at the beginning of the chapter. The calls to *MAPILogonEx*, *GetMsgStoresTable*, and *OpenMsgStore* execute code implemented in MAPI (MAPI32.DLL), but the *IMsgStore* pointer points to code implemented in the store provider DLL. In reality, there is no intervening layer between the client application and the provider in this case. But, even more importantly, the client isn't aware of this subtlety; all it cares about is that it has an *IMsgStore* interface and it can now access the message store provider.

To further underscore this point, consider the next call to *OpenAddressBook*. This method returns a pointer to the top-level address book interface, *IAddrBook*. *IAddrBook* is implemented by MAPI, not by a provider. Calls to *IAddrBook* methods execute inside MAPI32.DLL, which in turn calls the individual address book providers to do the work. Again, the distinction is immaterial to the client.

The *IAddrBook* interface provides almost every operation a client needs to access MAPI address book providers. There are methods for viewing a container's contents; resolving ambiguous names; creating and deleting entries in a writable address book provider such as the Microsoft personal address book provider; copying entries from one address book provider to another; displaying a recipient's address book provider database record (or details page); and obtaining its properties for addressing a message. MAPI provides dialog boxes in the *IAddrBook* methods, so the client doesn't even have to implement an address book provider UI if it doesn't want to. We call only a few of these methods to browse the address book and display a recipient's details page. For more advanced requirements, a client can also access individual address book containers.

The next call to *OpenIPMSubtree* retrieves the entry IDs of folders in the IPM subtree. All the IPM folders except the receive folder have predefined property tags. MAPI doesn't define a PR_IPM_INBOX_ENTRYID property tag because a session can have multiple receive folders for messages of different classes. Consequently, we set up a *SizedSPropTagArray* initialized to the property tags of each folder except the receive folder, which we initialize to PR_NULL. The call to *GetProps* returns the requested entry IDs in the *SPropValue* array with a spot reserved for the receive folder's ID. We get that entry ID explicitly through a call to *IMsgStore::GetReceiveFolder*, whose first parameter specifies the message class of the receive folder we're interested in—"IPM-.Note," in this case. We finish by opening the Inbox, Outbox, and Wastebasket folders and saving their interface pointers in the *CSession* object.

After returning from *OpenIPMSubtree*, we also cache a pointer to the spooler's status object in the call to *GetSpoolerStatus*. MAPI maintains a *status table* that contains information on the state of different components in the current session. A transport provider is required to supply a row to this table, although it's optional for address book providers and store providers. MAPI provides rows for the MAPI subsystem, the address book supercontainer, and the spooler. Components that support the status table also implement the *IMAPIStatus* interface to give clients a way to query or alter the components' current state. One method that is specific to transports and the spooler is *IMAPIStatus::FlushQueues*, whose purpose is to force the immediate delivery of inbound and/or outbound messages.

Our interest in the status object lies in the spooler's *FlushQueues* method, because this is how we implement the logic behind the Deliver Now button on the Inbox viewer. A call to *FlushQueues* on a specific transport causes any messages awaiting delivery through that transport to be delivered, whereas a call to *FlushQueues* on the spooler's status object causes messages pending in *all* transports to be delivered. To obtain this interface, we first get the session status table by calling *IMAPISession::GetStatusTable*. We then use *HrQueryAllRows* to return a view restricted to the single row occupied by the spooler, the row whose PR_RESOURCE_TYPE is equal to MAPI_SPOOLER. We obtain the spooler's entry ID from this row and pass it to a call to *OpenEntry*, requesting the *IMAPIStatus* interface and getting back the spooler's status object.

ShowDialog

This method is simply a wrapper for *DialogBoxParam* that creates a new *CContext* object—the "*Param*" in *DialogBoxParam*—and invokes the dialog box. The function decides which dialog resource and dialog procedure should be used based on the value of *ulCtx*.

ViewInbox

The helper function *InitDialog* sets up the *CContext* object and sets the dialog box's title bar. The *LoadListBox* function retrieves the contents table of the receive folder and formats a string that is a concatenation of each row's PR_SENT_REPRESENTING_NAME and PR_SUBJECT properties. Although we use *HrQueryAllRows* to retrieve the entire row set, you should use *SeekRowApprox* and *QueryRows* and read in only as many rows as are visible to the user at a given time. We need to emphasize that *you should not, in general, use* HrQueryAllRows *to view the Inbox contents table*. Folder contents tables can be potentially huge, and you waste memory by retrieving the entire row set when only a relatively small subset can be accessed. Furthermore, at least two copies of the data are likely to be in memory at the same time: the data backing the table and the view. A better choice would be to call *QueryRows* to load the list box with one page's worth of rows and then reposition the table cursor with *SeekRowApprox* and reload another page when the user scrolls or pages past the last viewable row.

The formatted string is added to the viewer list box, along with the message's entry ID and PR_MESSAGE_FLAGS property, which we save in the list box entry's item data. We keep these two pieces of data handy so that we can easily open the entry in the store provider when the user double-clicks a string in the list box, and so we know what context in which to display the corresponding message. The helper function *GetLBSelection* retrieves these two pieces of data.

The *DeleteMsg* method also calls *GetLBSelection* to retrieve the selected item's entry ID, but in this case the message is moved to the Wastebasket folder rather than opened. Notice that the message isn't deleted outright by calling *IMAPIFolder::DeleteMessages*, but instead by calling *IMAPIFolder::CopyMessages* with the MESSAGE_MOVE flag. Your application can provide an "Empty Wastebasket" button that permanently deletes everything in the Wastebasket. We omit this functionality to conserve space.

Since the logic of *ComposeNote* has already been covered, we won't dwell on it here except to mention that we pass NULL in the first argument to *CreateMessage* to indicate that we want the default interface (*IMessage*); and we pass 0 in the second argument to indicate that we want to create an ordinary message, not an associated message.

PopulateReadNote

The *PopulateReadNote* method is called to open an existing message in the Inbox and populate the IDD_READNOTE dialog box with its properties. We first call *IMsgStore::OpenEntry*, passing the size of the message's entry ID (*pCtx -> m__cbEID*); the entry ID (*pCtx -> m_pParentEID*); NULL, because we're requesting the default interface (*IMessage*); and MAPI_BEST_ACCESS, to indicate we want the highest access privilege on this message that the store provider is willing to grant us (in this case, read/write access). The object type and interface pointer are passed back in *ulObjType* and *pMsg*. Standard error handling is to check the return method's value using the *FAILED* macro and to verify in *ulObjType* that the object returned is indeed a MAPI_MESSAGE.

The call to *PopulateNote* gets properties from the open message and stuffs them into the appropriate dialog box controls. The global *SPropTagArray* *g_sptMsgProps* identifies the properties we want to retrieve, and the property array is returned in *pProps*. The message subject, body, and sender's name, if found, are set into the corresponding dialog box controls.

The PR_HASATTACH property is also checked. If the message has attachments, the attachment table is retrieved via a call to *OpenProperty* on PR_MESSAGE_ATTACHMENTS, which requests an *IMAPITable* interface. We use *HrQueryAllRows* to retrieve the attachment table rows and select the PR_ATTACH_FILENAME and PR_ATTACH_NUM columns. The first property is added to the Attachments list box; the second is inserted in the list box entry's item data. We don't support deleting attachments, but if we did, we'd use the attachment number to identify the attachment we want to delete in the call to *IMessage::DeleteAttach*.

After returning from *PopulateNote*, the last thing *PopulateReadNote* does is to add any recipients to the To line. We get the recipient information by calling *GetRecipientTable*, then *HrQueryAllRows*, using the column set given in *g_sptRecips*. The *ConcatRecips* helper function iterates through an *ADRLIST* or *SRowSet*, extracts each recipient's display name, and concatenates them into a single string of names separated by semicolons. The resulting string is displayed in the IDC_RECIP edit control. The *ConcatRecips* function allocates storage for the returned string, which is later freed after being displayed in the control. If the message has a nonempty recipient table, the Send button is enabled and the newly opened message object is passed back. On a failure, the message is released and an error code is returned.

AddRecips

This method invokes *IAddrBook::Address* to display the MAPI address book browser dialog box. Calling *IAddrBook::Address* displays several different dialog boxes, depending on how the *ADRPARM* parameter is initialized. *AdrParm.ulFlags* is set to a combination of DIALOG_MODAL and AB_RESOLVE, indicating that we want the dialog box to be modal to *hDlg*'s window and that any names the user selects will be returned as fully resolved entries.

The address book browser dialog box has a list box in the left pane for browsing an address book container. The right pane has from one to three edit controls (To, Cc, or Bcc) into which the user can move a recipient selected in the left pane. We set *AdrParm.cDestFields* to 1 to indicate we want a single right-pane edit control for To recipients only. The *nDestFieldFocus* member indicates which control has initial focus.

If successful, the call to *Address* returns an *ADRLIST* of resolved entries corresponding to the recipients selected by the user. Note that we can rely on *Address* to return fully resolved *ADRLIST*s because we don't allow the user to enter names manually in the IDC_RECIP edit control—we force him to browse instead. This is a simplifying assumption but not very realistic for a commercial product, where the user should be allowed to enter anything and let the program worry about validating the input string and resolving the names.

187

To support manually entered recipient names, a client must perform a few additional steps:

1. Parse the input string into individual recipient names. (The conventional delimiter is ";".)

2. Construct an unresolved *ADRLIST*. Each *ADRENTRY* in the *ADRLIST* represents a recipient and contains the recipient type in PR_RECIPIENT_TYPE and the name substring in PR_DISPLAY_NAME.

3. Call *IAddrBook::ResolveName*, passing the unresolved *ADRLIST*. If the name is ambiguous (i.e., it can match more than one name), *ResolveName* can display a dialog box for selecting one of the possible matches. It also displays a dialog box if the entry isn't found. The call can also be made without UI, in which case the *ADRLIST* comes back with error codes inserted for each offending recipient.

We overwrite the recipient table by the call to *ModifyRecipients*. Passing 0 in the first parameter indicates we want to replace the entire table with the *ADRLIST* passed in the second parameter. Other options are to append rows to the table (MODRECIP_ADD), replace certain rows with those passed in *ADRLIST* (MODRECIP_MODIFY), or remove rows (MODRECIP_REMOVE). The changes to the recipient table aren't committed until a *SaveChanges* or *SubmitMessage* call.

We use *ConcatRecips* again to format the IDC_RECIP string and, if the call is successful, enter it into the recipient's edit control and enable the Send button.

SenderDetails

A call to *SenderDetails* displays a details page for the sender, which typically includes the sender's name, email address, address type, and other miscellaneous information, depending on the address book provider from which the recipient record is taken. The *IAddrBook::Details* method does the address book lookup to find the recipient's database record based on the sender's entry ID, which we obtain by getting the PR_SENT_REPRESENTING_ENTRYID property.

The *Details* method allows the caller to add a button to the Details dialog box and have *IAddrBook* invoke a callback function when the button is clicked. Another option is to have a callback made when the dialog box is dismissed. We pass NULL for these options.

Save

The *Save* method calls the *GetUIData* helper function to extract the text from the IDC_SUBJECT and IDC_BODY edit controls. We update the message flags and call *SetProps* to copy the edit control data back onto the message. Calling *SaveChanges* with the KEEP_OPEN_READWRITE flag commits the updates to disk but keeps the object open for further use (e.g., if we decide to submit it).

AttachFile

A call to *GetOpenFileName* returns to us the full path and filename of a file that the user selects to attach to the message. We open an *IStream* interface on the selected file using the *OpenStreamOnFile* API, passing the MAPI allocation and free functions, STGM_READ to request read-only access, and the full path to the file. The *IStream* interface is returned in *pStrmSrc*. Next we create an attachment object with a call to *IMessage::CreateAttach* requesting the default interface, *IAttach*, by passing NULL in the first parameter. The attachment number and interface pointer are returned in the last two parameters. To create the destination stream, we open an *IStream* interface on the PR_ATTACH_DATA_BIN property of the attachment object, requesting read/write access.

Attachments can be accessed through several properties. PR_ATTACH_DATA_BIN gives you access to the attachment data as a stream of bytes that can be read or written using the *IStream* interface. Attachments can also be accessed as embedded OLE objects in the PR_ATTACH_DATA_OBJ property. (How this is accomplished is beyond the scope of this book.)

We use the *IStream::Stat* method to get the size of the source stream in the attachment file, and then call the *IStream::CopyTo* method to copy the file's data into the destination stream. The PR_ATTACH_FILENAME property is set to the filename returned by *GetOpenFileName*, excluding the path information. PR_ATTACH_METHOD is set to ATTACH_BY_VALUE to indicate that the attachment's data is part of the message and that it is found in PR_ATTACH_DATA_BIN. A file can be attached by reference also, meaning that only the path and filename are part of the message. In this case, the recipient is presumed to have access to the network resource where the attached file resides. Messages and OLE objects can also be attached. See the MAPI documentation for specifics.

The PR_RENDERING_POSITION property is set to (0xFFFFFFFF) −1 to indicate the attachment shouldn't be rendered in any way, and the attachment properties are set on the attachment object. The call to *SaveChanges* with a parameter of 0 means that we plan on releasing the object without further modification. Lastly, the IDC_ATTACHMENTS list box is updated.

SendNote

A call to *SendNote* prepares the message for submission and then submits it. As with *Save*, the first step is a call to *GetUIData*. Next we call *SetOutgoingProps*, which sets the PR_SUBJECT, PR_BODY, and PR_SENTMAIL_ENTRYID properties.

We set PR_SENTMAIL_ENTRYID to the entry ID of the Sent Items folder to tell the store provider to move the message to this folder after passing it to the spooler. The *SetOutgoingProps* method calls *SaveChanges*, keeping the message object open, to commit the new properties. After returning from *SetOutgoingProps*, we create a message in the Outbox and copy the reply message to the newly created message using *CopyTo*, call *IMessage::SubmitMessage* to start the outbound logic, and then delete the Inbox message using *DeleteMessages*.

A message can be created and submitted in any folder but is most often submitted in the Outbox. Which folder you create the message in is a design decision. Most applications create a message in the Outbox to eliminate the need to move it there on submission. This makes sense for the typical case in which a message is composed and sent without being saved, but it also adds some complexity to the logic. Creating the message in the Inbox simplifies processing of the Save command but typically introduces an extra move operation because saved messages should be kept in the Inbox folder.

There are two ways to handle this requirement: Either create and submit the message in the Outbox or create the message in the Inbox and then move it to the Outbox just before submission. If you create the message in the Outbox to avoid moving it there for submission, you have to create a copy of it in the Inbox if the user first saves the message. This means that instead of holding a single message object, you now have to maintain two message pointers—the Outbox message and the saved copy in the Inbox—and update both in parallel. If the user chooses to save many intermediate versions of the message before submission (the atypical case), this scheme becomes more expensive. One rather quick and dirty scheme would be to set a flag on the first Save command and "remember" to copy the message to the Inbox if it's released without being submitted. But this is not an acceptable solution because the saved message wouldn't be visible in the Inbox contents table until *after* the user released the message without submitting it. Your users would be left scratching their heads, wondering, "Gosh, I *know* I saved it; why don't I see it?"

We choose simplicity over performance in this case and opt for solution number two. Note that if the user opens a saved message in the Inbox and decides to submit it, the message must be copied to the Outbox anyway.

CreateReplyNote

The processing of a reply message is similar to that of a new message except that properties are copied from the original message to which we're replying. First, we create a new message object. If we are forwarding the original message, we invoke *IMessage::CopyTo* on the original message to copy it to *pNewMsg*. We exclude the message recipients from the reply message and the properties we intend to modify. This step is redundant in this case because we will overwrite these properties before we submit the message, but it illustrates how *CopyTo* works in the general case.

The properties we exclude include the following:

- PR_SUBJECT (because we add the "FW:" prefix)

- PR_BODY (because we add "- - - -")

- PR_MESSAGE_RECIPIENTS (because the user will explicitly select new recipients)

- PR_SENDER_XXX, PR_SENT_REPRESENTING_XXX (because the transport sets these anyway)

SetReplyRecips

If *pNewMsg* is a reply or reply-all to *pOrigMsg*, we call *SetReplyRecips* to update the recipient table automatically. First we get the PR_SENT_REPRESENTING-_XXX properties listed in *g_sptSender* and convert them to their equivalent recipient table columns. Notice that *g_sptSender* reserves a spot in the property array for the PR_RECIPIENT_TYPE property by passing PR_NULL (PR-_SENT_REPRESENTING_RECIP_TYPE). This lets the *GetProps* call allocate the *SPropValue* array with the required number of properties, even though there *isn't* a recipient type for the sender. We change the PR_SENT_REPRE-SENTING_XXX property tags to their corresponding PR_XXX tags, and *voila*, the sender is now a resolved recipient.

Next we get the PR_RECEIVED_BY_SEARCH_KEY property. This message property is the search key of the recipient that received *this copy* of the message, i.e., the user. If a message is addressed to Miles, John, and Julian, for example, PR_RECEIVED_BY_SEARCH_KEY will correspond to Miles on Miles's machine, John on John's machine, and Julian on Julian's machine. When the user chooses to reply-all to a message, a copy of his reply shouldn't come back to him. We use this property to know which row in the recipient table belongs to the user, and we exclude that recipient from reply-all messages.

If we are creating a reply message, our job is nearly finished: The reply goes to the sender. In this case there will be a single entry in the *palTo ADRLIST.* Otherwise, we must get the recipient table from the original message so we can figure out who our reply-all recipients are.

We iterate through the recipient table, being careful to exclude the sender (because we already have his entry), the user's entry (any entry whose search key matches PR_RECEIVED_BY_SEARCH_KEY), and any Bcc recipients. Along the way, we count the number of recipients accumulated in the filtered table, free the excluded rows, and mark the freed entries by setting *aEntries[i].cValues* to 0. We maintain the recipient type for the rows we keep so that To recipients retain MAPI_TO in the reply and Cc recipients stay MAPI_CC.

There are four cases we need to consider:

- *Reply.* Add the sender alone to the reply message's recipient table.

- *Reply-all.* The user is the only recipient, so handle this in the same way as reply.

- *Reply-all.* The sender is also the user, so don't add him to the reply recipients.

- *Reply-all.* The sender is not the user, and there are also other recipients. The PR_SENT_REPRESENTING_SEARCH_KEY property will be different from PR_RECEIVED_BY_SEARCH_KEY, and the filtered table will have one or more rows. Merge the filtered table entries with the sender's entry.

We add the sender to the reply recipients in all cases except the third above and keep track of this fact with the *fAddSndr* flag. If we must add the sender, we stick the sender in the first entry of a newly allocated *ADRLIST* and add the other recipients, if there are any, at the end. We scan the original list (*palTbl*), which consists of the rows from the filtered recipients table, and then copy each *ADRENTRY* structure into the new *ADRLIST.* At this point, any entries in *palTbl* will be shared between the two lists; specifically, each *ADRENTRY*'s properties member will be aliased by two pointers: an *rgPropVals* in *palTbl* and one in *palTo.* To avoid freeing the same memory twice, we decrement *palTbl*'s entry count. When the loop terminates, *cEntries* will be zero, since any entries not previously filtered will belong to *palTo* and any excluded entries will have already been freed. Our cleanup code can then call *FreePadrlist* on *palTo* without having to explicitly check its contents, because *FreePadrlist* frees only the enclosing *ADRLIST* structure if there are no entries.

Why do we iterate through the recipient table instead of simply setting up a restriction on PR_RECEIVED_BY_SEARCH_KEY? The reason is simple: Recipient tables aren't required to support restrictions.

The *ConcatRecips* method concatenates the new recipients' names into a semicolon-delimited string using each *ADRENTY*'s PR_DISPLAY_NAME value. We call *ModifyRecipients* to update the recipient table and then free the sender properties, both *ADRLIST*s, and release the table.

WINDS CASE STUDY AND IMPLEMENTATIONS

The remainder of this book is devoted to the study of MAPI service providers. We start by introducing service providers in a general way and then demonstrating the concepts in a case study of a working MAPI messaging system, WINDS. Many of the issues you'll face designing and implementing your own providers are best understood by taking a hands-on approach using actual working code. Many of the implementation details you'll have to worry about aren't necessarily described in the MAPI documentation; we've tried to address them here. Parts of the specification are open to interpretation; we've tried to distinguish what's mandatory from what's optional as we give you *our* reading of the specification in those cases where there isn't a rigid interpretation.

The insights you'll gain by studying the following chapters will help you understand the issues well enough to make informed decisions about your own design. However, the samples in this book don't represent the *only* way to implement MAPI service providers—maybe not even the best way—because each messaging system has its own idiosyncrasies and each project its own requirements. We operated under different constraints than you're likely to find in a commercial project, so there are instances where your solutions can be optimized considerably over what you'll find in this book. This is especially true for our database back-end implementation, where for a variety of reasons we found it more convenient to write our own database rather than use a commercial model. Occasionally we opted for clarity over efficiency or a general solution over an optimal one. So keep this in mind when you start work on your own project—take from these chapters what works for you, and cheerfully discard the rest.

MAPI Service Providers

Service providers occupy the lowest level of the MAPI architecture and are generally the most complex components in a MAPI messaging system. The complexity of *your* implementation will depend on the type of provider you are writing—message stores are usually the most complex and transports the simplest—and on the features you choose to support.

Providers are the components responsible for implementing most of the interfaces used by the MAPI subsystem and client applications. In this respect, service providers play a slightly different role in the MAPI subsystem than in other subsystems. For example, Microsoft uses the *application -> API -> subsystem -> SPI -> service provider* model in the Microsoft Windows NT security APIs and for the Winsock 2 API. In those technologies, an application makes a service request by calling an API; the request is passed to the subsystem which calls a service provider through a service provider interface (SPI). The service provider processes the request and passes the result back to the subsystem, which packages the data and returns it to the client through the API.

The situation is similar in MAPI except that, in many cases, the MAPI subsystem is not directly involved in the transaction. This is because the interface pointers returned to a client are frequently pointers to code that is implemented in the service provider DLL, not the MAPI subsystem. When a client calls an interface method through such a pointer, the call is serviced directly by the provider without MAPI's intervention. A provider services client requests either by doing the work itself or by forwarding the request to the messaging back end. The results are communicated directly to the client when the method returns or by asynchronous notifications generated by the service provider.

The MAPI specification is pretty flexible about what is and isn't required of a service provider implementation. Each provider must implement certain interfaces, but many interface methods are optional—the provider can support them or not support them depending on the implementation's requirements. This flexibility allows a vendor to make incremental releases of commercial providers and quickly bring MAPI providers to the market. For example, a developer creating a special-purpose message store provider could decide his implementation doesn't have to support messages with attachments, particularly if he defines a custom form or forms for the data in his message store provider. The same principle applies to address book providers and message transport providers.

It's important to point out that service providers can support features that go far beyond those described by the MAPI specification as well as those that fall somewhere short of it. Providers can add value by supporting more difficult and sophisticated features as well as by implementing features not specifically defined in MAPI. MAPI defines mechanisms by which providers can communicate their feature sets to clients.

What to Consider When Designing a Specific Provider

This question is rather broad and must be answered in the context of the problem or need that the system is being designed to address. Which type of provider you should implement depends on the data source you'll be accessing and what you'll be using it for. For example, if your provider will be accessing a document database or voicemail system, it might be convenient to write a message store provider to allow dynamic interaction between the client and the server where the data resides. If your provider will be accessing a directory of user information, an address book provider will be the best choice. Here are a few things to consider during the design of a MAPI service provider against an existing back end:

- *Can I use one or more existing service providers (the providers shipped with MAPI: the Personal Address Book and the Personal Folders message store, for example) so that the number or types of providers I need to write is minimized?* It is important that you, as a developer faced with the task of implementing one or more service providers, understand the trade-offs of writing one provider vs. another. Voicemail vendors, for example, typically have to decide whether to develop a store provider or a transport provider. The store provider lets them keep their data on the server for access via non-email interfaces such as telephones. On the other hand, a transport provider lets them present their messages in the default Inbox folder and is also easier to write than a store provider.

  Implementers of address book providers can usually choose among writing a full-fledged address book provider; writing a template-only address book provider and using the MAPI-supplied

Personal Address Book for storage of the recipient properties; or writing a read-only address book provider. In the case where a MAPI address book provider is designed to interface with an existing Personal Information Manager (PIM) application, writing a full address book provider is probably the best solution.

If you're writing a set of providers that talk to an existing message server, your choices include whether to write a tightly-coupled message store/transport provider, whether to write a message store provider at all, and whether to migrate existing messages to another MAPI store provider (e.g., the Personal Folders provider that ships with MAPI).

■ *Will the data for my service provider reside on a server or will it be local to the client machine?* If the data is located on a remote server, consider the speed of the link on the design of your service provider. For performance reasons, you might want to store the data locally; but for maximum data integrity, best use of system resources, and ease of administration, consider storing as much information as possible on a server. In other cases, the location of the data is dictated by an existing system you must interface with. Some server-based providers cache a local copy of the data to the user's hard drive and use the local cache for offline operators—for example, when the connection goes down or the link is slow.

■ *How can I increase the efficiency of my transport provider?* When writing a transport provider, if the link is slow, consider implementing the remote folder interface (discussed later in this chapter); otherwise, write a standard transport. If your development efforts also call for implementing a message store provider, consider writing a tightly-coupled store/transport provider.

■ *How much functionality should my provider offer the back-end messaging system?* Consider adding as much functionality as permitted. Doing so will make clients rely on the service provider for tasks that can be better implemented by the back end or service provider instead of forcing clients to simulate the functionality. If the back end supports a feature that your provider can expose to the client, you should expose it through the appropriate method instead of returning MAPI_E_NO_SUPPORT. An example would be notifications, which are used to update the client's user interface.

How Service Providers Are Implemented

A MAPI service provider is implemented as a standard DLL with a well-known entry point function. This allows the DLL to be loaded by MAPI in multiple processes and to be dynamically bound via *LoadLibrary* and *GetProcAddress*. The table in Figure 6-1 shows the names of the entry point functions that are called by MAPI for each provider.

Service Provider	Entry Point Function Name	MAPI Interface Returned
Address book	*ABProviderInit*	*IABProvider*
Message store	*MSProviderInit*	*IMSProvider*
Transport	*XPProviderInit*	*IXPProvider*

Figure 6-1.
Entry points and interfaces implemented by the different types of service providers that interact with the MAPI subsystem.

Note that these functions must be exported by name in the EXPORTS section of the project's DEF file. Following is an example of the DEF file for a message store provider DLL. (The *WizardEntry* and *ServiceEntry* functions in the file are discussed later.)

```
LIBRARY        MSLMS32
DESCRIPTION    'MAPI 1.0 PSS Sample Message Store Provider DLL'
CODE           SHARED READ EXECUTE
DATA           SHARED READ WRITE
EXPORTS
    MSProviderInit          @2
    WizardEntry             @3
    ServiceEntry            @4
```

The *XXXProviderInit* function handles two tasks: version negotiation between the service provider and MAPI and returning an instance of the interface appropriate to the provider. During the version negotiation, MAPI passes its internal version to the provider and the provider checks it against the version with which it is compatible. If the version of MAPI installed on the system is equal to or greater than the version of MAPI that the provider was written to work with, the provider creates a new instance of the *IXXXProvider* interface that it returns along with the version of the MAPI service provider interface (SPI) for which it was developed. If MAPI decides that it can handle that version of the SPI, it proceeds; otherwise, it releases the interface just obtained and unloads the provider DLL. From that point on, all interactions among MAPI, the client, and the service provider occur by calling methods on the interfaces obtained from the service provider. Figure 6-2 on pages 202–203 illustrates the interfaces available from each provider and how each interface is obtained.

Implementing Multiple Providers in a Single DLL

Sometimes it is convenient to create a single DLL for multiple providers. This is possible as long as each provider is of a different type. In other words, a single DLL can't have more than one transport provider, more than one store provider, or more than one address book provider.[1]

This limitation is due to the fact that MAPI relies on named entry points to bind to service providers. It is syntactically incorrect to define two functions with the same name within a single DLL (two *XPProviderInit* functions in a single DLL, for example), and MAPI does not provide a way to return different provider implementations within a single *XXXProviderInit* call.

A developer might get around this limitation to some extent by having a single entry point return service provider interfaces for different provider types based on information stored in the profile. The Microsoft Exchange Server is a good example: It has a single store provider entry point but recognizes three different provider subtypes with rather different characteristics (private, public, and delegate stores). However, this approach might not work well for completely unrelated provider types, which is why a future version of MAPI will eliminate this limitation.

---

1. Actually, a fourth provider type, the spooler hook provider, can be added to the DLL because the entry point for this kind of provider is *HPProviderInit*. However, spooler hooks are not in the scope of this book.

Address Book Providers

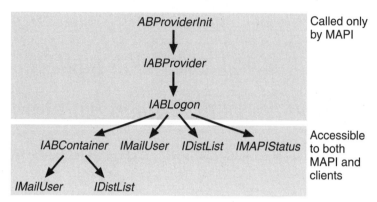

Transport Providers

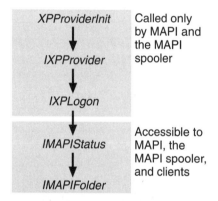

Figure 6-2. *(continued)*

The diagrams show how different interfaces are obtained from a service provider once MAPI calls its binding XXXProviderInit *function. Note that these trees are not interface inheritance maps and that they don't include the* IMAPITable *interface that is obtained from the different container interfaces such as* IABContainer, IMAPIFolder, *and so on.*

Figure 6-2. *continued*

Message Store Providers

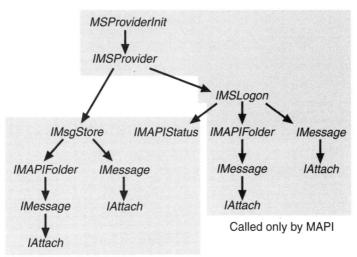

Available interfaces to MAPI
and client applications

How MAPI Interfaces Are Implemented

All MAPI service provider interfaces are derived from *IUnknown* and must implement all the basic COM functionality, such as reference counting, *QueryInterface*, and so on. To define a MAPI object in C++, you declare a class that inherits from the base class of the interface you want to implement. MAPI defines a set of macros to aid developers in the definition of the class's abstract methods. These macros are of the form *MAPI_XXX_METHODS(IMPL)*, where *XXX* is the name of the interface whose methods are being implemented. For example, let's assume we are defining the class *CABContainer*, which would be the implementation of the *IABContainer* interface. This is how it is done in C++:

```
class CABContainer : public IABContainer
{
public:
///////////////////////////////////////////////////////////////
// Interface virtual member functions
//
    MAPI_IUNKNOWN_METHODS(IMPL);
    MAPI_IMAPIPROP_METHODS(IMPL);
```

(continued)

```
    MAPI_IMAPICONTAINER_METHODS(IMPL);
    MAPI_IABCONTAINER_METHODS(IMPL);

//////////////////////////////////////////////////////////////
// Other member functions specific to this class
//
public:
    // Other functions here
    ⋮
private:
    // Other functions here
    ⋮


//////////////////////////////////////////////////////////////
// Constructors and destructors
//
public:
    CABContainer();
    ~CABContainer();

//////////////////////////////////////////////////////////////
// Data members
//
private:
    ULONG               m_ulRefCount;
    // Other members here
    ⋮
};
```

In the preceding example, the IMPL symbol is defined by MAPI and expands to nothing when the source code is compiled. It is common for the *IUnknown* interface to be declared in line, so the macro is not used. Using the MAPI macros or declaring the methods manually yields no difference in code size or performance, so it's up to you to decide which method to use. Note that when a class inherits from a MAPI interface, the implementation needs to support all the methods declared in the abstract class. For example, *IABContainer* derives from *IMAPIContainer*, which in turn derives from *IMAPIProp*, so we must implement all the methods of *IMAPIProp* and *IMAPIContainer* in addition to the methods of *IABContainer*. The reason for this is that the methods in the MAPI interfaces are declared *pure virtual*, so derived classes must define methods that override each of these pure virtual functions.

Using the class in the preceding example, when a client or the MAPI subsystem asks for an *IABContainer* interface, the provider will simply do something like this:

```
// Allocate a new object with a reference count set to 1
// during the construction of the object along with
// preparing the object for client consumption.
CABContainer * pMyABC = new CABContainer(…);
LPABCONTAINER pABC = (LPABCONTAINER)pMyABC;
// Return pABC to the caller.
⋮
```

The caller is then responsible for releasing the object that the service provider returns.

General Guidelines for Implementation

Some implementation issues are common to all service providers. In this section we make the most general recommendations we can, but be aware that each project might have unique requirements implying different choices. Rather than considering our suggestions as mandatory, use them as guidelines for your own design.

The Session Status Table and *IMAPIStatus*

MAPI maintains a table containing status information for each component in the current session. A client obtains the status table by calling *IMAPISession::GetStatusTable*. Each provider contributes a row to the table, as do the spooler, the *IAddrBook* supercontainer, and the session itself.

Service providers put their status information in the table by calling *IMAPISupport::ModifyStatusRow*. The following properties are required columns in the service provider's status row: PR_STATUS_CODE, PR_PROVIDER-_DISPLAY, and PR_RESOURCE_METHODS. PR_RESOURCE_METHODS is a bitmap that indicates which methods the provider supports in the *IMAPIStatus* interface. If you choose not to support *IMAPIStatus*, you must still provide this column, even though the value will be zero.

MAPI clients can query the status table for a particular row and examine its columns to determine the state of a particular component. For example, any service provider component can advertise its health by setting bits in PR_STATUS_CODE to STATUS_AVAILABLE or STATUS_FAILURE. The status code is particularly relevant to providers that make network connections. The state of the connection can be indicated by setting or clearing the STATUS-_OFFLINE bit, and clients can use this information to enable or disable functionality. Transport providers use the status code to indicate all kinds of conditions, including whether or not inbound or outbound delivery is enabled and whether the transport is in the process of sending or receiving a message or flushing its queues.

Other interesting columns are PR_STATUS_STRING, which gives a text string with information about the state of the provider; PR_PROVIDER_DIS-PLAY, which is the provider's display name; PR_PROVIDER_DLL_NAME, which is the filename of the provider DLL; and PR_RESOURCE_TYPE, which indicates the type of component—address book provider, transport provider, store provider, spooler, and so on.

The function of *IMAPIStatus* varies depending on the type of provider implementing it. *IMAPIStatus* is an optional interface that lets a client obtain additional information not available in the status table. Three methods are common to all providers: *SettingsDialog*, *ChangePassword*, and *ValidateState*. *SettingsDialog* displays a dialog that lets the user view and/or modify the current configuration settings. *ChangePassword* provides a way to change a provider's password programmatically. *ValidateState* allows the service provider to check its current state against the status table and if necessary to be reinitialized with the MAPI subsystem. Remote transports *must* support *IMAPIStatus::ValidateState* since this is the method that controls downloading and uploading messages in the remote mailbag. Chapter 8 describes both methods in detail.

IMAPIStatus::FlushQueues is used only by transports. Although this method is "officially" considered optional (like the entire *IMAPIStatus* interface itself), you're strongly encouraged to support it in transports because the status object is the only way a client can directly interact with a transport, which is ordinarily commanded only by the MAPI spooler. *IMAPIStatus::FlushQueues* lets a client command a specific transport to deliver queued messages immediately.

Clients obtain a component's *IMAPIStatus* interface by retrieving the PR_ENTRYID from the component's status table row and passing it to *IMAPISession::OpenEntry*. This property is computed by MAPI, is not supplied by the component, and is used to identify the component's status object—*not* the component supplying the interface.

Thread-Safe and Reentrancy Issues in Service Providers

When you develop an address book provider or message store provider, many of the interfaces implemented end up being called directly by client applications. These client applications might be using the interfaces obtained from the service providers in multiple threads. A service provider must protect itself from the dangers of reentrancy. Because a service provider cannot predict which thread will execute the methods in an interface, when an interface implementation manipulates internal data that might be modified in other methods, it should lock the data for exclusive access using the standard synchronization mechanism available in the Win32 API (e.g., critical sections, mutexes).

Transports deserve special attention. Most of their interfaces are called by the MAPI spooler. The MAPI spooler guarantees transports that all sending and receiving calls will occur in the thread where they were initialized in the call to *XPProviderInit*. Other methods such as *IXPLogon::TransportNotify* can occur on a separate thread. Some specific interfaces (*IMAPIStatus* and *IMAPI-Folder*) in transports can be directly accessed by clients. (We show how these interfaces are used by transports in Chapter 8.) However, these interfaces are remoted from the MAPI spooler process to the client process using the standard OLE marshaling mechanism. The marshaling mechanism spins off a separate thread, so marshaled interfaces must be thread-safe.

Parameter Validation

Robustness is one of the goals when developing service providers. Service providers need to be able to handle bad parameters that a client application might pass during a method call. Service provider interface implementations should validate the arguments a client passes to its methods. This includes checking the flags passed into the methods to detect conflicting values and verifying memory address and ranges for pointers and memory blocks.

MAPI supplies a set of functions to validate the parameters in all the methods of most of the interfaces published in the MAPI 1.0 specification. The functions that validate the method parameters come in the following forms: *Validate_XXX_YYY(this, …)* and *CheckParameters_XXX_YYY(this, …)*, where *XXX* is the name of the interface and *YYY* is the name of the method in the interface being tested. The *this* argument is C++'s *this* pointer to the object itself, which allows the function to validate the actual object. Here is a code fragment from a couple of sample interface method implementations that use the MAPI validation routines:

```
// Implementation of IMessage::GetProps on a store provider
STDMETHODIMP CMessage::GetProps(LPSPropTagArray  pPropTagArray,
                                ULONG            ulFlags,
                                ULONG *          pcValues,
                                LPSPropValue *   ppPropArray)
{
    Validate_IMAPIProp_GetProps(this,
                                pPropTagArray,
                                ulFlags,
                                pcValues,
                                ppPropArray);

    ⋮
}
```

(continued)

```
// Implementation of IABProvider::Logon on an address book provider
STDMETHODIMP CABProvider::Logon(LPMAPISUP      pSupObj,
                                ULONG          ulUIParam,
                                LPTSTR         pszProfileName,
                                ULONG          ulFlags,
                                ULONG *        pcbSecurity,
                                LPBYTE *       ppbSecurity,
                                LPMAPIERROR *  ppMAPIError,
                                LPABLOGON *    ppABLogon)
{
    CheckParameters_IABProvider_Logon(this,
                                pSupObj,
                                ulUIParam,
                                pszProfileName,
                                ulFlags,
                                pcbSecurity,
                                ppbSecurity,
                                ppMAPIError,
                                ppABLogon);

    ⋮

}
```

So what is the difference between using the *Validate_XXX_YYY* and the *CheckParameters_XXX_YYY* forms? Functionally speaking, they do the same thing, but the difference is that *CheckParameters_XXX_YYY* is present only during debug builds of your service provider. When the project is compiled without the debugging information, the *CheckParameters_XXX_YYY* form disappears from your code. The *Validate_ XXX_YYY* form, on the other hand, is present during debug and release builds of a project so that it always validates incoming parameters. The rule for using one rather than the other is simple: Always validate parameters on methods that will be called by client applications. For interfaces that are called only by MAPI and its components (e.g., the *IXXXLogon* and *IXXXProvider* interfaces), service provider implementation should use the *CheckParameters_XXX_YYY* form of the validating routines. In the previous code fragment, we always validate on methods from our *IMessage* implementation because the *GetProps* method might be called directly by a client application and we can't predict its behavior. The *CABProvider::Logon* implementation, on the other hand, does not interact with arbitrary client code—it is called only by MAPI, and the implementation can trust the incoming parameters.

Memory Management

Often a program's memory management code is the most time-consuming and difficult code to debug. Windows programs are particularly susceptible to memory management errors, which manifest themselves in memory leaks, heap corruption, and so forth.

MAPI service providers are subject to the same memory management problems experienced by other Windows programs, and they must follow MAPI's rules for allocating memory that will be freed by others. In Chapter 2 we discussed the semantics of the MAPI allocation functions and the benefits of using them. Another feature these functions provide is leak detection and debug traces that tell you the name of the function and module where the allocation took place. (Consult the "Guide" section of the *MAPI Programmer's Reference* for information on how to use this capability.) Although using the MAPI allocators is required *for any data a provider returns to MAPI,* a provider can choose any allocator for data that is only accessed internally. Although you can use *new* or *HeapAlloc* for your internal data structures, you'll get some great debugging aids if you use MAPI's allocators—at least for your debug builds. Doing so makes it much easier to track down memory leaks and heap-corruption problems.

Of course, this functionality doesn't come free. For this reason, we recommend that providers use the MAPI allocators for their internal needs during the debug development phase. When the code has been completely debugged and it is ready for a final release build, you can switch back to the system's native memory allocators such as *HeapAlloc, HeapFree,* and so on. This dual memory management can be achieved by creating a common memory manager object or by conditional compilation switches for debug and release targets. Most of the sample service providers we developed for this book use this approach. The following sample illustrates how we overload the *new* operator for debug and release builds:

```
// Global pointers to the MAPI memory allocation functions
// These pointers are initialized in some other place in a
// service provider (e.g., the XXXProviderInit function).
LPALLOCATEBUFFER gpfnMAPIAllocateBuffer = NULL;
LPALLOCATEMORE   gpfnMAPIAllocateMore   = NULL;
LPFREEBUFFER     gpfnMAPIFreeBuffer     = NULL;
```

(continued)

```
void * operator new(size_t size)
{
    #ifdef _DEBUG
    LPVOID pVoid;
    gpfnMAPIAllocateBuffer((ULONG)size, &pVoid);
    return pVoid;
    #else
    return HeapAlloc(GetProcessHeap(),
                     HEAP_ZERO_MEMORY,
                     (DWORD)size);
    #endif
}

void operator delete(void * pVoid)
{
    #ifdef _DEBUG
    gpfnMAPIFreeBuffer(pVoid);
    #else
    HeapFree(GetProcessHeap(), 0, pVoid);
    #endif
}
```

The *IMAPISupport* Interface

During a service provider's logon sequence (*IXXXProvider::Logon* method), MAPI passes a pointer to an instance of the *IMAPISupport* interface. This interface has helper methods used by the service provider to interact with the MAPI subsystem. MAPI passes a support object to the provider in several different methods; however, the support object passed in one method might not support the same methods as one passed in another method. The methods that the support object supports also depend on which type of provider it's being passed to.

For example, the *IMAPISupport::OpenEntry* method is not supported on the support object passed to the *ServiceEntry* entry point, but it is supported by the object passed to *IABProvider::Logon, IMSProvider::Logon,* and *IXPProvider::Logon.* Similarly, the *IMAPISupport::NewEntry* method is supported only on the object passed to an address book provider (i.e., the support object passed in *IABProvider::Logon*), so calling this method from a transport or store provider context returns MAPI_E_NO_SUPPORT. Some *IMAPISupport* methods don't make sense in certain contexts, and for those situations the methods will return MAPI_E_NO_SUPPORT. Be aware of this subtlety when using the support object in your provider implementation.

The support object is particularly useful to service providers implementing notifications in interfaces that require them (e.g., *IMAPITable, IMsgStore, IABLogon*). The *IMAPISupport::Subscribe, IMAPISupport::Unsubscribe,* and *IMAPISupport::Notify* methods are used by a provider to access MAPI's notification engine. The notification engine relieves providers of the burden of implementing a lot of the low-level details necessary for supporting notifications. In particular, the notification engine takes care of multithreading issues for clients that require multithread support and deals with the intricacies of passing data blocks across different process boundaries.

When using *IMAPISupport* for notifications, the calls to the *XXX::Advise* and *XXX::Unadvise* methods in the service provider will delegate mostly to the *IMAPISupport::Subscribe* and *IMAPISupport::Unsubscribe* methods. The sample providers in this book demonstrate how this is done.

Another important method in the *IMAPISupport* interface is *SetProviderUID*. From our discussion of how entry IDs are constructed, you might recall that the second member of the entry ID structure is a UID that MAPI uses to associate entry IDs with a particular service provider. When address book and message store providers that support opening objects are initialized, they call *IMAPISupport::SetProviderUID* to register the UID associated with the entry ID supplied in their tables and objects. If a provider needs to support multiple types of entry IDs (i.e., short-term and long-term entry IDs), then it must call *IMAPISupport::SetProviderUID* for each distinct UID that the service provider plans to use in its entry IDs.

The *IMAPIProp* Interface: A Generic Design

MAPI defines the *IMAPIProp* interface to be a generic data abstraction layer that presents a uniform way to access different types of data. This model offers great advantages to clients, but implementing *IMAPIProp* is also one of the most time-consuming and tedious tasks of writing a service provider. Because *IMAPIProp* is the base class of many interfaces returned by the provider (*IMessage, IMAPIFolder, IMsgStore, IABContainer, IDistList, IMailUser,* and *IMAPIStatus*, to mention just a few), you can save yourself a lot of work by defining a base *IMAPIProp* implementation and sharing the code among all the derived interfaces. (See Figure 6-3 on the following page.)

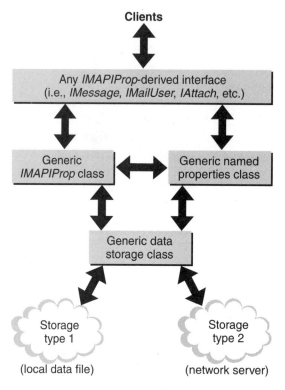

Figure 6-3.

Abstraction layers for a generic IMAPIProp *implementation that writes to multiple back ends. Note that this figure is not a derivation digraph. The arrows indicate calls made from one object to another—not inheritance.*

In our model, the base *IMAPIProp* implementation provides a generic way to store and retrieve properties that is independent of the back-end storage mechanisms and the various interfaces that will derive from it. The *IMAPIProp* methods of the derived interfaces delegate to the base implementation's methods, which do the work. In other words, the derived classes' *IMAPIProp* methods are usually stubs that just call the base class's methods. This model is what OLE calls *object containment,* and it's needed because COM imposes some restrictions on how objects can inherit from other objects. (COM doesn't support multiple inheritance, for example.) We examine this subject in detail in Chapter 9.

When the properties stored in the base *IMAPIProp* object need to be committed to permanent storage, a request is made to the generic data storage layer, which implements the details of saving the data to a nonvolatile device (e.g., a local database file or network server).

How Providers Are Installed, Registered, and Configured

Clients can connect to multiple messaging back ends concurrently in the same session. A client might need to use the services of one back end for some tasks and the services of another back end for other tasks. Which back-end system is accessed, and consequently which providers will be invoked, is usually driven by the end user's actions. For example, the user might read messages in a server-based store provider one moment and then decide to send a fax the next. The goal of the Universal Inbox discussed in Chapter 1 is (ideally) to make these multiple concurrent connections transparent to the user, or at least easy to manage.

MAPI uses the concept of *profiles* to aid in managing the various installable service providers and back-end systems. A profile is a logical group of one or more message services. Each message service is composed of one or more service providers that supply the necessary connectivity. When a client logs on to a messaging service using a specific profile, the client is running a *MAPI session of a profile;* in other words, you can think of a MAPI session as a running instance of the services in a profile.

Profiles are typically created by the end user using a configuration program such as the Microsoft Mail and Fax applet in the system's Control Panel. (MAPI also provides a set of interfaces for creating and managing profiles programmatically, but they are outside the scope of this book.) When a new profile is created, the user selects which messaging services will be included in it. The MAPI subsystem provides a list of installed and available messaging services from which the user selects services to add to the profile.

A message service is a DLL that provides a single entry point and some common code for configuring one or more providers. It's less confusing to the end user to be presented with all the service providers used to access a given back end as a single entity rather than to be presented with a configuration of each service provider on a provider-by-provider basis. For example, instead of presenting an address book provider for XYZ system, a store provider for XYZ system, and a transport provider for XYZ system, the vendor implements a single message service that contains the XYZ store, transport, and address book providers.

This grouping has some implications for developers of the different service providers that make up the message service. The most important characteristic of a messaging service is that users configure the message service, rather than the service's individual providers, so that the providers must convey the properties required for configuration into a single coherent interface that is presented to the user.

A message service can contain more than one provider of the same type. For instance, the ACME message service might consist of an address book provider, a personal folders store provider, a public folders store provider, and a transport provider.

MAPISVC.INF

The list of MAPI message services available on a given system is contained in the file MAPISVC.INF, which is found in the system directory (e.g., \WINNT-\SYSTEM32). The Control Panel Mail and Fax applet enumerates these services and presents them in a list box from which the user selects services to add to a profile. The MAPISVC.INF file contains all the information needed to add a selected message service to a user profile, including information such as the types of service providers in the message services, the names of the service provider DLLs, and some of the service provider capabilities. The Mail and Fax applet reads the MAPISVC.INF file and tries to locate each service provider DLL before displaying it in the list box of available message services. The DLLs must therefore be in a directory listed in the system PATH variable. If the message service DLL is not found, the service is not listed at all.

Adding a New Service to the System

A developer creating a new service provider must supply a small INF file for the message service containing its providers. When this INF file is merged with the system MAPISVC.INF file, the message service becomes visible to users (via the Mail and Fax applet) and can then be added to a profile.

The MERGEINI Utility

The MAPI SDK includes a utility that takes the name of a message service's INF file as an argument and merges its contents with the system's current MAPISVC.INF file, thus making available the new set of service providers in the message service. The tool is invoked from the command line like this:

```
C:\MYMSGSP> MERGEINI C:\MYMSGSP\MYMSGSP.INF -m
```

The line above merges the contents of MYMSGSP.INF with the system's MAPISVC.INF file.

Following is a fragment of an INF file taken from one of the code samples in this book:

```
[Services]
MSLMS=Sample Local Message Store

[MSLMS]
; Here we list the providers that compose this service.
Providers=MS_LMS
PR_SERVICE_DLL_NAME=MSLMS.DLL
PR_SERVICE_ENTRY_NAME=ServiceEntry
PR_SERVICE_SUPPORT_FILES=MSLMS.DLL
PR_SERVICE_DELETE_FILES=MSLMS.DLL
PR_RESOURCE_FLAGS=SERVICE_NO_PRIMARY_IDENTITY
WIZARD_ENTRY_NAME=WizardEntry

[MS_LMS]
PR_PROVIDER_DLL_NAME=MSLMS.DLL
PR_RESOURCE_TYPE=MAPI_STORE_PROVIDER
PR_RESOURCE_FLAGS=STATUS_DEFAULT_STORE
PR_PROVIDER_DISPLAY=PSS Message Store
PR_DISPLAY_NAME=Sample Mailbox
```

The INF file is composed of sections that start with the section name enclosed in square brackets, like so: [SECTION_NAME]. Each line in a section consists of a key and a string value in the form KEY_NAME={some string value}.

The [Services] section lists the message services being installed from the INF file, with each entry representing a different service. In this example, the only service installed is the Sample Local Message Store, whose information is listed in the [MSLMS] section of the file. The value of a key in the [Services] section gives the name of the service as it will appear in the Mail and Fax's list box of available services. (See Figure 6-4.) In this case, the service is called "Sample Local Message Store," but any string is valid.

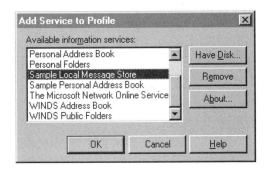

Figure 6-4.
After a message service is added to the system and its information added to MAPISVC.INF, the service is available and can be added to an existing or new profile.

The [MSLMS] section lists various attributes of the MSLMS service whose key was given in the [Services] section. These attributes include the PR_SERVICE_DLL_NAME key, which specifies the name of the DLL containing the service's code. When the value of the PR_SERVICE_DLL_NAME key is read, MAPI adds the *bitness* of the operating system to this string before attempting to load the DLL. For example, on Win32 systems (Windows NT and Windows 95), a service DLL named MSLMS.DLL would be concatenated with the string "32" so that MAPI would call a *LoadLibrary("MSLMS32.DLL")*. On Win16 systems, the string is taken as is without any suffix added to the name. Keep this in mind when generating the output file of a service provider project.

Each service section has the Providers key, which lists the individual MAPI service providers that are part of the service. This key can have multiple values, each of which is separated by a comma and corresponds to an individual service provider type (address book provider, store provider, transport provider, etc.) that is loaded and logged on to when the service is used in a profile. In the previous example, only one service provider is configured in this service: the provider specified in [MS_LMS]. The order is important here. Address book providers must come first, followed by message store providers and transport providers. (Spooler hook providers come last.)

Each provider in the service also has its own section in which we indicate to MAPI the name of the DLL where the service provider is actually implemented. The DLL name is given by the value of the PR_PROVIDER_DLL_NAME key, which follows the same naming conventions as PR_SERVICE_DLL_NAME. Other keys include the type of provider (PR_RESOURCE_TYPE), some of its capabilities (PR_RESOURCE_FLAGS), and its friendly name (PR_PROVIDER_DISPLAY).

Of these properties, only PR_PROVIDER_DLL_NAME, PR_PROVIDER_DISPLAY, and PR_RESOURCE_TYPE are required to properly install and register the component with MAPI, although including PR_RESOURCE_FLAGS in each provider section is highly recommended. PR_PROVIDER_DISPLAY can be used to programmatically recognize providers and should not be added in the different languages when the service is localized to a specific country. The order in which these properties appear in the file is not significant.

Adding and Configuring a Message Service in a Profile

When a service is added to a profile, MAPI reads the service properties (i.e., the values of the keys) directly from the MAPISVC.INF file. When the message service's section is read, MAPI looks for the PR_SERVICE_ENTRY_NAME key. The value of this key is the name of an exported function in the service's DLL whose name is given by the PR_SERVICE_DLL_NAME key. This function can have any name, but it must be exported *by name* (e.g., listed in the EXPORT section of the DEF file of the provider project) and must be of the *MSGSERVICEENTRY* prototype, as shown in the following code:

```
typedef HRESULT (STDAPICALLTYPE MSGSERVICEENTRY)(
    HINSTANCE         hInstance,
    LPMALLOC          lpMalloc,
    LPMAPISUP         lpMAPISup,
    ULONG             ulUIParam,
    ULONG             ulFlags,
    ULONG             ulContext,
    ULONG             cValues,
    LPSPropValue      lpProps,
    LPPROVIDERADMIN   lpProviderAdmin,
    LPMAPIERROR FAR   *lppMapiError
);
typedef MSGSERVICEENTRY FAR *LPMSGSERVICEENTRY;
```

The first time the message service is added to a profile, MAPI calls the *MSGSERVICEENTRY* function (or service entry) to configure the service's providers. The service entry function is also called whenever the user reconfigures or deletes the message service. To distinguish the multiple contexts in which this function is called, MAPI passes to the function an enumerated value in *ulContext* indicating the reason why the service entry function was invoked. Providers must also pay careful attention to the *ulFlags* parameter, which indicates whether the provider is allowed to display any UI to the end user. The service entry function might be invoked in situations where UI is not permitted, such as the configuration of a message service running in a Windows NT service, which typically does not allow UI. If the *ulFlags* parameter indicates that UI is prohibited, the message service must do a silent configuration. If the configuration cannot be performed without user input, the function must return the MAPI_E_UNCONFIGURED error. The service entry function might also be invoked in a situation where UI is required, such as when the provider logon sequence has failed because the service is not properly configured. In yet other situations, UI might be entirely optional (for example, displayed only if the configuration information is not complete).

The service entry function does not have to implement code to handle all the different contexts in which the function is called (UI is required, UI is forbidden, UI is optional). If the function is invoked in a context that is not supported, the message service should quietly return success to the caller (return S_OK back to the client).

We mentioned before that MAPI service providers are installed as a part of a message service. You can't install and configure a service provider unless it is part of a message service. The message service code controls the configuration process, so the service entry function represents the entry point of the configuration code for *all* the providers in a service. The job of this function is to display UI and collect data from the user. With this information, the service entry function is able to configure each individual service provider.

Adding a service using the Profile Wizard   The Control Panel's Mail and Fax applet also lets the user create and configure a profile through the Profile Wizard, an application that lets each message service display a series of property pages for gathering the configuration data. When a new profile is created using the Profile Wizard, MAPI reads the MAPISVC.INF in each service section as it looks for the WIZARD_ENTRY_NAME key. This key gives the name of the function that the wizard must invoke to interact with the message service through the MAPI Profile Wizard configuration protocol. The rules for declaring this function are the same as for the service entry function. If a service exports this entry point, MAPI adds it to a list of wizard-enabled services. The Profile Wizard displays these services in a list box from which the user may select the desired service. (See Figure 6-5.)

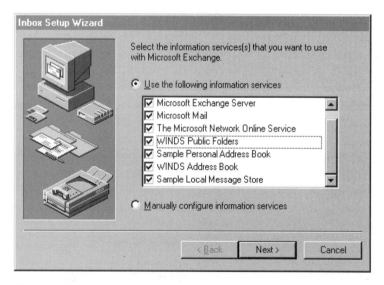

Figure 6-5.
When creating a new profile, the message services can be added with the Profile Wizard. All wizard-enabled message services will be added to this page, and the user selects the service to be added.

Once the services are selected, the Profile Wizard calls each service's wizard entry function to let it display its configuration property pages. Your wizard entry function is passed in an *IMAPIProp* interface, and you pass back a dialog procedure and the name of a dialog resource containing your configuration pages. Your dialog procedure is called to return the number of pages in your services configuration UI and to handle navigating through them. The dialog procedure extracts the configuration settings entered by the user and combines them into an *SPropValue* array. When all the configuration properties have been gathered, you call *SetProps* on the interface passed to you to save the configuration properties. After the last page of the provider's wizard pages is displayed and the data is retrieved from them, MAPI calls the service's service entry function, passing in an *SPropValue* array containing the saved properties. The service entry code uses these properties to configure the individual providers. So in order for a message service to support a configuration wizard, the message service must also support programmatic configuration via the *SPropValue* array passed to its service entry function with UI suppression (i.e., no user interaction).

Profile Sections

From the user's point of view, a profile is a group of message services. From a program's point of view, it's an object containing a database that lists the different services and profiles and stores their configuration properties. Each message service in a profile and each provider in a service has an area in this database known as a *profile section*. A profile section offers a programmatic interface, *IProfSect*, to access the values of the properties it holds. Each instance of a message service in a profile has its own unique *service profile section*. Each instance of a service provider in the profile has its own *provider profile section*. Each section is identified with a unique identifier (UID), so that if a user adds two instances of a message service XYZ to a profile, MAPI will allocate different profile sections for the instances.

Setting profile properties   A profile section is accessed programmatically using the *IProfSect* interface implemented by MAPI and available to service providers through the *IMAPISupport::OpenProfileSection* method. *IProfSect* is derived from *IMAPIProp*, so properties can be set and retrieved from the profile section in the same way as for any other object in MAPI. The *profile provider* [2]

---

2. This is another service provider used in the MAPI architecture. Only one profile provider is registered with MAPI and is supplied by Microsoft. The interfaces for developing a profile service provider are not documented in the MAPI 1.0 release.

implementation takes care of saving and loading these properties to and from the appropriate storage medium.

When a new service is added to a profile, MAPI creates the storage for each message service's section and for each provider section. Values of the PR_XXX keys in the MAPISVC.INF file for the added service are loaded and stored in the aforementioned sections. (See Figure 6-6.) You can't put arbitrary properties in the INF file using the PR_XXX strings, however. MAPI recognizes only a subset of these strings. You *can* put arbitrary MAPI properties in the INF file, but you must use the properties' numeric property tags instead.

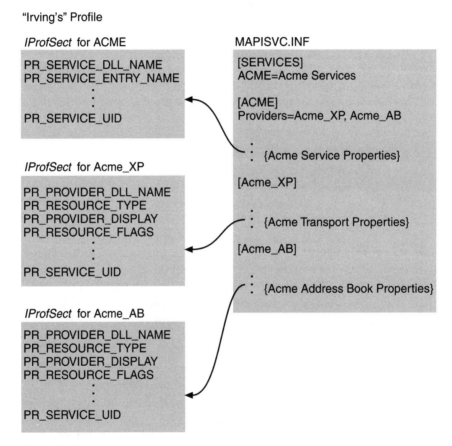

Figure 6-6.
A property import map from the MAPISVC.INF service section into the IProfSect *object. Each section in the system INF file maps to a new profile section object whose properties are available to the service provider in the service.*

Storing custom properties in the service profile section   Service providers can add arbitrary or custom properties to the INF file. When MAPI parses the file, these properties are read and added to the appropriate profile section and will then be accessible through the *IProfSect* interface. Custom properties (whose property IDs fall in the 0x6600 through 0x67FF range) or standard MAPI properties can be added to the service section or provider section of the file. You must use the hexadecimal representation of the property tag instead of a PR_XXX string.

The INF file can tell MAPI to create additional profile sections for storing properties that are not associated with either message services or providers. We mentioned that each profile section is labeled by MAPI with a unique identifier assigned by MAPI when the profile is created. This UID is used by the providers to identify which profile section to open. Message services might choose to assign a predetermined UID for one or more of their custom sections in the service so they can be accessed directly from the providers without having to browse the list of sections in a service. Only a custom section can have hard-coded identifiers. A standard profile section (e.g., a service profile section) cannot be assigned a UID; instead, MAPI allocates one and assigns it. MAPI *clients* can access these custom profile sections added by service providers. To access a custom profile section, the client application supplies the known UID of the custom profile section to the *IMsgServiceAdmin::OpenProfileSection* method. The following fragment of an INF file demonstrates how custom sections are added:

```
[Services]
ACME=Acme Services

[ACME]
Providers=ACME_MS, ACME_XP
; Create other subsections for this service.
Sections=ACME_Sect1, ACME_Sect2
; Standard properties for the service go here
; My custom PT_LONG property tag is below
66010003=3

[ACME_MS]
; Standard properties for the provider go here.
; Tell MAPI to use this PR_MDB_PROVIDER value instead.
34140102=79C2FA70AFF7234D9BC811BB002FC45A
```

(continued)

221

```
[ACME_XP]
; Standard properties for the provider go here.
; My custom PT_STRING8 property tag is below.
6602001E=My String Property

[ACME_Sect1]
UID=14DCC0C8AA05101A9BB000AA002FC630
66030003=1
66040003=2

[ACME_Sect2]
UID=17C220C8BB05101A9BB000AA002FC631
66050003=3
66060003=4
```

We must point out that when a message service uses hard-coded section UIDs in an INF file, the message service cannot support multiple instances of itself in a profile and must set the SERVICE_SINGLE_COPY flag on the service's PR_RESOURCE_FLAGS.

Accessing multiple profile sections   The MAPI subsystem controls access to the profile sections of message services in the different profiles available on a system. A message service's section is private to the service and the providers in the service. If two or more instances of the same service exist in the profile, each one has its *own* private sections that are not viewable by the other instances. This guarantees that service X won't overwrite service Y's data, or that X won't corrupt Y's data. Only members of a message service have access to the profile sections associated with that message service and only for that specific instance. A provider has access to its own section, the section of its service, and to the sections of the other providers in that service's instance. Profile sections of message services and their providers are protected from MAPI clients, too. Service provider writers often attempt to implement custom configuration UI or functionality on the client side. Clients can access only the custom profile sections added through the INF file, which have well-known UIDs. This could be used as a mechanism to detect when a provider is interacting with a specific message service and ultimately offer enhanced and additional capabilities to the end user.

Storing sensitive properties in profile sections   On Win32 systems (Windows NT and Windows 95), a profile section's property values are stored in the system's registry. On Win16 platforms (Windows 3.1*x*) the profile information is saved to a local file. Programmatically, the information contained in the profile section of a service is not accessible to client applications or to other message services even within the same profile. The registry, however, is open to any user or program with sufficient security privileges. Anyone can potentially modify or view the system registry (e.g., using REGEDIT) and modify or delete entries belonging to services in an active profile.

A provider that needs to store critical information in its profile section, such as a password to the database file, decryption keys, and so on, must use secure properties to store its sensitive data in the profile section. Secure properties provide a mechanism for storing configuration or credential properties and guarantee that no one will have access to this information other than the provider that stored it. On systems that offer security services natively (e.g., Windows 95 and Windows NT), MAPI relies on the operating system for the storage and encryption of this information. On platforms where these security services do not exist natively (e.g., Windows 3.1*x*), MAPI provides them.

To store a secure property in the profile section, define each property ID in the range (boundaries included) PROP_ID_SECURE_MIN (defined as 0x67F0) through PROP_ID_SECURE_MAX (defined as 0x67FF). *IProfSect* encrypts any property whose ID is in this range before writing it to the registry. Here is an example of how to define a custom property in the secure range:

```
#define PR_MY_PASSWORD PROP_TAG(PT_TSTRING,PROP_ID_SECURE_MIN)
#define PR_MY_FILE_PWD PROP_TAG(PT_TSTRING,PROP_ID_SECURE_MIN+1)
```

How the *IProfSect* interface is obtained   As we mentioned earlier, the different profile sections in a service are identified by a UID. To get an instance of a given profile section object during the service entry call, the service provider calls *IProviderAdmin::GetProviderTable*, which returns a table of the service providers in the message service. The UID for each service is found in PR_SERVICE_UID, and the UIDs for the providers are found in PR_PROVIDER_UID, both of which are columns in this table. The PR_SERVICE_UID, or the PR_PROVIDER_UID, or NULL can then be passed to *IMAPISupport::Open-ProfileSection* to gain access to a profile section. MAPI does security enforcement to control who can access the profile section, even if the caller passes the UID belonging to a section it does not own or should not have access to.

If NULL is passed for the UID in *OpenProfileSection*, MAPI opens the default profile section *for the context* in which the call was made. For example, the *IProviderAdmin* interface passed in the service entry function call accesses the service's profile section. After the provider has been logged on, any calls it makes to *IMAPISupport::OpenProfileSection* (where no UID is specified) returns the *provider's* profile section. A provider can gain access to the message service profile section by opening the provider profile section, getting the

PR_SERVICE_UID property, and using the property to open the service's profile section, as illustrated in the fragment below:

```
SPropTagArray sptService = { 1, { PR_SERVICE_UID } };
LPPROFSECT pProvProfSect = NULL, pSvcProfSect = NULL;
ULONG cValues;
LPSPropValue pProp;
// pSupObj is the support object passed in IXXXProvider::Logon.
HRESULT hResult = pSupObj -> OpenProfileSection(NULL,
                                                MAPI_MODIFY,
                                                &pProvProfSect);

if (hResult)
{
    // Fail the call.
    ⋮
}


hResult = pProvProfSect -> GetProps(&sptService,
                                    0,
                                    &cValues,
                                    &pProp);
if (SUCCEEDED(hResult))
{
    if (S_OK == hResult)
    {
        hResult = pSupObj -> OpenProfileSection
                            ((LPMAPIUID)pProp -> Value.bin.lpb,
                            MAPI_MODIFY, // READ/WRITE
                            &pSvcProfSect);
    }
    else
    {
        hResult = E_FAIL;
    }
    // Release the memory of pProp using the
    // provider's MAPI memory functions.
    gpfnMapiFreeBuffer(pProp);
}
if (pSvcProfSect)
{
    // Use the interfaces here.
    ⋮
}
// Cleanup goes here.
⋮
```

The MAPI Spooler

The MAPI spooler is an executable process that runs in the background whenever a MAPI session is activated by a client application logging on to a profile[3]. The spooler's main task is to sort the outgoing messages submitted in the message store providers and assign them to the appropriate transports for delivery. The spooler also handles requests from the different transports to create new inbound messages in the default store provider. These new messages are used to hold the data received by the transports.

The MAPI spooler is considered the administrator of all transports running in all MAPI sessions. The spooler loads the transport DLLs upon session initialization and logs on to them through the *IXPProvider* and *IXPLogon* interfaces. Since the spooler is the only application that logs on to the different transports in a profile, a client does not have to worry about figuring out which one should handle delivery of a specific message. And because the spooler is a separate process, delivery of outbound and inbound messages happens in the background without the client application interacting in the process or being bogged down by it.

The MAPI spooler provides a pseudo-multitasking environment for the heterogeneous transports that run concurrently in one or more MAPI sessions. The spooler arbitrates over access to shared system resources used by the transports to deliver or receive messages (e.g., communication ports and modem lines, pager cards, and so forth). The spooler guarantees that it will call only one transport at a time to deliver or receive messages so that the provider can gain exclusive access to the transmission channel. Transport provider developers must pay attention to these rules, particularly when a flush operation is requested by the client or spooler. When the spooler calls the transport to flush the transport's outbound and inbound queues, mechanisms exist so that the provider stays in a *flushing* state and the spooler won't activate any other transports. When the queues are empty, the transport indicates to the spooler that it wishes to be taken out of the flushing state. When the transport returns to its normal state, other transports can be activated.

When a message is addressed, the client application fills the recipient table with the properties of each intended recipient. To figure out which message transport delivers the message to each recipient, the MAPI spooler uses two columns from the recipient table of a message: PR_ENTRYID and PR_ADDRTYPE. The PR_ENTRYID property is the entry ID of the mail user

---

3. There is an exception to this rule: If the client logs on using the MAPI_NO_MAIL flag, the spooler is not started and none of the transport providers are activated.

object (*IMailUser* interface) in the address book provider that resolved a particular recipient for delivery. The PR_ADDRTYPE property is the address type string for each recipient in the table (e.g., X400 and SMTP). Each transport can register for any number of address types and any number of UIDs through *IXPLogon::AddressTypes*. The transports are ordered in the profile (the order can be changed through the Control Panel). The MAPI spooler assigns each recipient to a transport based on the UID in its entry ID first and then, if there is no match on the UID, on its address type. The UIDs are essentially a way of tightly coupling an address book provider and transport (or store provider that supports submission). It guarantees the transport first chance at its own address book provider's recipients.[4]

When a recipient in a message is delivered by a specific transport, the transport marks the recipient as *handled* by setting the PR_RESPONSIBILITY property equal to *TRUE* in the recipient table of the message. After all the recipients have been handled by the available transports, any recipient that still has the PR_RESPONSIBILITY property set to *FALSE* causes the spooler to generate a nondelivery report (NDR) message with the list of all failed recipients.

Message Paths During Sending and Receiving

This section describes what occurs when a message is submitted and received and explains the role of each component in both processes from the service provider perspective—we omit the client-side steps for creating the message, setting its properties, and so on. (See Chapter 5 for details.)

We also don't discuss how spooler hook providers work. These special providers are invoked by the message spooler for outbound messages (after the message is processed by the spooler) and for inbound messages (after the transport is finished with the new message). If you're interested in the spooler hook providers, look at the documentation included with the MAPI SDK for further information. In the following lists, to simplify the discussion, we purposely omitted a description of the process path in a tightly-coupled store/transport. (See the "Guide" section of the *MAPI Programmer's Reference* on message store provider development.)

---

4. The transport ordering mechanism in MAPI 1.0 does not provide sufficient flexibility and will probably be revised in a forthcoming version of MAPI.

Message Submission (Outbound)

The following list outlines the steps involved in outbound message processing. (The steps in the list correspond to those depicted in Figure 6-7 on the following page.)

1. A message is submitted by a client application using the *IMessage-::SubmitMessage* method. A submitted message must have, at least, a properly constructed recipient table—without it, the submission process won't even be started.

2. The message store provider calls the *IMAPISupport::PrepareSubmit* method. This function makes sure the MAPI spooler is ready to accept messages and that the client and spooler sessions are synchronized for this operation. After this is done, the message store provider calls *IMAPISupport::ExpandRecips*, which expands any personal distribution lists to their individual member recipients and adds any missing properties. For this operation, MAPI calls into the address book providers to expand recipients and collect mail user properties.

3. The *IMAPISupport::ExpandRecips* function also checks the recipient table against installed message preprocessors to verify whether the message needs to be preprocessed or not. A message preprocessor is a special kind of message transport that is called before the actual delivery transport is called for a message. See the MAPI SDK documentation for more details about this. For your reference, a preprocessor sample with the source code is supplied on the companion CD-ROM.

4. Once the message is processed and is ready to be delivered, the message store provider adds a row to the message store provider outgoing queue table. The row has the following properties: PR_INSTANCE_KEY, PR_ENTRYID, PR_SUBMIT_FLAGS, and PR_CLIENT_SUBMIT_TIME. The MAPI spooler has an advise on this table. As soon as the table is modified, the spooler is notified and the row is processed at the earliest convenience of the spooler.

5. The MAPI spooler calls *IMsgStore::OpenEntry* using the entry ID of the submitted message obtained from the outgoing queue table. The newly opened message is then locked for exclusive access (*IMsgStore::SetLockState*), and the spooler gets the message's recipient table. The spooler uses the recipient table to sort each recipient by the PR_ADDRTYPE property.

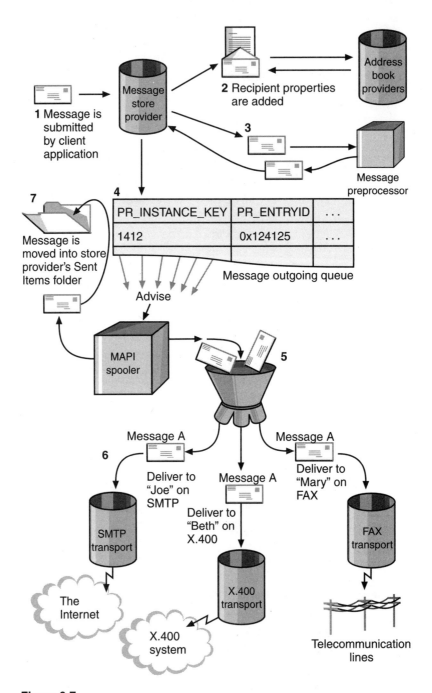

Figure 6-7.
The chronological path of a message when it is submitted and the components with which it interacts during the process.

6. The spooler gives the message to the different transports that handle the different address types. Each transport's *IXPLogon::SubmitMessage* and *IXPLogon::EndMessage* methods are called for each message to start the outbound logic.

7. After all the recipients are handled and any NDRs generated, the MAPI spooler *moves* each message to the Sent Items folder if the PR_IPM_SENTMAIL_ENTRYID property has been set in the submitted message. If PR_DELETE_AFTER_SUBMIT is set to *TRUE* or if the property is not set in the message at all, the message is deleted.

Message Reception (Inbound)

The following list is a step-by-step explanation of inbound message processing. (The steps in this list correspond to those depicted in Figure 6-8 on page 230.)

1. When a transport receives new mail from the foreign system, it notifies the MAPI spooler that it has pending incoming mail by calling *IMAPISupport::SpoolerNotify(NOTIFY_NEWMAIL, NULL)* or by changing its state with the spooler to "Inbound Flushing," which clears several incoming messages pending processing.

2. The spooler responds by calling into the default message store provider to request a new message. The message store provider creates an empty message object and returns it to the spooler.

3. The empty message received from the message store provider is wrapped into a private implementation in the MAPI spooler. This wrapped empty message is passed to the transport via *IXPLogon::StartMessage*. The transport then proceeds to translate the foreign system properties into MAPI properties that are set on this new message.

4. A transport might need to call into the address book provider to get additional recipient and/or sender information that will be added to the received message.

5. The transport calls *SaveChanges* on the wrapped message object and returns it. The spooler then performs some postprocessing to add certain properties. The processed message must have the PR_MESSAGE_CLASS property set. This property is used to decide into which folder the new message will be moved in the default message store provider.

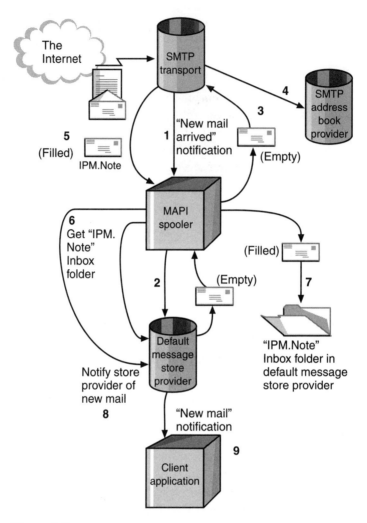

Figure 6-8.
The chronological path of a message as it is received from the transport provider and the components with which it interacts during this process.

6. The spooler calls *IMsgStore::GetReceiveFolder* to see if a default receive folder has been specified for the message class belonging to the inbound message.

7. The spooler calls *IMsgStore::OpenEntry* using the entry ID of the receive folder obtained from *GetReceiveFolder* to open the indicated folder. The new message is then *moved* to this folder, and the

changes made by the spooler and transport are committed to this new message.

8. After the message is saved in the Inbox folder, the spooler notifies the message store provider through *IMsgStore::NotifyNewMail* that a new message has arrived.

9. After the spooler notifies the message store provider of new mail, the message store provider constructs (or it might simply forward) a new mail notification to all mail clients that have set an *IMsgStore-::Advise(0, NULL, fnevNewMail,....)* notification link with the message store provider.

A Look Ahead

We have introduced many concepts throughout the first six chapters and now need to demonstrate how all the MAPI interfaces used by client applications are implemented by the different service providers. Chapter 7 gives a quick introduction about the kinds of service providers we will be demonstrating. Chapters 8 through 10 present the actual implementations.

Implementing Service Providers: A Case Study

In this and the next three chapters, we examine some specific implementations of MAPI service providers. Chapter 8 presents a case study of the XPWDS and XPWDSR transport providers; Chapter 9 presents the ABPAB and ABWDS address book providers, and Chapter 10 covers the MSLMS and MSWDS message store providers. We've implemented two classes of providers: local-based providers (MSLMS and ABPAB) that access databases stored in files residing on the user's hard drive and server-based providers (XPWDS, XPWDSR, ABWDS, and MSWDS) that access data on a remote server.

The remote server hosts the WINDS post office, which is our implementation of a generic back-end messaging system. We provide the WINDS post office because the server-based providers included in this book must have a back-end system to talk to, not because we want to demonstrate how to write a post-office server. We won't go into the internals of WINDS in any detail—except when absolutely necessary to explain how a provider interfaces to the server. This chapter presents a high-level description of the WINDS system, the WINDS server-based providers, and the local-based providers.

The WINDS Mail System

WINDS is a sample implementation of a client/server mail system in which each user has his own mailbox for receiving messages. (See Figure 7-1 on the following page.) WINDS is hosted on a server machine and administered by the WINDS Admin program. We devised this system to act as a back end (and test bed) for the service providers included in this book and to demonstrate, on a small scale, the potential of MAPI service providers and the technical issues involved in interfacing to a messaging-system back end. You are encouraged to study the providers presented here and adapt them to your own projects.

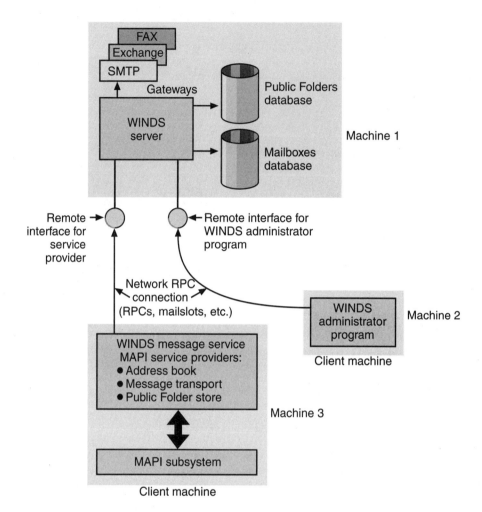

Figure 7-1.
Components of the WINDS messaging system.

The WINDS Server

The WINDS post office is a Microsoft NT–based server process that controls access to a database of mailboxes and distribution lists. Each mailbox represents a user of the system. The database of mailboxes serves as a temporary storage location for messages delivered to a user's mailbox. The public folders database stores a hierarchy of folders that are accessible concurrently by multiple clients. These public folders are used as a kind of bulletin board where any user can post a message that is viewable by other users. The author of a message posted in a public folder has total control over the disposition of the message; users have read-only access to messages posted by other users.

The WINDS server is implemented as an NT service that exposes two sets of remote procedure call (RPC) functions that are invoked by the WINDS MAPI service providers and by the WINDS Admin program. The RPC functions are exposed on the named pipe protocol family, so WINDS' clients (including the service providers and the WINDS Admin program) can run on any platform that supports named pipes (i.e., Windows NT or Microsoft Windows 95).

The WINDS Administrator

WINDS Admin is an application used to create and maintain mailboxes and distribution lists on one or more WINDS servers and to maintain the public folder database. This program communicates with the server through a special interface designed solely for the Admin program; the interface uses RPCs as the interprocess communications (IPC) mechanism. (See Figure 7-2.)

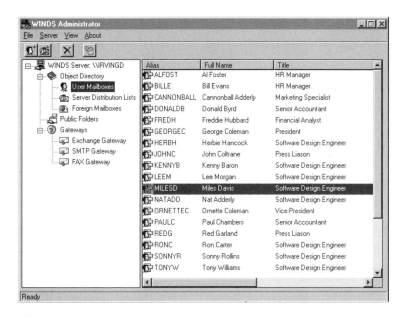

Figure 7-2.
The WINDS Admin program is used to manage the WINDS service running on multiple servers on a network.

Once WINDS is installed on a machine, the post-office administrator can use the Admin program to create accounts for users on the system. Figure 7-3 shows the property sheets that the administrator uses to add a new mailbox to the system. The administrator must communicate this account information (e.g., the server name and account name) to the end user, so the user can enter his account information when he configures the WINDS service providers.

Figure 7-3.
A new mailbox is created in the WINDS server using the WINDS Admin program.

The administrator can create a distribution list using the New Distribution List property sheet shown in Figure 7-4 on the facing page. A new entry is created in the distribution list's parent container, and members can then be added to it. Note that a distribution list can be created and saved without adding any members, but if a message is sent to an empty distribution list, the message is dropped.

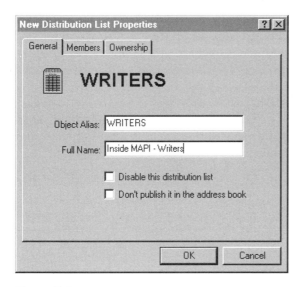

Figure 7-4.
A new distribution list is created. Members can be added immediately.

The WINDS Message Service

On the client side is the WINDS message service, which contains the set of MAPI service providers used to access the WINDS server. The message service is implemented as a single DLL[1] that exposes address book provider, public folder message store provider, and message transport service provider interfaces. Each provider interacts with a different component of the WINDS server. The message service can be configured for LAN or Remote/Off Line connections. A LAN connection is used by clients connected to the server through a normal network interface card (e.g., an ethernet adapter) with normal network bandwidth. A Remote/Off Line connection is useful when only a slow link or intermittent link to the WINDS server is available (e.g., dial-up Remote Access Service).

---

1. On the companion CD-ROM, we also include versions of these providers implemented as single and stand-alone providers that can be added to a profile. These individual versions of the WINDS service providers might be useful if you are trying to concentrate on a single provider and don't want to be overwhelmed by the extra details of a combined message service.

The WINDS message service is configured as a single entity. When the service is added to a MAPI profile, the server and the user identity must be specified. Figure 7-5 on the facing page shows the configuration property sheets for the WINDS message service. The following list explains the components of the User Account property sheet.

- *Server Name.* This is the network UNC (universal naming convention—i.e., \\HOST) name of the machine where the user account is located. The server machine must be running the WINDS service.

- *Mailbox Name.* The mailbox name is the name of the account on the remote server. To select a mailbox or change the current one, the user clicks the Browse button and selects a name from the list that appears. Once selected, the user is asked to enter the password for the mailbox. For new mailboxes, the default password is PASSWORD.

- *Full Name.* This is the complete name of the owner of the selected mailbox. This field is updated automatically when a new mailbox is selected. This information cannot be edited manually.

- *Change Mailbox Password.* This button brings up a dialog box to change the password for this mailbox. The user is asked to type the old password and a new password, and then confirm the new password.

- *Using Continuous Network Connection.* This is the option to use if the machine has a persistent LAN connection. If this option is selected, the service will create notification links with the remote system, which allows the providers to update internal data dynamically as the data changes on the server and to react to changes or commands from the server.

- *Using Remote/Intermittent Connection.* This setting instructs the service providers to use local data and to defer communications with the server until the user changes the connection mode. This mode is useful if the server or the client machine is not on a persistent LAN connection. If this option is selected, the server doesn't automatically update the providers' local data.

The different MAPI service providers that make up the WINDS message service are ABWDS, MSWDS, XPWDS, and XPWDSR.

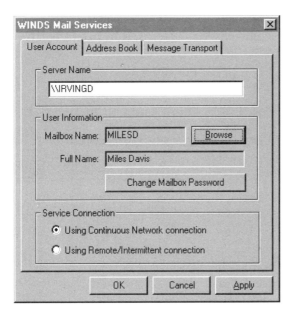

Figure 7-5.
Server location, user information, and connection configuration of the WINDS message service.

ABWDS

The WINDS address book provider exposes the lists of addressable recipients of a WINDS server. The addressable recipients are the mailboxes, distribution lists, addressable public folders, and recipients accessed through the installed gateways on the server. The foreign address book provider recipients are grouped in subcontainers corresponding to the gateways through which they are accessed. However, the entire list of addressable objects (native and foreign) is presented in the global address list. Figure 7-6 on the following page shows a screen shot of different containers exposed to MAPI clients in the WINDS address book provider.

The ABWDS address book provider is presented to MAPI as read-only, so entries cannot be created in it through the MAPI interfaces. However, when new items are added in the WINDS server to the directory of addressable objects (i.e., mailboxes or distribution lists) using the WINDS Admin program, the ABWDS address book providers running on each client machine are notified and the providers' internal tables are updated. The address book provider is available when the connection is via LAN or Remote/Off Line. During Remote/Off Line connections, the ABWDS uses a local file that holds most of the information for address book provider objects so that addresses can be resolved. If the connection to the server is broken or the server goes temporarily off line, the ABWDS automatically switches to using the local cache of addressable objects.

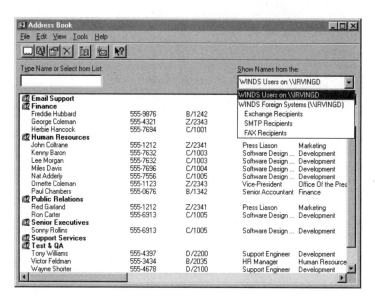

Figure 7-6.
WINDS server containers presented to MAPI clients.

MSWDS

The WINDS public folder store provider affords access to the public folder database, enabling a client to post and read messages available in the hierarchy of folders accessible to all users of the WINDS server. MSWDS can't be chosen as the default by a MAPI client because it does not support several features required of the default store provider—specifically, it does not support message submission. Since the folder hierarchy is stored on the server, when a LAN connection to a WINDS server machine is not available, the public folder store provider is off line and inaccessible.

XPWDS, XPWDSR

The WINDS message transport is responsible for delivering messages to and from a user's mailbox on the WINDS server. The message transport is, by default, configured to deliver mail immediately after a client submits a message, provided that the server is available and accepting connections. If the server is down or a network error occurs, the message delivery is automatically deferred. Alternatively, if the user connects to the WINDS server over a slow link (for example, a RAS dial-up link), the transport might be configured so that the remote folder interface for transports is used. This interface allows the end user to manually download the headers of available messages and select which message should be downloaded and which message should be deleted. When the WINDS transport is configured for remote operation, automatic tasks might be scheduled to happen without user interaction (e.g., connect every day at midnight to get the new message headers). XPWDS is the transport provider that handles immediate delivery, and XPWDSR is the remote transport provider.

MSLMS: A Personal Message Store Provider

The Local Message Store sample is an implementation of a local-based message store provider. This implementation fulfills all the requirements of a default message store provider. Among the features supported in this implementation are the following:

- As a read/write message store provider, MSLMS allows the creation and modification of message store objects such as folders and messages.

- Supports the creation of attachments in messages. Attachments can assume one of the following forms:

  - ❑ Binary data (i.e., PR_ATTACH_DATA_BIN with IID_IStream)

  - ❑ OLE embedded objects (i.e., PR_ATTACH_DATA_OBJ with IID_IStorage)

  - ❑ MAPI embedded messages (i.e., PR_ATTACH_DATA_OBJ with IID_IMessage)

- Supports message submission to the MAPI spooler.

- Supports notifications on its tables and other message store provider objects.

- Allows clients to set multivalue properties on its objects.

- Supports sorting and restrictions on its contents and hierarchy tables.

- Supports creating associated messages which are exposed through the associated contents tables on folder objects.

- Supports named properties. All objects share a common mapping, which is done at the message store provider level. This facilitates using the message store provider with MAPI forms and custom messages that require named properties support.

Other interesting features of the Local Message Store include native RTF support, search capabilities, and categorization support on the contents and hierarchy tables.

CDataBase

The message store provider implementation (MSLMS) and the Personal Address Book service provider (ABPAB) both use a local file for their database storage. The database implemented on top of this file was developed from scratch to provide a freely distributable database back end for the Personal Address Book and the Local Message Store samples. The database storage mechanism supports the specific needs of MAPI service providers, such as concurrent multiprocess access on a single machine (record level locking, for example).

CDataBase was designed to encapsulate the details of accessing specific database records and keep the database access mechanism separate from the MAPI-specific code. This interface manages how data is read and written to disk using a small and coherent set of functions that can be adapted and used by the different MAPI service providers. *CDataBase* provides a record-oriented way to access a file without handcuffing the caller to a specific record or file structure. To achieve this, it makes use of OLE *IStream* interfaces to access the data stored in its records. A record is a group of five fields. Each field is a separate stream of data in a particular MAPI object. Each record in the database is identified by a unique ID that serves as the search key for finding a particular record. (See Figure 7-7.)

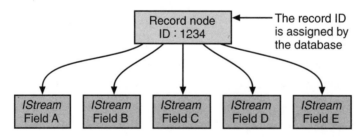

Figure 7-7.
A record in the database is a collection of five fields that represent the data contents of MAPI objects. To access an object's data, a client simply supplies the database with the record ID of the object and specifies which data fields it needs to access. The data in a field is accessed using the IStream *interface.*

The *CDataBase* object allocates a new record ID when either *CDataBase::CreateEmptyRecord* or *CDataBase::CreateRecord* is called. These methods create a record that has no streams on it yet. Before you can read or write data to an empty record, you must create or open a stream against a record field. The newly opened stream is associated with the record by a call to *CDataBase::OpenRecordField*. The caller can use an open stream for storing any kind of data; the database doesn't impose any structure at all on the stream. For example, the ABPAB and MSLMS service provider samples write the property data of their MAPI objects to one of the streams in a record.

Internally, the data in the database file is stored on disk in blocks of 2 KB, which is the smallest allocation unit stored in the file. The data blocks belonging to the same stream are kept together in a linked list within the file—each data block contains a header with the disk file offset of the next block in the stream. Figure 7-8 shows how data blocks are organized in a database file.

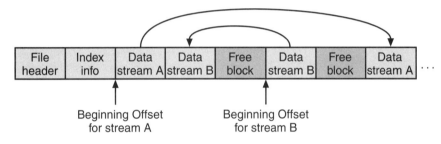

Figure 7-8.
Typical organization of the data blocks in the database file. The data for a stream might not be contiguous. The IStream *object deals with that. When a data block is freed, it is marked as such and the next time a stream needs to grow, a freed node is used before growing the file. This helps fill in the fragmentation holes in the database file.*

The stream grows or shrinks by dynamically adding or removing blocks from this list. The *IStream* implementation returned by *CDataBase::OpenRecordField* or *CDataBase::OpenRecord* is responsible for managing the disk file and calling internal database functions to grow and shrink the number of nodes in a stream.

ABPAB: A Personal Address Book Provider

The sample Personal Address Book provider is a full implementation of what MAPI designates as a personal address book provider. This address book provider implements all the features writable address book providers must support.

Among the features supported in this implementation are the following:

- Provides read/write access to allow the creation and modification of address book provider objects such as distribution lists and mail users.

- Allows entries to be copied from foreign address book providers. Custom properties and the details page of the foreign entry are preserved.

- Supports named properties. The mapping is done at the address book provider level, so all objects share a common named property mapping.

- Supports notifications on its tables as well as on the different address book provider objects.

- Supports sorting and restrictions on its contents and hierarchy tables.

- Supports name resolution in the container object (*IABContainer::ResolveNames*) and restrictions on the contents tables for ambiguous name resolution (PR_ANR).

- Supports help file mapping in the details page.

The ABPAB address book provider uses the same database file format as the MSLMS, so it uses the *CDataBase* object to manage the low-level interaction with the physical storage medium.

Message Transport Providers

Transport providers are DLLs that provide connectivity to a back-end messaging system. In our representation of the layers of the MAPI architecture (in Figure 1-4 on page 15), you'll notice that the service provider interface between the transport provider and MAPI shows the transport communicating exclusively with the MAPI spooler. You can visualize a transport's lower half as a link of some kind to the back-end system and the upper half as a set of MAPI interfaces that are manipulated by the spooler, or by the spooler on the client's behalf. Although transports can communicate indirectly with MAPI clients, almost all transport activity is driven by the spooler.

We use the terms "message transport," "transport provider," and "transport" interchangeably to mean the MAPI message transport provider component. In networking terminology, "transport" denotes a layer of a network protocol stack, but in MAPI it describes the component that translates MAPI properties to and from the back-end system's native data format and sends and receives messages. The MAPI specification doesn't tie a transport provider to a particular network transport protocol: A transport provider can use any network protocol or none at all.

Transport providers make MAPI systems easily extensible because the message delivery code for each back-end system is isolated within the transport provider module, effectively decoupling message delivery from message storage, addressing, and other client-side functions. This means that the user has only to install and configure a new transport when connectivity to a different back-end system is required, which makes it easier and cheaper to replace or upgrade components as the need arises.[1] We mentioned in Chapter 1 that one of the features driving the MAPI architecture was the idea of a Universal

---

1. MAPI also permits transports to be *tightly coupled* to another provider (typically a message store provider) for those systems where the back end provides storage and/or addressing functionality and where it's desirable to have the client-to-back-end connection managed by a single component. Tightly-coupled transports can bypass the MAPI spooler and run directly in the client's context.

Inbox on the user's desktop. Transport providers are the components that make the Universal Inbox possible.

Any number of transports can be installed in a profile and can run concurrently in a MAPI session, enabling a client to talk to more than one messaging system at the same time. Transports make MAPI systems highly interoperable because the *lingua franca* of a MAPI transport is always composed of MAPI messages that can be manipulated by any MAPI-compliant store provider or client. In other words, a message from any client can (in theory) be delivered by any transport that handles the message recipient's address type, and a message from any transport can be placed in any store provider that can be the default store provider. Transports also make MAPI systems highly extensible because the transport component can be changed or added anytime you need connectivity to a different back-end system.

How Transports Interact with the MAPI Subsystem

A transport runs in the spooler's context. The spooler process is designed to allow potentially lengthy delivery operations to appear to occur in the background while MAPI clients run in the foreground. The goal is to let a client call to *IMessage::SubmitMessage* return quickly, making the client as responsive as possible to the user. In the meantime, the spooler churns away in the background, routing the submitted message to one or more transports for delivery.

The spooler has the job of managing the various transports running in the current session. Its responsibilities include the following:

- Loading each transport provider DLL in the current profile
- Logging on to the installed transports and calling each one's initialization routines
- Queuing outbound messages from multiple store providers
- Selecting an appropriate transport to deliver a message to a given recipient
- Passing submitted message objects from the store provider to the transport (outbound)
- Passing received message objects from the transport to the store provider (inbound)
- Collating outbound messages so they are delivered in the order submitted
- Servicing transport requests to accept inbound messages

The spooler responds to client-side requests that pass through either the store provider or the session status object. These requests cause the spooler to call methods on a transport provider's interfaces. The spooler also monitors each transport's row in the session status table, and a transport can change its status row to request services from the spooler.

Outbound Logic

The spooler loads each transport provider DLL and logs on to each transport in the profile when the session is started. After logon, the spooler calls each transport's *IXPLogon::AddressTypes* method to let the transport register the address types it supports. An address type is a string or a GUID that tells the spooler what type of back-end system a transport can connect to. Recipients also expose the address type property PR_ADDRTYPE, which tells the spooler the type of back-end system on which the recipient receives mail. The spooler uses this information to choose which transport provider should deliver a message destined for a particular recipient. For example, an Internet transport can deliver messages to recipients whose address type is "SMTP" and advertises that fact by returning "SMTP" in *IXPLogon::AddressTypes*. The Microsoft Mail transport handles recipients of type "MS"; a fax transport would register the "FAX" address type, and so on. Microsoft publishes a list of the common or standard address types in use today, but a vendor can create a custom address type if the implementation requires it. Address types can also be specified by a GUID if uniqueness is required.

The spooler keeps an ordered list of transports and the address types each one supports. When a message is submitted, the spooler checks the address type of each recipient against its list and passes a copy of the message to the first transport that has registered for that address type. If the address type is unique among all the registrations, there can never be more than one transport that handles recipients of that type. A transport can ensure this state of affairs by registering for a custom address type or, better yet, a GUID address type. The spooler searches its list of GUID address types first, looking for a match on the GUID embedded in the recipient's PR_ENTRYID property. If no match is found, the list of string address types is searched for the recipient's PR_ADDRTYPE property. Since the GUID is unique, a transport that registers for a GUID address type will always be chosen over any competitors. Transport providers that connect to a server-based post office can use this technique to guarantee that they are always chosen to handle messages to recipients who have mailboxes on the post office.

The spooler passes the message object to the chosen transport in the *IXPLogon::SubmitMessage* method. If the transport decides it can deliver the message, it accepts responsibility for the outbound message by setting the recipient table's PR_RESPONSIBILITY column to *TRUE* for that recipient. If the transport can't deliver the message, it doesn't modify PR_RESPONSIBILITY and the spooler searches its list for the next transport that handles that address type. If the transport accepts the message, it translates the message's properties into the back end's native data format and sends the stream out over the wire. Before the transport returns from *SubmitMessage*, it calls *SaveChanges* to mark the message as having been delivered to that recipient.

Sometime afterwards, the spooler will call *IXPLogon::EndMessage* to determine the final disposition of the message. The transport can instruct the spooler to remove the message from the outbound queue—if it's been delivered, for example—or the transport can request the spooler to requeue the message and try again later. This latter scenario is called *deferred delivery*, and it is used to schedule delivery for a certain time of day or to queue messages created "off line" until a connection is established with the back end. If the transport returns from *EndMessage* without deferring the message, the spooler removes the message from its outbound queue and either deletes it or moves it to another folder, depending on the values of the message's PR_DELETE_AFTER_SUBMIT and PR_SENTMAIL_ENTRYID properties. If the spooler can't find a transport to deliver the message to the recipient, it generates a nondelivery report.

Inbound Logic

A transport can choose to notify the spooler when inbound mail arrives, or it can ask the spooler to poll it periodically. The transport tells the spooler which mechanism to use by passing back a bitmap of flags in *IXPProvider::TransportLogon*. If the transport is polled, the spooler will call its *IXPLogon::Poll* method periodically. The transport notifies the spooler of inbound mail by passing back a nonzero number in *Poll*'s single parameter. A transport can also choose to notify the spooler when mail arrives (instead of being polled) by calling *IMAPISupport::SpoolerNotify* the next time the transport has control and there is inbound mail.

Either way, the spooler responds by calling *IXPLogon::StartMessage* to begin the inbound logic. The spooler creates a new message object in the store provider's receive folder and passes it to the transport in the *StartMessage* call. The transport decodes the inbound stream into MAPI properties and sets them on the message object. When the transport has finished encoding the inbound stream into the MAPI message, it calls *SaveChanges* on the message object and returns. The spooler responds by calling *IMsgStore::NotifyNewMail* to tell the client-side instance of the store provider that an inbound message has arrived. The store provider then notifies any clients that have advised on *fnevNewMail*.

How Transports Interact with Message Store Providers and Address Book Providers

Message transports interact with the message store provider indirectly. The spooler acts as the intermediary by creating new inbound message objects in the store provider and by passing outbound messages from the store provider to the transport. Here's how this works for an outbound message.

1. The client calls *IMessage::SubmitMessage*, and the store provider adds a row to its outgoing queue table.

2. The spooler gets a notification on changes to the store provider's outgoing table and places the new outbound message in the spooler's outbound queue.

3. The spooler gets the entry ID of the next outbound message from the outbound queue and opens it.

4. The spooler can call into the address book provider to resolve recipients or add properties to the recipient table.

5. The spooler chooses a transport to deliver the message and passes the message object to the chosen transport in a call to *IXPLogon::SubmitMessage*.

For inbound messages, the spooler calls *IMsgStore::NotifyNewMail* after the transport calls *IMessage::SaveChanges* on the message object passed in *StartMessage*.

Message transports can call into an address book provider to get additional properties for the sender or recipients. A transport might do this to compute the PR_SENDER_XXX properties, for example, for a sender that has an entry in one of the installed address book providers. Transports are responsible for setting the PR_SENDER_XXX and PR_SENT_REPRESENTING_XXX properties on outbound messages so that a client can reply to the message. (See Figure 8-1 on pages 252 through 254 and Chapter 5 for an explanation of the PR_SENT_REPRESENTING_XXX properties.)

General Requirements for All Message Transports

All MAPI transport providers must obey certain conventions to be fully compliant. Although some of these should be obvious, we list them all for completeness.

Transports must provide the connectivity to the back-end messaging system. The connection can be persistent, or it can be opened on demand. Persistent connections are opened at logon time and exist for the duration of the session. XPWDS is such a transport: It establishes a connection to the WINDS server by creating a mailslot that is closed only when the provider logs off. When the cost of maintaining the connection is low and the bandwidth high—a corporate LAN, for example—this type of transport will provide a highly responsive messaging system.

Transports that connect on demand are commonly called *remote transports.* They connect to the back-end system at scheduled times or when commanded by the client. In the "between" times, a remote transport will defer all outbound messages until the scheduled upload time occurs or until the client flushes the outbound or inbound queues. This type of transport is advantageous when the connection costs are high or the link is slow, e.g., connecting to an online service where the user pays for connect time by the minute.

Transports must provide secure access (where applicable) to the underlying system. Because the transport is the link between the user and the back-end system, the task of authenticating the user to the system usually falls on the transport. Transports can obtain a user's security attributes from the operating system; they can rely on the MAPI logon to provide credentials; or they can obtain password or other authenticating information from the user when the transport is configured. A transport also can provide the MAPI subsystem with the logged-on user's identity properties.

A transport must understand the back end's native data representation and be able to translate MAPI properties to and from the native data format.

A transport must accept responsibility for messages it chooses to deliver.

All transport providers must implement a set of required APIs and interfaces, namely the following:

- *XPProviderInit.* The initialization API

- *IXPProvider.* The interface that contains the *TransportLogon* method, which is called when the provider is logged on

- *IXPLogon.* Contains methods for submitting outbound messages and delivering inbound messages

- *IMAPIStatus.*

Transports must compute some required properties and add them to messages. (See Figure 8-1 on pages 252 through 254.)

Transport interfaces and APIs must be thread-safe in some situations. This requirement isn't as strict for transports as it is for store providers and address book providers because most of the calls to the transport are guaranteed to happen on a single thread. The transport session is managed by the spooler through the *IXPLogon* object, and the spooler calls most *IXPLogon* methods on the same thread from which *XPProviderInit* was called. The spooler loads a single instance of a transport provider's DLL and acquires a single instance of the *IXPProvider* interface regardless of the number of sessions the transport is logged on to.

The exception to this rule is the *IXPLogon::TransportNotify* method, which can be called from a different thread. In addition, a transport's *IMAPIStatus* interface must be thread-safe because the interface is marshaled from the spooler process to the client process and the OLE marshaling code creates a separate thread on the spooler side.

Of course, if your implementation creates worker threads to handle some processing chores, you must also ensure that access to shared data objects (e.g., global data or static data members) is synchronized. You are also prohibited from calling any *IMAPISupport* methods on a worker thread. All calls from the transport that are serviced in the spooler must be made from the same thread from which *XPProviderInit* was called. The single exception to this rule is *IMAPISupport::SpoolerNotify,* which can be called from a different thread.

Transports should occasionally yield control during lengthy operations. The spooler creates a hidden window and enters a message loop as part of its initialization. When the spooler calls into an *IXPLogon* method, the message loop hangs until the call returns. When a transport is in the middle of a lengthy operation, such as sending or receiving a message, it should occasionally yield control to the spooler so that the message loop can run and process window messages. The MAPI specification recommends that transports yield to the spooler at approximately 0.2-second intervals by periodically calling *IMAPI-Support::SpoolerYield.*

A transport should inform the MAPI subsystem of its activity and changes in state. When a transport changes state in order to process a request or handle an event, it should tell the MAPI subsystem of the new state by updating its status row in the session status table. Transports should set PR_STATUS_CODE and PR_STATUS_STRING in their status row property set and use *IMAPI-Support::ModifyStatusRow* to update the table.

Required Properties on Inbound and Outbound Messages

Property Tag	Description
Required Properties for Both Message Types	
PR_SENDER_NAME	The sender's display name.
PR_SENDER_EMAIL_ADDRESS	The sender's email address.
PR_SENDER_ADDRTYPE	The sender's address type.
PR_SENDER_ENTRYID	The sender's entry ID.
PR_SENDER_SEARCH_KEY	The sender's search key.
PR_SENT_REPRESENTING_NAME	The name of the party on whose behalf the sender is sending the message. If the sender has been delegated to send the message by another user (a secretary might be delegated to send mail on behalf of the boss, for example), this property will contain the name of the person delegating authority to the sender. In other words, PR_SENDER_XXX represents the person who clicked the Send button; PR_SENT_REPRE-SENTING_XXX represents whomever the message is from. If the message wasn't sent by a delegate, PR_SENT_REPRESENTING_XXX will be the same as PR_SENDER_XXX.
PR_SENT_REPRESENTING-_SEARCH_KEY	The delegator's search key. If the sender isn't a delegate, this property will be the same as PR_SENDER_SEARCH_KEY.
PR_SENT_REPRESENTING-_ADDRTYPE	The delegator's address type. If the sender isn't a delegate, this property will be the same as PR_SENDER-_ADDRTYPE.
PR_SENT_REPRESENTING-_EMAIL_ADDRESS	The delegator's email address. If the sender isn't a delegate, this property will be the same as PR_SENDER_EMAIL-_ADDRESS.

Figure 8-1. *(continued)*

The properties that transports are required to compute for inbound and outbound messages.

Figure 8-1. *continued*

Property Tag	Description
Required Properties on Outbound Messages Only	
PR_MESSAGE_DELIVERY_TIME	The date and time the message was actually delivered by the transport.
PR_PROVIDER_SUBMIT_TIME	The date and time the transport received the message in *IXPLogon-::SubmitMessage*. The submit time should be close to the delivery time unless the message is deferred.
Required Properties on Inbound Messages Only	
PR_RECEIVED_BY_ENTRYID	The PR_RECEIVED_BY_XXX properties identify the message recipient. PR_RECEIVED_BY_ENTRYID is the recipient's entry ID in one of the installed address book providers.
PR_RECEIVED_BY_NAME	The recipient's name.
PR_RECEIVED_BY_SEARCH_KEY	The recipient's search key: a concatenation of the address type, a colon character, and the email address.
PR_RECEIVED_BY_ADDRTYPE	The recipient's address type.
PR_RECEIVED_BY_EMAIL_ADDRESS	The recipient's email address.
PR_RCVD_REPRESENTING_ENTRYID	If the recipient is a delegate, i.e., a user receiving mail on another's behalf, the PR_RCVD_REPRESENTING_XXX properties identify the delegator, i.e., the party for whom the recipient is receiving the message. If the recipient isn't a delegate, the delegator and delegate will be the same user, so the PR_RCVD_REPRESENTING_XXX properties will be the same as their PR_RECEIVED_BY_XXX counterparts. This property is the delegator's entry ID.
PR_RCVD_REPRESENTING_NAME	The delegator's name.

(continued)

Figure 8-1. *continued*

Property Tag	Description
Required Properties on Inbound Messages Only (continued)	
PR_RCVD_REPRESENTING__SEARCH_KEY	The delegator's search key.
PR_RCVD_REPRESENTING__ADDRTYPE	The delegator's address type.
PR_RCVD_REPRESENTING__EMAIL_ADDRESS	The delegator's email address.

Transports must exclude nontransmittable properties. Outbound messages shouldn't contain any properties with IDs in the so-called "nontransmittable" range. These are properties that have meaning only to the sender's system—such as PR_SENTMAIL_ENTRYID, which tells the spooler where to move the message after submission—or properties that, for reasons of security, shouldn't be sent over the wire. MAPI defines a macro, *FIsTransmittable*, that is used to check whether or not the property can be transmitted.

Using TNEF for Message Data Encapsulation

The *Transport Neutral Encapsulation Format* (TNEF) is a protocol for encapsulating MAPI messages into a binary file. TNEF lets transport providers send MAPI messages through any type of intermediate system such that the receiver can access all the message's properties. A transport does this by encoding some or all of the message's properties into a TNEF file, which is then transmitted on the outbound stream. If the receiver supports TNEF, it decodes the inbound stream and extracts some or all of the message's properties from it. Note that neither the sender nor the receiver *has* to be MAPI-compliant to use TNEF, but non-MAPI systems that want to use TNEF must write their own software for interpreting TNEF. Microsoft publishes the format of the TNEF file for the benefit of those vendors interested in writing their own software.

TNEF makes it possible to transmit messages that have rich content (i.e., anything more complicated than plaintext) through systems that might not fully support rich content. Keep in mind that a message will likely pass through one or more gateways before arriving at its destination, and each gateway will copy the message, determine the routing to the next hop, and then retransmit the message. (This model is known as "store and forward" in Netspeak.) The odds are high that one or more of these intermediate hops will *not* understand MAPI, but the sender would like the rich content of his message preserved even if it is handled by a non-MAPI system.

Any system that is capable of sending a binary file or a text message with one or more attachments can transmit MAPI messages containing OLE objects, named properties, rich text, attachments, and embedded messages. TNEF handles the sundry details of encoding and decoding these objects, such as remapping named properties from the sender's to the recipient's system. (See Appendix A for a discussion of named properties.) TNEF lets the sender encode the entire message or only some of its properties. A transport might decide to encode only those properties that are likely to be lost in transmission, such as formatted text information. For example, an SMTP transport could map the message's generic envelope properties to the corresponding SMTP headers and the body to a clear text string and then TNEF encode the rest. In this case, the TNEF stream is attached to the plaintext message as a single attachment called WINMAIL.DAT.

If the WINMAIL.DAT attachment gets dropped somewhere along the way, the recipient will still get the headers and the body. If the WINMAIL.DAT attachment makes it to the recipient's gateway and the gateway understands TNEF, it can decode the WINMAIL.DAT into MAPI properties and completely reconstruct the message. (Again, a non-MAPI gateway could also decode the TNEF file.)

The transport can also encode the entire message into a TNEF file and send the binary blob over the wire. When the receiving end decodes the TNEF blob, it gets back a MAPI message complete with all attachments, embedded messages, OLE objects, and so on. The receiving end doesn't have to explicitly decode individual MAPI properties and set them into a MAPI message. TNEF takes care of all the details!

Client Access to Message Transports

We've mentioned this before, but we say it again: Clients don't interact directly with transports, only the spooler does. So how does a client communicate with the spooler or the installed transports? Clients can query the system status table to find out the state of any transport provider and thereby determine what it's doing at any given time. A transport makes its state visible to the client by updating its status row through a call to *IMAPISupport::ModifyStatusRow*. A transport is required to modify its status row when it completes its initialization, whenever it starts to deliver an inbound or outbound message, when the inbound or outbound delivery is finished, when inbound or outbound transmission is enabled or disabled, when the connection status changes, when the transport enters flush mode, if the transport supports the remote mail viewer, or if an error occurs. These criteria correspond to the following possible bit values of the PR_STATUS_CODE property, a required property in the transport's status row:

- STATUS_AVAILABLE
- STATUS_INBOUND_ACTIVE
- STATUS_OUTBOUND_ACTIVE
- STATUS_INBOUND_ENABLED
- STATUS_OUTBOUND_ENABLED
- STATUS_OFFLINE
- STATUS_INBOUND_FLUSH
- STATUS_OUTBOUND_FLUSH
- STATUS_REMOTE_ACCESS
- STATUS_FAILURE

Clients can also indirectly command the transport through the *IMAPIStatus* interface, which is obtained by calling *IMAPISession::OpenEntry* on the spooler's (or an individual transport's) status entry ID obtained from the session status table. A client can force immediate delivery of inbound and outbound messages, for example, by calling *IMAPIStatus::FlushQueues.* (The HelloMAPI mail client presented in Chapter 5 demonstrates how to do this.) Calls to *IMAPIStatus* are remoted (via *lightweight remote procedure calls,* or LRPC) to the transport provider by the MAPI spooler. The client doesn't call directly into the transport code—it's in a different process.

Developing a Message Transport: The WINDS Transport (XPWDS)

In this section, we describe the techniques we used to develop the sample transport providers, XPWDS and XPWDSR. There is no single "right" way to develop a transport, so consider the following to be our recommendations only.

1. Start by implementing stub interfaces that return MAPI_E_NO-_SUPPORT.

2. Edit the MAPISVC.INF file.

3. Implement the transport configuration code. This will include *ServiceEntry* if the provider is also a message service.

4. Add the transport to a profile and configure it.

5. Implement *XPProviderInit*.

6. Implement *IXPProvider*.

7. Implement *IXPLogon*.

8. Implement *IMAPIStatus*.

Implementing Stub Interfaces

Before you begin implementing specific methods, you should create and compile a skeleton provider DLL that can be loaded and run in the debugger. Your skeleton should define all the required interfaces by using stubs for each method. We recommend that your stubs include parameter validation code and a debug trace and that they return MAPI_E_NO_SUPPORT. As you code each interface, you replace the stub method with its actual implementation until you have a complete provider. This method of program development (which is sometimes called the "KIWI"[2] methodology) has some advantages when it comes to writing providers:

■ You always have a loadable DLL that you can set breakpoints in and step into in the debugger.

■ You can see where you're being called. This will give you an idea of the sequence of events that each client action triggers. The debug traces are also great for doing postmortem debugging.

■ You can make incremental changes, making it easier to test and debug your provider.

---

2. KIWI—"Keep It Working, Idiot!"—is closely related to that other famous methodology, KISS ("Keep It Simple, Stupid"). Both are based on that immutable axiom of all software development, Murphy's Law.

The following code fragment illustrates how the *IXPLogon* interface would be implemented in your skeleton:

```
STDMETHODIMP CXPLogon::AddressTypes(ULONG *      pulFlags,
                                    ULONG *      pcAdrType,
                                    LPTSTR **    pppAdrTypeArray,
                                    ULONG *      pcMAPIUID,
                                    LPMAPIUID ** pppMAPIUIDArray)
{

    InfoTrace("CXPLogon::AddressTypes method called");
    CheckParameters_IXPLogon_AddressTypes(this,
                                    pulFlags,
                                    pcAdrType,
                                    pppAdrTypeArray,
                                    pcMAPIUID,
                                    pppMAPIUIDArray);

    return MAPI_E_NO_SUPPORT;
}

STDMETHODIMP CXPLogon::RegisterOptions(ULONG *        pulFlags,
                                       ULONG *        pcOptions,
                                       LPOPTIONDATA * ppOptions)
{
    InfoTrace("CXPLogon::RegisterOptions method called");
    CheckParameters_IXPLogon_RegisterOptions(this,
                                       pulFlags,
                                       pcOptions,
                                       ppOptions);
    return MAPI_E_NO_SUPPORT;
}
    ⋮
```

Editing the MAPISVC.INF File

You'll need to add entries to the MAPISVC.INF file before you can configure your provider and use it in a MAPI session. You can do this manually, or you can write a short INF file and use the MERGEINI utility to copy it into MAPISVC.INF. Figure 8-2 shows XPWDS's INF file.

The XPWDS service sets the SERVICE_SINGLE_COPY flag, which means that a user can add the provider only once to a profile. XPWDS provides the user's primary identity to the MAPI subsystem. Other providers can also supply primary identity (store providers and address book providers), but transports are good choices since they are the only components that are *required* to connect to the back end—the WINDS server, in this case—and because they must provide the user's identity in the PR_SENDER_XXX properties on all outbound messages. Notice that XPWDS is both a service provider and a message service DLL, so we will implement *ServiceEntry*, our message service configuration entry point.

```
[Services]
XPWDS=WINDS Transport

[XPWDS]
Providers=XP_WDS
PR_SERVICE_DLL_NAME=XPWDS.DLL
PR_SERVICE_SUPPORT_FILES=XPWDS.DLL
PR_SERVICE_DELETE_FILES=XPWDS.DLL
PR_SERVICE_ENTRY_NAME=ServiceEntry
PR_RESOURCE_FLAGS=SERVICE_SINGLE_COPY
PR_DISPLAY_NAME=WINDS Transport
WIZARD_ENTRY_NAME=WizardEntry

[XP_WDS]
PR_PROVIDER_DLL_NAME=XPWDS.DLL
PR_PROVIDER_DISPLAY=WINDS Transport
PR_RESOURCE_TYPE=MAPI_TRANSPORT_PROVIDER
PR_RESOURCE_FLAGS=STATUS_PRIMARY_IDENTITY
```

Figure 8-2.
The XPWDS.INF file contains entries specific to the XPWDS provider. It is merged with the MAPISVC.INF file using the MERGEINI utility.

Implementing *ServiceEntry*

Your next task should be to write the code that gets called when a user adds your service to a profile or configures your provider. Notice that this code isn't called from the spooler's context but by a setup program, the Control Panel's Mail and Fax applet, the Profile Wizard, or a client. You must provide an entry point function that uses the MSGSERVICEENTRY prototype, and it must be properly exported. The name of this entry point is given in the PR_SERVICE-_ENTRY_NAME property found in the [Services] section of the MAPISVC.INF file. For XPWDS, the message service is implemented in the provider DLL and the function is called *ServiceEntry*.

Figure 8-3 shows the *ServiceEntry* code.[3] The *ulContext* flag in *ServiceEntry* tells you whether you are being called to create, configure, install, uninstall, or delete your message service. XPWDS doesn't do any special processing for the install, uninstall, and delete cases, so it returns right away if one of these values is passed in *ulContext*. We handle only the cases where *ulContext* is equal to MSG_SERVICE_CREATE or MSG_SERVICE_CONFIGURE.

First we save the MAPI memory allocation functions to global variables. We then open the service's profile section by calling *IProviderAdmin::Open-ProfileSection*, passing NULL for the first parameter (*lpUID*). If the service is being added to a profile, *ulContext* will contain MSG_SERVICE_CREATE, in which case PR_SMP_CONNECT_TYPE is set to LAN_CONNECT, meaning we will maintain a continuous, live connection to the server.

We retrieve any properties written to the profile section the last time the message service was configured. These include the server name, the user's account name, and the user's friendly name and password. If the user's account name already exists in the profile, we save it to a local variable in case the user changes it. We do this because XPWDS creates a directory in the user's TEMP directory to hold temporary TNEF files we create for inbound messages. If the user changes the account name or deletes the service from the profile (as indicated by *ulContext* being equal to MSG_SERVICE_DELETE), we must remove the temporary directory.

The *pCfgProps* parameter will contain an array of *SPropValue* structures with configuration properties if *ServiceEntry* is called from *IMsgServiceAdmin-::ConfigureMsgService*. *ConfigureMsgService* lets the caller pass an array of properties (in the *lpProps* parameter) that are passed to *ServiceEntry* for display in the service's configuration dialog box. If the service is being configured by the Profile Wizard, *pCfgProps* will contain the configuration properties the user entered in the wizard's property sheets. Either way, if *pCfgProps* is non-NULL, we merge the *pCfgProps* properties with those already in the profile section by calling *MergeConfigProps*, which overwrites any existing properties with the new values.

Next we check the *ulFlags* parameter to see whether we are allowed to display our configuration property sheets. If we are, we copy the configuration properties and some other handy data (such as the support object and the handle to the parent window) into a structure called *CfgDialog* and call

---

3. In the interest of brevity, we've omitted a lot of important details (such as error handling and parameter validation) from the code fragments we show in the book. We don't mean to imply that these details are "optional" or any less important, but simply that they don't necessarily relate directly to the subject matter at hand. You should be diligent about putting them in your implementation. To see the complete source code, refer to the companion CD-ROM.

DoLogonDlg to display our configuration UI. (The code for *DoLogonDlg* is shown in Figure 8-4 on pages 265 through 267; we'll talk about how it works in a moment.)

When *DoLogonDlg* returns, *pProps* will contain the configuration properties as set by the user. We call *PingRemoteServer* to try to connect to the server specified in the dialog. If the server is on line, *PingRemoteServer* calls *LogonServer-Mailbox* (passing the server name and the user's account name and password) to connect to the server and authenticate the user's credentials. These configuration properties are found in the PR_SMP_SERVER_NAME, PR_SMP_MAIL-BOX_NAME, and PR_SMP_MAILBOX_PASSWORD properties, respectively.

The section of code after the call to *PingRemoteServer* checks whether the user's account name has changed from the last time the service was configured. If it has, we must delete the TNEF download subdirectory in the user's TEMP directory and create a new subdirectory for the new account.

```
HRESULT STDAPICALLTYPE ServiceEntry(HINSTANCE        hInstance,
                                    LPMALLOC          pMallocObj,
                                    LPMAPISUP         pSupObj,
                                    ULONG             ulUIParam,
                                    ULONG             ulFlags,
                                    ULONG             ulContext,
                                    ULONG             ulCfgPropCount,
                                    LPSPropValue      pCfgProps,
                                    LPPROVIDERADMIN   pAdminProvObj,
                                    LPMAPIERROR *     ppMAPIError)
{
    HRESULT       hResult = S_OK;
    LPPROFSECT    pProfileObj = NULL;
    ULONG         ulPropCount;
    LPSPropValue  pProps = NULL;
    HANDLE        hUIMutex = NULL;

    // Temporary storage for previous account name
    char szOldAccount[64] = { 0 };

    // What context were we called in?
    if (MSG_SERVICE_INSTALL          == ulContext ||
        MSG_SERVICE_UNINSTALL        == ulContext ||
        MSG_SERVICE_PROVIDER_CREATE  == ulContext ||
        MSG_SERVICE_PROVIDER_DELETE  == ulContext)
```

Figure 8-3.   *(continued)*

The ServiceEntry *code is called by a configuration utility, such as the Control Panel's Mail and Fax applet, a setup program, or a client, to get the service's configuration settings from the user and save them in the profile section.*

Figure 8-3. *continued*

```
{
    goto ErrorExit;
}


// Get the MAPI memory allocation routines we'll be needing.
hResult = pSupObj -> GetMemAllocRoutines(&gpfnAllocateBuffer,
                                         &gpfnAllocateMore,
                                         &gpfnFreeBuffer);
⋮

// Open the profile section for this service.
hResult = pAdminProvObj -> OpenProfileSection(NULL,
                                              NULL,
                                              MAPI_MODIFY,
                                              &pProfileObj);
// Error handling omitted
if (MSG_SERVICE_CREATE == ulContext)
{
    SPropValue spvProps[1] = { 0 };
    spvProps[0].ulPropTag = PR_SMP_CONNECTION_TYPE;
    spvProps[0].Value.l = LAN_CONNECT;
    hResult = pProfileObj ->
                  SetProps(sizeof(spvProps)/sizeof(SPropValue),
                           spvProps, NULL);
}


// The profile section is open; get the properties out of it.
hResult = pProfileObj -> GetProps((LPSPropTagArray)&sptLogonProps,
                                  …, &pProps);
⋮
// Save the current account name.
if (PR_SMP_MAILBOX_NAME == pProps[MAILBOX_NAME].ulPropTag)
    lstrcpy(szOldAccount, pProps[MAILBOX_NAME].Value.lpszA);


if (MSG_SERVICE_DELETE == ulContext)
{
    // If the service is being removed from a profile, clean up.
    TCHAR   szTmpDir[_MAX_PATH],
            szDownloadDir[_MAX_PATH];

    GetTempPath(_MAX_PATH, szTmpDir);
    lstrcat(szTmpDir, WINDS_DATA_DIRECTORY);
```

```
            if (PR_SMP_MAILBOX_NAME == pProps[MAILBOX_NAME].ulPropTag)
            {
                wsprintf(szDownloadDir,
                        WINDS_DOWNLOAD_DIR_NAME_FORMAT,
                        szTmpDir,
                        pProps[MAILBOX_NAME].Value.LPSZ);
                RemoveDirectory(szDownloadDir);
            }
            RemoveDirectory(szTmpDir);
            // We are finished.
            hResult = S_OK;
            goto ErrorExit;
        }

        // Merge setup wizard properties with those from profile section.
        if (pCfgProps && ulCfgPropCount)
            hResult = MergeConfigProps(ulCfgPropCount, pCfgProps, pProps);

        // If we can, display the UI.
        if (SERVICE_UI_ALWAYS & ulFlags || SERVICE_UI_ALLOWED & ulFlags)
        {
            CFGDLG CfgDialog = { 0 };
            hUIMutex = CreateMutex(NULL, FALSE, CONFIG_UI_MUTEX);
                :

            // Wait for .25 second for mutex.
            if (WAIT_TIMEOUT == WaitForSingleObject(hUIMutex, 250))
            {
                hResult = MAPI_E_BUSY;
                goto ErrorExit;
            }

            // Fill in the logon UI structure.
            CfgDialog.hInst    = hInstance;
            CfgDialog.hWnd     = (HWND)ulUIParam;
            CfgDialog.ppProps  = &pProps;
            CfgDialog.pSupObj  = pSupObj;
            CfgDialog.ulFlags  = MSG_SERVICE_UI_READ_ONLY & ulFlags ?
                                    UI_READONLY : 0;
            CfgDialog.hUIMutex = NULL; // So DoLogonDlg won't have to wait
ShowPropsAgain:
            hResult = DoLogonDlg(&CfgDialog);
                :
```

(continued)

Figure 8-3. *continued*

```
        if (!PingRemoteServer ((HWND)ulUIParam, pProps))
            goto ShowPropsAgain;
    }

    if (PR_SMP_MAILBOX_NAME == pProps[MAILBOX_NAME].ulPropTag)
    {
        char szTmpDir[512], szDownloadDir[512];
        GetTempPath(512, szTmpDir);
        lstrcat(szTmpDir, WINDS_DATA_DIRECTORY);

        // If the account name changed, we must delete the old account's
        // download directory.
        if (lstrlen(szOldAccount) &&
            lstrcmpi(szOldAccount, pProps[MAILBOX_NAME].Value.LPSZ))
        {
            wsprintf(szDownloadDir, WINDS_DOWNLOAD_DIR_NAME_FORMAT,
                    szTmpDir, szOldAccount);
            RemoveDirectory(szDownloadDir);
        }
        wsprintf(szDownloadDir,
                WINDS_DOWNLOAD_DIR_NAME_FORMAT,
                szTmpDir,
                pProps[MAILBOX_NAME].Value.LPSZ);
        CreateDirectory(szDownloadDir, NULL);
    }

    hResult = pProfileObj ->
                SetProps(NUM_LOGON_PROPERTIES, pProps, NULL);

ErrorExit:
    // Clean up; Release mutex.
    :
    return hResult;
}
```

The code for *DoLogonDlg*, shown in Figure 8-4, is interesting mainly because it uses display tables and the *IMAPISupport::DoConfigPropsheet* method. We'll cover display tables in detail in Chapter 9 when we talk about address book providers, but for now, consider a display table to be an *IMAPITable* object whose rows describe a dialog box that is displayed by MAPI. *DoConfigPropsheet* displays a property sheet dialog whose controls are specified by a display table passed in its *lpDisplayTable* parameter. (See Figure 8-5 on page 267.) *DoConfigPropsheet* populates these controls by calling *GetProps* on an *IMAPIProp* interface passed in its *lpConfigData* parameter. When the user enters data into a control on the property sheet and dismisses the dialog, *DoConfigPropsheet* calls *lpConfigData -> SetProps* to update the properties embodied in the *IMAPIProp* interface. In this case, we must create a new object derived from *IMAPIProp*, *CUIMAPIProp*, to pass in *lpConfigData*.

Next we initialize the *DTPAGE* data structure required by *BuildDisplay-Table*. *DTPAGE* contains an array of structures that describe the controls we want included in our property page. We'll have more to say about these structures in Chapter 9. For now, notice that *DtPropPages[0].lpszResourceName* contains the name of a dialog resource that describes the overall appearance of the page and gives the location of each control. We can enable and disable specific controls depending on whether we are called here to display the property sheets in read/write or read-only mode. Finally, we call *BuildDisplayTable*, save the *ITableData* interface passed back in *pTableData* to a member variable (by calling *SetTableData*), and display the property sheets in a call to *DoConfig-Propsheet*.

When *DoConfigPropsheet* returns, the data extracted from the dialog's controls can be retrieved from the *IMAPIProp* interface by calling *pPropObj -> GetProps*. The *IsValidServerName* function validates the server name string entered by the user; if the name is invalid, the configuration dialog is displayed again.

```
HRESULT WINAPI DoLogonDlg(PCFGDLG pCfgDialog)
{
    HRESULT hResult;

    // Take ownership of property value array so that calling code
    // will not leak memory.
    LPSPropValue pProps = *pCfgDialog -> ppProps;
    ⋮


    pPropObj = new CUIMAPIProp(pCfgDialog -> hInst,
                               gpfnAllocateBuffer,
                               gpfnAllocateMore,
                               gpfnFreeBuffer,
                               pCfgDialog -> ulFlags & UI_READONLY);
    ⋮


    hResult = pPropObj -> SetProps(NUM_LOGON_PROPERTIES, pProps, NULL);
    ⋮
    DTPAGE DtPropPages[1];
    DtPropPages[0].cctl = NUM_CFG_USERINFO_PAGE_CTLS;
```

Figure 8-4. *(continued)*

DoLogonDlg *uses a display table and* IMAPISupport::DoConfigPropsheet *to display the configuration property sheets.*

Figure 8-4. *continued*

```
    DtPropPages[0].lpszComponent = szBlank;
    DtPropPages[0].lpszResourceName = MAKEINTRESOURCE(IDD_CFG_USERINFO);
    DtPropPages[0].lpctl = UserConfigPage;

    // If UI_READONLY, disable all controls on property sheets.
    if (pCfgDialog -> ulFlags & UI_READONLY)
    {
        // Disable the controls (make them read-only).
        DtPropPages[0].lpctl[1].ulCtlFlags &=
            ~(DT_EDITABLE | DT_SET_IMMEDIATE);
        DtPropPages[0].lpctl[6].ulCtlFlags &=
            ~(DT_EDITABLE | DT_SET_IMMEDIATE);
    }
    else
    {
        // Enable the controls (make them read/write).
        DtPropPages[0].lpctl[1].ulCtlFlags |=
            (DT_EDITABLE | DT_SET_IMMEDIATE);
        DtPropPages[0].lpctl[6].ulCtlFlags |=
            (DT_EDITABLE | DT_SET_IMMEDIATE);
    }


    // Create the display table for logon dialog. It's based on dialog
    // resources plus the static information at the head of this module.
    LPTABLEDATA pTableData;
    hResult =
        BuildDisplayTable(…, DtPropPages, …, &pTableObj, &pTableData);

    if (!hResult)
    {
        pPropObj -> SetTableData(pTableData);
        pTableData -> Release();

        // Display the dialog/property sheets.
DisplayPropsAgain:
        hResult = pCfgDialog -> pSupObj ->
                    DoConfigPropsheet(…, pTableObj, pPropObj, 0);
        if (!hResult)
        {
            // Retrieve the altered data.
            gpfnFreeBuffer(pProps);
            pProps = NULL;
```

```
                hResult = pPropObj ->
                            GetProps((LPSPropTagArray)&sptLogonProps,
                                ...,
                                &pProps);
            ⋮

            // Check the server name.
            if (!IsValidServerName(pProps[SERVER_NAME].Value.LPSZ))
                goto DisplayPropsAgain;

            // Return the new property array.
            *pCfgDialog -> ppProps = pProps;
            pProps = NULL;        // Do not free this in cleanup code
                                  // below.
        }
    }

ErrorExit:

    // Clean up.
    ⋮
    return hResult;
}
```

Figure 8-5.
The XPWDS configuration property sheet.

Once you have implemented the *ServiceEntry* code, you can add the service to a user profile and configure the service's providers—which in the case of the XPWDS service is the single XPWDS transport provider. Before you can configure XPWDS, you will need to set up the WINDS post office on a machine connected to the same LAN as the machine hosting the XPWDS service. The README.WRI file on the companion CD-ROM describes how to set up the post office and configure the service.

Implementing *XPProviderInit*

The *XPProviderInit* function is the spooler's entry point into the transport provider and the first call in the logon sequence. The function's main task is to create an instance of the *IXPProvider* object and return a pointer to it to the caller. This function must be named *XPProviderInit*, and it must be properly exported if the spooler is to find it and log on to your provider. The spooler passes the current version number of the MAPI subsystem installed on the host machine. The *CURRENT_SPI_VERSION* macro gives the version of the MAPI SDK under which the provider was compiled. If the version of the MAPI subsystem installed on the user's machine is older than *CURRENT_SPI_VERSION*, *XPProviderInit* returns MAPI_E_VERSION because XPWDS can't run with older versions of MAPI. If the version of the MAPI subsystem is newer (or identical), the spooler decides whether it can run the transport by checking the version passed back in *pulProviderVer*. Next, the MAPI allocation functions passed to *XPProviderInit* are saved in *gpfnAllocateBuffer*, *gpfnAllocateMore*, and *gpfnFreeBuffer*, and the newly created *IXPProvider* object is returned in *ppXPProviderObj*:

```
STDINITMETHODIMP XPProviderInit(HINSTANCE       hInstance,
                                LPMALLOC        pMallocObj,
                                LPALLOCATEBUFFER  pfnAllocateBuffer,
                                LPALLOCATEMORE    pfnAllocateMore,
                                LPFREEBUFFER      pfnFreeBuffer,
                                ULONG           ulFlags,
                                ULONG           ulMAPIVer,
                                ULONG *         pulProviderVer,
                                LPXPPROVIDER *  ppXPProviderObj)
{
    *pulProviderVer = CURRENT_SPI_VERSION;

    if (ulMAPIVer < CURRENT_SPI_VERSION)
        return MAPI_E_VERSION;

    // Save the pointer to the allocation routines in global variables.
    gpfnAllocateBuffer = pfnAllocateBuffer;
    gpfnAllocateMore   = pfnAllocateMore;
```

```
gpfnFreeBuffer      = pfnFreeBuffer;
ghInstance          = hInstance;

// Allocate a new XPProvider object. The constructor will initialize
// the data member.
CXPProvider * pXPProvider = new CXPProvider(hInstance);

if (!pXPProvider)
    return E_OUTOFMEMORY;

// Copy the pointer to the allocated object back into the return
// IXPProvider object pointer.
*ppXPProviderObj = (LPXPPROVIDER)pXPProvider;
return S_OK;
}
```

Implementing *IXPProvider*

The spooler logs on to a transport provider by making a call to *IXPProvider-::TransportLogon*, which returns an *IXPLogon* object if the logon is successful. XPWDS's *TransportLogon* opens the service's profile section and gets the configuration properties stored there. If the configuration properties are valid, XPWDS uses them to try and connect to the WINDS server. If the configuration properties are invalid, incomplete, or missing entirely, *TransportLogon* displays the configuration property pages by calling *DoLogonDlg* and attempts to get a set of valid configuration properties.

Once the provider has a valid set of configuration properties, it tries to connect to the WINDS server by calling *DoServerLogon*. If the connect fails, *TransportLogon* displays the configuration property sheets and retries the logon. This process is repeated until the connection succeeds or until the user cancels the configuration dialog.

DoServerLogon uses the server name passed in the PR_SMP_SERVER-_NAME property in *pProps* to bind to the WINDS server. If the *Bind* call succeeds, a remote procedure call (RPC) is made to the server, passing the user's account name, mailbox ID, password and display name, and the name of the XPWDS host computer. If the server is able to validate the user's account name and password, it responds by returning a connection ID to the transport and filling in a *MAILBOX_INFO* structure with data about the user's mailbox. The transport uses the connection ID to compose a name string for a Win32 mailslot. The mailslot is created by the transport (the mailslot server) in the constructor of the *CXPLogon* object and used by the WINDS post office (the mailslot client) to broadcast notifications from the post office to the XPWDS transport provider. The WINDS post office sends notifications to XPWDS when new mail arrives in the user's mail box or when the server is shutting down or starting up. XPWDS creates a background thread that listens on the mailslot for these notifications.

If *DoServerLogon* succeeds, a new *CXPLogon* object is created, the user's identity properties (the PR_SENDER_XXX properties we stamp on all outbound messages) are set, and the transport's row in the session status table is initialized. (Figures 8-7 and 8-8 on pages 275 and 276 show the code for *SetIdentityProps* and *InitializeStatusRow*, respectively.)

Notice that XPWDS doesn't set *pulFlags* to ask the spooler to poll it for new mail but instead creates the notification mailslot and the background thread that listens on the mailslot. This design is more elegant than polling because the spooler doesn't waste time calling XPWDS unless there's inbound mail to deliver. Instead, XPWDS calls the spooler by calling *SpoolerNotify(NOTIFY_NEWMAIL,...)* when the WINDS post office tells it that there is indeed new mail in the user's mailbox. We mentioned earlier that *SpoolerNotify* was the only *IMAPISupport* method that could be called from multiple threads; here's an example of when you'd want to do just that. The notification thread incurs very little overhead because it's reading from the mailslot and therefore blocked most of the time; it unblocks only when the post-office server broadcasts a notification to the XPWDS mailslot. (See the *XPMailslotListenThreadProc* function in XPPROV.CPP on the companion CD-ROM for details.) Figure 8-6 shows the *TransportLogon* code.

```
STDMETHODIMP CXPProvider::TransportLogon(LPMAPISUP      pSupObj,
                                         ULONG          ulUIParam,
                                         LPTSTR         pszProfileName,
                                         ULONG *        pulFlags,
                                         LPMAPIERROR *  ppMAPIError,
                                         LPXPLOGON *    ppXPLogon)
{
    CheckParameters(IXPProvider_TransportLogon, pSupObj);

    CXPLogon     * pXPLogon = NULL;
    ULONG          ulPropCount;
    LPSPropValue   pProps = NULL;
    MAILBOX_INFO   UserMBInfo = { 0 };
    CFGDLG         CfgDialog = { 0 };
    LPPROFSECT     pProfileObj;
    DWORD          dwConnectionID;
```

Figure 8-6. *(continued)*

The IXPProvider::TransportLogon *method initializes the transport provider and returns an* IXPLogon *object.*

270

Figure 8-6. *continued*

```
HRESULT hResult = OpenServiceProfileSection(pSupObj,
                                            &pProfileObj,
                                            gpfnFreeBuffer);
    ⋮

HANDLE hUIMutex = CreateMutex(NULL, FALSE, CONFIG_UI_MUTEX);
    ⋮

hResult = pProfileObj -> GetProps((LPSPropTagArray)&sptLogonProps,
                                  …, &pProps);
    ⋮

// Fill in the logon UI structure.
CfgDialog.hInst    = m_hInstance;
CfgDialog.hWnd     = (HWND)ulUIParam;
CfgDialog.ppProps  = &pProps;
CfgDialog.pSupObj  = pSupObj;
CfgDialog.hUIMutex = hUIMutex;

// In case we get MAPI_W_ERRORS_RETURNED, ignore it and reset
// to S_OK. Now display the logon configuration dialog.
if (MAPI_W_ERRORS_RETURNED == hResult)
{
    if (PR_SMP_MAILBOX_ID      != pProps[MAILBOX_ID].ulPropTag ||
        PR_SMP_CONNECTION_TYPE != pProps[NET_CON].ulPropTag)
    {
        hResult = MAPI_E_UNCONFIGURED;
        ⋮
        goto ErrorExit;
    }

    if (PR_SMP_REMOTE_SERVER != pProps[SERVER_NAME].ulPropTag ||
        PR_SMP_MAILBOX_NAME != pProps[MAILBOX_NAME].ulPropTag ||
        PR_SMP_USER_NAME != pProps[USER_NAME].ulPropTag ||
        PR_SMP_MAILBOX_PASSWORD != pProps[PASSWORD].ulPropTag)
    {
        if (LOGON_NO_DIALOG & *pulFlags)
        {
            hResult = MAPI_E_UNCONFIGURED;
            goto ErrorExit;
        }
```

(continued)

Figure 8-6. *continued*

```
ReStartLogonDlg :
        if ((hResult = DoLogonDlg(&CfgDialog)))
            goto ErrorExit;

        hResult = pProfileObj -> SetProps(4, pProps, NULL);

        if (hResult)
            goto ErrorExit;
    }
}

if (LAN_CONNECT == pProps[NET_CON].Value.l)
{
    // Connect to the host server. If necessary (and allowed),
    // display UI.
    hResult = DoServerLogon(&UserMBInfo,
                            pProps,
                            pProfileObj,
                            !(LOGON_NO_DIALOG & *pulFlags),
                            (HWND)ulUIParam,
                            TRUE,
                            WINDS_NOTIF_ON_XP | WINDS_NOTIF_ON_USER,
                            &dwConnectionID,
                            FALSE);
    if (S_FALSE == hResult)
    {
        goto ReStartLogonDlg;
    }
}

if (OFFLINE_CONNECT == pProps[NET_CON].Value.l ||
    MAPI_W_NO_SERVICE == hResult ||        // The error returned in
                                           // CLIENT context
    MAPI_E_NETWORK_ERROR == hResult)       // The error returned in
                                           // SPOOLER context
{
    hResult = S_OK;
    pProps[NET_CON].Value.l = OFFLINE_CONNECT;
    // To avoid creating a mailslot notification sink in the
    // CXPLogon constructor
    dwConnectionID = 0;
}
    :
```

```
try
{
    // Allocate the IXPLogon-derived object. Initialize its data
    // members.
    pXPLogon = new CXPLogon(…, dwConnectionID);

    if (!pXPLogon)
        // New failed, probably due to memory shortage.
        hResult = E_OUTOFMEMORY;
}
catch (CException & Exception)
{
    hResult = Exception.GetError();
}
if (hResult)
    goto ErrorExit;

// To avoid closing this in the cleanup code
hUIMutex = NULL;

// Lock other threads because we are going to work on data that is
// global to all threads (sessions) using this transport.
EnterCriticalSection(&m_csObj);

// Check the mode in which MAPI is logging on to our transport, and
// set the appropiate internal transport session flags (this CXPLogon
// object).
pXPLogon -> InitializeTransportStatusFlags(*pulFlags);

// Initialize the transport ID prop array for this session.
hResult = pXPLogon -> SetIdentityProps();
if (!hResult)
{
    // Build the transport status row for this session.
    hResult = pXPLogon -> InitializeStatusRow();
    if (!hResult)
    {
        // Set the session flags returned to MAPI by the transport.
        pXPLogon -> SetSessionFlags(pulFlags);
        // Copy our allocated object back to the returned MAPI object
        // pointer.
        *ppXPLogon = (LPXPLOGON)pXPLogon;
    }
}
```

(continued)

273

Figure 8-6. *continued*

```
    // Release the critical section.
    LeaveCriticalSection(&m_csObj);


ErrorExit:
    // Clean up.
    ⋮
    return hResult;
}
```

We store the user's identity properties for two purposes: First, because as a transport we need to set the user's PR_SENDER_XXX properties on all outbound mail; and second, because we provide the user's primary identity to the MAPI subsystem. We mentioned earlier that transports are especially well suited to providing primary identity for those reasons; Figure 8-7, which contains the code for *SetIdentityProps*, shows how it's done.

Recall that *DoServerLogon* returns information about the user's account, including a numeric ID that uniquely identifies the user's mailbox on the WINDS post office and some other miscellaneous information such as the user's job title, name, and password. The mailbox ID is passed to the *CXPLogon* constructor, which computes the user's entry ID as it exists in the WINDS address book. We can do this because we have some "inside" knowledge of the format of WINDS address book provider entry IDs. The entry ID is passed in a call to *IMAPISupport::OpenEntry*, which succeeds if the user does, in fact, have an entry in the WINDS address book provider. Notice that we're calling *OpenEntry* only to test the validity of the entry ID we computed and to find out if the address book provider is available. Although we could also use the *IMailUser* interface returned in *pUser* to call *GetProps* and retrieve the user's identity properties, this is unnecessary because we already have all the information we need from the configuration properties and the information returned by the *DoServerLogon* call. We use this information to create the user's identity properties, which we save to some data members and also place in the status row.

What's a One-off?

A *one-off* is a recipient object (i.e., a mail user or distribution list) that doesn't have a corresponding entry in any address book provider. A one-off can be created in two ways: on the fly by MAPI in order to add a recipient to a message and by an address book provider when it creates a new entry that hasn't been saved yet. We discuss one-off entries in detail in Chapter 9, particularly as they relate to address book providers.

If the WINDS address book provider isn't available or the user doesn't have an entry in it, MAPI has to create a one-off for the user so that we can associate a meaningful entry ID with this user since the entry ID *we* constructed didn't map to an address book provider entry. (See the sidebar on the facing page for an explanation of a one-off.) We save the entry ID in the *m_pIdentityProps* array along with the rest of the user's identity properties.

```
STDMETHODIMP CXPLogon::SetIdentityProps()
{
    // Allocate the property array for transport. This memory block is
    // freed in the destructor of the CXPLogon object.
    HRESULT hResult = gpfnAllocateBuffer(…, (LPVOID *)&m_pIdentityProps);
    ⋮
    LPMAILUSER  pUser;
    ULONG       ulObjType;
    TCHAR       szSearchKey[128];
    LPTSTR      pStr;

    // Try to open our entry ID in the ABWDS address book. (See if it is
    // around.) If the call fails, we must create a one-off for our
    // identity.
    hResult = m_pSupObj -> OpenEntry(…, (LPENTRYID)&m_UserEID,
                                     …, (LPUNKNOWN *)&pUser);

    if (S_OK == hResult)
    {
        m_fABWDSInstalled = TRUE;
        m_pIdentityProps[XPID_NAME].ulPropTag = PR_SENDER_NAME;
        m_pIdentityProps[XPID_NAME].Value.LPSZ = m_UserInfo.szFullName;
        m_pIdentityProps[XPID_EID].ulPropTag = PR_SENDER_ENTRYID;
        m_pIdentityProps[XPID_EID].Value.bin.cb = CB_PRIVATE_EID;
        m_pIdentityProps[XPID_EID].Value.bin.lpb = (LPBYTE)&m_UserEID;

        wsprintf(szSearchKey,
                 TEXT("%s:%s\\%s"),
                 WINDS_ADDRESS_TYPE,
                 m_szServer,       // This is already in the format
                                   // "\\<servername>".
                 m_UserInfo.szMailboxName);
        CharUpper(szSearchKey);
        hResult = gpfnAllocateMore(…, m_pIdentityProps, (LPVOID *)&pStr);
```

Figure 8-7.   *(continued)*

The user's identity is created from information supplied by the server. If the WINDS address book provider isn't available or the user doesn't have an entry in it, we ask MAPI to create a one-off entry ID for the user. The other identity properties are copies of the PR_SENDER_XXX properties we set on outgoing messages.

Figure 8-7. *continued*

```
        ⋮
        lstrcpy(pStr, szSearchKey);
        m_pIdentityProps[XPID_SEARCH_KEY].ulPropTag =
            PR_SENDER_SEARCH_KEY;
        m_pIdentityProps[XPID_SEARCH_KEY].Value.bin.cb = Cbtszsize(pStr);
        m_pIdentityProps[XPID_SEARCH_KEY].Value.bin.lpb = (LPBYTE)pStr;


        pUser -> Release();
        return hResult;
    }


    // No address book provider entry. Set the PR_SENDER_ENTRYID property
    // by creating a one-off based on the user's name and address.
    m_pIdentityProps[XPID_EID].ulPropTag = PR_SENDER_ENTRYID;
    hResult = m_pSupObj ->
        CreateOneOff(m_UserInfo.szFullName,
                     WINDS_ADDRESS_TYPE,
                     m_szAddress,
                     fMapiUnicode,
                     &m_pIdentityProps[XPID_EID].Value.bin.cb,
            (LPENTRYID *)&m_pIdentityProps[XPID_EID].Value.bin.lpb);
        ⋮


    // Set the PR_SENDER_NAME property.
    m_pIdentityProps[XPID_NAME].ulPropTag = PR_SENDER_NAME;
    // Etc.
        ⋮
    // Set the PR_SENDER_SEARCH_KEY property.
    m_pIdentityProps[XPID_SEARCH_KEY].ulPropTag = PR_SENDER_SEARCH_KEY;
    // Etc.
        ⋮
    return hResult;
}
```

To complete the transport logon, the transport's row in the session status table needs to be updated. Figure 8-8 shows the code.

```
STDMETHODIMP CXPLogon::InitializeStatusRow(ULONG ulFlags)
{
    #define NUM_STATUS_ROW_PROPS    8
    SPropValue spvStatusRow[NUM_STATUS_ROW_PROPS] = { 0 };
```

Figure 8-8.   *(continued)*
The code to initialize our row in the status table. Notice that the PR_IDENTITY_XXX properties are the same as our PR_SENDER_XXX properties.

Figure 8-8. *continued*

```
    ULONG i = 0;
    spvStatusRow[i].ulPropTag = PR_PROVIDER_DISPLAY;
    spvStatusRow[i++].Value.LPSZ = TRANSPORT_DISPLAY_NAME_STRING;

    // Set PR_RESOURCE_METHODS property. These are the methods implemented
    // in the IMAPIStatus implementation (CXPMAPIStatus class).
    spvStatusRow[i].ulPropTag = PR_RESOURCE_METHODS;
    // We support ALL methods in IMAPIStatus interface (except the
    // WRITABLE ones).
    spvStatusRow[i++].Value.l = STATUS_SETTINGS_DIALOG |
                                STATUS_FLUSH_QUEUES |
                                STATUS_VALIDATE_STATE |
                                STATUS_CHANGE_PASSWORD;

    spvStatusRow[i].ulPropTag = PR_STATUS_CODE;
    spvStatusRow[i++].Value.l = GetTransportStatusCode();

    TCHAR szStatus[128];
    LoadStatusString(szStatus, sizeof(szStatus));
    spvStatusRow[i].ulPropTag = PR_STATUS_STRING;
    spvStatusRow[i++].Value.LPSZ = szStatus;

    TCHAR szDisplayName[64];
    wsprintf(szDisplayName, TEXT("%s (%s)"),
            TRANSPORT_DISPLAY_NAME_STRING, m_szServer);
    spvStatusRow[i].ulPropTag = PR_DISPLAY_NAME;
    spvStatusRow[i++].Value.LPSZ = szDisplayName;

    spvStatusRow[i].ulPropTag = PR_IDENTITY_ENTRYID;
    spvStatusRow[i++].Value = m_pIdentityProps[XPID_EID].Value;

    spvStatusRow[i].ulPropTag = PR_IDENTITY_DISPLAY;
    spvStatusRow[i++].Value.LPSZ = m_pIdentityProps[XPID_NAME].Value.LPSZ;

    spvStatusRow[i].ulPropTag = PR_IDENTITY_SEARCH_KEY;
    spvStatusRow[i++].Value = m_pIdentityProps[XPID_SEARCH_KEY].Value;
    ASSERT(NUM_STATUS_ROW_PROPS == i);

    // Write the entries on the provider's session status row.
    HRESULT hResult = m_pSupObj -> ModifyStatusRow(i, spvStatusRow,
                                                   ulFlags);

    return hResult;
}
```

We set the following columns in the transport's status row:

- *PR_PROVIDER_DISPLAY*. The display name of our provider.

- *PR_RESOURCE_METHODS*. A bitmap of flags that advertise which *IMAPIStatus* methods we support. Our transport supports *SettingsDialog, FlushQueues, ValidateState*, and *ChangePassword*.

- *PR_STATUS_CODE*. A bitmap of flags telling our current state. On initialization, we set STATUS_INBOUND_ENABLED ¦ STATUS_OUTBOUND_ENABLED unless the spooler explicitly disables inbound or outbound operations in *TransportLogon*.

- *PR_STATUS_STRING*. A textual description of our current state, i.e., a descriptive version of the information in PR_STATUS_CODE.

- *PR_IDENTITY_DISPLAY*. The same as PR_SENDER_NAME, the user's display name.

- *PR_IDENTITY_ENTRYID*. The same as PR_SENDER_ENTRYID, the user's entry ID.

- *PR_IDENTITY_SEARCH_KEY*. The same as PR_SENDER_SEARCH_KEY, the user's search key.

Then we call *IMAPISupport::ModifyStatusRow* to add them to the session status table.

IXPProvider::Shutdown

IXPProvider::Shutdown is called by the spooler as part of the logoff process. The spooler first releases any *IXPLogon* objects, then calls *Shutdown* and releases the *IXPProvider* interface. The transport DLL is then unloaded. You can do any logoff or cleanup operations in this method. For XPWDS, this is just a stub.

Implementing *IXPLogon*

IXPLogon is the meat of a transport provider. This is the interface that does most of the work, including connecting to the back-end system, sending and receiving messages, notifying the spooler of changes in state, and generating delivery or nondelivery reports. The spooler calls *XPProviderInit* only once to obtain a single *IXPProvider* object, regardless of how often your transport is logged on to. Each logon triggers a call to *IXPProvider::TransportLogon*, which returns an instance of the *IXPLogon* object.

We recommend that you instantiate a new *IXPLogon* object for each *TransportLogon* call. This is what XPWDS does, and it makes your implementation simpler and less error prone. Alternatively, you can maintain a single *IXPLogon* object, but then you must keep separate data for each logon instance.

IXPLogon::RegisterOptions

This method is called by the spooler to register per-message or per-recipient options. A per-message option is a way for the sender to request special handling of an outbound message. Examples of per-message options include setting the sensitivity (PR_SENSITIVITY) or importance (PR_IMPORTANCE) of a message to higher or lower values in relation to the default and requesting delivery or nondelivery reports be sent for a given message. Per-message options are specific to a given transport and global to all recipients. In other words, the set of available options is determined by your transport and returned in *RegisterOptions*; if the message is delivered to more than one recipient through your transport, each recipient's message will be delivered using the same per-message options.

Per-recipient options are specific to an address type and can be set to different values for different recipients on the same message. Being "specific to an address type" means that the recipient options presume some knowledge of the messaging system receiving the message. For example, a recipient who gets messages via a modem connection might have properties advertising his modem speed, whether or not the modem supports compression, and the delay between redial attempts. When the user sends a message to that recipient, the user can request that the transport use this information to customize delivery of the message to that recipient.

We don't support delivery options in XPWDS, so our *RegisterOptions* method looks like the following code:

```
STDMETHODIMP CXPLogon::RegisterOptions(ULONG *       pulFlags,
                                       ULONG *       pcOptions,
                                       LPOPTIONDATA * ppOptions)
{
    *pulFlags = 0;
    *pcOptions = 0;
    *ppOptions = NULL;
    return S_OK;
}
```

If you want to support delivery options, you should pass back an array of *OPTIONDATA* structures in **ppOptions*. The number of elements in the array is given in *pcOptions*, and is either 0, 1, or 2, depending on whether you support no options (as is the case with XPWDS), support either per-message *or* per-recipient options, or support both per-message *and* per-recipient options. The *OPTIONDATA* structure looks like the following:

```
typedef struct _OPTIONDATA
{
    ULONG       ulFlags;
    LPGUID      lpRecipGUID;
    LPTSTR      lpszAdrType;
    LPTSTR      lpszDLLName;
    ULONG       ulOrdinal;
    ULONG       cbOptionsData;
    LPBYTE      lpbOptionsData;
    ULONG       cOptionsProps;
    LPSPropValue        lpOptionsProps;
} OPTIONDATA, FAR *LPOPTIONDATA;
```

The *ulFlags* member is set to MAPI_MESSAGE or MAPI_RECIPIENT, depending on whether the data in the structure applies to per-message or per-recipient options. The *lpRecipGUID* member points to a GUID address type that uniquely identifies the recipient's back-end system. The value of *lpRecipGUID* can be NULL. The *lpszAdrType* member is a string address type identifying the recipient's messaging system (e.g., "SMTP"). The *cOptionsProps* and *lpOptions-Props* members contain a counted array of *SPropValue*s that will contain the message's or recipient's requested delivery options.

The *lpszDLLName* and *ulOrdinal* members are used to load a DLL and link to a callback function exported from the DLL. The DLL's filename is in *lpszDLLName* and has no platform-specific decoration ("32" for Microsoft Windows 95 and Microsoft NT). The member *ulOrdinal* is the callback function's ordinal number as given in the DLL's DEF file. The callback function is used to return an *IMAPIProp* interface to the spooler. Here's how it works:

1. A client calls *IAddrBook::RecipOptions* or *IMAPISession::Message-Options*. These methods display dialog boxes that let the user set per-recipient and per-message options, respectively. *RecipOptions* takes an *ADRENTRY* parameter that describes the recipient to whom the message will be delivered. *MessageOptions* takes the address type of the back-end system whose delivery options you want to apply to an *IMessage* object that is passed as a parameter.

2. MAPI checks the set of options registered by the installed transports. If MAPI finds a registration for the recipient's address type (in the case of *IAddrBook::RecipOptions*) or the back-end system's

address type (*MessageOptions*), it loads the DLL and calls the call-back function.

3. The callback function returns an *IMAPIProp* interface whose only purpose is to handle *IMAPIProp::OpenProperty* on PR_DETAILS-_TABLE. You can return an existing *IMAPIProp* interface that is "wrapped" to handle the *OpenProperty* method. By this we mean that the calls to all *IMAPIProp* methods *except OpenProperty* are simply stubs that delegate to the existing *IMAPIProp* interface. Calls to *SetProps* and *GetProps*, for example, are handled by the existing inter-face. The *OpenProperty* call isn't delegated: It handles the PR_DE-TAILS_TABLE request by constructing a display table that describes the option dialog box that *RecipOptions* or *MessageOptions* will display to the user.

4. MAPI uses the display table to pop up a dialog box displaying the available delivery options. The user enters data in the dialog box controls and dismisses the dialog. MAPI extracts the data entered by the user from each control and saves it in the form of properties. If the call was to *MessageOptions*, the properties are written to the message object when the client calls *IMessage::SaveChanges*. If the call was to *RecipOptions*, the properties are stuffed into the *ADRENTRY* structure that was passed as a parameter.

5. Eventually, the transport that registered the options is passed the message for delivery. It checks the message and/or the recipients for the presence of one or more delivery option properties and uses the property values to perform specialized delivery of the message.

IXPLogon::AddressTypes

Every transport connects to one or more back-end systems, and each back-end system is associated with a GUID or an address type string. When a message is submitted, MAPI uses the entry ID or PR_ADDRTYPE property of each recipi-ent to identify the back-end system that will receive the message and, conse-quently, which transport provider to pass it to. Transports advertise which back-end systems they can connect to by registering one or more address types. MAPI keeps an ordered list of the transports in the profile as well as the address types they have registered. The default order is the order in which the trans-ports were installed in the profile, but the order can be set explicitly by a client that calls *IMsgServiceAdmin::MsgServiceTransportOrder* or set implicitly by the trans-port setting the STATUS_XP_PREFER_LAST bit in the PR_RESOURCE-_FLAGS of the session status table. When the spooler is searching for a transport that will handle an outbound message, it first checks the MAPIUID field of the recipient's entry ID for a match on the MAPIUIDs registered by each transport. If no match is found, the spooler searches for a match on the PR_ADDRTYPE string. A transport connecting to a gateway that handles multiple recipient types can pass NULL in *pppAdrTypeArray*, and the spooler will pass it all messages, regardless of the address type.

Registering MAPIUIDs is optional in *AddressTypes*; a transport can set *pppMAPIUIDArray*, *pppAdrTypeArray*, or both. The XPWDS transport registers the WINDS address book provider UID because we want to handle delivery of any messages that have recipients with mailboxes on the WINDS server. If another transport in the profile registers for the WINDS address type (by returning "WINDS" in *IXPLogon::AddressTypes*), the spooler will give XPWDS the first shot at delivering it, even if the other transport is before XPWDS in the transport order. Here's the code for *AddressTypes*:

```
STDMETHODIMP CXPLogon::AddressTypes(ULONG *      pulFlags,
                                    ULONG *      pcAdrType,
                                    LPTSTR **    pppAdrTypeArray,
                                    ULONG *      pcMAPIUID,
                                    LPMAPIUID ** pppMAPIUIDArray)
{
    // Count of strings we return in *pppAdrTypeArray
    *pcAdrType = 1;

    // Copy address types back to the MAPI pointer.
    gpszXPAddressTypes = &gszWINDSAddressType;
    *pppAdrTypeArray = gpszXPAddressTypes;
    *pulFlags = fMapiUnicode;

    // The UID for routing messages is set here. If not used, set it NULL.
    // We register support for UID of WINDS address book's entry ID.
    puidWINDSEntries = &guidABEntries;
    *pcMAPIUID = 1;
    *pppMAPIUIDArray = &puidWINDSEntries;
    return S_OK;
}
```

IXPLogon::FlushQueues

This method is called by the spooler when a client calls *IMAPIStatus::FlushQueues* on the spooler's status object. The spooler's *IMAPIStatus::FlushQueues* method takes an entry ID as a parameter. Passing NULL for the entry ID causes the spooler to call each installed transport's *IXPLogon::FlushQueues* method in turn. A client can also pass the status table entry ID column for a specific transport to the spooler's *IMAPIStatus::FlushQueues*; the spooler responds by calling that single transport's *IXPLogon::FlushQueues* method.

The spooler asks the transport to make a transition from its current state to the flush state by calling *FlushQueues*. If and when the transport can make the transition, it responds by setting the STATUS_INBOUND_FLUSH or STATUS_OUTBOUND_FLUSH bits in PR_STATUS_CODE and modifying its row in the session status table. When a transport enters the flush state, it's expected to deliver any inbound or outbound messages as quickly as possible. If the spooler is called to flush all transports, it will call *FlushQueues* in turn on each transport as listed in the transport order. A transport that is currently flushing must leave the flush state before the next one will be called, so two transports can never be in the flush state concurrently. Although this guarantees that transports won't compete for resources, it also means that if the flushing transport is waiting for a resource held by another *process*, all the other transports will wait too. For this reason, a transport that needs to acquire resources to deliver the messages should acquire them upon entry to the flush state and hold them until it leaves.

Entering outbound flush mode means that the spooler calls *IXPLogon::SubmitMessage* and *IXPLogon::EndMessage* for each message held in the spooler's outbound queue. The outbound queue contains any messages submitted by the client that haven't been delivered yet. The spooler detects the transport's transition to the outbound flush state by watching the transport's status row. When the STATUS_OUTBOUND_FLUSH bit appears in the PR_STATUS_CODE column, the spooler starts emptying its outbound queue. The spooler calls *IXPLogon::SubmitMessage* for each message in the outbound queue until the queue is empty or until the transport ends the outbound flush by changing state. When the last outbound message has been pumped through the *SubmitMessage/EndMessage* loop, the spooler calls *IXPLogon::TransportNotify* to command the transport to transition out of the flush state.

A transport should also send any deferred messages when it enters outbound flush mode. Deferred messages are those messages that aren't delivered immediately but will be delivered at some point in the future. Transports can defer messages until a scheduled delivery time (a remote transport) or until a connection can be made to the back-end server. The spooler queues the deferred messages separately from the nondeferred messages, and the flush mode state doesn't automatically empty the deferred queues. Instead, a transport must explicitly ask the spooler to send the deferred messages by calling *SpoolerNotify(NOTIFY_SENTDEFERRED, ...)*. You can ask the spooler to dequeue a specific message by passing its entry ID in the second parameter of *SpoolerNotify* or to dequeue all deferred messages by passing NULL.

FlushQueues is really more useful to remote transports than to transports that maintain persistent connections. Because the nonremote transport delivers messages as they are submitted, or as they arrive from the server, the spooler queues are usually empty. A remote transport, however, frequently has deferred messages waiting in the outbound queue and inbound messages waiting on the back-end server. For remote transports, *FlushQueues* gives the user a way to force upload and download of these pending messages, even if the scheduled delivery time hasn't arrived. The spooler might still call *FlushQueues* on a nonremote transport if there are queued messages pending at logon time. This frequently happens if the user logs off one session with mail still waiting in the Outbox and then logs on to a new session.

Nonremote transports also defer messages in some circumstances. XPWDS, for example, defers messages that are submitted while the transport is off line. When the connection is restored and the transport goes back on line, we request that the spooler start emptying its outbound queues of any pending messages. The call to *IsWINDSServerAvailable* determines the connection status. If the connection is valid, we set the STATUS_OUTBOUND_FLUSH bit in PR_STATUS_CODE by a call to *AddStatusBits*, which puts us in outbound flush mode. We also call *SpoolerNotify*, passing NOTIFY_SENTDEFERRED and NULL, to request all previously deferred messages.

The inbound flush works the same way: We first check the server to see whether a live connection exists and, if so, whether there are any messages in our mailbox. If both conditions are true, *CheckForPendingMessages* returns S_OK and a nonzero value in *ulMsgWaiting*. We respond by setting the STATUS_IN-BOUND_FLUSH bit in PR_STATUS_CODE to start the transition to the inbound flush mode state. As long as we're in the inbound flush mode, the spooler will repeatedly call *IXPLogon::StartMessage* to retrieve inbound messages until we end the flush mode or until we indicate that we've downloaded the last message. If the connection doesn't exist or there are no pending messages, we clear the STATUS_INBOUND_FLUSH bit, which takes us out of flush mode. The code for *FlushQueues* is as follows:

```
STDMETHODIMP CXPLogon::FlushQueues(ULONG       ulUIParam,
                                   ULONG       cbTargetTransport,
                                   LPENTRYID   pTargetTransport,
                                   ULONG       ulFlags)
{
    HRESULT hResult = S_OK;
    // Update status flags, and then update the transport
    // status rows.
    if (ulFlags & FLUSH_UPLOAD)
```

```
    {
        // If the server is off line, the transport can't send any
        // deferred messages.
        if (TRUE == IsWINDSServerAvailable(m_szServer))
        {
            // If the server was off line, set the transport state back to
            // on line.
            SetTransportState(READY);
            AddStatusBits(STATUS_OUTBOUND_FLUSH); // Add these bits to the
                                                  // status code.
            // We pass NULL for the entry ID so that the spooler will
            // resend ALL the deferred messages. Transport might pass
            // individual entry IDs for specific messages.
            hResult = m_pSupObj -> SpoolerNotify(NOTIFY_SENTDEFERRED,
                                                 NULL);
        }
        else
            RemoveStatusBits(STATUS_OUTBOUND_FLUSH);
    }
    // Update status flags, and then update the transport status rows.
    if (ulFlags & FLUSH_DOWNLOAD)
    {
        // If the server was off line, set the transport state back to
        // on line.
        SetTransportState(READY);
        ULONG ulMsgWaiting = 0;
        if (S_OK == CheckForPendingMessages(m_szServer,
                                            m_UserInfo.szMailboxName,
                                            &ulMsgWaiting)
                && ulMsgWaiting)
            AddStatusBits(STATUS_INBOUND_FLUSH);
        else
            RemoveStatusBits(STATUS_INBOUND_FLUSH);
    }
    UpdateStatus();
    return hResult;
}
```

IXPLogon::TransportNotify

The spooler calls this method to notify the transport of events that are of interest to the transport. The transport responds by modifying its PR_STATUS-_CODE and PR_STATUS_STRING properties and then updating its row in the session status table. The spooler can use *TransportNotify* to command the transport to change state or cancel transmission of a message.

The spooler will call *TransportNotify* with NOTIFY_BEGIN_INBOUND sometime after we complete our initialization. This is a wake-up call from the spooler to the transport telling the transport to enable its inbound message logic. We modify our status row to advertise to the spooler that we are ready to receive incoming messages and to ask it to respond to our *IMAPISupport-::SpoolerNotify(NOTIFY_NEWMAIL, ...)* calls. We also put ourselves in inbound flush mode to download any messages that have accumulated in the user's mailbox since the last logon. Sometime after we enter inbound flush mode, the spooler calls *FlushQueues.* From *FlushQueues* we call *CheckForPendingMessages* to find out from the server whether there's mail waiting in the user's mailbox. If the mailbox is empty, we transition out of inbound flush mode by clearing the STATUS_INBOUND_FLUSH bit in PR_STATUS_CODE and returning. If there is mail in the mailbox, we remain in inbound flush mode and the spooler will start calling our *StartMessage* method. The inbound logic is disabled when the spooler passes NOTIFY_END_INBOUND. We clear the STATUS-_INBOUND_ENABLED bit in PR_STATUS_CODE and modify our status row.

Enabling the outbound logic works the same way: We simply add the STATUS_OUTBOUND_ENABLED bit to the PR_STATUS_CODE column in the status table and update the table. This advertises to the spooler that we are ready to start transmitting outbound messages. Any messages left in the outbound queue from the last session will be pumped through the *SubmitMessage/ EndMessage* loop. The spooler can also disable outbound message delivery by passing the NOTIFY_END_OUTBOUND flag.

The spooler also calls *TransportNotify* if the user opens or deletes a deferred message waiting in the Outbox. Any attempt to delete or modify a pending message causes the spooler to remove the message from its outbound queue. The transport is notified of this change so that it knows not to ask the spooler for that message in a subsequent call to *SpoolerNotify(NOTIFY-_SENT_DEFERRED, ...).* In that case, *pulFlags* contains NOTIFY_ABORT-_DEFERRED and *ppvData* contains the entry ID of the message in question. A transport that calls *SpoolerNotify* on individual messages might maintain a list of entry IDs for messages it's deferred. When the NOTIFY_ABORT-_DEFERRED call occurs, it can delete the entry ID passed in *ppvData* from its list and *SpoolerNotify* won't be called for that message. XPWDS doesn't track individual messages this way but instead requests *all* deferred messages by passing NULL in *SpoolerNotify.* Since the spooler will have already removed the modified message from its queue, we don't have to do any special processing for this case.

NOTIFY_CANCEL_MESSAGE is used to abort a message that is in the process of being delivered. The transport assigns a reference number to each outbound message in *IXPLogon::SubmitMessage* and to each inbound message in *IXPLogon::StartMessage.* Each of these calls passes the reference number to the spooler through a pointer argument. The spooler can abort delivery of a message by passing the reference number in *ppvData* in the call to *Transport-Notify*. This implies that the *TransportNotify* call can occur on a thread different from the thread of *SubmitMessage* and *StartMessage*; if the call occurred on the same thread, the spooler couldn't pass the reference number to *Transport-Notify* until after the *SubmitMessage* or *StartMessage* call had returned, and by that time the message would have been delivered. Because *TransportNotify* can be called from a different thread, a transport that supports NOTIFY_CANCEL-_MESSAGE should periodically check for this event during the *SubmitMessage* and *StartMessage* calls and abort the delivery if the message is canceled. (An alternative is to copy the message to a temporary file, return from *Submit/StartMessage* right away, and then do the delivery on a separate thread that checks for the NOTIFY_CANCEL_MESSAGE event. Copying the message means that you must accept responsibility for it first and then figure out if you can actually deliver it.) In XPWDS, the message delivery happens synchronously in the *Submit/StartMessage* call and we don't check for NOTIFY-_CANCEL_MESSAGE. Therefore, we ignore this event in *TransportNotify*.

The code for all this is relatively simple, and it is as follows:

```
STDMETHODIMP CXPLogon::TransportNotify(ULONG * pulFlags, LPVOID * ppvData)
{
    ULONG ulOldStatus = GetTransportStatusCode();

    // Set appropriate status flags, and reregister status row.
    if (*pulFlags & NOTIFY_BEGIN_INBOUND)
        // We put ourselves in flush mode and download any messages in
        // our mailbox as soon as the inbound logic is enabled.
        AddStatusBits(STATUS_INBOUND_ENABLED | STATUS_INBOUND_FLUSH);

    if (*pulFlags & NOTIFY_END_INBOUND)
        RemoveStatusBits(STATUS_INBOUND_ENABLED);

    if (*pulFlags & NOTIFY_BEGIN_OUTBOUND)
        AddStatusBits(STATUS_OUTBOUND_ENABLED);

    if (*pulFlags & NOTIFY_END_OUTBOUND)
        RemoveStatusBits(STATUS_OUTBOUND_ENABLED);

    if (*pulFlags & NOTIFY_BEGIN_OUTBOUND_FLUSH)
    {
        // If the spooler needs to flush us, we put ourselves in flush
        // mode and tell the spooler to give us any deferred messages
        // queued for us.
```

(continued)

287

```
                    AddStatusBits(STATUS_OUTBOUND_FLUSH); // Add this bit to the
                                                          // status code.
                    SetTransportState(READY);
                    m_pSupObj -> SpoolerNotify(NOTIFY_SENTDEFERRED, NULL);
            }

            if (*pulFlags & NOTIFY_END_OUTBOUND_FLUSH)
                    if (GetTransportStatusCode() & STATUS_OUTBOUND_FLUSH)
                            // The spooler finished sending messages through our
                            // SubmitMessage method. It calls us here to end flush mode.
                            // We need to reset our status to tell the spooler to end the
                            // outbound flush.
                            RemoveStatusBits(STATUS_OUTBOUND_FLUSH);

            if (*pulFlags & NOTIFY_BEGIN_INBOUND_FLUSH)
            {
                    AddStatusBits(STATUS_INBOUND_FLUSH); // Add this bit to the
                                                         // status code.
                    SetTransportState(READY);
            }

            if (*pulFlags & NOTIFY_END_INBOUND_FLUSH)
                    RemoveStatusBits(STATUS_INBOUND_FLUSH); // Add this bit to the
                                                            // status code.

            // We get called here if user deletes/modifies queued msg in Outbox.
            // If the user modifies and resends it, we get called again at
            // SubmitMessage. If the user closes the message viewer or just saves
            // it, it's removed from the spooler queue and discarded.
            if (*pulFlags & NOTIFY_ABORT_DEFERRED)
                    InfoTrace("CXPLogon::TransportNotify: Abort deferred message");

            if (*pulFlags & NOTIFY_CANCEL_MESSAGE)
                    InfoTrace("CXPLogon::TransportNotify: Cancel message");

            if (ulOldStatus != GetTransportStatusCode())
                    UpdateStatus();

            return S_OK;
    }
```

IXPLogon::SubmitMessage

IXPLogon::SubmitMessage starts the logic for delivering an outbound message. The spooler calls *SubmitMessage* only if the message has recipients of your registered address type whose PR_RESPONSIBILITY flags are *FALSE*. The outbound message loop works like this:

1. The spooler dequeues a message from the outbound queue.

2. The message is passed to *SubmitMessage* for delivery.

3. *SubmitMessage* delivers the message or defers it.

4. The spooler calls *IXPLogon::EndMessage.*

5. Steps 1 through 4 are repeated until the queue is empty.

Transports such as XPWDS, which maintain a persistent connection to the back end, will typically deliver the message before returning from *SubmitMessage.* Transports that defer delivery will return S_OK immediately from *SubmitMessage* and flag the message as deferred in the subsequent *EndMessage* call. At some later time, the transport requests the deferred message (or messages) by calling *SpoolerNotify(NOTIFY_SENTDEFERRED, ...)* and the spooler again calls *SubmitMessage.* The transport then delivers the message and returns.

Message delivery includes connecting to the back-end system, transmitting the message over the wire, setting PR_RESPONSIBILITY to *TRUE* for the recipients to whom we've sent the message, calling *SaveChanges* on the message object, and returning. If the transport supports the NOTIFY_CANCEL-_MESSAGE event, it should place a nonzero message reference number in *pulMsgRef* so that the spooler can cancel the message should the need arise.

We don't support canceling outbound messages, so our first step is to check the status of the WINDS server. If we already know the server is off line, we return immediately and expect to be called at *EndMessage,* where we'll defer the message until the server comes back on line. If our internal state indicates a live connection, we ping the server; if we get no response, we set our internal state to SERVER_UNAVAILABLE. We then update our status row to STATUS_OFFLINE and return S_OK to defer the message in *EndMessage.*

If the connection is intact, we get the message's recipient table, first yielding to the spooler. Next we set up a property restriction on PR_RESPONSIBILITY==FALSE so that we can filter the recipient table to include only recipients that haven't already been claimed by another transport.[4] We call *HrAddColumns* to reserve space in the recipient table for some properties we will need to access later. These properties include PR_ROWID, PR_DELIVER_TIME, PR_REPORT_TIME, and PR_REPORT_TEXT. None of these properties are typically found in a message's recipient table, but they are all required in an *ADRLIST* passed to *StatusRecips,* which creates delivery and

---

4. We mentioned in Chapter 5 that a message's recipient table isn't required to support restrictions. However, the messages passed from the spooler to the transport are "wrapped" by MAPI, and the wrapped message's recipient table supports restrictions.

nondelivery reports for a particular recipient. The call to *HrAddColumns* lets
MAPI allocate the extra columns so that we can later fill in the properties, cast
the *SRowSet* to an *ADRLIST*, and pass it to *StatusRecips*.

Next we yield to the spooler and then call *SendMailMessage* to deliver the
message to the WINDS server. If the delivery was successful, we call *SaveChanges*
on the message to update the recipient table and return. If we encountered an
error, we return MAPI_E_NOT_ME, which tells the spooler to try another
transport for this message. Alternatively, *SubmitMessage* can return S_OK without accepting responsibility for the message. The code for *SubmitMessage* is as
follows:

```
STDMETHODIMP CXPLogon::SubmitMessage(ULONG      ulFlags,
                                     LPMESSAGE pMsgObj,
                                     ULONG *   pulMsgRef,
                                     ULONG *   pulReturnParm)
{

    // If the server is not available, defer submission on the message
    // until later.
    if (SERVER_UNAVAILABLE == GetTransportState())
        return S_OK;

    if (!IsWINDSServerAvailable(m_szServer))
    {
        SetConnectionType(CONNECTION_BROKEN);
        AddStatusBits(STATUS_OFFLINE);
        UpdateStatus();
        SetTransportState(SERVER_UNAVAILABLE);
        return S_OK;
    }

    // Initialize the timer for yielding to the spooler.
    CheckSpoolerYield(TRUE);

    // Notify the spooler that the transport is going to flush any queued
    // msgs and submit them. If the transport is going to use shared
    // resources, e.g., COM ports, it should put itself into flush mode
    // when submitting a batch of messages. This gives the transport the
    // advantage of locking shared resources across submitted messages
    // and ensures that the spooler does not call other transports while
    // another is flushing (because it could have something locked). This
    // transport does not use any shared resources that we would need to
    // lock, but for the purpose of demonstration, we put ourselves into
    // flush mode until the spooler tells us to step down.
```

```
AddStatusBits(STATUS_OUTBOUND_ACTIVE | STATUS_OUTBOUND_FLUSH);
UpdateStatus();

// Get the recipient table from the message.
LPMAPITABLE pTable = NULL;
HRESULT     hResult = pMsgObj -> GetRecipientTable(fMapiUnicode,
                                                   &pTable);

    ⋮

// The spooler marks all the message recipients that this transport
// has to handle with PR_RESPONSIBILITY set to FALSE.
SPropValue spvRecipUnsent;
spvRecipUnsent.ulPropTag                    = PR_RESPONSIBILITY;
spvRecipUnsent.Value.b                      = FALSE;

SRestriction srRecipientUnhandled;
srRecipientUnhandled.rt                       = RES_PROPERTY;
srRecipientUnhandled.res.resProperty.relop    = RELOP_EQ;
srRecipientUnhandled.res.resProperty.ulPropTag = PR_RESPONSIBILITY;
srRecipientUnhandled.res.resProperty.lpProp   = &spvRecipUnsent;

hResult = HrAddColumns(pTable,
                       (LPSPropTagArray)&sptRecipTable,
                       gpfnAllocateBuffer,
                       gpfnFreeBuffer);
    ⋮

// Let the MAPI spooler do other things.
CheckSpoolerYield();

LPSRowSet pRecipRows;
hResult = HrQueryAllRows(pTable,
                         NULL,
                         &srRecipientUnhandled,
                         NULL,
                         0,
                         &pRecipRows);
if (!hResult)
{
    // Let the MAPI spooler do other things.
    CheckSpoolerYield();
    // Send message to the recipients we can reach, and generate NDRs
    // for the ones we can't.
    hResult = SendMailMessage(pMsgObj, pRecipRows);
    FreeProws(pRecipRows);
    if (!hResult)
```

(continued)

```
        {
            // Now we need to save changes on the message and close it.
            // After this, the message object can't be used.
            hResult = pMsgObj -> SaveChanges(0);
        }
    }

ErrorExit:
    // Clean up.
    ⋮
    // In case there is a warning or error floating around, don't let it
    // escape to the spooler.
    if (FAILED(hResult))
        // We default to MAPI_E_NOT_ME so that the spooler attempts to
        // hand the message to another transport (currently running in
        // this profile) that handles the same address type as ours.
        hResult = MAPI_E_NOT_ME;
    else
        hResult = S_OK;

    RemoveStatusBits(STATUS_OUTBOUND_ACTIVE);
    UpdateStatus();
    return hResult;
}
```

CXPLogon::SendMailMessage

This method handles the details of transmitting the message to the WINDS server. The logic is as follows:

1. Create a temporary file to hold the outbound message's data.

2. Open a TNEF stream on the temporary file.

3. Set the properties that the transport is required to supply on the outbound message.

4. Encode all the transmittable properties, including PR_MESSAGE-_RECIPIENTS, into the TNEF stream.

5. Create a message header that identifies the message to the WINDS server (for the remote transport).

6. Create a named pipe connected to the WINDS server, and send the TNEF stream over the pipe to the server.

7. Tell the WINDS server to place a copy of the uploaded message in each recipient's mailbox.

8. For each recipient to whom the message was successfully delivered, set PR_RESPONSIBILITY to *TRUE* and generate a delivery report if one was requested.

9. For each failed recipient, generate a nondelivery report if one was requested.

10. Delete the temporary file.

The call to *GetMsgTempFileName* opens a subdirectory in the user's TEMP directory and a temporary file in the subdirectory. (The subdirectory is created if it doesn't already exist.) The temporary file will hold the message's data in the form of a TNEF encoded file. We create the name of the TNEF file dynamically, using the system time to compose a pseudorandom filename.

Next we call *OpenStreamOnFile* to create an OLE *IStream* interface on top of the temporary file and wrap the OLE *IStream* with our own *IStream* implementation (*CCachedStream*), which buffers read and write operations. We open a TNEF stream on top of the cached *IStream* by calling *OpenTnefStream*, which returns an *ITnef* object in **pTNEFObj*. The *OpenTnefStream* API takes a pointer to the *IMAPISupport* object, the destination stream (*lpStream*), the name of the TNEF attachment file holding the encapsulated data (*lpszStreamName*), some flags (*ulFlags*) that specify the semantics of the call, a pointer to the source message, a unique key used by the *ITnef* object, and a pointer to the returned *ITnef* object. The *OpenTnefStream* function prototype follows:

```
HRESULT OpenTnefStream(LPMAPISUP lpMapiSup,
                       LPSTREAM lpStream,
                       LPTSTR lpszStreamName,
                       ULONG ulFlags,
                       LPMESSAGE lpMessage,
                       WORD wKey,
                       LPITNEF FAR * lppTNEF)
```

We pass TNEF_ENCODE | TNEF_PURE in the *ulFlags* parameter to indicate that we're encoding the message in **lpMessage* into the TNEF stream.

We get the system time and convert it to a *FILETIME* structure, which we then pass in the call to *SetOutgoingProps*. *SetOutgoingProps* sets the required transport-supplied properties on the outbound message. The *FILETIME* structure is used to set PR_MESSAGE_DELIVERY_TIME and PR_PROVIDER_SUBMIT_TIME, whose values are the same since the message isn't being deferred. Other required properties we set at this time are the PR_SENDER_XXX properties and the PR_SENT_REPRESENTING_XXX properties. We check first whether the PR_SENDER_ENTRYID and PR_SENT_REPRESENTING_NAME properties have already been set. If they haven't, we create them from the user's identity information, which we saved at logon time.

The call to *GetPropList* returns a list of property tags for all the properties set on the message object. We walk this list and save all the tags belonging to nontransmittable properties *except* PR_MESSAGE_RECIPIENTS and PR_ATTACHMENTS. We merge these tags with the front of the *pTags* list, so that when the for loop terminates, we have a list of all the nontransmittable properties (except PR_MESSAGE_RECIPIENTS and PR_ATTACHMENTS) set on the object. This is the list of properties we want to exclude from the TNEF stream. Calling *ITnef::AddProps* with TNEF_PROP_EXCLUDE tells the *ITnef* object to exclude the properties in *pTags* from the encoded stream. We encode every transmittable property plus the attachment and recipient tables. A transport that handles address types for foreign systems might encode only those properties that are likely to be dropped somewhere en route. For example, if XPWDS handled SMTP recipients, we would probably encode all the properties that don't map directly to an SMTP header field or the message body and send the rest as text. *ITnef::Finish* encodes the source message (*lpMessage* in *OpenTnefStream*) onto the destination stream.

The call to *CreateFile* opens the temporary file containing the TNEF encoded message and saves the file handle for use later. The *GetProps* call retrieves some properties from the message that we will need later. Among these properties is PR_ORIGINATOR_DELIVERY_REPORT_REQUESTED, which will be *TRUE* if the sender wants us to create a delivery report upon successful transmission of the message. The other properties are passed to *CreateMsgHeaderTextLine*, which composes a string containing a comma-separated list of substrings that describe the message that is about to be delivered and the user's accounts for which it's destined. For example, the string

```
"13,John Coltrane,28,\\MAPLE\LEEM;\\MAPLE\WYNKEL,10,Blue
Trane,IPM.NOTE,0,1122,0,1,0,1709625744,29048386,"
```

describes a message from sender "John Coltrane" to recipients "\\MAPLE\LEEM" and "\\MAPLE\WYNKEL." The subject is "Blue Trane," and the message is an IPM.Note message of 1122 bytes. The last two fields contain the delivery time represented as two 32-bit integers. Each message in the user's mailbox has a companion string—the message header string—associated with it. The WINDS server returns these strings when the remote transport, XPWDSR, downloads the list of message headers in a user's mailbox and displays them in the remote mail viewer, which lets the local user selectively download messages from the mailbox. Even though the sender (John Coltrane) might be connecting via XPWDS, the recipients (Lee Morgan and Wynton Kelly) might be using XPWDSR, so we need to update each mailbox's list of headers.

The next call to *OpenServerUploadPipe* makes an RPC to the WINDS server to open the link for sending the message. The server creates a named pipe whose name is passed back in the RPC. *OpenServerUploadPipe* opens the named pipe and writes the data from the open TNEF file to the pipe. The server saves the incoming stream to its own local file. We walk the list of recipients (*pRecipRows*) and call *SendMsgToAccount* for each one. *SendMsgToAccount* makes another RPC to the server to tell WINDS to place a copy of the new message in the user's mailbox and update the header list.

We accept responsibility for the message even if a transmission error occurred, because we're the only transport that knows how to handle the WINDS address type. Alternatively, we could have set PR_RESPONSIBILITY to *FALSE* and let the spooler create an NDR when it couldn't find a transport to deliver the message. But instead we call *StatusRecips* ourselves if an error exists—a much better and more efficient method because the spooler doesn't have to search for another transport and because we can put specific error information in the NDR instead of relying on the spooler's default "no transport available for this address type" description.

The following *if...else* statement sets up the recipient properties required for the call to *StatusRecips*:

```
if (!fSentSuccessfully)
{ //…
}
else
{ //…
}
```

The if clause adds the specific error information in PR_REPORT_TEXT; the else clause sets the PR_DELIVER_TIME property. We maintain pointers to two *ADRLIST*s, *pAdrList* and *pAdrListFailed*, and add the recipient properties to one or the other depending on whether or not the message was delivered. When we finish processing all the recipients, we call *IMessage::ModifyRecipients*, passing *pAdrList* so that the PR_RESPONSIBILITY flag is updated for those recipients to whom we were able to deliver the message. If the sender requested delivery reports, we ask the spooler to generate one for each successful recipient by calling *StatusRecips* and passing *pAdrList*. We do the same for *pAdrListFailed*, except that we generate nondelivery reports unconditionally for each failed recipient in *pAdrListFailed*. The code for *SendMailMessage* follows:

```
STDMETHODIMP CXPLogon::SendMailMessage(LPMESSAGE pMsgObj,
                                       LPSRowSet pRecipRows)
```

(continued)

```
{
    LPSPropValue pMsgProps = NULL;
    LPADRLIST pAdrList = NULL, pAdrListFailed = NULL;
    LPSTnefProblemArray pProblems = NULL;
    CCachedStream * pStream = NULL;
    LPSTREAM pFileStream;
    HANDLE hMsgFile = NULL;
    HRESULT hOpenConnect, hUploadError;
    BOOL fErrorInServer, fSentSuccessfully;
    ULONG ulRow, ulCount1 = 0, ulCount2 = 0;
    LPTSTR pszServer, pszMailbox;
    LPSPropValue pProps;
    TCHAR szNDRInfo[1024], szHeaderText[1024], szTmpFile[_MAX_PATH],
        szConnectInfo[MAX_STRING_SIZE+1] = { 0 };

    if (!GetMsgTempFileName(szTmpFile))    // Not the Win32 API, but an
                                           // internal implementation
    {
        return E_FAIL;
    }

    // Create a stream where all message information will be saved.
    HRESULT hResult = OpenStreamOnFile(gpfnAllocateBuffer,
                                       gpfnFreeBuffer,
                                       STGM_CREATE | STGM_READWRITE,
                                       szTmpFile,
                                       NULL,
                                       &pFileStream);
    ⋮

    pStream = new CCachedStream(pFileStream, XPSOF_READWRITE);
    ⋮

    // The wKey is a key used to identify the TNEF property stream.
    // Transports should generate a pseudorandom number for this field.
    // Here we get a number based upon the system's tick count. Note that
    // this number cannot be zero or the OpenTnefStream call will fail.
    WORD wKey = LOWORD(GetTickCount());

#pragma warning (disable : 4127)
    if (!wKey)
    {
        ASSERTMSG(FALSE, "I'll be darn! It's zero!!!");
        wKey = (WORD)(LOWORD(GetTickCount()) + 1);
        ASSERTMSG(0 != wKey, "No way! What is going on!?!?");
    }
#pragma warning (default : 4127)
```

```
LPITNEF pTNEFObj = NULL;
hResult = OpenTnefStream(m_pSupObj,
                         pStream,
                         TNEF_FILE_NAME,
                         TNEF_ENCODE | TNEF_PURE,
                         pMsgObj,
                         wKey,
                         &pTNEFObj);
    ⋮

// Let the MAPI spooler do other things.
CheckSpoolerYield();

// Get the current time. We need to set some properties that require
// the time.
SYSTEMTIME st;
FILETIME ft;
GetSystemTime(&st);
SystemTimeToFileTime(&st, &ft);

SetOutgoingProps(pMsgObj, ft);

// Check which properties there are, and exclude the nontransmittable
// ones.
LPSPropTagArray pTags;
hResult = pMsgObj -> GetPropList(fMapiUnicode, &pTags);

    ⋮

// Let the MAPI spooler do other things.
CheckSpoolerYield();

// In this sample transport, we opted to let TNEF encapsulate
// the table of recipients of this message. This has a side effect:
// The addresses of the recipients get merged into the TNEF stream.
// So, for example, a foreign mail system will not be able to
// translate addresses of the recipients. A transport that uses TNEF
// and transmits messages to a foreign mail system must do custom
// processing of the recipients and their addresses so that the
// receiving side will understand them. This sample code must be
// modified if you want it as the base code for a gateway transport.
// Here we also let TNEF encode all the attachments we want to send.
ULONG cValues, i;
cValues = 0;
for (i = 0; i < pTags -> cValues; i++)
```

(continued)

```
    {
        // Use the FIsTransmittable macro in MAPI to determine whether a
        // property is transmittable.
        if (!FIsTransmittable(pTags -> aulPropTag[i]) &&
            PR_MESSAGE_RECIPIENTS != pTags -> aulPropTag[i] &&
            PR_MESSAGE_ATTACHMENTS != pTags-> aulPropTag[i])
        {
            pTags -> aulPropTag[cValues++] = pTags -> aulPropTag[i];
        }
    }
}
pTags -> cValues = cValues;

// Encode the properties now.
hResult = pTNEFObj -> AddProps(TNEF_PROP_EXCLUDE, 0, NULL, pTags);
gpfnFreeBuffer(pTags);

    ⋮

hResult = pTNEFObj -> Finish(0, &wKey, &pProblems);
    ⋮

hMsgFile = CreateFile(szTmpFile,
                      GENERIC_READ,
                      0,
                      NULL,
                      OPEN_EXISTING,
                      FILE_ATTRIBUTE_TEMPORARY |
                      FILE_FLAG_DELETE_ON_CLOSE |
                      FILE_FLAG_SEQUENTIAL_SCAN,
                      NULL);
    ⋮

// Get some properties in the message. Need to send the message
// and delivery report information.
hResult = pMsgObj -> GetProps((LPSPropTagArray)&sptPropsForHeader, …,
                              &pMsgProps);

    ⋮

// We need to check whether the sender requested a delivery report.
BOOL fNeedDeliveryReport;

if (PR_ORIGINATOR_DELIVERY_REPORT_REQUESTED ==
    pMsgProps[MSG_DR_REPORT].ulPropTag &&
    pMsgProps[MSG_DR_REPORT].Value.b)
    fNeedDeliveryReport = TRUE;
else
    fNeedDeliveryReport = FALSE;
```

```
// Create the header that we transmit to the server. The remote host
// will store this information and make it available to us when the
// message recipients ask for a headers update on their remote
// mailboxes.
CreateMsgHeaderTextLine(pMsgProps, szHeaderText, ft);

// Let the MAPI spooler do other things.
CheckSpoolerYield();

hOpenConnect = OpenServerUploadPipe(m_szServer,
                                    m_UserInfo.szMailboxName,
                                    hMsgFile,
                                    szConnectInfo,
                                    &fErrorInServer);
for (ulRow = 0; ulRow < pRecipRows -> cRows; ulRow++)
{
    pProps = pRecipRows -> aRow[ulRow].lpProps;

    // Assume the worst. If hOpenConnect is not S_OK, then
    // fSentSuccessfully must be FALSE in order to generate NDR for
    // each recipient.
    fSentSuccessfully = FALSE;
    if (S_OK == hOpenConnect)
    {
        if (IsValidAddress(pProps[RECIP_EMAIL_ADR].Value.LPSZ,
            &pszServer, &pszMailbox))
        {
            // pszServer should be the same as m_szServer.
            hUploadError = SendMsgToAccount(pszServer,
                                        pszMailbox,
                                        szHeaderText,
                                        szConnectInfo,
                                        &fErrorInServer);
            if (!hUploadError)
                // If we got here, we assume the message has been
                // received in the server.
                fSentSuccessfully = TRUE;
        }
        else
            hUploadError = MAKE_HRESULT(1, FACILITY_WIN32,
                                        ERROR_INVALID_ADDRESS);
    }
    else
        hUploadError = hOpenConnect;

    // Let the MAPI spooler do other things.
    CheckSpoolerYield();
```

(continued)

```
// Set the PR_RESPONSIBILITY flag to indicate we have handled this
// recipient. If the flag is not modified, MAPI will pass this
// message to the next transport in the profile that knows how to
// handle the same address types.
// In this case, we want to be the last to handle the message. If
// we fail the submission, we should tell MAPI to generate an NDR.
pProps[RECIP_RESPONSIBILITY].ulPropTag = PR_RESPONSIBILITY;
pProps[RECIP_RESPONSIBILITY].Value.b = TRUE;

// Set the report time for DRs and NDRs.
pProps[RECIP_REPORT_TIME].ulPropTag = PR_REPORT_TIME;
pProps[RECIP_REPORT_TIME].Value.ft = ft;

if (!fSentSuccessfully)
{
    // Make the spooler generate an NDR instead of a DR.
    pProps[RECIP_DELIVER_TIME].ulPropTag = PR_NULL;

    // The spooler will generate an NDR report and will fill in
    // all required properties in the StatusRecips call. The only
    // thing we need to do is to fill in a specific per-recipient
    // text description of the problem. It's good to have info
    // from the transport indicating the cause for the failure.
    ⋮
    if (fErrorInServer && hUploadError)
    {
        DWORD dwServerErrorIDS = 0;
        switch (hUploadError)
        {
            case HRESULT_FROM_WIN32(ERROR_INVALID_ACCOUNT_NAME) :
                dwServerErrorIDS =
                    IDS_DELIVERY_ERROR_INVALID_ACCT;
                break;
            case HRESULT_FROM_WIN32(ERROR_NO_SUCH_USER) :
                ⋮
        }
        if (!dwServerErrorIDS &&
            FACILITY_STORAGE == HRESULT_FACILITY(hUploadError))
            dwServerErrorIDS = IDS_DELIVERY_ERROR_ISTORAGE;

        if (!dwServerErrorIDS &&
            FACILITY_WIN32 == HRESULT_FACILITY(hUploadError))
            dwServerErrorIDS = IDS_DELIVERY_ERROR_WIN32;

        if (dwServerErrorIDS)
```

```
        {
            TCHAR szBuffer[256];
            if (LoadString(m_hInstance, dwServerErrorIDS,
                        szBuffer, 255))
            {
                lstrcat(szNDRInfo, TEXT("\r\n\t"));
                lstrcat(szNDRInfo, szBuffer);
            }
        }
    }
    LPTSTR pStr;
    hResult = gpfnAllocateMore(Cbtszsize(szNDRInfo), pProps,
                        (LPVOID *)&pStr);
    if (SUCCEEDED(hResult))
    {
        // Copy the formatted string, and hook it into the
        // preallocated (by MAPI) column.
        lstrcpy(pStr, szNDRInfo);
        pProps[RECIP_REPORT_TEXT].ulPropTag = PR_REPORT_TEXT;
        pProps[RECIP_REPORT_TEXT].Value.LPSZ = pStr;
    }
    else
    {
        pProps[RECIP_REPORT_TEXT].ulPropTag =
            PROP_TAG(PT_ERROR, PROP_ID(PR_REPORT_TEXT));
        pProps[RECIP_REPORT_TEXT].Value.err = hResult;
        ⋮
    }
}
else
{
    // For delivery report, each recipient must have this property
    // set. Otherwise the spooler will default to generate an NDR
    // instead.
    pProps[RECIP_DELIVER_TIME].ulPropTag = PR_DELIVER_TIME;
    pProps[RECIP_DELIVER_TIME].Value.ft = ft;

    pProps[RECIP_REPORT_TEXT].ulPropTag =
        PROP_TAG(PT_ERROR, PROP_ID(PR_REPORT_TEXT));
    pProps[RECIP_REPORT_TEXT].Value.err = S_OK;
}

// Based on the result of the submission to the remote host, we
// determine to which address list we should add this recipient.
LPADRLIST * ppTmpList = (fSentSuccessfully ?
                        &pAdrList : &pAdrListFailed);
ULONG ulTmpCount = (fSentSuccessfully ? ulCount1 : ulCount2);
```

(continued)

```
                // Does the list where this recipient belongs have enough room for
                // one more entry? If not, resize the address list to hold
                // QUERY_SIZE more entries.
                if (!(*ppTmpList) || ((*ppTmpList) -> cEntries + 1 > ulTmpCount))
                {
                    hResult= GrowAddressList(ppTmpList, 10, &ulTmpCount);
                     ⋮

                    ulCount1 = (fSentSuccessfully ? ulTmpCount : ulCount1);
                    ulCount2 = (!fSentSuccessfully ? ulTmpCount : ulCount2);
                }

                // We have room now, so store the new ADRENTRY. As part of the
                // storage, we're going to copy the SRow pointer from the SRowSet
                // into the ADRENTRY. Once we've done this, we won't need the
                // SRowSet anymore, and the SRow will be released when
                // we unwind the ADRLIST.
                (*ppTmpList) -> aEntries[(*ppTmpList) -> cEntries].cValues =
                    pRecipRows -> aRow[ulRow].cValues;
                (*ppTmpList) -> aEntries[(*ppTmpList) -> cEntries].rgPropVals =
                    pRecipRows -> aRow[ulRow].lpProps;

                // Increase the number of entries in the address list.
                (*ppTmpList) -> cEntries++;

                // Now that we are finished with this row (it is in the right
                // ADRLIST), we want to disassociate it from the row set
                // so that we don't delete this before modifying the recipients
                // list.
                pRecipRows -> aRow[ulRow].lpProps = NULL;
                pRecipRows -> aRow[ulRow].cValues = 0;
        }

        // Let the MAPI spooler do other things.
        CheckSpoolerYield();

        // Do we have some recipients who received the message?
        if (pAdrList)
        {
            hResult = pMsgObj -> ModifyRecipients(MODRECIP_MODIFY, pAdrList);
            hResult = S_OK; // We'll drop the error code from the modify
                            // recipients call.
            if (fNeedDeliveryReport)
            {
                hResult = m_pSupObj -> StatusRecips(pMsgObj, pAdrList);
                if (!hResult)
```

```
        {
            // If we were successful, we should NULL out the pointer
            // because MAPI released the memory for this structure. We
            // should not try to release it again in the cleanup code.
            pAdrList = NULL;
        }
    }
}
// Do we have some recipients who did not receive the message?
if (pAdrListFailed)
{
    hResult = pMsgObj ->
                ModifyRecipients(MODRECIP_MODIFY, pAdrListFailed);
    // We'll drop the error code from the modify recipients call.
    // The address list has the entries with the PR_RESPONSIBILITY
    // set, so the spooler will know if it has to generate NDR
    // reports.
    hResult = m_pSupObj -> StatusRecips(pMsgObj, pAdrListFailed);

    if (!hResult)
    {
        // If we were successful, we should NULL out the pointer
        // because MAPI released the memory for this structure. And we
        // should not try to release it again in the cleanup code.
        pAdrListFailed = NULL;
    }
}

ErrorExit:
    // Clean up.
    ⋮
    return hResult;
}
```

IXPLogon::EndMessage

EndMessage is the mate to *SubmitMessage*. Unless the message is canceled
through a call to *TransportNotify*, the spooler guarantees that *EndMessage* will
be called next after *SubmitMessage* returns. We already described how *Submit-
Message* defers the message by returning immediately if the connection to the
server goes down, as the following code illustrates:

```
if (SERVER_UNAVAILABLE == GetTransportState())
    return S_OK;
```

When *EndMessage* is called for a deferred message, the *ulMsgRef* parameter will
contain the reference number we previously assigned to the message in

SubmitMessage. Passing back END_DONT_RESEND in **pulFlags* tells the spooler to put the message in its deferred queue. Passing back 0 (zero) indicates that we're finished delivering the message. Here's the code:

```
STDMETHODIMP CXPLogon::EndMessage(ULONG ulMsgRef, ULONG * pulFlags)
{
    if (SERVER_UNAVAILABLE == GetTransportState())
        // Tell spooler to queue msg for deferred delivery.
        *pulFlags = END_DONT_RESEND;
    else
        *pulFlags = 0;

    return S_OK;
}
```

IXPLogon::StartMessage

This method implements the inbound message logic. The inbound message loop is similar to the outbound loop except that the transport starts the process by calling *SpoolerNotify* (or by being called at *Poll*) and ends the process by returning from *StartMessage* without calling *SaveChanges* on the object in the *pMsgObj* parameter. The processing is described in the following steps:

1. The transport calls *SpoolerNotify(NOTIFY_NEWMAIL, ...)* to start the inbound message loop.

2. The spooler responds by calling *StartMessage*, passing a blank *IMessage* object to hold the incoming data.

3. If there are no more inbound messages, clear the STATUS_INBOUND_ACTIVE bit in PR_STATUS_CODE and return; the loop terminates. Otherwise, set the STATUS_INBOUND_ACTIVE bit in PR_STATUS_CODE to indicate that a download is in progress.

4. Translate the inbound stream into MAPI properties. Set the properties on the blank *IMessage* object, call *IMessage::SaveChanges*, and return. The loop repeats from Step 2.

We described how XPWDS calls *SpoolerNotify(NOTIFY_NEWMAIL, ...)* from a worker thread when it gets a new mail notification from the WINDS server. Sometime after the *SpoolerNotify* call returns, we get called at *StartMessage* and the inbound loop starts as described above. We add the STATUS_INBOUND_ACTIVE bit to our status row to indicate that we're in the process of handling incoming mail.

The call to *GetMsgTempFileName* creates a zero-length temporary file in the user's "temp" directory. This file stores the contents of the TNEF file that we download from the WINDS server when we call *GetNextMailboxMsg*. We use the same mechanism for downloading inbound mail as we do for uploading outbound messages: We make an RPC to the WINDS server to request that it create a named pipe. The server creates the pipe and starts writing the TNEF stream containing the inbound message to it. The RPC returns the pipe's name, we open the pipe on our side, and we then start reading the inbound TNEF stream. We do a blocking *ReadFile* on the pipe to synchronize the operation with the WINDS server's *WriteFile*. Each call to *ReadFile* reads a chunk of the TNEF stream into a buffer, which we then write to the temporary file with a call to *WriteFile*. When the server has downloaded the entire TNEF file, it closes the connection; we close the pipe and return from *GetNextMailboxMsg*.

The next task is to translate the TNEF file into a MAPI message. TNEF makes this extremely easy—all we have to do is call *OpenTnefStream* to obtain an *ITnef* object and then ask the *ITnef* interface to decode the TNEF stream into MAPI properties and set those properties on an open *IMessage* object. The spooler passes us a blank message object for this purpose in the *pMsgObj* parameter.

We've seen the *OpenTnefStream* API previously in the *SendMailMsg* method. The arguments are almost the same for decoding as they are for encoding, except that now we must pass TNEF_DECODE in the fourth parameter (*ulFlags*) and we don't need to pass a key in the sixth parameter (*wKey*). We again use *OpenStreamOnFile* to create an OLE *IStream* interface on the TNEF file and wrap the OLE *IStream* with our own implementation that buffers reads and writes.

The call to *ITnef::ExtractProps* tells the *ITnef* interface to decode the TNEF stream into MAPI properties and to set them on the message object passed in the call to *OpenTnefStream*. You can explicitly specify which properties you want to decode by passing their property tags in the second parameter and TNEF_INCLUDE in the first. Only those properties will be decoded and written to the message object. You can also pass a list of properties to exclude by passing TNEF_EXCLUDE in the first parameter. In that case, all the properties *except* those you specify will be decoded and saved to the message object. We don't exclude any properties, so we pass TNEF_EXCLUDE and a zero-sized *SPropTagArray*.

The last step is to compute any required properties that the transport must set and set them on the message. The most important of these properties are PR_SENDER_XXX and PR_SENT_REPRESENTING_XXX—especially the entry IDs. The code for *SetIncomingProps* handles adding the required properties to the inbound message. (See the companion CD-ROM for details.) If there are no errors, we call *SaveChanges* on the message, clear the STATUS-_INBOUND_ACTIVE and STATUS_INBOUND_FLUSH bits from our status row, and return.

Clearing the STATUS_INBOUND_FLUSH bit is necessary because we might be getting called at *StartMessage* as a result of the spooler putting us in the inbound flush state and not because we called *SpoolerNotify*. Once the transport enters the inbound flush state, the spooler will repeatedly call *StartMessage* until the transport ends the inbound flush operation. The transport is responsible for ending the inbound flush state because only it knows when there are no more messages to download. The transport stops inbound flushing by clearing the STATUS_INBOUND_FLUSH bit in the status row and returning from *StartMessage* without calling *SaveChanges* on the message object. The *goto ErrorExit* statement following *GetNextMailboxMsg* (which returns S_FALSE if the mailbox is empty) handles this case.

The inbound flush scenario isn't as important for XPWDS as it is for the remote transport, XPWDSR. Doing an inbound flush is really a command to the transport that says, "Connect to your server, and download any messages sitting in the user's mailbox. Do this in the foreground, and don't stop until you're finished." XPWDS doesn't typically flush the inbound message because the server initiates the downloads automatically. We put ourselves in the inbound flush mode shortly after logon, however, so we still need to handle the STATUS_INBOUND_FLUSH case. We'll describe how a remote transport uses the inbound flush state when we discuss XPWDSR later in this chapter. The *StartMessage* code follows:

```
STDMETHODIMP CXPLogon::StartMessage(ULONG      ulFlags,
                                    LPMESSAGE  pMsgObj,
                                    ULONG *    pulMsgRef)
{
    // Initialize the pseudotimer for the SpoolerYield call.
    CheckSpoolerYield(TRUE);

    LPSTREAM pFileStream = NULL;
    CCachedStream * pStream = NULL;
    LPITNEF pTNEFObj = NULL;
    SPropTagArray sptExcludedProps = { 0 };

    AddStatusBits(STATUS_INBOUND_ACTIVE);
    UpdateStatus();

    HRESULT hResult;
    TCHAR szFileName[_MAX_PATH] = { 0 };
```

```
if (!GetMsgTempFileName(szFileName))
    hResult = E_FAIL;

hResult = GetNextMailboxMsg(m_szServer, m_UserInfo.szMailboxName,
                            szFileName);
if (hResult)
    goto ErrorExit;

  ⋮


// Open the stream where the message properties are.
hResult = OpenStreamOnFile(gpfnAllocateBuffer,
                           gpfnFreeBuffer,
                           STGM_READ,
                           szFileName,
                           NULL,
                           &pFileStream);
  ⋮


// Create a buffered IStream interface for the TNEF decoding.
pStream = new CCachedStream(pFileStream, XPSOF_READ);
  ⋮


hResult = OpenTnefStream(m_pSupObj,
                         pStream,
                         TNEF_FILE_NAME,
                         TNEF_DECODE,
                         pMsgObj,
                         0,    // Not needed when decoding TNEF
                         &pTNEFObj);
  ⋮


// Let the MAPI spooler do other things.
CheckSpoolerYield();

// Get the properties for the message that are encoded in the TNEF
// message stream. The sptExcludedProps argument is just a stub.
// We are not excluding any properties.
LPSTnefProblemArray pProblems;
pProblems = NULL;
hResult = pTNEFObj -> ExtractProps(TNEF_PROP_EXCLUDE,
                                   &sptExcludedProps, &pProblems);

  ⋮


SetIncomingProps(pMsgObj);
```

(continued)

307

```
    // Save all changes and new properties back on the message.
    // Don't release the message object. The spooler is still using it.
    // After this, the message object can't be used by this transport.
    hResult = pMsgObj -> SaveChanges(0);

ErrorExit:
    // Clean up.
    ⋮

    if (S_FALSE == hResult)
    {
        RemoveStatusBits(STATUS_INBOUND_FLUSH);
        hResult = S_OK;
    }

    // Delete the file only if we were successful putting the
    // file data into the message. Otherwise, leave the file in
    // the directory and it will be picked up later.
    if (S_OK == hResult)
        DeleteFile(szFileName);

    RemoveStatusBits(STATUS_INBOUND_ACTIVE);
    UpdateStatus();
    return hResult;
}
```

IXPLogon::TransportLogoff

The spooler calls *TransportLogoff* to end the session with the transport—for example, when the user logs off. The transport can do any housekeeping or cleanup chores at this time, such as releasing objects and freeing memory. The following code illustrates *TransportLogoff*:

```
STDMETHODIMP CXPLogon::TransportLogoff(ULONG ulFlags)
{
    if (m_pStatusObj)
    {
        m_pStatusObj -> Release();
        m_pStatusObj = NULL;
    }

    return S_OK;
}
```

IXPLogon::Idle, IXPLogon::Poll

Because the transport runs in the spooler's context, control passes to the transport only when the spooler calls into the transport code. But a transport must also respond to events occurring at any time on the back-end server. The spooler occasionally yields control to the transport by calling the *Idle* and *Poll* methods. The *Idle* method is a general-purpose way to occasionally give the CPU to the transport. It is called only when there is no other activity on the spooler nor on any running transport. Transports can do any housekeeping chores or other processing in the *Idle* call.

Poll is also called periodically by the spooler to give control to the transport, but in this case, the purpose of the call is very specific: to check for inbound messages. The transport indicates the presence of new inbound mail by returning a nonzero value in *Poll's* single parameter (*pulIncoming*). The spooler responds by starting the inbound *StartMessage* loop. The transport requests that the spooler make these calls by setting the LOGON_SP_POLL or LOGON_SP_IDLE bits in a bitmap, which is passed back in the *IXPProvider- ::TransportLogon* method call at logon time.

IXPLogon::ValidateState

IXPLogon::ValidateState is triggered by a client call to *IMAPIStatus::ValidateState* on the spooler's status object (obtained from the status table by a call to *OpenEntry* on the spooler's entry ID). The transport compares the configuration data it's using with the data supplied by the user when the provider was configured and calls *SpoolerNotify* if the two sets of data don't match. The effect of *SpoolerNotify(NOTIFY_CONFIG_CHANGED, …)* is to trigger a call to *IXPLogon::AddressTypes* and *IXPLogon::RegisterOptions*.

```
STDMETHODIMP CXPLogon::ValidateState(ULONG ulUIParam, ULONG ulFlags)
{
    // Try to open the transport profile section.
    LPPROFSECT    pProfileObj;
    HRESULT       hResult;
    LPSPropValue  pProps = NULL;
    ULONG         ulPropCount;
    // Open the service's profile section.
    hResult = OpenServiceProfileSection(m_pSupObj, &pProfileObj,
                                        gpfnFreeBuffer);
    ⋮

    // Read the properties stored in the profile of this user.
    hResult = pProfileObj -> GetProps((LPSPropTagArray)&sptLogonProps,
                                      fMapiUnicode,
                                      &ulPropCount,
                                      &pProps);
```

(continued)

309

```
    if (!hResult)
    {
        // Now compare what the transport thinks the information in the
        // profile is to the real data. If the data are different, tell
        // the spooler the transport would like to be reloaded.
        if (lstrcmp(m_UserInfo.szMailboxName,
                    pProps[MAILBOX_NAME].Value.LPSZ)                    ||
            lstrcmp(m_UserInfo.szPassword, pProps[PASSWORD].Value.LPSZ) ||
            lstrcmp(m_UserInfo.szFullName, pProps[USER_NAME].Value.LPSZ)||
            lstrcmpi(m_szServer, pProps[SERVER_NAME].Value.LPSZ))
        {
            hResult = m_pSupObj -> SpoolerNotify(NOTIFY_CONFIG_CHANGE,
                                                 NULL);
        }
    }
    pProfileObj -> Release();
    gpfnFreeBuffer(pProps);

    return hResult;
}
```

IXPLogon::OpenStatusEntry

The *OpenStatusEntry* method is called by the spooler when a client calls *IMAPISession::OpenEntry* on the transport's status table entry ID. This entry ID is computed by MAPI—not the transport—and is found only as a column in the session status table. The transport creates an *IMAPIStatus* object, which is returned in **ppEntry*. The spooler returns the *IMAPIStatus* object to MAPI, and MAPI returns it to the client. MAPI handles marshaling the interface across the two process boundaries. The following code returns a cached pointer to a *CXPMAPIStatus* object or returns a newly created object (and caches it) if it doesn't already exist. We call *OpenProfileSection* to retrieve the provider's profile section and pass it to the *CXPMAPIStatus* constructor. *CXPMAPIStatus* uses the profile section object to retrieve the provider's configuration properties. Nonremote transports aren't technically required to support *OpenStatusEntry* nor to provide an *IMAPIStatus* object, but they should because the status object is the only way a client application can communicate with the transport provider.

```
STDMETHODIMP CXPLogon::OpenStatusEntry(LPCIID        pInterface,
                                       ULONG         ulFlags,
                                       ULONG *       pulObjType,
                                       LPMAPISTATUS * ppEntry)
```

```
{
    ⋮
    HRESULT hResult = S_OK;
    // Now, if we already have created a status object on this logon
    // context, we'll just use QueryInterface to get a new copy
    // (AddRef it) of the object.

    if (!m_pStatusObj)
    {
        // Get the profile section of the provider so that we can get some
        // properties, assigned by MAPI to this provider, directly on the
        // status object.
        LPPROFSECT pProfileObj = NULL;
        m_pSupObj -> OpenProfileSection(NULL, 0, &pProfileObj);
        // If we don't have an object, create it, and save a copy in the
        // logon object.
        m_pStatusObj = new CXPMAPIStatus(this, pProfileObj);
        ⋮

        // The constructor of CXPMAPIStatus AddRef'ed this object.
        if (pProfileObj)
            pProfileObj -> Release();
    }

    if (!hResult)
    {
        // Return *ppEntry == NULL or a pointer to the object.
        m_pStatusObj -> AddRef();
        *ppEntry = m_pStatusObj;
        *pulObjType = MAPI_STATUS;
    }
    return hResult;
}
```

Implementing *IMAPIStatus*

We demonstrated how to use the spooler's status object to implement the *Deliver Now* functionality in HelloMAPI, the sample client we discussed in Chapter 5. In Chapter 6, we described how MAPI builds the session status table from the rows contributed by each provider's call to *ModifyStatusRow*. And in this chapter, we've seen how we update the PR_STATUS_CODE column in the status table when we change state—for example, when we go into flush mode. By now you should understand the purpose of the provider's status object and how it's used, so we'll cover the implementation details at warp speed.

The transport must provide the columns shown on the following page.

Status Table Columns Provided by the Transport

Property	Description
PR_DISPLAY_NAME	The provider's friendly name.
PR_PROVIDER_DLL_NAME	The filename of the provider DLL excluding the platform suffix (e.g., "32" for Windows 95 and NT).
PR_STATUS_CODE	A bitmap of flags indicating transport state.
PR_RESOURCE_TYPE	MAPI_TRANSPORT_PROVIDER.
PR_RESOURCE_METHODS	A bitmap of flags that indicate which *IMAPIStatus* methods the transport supports. Possible bit values are STATUS_VALIDATE_STATE, STATUS_SETTINGS_DIALOG, STATUS_CHANGE_PASSWORD, STATUS_FLUSH_QUEUES (in any combination).

The following columns are computed by MAPI:

Status Table Columns Computed by MAPI

Property	Description
PR_OBJECT_TYPE	Identifies the type of interface represented by the table row. MAPI_STATUS is the only possible value.
PR_RESOURCE_FLAGS	A bitmap of flags indicating basic functionality, such as whether the transport provides primary identity (STATUS_PRIMARY_IDENTITY) and whether the provider should be last in the transport order (STATUS_XP_PREFER_LAST). (See the MAPI documents for details.) PR_RESOURCE_FLAGS is set initially by MAPI and is based on values provided in the MAPISVC.INF file but might be changed programmatically by MAPI via calls such as *IMsgServiceAdmin::MsgServiceTransportOrder*.
PR_ENTRYID	An entry ID, created by MAPI, that a client can pass to *OpenEntry* in order to retrieve the transport's *IMAPIStatus* object.
PR_INSTANCE_KEY	Identifies the row in the table.
PR_ROWID	Identifies the row in the table.

These columns are optional and set by the transport:

Optional Status Table Columns Set by the Transport

Property	Description
PR_IDENTITY_DISPLAY	The PR_IDENTITY_XXX properties represent the user's identity as provided by this transport. We compute the identity properties from information concerning the user's account on the WINDS server and cache them in the logon object. This property is the user's display name.
PR_IDENTITY_ENTRYID	The user's entry ID in the WINDS address book provider. This property uniquely identifies every XPWDS user, since a user must have an account on the WINDS server and an address book entry is created for each account.
PR_IDENTITY_SEARCH_KEY	The user's search key from the WINDS address book provider.
PR_STATUS_STRING	A text description of the transport's state as set in PR_STATUS_CODE.
PR_CURRENT_VERSION	The current version of the provider code.

The *IMAPIStatus::GetProps* method returns all properties listed in the previous three tables. Some are computed on the fly, others we get from the provider's profile section, and some (such as the PR_IDENTITY_XXX properties) are supplied by the WINDS server.

IMAPIStatus::SettingsDialog

This method displays the current configuration properties as set by the user and saved in the profile section. The code is essentially the same as the UI code in *ServiceEntry*: The current configuration properties are retrieved from the service's profile section and displayed on the same configuration property sheets as in *ServiceEntry* by calling *DoLogonDlg*. About the only difference is that *SettingsDialog* doesn't take an array of property tags as a parameter; its purpose is to display or change the settings of a specific provider, not a message service containing (potentially) multiple providers. Also, we call *ModifyStatus-Row(..., STATUSROW_UPDATE)* to tell MAPI to add the new configuration properties to the status table. Since the code is so similar to *ServiceEntry*, we won't reproduce it here. See the companion CD-ROM for details.

IMAPIStatus::FlushQueues

This *FlushQueues* method is triggered by a client call to *IMAPIStatus::Flush-Queues* on the transport's status object obtained by calling *IMAPISession::Open-Entry*, passing the entry ID column from this transport's status table row. The semantics and implementation are the same as for *IXPLogon::FlushQueues*.

IMAPIStatus::ChangePassword

A client can call this method to change the user's password on the server. The implementation passes the old password and the new password found in *pszOldPass* and *pszNewPass* to a single RPC. The server does a simple string comparison of *pszOldPass* against the mailbox user's password stored on the server. If the two match, the server updates the user's password to *pszNewPass* and returns success; otherwise, it returns failure, as shown in the following code:

```
STDMETHODIMP CXPMAPIStatus::ChangePassword(LPTSTR pszOldPass,
                                           LPTSTR pszNewPass,
                                           ULONG  ulFlags)
{
    HRESULT hResult = ChangeMBServerPassword(m_pLogon -> GetServerName(),
                                             m_pLogon -> GetAccountName(),
                                             pszOldPass,
                                             pszNewPass);
    if (hResult)
        if (HRESULT_FROM_WIN32(ERROR_INVALID_PASSWORD) == hResult)
            hResult = E_ACCESSDENIED;

    return .hResult;
}
```

Remote Transports

A remote transport is a transport provider that doesn't maintain a continuous connection to the back end. Remote transports are useful when the cost of maintaining a persistent connection is prohibitive, the link is slow, or both. Instead of keeping the link open continually, a remote transport will connect to the back-end system only at a scheduled time or when explicitly commanded to do so by the client. Whereas a nonremote transport downloads all inbound mail to the local machine, a remote transport lets the client selectively download messages from the user's mailbox. The remote transport implements an

IMAPIFolder interface whose contents table provides a view of the contents of the user's mailbox. Each message waiting in the user's mailbox is represented in the table by a "header," which contains summary information about a pending message—for example, the subject, the sender, and the message size.

The user can preview the message headers in a *remote viewer* provided by the client and decide which messages to download and which to delete. (See Figure 8-9.) Allowing the user to selectively download messages saves time and money because she doesn't have to retrieve the message first to decide if she wants to read it (e.g., junk email).

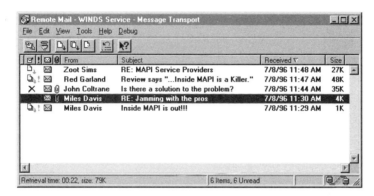

Figure 8-9.
The Microsoft Exchange client's remote mailbag viewer.

General Requirements

Remote transports must expose the same interfaces as nonremote transports, including the *IMAPIFolder* interface. Most of the *IMAPIFolder* methods can be stubs, though, because only *SetMessageStatus*, *GetProps*, and *GetContentsTable* are required. Remote transports must also set the STATUS_REMOTE_ACCESS bit in PR_STATUS_CODE and the STATUS_VALIDATE_STATE bit in PR_RE-SOURCE_METHODS. The client application looks for these bits to determine whether the provider supports remote operations; if they're not found, the client application can disable its remote viewer capability. (Of course, *IMAPIStatus::ValidateState* must also be supported.)

Remote transports must also support the same properties as nonremote transports, in addition to those listed in the table on the following page.

Required Property	Description
PR_HEADER_FOLDER_ENTRYID	The entry ID of the folder whose contents table provides the view of the remote mailbag. This property appears in the status table.
PR_REMOTE_PROGRESS	A number from 0 through 100 that indicates how far along in the download or upload operation we are. The number is expressed as a percentage. When no transfer is in progress, this value is set to −1. This property appears in the status table.
PR_REMOTE_PROGRESS_TEXT	A string that represents what percentage of the download or upload operation is complete. This property appears in the status table.
PR_REMOTE_VALIDATE_OK	Setting this property to *TRUE* tells the client application that it can make repeated calls to *IMAPIStatus::ValidateState*. This property is found in the status table.

Our Remote Transport Implementation: XPWDSR

At configuration time the user sets the scheduled connect time. When we log on, we calculate the difference between the scheduled delivery time and the current time and set a one-shot timer to go off after that interval has elapsed. We maintain a state variable that helps us keep track of which operations we are conducting at any time. Our state is initialized to WAITING in the *CXPLogon* constructor, which means that we're waiting for our delivery time to occur.

When the one-shot timer goes off, it calls a callback function, *UploadTimerProc*, which puts us in inbound and outbound flush mode. We change from the WAITING state to the PROCESSING_TIMER_EVENT state, confirming that we're doing our scheduled delivery and not being flushed by the client or updating the headers. We then get called at *IXPLogon::FlushQueues* with *ulFlags* set to FLUSH_UPLOAD. We call *SpoolerNotify(NOTIFY_SENT-DEFERRED, …)* to flush the outbound queue and reset the timer to go off again in 24 hours. If there are any deferred messages, they're pumped through our *SubmitMessage/EndMessage* cycle. In *SubmitMessage*, we check our state. Since we're not in the WAITING state anymore, we go ahead and send each message instead of deferring it as we would do if we were waiting for the timer to expire. The *EndMessage* call also checks the state and defers the message by passing back END_DONT_RESEND in **pulFlags* if the state is WAITING or 0 if not.

Next we get called at *FlushQueues* for FLUSH_DOWNLOAD. In the
PROCESSING_TIMER_EVENT state, we download only the headers—we
don't fetch any new mail in the user's mailbox. Remember, the user must explicitly download inbound mail by marking messages for retrieval via the remote viewer. Of course, it's possible that the downloading of marked messages
and the timer event can occur at about the same time. This is why we check our
state and finish one operation before changing state and starting another.

If we're not servicing the timer event and we're being called with
FLUSH_DOWNLOAD, either we're handling a client command to "Deliver
Now" *or* we're being asked to download messages that the user marked for
retrieval via the remote viewer. We ignore the first case, as mentioned above.
We detect the second case by checking a list we maintain that has a reference
to each marked message. If the list is empty, we have no work to do; otherwise,
we enter the inbound flush state and let the spooler call us at *StartMessage*. In
StartMessage, we connect to the server and ask it to send us each message in the
download list. The inbound processing at that point is the same as for XPWDS.

The *IXPLogon::FlushQueues* method has been modified slightly from the
XPWDS code to implement the new logic, as shown in the following code:

```
STDMETHODIMP CXPLogon::FlushQueues(ULONG      ulUIParam,
                                   ULONG      cbTargetTransport,
                                   LPENTRYID  pTargetTransport,
                                   ULONG      ulFlags)
{
    HRESULT hResult = S_OK;
    // Update status flags, and then update the transport status rows.
    if (ulFlags & FLUSH_UPLOAD)
    {
        // If the server is off line, the transport won't send deferred
        // messages.
        if (TRUE == IsWINDSServerAvailable(m_szServer))
        {
            // If we're already delivering, submitted messages won't be
            // deferred, so don't bother asking the spooler for deferred
            // messages.
            if (READY != GetTransportState())
            {
                // Guard against reentrancy from timer callback on
                // different thread.
                if (PROCESSING_TIMER_EVENT != GetTransportState())
                    SetTransportState(READY);
```

(continued)

317

```
                      // We pass NULL for the entry ID so spooler will resend
                      // ALL the deferred messages. We can also pass specific
                      // msgs' entry IDs.
                      hResult = m_pSupObj -> SpoolerNotify(NOTIFY_SENTDEFERRED,
                                                           NULL);
               }
        }
}
if (ulFlags & FLUSH_DOWNLOAD)
{
    if (HEADERS_AND_DOWNLOAD == GetTransportState())
    {
        m_hRemoteActionErr = ProcessHeaders();
        if (!m_hRemoteActionErr && !m_fCancelPending)
        {
            m_pSupObj -> SpoolerYield(0);
            if (m_List.AreTherePendingDownloads())
                // Put ourselves in flush mode. Spooler will call us
                // until we finish putting downloaded messages into
                // the default store.
                AddStatusBits(DOWNLOADING_MESSAGES);

            if (!m_fCancelPending)
            {
                // Upload any deferred messages the spooler has for
                // our transport.
                if (IsWINDSServerAvailable(m_szServer))
                    m_pSupObj -> SpoolerNotify(NOTIFY_SENTDEFERRED,
                                                        NULL);

                if (!m_fCancelPending)
                {
                    m_hRemoteActionErr = DownloadMessageHeaders();

                    if (!m_hRemoteActionErr &&
                        !(GetTransportStatusCode() &
                          DOWNLOADING_MESSAGES))
                    {
                        RemoveStatusBits(STATUS_INBOUND_FLUSH);
                        UpdateStatus(TRUE, TRUE);
                        m_pSupObj -> SpoolerYield(0);
                    }
                }
            }
        }
    }
```

```
                SetTransportState(PENDING_RETURN_CODE);
                AddStatusBits(STATUS_OFFLINE);
                if (m_hRemoteActionErr)
                {
                    RemoveStatusBits(STATUS_INBOUND_FLUSH);
                    UpdateStatus(TRUE, TRUE);
                }
                else
                {
                    if (m_fCancelPending)
                        UpdateStatus(TRUE, TRUE);
                    else
                        UpdateStatus();
                }
            }
            else
            {
                if (PROCESSING_TIMER_EVENT == GetTransportState())
                {
                    if (m_fGetHeaders)
                    {
                        RemoveStatusBits(STATUS_OFFLINE);
                        UpdateStatus();
                        DownloadMessageHeaders();
                        AddStatusBits(STATUS_OFFLINE);
                        UpdateStatus();
                    }
                }
                else
                    if (m_List.AreTherePendingDownloads())
                    {
                        // Put ourselves into flush mode. Spooler will call us
                        // until we are finished putting inbound messages into
                        // the default store.
                        AddStatusBits(DOWNLOADING_MESSAGES);
                        UpdateStatus();
                    }
            }
        }
    return hResult;
}
```

IXPLogon::SubmitMessage looks almost the same as the code for XPWDS. The only difference is the first couple of lines that check for the WAITING state and the UPLOADING_MESSAGES state, as shown here:

```
STDMETHODIMP CXPLogon::SubmitMessage(ULONG      ulFlags,
                                     LPMESSAGE pMsgObj,
                                     ULONG *   pulMsgRef,
                                     ULONG *   pulReturnParm)
{

    // Lock the object against timer thread reentrancy. Timer events are
    // handled in a separate thread. This section gets unlocked in
    // CPXLogon::EndMessage.
    if (WAITING == GetTransportState())
        return S_OK;

    CheckSpoolerYield(TRUE);

    // Notify spooler that we'll flush any queued-up messages and submit
    // them. XPs that use shared resources (e.g., COM ports) should go
    // into flush mode when submitting a batch of messages. This lets the
    // transport lock shared resources across submitted messages. It
    // ensures that the spooler doesn't call other transports while we're
    // flushing, because the spooler could have something locked. This
    // transport doesn't use any resources we would need to lock, but for
    // the purpose of demonstration, we go into flush mode until the MAPI
    // spooler tells us to step down.
    if (!(GetTransportStatusCode() & UPLOADING_MESSAGES))
    {
        AddStatusBits(UPLOADING_MESSAGES);
        UpdateStatus();
    }

    // Same as XPWDS
    :
}
```

We also check for the WAITING state in *EndMessage* to decide whether we'll defer the message or process it, as shown in the following code:

```
STDMETHODIMP CXPLogon::EndMessage(ULONG ulMsgRef, ULONG * pulFlags)
{
    if (WAITING == GetTransportState())
        // Tell spooler to queue msg for deferred delivery.
        *pulFlags = END_DONT_RESEND;
```

```
    else
        *pulFlags = 0;

    return S_OK;
}
```

StartMessage should look very familiar. The only difference between the non-remote and remote versions is that we check our list of messages selected for download (*m_List*) before we decide whether we want to proceed (i.e., connect to the WINDS server and request the message) or terminate the flush mode. We terminate the flush if the list is empty by changing state back to WAITING and returning without calling *SaveChanges* on the message in *pMsgObj*:

```
STDMETHODIMP CXPLogon::StartMessage(ULONG     ulFlags,
                                    LPMESSAGE pMsgObj,
                                    ULONG *   pulMsgRef)
{

    // Initialize the pseudotimer for the SpoolerYield call.
    CheckSpoolerYield(TRUE);

    HRESULT         hResult = S_OK;
    LPSTREAM        pFileStream = NULL;
    CCachedStream * pStream = NULL;
    LPITNEF         pTNEFObj = NULL;
    SPropTagArray   sptExcludedProps = { 0 };

    PLIST_NODE      pNode = m_List.GetDownloadNode();

    if (!pNode)
    {
        RemoveStatusBits(DOWNLOADING_MESSAGES);
        UpdateStatus();

        if (READY == GetTransportState())
            SetTransportState(WAITING);
        goto ErrorExit;
    }

    // Close the file so that we can open it in the call below.
    if (pNode -> hFile)
    {
        CloseHandle(pNode -> hFile);
        // NULL the handle to avoid closing the file again during cleanup.
        pNode -> hFile = NULL;
    }
```

(continued)

```
            // Open the stream where the message properties are.
            hResult = OpenStreamOnFile(gpfnAllocateBuffer,
                                       gpfnFreeBuffer,
                                       STGM_READ,
                                       pNode -> szFileName,
                                       NULL,
                                       &pFileStream);
        // Same as XPWDS
        ⋮
    }
```

Implementing *IMAPIFolder*

A remote transport must implement a minimal *IMAPIFolder* interface. The folder, which represents the user's remote mailbox, returns a contents table that provides a view of the messages waiting in the mailbox. A client can display the folder's contents table in its remote viewer to let users select messages to be either deleted from the remote mailbox or downloaded to the local machine. The folder is accessed through the transport's *IMAPIStatus* interface, which is obtained from the session status table. For example, a client wanting to view the remote mailbox would make the following calls:

1. *IMAPISession::GetStatusTable(…, &pStatTbl)*.

2. *pStatTbl -> Restrict* on (PR_RESOURCE_TYPE == MAPI_TRANS-PORT && (PR_STATUS_CODE & STATUS_REMOTE_ACCESS)) to find all the remote transports in the session.

3. *pStatTbl -> QueryRows(…, &pRows)*.

4. Select a transport from the returned rows and get its PR_ENTRYID column.

5. *IMAPISession::OpenEntry(…, eidTransport, &IID_IMAPIStatus, …, &pStatObj)* to obtain the desired transport's *IMAPIStatus* object.

6. *pStatObj -> QueryInterface(IID_IMAPIFolder, &pFolder)* to obtain the folder representing the remote mailbox.

7. *pFolder -> GetContentsTable(…, &pHeaderTbl)*.

8. Call methods on *pHeaderTbl* to display the contents table. Save the entry ID column for each message the user wants to download or delete.

9. Call *pFolder -> SetMessageStatus* for each message the user selected in Step 8. Passing MSGSTATUS_REMOTE_DOWNLOAD | MSGSTAT-US_REMOTE_DELETE will move the message from the mailbox to

the default store's Inbox; passing MSGSTATUS_REMOTE_DOWN-LOAD will copy it to the Inbox, and passing MSGSTATUS_REMOTE-_DELETE will delete the message from the mailbox.

10. Call *pStatObj -> ValidateState* to update the remote mailbox. The caller passes the requested action in the *ulFlags* parameter. PROCESS_XP-_HEADER_CACHE updates the remote mailbox by carrying out the action specified by *SetMessageStatus* for each message. REFRESH-_XP_HEADER_CACHE updates the contents table to reflect the current state of the remote mailbox. You can OR both values together.

The client-side calls map one-to-one with the same methods implemented by the transport provider. For example, *IMAPISession::OpenEntry* is serviced in *IXPLogon::OpenStatusEntry*, and the client calls to *IMAPIStatus* (e.g., *QueryInterface, ValidateState*) end up in the transport's *IMAPIStatus* methods. The same is true for *IMAPIFolder* and *IMAPITable*. MAPI marshals these interfaces from the spooler process to the client process, but this is done transparently to both the client and the provider.

IMAPIFolder::GetContentsTable

The header contents table is backed by some type of storage that reflects the contents of the user's mailbox the last time the remote transport queried the server. This storage is called the *header cache* in the MAPI documentation. XPWDSR saves the header information in a local file that backs an *ITableData* object used to service requests for the header contents table. So our header cache is an *ITableData* object backed by a disk file. When the client asks us to refresh the header cache, we connect to the server and download the list of headers into our local file and then modify the *ITableData* object accordingly. This scheme means that any open views (the contents table) get notifications automatically when we update the headers.

The *GetContentsTable* code shows how we create the *ITableData* object and cache it in the *CXPMAPIFolder* object the first time we're asked for a view of the remote folder. Thereafter, we just return the cached pointer. The *FillContentsTable* function reads the disk file, copies each header record into an *SRow*, and passes the records to *ITableData::HrModifyRow* to update *ITableData*:

```
STDMETHODIMP CXPMAPIFolder::GetContentsTable(ULONG ulFlags,
                                             LPMAPITABLE * ppTable)
{
    HRESULT hResult;
    :
    if (MAPI_ASSOCIATED & ulFlags)
        return MAPI_E_NO_SUPPORT;
```

(continued)

```
    // If we don't have an ITableData interface pointer instantiated,
    // create one.
    if (!m_pTableData)
    {
        EnterCriticalSection(&m_csObj);

        hResult = CreateTable(…, &m_pTableData);
        ⋮
        // Populate the data for the table here.
        hResult = FillContentsTable(m_pLogon -> GetLocalHeadersCache());

        if (hResult)
            return hResult;
        LeaveCriticalSection(&m_csObj);
    }
    hResult = m_pTableData -> HrGetView(NULL, NULL, 0, ppTable);
    ⋮
    return hResult;
}
```

Required columns in the remote mailbox contents table are given in the following list. We've discussed most of these in this chapter and in Chapter 5.

- *PR_ENTRYID.* The entry ID in this case is simply a unique identifier for the header. It doesn't map to an entry in any store provider, and it can't be used in *OpenEntry*, for example. Its only purpose is to identify a row in the table in a call to *SetMessageStatus*.

- *PR_SENDER_NAME.*

- *PR_SENT_REPRESENTING_NAME.*

- *PR_DISPLAY_TO.*

- *PR_SUBJECT.*

- *PR_MESSAGE_CLASS.*

- *PR_MESSAGE_FLAGS.*

- *PR_MESSAGE_SIZE.*

- *PR_PRIORITY.*

- *PR_IMPORTANCE.*

- *PR_SENSITIVITY.*

- *PR_MESSAGE_DELIVERY_TIME.* The date and time the message was delivered.

- *PR_MSG_STATUS.*

- *PR_MESSAGE_DOWNLOAD_TIME.* The estimated time (in seconds) needed to download the message in question.

- *PR_HASATTACH.*

- *PR_OBJECT_TYPE.*

- *PR_INSTANCE_KEY.*

- *PR_NORMALIZED_SUBJECT.* The subject string with any "RE:" or "FW:" prefixes removed.

IMAPIFolder::SetMessageStatus

SetMessageStatus is used to mark a message for downloading or deletion from the remote mailbox. When the client wants to mark a message, it obtains the target message's entry ID column from the remote header contents table and passes it to *SetMessageStatus.* The caller also passes a bitmap of flags containing the bit values to be set and a bitmask that masks the bits that don't change. When the call returns, the target row has its PR_MSG_STATUS column updated to include the new bit values, and the old value of PR_MSG_STATUS is passed back in *pulOldStatus.*

Possible values for *ulNewStatus* and their meanings are as follows:

ulNewStatus Values	Meaning
MSGSTATUS_REMOTE_DOWNLOAD	Copy the message from the remote mailbox to the default store Inbox.
MSGSTATUS_REMOTE_DELETE	Delete the message from the remote mailbox.
MSGSTATUS_REMOTE_DOWNLOAD- ¦ MSGSTATUS_REMOTE_DELETE	Move the message from the remote mailbox to the default store Inbox.

The *ulNewStatusMask* has a 1 in each bit you want to set or clear. The *ulNewStatus* has a 1 in each bit you want to set and a 0 in each bit you want to clear. For example, if the caller wanted to mark a message for deletion, it would pass MSGSTATUS_REMOTE_DELETE in *ulNewStatus* and MSGSTATUS_REMOTE_DELETE ¦ MSGSTATUS_REMOTE_DOWNLOAD in *ulNewStatusMask*:

```
STDMETHODIMP CXPMAPIFolder::SetMessageStatus(ULONG     cbEntryID,
                                             LPENTRYID pEntryID,
                                             ULONG     ulNewStatus,
                                             ULONG     ulNewStatusMask,
                                             ULONG *   pulOldStatus)
```

(continued)

325

```
{
    SPropValue spvSearchProp;
    LPSRow psrTargetRow;
    EnterCriticalSection(&m_csObj);
    spvSearchProp.ulPropTag     = PR_ENTRYID;
    spvSearchProp.Value.bin.cb  = cbEntryID;
    spvSearchProp.Value.bin.lpb = (LPBYTE)pEntryID;

    HRESULT hResult = m_pTableData -> HrQueryRow(&spvSearchProp,
                                          &psrTargetRow, NULL);
    if (hResult)
        // Error
        ⋮
    else
    {
        BOOL bFound = FALSE;
        ULONG ulOldStatus;
        for (ULONG i = 0; i < psrTargetRow -> cValues; i++)
        {
            if (PR_MSG_STATUS == psrTargetRow -> lpProps[i].ulPropTag)
            {
                bFound = TRUE;
                ulOldStatus = psrTargetRow -> lpProps[i].Value.l;

                if (pulOldStatus)
                    *pulOldStatus = ulOldStatus;

                ulOldStatus &= ulNewStatusMask;
                ulNewStatus &= ulNewStatusMask;
                if (ulNewStatus != ulOldStatus)
                {
                    psrTargetRow -> lpProps[i].Value.l &=
                        ~ulNewStatusMask;
                    psrTargetRow -> lpProps[i].Value.l != ulNewStatus;
                    hResult= m_pTableData -> HrModifyRow(psrTargetRow);
                }
                break; // Out of the loop
            }
        }
        ⋮
        gpfnFreeBuffer(psrTargetRow);
    }
    LeaveCriticalSection(&m_csObj);
    return hResult;
}
```

Our implementation uses the entry ID in *pEntryID* as the index column in the *ITableData* backing the contents table. We call *HrQueryRow* to find the row, iterate through the columns to find PR_MSG_STATUS, set the bits, and then call *HrModifyRow* to update the underlying table.

Implementing *IMAPIStatus* on Remote Transports

The first step in supporting the *IMAPIFolder* interface is to support IID_IMAPI-Folder in *IMAPIStatus::QueryInterface,* as shown in the following code:

```
STDMETHODIMP CXPMAPIStatus::QueryInterface(REFIID riid, LPVOID * ppvObj)
{
    HRESULT hResult = S_OK;

    *ppvObj = NULL;

    if (riid == IID_IMAPIStatus ||
        riid == IID_IMAPIProp   ||
        riid == IID_IUnknown)
    {
        *ppvObj = (LPVOID)this;
        AddRef();
    }
    else
    {
        // If the transport has not been configured for the remote
        // interface, then don't support this interface.
        if (OFFLINE_CONNECT != m_pLogon -> GetConnectionType())
            return E_NOINTERFACE;

        if (riid == IID_IMAPIFolder)
        {
            EnterCriticalSection(&m_csObj);
            // If we already have a folder, return the same object to the
            // caller.
            if (!m_pHeaderFolder)
                m_pHeaderFolder = new CXPMAPIFolder(this, m_pLogon);
            ⋮

            if (!hResult)
            {
                m_pHeaderFolder -> AddRef();       // One for the caller
                                                   // requesting it
                *ppvObj = (LPVOID)m_pHeaderFolder;
            }
            LeaveCriticalSection(&m_csObj);
        }
```

(continued)

```
        else
            // This object does not support the interface requested.
            hResult = E_NOINTERFACE;
    }
    return hResult;
}
```

The code is completely straightforward: We return a cached *IMAPIStatus* object, or create a new one if it doesn't already exist, and return it to the caller. One subtlety we should point out here is that *IMAPIFolder::QueryInterface* must return *CXPMAPIStatus* if IID_IUnknown is requested. These semantics are required by the reflexive rule of OLE COM: If *QueryInterface* on A returns B, then *QueryInterface* on B must return A. Not only must each call return the correct object, but it must return a pointer to the *same instance* of the object.

IMAPIStatus::ValidateState: Processing the Header Cache

The client calls *ValidateState* to download the headers, process any messages marked in the remote header table, or cancel an operation already in progress. The *ulFlags* parameter contains a bitmap of flags indicating the requested operation. If the PROCESS_XP_HEADER_CACHE bit is set in *ulFlags*, the client is commanding us to check the header table and download any messages whose rows are marked for download and delete any messages marked for deletion. If the REFRESH_XP_HEADER_CACHE bit is set, we are being commanded to connect to the server and retrieve header information for any messages waiting in the user's mailbox. Anytime that we're asked to process the headers (i.e., download the marked messages), we go ahead and refresh the headers. The download operation is relatively expensive compared to the refresh operation, so if we have to go to the trouble of connecting to the server, we might as well do both operations at the same time. The code that initiates this action is as follows:

```
STDMETHODIMP CXPMAPIStatus::ValidateState(ULONG ulUIParam, ULONG ulFlags)
{
    HRESULT hResult = S_OK;
    :
    // Get headers or process marked messages, and upload deferred
    // messages.
    if (ulFlags & (PROCESS_XP_HEADER_CACHE ¦ REFRESH_XP_HEADER_CACHE))
    {
        if (PENDING_RETURN_CODE == m_pLogon -> GetTransportState())
        {
            m_pLogon -> SetTransportState(WAITING);
            m_pLogon -> UpdateStatus(TRUE, FALSE);
```

```
            // Reset PR_REMOTE_PROGRESS_TEXT.
            m_pLogon -> UpdateProgress(-1, REMOTE_ACTION_IDLE);
            return m_pLogon -> m_hRemoteActionErr;
        }
        if (HEADERS_AND_DOWNLOAD == m_pLogon -> GetTransportState())
            return MAPI_E_BUSY;

        m_pLogon -> m_fCancelPending = FALSE;

        // Fire up a request to the spooler to flush the INBOUND logic,
        // which in turn will also get new headers.
        m_pLogon -> SetTransportState(HEADERS_AND_DOWNLOAD);
        m_pLogon -> AddStatusBits(DOWNLOADING_MESSAGES);
        m_pLogon -> RemoveStatusBits(STATUS_OFFLINE);
        m_pLogon -> UpdateStatus(TRUE, FALSE);
        return MAPI_E_BUSY;
    }
    return S_OK;
}
```

We first check our internal state to see whether we're already in the PENDING_RETURN_CODE state—that is, to see whether we're processing a previous download request and whether we're at the stage where we've downloaded all the messages into temporary files but the *StartMessage* loop hasn't begun yet. If we're in the PENDING_RETURN_CODE state, we reset our internal state to WAITING, reset the PR_REMOTE_PROGRESS_XXX properties, and then return. This test prevents us from reentering the HEADERS-_AND_DOWNLOAD state if messages are being pumped through our *SubmitMessage/StartMessage* logic from the last time we were in the HEADERS_AND_DOWNLOAD state. If we're already in the HEADERS-_AND_DOWNLOAD state, we're preparing to download the headers and/or incoming messages, so we return MAPI_E_BUSY.

Next we initialize a flag (*m_fCancelPending*), which we can check later in *FlushQueues* if we are asked to abort the operation, and then transition to the HEADERS_AND_DOWNLOAD state. This state means that we will ask the spooler to put us in inbound flush mode and update the remote headers. We do the first by changing our PR_STATUS_CODE column in the session status table to STATUS_INBOUND_FLUSH ¦ STATUS_INBOUND_ACTIVE (the inbound flush mode) and then setting our internal state variable to HEADERS_AND_DOWNLOAD. The result is seen in the next call to *IXPLogon::FlushQueues*, which occurs when the status table changes, as shown on the following page.

```
STDMETHODIMP CXPLogon::FlushQueues(ULONG     ulUIParam,
                                   ULONG     cbTargetTransport,
                                   LPENTRYID pTargetTransport,
                                   ULONG     ulFlags)
{
    HRESULT hResult = S_OK;
    ⋮

    if (ulFlags & FLUSH_DOWNLOAD)
    {
        if (HEADERS_AND_DOWNLOAD == GetTransportState())
        {
            m_hRemoteActionErr = ProcessHeaders();

            if (!m_hRemoteActionErr && !m_fCancelPending)
            {
                m_pSupObj -> SpoolerYield(0);
                if (m_List.AreTherePendingDownloads())
                {
                    // Go to inbound flush mode. Spooler will call us
                    // until we are finished downloading messages into
                    // default store.
                    AddStatusBits(DOWNLOADING_MESSAGES);
                }
                if (!m_fCancelPending)
                {
                    // Upload any deferred messages the spooler has
                    // for us.
                    if (IsWINDSServerAvailable(m_szServer))
                    {
                        m_pSupObj -> SpoolerNotify(NOTIFY_SENTDEFERRED,
                                                   NULL);
                    }
                    if (!m_fCancelPending)
                    {
                        m_hRemoteActionErr = DownloadMessageHeaders();
                        if (!m_hRemoteActionErr &&
                            !(GetTransportStatusCode() &
                              DOWNLOADING_MESSAGES))
                        {
                            RemoveStatusBits(STATUS_INBOUND_FLUSH);
                            UpdateStatus(TRUE, TRUE);
                            m_pSupObj -> SpoolerYield(0);
                        }
                    }
                }
            }
        }
        ⋮
```

```
        SetTransportState(PENDING_RETURN_CODE);
        AddStatusBits(STATUS_OFFLINE);
        ⋮
        UpdateStatus();
    }
}
⋮
return hResult;
}
```

The spooler passes us *ulFlags* with the FLUSH_DOWNLOAD bit set to honor our request in *ValidateState* to enter the inbound flush mode. We check our internal state to see if we're in the HEADERS_AND_DOWNLOAD state.

The call to *ProcessHeaders* gets the header contents table and restricts it to rows whose PR_MSG_STATUS columns have the MSGSTATUS_REMOTE-_DOWNLOAD or MSGSTATUS_REMOTE_DELETE (or both) bits set. These are the messages the user marked to *move* from the mailbox to the local machine (MSGSTATUS_REMOTE_DOWNLOAD ¦ MSGSTATUS_REMOTE_DELETE), to *copy* to the local machine (MSGSTATUS_REMOTE_DOWNLOAD), or to *delete* from the mailbox (MSGSTATUS_REMOTE_DELETE).

ProcessHeaders constructs a linked list in which each node contains the message's ID number on the server and a command that tells WINDS whether to move, copy, or delete the message. We call this list the TO-DO list. We connect to the server and ask it to create a named pipe for the download stream. Data, server commands, and control information are passed over the pipe. The server creates the pipe and passes us back its name in an RPC. We open the pipe, walk the TO-DO list, get the message ID and the requested action from each node, and send a command over the pipe to the server. The server examines the command and the message ID and sends an acknowledgment (ACK) if it can service the request. If the server can't service the request or we encounter an error, we go to the next message in the list. If the command was to delete the message, we assume the ACK from the server means that the message was successfully deleted. If the command was to download the message, the ACK means that the server will start streaming the message's data over the pipe. We read the data from the pipe into a temporary file we create on the local machine to hold the incoming message.

After successfully downloading a message, we remove its node from the TO-DO list and insert it in the DONE list. (We'll use the DONE list later to control the inbound flush in *StartMessage.*) Note that deleted messages aren't inserted in the DONE list. We also advertise our progress by updating the PR_REMOTE_PROGRESS property in the status table with the percent completion of the total download. Finally, we update the *ITableData* backing the header contents table to reflect the new contents of the remote mailbox. This means that if a message was deleted or moved from the mailbox, we delete the corresponding row from the *ITableData* table, causing any open views (the contents table, for example) to be notified.

We then call *SpoolerNotify(NOTIFY_SENTDEFERRED, ...)* to start the outbound message pump and *DownloadMessageHeaders* to update the local header file that backs the header *ITableData*. *DownloadMessageHeaders* uses the same scheme for communicating with the server as the message download logic does. It makes an RPC to the server asking for the name of a pipe. The server returns the name, both the server and XPWDSR open the pipe, the server streams the header data over the pipe, and XPWDSR reads the stream into a local file (more on this subject later). Finally, we transition out of the HEADERS_AND_DOWNLOAD state to the PENDING_RETURN_CODE state and update the status row.

PENDING_RETURN_CODE means that we're in inbound and outbound flush mode and are being called in the *SubmitMessage* or *StartMessage* loops. In the PENDING_RETURN_CODE state, we transfer the contents of the temporary files into the user's default store provider (inbound) and deliver any deferred messages.

You probably noticed that we frequently checked a member variable called *m_fCancelPending* during *FlushQueues*. We do this to check whether the processing of the header cache has been canceled by the client application in a call to *ValidateState* with ABORT_XP_HEADER_OPERATION. If *m_fCancel-Pending* is *TRUE*, we don't proceed to the next step. You might wonder whether the call to *ValidateState* can occur on a different thread than the one that called *FlushQueues*. The answer is that MAPI reserves the right to call *ValidateState* from multiple threads, so the value of *m_fCancelPending* could conceivably change before the *FlushQueues* method returns.[5] The following code sets the flag:

---

5. Notice that we don't bother protecting *m_fCancelPending* with a critical section because it's read-only in *FlushQueues*—the only consequence of a race condition on this variable would be that a canceled message might slip through and be delivered. ABORT_XP_HEADER_OPERATION doesn't give the caller the ability to abort the operation in real time, only to end the operation as soon as possible.

```
STDMETHODIMP CXPMAPIStatus::ValidateState(ULONG ulUIParam, ULONG ulFlags)
{
    HRESULT hResult = S_OK;
    ⋮
    if (ulFlags & ABORT_XP_HEADER_OPERATION)
    {
        // If we are called to cancel an operation and can't cancel, we
        // will set a flag so when current operation finishes, we
        // won't continue.
        if (HEADERS_AND_DOWNLOAD == m_pLogon -> GetTransportState())
        {
            m_pLogon -> m_fCancelPending = TRUE;
            return MAPI_E_BUSY;
        }
        // The cancel occurred while we were flushing the inbound queue.
        // We can cancel this by telling the spooler to stop flushing us.
        // Note that at this point ALL the messages have been downloaded
        // to temporary files and are simply waiting to be placed in the
        // default Inbox.
        if (DOWNLOADING_MESSAGES & m_pLogon -> GetTransportStatusCode())
        {
            // Tell the spooler to take us off from inbound flush.
            m_pLogon -> RemoveStatusBits(DOWNLOADING_MESSAGES);

            // The transport is now off line.
            m_pLogon -> AddStatusBits(STATUS_OFFLINE);
            // Set PR_REMOTE_VALIDATE_OK to TRUE.
            m_pLogon -> UpdateStatus(TRUE, TRUE);
            m_pLogon -> SetTransportState(WAITING); // The transport is
                                                    // now IDLE.
        }
        return S_OK;
    }
    ⋮
}
```

C H A P T E R   N I N E

Developing Address Book Providers

Address book providers manipulate databases of message recipients for the purpose of adding address information to message envelopes. A client views the recipient database as a hierarchy of containers, subcontainers, and recipients, even though the data might or might not be represented that way internally. You can arrange the container hierarchy in any way that is convenient for your implementation and makes sense for your specific application. Some possibilities include grouping recipients according to the following criteria:

- *Address type.*

- *Locality.* For example, by physical site.

- *Routing information.* Recipients on different subnets or domains or residing on different servers can be grouped into different containers.

- *Data source.* For example, implementing separate containers for each database backing your address book provider.

- *Department or work group.* For example, accounting in one subcontainer, research and development in another, and so on.

The two implementations we describe in this chapter demonstrate how the container hierarchy can differ depending on the design of the provider and the back-end database it communicates with. The first, ABPAB, is a personal address book provider that provides a single subcontainer for all entries. The second, ABWDS, is a server-based implementation that has separate subcontainers for an enterprisewide "global address list" and for recipients reachable through gateways.

General Requirements

Address book providers are expected to adhere to the requirements MAPI imposes on all providers, namely the following:

- They are implemented in DLLs.
- They must be thread-safe.
- They can return MAPI_E_NO_SUPPORT for unsupported methods.
- They export an *XXXProviderInit* function, *ABProviderInit* in this case.
- They have private profile sections.
- They are configured through a message service's *ServiceEntry* routine.

We cover the implications of these requirements in detail in Chapter 6.

Address book providers also have much in common with message store providers. Like store providers, they can be local like ABPAB or server-based like ABWDS. They can be read/write (like ABPAB) or read-only (like ABWDS). An address book provider database can be viewable by a single user—a personal address book provider, or PAB—or it can be shared by many users. And like all providers, an address book provider must implement a set of prescribed interfaces.

Address book providers also have some special requirements not shared by other providers. The most obvious difference, of course, is that they implement different interfaces. Address book providers are also called by MAPI when MAPI creates the address book supercontainer and when clients access the supercontainer through the *IAddrBook* interface. In addition, a client can use *IAddrBook* to open address book provider interfaces directly.

The supercontainer was designed to give the illusion of a single address book provider regardless of the number of providers in a session. It does this by merging the root containers of each address book provider into a single hierarchy that is uniformly accessible through the *IAddrBook* interface. Maintaining this illusion depends on providing a consistent user interface, regardless of the data source of a particular entry. For this reason, address book providers don't do their own UI but instead provide *display tables* that describe dialog boxes. *IAddrBook* uses these display tables to create the dialog boxes the user sees when *IAddrBook::Details* is called. The use of display tables allows an entry copied from one provider to another to be displayed in the same UI in the destination container as it was in the native address book provider. We'll examine the design implications of these issues later in this chapter.

Address Book Provider Interfaces

Address book providers must implement the following interfaces:

- *IABProvider.* This is used to log on to the provider, initialize it, and return an *IABLogon* object. It also has a method for uninitializing the provider on logoff.

- *IABLogon.* This object is returned after a successful logon. It provides access to address book provider objects and manages data used by them. It also includes some important support functions. A single instance of *IABLogon* exists per logon.

- *IABContainer.* This is the address book provider–specific implementation of *IMAPIContainer.* Address book containers can have children that are containers, distribution lists, or mail users. *IABContainer* provides methods for creating, copying, and deleting entries and for resolving ambiguous names. Address book containers are not addressable entities.

- *IDistList.* Distribution lists are special cases of *IABContainer* objects. *IDistList* has no unique methods. The difference between *IABContainer* and *IDistList* is that a distribution list can contain only distribution lists and mail users, not containers. Hence, distribution lists never have a hierarchy table. Distribution lists are addressable, i.e., you can send a message to a distribution list, but you can't send one to a container.

  Distribution lists can be of two types: those that have email addresses like any recipient and those that don't. A message addressed to the first type of DL will have a single row in its recipient table that represents all the members. The server is responsible for expanding this single address into a list of recipients and distributing the message to each member.

  The second type is known as a personal distribution list, or PDL. A message addressed to a PDL will have a row in its recipient table for each member of the distribution list. In other words, a PDL is expanded locally by the store provider when the message is submitted. Personal distribution lists don't have email addresses.

- *IMailUser.* This interface represents a single, addressable user. *IMailUser* is directly derived from *IMAPIProp* and has no unique methods.

- *IMAPITable.* An address book provider must provide hierarchy and contents tables for its containers.

Notice that because neither the *IDistList* nor *IMailUser* interfaces define any new methods, they are essentially aliases for *IABContainer* and *IMAPIProp*, respectively. So why are they defined? In the first place, the naming convention is self-documenting. It's immediately obvious you're talking about a distribution list—as opposed to a container—if the object is named *IDistList* instead of *IABContainer*. In the second place, having separate interfaces also means that unique GUIDs are defined for each class, which means you can provide completely different implementations of each class if you choose,[1] and of course there's always the possibility that the interfaces might be extended in later versions of the MAPI specification.

But the differences between address book containers and distribution lists turn mostly on how they're used and what properties they're expected to support. We mentioned some of these differences in passing—distribution lists are addressable and don't have hierarchy tables, for example—and we'll have more to say about them when we look at the sample code.

The Provider-to-Database Interface

MAPI terminology is intended to be general enough to avoid connotations of a particular schema. An address book provider entry, for example, is an abstraction of a database record. An entry ID is an abstraction of a database record number, and an entry's properties map (roughly) to a record's fields. The vagueness of these mappings underscores the fact that the provider-to-MAPI interface is explicit, while the provider-to-back-end interface is implementation-defined. Whereas MAPI doesn't specify at all how the provider communicates with the recipient database, the specification does impose certain requirements about how an address book provider should behave, and you'll need to consider these when you design the interface between the provider and the back-end database.

MAPI requires only that the provider supply a hierarchy of containers, DLs, and recipients. Mapping the underlying database schema to this hierarchy is one of the main tasks you undertake when writing an address book provider. In essence, your provider manifests this hierarchy through its hierarchy tables and contents tables, which enumerate each container's children. The following rules apply:

---

1. For ABPAB and ABWDS, the distinction *isn't* important—at least from a class derivation point of view. Of course, it's important to distinguish between objects of one type or the other, but it's not necessary in our implementation to override most of *IABContainer*'s methods for *IDistList* objects. We choose to deal with any differences between the two classes on an *ad hoc* basis, by relying on flags (in the entry ID, for example) to tell them apart.

- The database is represented as a hierarchy, or tree structure.

- There is a single root container; all other entries descend from this entry.

- Entries can be of three distinct types: containers, distribution lists, or mail users.

- The root container's children can only be containers.

- Containers and distribution lists can have any number of children.

- A mail user can only be a child.

- Every entry has at least one parent, possibly more.

Figure 9-1 illustrates these relationships.

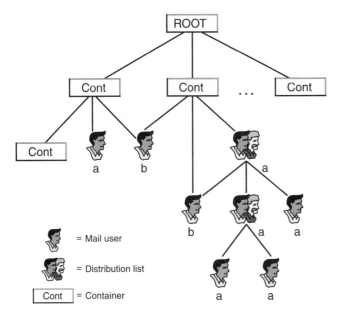

Figure 9-1.
An address book provider's container hierarchy. The root container can have multiple subcontainers but no mail users or distribution lists. All recipients have at least one parent (b) but can have more (a).

So your database must be capable of maintaining these parent-child relationships, and your provider must be capable of querying the database for this information and returning it in the appropriate *IMAPITable* interface.

Writable Address Book Providers

A writable address book provider is a provider in which one or more objects can be modified by a client application. Because permissions are specified on an object-by-object basis, there are varying degrees of "writability" among address book provider objects. For example, an address book provider might allow clients to create, delete, and modify mail users and distribution lists but not to create or delete containers. Other possibilities include the following:

- Existing objects can be modified (i.e., *SetProps* will succeed) but creating or deleting entries in a container is prohibited.

- Entries can be added, deleted, or modified in some containers but not in others.

- Members can be added to or deleted from a distribution list, but the distribution list's properties and/or its members' properties can't be changed.

- Some properties on an object can be modified; others are read-only.

PR_CONTAINER_FLAGS tells a client if entries can be created or deleted within a given container and if subcontainers can exist in it. Keep in mind that how the object was opened (that is, what flags were passed in *OpenEntry*) also determines which permissions are available. And, of course, individual properties have implied permissions that are specified by MAPI and enforced by methods, such as *SaveChanges*, that return MAPI_E_NO_ACCESS when those permissions are violated. So when we talk about writable address book providers, we are really talking about the general case where a client can freely create, delete, and modify containers and their entries. Most real-life implementations will restrict access to some (or all) objects.

Writable address book providers have a few additional requirements that don't apply to their read-only cousins. For example, the underlying database must let your provider create, delete, and modify database records. The ability to create and delete records implies you must be able to update the parent-child relationships of the entries involved. Creating a new mail user, for example, implies making it a child of a container or distribution list entry. Deleting an entry implies disinheriting it from another entry. Notice that an entry is created in, or deleted from, a specific container—not the database at large.

Since a given entry can simultaneously exist as a child of more than one container (or DL), deleting an entry is equivalent to purging its record from the database *only* if the entry has no other parents. If the entry is itself a container (or a DL), it will have children that might or might not be orphaned by the deletion. In this case, the same rule applies: The children can be purged from the database only if they have no other parents.

Whenever an entry is created, deleted, copied, or modified, the contents table of the entry's parent container (or DL) is modified. If an open view of this table exists, a good provider should notify whoever holds the view that the table's underlying data has changed. A client displaying a container's contents should be able to update its UI dynamically when an entry is added, deleted, or modified. Even providers that don't support direct modification of a container's objects should notify on changes to a container's contents—when an administrator adds or deletes entries, for example—so that the client application can display the changes.

Writable address book providers must also support the *SaveChanges* transaction model for mail users and DLs. In other words, you can't commit changes to an existing mail user or DL database record until the *SaveChanges* call. Alternatively, you can write the changes to the database but you must be able to back out of any modifications later if the object is released without *SaveChanges* being called.

Entry IDs

Only your provider has to interpret your entry IDs, so you should choose a representation that makes sense for your implementation. Keep in mind that an entry ID must be unique among all objects returned by all providers. Just the record ID isn't enough because two databases can contain different records whose record numbers are the same. The entry ID must unambiguously differentiate two entries, {n,D,p} and {n',D',p'}, where *n* is the record number, *D* is the database, and *p* is the provider. Notice that ambiguity can exist even within the same provider where entries are backed by more than one database.

The solution is to plop a *MAPIUID* (MUID) into your entry ID structure. The MUID is a GUID you generate that occupies bytes 4 through 20 of the entry ID. If you have entries from more than one database, you can create a separate MUID for each one. ABPAB, for example, generates a MUID whenever the user creates a new database file, so the MUID associates the entry with the database file in which it resides. You register the MUID with MAPI through a call to *SetProviderUID*. Now when a call to *OpenEntry* is made, MAPI can examine the entry ID's MUID field and know which provider's *XXXLogon::OpenEntry* to call. (See Figure 9-2 on the following page.)

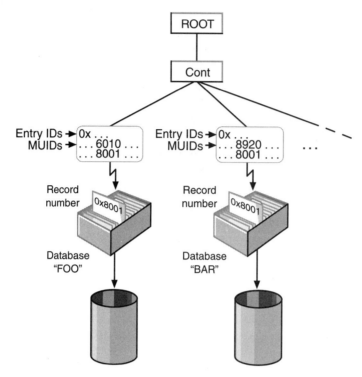

Figure 9-2.
The MUID field of the entry ID guarantees that entry IDs are unique even if the record numbers are not.

The Database Implementation

In general, there are three ways to implement the database back end:

- *Write the database from scratch.* This solution involves the most work but gives you complete control of the design and functionality. It also means you don't have to worry about licensing and redistributing another vendor's product.

- *Use a commercial database back end, such as Microsoft Access, Microsoft FoxPro, or Microsoft SQL Server.*[2] This solution is (potentially) easier, especially if you're already familiar with the product's data manipulation language, but it limits you to whatever functionality the product

---

2. OK, we're biased. Other vendors have similar products, too!

supports.[3] And you might have to pay licensing fees if you intend to redistribute the product to customers.

■ *Write your provider to talk to an existing database.* This might be your only option if you're pulling data out of an existing database—for example, a central corporate database. This is also an attractive solution for adding messaging capability to an application that manipulates an existing database of people.

Case Study of Two
Implementations: ABPAB and ABWDS

The remainder of this chapter is a case study of the two address book providers included in the WINDS messaging system, ABPAB and ABWDS. The complete source code is included on the companion CD-ROM, so the code fragments you see in this chapter might be excerpted from the full source to save space. We'll start by describing those aspects of the implementation that are applicable to all address book providers, then study those features specific to writable providers. We'll use fragments of the code from ABPAB where examples are needed.

Next we'll shift gears and devote the remainder of the chapter to examining a server-based implementation, ABWDS. We'll focus on only those elements of the design that are necessarily different from the local provider, or on those cases where ABWDS implements a given feature differently from ABPAB.

Our principle objective in these samples is to demonstrate how to write MAPI address book providers. Clarity and readability were higher priorities than performance, so in some cases you might be able to save yourself some work or come up with more optimal solutions. Because we distribute the complete source code, we also had to write everything ourselves—the database, for example—something you probably won't have to do.

ABPAB is a personal address book provider, or PAB. It's a local-based, writable address book provider that can contain a user's most frequently accessed recipients. The database is stored in a file on the user's hard disk, and the provider reads and writes this file when it accesses recipient records.

---

3. For example, some commercial RDBMSs limit the size of a field's data or support only predefined data types.

ABWDS is a read-only address book provider in which the database resides on a server, in this case, the WINDS post-office server. This implementation is typical of a post-office address book provider shared by multiple users and contains separate address lists for users reachable through different gateways and a global address list containing both gateway recipients and users with accounts on the WINDS post office.

Common Design Features

Both implementations share many common design features. For example, both have a layer of software between the MAPI-specific code and the database back end. For ABPAB, this layer comprises a set of APIs that are supposed to look like generic commands for manipulating some hypothetical database. For ABWDS, this layer is embodied in an object, *CABServerBackEnd*, which contains methods for accessing the remote database.

CABServerBackEnd methods return MAPI objects and tables that are ready for immediate consumption by the client. *CABServerBackEnd* methods access the database through RPCs, named pipes, and mailslots.

The database commands used by ABPAB hide the details of the underlying database from the implementation. In reality, they map to method calls on a lower-level object that manages the local storage but could just as easily be replaced by commands to a real-life database management system (DBMS). We mention this here because this object, *CDataBase*, is also used by the sample message store provider we discuss in Chapter 10. (See Chapter 7 for a description of *CDataBase*'s design.)

Caching an Object's Properties in Memory

Both implementations also cache an object's properties in memory rather than read them repeatedly from the database. The cache is a separate class that manages an object's properties. An instance of the cache is created and initialized for each newly opened object and saved in a member variable.

Properties are saved in the cache in a linked list of property values. Each node contains an *SPropValue* that has been "flattened," or serialized, so that it can be easily read or written to a stream. There is a separate node for each property on the object. These flattened property nodes are "unflattened" into conventional *SPropValue*s before they are returned to MAPI.

ABPAB, because it's writable, also maintains a "dirty flag" to keep track of whether we must write cached properties back to the database at *SaveChanges* time. This is how we support the transaction model: by flushing the cache to disk during *SaveChanges*. (See Figure 9-10 on page 371 and Figure 9-11 on page 372.)

Table Implementation

ABPAB and ABWDS also use a similar table implementation. Each container object (DLs, too) has member variables that point to one or more *ITableData* interfaces. When the object's hierarchy or contents table is first requested, we create the *ITableData*, populate it with data, and return a view to the caller. We dynamically maintain the *ITableData* by adding, modifying, or deleting rows as required. Subsequent requests for a table interface are honored by returning a new view on the cached *ITableData*. While this scheme is convenient and easy to implement, it requires that we keep the entire data set for the table in memory at one time. You might want to design a more sophisticated caching mechanism if your requirements call for large tables or you're targeting platforms such as Win16 that don't provide gigabytes of virtual address space.

The view we return is a pointer to our *IMAPITable* implementation. This *IMAPITable* is a wrapper which mostly just calls the MAPI implementation's methods. We wrap MAPI's table to take care of the single case of a restriction on PR_ANR for a container's contents table. The semantics of PR_ANR are implementation-defined, so naturally MAPI's table implementation can't handle restrictions on this property.

Logging On to an Address Book Provider

In this section we describe the code that gets called when your provider is configured and logged on to. Before you begin implementing specific methods, you should create and compile a skeleton provider DLL that can be loaded and run in the debugger. Your skeleton provider DLL should define all the required interfaces using stubs for each method. We recommend that your stubs include parameter validation code and a debug trace and that they return MAPI_E_NO_SUPPORT. As you code each interface, you replace the stub method with its actual implementation until you have a complete provider. The fragment below gives an example of how the *IABProvider* interface would be implemented in your skeleton:

```
STDMETHODIMP CABProvider::Logon(LPMAPISUP        lpMAPISup,
                                ULONG            ulUIParam,
                                LPTSTR           lpszProfileName,
                                ULONG            ulFlags,
                                ULONG *          lpulpcbSecurity,
                                LPBYTE *         lppbSecurity,
                                LPMAPIERROR *    lppMAPIError,
                                LPABLOGON *      lppABLogon)
```

(continued)

```
{
    TraceMessage("CABProvider::Logon");

    CheckParameters_IABProvider_Logon(this,
                                      lpMAPISup,
                                      ulUIParam,
                                      lpszProfileName,
                                      ulFlags,
                                      lpulpcbSecurity,
                                      lppbSecurity,
                                      lppMAPIError,
                                      lppABLogon);

    return MAPI_E_NO_SUPPORT;
}

STDMETHODIMP CABProvider::Shutdown(ULONG * pulFlags)
{
    TraceMessage("CABProvider::Shutdown");
    CheckParameters_IABProvider_Shutdown(this, pulFlags);
    return MAPI_E_NO_SUPPORT;
}
⋮
```

Service Configuration

Next you should tackle the provider configuration code. This is the code that gets called from the entry point function of the message service that configures your provider. The entry point function is invoked when a user adds your service to a profile via the Profile Wizard or configures your provider via the Control Panel Mail and Fax applet or the *IMsgServiceAdmin* interface. For ABPAB, the message service and the service provider are one and the same, and the function is called *ServiceEntry*. The entry point function must conform to the MSGSERVICEENTRY prototype, and it must be properly exported, but it can be given any legal C name. The function's name is added to the MAPISVC.INF file in the PR_SERVICE_ENTRY_NAME property, which can be found in the [Services] section for the service that configures your provider.

The *ulContext* flag tells you whether your service entry is being called to create, configure, install, uninstall, or delete your message service. ABPAB doesn't do any special processing for the install, uninstall, and delete cases, so we handle only the cases where *ulContext* is equal to MSG_SERVICE_CREATE or MSG_SERVICE_CONFIGURE.

Our first task is to save the MAPI memory allocation functions to global variables. We then open this provider's private profile section and retrieve any properties written there the last time we were configured. If you need to preserve configuration data so that it persists across sessions, you should save it to the profile section. ABPAB saves the name of the local database file, the service's display name, and a comment, but a server-based provider might want to save the user's password, his account name, the name of the remote server, and information about whether the connection will be over a LAN (continuous) or over a slow link (connect-on-request). The code in *ConfigObj::Init* shows how to open the profile section:

```
STDMETHODIMP ConfigObj::Init(LPSPropTagArray pLogonTags)
{
    LPPROFSECT      pProfSecn      = NULL;
    LPMAPITABLE     pProvTbl       = NULL;
    LPSPropValue    pProps         = NULL;
    SPropTagArray   sptProvider    = { 1, { PR_PROVIDER_UID } };
    LPSRowSet       pRows          = NULL;
    ULONG           ulPropCnt;

    // Get the provider table where the settings are stored.
    if (FAILED(hRes = m_pAdminProv -> GetProviderTable(0, &pProvTbl)))
        return hRes;

    if (FAILED(hRes = HrQueryAllRows(pProvTbl,
                                     &sptProvider,
                                     NULL,
                                     NULL,
                                     1,
                                     &pRows)))
        goto Quit;

    // Error checking omitted
    ⋮
    if (!pRows -> cRows ||
        PR_PROVIDER_UID != pRows -> aRow -> lpProps[0].ulPropTag)
    ⋮

    // If we can't open profile section, bail.
    if (FAILED(hRes = m_pAdminProv ->
                          OpenProfileSection((LPMAPIUID)pRows -> aRow ->
                                                 lpProps -> Value.bin.lpb,
                                             NULL,
                                             MAPI_MODIFY,
                                             &pProfSecn)))
        goto Quit;
```

(continued)

```
                // Get the current config settings.
                if (FAILED(hRes = pProfSecn -> GetProps(pLogonTags,
                                                        0,
                                                        &ulPropCnt,
                                                        &pProps)))
                    goto Quit;

                ⋮
        }
```

Since our message service contains only a single provider, ABPAB, we can assume that the call to *HrQueryAllRows* on the provider table will return our row. If our service configured multiple providers, we would pass a restriction to *HrQueryAllRows* to limit the view to the desired provider's row. The section we want to open is identified by PR_PROVIDER_UID.

If we've never been configured before, the profile section for our provider will be blank, so we use defaults for the required properties. At this point we would like to display a dialog box and let the user overwrite the current configuration. But before we do, we check the *ulFlags* parameter to be sure that UI is allowed. If it is, we display a dialog box and let the user enter data for the configuration properties. You can use standard Windows APIs to bring up your dialog box, or you can do what we did: Create a display table with *BuildDisplay-Table* and call *DoConfigPropsheet* to let MAPI do the UI. Figure 9-3 on page 350 shows the configuration property page displayed by *DoConfigPropsheet*.

DoConfigPropsheet takes pointers to the display table and to an *IMAPIProp* interface as parameters. We describe display tables in detail later in the chapter. For now, suffice it to say that a display table contains a row for each control on the dialog, and each control has a property tag associated with it. *DoConfig-Propsheet* displays a property sheet containing the controls given by the display table rows. It extracts the data from each control and the property tag from the corresponding row and stuffs them into an *SPropValue* array. When the dialog is dismissed, *DoConfigPropsheet* calls the *IMAPIProp* interface's *SetProps* method, passing it the property array. To make this work, we provide an *IMAPIProp* interface (*ConfigObj*, in this case) and then call *GetProps* after the call to extract the properties set by the user:

```
STDMETHODIMP ConfigObj::DoLogonDlg()
{
    LPSPropValue    pTemp = NULL;
    HRESULT         hRes  = S_OK;
    ULONG           ulPropCnt;

    ⋮
```

```
        // Set any existing values.
        if (FAILED(hRes = SetProps(LOGON_NUM_PROPS, m_pProps, NULL)))
            goto Quit;

        // Create the display table for the logon dialog. It's based
        // on dialog resources plus display table structure.
        if (FAILED(hRes = BuildDisplayTable(gAllocBuff,
                                            gAllocMore,
                                            gFreeBuff,
                                            NULL,
                                            m_hInst,
                                            1,
                                            m_pDTPage,
                                            0,
                                            &m_pDispTbl,
                                            &m_pDispTblData)))
            goto Quit;

        // Display the dialog/property sheets.
        if (FAILED(hRes = m_pSupObj -> DoConfigPropsheet((ULONG)m_hWnd,
                                            0,
                                            SZ_PSS_SAMPLE_AB,
                                            m_pDispTbl,
                                            (LPMAPIPROP)this,
                                            0)))
            goto Quit;

        // Get any changes.
        hRes = GetProps((LPSPropTagArray)&sptLogonTags,
                        0,
                        &ulPropCnt,
                        &pTemp);

Quit:
    // Cleanup omitted
    ⋮
}
```

You can also be called to configure your service silently, i.e., without UI. In that case, the SERVICE_UI_ALWAYS ¦ SERVICE_UI_ALLOWED bits will be clear in *ulFlags*, and you will be passed an array of configuration properties in *pCfgProps*. This is how setup programs like the Profile Wizard call your service entry. The wizard, for example, does its own UI to obtain data from the user and then copies the data into an *SPropValue* array that it passes to your service entry. You can define what the configuration properties are (by publishing their property tags in header files, for example), and the application calculates the values and passes them to your provider.

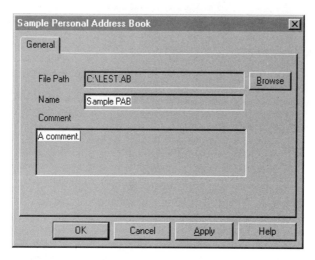

Figure 9-3.
The ABPAB configuration property sheet.

Finally, we try to open the database file, or create it if it doesn't exist. If all goes well, we write the new configuration settings back to the profile section and return:

```
STDMETHODIMP ConfigObj::UpdateProfile()
{
    HRESULT hRes;

    if (FAILED(hRes = m_pProfSecn -> SetProps(LOGON_NUM_PROPS,
                                              m_pProps,
                                              NULL)))
        return hRes;

    return m_pProfSecn -> SaveChanges(0);
}
```

Provider Logon

When a client logs on to a MAPI session, each address book provider's DLL is loaded and its logon code is executed. Each provider executes its initialization code and returns an *IABLogon* object. MAPI constructs a list of these objects for use later when the *IAddrBook* supercontainer is created. From the provider's point of view, logon is a two-step process:

1. The *ABProviderInit* function is called, and it returns an *IABProvider* object.

2. The *IABProvider::Logon* method is called, and an *IABLogon* object is returned.

Step 1: *ABProviderInit*

ABProviderInit is the entry point of an address book DLL. This function must be named *ABProviderInit,* and it must be properly exported. Its main job is to do version checking and return the *IABProvider* object, but since this is the only time your provider is passed the MAPI allocation functions, it's also a convenient time to save them somewhere. (Alternatively, you can call *IMAPISupport-::GetMemAllocRoutines* anytime you're passed an *IMAPISupport* interface, but why make a method call when they're handed to you?) Following is the *ABProviderInit* function:

```
STDINITMETHODIMP ABProviderInit(HINSTANCE        hInst,
                                LPMALLOC         pMalloc,
                                LPALLOCATEBUFFER pAllocBuff,
                                LPALLOCATEMORE   pAllocMore,
                                LPFREEBUFFER     pFreeBuff,
                                ULONG            ulFlags,
                                ULONG            ulMAPIVers,
                                ULONG          * pulABVers,
                                LPABPROVIDER   * ppABProvider)
{
    HRESULT     hRes     = S_OK;
    LPCABProv   pABProv  = NULL;

    *ppABProvider = NULL;

    ⋮

    // This must come before first use of new, since the debug
    // version overloads new with MAPI allocators (for leak detection).
    gAllocBuff = pAllocBuff;
    gAllocMore = pAllocMore;
    gFreeBuff  = pFreeBuff;

    if (ulMAPIVers < CURRENT_SPI_VERSION)
    {
        *pulABVers = CURRENT_SPI_VERSION;
        return MAPI_E_VERSION;
    }
```

(continued)

```
*pulABVers = CURRENT_SPI_VERSION;
pABProv = new CABProvider(hInst);
if (!pABProv)
    hRes = MAPI_E_NOT_ENOUGH_MEMORY;

if (SUCCEEDED(hRes))
{
    pABProv -> AddRef();
    *ppABProvider = (LPABPROVIDER)pABProv;
}

return hRes;
}
```

We first save the MAPI memory management functions in global variables. Since we use these functions to overload the *new* operator, the code to save them must come before the creation of the *CABProvider* object. The version negotiation works like this: If the version of MAPI we compiled with is newer than the version of MAPI installed on this system (that is, we have a larger version number), *we* decide whether we can run with this older version. If we can, we return MAPI's version number. However, our implementation can't, so we return our version number and an error—MAPI_E_VERSION. If we're older or the same age (that is, our version number is less than or equal to MAPI's), we create a *CABProvider* object and return it in **ppABProvider*, along with our version number in **pulABVers*, and let *MAPI* decide if it can call us. If MAPI determines that the versions are incompatible, it immediately releases the *CABProvider* object and we aren't logged on. You should return NULL in **ppABProvider* and an appropriate error code if something fails. This function is called in both the client context and the spooler context.

Step 2: *IABProvider::Logon*

The next step in the logon process is the call to *IABProvider::Logon*. This method's main task is to initialize the provider, register our UID, and return an *IABLogon* object:

```
STDMETHODIMP CABProvider::Logon(LPMAPISUP        lpMAPISup,
                                ULONG            ulUIParam,
                                LPTSTR           lpszProfileName,
                                ULONG            ulFlags,
                                ULONG *          lpulpcbSecurity,
                                LPBYTE *         lppbSecurity,
                                LPMAPIERROR *    lppMAPIError,
                                LPABLOGON *      lppABLogon)
{
    HRESULT      hRes      = S_OK;
    LPCABLogon   pLogonObj = NULL;
```

```
MAPIUID     UID       = {0};
PDATABASE   pDB       = NULL;

    ⋮

*lppABLogon  = NULL;
*lppMAPIError = NULL;

// IAddrBook expects us to AddRef, even though we don't
// keep it around.
lpMAPISup -> AddRef();

// This opens/creates database and root and DIR records.
if (FAILED(hRes = OpenDatabase(ulFlags,
                               (HWND)ulUIParam,
                               UID,
                               lpMAPISup,
                               &pDB)))
    goto Quit;

pLogonObj = new CABLogon(ulFlags,
                         m_hInst,
                         lpMAPISup,
                         UID,
                         pDB);

    ⋮

if (FAILED(hRes = pLogonObj -> Init(&GDLDetailsPage,
                                    &GConfigDetailsPage,
                                    &GUserDetailsPage)))
    goto Quit;


if (FAILED(hRes = lpMAPISup -> SetProviderUID((LPMAPIUID)&UID, 0)))
    goto Quit;

hRes = pLogonObj -> SetStatusRow(TRUE);

    ⋮

}
```

First we attempt to connect to our database, which for a local provider means trying to open the database file. A server-based address book provider would attempt to connect to the server and open the remote database. The details of how we accomplish this are inside the call to *OpenDatabase*. First we open the profile section and get the configuration properties we stored there during the *ServiceEntry* call. If the configuration data is missing or invalid, we check the *ulFlags* parameter for the AB_NO_DIALOG bit. If this bit is set, we fail the call; otherwise, we display a dialog box and try to get the required settings from the user. The only property that is absolutely essential is the name of the database file, so our dialog is essentially a wrapper that tries to open the file and calls *GetOpenFilename* if it can't be found.

Once we have a valid filename, we open the file. If the file doesn't exist, this must be our first logon, so we create it and write the root and DIR container records to it. Our database storage object, *CDataBase*, manages creating UIDs on behalf of our provider and automatically creates a new UID and writes it to the file whenever a new database is created. If the file already exists, opening it returns the UID.

The UID is tied to the database file to distinguish between entries that are created by our provider but that live in different databases. If we used a fixed UID, there would be no way for MAPI to differentiate between entries that live in distinct files. We might even be asked to open an entry that exists on another machine (a recipient in a message, for example) whose user happened to be running our provider. Needless to say, the likelihood of the entry ID referring to the same entry in this scenario is pretty remote. We create and initialize the logon object in separate steps to avoid making calls that can fail inside the constructor. We must register our UID with MAPI by calling *SetProviderUID* to ensure that we receive *OpenEntry* calls only for objects belonging to our provider and living in our database. And finally, if all goes well, we advertise our health by adding a row to the session status table.

Editing the MAPISVC.INF File

The last thing you'll need to do before you can log on to your provider is add the service to a profile. Before you can add the service to a profile, you must add sections to the MAPISVC.INF file for the message service and the provider. You can do this manually, or you can write an INF file and use the MERGEINI utility to copy it into MAPISVC.INF. Figure 9-4 shows ABPAB's INF file:

```
[Services]
SPAB=Sample Personal Address Book

[Help File Mappings]
ABPAB Help=c:\temp\ABPAB.hlp
```

Figure 9-4. *(continued)*
The ABPAB.INF file.

Figure 9-4. *continued*

```
[SPAB]
Providers=S_PAB
PR_SERVICE_DLL_NAME=abpab.dll
PR_SERVICE_SUPPORT_FILES=abpab.dll
PR_SERVICE_DELETE_FILES=abpab.dll
PR_SERVICE_ENTRY_NAME=ServiceEntry
PR_RESOURCE_FLAGS=SERVICE_SINGLE_COPY : SERVICE_NO_PRIMARY_IDENTITY
WIZARD_ENTRY_NAME=WizardEntry

[S_PAB]
PR_RESOURCE_TYPE=MAPI_AB_PROVIDER
PR_PROVIDER_DLL_NAME=abpab.dll
PR_PROVIDER_DISPLAY=Sample Personal Address Book
PR_DISPLAY_NAME=Sample PAB
```

Address Book Provider Properties

Address book providers support configuration properties, container properties, distribution list properties, and mail user properties. Before we continue developing the sample, we'll take a moment to list some of these properties and describe what they do. Figure 9-5 contains ABPAB's configuration properties.

Property Tag	Description
PR_COMMENT	A descriptive string set by the user for informational purposes. This property isn't required and isn't processed in any way.
PR_DISPLAY_NAME	The provider's user-defined name as seen on the configuration property page.
PR_SMP_AB_PATH	A custom property containing the full path to the database file. Server-based address book providers should define custom properties for the server name and user password (if required) and any other properties that you might need to connect to the remote database.

Figure 9-5.
Configuration properties used by ABPAB. These properties are specific to the implementation and are saved in the profile section.

The properties in Figure 9-6 on the following page are required columns in a hierarchy table. These are properties of the containers that are represented by rows in the hierarchy table, not of the container providing the hierarchy table.

Property Tag	Description
PR_CONTAINER_FLAGS	Describes the basic attributes of a container. Setting the AB_RECIPIENTS bit doesn't say that the container has recipients, only that it is capable of having them. Clear this bit if the container can have only subcontainers.
	Set the AB_MODIFIABLE or AB_UNMODIFIABLE bit depending on whether you can create entries in this container.
	Set the AB_SUBCONTAINERS bit if the container in this row will provide a hierarchy table.
PR_ENTRYID	The entry ID of the container in this row.
PR_OBJECT_TYPE	Set to MAPI_ABCONT.
PR_DISPLAY_TYPE	This property lets the UI code know what type of icon to use to represent the container in this row. Possible values for address book providers are DT_MODIFIABLE, DT_GLOBAL, DT_LOCAL, DT_WAN, DT_NOT_SPECIFIC. ABPAB sets this property to DT_MODIFIABLE because it's a writable container.
PR_DEPTH	This property represents the level of nesting of the container in this row with respect to the container providing this hierarchy table.
	Immediate children are at depth 0, grandchildren are at depth 1, great-grandchildren are at depth 2, and so on. This property is used to construct tree-views of the hierarchy.
PR_DISPLAY_NAME	The name of the container represented by this row.
PR_DETAILS_TABLE	This property is of type PT_OBJECT and represents a *display table* that is used by MAPI to create a dialog box showing properties of an address book provider entry. These properties are called the entry's *details,* and the dialog box is called the *details page.* (We'll see how display tables are created later in the chapter.)
PR_CONTAINER_CONTENTS	*OpenProperty* on this property returns the container's contents table.

Figure 9-6.

Required columns in a hierarchy table.

Figure 9-7 lists some properties that might or might not be columns in a hierarchy table. The last three, PR_DEF_CREATE_MAILUSER, PR_DEF-_CREATE_DL, and PR_CREATE_TEMPLATES, are applicable only to writable address book providers such as ABPAB.

Property Tag	Description
PR_AB_PROVIDER_ID	The MUID of the provider that this container belongs to. It's the same value passed to *SetProviderUID*.
PR_DEF_CREATE_MAILUSER	The entry ID of the default template used to create mail user entries in a writable address book provider. The value in this column can be passed to *IAddrBook::NewEntry* or *IABContainer::CreateEntry*.
PR_DEF_CREATE_DL	The entry ID of the default template used to create distribution list entries in a writable address book provider. The value in this column can be passed to *IAddrBook::NewEntry* or *IABContainer::CreateEntry*.
PR_CREATE_TEMPLATES	A table of one-off template entry IDs used for creating different entries in a writable address book provider. You will normally have a row in this table for each type of entry that can be created in your database. For example, if your database can contain X.400, FAX, SMTP, and CompuServe recipients, you'd probably want to supply six rows: one for a default mail user, one for a default distribution list, and one each for X.400, FAX, SMTP, and CompuServe entries. The value in this column can be passed to *IAddrBook::NewEntry* or *IABContainer::CreateEntry*. Your address book provider can know what type of entry is being created by examining this value.

Figure 9-7.
Optional hierarchy table properties.

Common recipient properties are listed in Figure 9-8 on the following page. Most of these properties are found on both mail users and distribution lists and can be columns in a container's contents table.

Common Recipient Properties
(Mail Users and Distribution Lists)

Property Tag	Description
PR_ENTRYID	A required property for all entries. Both ABPAB and ABWDS use long-term entry IDs exclusively.
PR_OBJECT_TYPE	The value is either MAPI_MAILUSER or MAPI-_DISTLIST, as appropriate. Required.
PR_DISPLAY_TYPE	The value can be DT_MAILUSER, DT_DISTLIST, or DT_PRIVATE_DISTLIST. DT_DISTLIST is for server-based distribution lists that have an account or mailbox on the server. DT_PRIVATE_DISTLIST is for personal distribution lists that are created and managed locally by a personal address book provider. (We'll discuss the differences later in this chapter.)
PR_EMAIL_ADDRESS	A string representation of the entry's email address, e.g., *brownie@joyspring.com*. This is a required property for mail users and server-based distribution lists, although personal distribution lists (PDLs) don't have email addresses.
PR_SEARCH_KEY	A normalized version of the concatenation of the entry's address type, a colon, and the email address, e.g., *SMTP:MILESD@ESP.COM*. Normalizing the string means stripping leading and trailing white space and converting to uppercase. This is a required property for mail users and server-based distribution lists. Although this property isn't relevant to personal distribution lists, ABPAB sets it to a PDL's entry ID to simplify processing.
PR_ADDRTYPE	Describes the messaging system on which the recipient resides: EX for Exchange recipients, FAX for fax recipients, SMTP, and so on. Possible values are published by Microsoft. Personal distribution lists have an address type of *MAPIPDL*. This is a required property.
PR_DETAILS_TABLE	A display table obtainable from *OpenProperty* for this entry's details page.

Figure 9-8.   *(continued)*

Properties of mail users, distribution lists, and personal distribution lists.

Figure 9-8. *continued*

Property Tag	Description
PR_TRANSMITTABLE-_DISPLAY_NAME	A string containing the recipient's display name that is seen on messages. Usually this property is the same as PR_DISPLAY_NAME, but it can be different if you want the entry to have one name in the address book and another in the outside world. For example, the display name for your significant other might be "Ducky Face" in your PAB, but he or she might be slightly embarrassed to see mail circulating with the To line containing "Ducky Face."
PR_SEND_RICH_INFO	A Boolean property that indicates whether the recipient's email system can support formatted text (RTF). This property isn't required, but including it makes message submission more efficient.
PR_7BIT_DISPLAY_NAME	The entry's display name represented by a string comprised only of low-value ASCII characters (i.e., those whose ASCII value is less than 128). This property is provided for compatibility with older email systems and isn't required, although including it will make message submission more efficient.

Returning the Root Hierarchy

At this point, your address book provider can be configured and logged on to, but that's about all. It's time to add some code to the implementation that lets it do something useful, like display its root hierarchy. Before we get to the implementation details, though, we need to talk about the *IAddrBook* supercontainer and our database implementation.

Database Primitives

We didn't have the luxury of using an existing database for our back end. To make our design more modular and to decouple the data storage mechanism from the provider code, we wrote a set of APIs that the provider calls to access the underlying database object, *CDataBase*. The motivation was to provide a layer between our database implementation and the MAPI-specific code. This layer translates the data representation used by the back end, which in our case is based on OLE streams, into a form usable by the provider, which is based on linked lists of MAPI properties.

These APIs include some common database operations that might be found in a hypothetical database system. Although the names might sound familiar, the semantics of each function don't necessarily match similarly named commands in any existing data manipulation language. In other words, any resemblance to real RDBMS commands, living or dead, is purely coincidental. These primitives are called *Open*, *Fetch*, *Update*, *Close*, *DeleteRec*, and *InsertRec*.

The first of these APIs is the *Open* command:

```
STDMETHODIMP Open(CDataBase      * pDB,
                  ULONG            ulFlags,
                  const ABPAB_ID & ID,
                  RECORD_NUMBER  & RecNum);
```

This function opens a database record and makes it available for reading and writing. *Open* takes a pointer to the database back-end object, *CDataBase*; some flags that specify the mode in which to open the record (CREATE_IF_NOT_EXIST or OPEN_ONLY); and the record's ID number as input parameters. It returns an initialized *RECORD_NUMBER* structure. *RECORD_NUMBER* is an opaque data structure that contains the entry's record ID and an array of pointers to *IStream* interfaces. *Open* creates *IStream* objects for each valid field of the record and saves pointers to them in *RECORD_NUMBER*'s *IStream* pointer array. The other database APIs are passed an open *RECORD_NUMBER* and can use the pointer array to read and write the record's fields by accessing the open *IStream* objects. Notice that not all fields are applicable to all records. A mail user, unlike a container or DL, can't have children, for example, so opening a mail user's record returns a NULL pointer in the "children" stream (RECFLD_CHILDREN). Of course, all of this happens internally and is hidden from the caller.

Fetch retrieves a given field's data and returns it in a list; the type of list depends on the field being returned. To retrieve an entry's properties, for example, you'd call *Fetch* on the RECFLD_PROPS field and get back a pointer to a *CFlatPropList*:

```
STDMETHODIMP Fetch(RECORD_NUMBER & RecNum,
                   FIELD             Field,
                   CFlatPropList * pFlatProps);
```

The first parameter is a *RECORD_NUMBER* structure previously opened by a call to *Open*. The *Field* parameter specifies the field whose data we want (it's actually an index into the array of *IStream*s in *RECORD_NUMBER*) and can be one of RECFLD_PROPERTIES, RECFLD_CHILDREN, RECFLD_PARENTS, or RECFLD_TABLEROWS. The third parameter is a pointer to either a *CFlatPropList* (if properties are requested), a *CList<ABPAB_ID>* (if either parents or children are requested), or an *SRowSet* (if the request is for a foreign entry's details table—more on this later). *Fetch* is overloaded to accommodate these different list types. It is an error to call *Fetch* on a field that doesn't exist[4] for the given record; fetching RECFLD_CHILDREN for a mail user, for example, is illegal.

There are matching *Update* commands for every *Fetch* overload, and their parameter lists are identical. Where *Fetch* reads a record's fields, *Update* writes them. Internally, *Update* walks the list passed in its third parameter and writes each node in that list to the appropriate stream. It is an error to call *Update* on a field that doesn't exist for the given record.

```
STDMETHODIMP Update(RECORD_NUMBER & RecNum,
                    FIELD             Field,
                    CFlatPropList * pFlatProps);
```

The last three commands are pretty straightforward:

```
STDMETHODIMP Close(RECORD_NUMBER & RecNum);
STDMETHODIMP DeleteRec(PDATABASE pDB, RECORD_NUMBER & RecNum);
STDMETHODIMP InsertRec(PDATABASE        pDB,
                       RECORD_NUMBER  & rnDest,
                       RECORD_NUMBER  & rnSrc);
```

Close closes an open record and releases all the resources acquired in opening it—specifically, the record's streams. It's not an error to close an already closed record, i.e., to make two calls to *Close* without an intervening call to *Open*. *Close* releases the record's non-NULL stream pointers and resets them to NULL or ignores them if they are already NULL. *DeleteRec* irrevocably purges a record from the database, and *InsertRec* makes *rnSrc* a child of *rnDest*.

---

4. Just to be clear, we mean "it can't possibly exist" because of the intrinsic properties of the object that the record represents. We *don't* mean that the field is empty of data, i.e., that it hasn't been updated yet.

IABLogon::OpenEntry

Now we can begin to look at how our *OpenEntry* implementation is called in the context of the *IAddrBook* supercontainer. We stress again that this is only one of many possible implementations: You must decide what is and isn't applicable to your requirements. In any case, the sequence of events will remain the same regardless of how you choose to implement your address book provider.

MAPI creates the address book supercontainer the first time a client calls an *IAddrBook* method that needs to access an installed address book provider. We mentioned earlier that *IAddrBook* maintains a list of logon objects belonging to each logged-on provider. When the supercontainer is created, MAPI walks this list and calls each provider's *IABLogon::OpenEntry* method on the provider's root container and gets the provider's root hierarchy table. The subcontainers found in each hierarchy table are merged into the supercontainer's hierarchy to create the illusion of a unified address book provider. Figure 9-9 illustrates how the supercontainer hierarchy might look:

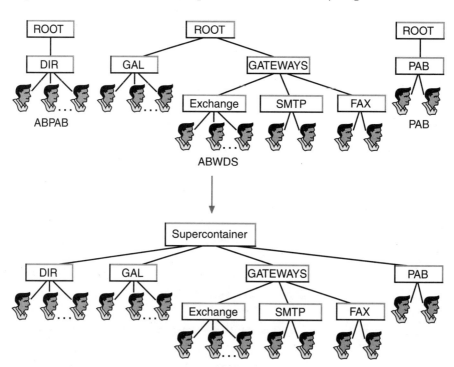

Figure 9-9.
Each provider's root hierarchy becomes a subtree of the supercontainer.

The provider sees the creation of the supercontainer as two calls, first to *OpenEntry*:

```
pMyLogonObj -> OpenEntry(0, NULL, …, &pRoot);
```

and then to

```
pRoot -> GetHierarchyTable(…);
```

Passing a NULL argument for an entry ID (the second parameter of *OpenEntry*) is a MAPI convention for requesting the object's root container. *OpenEntry* creates a *CABContainer* object for the root container the first time it's called or returns a pointer to a cached object in *pRoot* if ROOT has already been created. We cache the ROOT and DIR containers only; all other entries are created on the fly:

```
STDMETHODIMP CABLogon::OpenEntry(ULONG          cbEntryID,
                                 LPENTRYID      pEntryID,
                                 LPCIID         pInterface,
                                 ULONG          ulFlags,
                                 ULONG    *     pulObjType,
                                 LPUNKNOWN *    ppUnk)
{
    HRESULT         hRes      = S_OK;
    PABPAB_EID      pEID      = (PABPAB_EID)pEntryID;
    ULONG           ulEntryType;

    CheckParameters_IABLogon_OpenEntry(this,
                                       cbEntryID,
                                       pEntryID,
                                       pInterface,
                                       ulFlags,
                                       pulObjType,
                                       ppUnk);

    if (NULL                 != pInterface             &&
        IID_IMAPIContainer   != (REFIID)*pInterface &&
        IID_IABContainer     != (REFIID)*pInterface &&
        IID_IDistList        != (REFIID)*pInterface &&
        IID_IMailUser        != (REFIID)*pInterface &&
        IID_IMAPIProp        != (REFIID)*pInterface)
        return MAPI_E_INTERFACE_NOT_SUPPORTED;

    // Validate that the EID is one of ours.
    // If it's NULL, *pulObjType - MAPI_ABCONT.
    ulEntryType = CheckEID(cbEntryID, pEntryID);
    EnterCriticalSection(&m_cs);
```

(continued)

```
            switch (ulEntryType)
            {
                case PSS_ABCONT:
                    if (!pEID || ROOT_ID_NUM == pEID -> ID.Num)
                    {
                        if (m_pRootCont)
                        {
                            m_pRootCont -> AddRef();
                            *ppUnk = (LPUNKNOWN)(LPCABCont)m_pRootCont;
                            *pulObjType = MAPI_ABCONT;
                        }
                        else
                            M_FAIL(hRes = OpenRoot(pulObjType, ppUnk));
                        break;
                    }

                        ⋮


                default:
                    M_FAIL(hRes = MAPI_E_INVALID_ENTRYID);
            }

        LeaveCriticalSection(&m_cs);

            ⋮

        return hRes;
    }
```

We've stripped out everything that doesn't relate to the root container from the preceding *OpenEntry* code fragment. The first thing we do is call the MAPI-defined parameter validation macro *CheckParameters_IABLogon_OpenEntry.*

If the parameter validation succeeds, we then check what interface we're being asked to supply. We fail a request for any interface that doesn't apply to an address book provider entry; a request for an *IMAPITable* or *IMAPIFolder* interface, for example, should raise a red flag that says, "the caller is confused." Your provider should be robust enough to handle being called by misbehaving clients, so it's important to provide ample error checking in each method. In this particular instance we're being called by MAPI, but we shall see other situations where the client calls directly into your provider, and in those cases, it's wise to heed Murphy's Law and cover any reasonable contingency. In the interest of saving paper, we won't show the parameter validation and error-checking code in subsequent code fragments given in this chapter, but you should make it a practice to use *at least* the MAPI-defined *Validate_XXX* or *CheckParameters-_XXX* macros for every interface method.

The call to *OpenRoot* handles the details of creating the new *CABContainer*:

```
STDMETHODIMP CABLogon::OpenRoot(ULONG       *  pulObjType,
                                LPUNKNOWN  *  ppUnk)

{
    HRESULT         hRes  = S_OK;
    PABPAB_EID      pEID  = NULL;
    LPCABCont       pCont = NULL;
    DECLARE_REC_NUM(RecNum);

    if (M_FAIL(hRes = NewEID(0,
                             ROOT_ID_NUM,
                             MAPI_ABCONT,
                             NULL,
                             &pEID)))
        goto Quit;

    pCont = new CABContainer(this, NULL, pEID, 0);

    if (!pCont)
    {
        hRes = MAPI_E_NOT_ENOUGH_MEMORY;
        goto Quit;
    }

    if (FAILED(hRes = pCont -> Init()))
        goto Quit;

    if (FAILED(hRes = Open(m_pDB,
                           OPEN_ONLY,
                           pEID -> ID,
                           RecNum)))
        goto Quit;

    if (FAILED(hRes = pCont -> m_pPropCache -> Load(RecNum)))
        goto Quit;

Quit:
    Close(RecNum);
    gFreeBuff(pEID);

    if (FAILED(hRes))
    {
        delete pCont;
        return hRes;
    }
```

(continued)

```
    // Once for us
    m_pRootCont = pCont;
    m_pRootCont -> AddRef();

    *pulObjType = MAPI_ABCONT;
    *ppUnk = (LPUNKNOWN)pCont;
    return hRes;
}
```

NewEID creates our implementation-defined entry ID, given a record number and the type of object. A *CABContainer* object is constructed and its database record is opened. Next we initialize ROOT's internal property cache by calling *pCont -> m_pPropCache -> Load. Load* simply calls *Fetch(..., RECFLD-_PROPERTIES, ...)* to initialize the cache. We call *AddRef* twice on the new container object—once for the caller in *IABContainer::Init* and once in *OpenRoot* for the copy we cache in *m_pRootCont*. Finally, we clean up and return the new container object.

We get called next at ROOT's *GetHierarchyTable*:

```
STDMETHODIMP CABContainer::GetHierarchyTable(ULONG        ulFlags,
                                             LPMAPITABLE * ppTable)
{

    HRESULT        hRes  = S_OK;
    LPMAPITABLE    pTable = NULL;

    ⋮

    *ppTable = NULL;

    if (ROOT_ID_NUM != m_MyEID.ID.Num)
        return MAPI_E_NO_SUPPORT;

    EnterCriticalSection(&m_cs);

    if (m_pHierTblData)
    {
        if (FAILED(hRes = HrGetView(m_pHierTblData,
                              NULL,
                              NULL,
                              0,
                              &pTable)))
            goto Quit;
    }
    else
        if (FAILED(hRes = CreateRootHTbl(&pTable)))
            goto Quit;
```

```
    *ppTable = pTable;

Quit:
    LeaveCriticalSection(&m_cs);

    if (FAILED(hRes))
        if (pTable)
            pTable -> Release();

    return hRes;

}
```

The *ITableData* backing the table is cached in the *CABContainer::m_pHier-TblData* member, which is initialized to NULL when the container is created. The first call to *GetHierarchyTable* causes the *ITableData* to be created, filled with data, and then cached. Subsequent calls to *GetHierarchyTable* just return a view of the cached data. Notice that we cache the *ITableData* but always return a new view. This is the required behavior of *GetHierarchyTable* and *GetContentsTable*: The view returned by each call is a separate, independent interface. Suppose a client calls *GetXXXTable* twice in succession and is returned two *IMAPITable* pointers, then calls *SetColumns* through the first pointer and *QueryRows* through the second pointer. The call to *QueryRows* (on the second pointer) will return rows containing the default column set. A subsequent call to *QueryRows* through the first pointer will return rows containing the caller-defined column set. If your provider returns the same pointer for each view, changes made in one instance are reflected in *all* instances.

CreateRootHTbl handles the task of creating and initializing the *ITableData* that backs the table. It does so by opening each child container's database record, querying the database for certain properties of the child, and adding these properties to the child's row in the underlying *ITableData*. The requested properties comprise the default column set of the hierarchy table:

```
STDMETHODIMP CABContainer::CreateRootHTbl(LPMAPITABLE *ppHTbl)
{

    LPMAPITABLE    pHTbl      = NULL;
    LPTABLEDATA    pTblData   = NULL;
    HRESULT        hRes       = S_OK;
    LPSPropValue   pProps     = NULL;
    ABPAB_ID       ID         = {DIR_ID_NUM, MAPI_ABCONT};
    ULONG          i;
    SRow           sr;
```

```
CFlatPropList fplDirProps;
DECLARE_REC_NUM(RecNum);

if (FAILED(hRes = gAllocBuff(sptHierTbl.cValues * sizeof(SPropValue),
                            (LPVOID *)&pProps)))
    goto Quit;

// ROOT has a single container, DIR. Open DIR's record.
if (FAILED(hRes = Open(m_pLogon -> m_pDB,
                       OPEN_ONLY,
                       ID,
                       RecNum)))
    goto Quit;

// Get DIR's properties.
if (FAILED(hRes = Fetch(RecNum, fldPROPS, &fplDirProps)))
    goto Quit;

for (i = 0; i < sptHierTbl.cValues; i++)
{
    PFlatPropNode    pFlatPropNode = NULL;

    pFlatPropNode = fplDirProps.Find(sptHierTbl.aulPropTag[i]);

    if (pFlatPropNode)
    {
        hRes = UnFlatten(pFlatPropNode,
                         pProps,
                         pProps[i]);
    }
    else
        hRes = MAPI_E_NOT_FOUND;

    if (hRes)
        hRes = HrPropNotFound(pProps[i], sptHierTbl.aulPropTag[i]);
}

// Create a table.
if (FAILED(hRes = CreateTable(&IID_IMAPITableData,
                             gAllocBuff,
                             gAllocMore,
                             gFreeBuff,
                             NULL,
                             TBLTYPE_DYNAMIC,
                             PR_INSTANCE_KEY,
                             (LPSPropTagArray)&sptHierTbl,
                             &pTblData)))
    goto Quit;
```

```
        sr.cValues = NUM_HTBL_PROPS;
        sr.lpProps = pProps;

        // Populate the table with DIR's properties: voila, an HTbl.
        if (FAILED(hRes = pTblData -> HrModifyRow(&sr)))
            goto Quit;

        // We can return a view if asked to.
        if (ppHTbl)
            hRes = HrGetView(pTblData, NULL, NULL, 0, &pHTbl);

Quit:
    Close(RecNum);
    gFreeBuff((LPVOID)pProps);

    if (FAILED(hRes))
    {
        if (pTblData)
            pTblData -> Release();

        if (pHTbl)
            pHTbl -> Release();

        return hRes;
    }

    if (ppHTbl)
        *ppHTbl = pHTbl;

    m_pHierTblData = pTblData;

    return hRes;
}
```

Since we support only a single child container, DIR, we do a single call to *Open* on its hard-coded record ID. If we supported the more general case of multiple containers under ROOT, we would have to query the database to find the record IDs of the child containers, open each one, obtain its default column set properties, and add them to the *ITableData*. An implementation supporting the optional CONVENIENT_DEPTH flag in its hierarchy table and having multiple containers would also have to recursively descend the tree of subcontainers to get information on each container in the hierarchy. (Since ABPAB has only a single subcontainer, we ignore this flag.)

The *Fetch* call gets the list of DIR's properties; *Find* walks this list looking for default column set properties, and if found, *UnFlatten* places each one in an *SPropValue* array. The *ITableData* is created and cached in ROOT's *m_pHierTblData* member by a call to *CreateTable*, and a row containing the "unflattened" properties is added via *HrModifyRow*. *CreateRootHTbl* can also return a view if the caller passes a non-NULL argument in **ppHTbl*.

Returning Recipient Entries

At this point we have a provider that can be configured and logged on to and that can return a hierarchy table with a single child container. Next we turn our attention to retrieving and displaying recipients' entries from the address book provider. It's a little awkward to explain how to view entries when we haven't yet explained how to create any entries to view, but we present this material first because its applicable to both writable and read-only implementations. If you're writing a read-only address book provider, we'll assume you've already figured out a method of populating your underlying database. If you're writing a PAB, then you'll have to find a way to put some "debug" entries into your database, or persevere until the next section, where we cover creating entries.

Implementing *IMAPIProp*

Before we begin, we have to take a slight detour here and explain some of the dirty implementation details of our *IMAPIProp* interfaces. Both ABPAB and ABWDS implement a base class that provides the "meat" of the *IMAPIProp* interface. The ABPAB version is called *CBaseProp*; ABWDS's is called *CGenericProp*. These classes implement all of the common code shared by any *IMAPIProp* derivatives—specifically, *IABContainer*, *IMailUser*, and *IDistList*. The semantics of most *IMAPIProp* methods will be identical for all derived classes; *GetProps*, for example, works the same regardless of whether the object is a DL or a mail user, so most of the derived class's methods are stubs that call the base class method. Where the semantics of the call depend on the type of object being referenced—*OpenProperty*, for example—the derived class defines its own method that overrides the base class's implementation.

CPropCache

IMAPIProp objects in both ABWDS and ABPAB store their properties in a member object that implements an internal property cache. Once the cache is loaded, all property manipulations are operations against the cache and occur in memory. Only a call to *SaveChanges* (in ABPAB) flushes the cache to persistent storage.

Both cache implementations are essentially the same; we describe *CPropCache*, which is ABPAB's version, but aside from the identifier names, most everything we say about one cache applies equally to the other. For example, both caches store the properties in a linked list that is a member of the cache object. Each node in this linked list contains a flattened property value, which consists of an *SPropValue* plus a variable-length array of bytes that can contain data referenced through an *SPropValue* pointer:

```
typedef struct _FlatPropValue
{
    ULONG       cbTotal,
                cbData;
    SPropValue  spv;
    BYTE        Data[FPN_BYTES];
} FlatPropValue, *PFlatPropValue;
```

*(SPropValue::Value.bin.lpb) and **(SPropValue::Value.lpszA)* are examples of data that would live in a separate allocation in an ordinary property but reside in the *FlatPropValue::Data* buffer in a flat property. Figure 9-10 shows how a MAPI *SPropValue* looks before and after being flattened.

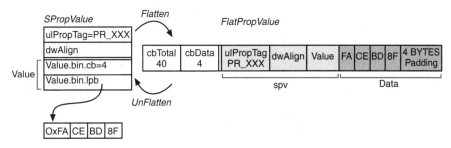

Figure 9-10.
A MAPI SPropValue *and a* FlatPropValue.

We unflatten these *FlatPropValues* only when we need to pass them to MAPI in an *SPropValue* array returned by *GetProps* or when we add rows to *ITableData*, for example. Likewise, any *SPropValues* passed to us *from* MAPI have to be flattened before they can be added to the cache. This is illustrated in Figure 9-11 on the following page.

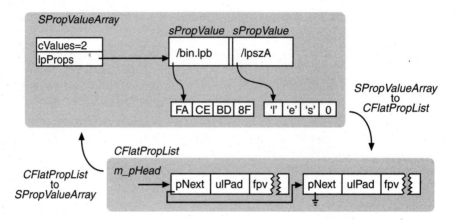

Figure 9-11.
We convert SPropValue*s into* FlatPropValue*s when MAPI passes them to us. We convert* FlatPropValue*s to* SPropValue*s when we must return properties to MAPI.*

We use this scheme to make it easier to read and write properties from and to streams. You *must* serialize the data like this anyway if you write complex data structures to disk or over a named pipe; we have just formalized this process and are using the serialized version for our internal representation.

CPropCache provides methods for inserting, deleting, enumerating, searching, and queuing nodes in the property cache's linked list. We use the property ID as the key, or basis of comparison, in searching and replacing nodes. A few of the more widely used *CPropCache* methods include the following:

- *Insert.* Inserts a node in the list, replacing any existing node with the same property ID. If the property ID doesn't exist in the list, the new node is added in FIFO order.

- *Find. Find* walks the list searching for a target property ID. It returns a pointer to the node, if found, or NULL if it's not found. This method doesn't disturb the list.

- *Scan. Scan* is an enumerator. The first call to *Scan* returns a pointer to the first node in the list, the second call returns the second node, and so on. When the end of the list is reached, *Scan* returns NULL.

- *Delete. Delete* searches for the node containing the target ID and returns a pointer to the node, if found, or NULL if it is not found. The found node is unlinked from the list. The caller is responsible for destroying the node.

Most of the *CBaseProp* methods work by simply calling methods on the cache object. We'll take a moment now to explain each.

GetProps

If the *LPSPropTagArray* parameter is NULL, we call the *GetAllProps* method, which allocates an *SPropValue* array, scans the property cache, unflattens each node, and copies it into a slot of the *SPropValue* array. Otherwise, *GetProps* allocates an *SPropValue* array large enough to hold the set of requested properties, then walks the *SPropTagArray* of requested properties and calls *CPropCache::Find* for each. If the requested property isn't in the cache, we mark that element of the *SPropValue* array as NOT_FOUND. If the property is found in the cache, we unflatten it and copy it into the next slot in the array.

```
STDMETHODIMP CBaseProp::GetProps(LPSPropTagArray lpPropTagArray,
                                 ULONG           ulFlags,
                                 ULONG         * lpcValues,
                                 LPSPropValue  * lppPropArray)
{
    HRESULT         hRes = S_OK;
    PFlatPropNode   pFlatPropNode = NULL;
    LPSPropValue    pProps = NULL;
    ULONG           cValues = 0;
    BOOL            bFound;
    int             i;

    :

    EnterCriticalSection(&m_cs);

    if (!lpPropTagArray)
    {   // Doesn't depend on order like GetPropList so scans once
        hRes = GetAllProps(&cValues, &pProps);
        goto Quit;
    }

    // Allocate the SPropValue array.
    :

    cValues = lpPropTagArray -> cValues;

    for (i = 0; i < (int)cValues; i++)
    {
        if (PR_NULL == lpPropTagArray -> aulPropTag[i])
            pProps[i].ulPropTag = PR_NULL;
```

(continued)

```
            else
            {
                bFound = FALSE;

                // Exclude PR_INSTANCE_KEY from returnable props.
                if (PROP_ID(PR_INSTANCE_KEY) !=
                    PROP_ID(lpPropTagArray -> aulPropTag[i]))
                {
                    pFlatPropNode = m_pPropCache ->
                                    m_pProps      ->
                                    Find(lpPropTagArray -> aulPropTag[i]);

                    if (pFlatPropNode)
                    {
                        if (M_FAIL(UnFlatten(pFlatPropNode,
                                             pProps,
                                             pProps[i])))
                        {
                            hRes = MAPI_E_NOT_ENOUGH_MEMORY;
                            goto Quit;
                        }
                        bFound = TRUE;
                    }

                if (!bFound)
                    hRes = HrPropNotFound(pProps[i],
                                 lpPropTagArray -> aulPropTag[i]);
            }
        }

Quit:
    LeaveCriticalSection(&m_cs);

    if (SUCCEEDED(hRes))
    {
        *lppPropArray = pProps;
        *lpcValues = cValues;
    }
    else
        :
}
```

The semantics of *GetProps* dictate that the array returned in **lppPropArray*
must be in the same order as the *SPropTagArray* passed in *lpPropTagArray*, unless of course *lpPropTagArray* is NULL. The caller might ask us to reserve a slot

374

in the *SPropValue* array for its own use by passing PR_NULL in the *SPropTag-Array*. We ignore any requests for PR_NULL properties. We might have some properties in the cache that are for our internal use, but we don't return them even if requested. PR_INSTANCE_KEY is the only example; we mark requests for this property as NOT_FOUND. Notice that we use the *PROP_ID* macro when comparing property tags. The caller might request a property without knowing its type by passing a property tag composed of the ID and the PT_UNSPECIFIED property type. The implementation must honor these requests and return the property with the type properly specified.

SetProps

For each property passed in *lpPropArray*, we call *HrSetOneProp*, which calls *CPropCache::Insert* to add the property to the cache. *Insert* is overloaded to take an *SPropValue* or a node containing a *FlatPropValue*. If an *SPropValue* is passed to *Insert*, it will call *Flatten* to serialize the *SPropValue* into a *FlatPropNode* that can be inserted in the cache. *HrSetOneProp* must update any properties in the cache that are computed from other properties. PR_SEARCH_KEY is an example—it's derived from PR_ADDRTYPE and PR_EMAIL_ADDRESS. It's an error to set computed properties such as PR_SEARCH_KEY, so *HrSetOneProp* also checks the property tag and returns MAPI_E_COMPUTED if the tag belongs to a computed property.

If the caller passes a non-NULL pointer in *lppProblems*, we allocate an *SPropProblemArray* big enough for the worst-case scenario: We can't set any of the requested properties. *HrSetPropProblem* sets individual elements of this array when a given property can't be set.

```
STDMETHODIMP CBaseProp::SetProps(ULONG                 cValues,
                                 LPSPropValue          lpPropArray,
                                 LPSPropProblemArray * lppProblems)
{
    HRESULT              hRes = S_OK;
    LPSPropProblemArray  pProblems = NULL;
    ULONG                ulBufLen;
    BOOL                 bProblems = FALSE;

    if (lppProblems)    // Caller passes NULL if doesn't care
                        // about problems.
    {
    // Allocate and initialize an SPropProblemArray.
        :
    }
```

(continued)

```
        EnterCriticalSection(&m_cs);

        for (ULONG i = 0; i < cValues; i++)
        {
            if (M_FAIL(hRes = HrSetOneProp(&lpPropArray[i])))
            {
                HrSetPropProblem(pProblems, i, lpPropArray[i].ulPropTag,
                                 hRes);
                bProblems = TRUE;
            }
        }

        if (lppProblems)
        {
            if (bProblems)
                *lppProblems = pProblems;
            else
                gFreeBuff((LPVOID)pProblems);
        }

        m_fDirtyFlags |= PROPS;
        LeaveCriticalSection(&m_cs);
        return S_OK;
}
```

We also set the PROPS bit in the *m_fDirtyFlags* member, which is examined later by *SaveChanges* to determine whether the cache should be flushed to disk.

GetPropList

This method allocates an *SPropTagArray* and then scans the property cache and copies each node's property tag to an element of the array.

```
STDMETHODIMP CBaseProp::GetPropList(ULONG                 ulFlags,
                                    LPSPropTagArray * lppPropTagArray)
{
    HRESULT         hRes         = S_OK;
    ULONG           ulCnt;
    LPSPropTagArray pTags        = NULL;
    PFlatPropNode   pFlatPropNode = NULL;

    ⋮
    ulCnt = m_pPropCache -> m_pProps -> Size();

    if (M_FAIL(hRes = gAllocBuff(CbNewSPropTagArray(ulCnt),
                                 (LPVOID *)&pTags)))
    {
        ⋮
    }
```

```
        pTags -> cValues = ulCnt;
        ulCnt = 0;

        for (pFlatPropNode = m_pPropCache -> m_pProps -> Scan(0);
             pFlatPropNode;
             pFlatPropNode = m_pPropCache -> m_pProps -> Scan())
        {
            // Don't list PR_INSTANCE_KEY.
            if (PROP_ID(PR_INSTANCE_KEY) !=
                PROP_ID(pFlatPropNode -> fpv.spv.ulPropTag))
            {
                pTags -> aulPropTag[ulCnt] =
                    pFlatPropNode -> fpv.spv.ulPropTag;
                ulCnt++;
            }
        }

Quit:
    ⋮
}
```

DeleteProps

We create an *SPropProblemArray* if *lppProblems* is non-NULL. The semantics are the same as for *SetProps*. This method calls *CPropCache::Delete* for each property tag in the *SPropTagArray*, which removes the property from the cache. The *Delete* method on the cache's property list searches the list for a node whose property ID matches the target tag's ID. We ignore the property type since the caller can pass tags of type PT_UNSPECIFIED. We set the PROPS bit in *m_fDirtyFlags* to indicate that the cache has changed and must be flushed to disk at the next *SaveChanges* call.

```
STDMETHODIMP CBaseProp::DeleteProps(LPSPropTagArray      lpPropTagArray,
                                    LPSPropProblemArray * lppProblems)
{
    HRESULT             hRes = S_OK;
    PFlatPropNode       pFlatPropNode = NULL;
    LPSPropProblemArray pProblems = NULL;
    ULONG               ulBufLen,
                        i;
    BOOL                bProblems = FALSE;

    ⋮
```

(continued)

```
        if (lppProblems)   // NULL if caller doesn't care about problems
        {
            // Allocate and initialize an SPropProblemArray.
            ⋮
        }

        EnterCriticalSection(&m_cs);

        for (i = 0; i < lpPropTagArray -> cValues; i++)
        {
            m_pPropCache ->
            m_pProps      -> Delete(lpPropTagArray -> aulPropTag[i],
                                    &pFlatPropNode);
            if (!pFlatPropNode)
               if (pProblems)
               {
                    HrSetPropProblem(pProblems,
                                     i,
                                     lpPropTagArray -> aulPropTag[i],
                                     MAPI_E_NOT_FOUND);
                    bProblems = TRUE;
               }
            delete pFlatPropNode;
        }

        if (lppProblems)
        {
            if (bProblems)
                *lppProblems = pProblems;
            else
                gFreeBuff((LPVOID)pProblems);
        }

        m_fDirtyFlags |= PROPS;
        LeaveCriticalSection(&m_cs);
        return S_OK;
}
```

CopyProps

This method is a wrapper for the MAPI method *IMAPISupport::DoCopyProps,* which makes a sequence of calls on the destination interface to do the copy.

SaveChanges

We'll discuss how this method is implemented when we examine how we support operations on writable address book providers.

OpenProperty

This method is overloaded for DL objects and mail user objects. ABPAB containers and distribution lists support *OpenProperty* on PR_CREATE_TEMPLATES, PR_DETAILS_TABLE, PR_CONTAINER_CONTENTS, and PR_EDIT_BUTTON, while mail user objects support only the PR_DETAILS case.

```
STDMETHODIMP CABContainer::OpenProperty(ULONG         ulPropTag,
                                        LPCIID        piid,
                                        ULONG         ulInterfaceOptions,
                                        ULONG         ulFlags,
                                        LPUNKNOWN * ppUnk)
{
    HRESULT      hRes = S_OK;
    LPMAPITABLE pTbl = NULL;

    ⋮

    *ppUnk = NULL;

    EnterCriticalSection(&m_cs);

    switch (ulPropTag)
    {
        case PR_CREATE_TEMPLATES:
            if (IID_IMAPITable != *piid)
            {
                hRes = MAPI_E_INTERFACE_NOT_SUPPORTED;
                break;
            }

            hRes = m_pLogon -> OpenTemplates(0, &pTbl);
            *ppUnk = (LPUNKNOWN)pTbl;
            break;

        case PR_DETAILS_TABLE:
            // Return details table of directory container or DL.
            if (IID_IMAPITable != *piid)
            {
                hRes = MAPI_E_INTERFACE_NOT_SUPPORTED;
                break;
            }

            if (DIR_ID_NUM == m_MyEID.ID.Num)
                hRes = m_pLogon -> m_pRootDetails ->
                        BuildDisplayTable(&pTbl);
```

(continued)

```
        else
            hRes = m_pLogon -> m_pDLDetails ->
                        BuildDisplayTable(&pTbl);
        *ppUnk = (LPUNKNOWN)pTbl;
        break;

    case PR_CONTAINER_CONTENTS:
        if (IID_IMAPITable != *piid)
        {
            hRes = MAPI_E_INTERFACE_NOT_SUPPORTED;
            break;
        }

        hRes = GetContentsTable(ulInterfaceOptions, &pTbl);
        *ppUnk = (LPUNKNOWN)pTbl;
        break;

    case PR_EDIT_BUTTON:
        {
            CMembersButton * pDLMembersButton =
                new CMembersButton(this);

            if (!pDLMembersButton)
                hRes = MAPI_E_NOT_ENOUGH_MEMORY;
            else
            {
                *ppUnk = (LPUNKNOWN)pDLMembersButton;
                (*ppUnk) -> AddRef();
            }
        }
        break;

    default:
        hRes = MAPI_E_NO_SUPPORT;
        break;
    }

    LeaveCriticalSection(&m_cs);
    return hRes;
}
```

Each case returns a different interface. The PR_CREATE_TEMPLATES case returns a table of one-off template entry IDs that lists the types of entries that can be created in the parent container. Each row gives the name, address type, and entry ID of a one-off template that is subsequently passed to the

IABContainer::CreateEntry call. *OpenProperty* on PR_DETAILS returns a display table for the object's details, whereas PR_CONTAINER_CONTENTS returns the object's contents table. PR_EDIT_BUTTON is an implementation-defined property that is opened when the user clicks a button on the object's details page. We'll have more to say about what each of these calls does later in the chapter.

Derived Classes

We derive four classes from *CBaseProp*: *CMailUser*, *CABContainer*, *CTemplateUser*, and *CTemplateDL*. *CMailUser* defines our implementation of mail user objects, and *CABContainer* defines containers and distribution lists. *CTemplateUser* and *CTemplateDL* are for objects copied from foreign address book providers; we defer discussion of them until we talk about writable address books. Each class overrides the *CBaseProp::OpenProperty* method and provides initialization specific to the type of entry it represents. The following sections provide examples.

CMailUser : public CBaseProp

This is our definition of a mail user object. We initialize a newly created *CMailUser* object with a set of default properties that includes PR_ENTRYID, PR_INSTANCE_KEY, PR_RECORD_KEY, PR_SEARCH_KEY, PR_OBJECT-_TYPE, PR_DISPLAY_TYPE, and PR_MAPPING_SIGNATURE. Some of these properties will be overwritten by actual values when the object is saved. Some properties (PR_INSTANCE_KEY, for example) are provided for the convenience of our implementation even though they have no intrinsic meaning to a mail user entry. We override the *CBaseProp::OpenProperty* method to support opening a single property, PR_DETAILS; all other methods are stubs that call (or *delegate to)* the corresponding *CBaseProp* methods.

CABContainer : public CBaseProp, public : IABContainer

We use the same class definition for distribution lists and containers. Since we produce only two containers, ROOT and DIR, we deal with any differences in initializing each object on an ad hoc basis. All methods are stubs that delegate to the *CBaseProp* base class except *OpenProperty*, which must handle PR_DE-TAILS, PR_CONTAINER_CONTENTS, and PR_CREATE_TEMPLATES.

You might wonder why we define stubs for every method and delegate to the base *CBaseProp* instead of deriving *CBaseProp* from *IMAPIProp* and defining only the overridden methods such as *OpenProperty*. The reason is that COM objects don't really support multiple inheritance. The problem has to do with the way each COM object is declared in the abstract base class's header file. Suppose, for example, that we wanted to declare our *CABContainer* as follows:

```
CBaseProp : public virtual IMAPIProp {…};
CABContainer : public IABContainer, public CBaseProp {…};
```

What we'd get would be a derivation tree that looks like Figure 9-12.

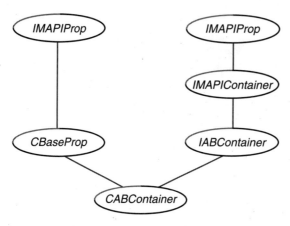

Figure 9-12.
Derivation tree of CABContainer *showing ambiguities.*

What we really want, however, is something more like Figure 9-13.

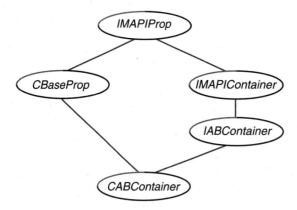

Figure 9-13.
Derivation tree of CABContainer *without ambiguities.*

You can see from derivation tree in Figure 9-12 that there are ambiguities resulting from the fact that *CBaseProp* and *IABContainer* are both derived from *IMAPIProp*. These ambiguities could be eliminated if *IABContainer* were declared in the following way:

```
IMAPIContainer : public virtual IMAPIProp;
IABContainer : public IMAPIContainer;
⋮
```

But the declaration of *IMAPIContainer* doesn't include the *virtual* keyword, so we can have only a single base class derived from *IMAPIProp*.

IABLogon::OpenEntry, Revisited

Now that we've examined the low-level implementation details of our *CBaseProp* class, it's time to conclude our detour and get back to the next order of business: returning the DIR container's contents table. Imagine for a moment that our provider has been loaded and initialized, and the *IAddrBook::Address* method has just been called. A log of the calls to our address book provider would look something like Figure 9-14.

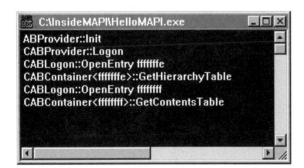

Figure 9-14.
The sequence of calls to the address book provider when a client logs on and calls IAddrBook::Address. *(We assume our DIR container is the default directory.)*

IAddrBook calls *OpenEntry* to obtain our ROOT container, gets our root hierarchy table, creates the supercontainer, opens our DIR container, gets DIR's contents table, and uses it to populate the Address Book dialog box shown in Figure 9-15 on the following page.

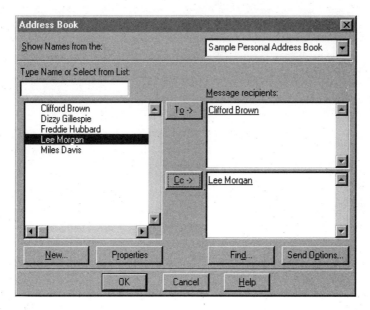

Figure 9-15.
The IAddrBook::Address *dialog box showing entries from our DIR container's contents table.*

To support these calls, we need to add some code to *OpenEntry* and implement *IABContainer::GetContentsTable*.

```
STDMETHODIMP CABLogon::OpenEntry(ULONG          cbEntryID,
                                 LPENTRYID      pEntryID,
                                 LPCIID         pInterface,
                                 ULONG          ulFlags,
                                 ULONG     *    pulObjType,
                                 LPUNKNOWN *    ppUnk)
{
    HRESULT         hRes       = S_OK;
    PABPAB_EID      pEID       = (PABPAB_EID)pEntryID;
    ULONG           ulEntryType;

    ulEntryType = CheckEID(cbEntryID, pEntryID);
    EnterCriticalSection(&m_cs);

    switch (ulEntryType)
    {
        case PSS_ABCONT:
        case PSS_DISTLIST:
        case PSS_ONEOFF_DL:
            if (!pEID || ROOT_ID_NUM == pEID -> ID.Num)
```

```
            {
                 ⋮
            }

            if (DIR_ID_NUM == pEID -> ID.Num)
                if (m_pDirCont)
                {
                    m_pDirCont -> AddRef();
                    *ppUnk = (LPUNKNOWN)(LPCABCont)m_pDirCont;
                    *pulObjType = MAPI_ABCONT;
                    break;
                }
            M_FAIL(hRes = OpenContainer(pEID, pulObjType, ppUnk));
            break;

        ⋮


        default:
            M_FAIL(hRes = MAPI_E_INVALID_ENTRYID);
    }

    LeaveCriticalSection(&m_cs);

    ⋮

    return hRes;
}
```

This time we're called with the entry ID of our DIR container that contains the hard-coded record ID, DIR_ID_NUM. We cache the DIR container's interface pointer when we create it and simply call *AddRef* on it and return it on subsequent requests. *OpenContainer* does the work of creating a DL or container object:

```
STDMETHODIMP CABLogon::OpenContainer(PABPAB_EID   pEID,
                                     ULONG      *  pulObjType,
                                     LPUNKNOWN *  ppUnk)
{
    HRESULT         hRes  = S_OK;
    LPCABCont       pCont = NULL;
    DECLARE_REC_NUM(RecNum);

    *pulObjType = 0;
    *ppUnk      = NULL;
    pCont       = new CABContainer(this, NULL, pEID, 0);
```

(continued)

```
if (!pCont)
    return MAPI_E_NOT_ENOUGH_MEMORY;

if (FAILED(hRes = pCont -> Init()))
    goto Quit;

if (ONEOFF_ENTRY & pEID -> ID.Type)
{
    hRes = pCont -> SetDefaultProps(pEID);
    *ppUnk = pCont;
    *pulObjType = OBJECT_TYPE(pEID -> ID.Type);

    return hRes;
}

if (FAILED(hRes = Open(m_pDB,
                        OPEN_ONLY,
                        pEID -> ID,
                        RecNum)))
    goto Quit;

hRes = pCont -> m_pPropCache -> Load(RecNum);

    ⋮

// Create a connection so this object can listen
// for changes to its children.
if (FAILED(hRes = pCont -> Subscribe()))
{
    Close(RecNum);
    goto Quit;
}

if (DIR_ID_NUM == pEID -> ID.Num)
{
    // Cache DIR container, AddRef for us.
    m_pDirCont = pCont;
    pCont -> AddRef();
}

Close(RecNum);

Quit:
    if (FAILED(hRes))
    {
        if (pCont)
            delete pCont;
        return hRes;
    }
```

```
    *ppUnk = pCont;
    *pulObjType = OBJECT_TYPE(pEID -> ID.Type);


    return hRes;
}
```

We create and initialize the *CABContainer* in separate steps because the initialization code creates an advise sink object, and we don't want to make any calls inside our constructor that can fail. Next we check whether the object we're trying to open is a one-off. Remember that one-offs exist only in memory; they don't have entries in the database, so if the entry ID belongs to a one-off, we set some default properties and we're finished.

Otherwise, we open the database record belonging to the requested entry, retrieve its properties, and load them into the property cache. Notice that for *OpenEntry*, the entry ID must point to a one-off or an existing record in our database. Any other possibility is an error, so if a call to *Open* fails (the record can't be found, for example), we return.

Next we register for notifications of changes to any child of the newly created container. The container's advise sink object found in *m_pAdviseSink* will be called at *OnNotify* if an entry is added, deleted, or modified in this container. This code is used mainly to update the container's contents table when entries are created or deleted. If the object we just created is the DIR container, we call *AddRef* on it and cache its pointer in *m_pDirCont*.

CABContainer::GetContentsTable

```
STDMETHODIMP CABContainer::GetContentsTable(ULONG          ulFlags,
                                            LPMAPITABLE * ppTable)
{

    HRESULT         hRes   = S_OK;
    LPMAPITABLE     pTable = NULL;

    DECLARE_REC_NUM(RecNum);
    SizedSSortOrderSet(1, SortOrder) =
        {1, 0 , 0, {PR_DISPLAY_NAME, TABLE_SORT_ASCEND}};

    :

    *ppTable = NULL;

    EnterCriticalSection(&m_cs);

    if (m_pCntsTblData)
```

(continued)

```
        {
            if (M_FAIL(hRes = HrGetView(m_pCntsTblData, …, &pTable)))
                goto Quit;
        }
        else
        {
            if (FAILED(hRes = Open(m_pLogon -> m_pDB, OPEN_ONLY,
                                    m_MyEID.ID, RecNum)))
            {
                if (MAPI_E_NOT_FOUND == hRes)
                {   // Create an empty table.
                    Close(RecNum);

                    if (M_FAIL(hRes = CreateTable(…)))
                        goto Quit;

                    if (M_FAIL(hRes = HrGetView(m_pCntsTblData, …, &pTable)))
                        goto Quit;
                }
            }
            else
            {   // Create m_pCntsTbl and populate it from DB.
                hRes = CreateCTbl(&pTable, RecNum);
                Close(RecNum);

                if (M_FAIL(hRes))
                    goto Quit;
            }
        }

        if (M_FAIL(hRes = pTable ->
                            SortTable((LPSSortOrderSet)&SortOrder, 0)))
            goto Quit;

        *ppTable = pTable;

Quit:
    LeaveCriticalSection(&m_cs);
    if (FAILED(hRes))
        if (pTable)
            pTable -> Release();

    return hRes;
}
```

GetContentsTable uses the same lazy evaluation scheme as *GetHierarchyTable*: The *ITableData* object backing the contents table is created and cached in the container object the first time *GetContentsTable* is called. If the *ITableData* has been created, we simply return a view to the caller; otherwise, we try to open the container's database record.

If there's no record in the database for this container, *Open* will fail with MAPI_E_NOT_FOUND, which means that the container has just been created but doesn't yet have a contents table. In other words, we're being called here for the first time *ever* for this container. In that case, we create and cache the *ITableData* and return a view of the empty table.

If the *Open* call succeeds, we know there is an existing database record for this container. Since the *ITableData* hasn't been cached yet, we know that we're being called for the first time *in this session* for this container. We call *CreateCTbl* to create the cached *ITableData* and then fetch the list of our children's IDs. We walk the ID list, opening each child and fetching its properties; merge the properties into an *SRow*, and call *HrModifyRow* to add each row to the *ITableData*. Again we should point out that our implementation is illustrative: Walking the list of children, opening each one, and retrieving its properties would be prohibitively expensive for anything but relatively small containers. You might consider caching some of these properties on disk or, better yet, use a true RDBMS back end and let the database do the work. The following code shows the *CreateCTbl* implementation:

```
STDMETHODIMP CABContainer::CreateCTbl(LPMAPITABLE   * ppTable,
                                       RECORD_NUMBER & RecNum)
{
    LPMAPITABLE         pCTbl       = NULL;
    HRESULT             hRes        = S_OK;
    PFlatPropNode       pFlatNode   = NULL;
    CPropCache        * pPropCache  = NULL;
    LPTABLEDATA         pTblData    = NULL;
    SRow                sr;
    ABPAB_ID          * pChildID;
    ABPAB_EID           EIDChild;
    CList<ABPAB_ID>     ChildIDList;
    CFlatPropList       FlatPropList;

    DECLARE_REC_NUM(ChildRecNum);

    if (FAILED(hRes = Fetch(RecNum, fldCHILDREN, &ChildIDList)))
        goto Quit;

    if (FAILED(hRes = CreateTable(…, &pTblData)))
        return hRes;

    // Get each child's row data.
    if (ChildIDList.Size())
```

(continued)

389

```
    {
        for (pChildID = ChildIDList.Scan(0);
             pChildID;
             pChildID = ChildIDList.Scan())
        {
            EIDChild.ID = *pChildID;
            sr.cValues  = NUM_CTBL_COLS;
            sr.lpProps  = NULL;

            if (SUCCEEDED(hRes = Open(…, EIDChild.ID, ChildRecNum)))
            {
                FlatPropList.Destroy();
                hRes = Fetch(ChildRecNum, fldPROPS, &FlatPropList);
                Close(ChildRecNum);

                if (SUCCEEDED(hRes))
                    if (SUCCEEDED(hRes = m_pLogon ->
                                              GetCTblRow(&FlatPropList,
                                                         &sr.lpProps)))
                        hRes = pTblData -> HrModifyRow(&sr);
            }

            gFreeBuff(sr.lpProps);
        }
    }

    // Return a view.
    if (ppTable)
    {
        if (FAILED(hRes = HrGetView(pTblData, NULL, NULL, 0, &pCTbl)))
            goto Quit;
        *ppTable = pCTbl;
    }

    // Cache the underlying data.
    if (m_pCntsTblData)
        m_pCntsTblData -> Release();

    m_pCntsTblData = pTblData;
    return hRes;

Quit:
    if (pTblData)
        pTblData -> Release();

    return hRes;

}
```

Viewing an Entry

So far, we can log on to our provider, get its root hierarchy, open the DIR container, and return the container's contents table. Next we would like to be able to view an entry's *details page,* which is a property sheet that displays some of the entry's properties. Address book providers don't supply the UI for displaying an entry's details: MAPI does, based on information provided by the container supplying the entry. This information is in the form of a MAPI table that, along with a dialog resource you create, specifies what controls will appear on the dialog box, their approximate position on the sheet, and the source of the data used to populate them.

Display Tables

MAPI calls these tables *display tables,* and they are returned when the client (or *IAddrBook*) calls *IMAPIProp::OpenProperty* on PR_DETAILS. Using display tables lets the supercontainer control the appearance of the property pages so that entries from different providers won't look radically different from container to container. We briefly mentioned display tables when we presented our configuration code and discussed the *DoConfigPropSheet* method (on page 348). Use of display tables is optional for provider configuration but is required for PR_DETAILS. In a moment we'll discuss another situation in which the details table is useful.

Display tables don't let you do everything you can with Windows APIs. For example, you *can't* do any of the following:

- Send arbitrary notifications to controls on the property sheet

- Set focus to a control on the property sheet

- Display icons or bitmaps on the property sheet

- Display arbitrary controls (e.g., tree-views) on the property sheet

What you *can* do is the following:

- Put some standard controls on the property sheet, such as the following:
  - ❏ Label
  - ❏ Edit box
  - ❏ List box
  - ❏ Combo box

- ❑ Drop-down list box

- ❑ Check box

- ❑ Group box

- ❑ Button control

- ❑ Tabbed page

- ❑ Radio button

- ❑ Ink-aware edit box

- ❑ Multivalued list box

- ❑ Multivalued drop-down list box

- ▨ Get notified when data is entered in a control on the property sheet

- ▨ Send some basic notifications

- ▨ Populate the controls

- ▨ Link a HLP file to a Help button on the details page

We mentioned earlier that each row in the display table corresponds to a control, and each control has a property tag associated with it. MAPI uses the *GetProps* and *SetProps* methods to pass data to the controls and to extract data from them. For this reason, the interface that returns the display table to MAPI must be one derived from *IMAPIProp*. To populate the controls on the property sheet, MAPI calls *GetProps* on this interface, passing the property tags associated with each control, and the values returned are stuffed into the corresponding control. You can designate whether a control can accept user input by making the control editable when you create the display table. MAPI extracts any user input from each editable control and stuffs the values into an *SPropValue* array, which it passes to *SetProps* when the dialog is dismissed.

Creating a Display Table

There are two ways to create a display table: the hard way and the not-as-hard way. The hard way is to create the table manually and then return a view. For example, you might call *CreateTable* to obtain an *ITableData* interface, then call *ITableData::HrModifyRows* to add rows to the underlying data, and finally call *ITableData::HrGetView* to return the *IMAPITable* interface. This method gives you the most flexibility because the table is created dynamically and the property sheets it describes can be changed at run time. A server-based address book provider might want to use this technique if the property sheets are expected to change periodically—for example, to add a control when a field is added or deleted in the database. The data backing the display table can be maintained on the server and downloaded by the provider whenever the details page is changed.

The second method is more convenient but requires you to recompile your provider if the property sheets change. In this method, you create a dialog in your favorite resource editor, set up some peculiar data structures, and pass them to *BuildDisplayTable*. *BuildDisplayTable* creates the table for you and returns an *IMAPITable* interface that you then pass back in *OpenProperty*. The data structures contain information about the property sheets you want displayed and the controls you want placed on each property sheet. The following code fragment shows how to initialize the data structures required to display the ABPAB distribution list details page:

```
#define ABPAB_HLP "ABPAB Help"

// Display table controls for DistList details page
DTBLLABEL   DLLabel      = {sizeof DTBLLABEL, 0};
DTBLPAGE    DLPage       = {sizeof DTBLPAGE, 0, 0, IDH_CREATE_DL};
DTBLLBX     DLMembers    = {0, PR_NULL, PR_CONTAINER_CONTENTS};
DTBLEDIT    DLName       = {sizeof DTBLEDIT, 0, MAX_PATH,
                            PR_DISPLAY_NAME};
DTBLBUTTON  DLEditButton = {sizeof DTBLBUTTON, 0, PR_EDIT_BUTTON};


DTCTL  GDLControls[] =
    {
        {DTCT_PAGE, 0, NULL, 0, NULL, 0, &DLPage},
        {DTCT_EDIT, DT_EDIT_FLAGS, NULL, 0, "*", IDC_EDIT_NAME, &DLName},
        {DTCT_LBX,  DT_EDIT_FLAGS, NULL, 0, "*", IDC_LIST_MEMBERS,
         &DLMembers},
        {DTCT_LABEL,  0, NULL, 0, NULL, IDC_STATIC1, &DLLabel},
        {DTCT_LABEL,  0, NULL, 0, NULL, IDC_STATIC2, &DLLabel},
        {DTCT_BUTTON, 0, NULL, 0, NULL, IDC_BUTTON_EDIT, &DLEditButton},
    };

DTPAGE  GDLDetailsPage = {6, MAKEINTRESOURCE(IDD_DL_DETAILS), ABPAB_HLP,
                          GDLControls};
```

A call to *BuildDisplayTable(..., (LPDTPAGE)&GDLDetailsPage, ...)* returns an LPMAPITABLE that represents the property sheet shown in Figure 9-16 on the following page.

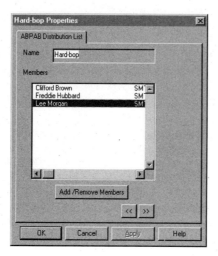

Figure 9-16.
This is what the property sheet based on GDLDetailsPage *looks like.*

You must declare and initialize three sets of data structures to use *BuildDisplayTable*. The first set comprises the *DTBLXXX* structures representing individual controls that are to appear on the property sheet. The second is an array of *DTCTL* structures that is used to create the display table rows. Each *DTCTL* in this array represents a row in the table and specifies the type of control, some flags that control its behavior, the control's ID in the resource script, and a pointer to the *DTBLXXX* structure defining the control. The third structure is the *DTPAGE* structure that includes a count of the number of controls, the dialog's ID in the resource script, the name of an entry in the MAPISVC.INF file that points to a help file, and a pointer to the DTCTL array. The DTCTL structure is declared as follows:

```
typedef struct {
    ULONG           ulCtlType;      // DTCT_LABEL, etc.
    ULONG           ulCtlFlags;     // DT_REQUIRED, etc.
    LPBYTE          lpbNotif;       // Pointer to notification data.
    ULONG           cbNotif;        // Count of bytes of notification data.
    LPTSTR          lpszFilter;     // Character filter for edit/combobox.
    ULONG           ulItemID;       // Used to validate parallel dlg
    union {                         // template entries (ulCtlType
        LPVOID          lpv;        // discriminates). Initialize this to
        LPDTBLLABEL     lplabel;    // avoid warnings.
        LPDTBLEDIT      lpedit;
        LPDTBLLBX       lplbx;
        LPDTBLCOMBOBOX  lpcombobox;
        LPDTBLDDLBX     lpddlbx;
```

```
        LPDTBLCHECKBOX      lpcheckbox;
        LPDTBLGROUPBOX      lpgroupbox;
        LPDTBLBUTTON        lpbutton;
        LPDTBLRADIOBUTTON   lpradiobutton;
        LPDTBLMVLISTBOX     lpmvlbx;
        LPDTBLMVDDLBX       lpmvddlbx;
        LPDTBLPAGE          lppage;
    } ctl;
} DTCTL, FAR *LPDTCTL;
```

The *ulCtlType* field contains a MAPI-defined constant that identifies the type of control: DTCT_EDIT for an edit field, DTCT_LBX for a list box, and so on. Controls that accept user input, such as edit fields, radio buttons, and check boxes, can set bits in the *ulCtlFlags* field to enable the control (DT_EDIT-ABLE), require a value to be entered (DT_REQUIRED), or cause the *SetProps* call as soon as the control loses focus (DT_SET_IMMEDIATE).

Display Table Notifications

You can refresh a control on the page by sending a notification to the display table. You must identify the row whose control you want refreshed. MAPI responds by calling *GetProps* with that control's property tag. You use the data in **DTCTL::lpbNotif* to identify the row. The *lpNotif* member points to a binary blob that contains a "key" value that is unique to the row to be refreshed, and *cbNotif* is the byte count of **lpbNotif.* You initialize **DTCTL::lpbNotif* to point at the key value before you call *BuildDisplayTable.* Later when you want to refresh the control, you must retrieve the key from the display table's PR_CONTROL column and pass its value to *ITableData::HrNotify,* which causes a window notification message to be sent to the corresponding control. The specific message sent depends on the type of control, but in most cases the net effect is a call to *GetProps.* The following code fragment shows how to notify a display table to reload its controls:

```
    ⋮
// Walk rows in display table's data.
for (int iRow = 0; ; iRow++)
{
    LPSRow         pRow = NULL;
    LPSPropValue pControlID;

    hRes = pDispTblData -> HrEnumRow(iRow, &pRow);
```

(continued)

continued

```
        if (!pRow || M_FAIL(hRes))
            goto Quit;

        // Get control ID.
        pControlID = PpropFindProp(pRow -> lpProps,
                                   pRow -> cValues,
                                   PR_CONTROL_ID);

        // If control has notification key (control ID non-NULL), notify.
        if (pControlID -> Value.bin.cb)
            m_pConfig -> m_pDispTblData -> HrNotify(0, 1, pControlID);

        gFreeBuff(pRow);
    }
    ⋮
```

The *lpszFilter* member points to a string that specifies what characters can be legally entered in an edit field or combo box. For example, if the property value associated with the control is a number, *lpszFilter* would allow only digits to be entered in the edit control. The *ulItemID* member is the identifier for the control, as defined in your resource script, and *ctl* is a union that contains the specific control data structure.

MAPI defines some strange-looking structures for specifying each control. These structures are named *DTBLXXX*, where *XXX* is *LBX* for a listbox, *EDIT* for an edit control, and so on. The *DTCTL.ctl.lpXXX* union points to one of these *DTBLXXX* data structures. The most important member of a *DTBLXXX* structure is the field where you specify the property that's associated with the control. We refer you to the MAPI documentation and MAPIDEFS.H for more information on each *DTBLXXX* structure.

Some *DTBLXXX* structures have members that give a byte offset from the beginning of the structure to a buffer containing extra data. *DTBLPAGE::ulbLpszLabel* and *DTBLPAGE::ulbLpszComponent* are examples:

```
typedef struct _DTBLPAGE
{
    ULONG ulbLpszLabel;
    ULONG ulFlags;
    ULONG ulbLpszComponent;
    ULONG ulContext;
} DTBLPAGE, FAR *LPDTBLPAGE;
```

If you use *BuildDisplayTable* to create your display table, these members are ignored.

The *DTBLPAGE* structure lets you associate a help file with the property sheet. The *ulContext* member is a topic number in your help file—IDH-_CREATE_DL, in this example. MAPI creates a help button at the bottom of the dialog box that calls WINHELP to display the help file topic given in *ulContext*. The name of the help file is given in the [Help File Mappings] section of the MAPISVC.INF file, which for ABPAB looks like this:

```
[Help File Mappings]
⋮
ABPAB Help=abpab.hlp
⋮
```

The help file mapping entry—"ABPAB Help", in our case—must also be specified in the *lpszComponent* member of the *DTPAGE* structure. *DTPAGE* is the third data structure you must initialize.

```
typedef struct {
    ULONG           cctl;
    LPTSTR          lpszResourceName; /* as usual, may be an integer ID */
    union {
        LPTSTR          lpszComponent;
        ULONG           ulItemID;
    };
    LPDTCTL         lpctl;
} DTPAGE, FAR *LPDTPAGE;
```

This structure is initialized with an array of *DTCTL* structures in *lpctl*, the count of elements in the *DTCTL* array in *cctl*, the name of a dialog resource to be used in *lpszResourceName*, and the aforementioned help-file–mapping string in *lpszComponent*.

The display table data structures are tricky to initialize, hard to maintain, and error prone. Display tables also give you only rudimentary control over the details dialog. Then why does MAPI require their use? The first reason is that the look of the user interface is consistent regardless of which container is supplying the entry being viewed. The illusion of the single supercontainer is more credible if MAPI has control of the UI instead of the individual providers. Also, an entry copied from provider *A* to provider *B* can be made to look the same when viewed from *B* as it did when viewed from *A*. Provider *B* has only to copy *A*'s display table data along with the entry when the entry is saved. Then when a call to *OpenProperty(PR_DETAILS, …)* is handled for that entry, *B* reconstructs and returns *A*'s display table. We'll see how this is done when we discuss writable address book providers.

Resolving Names

Address book providers relieve the user of having to memorize cryptic email addresses like *lthaler@cs.csu.pomona.edu* or */o=Microsoft/ou=PSS/cn=....* Instead the user can enter a friendly name to identify the recipient. The client queries the installed address book providers to try and find a match for the friendly name. If a match can be found, the addressing properties that the system needs to deliver the message can be retrieved and added to the message's recipient table. This process is known as name resolution. Its purpose is to transform a recipient's name, as entered by the user, into an unambiguous set of recipient properties.

A client resolves names against the installed address book providers by calling *IAddrBook::ResolveName. ResolveName* takes a list of names (an *ADRLIST*) in which each name is incompletely specified by one or more properties that are used to search for a matching entry. PR_DISPLAY_NAME is the most common choice, but other properties can be used as well. If the name is successfully resolved, the call returns the *ADRLIST* with each name completely specified. "Completely specified" might mean that each entry had only the display name property on input but was returned with all the properties required for delivery.

IAddrBook::ResolveName works by calling *IABContainer::ResolveNames* for each container in the *search path*. The search path is analogous to the PATH environment variable; PATH is an ordered list of file system directories, whereas the search path is an ordered list of address book containers in the current session. *IAddrBook::ResolveName* walks this list and calls each container's *IABContainer::ResolveNames* method until the name is resolved or the end of the list is reached.

Notice that finding a match doesn't necessarily mean the name is resolved. If the user entered "Trane" and there was more than one "Trane" in the container, the name would be considered ambiguous. In fact, exactly what constitutes a match is implementation-defined. ABPAB defines a match in terms of the PR_DISPLAY_NAME property, while ABWDS uses the PR_DISPLAY-_NAME and the PR_ACCOUNT_NAME properties.

The *IABContainer::ResolveNames* method has the following signature:

```
HRESULT ResolveNames(LPSPropTagArray lpPropTagArray,
                     ULONG           ulFlags,
                     LPADRLIST       lpAdrList,
                     LPFlagList      lpFlagList)
```

The first parameter, *lpPropTagArray*, tells the implementation which properties the caller would like returned in each *ADRENTRY* in *lpAdrList*. The *lpAdrList* member is the list of names to be resolved, and *lpFlagList* is an array of flags in which each element corresponds to an *ADRENTRY*. The implementation sets *lpFlagList[i]* to signal whether the entry in *lpAdrList[i]* was resolved or not.

The search algorithm (*IABContainer::ResolveNames*) goes like this:

```
for each entry i in lpAdrList
    if entry i is marked MAPI_RESOLVED or MAPI_AMBIGUOUS in lpFlagList[i]
        skip this entry
    search container for a match using our criteria
    if exactly one match exists
        mark name i as MAPI_RESOLVED in lpFlagList[i]
        fill the ADRENTRY with all requested properties
    if more than one match exists
        mark name i as MAPI_AMBIGUOUS in lpFlagList[i]
    if no matches are found, do nothing
return
```

Notice that any names in the *ADRLIST* that are marked MAPI-_RESOLVED or MAPI_AMBIGUOUS aren't considered—that is, only one container can mark an entry as resolved or ambiguous. Once all the containers have been searched, any unmarked entries are considered unresolved. *IAddrBook::ResolveName* displays a dialog box that tells the user the names couldn't be found and lets him browse the containers manually for the entries.

If a container marks an entry as ambiguous, *IAddrBook* will call *Restrict* (specifying PR_ANR) on that container's contents table. *Restrict* returns a view of the contents table that contains only the ambiguous names. Again, what constitutes a match in the context of PR_ANR is provider-dependent. The only requirement for ambiguity is that there must be two or more entries that match the target name. Notice that the criteria for matching names in *Restrict* isn't necessarily the same as that for *ResolveNames*.

The ABPAB implementation shows one of many possible schemes. The *DoANR* method does most of the work. This method is called from the *Resolve-Names* method for each *ADRENTRY* that is marked MAPI_UNRESOLVED:

```
STDMETHODIMP CABContainer::ResolveNames(LPSPropTagArray lpPropTagArray,
                                        ULONG           ulFlags,
                                        LPADRLIST       lpAdrList,
                                        LPFlagList      lpFlagList)
{
    HRESULT           hRes    = S_OK;
    LPMAPITABLE       pCntTbl = NULL;
    LPSPropTagArray   pCols;
    int               i;
```

(continued)

```
pCols = (!lpPropTagArray ?
        (LPSPropTagArray)&g_sptCntTbl : lpPropTagArray);

    ⋮

// Contents table is also sorted.
if (M_FAIL(hRes = GetContentsTable(0, &pCntTbl)))
    goto Quit;

if (M_FAIL(hRes = pCntTbl -> SetColumns(pCols, TBL_BATCH)))
    goto Quit;

// If a name is unresolved, try to parse it.
for (i = 0; i < (int)lpFlagList -> cFlags; i++)
{
    if (MAPI_UNRESOLVED == lpFlagList -> ulFlag[i])
    {

        ⋮

        hRes = DoANR(pProp -> Value.lpszA,
                    pCntTbl,
                    &ResolvedRow,
                    0);
        switch (hRes)
        {
            case S_OK: // Copy props to ADRENTRY.
                lpFlagList -> ulFlag[i] = MAPI_RESOLVED;
                hRes = CopyAdrEntry(pCols,
                                    &ResolvedRow,
                                    &(lpAdrList -> aEntries[i]));
                break;

            case MAPI_E_AMBIGUOUS_RECIP:
                lpFlagList -> ulFlag[i] = MAPI_AMBIGUOUS;
                hRes = S_OK;
                break;

            case MAPI_E_NOT_FOUND:
                hRes = S_OK;
                break;

            default:
                break;
        }
    }
}
```

```
Quit:
    ⋮
}

STDMETHODIMP  DoANR(LPTSTR        szTarget,
                    LPMAPITABLE    pSearchTbl,
                    LPSRow         psrResolved,
                    ULONG          ulNameCol)
{
    HRESULT        hRes               = S_OK;
    LPSRowSet      pHitRow            = NULL;
    BOOL           bSearch            = TRUE;
    TCHAR          szBuf[MAX_PATH];
    LPSTR          szTemp             = szBuf;
    ULONG          ulMatches          = 0,
                   ulState,
                   ulAmbig = 0;
    int            i, idxMatch = -1;
    SPropValue     spTemp;
    SRestriction   SRes;


    lstrcpyn(szTemp, szTarget, MAX_PATH);
    szTemp[MAX_PATH - 1] = '\0';
    spTemp.ulPropTag   = PR_DISPLAY_NAME;
    spTemp.Value.lpszA = GetNextToken(&szTemp);

    // Find all rows with the target string's first token.
    SRes.rt = RES_CONTENT;
    SRes.res.resContent.ulPropTag = PR_DISPLAY_NAME;
    SRes.res.resContent.lpProp = &spTemp;
    SRes.res.resContent.ulFuzzyLevel = FL_SUBSTRING | FL_IGNORECASE;

    if (FAILED(hRes = HrQueryAllRows(pSearchTbl,
                                     NULL,
                                     &SRes,
                                     NULL,
                                     0,
                                     &pHitRow)))
        goto Quit;

    for (bSearch = TRUE, i = 0; i < (int)pHitRow -> cRows && bSearch; i++)
    {
        // Run our parser and see if it matches.
        switch (ulState = RunStringState(PR_DISPLAY_NAME,
                                         szTarget,
                                         &pHitRow -> aRow[i]))
```

(continued)

```
    {
        case MATCH:
            if (++ulMatches > 1)
                bSearch = FALSE;

            idxMatch = i;
            break;

        case AMBIG:
            ulAmbig++;
            break;

        case NOMATCH:
            break;
    }
    }

Quit:
    if (1 == ulMatches || !ulMatches && 1 == ulAmbig)
    {   // Pull matching row out of row set; save it.
        *psrResolved = pHitRow -> aRow[idxMatch];
        pHitRow -> aRow[idxMatch].cValues = 0;
        pHitRow -> aRow[idxMatch].lpProps = NULL;
        hRes = S_OK;
    }
    else
    {   // If we have a single ambiguous hit
        if (ulAmbig > 1 || ulMatches > 1)
            hRes = MAPI_E_AMBIGUOUS_RECIP;
        else
            hRes = MAPI_E_NOT_FOUND;
    }
    FreeProws(pHitRow);
    return hRes;
}
```

DoANR breaks the display name into white-space delimited substrings, or "tokens." It restricts the container's contents table to any rows containing the first token as a substring by using a case-insensitive RES_CONTENT restriction. The rows returned from the restricted table are further examined to determine the quality of the match.

RunStringState is a simple parser that compares the tokens in the entry's display name against those in each row's display name and returns one of three possible results: MATCH, AMBIG, or NOMATCH. An exact match is one in which the entry and the row each have the exact same sequence of tokens. An ambiguous match is one in which all the entry's tokens appear in the row in the correct order, although the row might have more tokens interspersed between the entry's tokens.

If, after parsing the rows, we don't find any matches, *DoANR* returns MAPI_E_NOT_FOUND and *ResolveNames* ignores the entry. If we find more than one exact match or more than one inexact match, we return MAPI_E-_AMBIGUOUS_RECIP and *ResolveNames* marks the entry as ambiguous. We treat a single inexact match like a single exact match by returning the matching row.

The call to *SetColumns* in *ResolveNames* guarantees that our contents table will contain all requested properties that exist for each entry and that they will be in the same order as given in the *lpPropTagArray* parameter. Any requested properties that don't exist for an entry will be marked by *SetColumns* as type PT_ERROR. If *lpPropTagArray* is NULL, we call *SetColumns* using a default set of properties that should be included in a resolved name. These include the following required properties:

- PR_ENTRYID
- PR_SEARCH_KEY
- PR_ADDRTYPE

In addition, we return the following for performance reasons:

- PR_DISPLAY_NAME
- PR_EMAIL_ADDRESS
- PR_DISPLAY_TYPE
- PR_OBJECT_TYPE
- PR_TRANSMITTABLE_DISPLAY_NAME
- PR_INSTANCE_KEY
- PR_SEND_RICH_INFO
- PR_7BIT_DISPLAY_NAME

Returning these additional properties precludes a subsequent call to *PrepareRecips* when a message containing this recipient is submitted. Remember that *IAddrBook::ResolveName* is usually called by the client before *IMessage-::ModifyRecipients* prepares to send the message, and since we're getting properties for the entry anyway, we can save ourselves a little work by returning the complete set.

PR_ANR

If your container marks an entry as ambiguous in *ResolveNames*, you should expect a call to *IMAPITable::Restrict* on the container's contents table. *Restrict* will pass you a property restriction based on PR_ANR, which is a string property whose value is the name your container flagged as ambiguous. The result of the restriction is a table whose rows contain recipients that match the name. As in the case of *ResolveNames*, the implementation decides what constitutes a match, and the algorithm used for PR_ANR doesn't have to be the same as for *ResolveNames*, although the results should be consistent. ABPAB's *ResolveNames* uses a token parsing scheme to find matches, but applying the same algorithm to an existing table is impractical, so we use a slightly different criteria for *Restrict*.

This discrepancy doesn't present a problem, though, because the *Resolve-Names* method just tells the caller whether or not the name is ambiguous, not what entries made it ambiguous. Besides, the user typically ends up resolving the ambiguity by choosing one of the names from the restricted table. The ABPAB implementation is shown below:

```
STDMETHODIMP CMAPITable::Restrict(LPSRestriction  lpRestriction,
                                  ULONG           ulFlags)
{
    HRESULT        hRes = S_OK;
    LPSRestriction pRes = lpRestriction;
    SRestriction   SRes;
    SPropValue     spTemp;

    if (lpRestriction && (lpRestriction -> rt == RES_PROPERTY))
        if (PROP_ID(PR_ANR) == PROP_ID(lpRestriction ->
                                        res.resProperty.ulPropTag))
        {

            TCHAR szBuf[MAX_PATH];
            LPSTR szTemp = szBuf;

            ⋮

            lstrcpyn(szTemp,
                    lpRestriction -> res.resProperty.lpProp ->
                        Value.lpszA, MAX_PATH);
            szTemp[MAX_PATH - 1] = '\0';

            spTemp.ulPropTag = PR_DISPLAY_NAME;
            spTemp.Value.lpszA = GetNextToken(&szTemp);
```

```
                SRes.rt = RES_CONTENT;
                SRes.res.resContent.ulPropTag   = PR_DISPLAY_NAME;
                SRes.res.resContent.lpProp      = &spTemp;
                SRes.res.resContent.ulFuzzyLevel =
                    FL_SUBSTRING | FL_IGNORECASE;
                pRes = &SRes;
            }

    hRes = m_pTbl -> Restrict(pRes, ulFlags);
    return hRes;
}
```

We use a content restriction based on the first token in the offending name. This method will return more "hits" than the *ResolveNames* algorithm, which compares the names token-by-token. The *CMAPITable* class exists only to trap PR_ANR; all other restrictions are passed as is to the MAPI table implementation which *CMAPITable* wraps.

IABLogon::PrepareRecips

PrepareRecips is called by *IAddrBook::PrepareRecips* as part of the submission process to ensure that each recipient in an outgoing message has the properties needed for delivery. *PrepareRecips* also converts short-term entry IDs to long-term entry IDs. The caller passes in an *SPropTagArray* of the requested properties and a list of recipients in an *ADRLIST*. The *PrepareRecips* method retrieves the requested properties for each recipient and passes them back in the *ADRLIST*. Notice that adding properties to the *ADRENTRY* in the list will require *PrepareRecips* to free the *ADRENTRY.rgProps* member and reallocate a new *SPropValue* array in order to hold the entry's existing properties *plus* any requested properties.

```
STDMETHODIMP CABLogon::PrepareRecips(ULONG            ulFlags,
                                     LPSPropTagArray  lpPropTagArray,
                                     LPADRLIST        lpRecipList)
{
    HRESULT         hRes = S_OK;
    CFlatPropList   fplDBProps;
    ULONG           i;

    ⋮

    // No work to do
    if (!lpPropTagArray)
        return hRes;
```

(continued)

```
for (i = 0; i < lpRecipList -> cEntries; i++)
{

    PABPAB_EID      pEID    = NULL;
    LPSPropValue    pProps  = NULL,
                    pspvTmp = NULL;
    ULONG           cAEVals = lpRecipList -> aEntries[i].cValues,
                    cPTVals = lpPropTagArray -> cValues,
                    ulCnt   = 0,
                    j, k;

    DECLARE_REC_NUM(RecNum);

    // Find this recip's entry ID.
    pspvTmp = PpropFindProp(lpRecipList -> aEntries[i].rgPropVals,
                            cAEVals,
                            PR_ENTRYID);
    if (pspvTmp)
        pEID = (PABPAB_EID)pspvTmp -> Value.bin.lpb;

    // Make sure it's ours and a valid recipient.
    switch (CheckEID(pspvTmp -> Value.bin.cb,
                    (LPENTRYID)pspvTmp -> Value.bin.lpb))
    {
        case PSS_MAILUSER:
        case PSS_DISTLIST:
        case FOREIGN_DL:
        case TEMPLATE_DL:
        case FOREIGN_USER:
        case TEMPLATE_USER:
            break;

        default:            // Not mine, skip it.
            continue;
    }

    // Open this entry's DB record.
    if (FAILED(hRes = Open(m_pDB, OPEN_ONLY, pEID -> ID, RecNum)))
        goto NextEntry;

    // Get stored properties.
    if (FAILED(hRes = Fetch(RecNum, fldPROPS, &fplDBProps)))
        goto NextEntry;

    // Allocate an SPV array big enough for the worst case.
    if (FAILED(hRes = gAllocBuff((cAEVals + cPTVals) *
                                sizeof(SPropValue),
                            (LPVOID *)&pProps)))
```

```
        goto NextEntry;

// Get requested props from database, and put at front of list.
// If it's not in the database, see if it's in the ADRENTRY.
for (j = 0; j < lpPropTagArray -> cValues; j++)
{
    PFlatPropNode pFlatPropNode = NULL;

    fplDBProps.Delete(lpPropTagArray -> aulPropTag[j],
                      &pFlatPropNode);

    if (pFlatPropNode)              // We found it in the database.
    {
        if (FAILED(UnFlatten(pFlatPropNode,
                             pProps,
                             pProps[j])))
            pProps[j].ulPropTag =
                CHANGE_PROP_TYPE(pProps[j].ulPropTag,
                                 PT_ERROR);
        AE_Delete(lpPropTagArray -> aulPropTag[j],
                  &lpRecipList -> aEntries[i],
                  NULL,
                  NULL);

        delete pFlatPropNode;
    }
    else
        AE_Delete(lpPropTagArray -> aulPropTag[j],
                  &lpRecipList -> aEntries[i],
                  pProps,
                  &pProps[j]);
    ulCnt++;
}

// Add original props from ADRENTRY that weren't requested.
for (k = 0; k < cAEVals; k++)
    if (MAPI_E_OBJECT_DELETED !=
        lpRecipList -> aEntries[i].rgPropVals[k].ulPropTag)
        AE_Delete(lpRecipList ->
                      aEntries[i].rgPropVals[k].ulPropTag,
                  &lpRecipList -> aEntries[i],
                  pProps,
                  &pProps[ulCnt++]);
```

(continued)

407

```
        gFreeBuff((LPVOID)lpRecipList -> aEntries[i].rgPropVals);
        lpRecipList -> aEntries[i].rgPropVals = pProps;
        lpRecipList -> aEntries[i].cValues    = ulCnt;

NextEntry:
        Close(RecNum);
        fplDBProps.Destroy();

            ⋮
    }
        ⋮
}
```

The semantics of *PrepareRecips* make it appear more complicated than it really is. The first step is to convert short-term entry IDs to long-term entry IDs. Since ABPAB entry IDs are always long-term, we have to worry only about any requested properties. If no additional properties are requested, we're done. If the caller requests additional properties, they must be returned in each *ADRENTRY* in the order requested and they must appear before any properties that were originally present. The original properties must also be preserved in each *ADRENTRY*, and there shouldn't be any duplicates. In other words, if {A, B, C} is the list of requested properties and {C, D, E} is the list of properties on an *ADRENTRY*, your implementation should retrieve the values of A, B, and C from the database and D and E from the *ADRENTRY*; append D and E to {A, B, C}; and return {A, B, C, D, E} in the *ADRENTRY*.

We loop through the *ADRLIST* and get each *ADRENTRY*'s entry ID. If the entry is one of ours, we fetch its properties (A, B, and C in our example above). We allocate an *SPropValue* array big enough for all the requested properties plus the original properties found in the *ADRENTRY* (the worst case, since there will probably be some properties in common between the two sets). We mark any properties in the *ADRENTRY* that are also found in the requested set retrieved from the database (C in our example), using *AE_Delete* for this purpose. Any properties not marked are copied to the end of the *SPropValue* array. We then free the *ADRENTRY*'s properties and plug the *SPropValue* array in its place.

One-offs and the Session One-off Table

We've used the terms *one-off, one-off template,* and *one-off template entry ID* earlier in the chapter without defining exactly what they mean. To review, a one-off is a recipient that doesn't have an entry in an address book provider and must therefore be created on the fly instead of retrieved from the address book provider's database. The term *one-off* refers to both the recipient and an object representing the recipient (an *IMailUser* interface, for example), and has a slightly different meaning from the client's perspective than from the provider's perspective.

From the client's point of view, a one-off is used to address a message to a recipient who doesn't exist in any installed address book provider. If you type *[SMTP:lmorgan@ceora.com]* on the To line of the Microsoft Exchange client, you can send mail to Lee Morgan even though he doesn't have an entry in any of your address book providers. The client must add Lee Morgan's information to the message's recipient table to make the messages addressed to him deliverable. Recall that each recipient in the recipient table has a set of required properties, which includes the entry ID. But a one-off entry doesn't have an address book provider entry, so where does its entry ID come from? The answer is "from MAPI" via a call to *CreateOneOff*.

In the context of an address book provider, a one-off is an entry that doesn't have a record in the underlying database; it exists only in memory. This situation occurs when a client creates a new entry in the address book provider. The address book provider returns the appropriate interface (an *IMailUser*, say), but until the call to *SaveChanges*, the new entry isn't committed to permanent storage.

The term *template* is also fraught with ambiguity. A one-off template is a set of properties possessed by an entry of a given type and can be thought of as a template for a database record where each property maps to a record field. An address book provider database can have more than one type of record, and each record type will probably have a different set of fields, hence a different template. For example, an address book provider that contains Microsoft Mail, SMTP, and FAX recipients will probably have different types of records in its database because the fields that make sense for Microsoft Mail records might not make sense for SMTP or FAX recipients. In this example, the Microsoft Mail record might have fields for the email alias, the mailbox or account name, and the post office, while a FAX record might have a field for the number of times to redial on a busy signal, the time between redial attempts, and so on.

One-off templates are used for creating entries in a writable address book provider. In this case, a client calls *IAddrBook::NewEntry* or *IABContainer::CreateEntry*, both of which are passed the entry ID of the one-off template that the new entry is to be based upon. *CreateEntry* returns a one-off—i.e., an interface for the newly created entry that exists only in memory—on which the client can set and get properties. A call to *SaveChanges* turns the one-off into a persistent entry in the address book provider.

Each address book provider is given an opportunity to expose its one-off templates in its one-off table, which contains a row for each template available from the provider. A provider's one-off table is returned to MAPI via the *IABLogon::GetOneOffTable* method, which is called on each provider when MAPI creates the *IAddrBook* supercontainer. Each row in this table contains a different template for a one-off entry that can be returned by the address book provider. The following list shows the required columns in the one-off table. Some of these properties are intrinsic to the template, like PR_ENTRYID and PR_DISPLAY_NAME, but some are useful only for displaying UI that lists these templates.

Required Columns in the One-off Table

Property	Description
PR_ENTRYID	The entry ID of the one-off template. A client can pass this value to *IABContainer::CreateEntry*, for example.
PR_DISPLAY_NAME	The value should indicate what kind of entry the template represents—for example, "Generic Mail User," or "X.400 Recipient."
PR_SELECTABLE	Some rows in the table can be used to group different templates together. These rows aren't templates themselves but are viewed as *headings* when the table UI is displayed. The PR_SELECTABLE flag indicates whether the entry in the row contains a template or a heading (only templates are selectable).
PR_DEPTH	Indicates how far the entry in the row should be indented when the table UI is displayed. For example, if a heading row is at PR_DEPTH == 0, any templates included under that heading might be at PR_DEPTH==1, or indented by one tab stop.
PR_ADDRTYPE	The address type of an entry created using this template. This property is optional.
PR_DISPLAY_TYPE	This property tells the UI what kind of icon should be displayed for the entry in this row.
PR_INSTANCE_KEY	A unique value for this row.

The MAPI subsystem creates a session one-off table that shows the kind of entries that can exist in the supercontainer. Each provider contributes its rows to this table when the *IABLogon::GetOneOff Table* method is called, and the rows are merged into the session table. ABPAB contributes two rows, a generic recipient and a personal distribution list, but an address book provider can also contribute none of its own templates and use the templates in the session table instead, or it can use a combination of both. (The Microsoft Personal Address Book has no templates of its own, whereas ABPAB uses both, as we shall see in a moment.)

```
STDMETHODIMP CABLogon::GetOneOffTable(ULONG           ulFlags,
                                      LPMAPITABLE * lppTable)
{
    HRESULT      hRes;
    SRow         sRow;
    ULONG        i,
                 ulCnt = 0;
    LPTABLEDATA  pMyTbl = NULL;
    PABPAB_EID   pEID   = NULL;

    enum {NAME, EID, DEPTH, SELECT, ADDR_TYPE, DISP_TYPE, INST_KEY,
        NUM_ONEOFF_PROPS};
    static const SizedSPropTagArray(NUM_ONEOFF_PROPS, OneOffTags) =
    {
        NUM_ONEOFF_PROPS,
        {
            PR_DISPLAY_NAME,
            PR_ENTRYID,
            PR_DEPTH,
            PR_SELECTABLE,
            PR_ADDRTYPE,
            PR_DISPLAY_TYPE,
            PR_INSTANCE_KEY
        }
    };

    SPropValue rgsPropValue[NUM_ONEOFF_PROPS];

    ⋮

    if (M_FAIL(hRes = CreateTable(…, &pMyTbl)))
        goto Quit;

    sRow.cValues = NUM_ONEOFF_PROPS;
    sRow.lpProps = rgsPropValue;

    for (i = NAME; i < NUM_ONEOFF_PROPS; i++)
        rgsPropValue[i].ulPropTag = OneOffTags.aulPropTag[i];
```

(continued)

411

```
    if (M_FAIL(hRes = NewEID(0,
                             ONEOFF_USER_ID,
                             PSS_MAILUSER | ONEOFF_ENTRY,
                             NULL,
                             &pEID)))
        goto Quit;

    rgsPropValue[NAME].Value.LPSZ        = "ABPAB Address";
    rgsPropValue[EID].Value.bin.cb       = sizeof(ABPAB_EID);
    rgsPropValue[EID].Value.bin.lpb      = (LPBYTE)pEID;
    rgsPropValue[DEPTH].Value.l          = 0;
    rgsPropValue[SELECT].Value.b         = TRUE;
    rgsPropValue[ADDR_TYPE].Value.LPSZ   = "";
    rgsPropValue[DISP_TYPE].Value.l      = DT_MAILUSER;
    rgsPropValue[INST_KEY].Value.bin.cb  = sizeof(ULONG);
    rgsPropValue[INST_KEY].Value.bin.lpb = (LPBYTE)&pEID -> ID.Num;

    if (M_FAIL(hRes =  pMyTbl -> HrModifyRow(&sRow)))
        goto Quit;

    gFreeBuff(pEID);
    pEID = NULL;

    if (M_FAIL(hRes = NewEID(0,
                             ONEOFF_DL_ID,
                             PSS_DISTLIST | ONEOFF_ENTRY,
                             NULL,
                             &pEID)))
        goto Quit;

    rgsPropValue[EID].Value.bin.lpb      = (LPBYTE)pEID;
    rgsPropValue[NAME].Value.LPSZ        = "ABPAB Distribution List";
    rgsPropValue[ADDR_TYPE].Value.LPSZ   = "MAPIPDL";
    rgsPropValue[DISP_TYPE].Value.l      = DT_DISTLIST;
    rgsPropValue[INST_KEY].Value.bin.lpb = (LPBYTE)&pEID -> ID.Num;

    if (M_FAIL(hRes =  pMyTbl -> HrModifyRow(&sRow)))
        goto Quit;

    hRes = pMyTbl -> HrGetView(…, (LPMAPITABLE *)lppTable);
Quit:
    ⋮
    return hRes;
}
```

One of the ways a client can create a one-off recipient on a message is by using *IAddrBook::NewEntry. NewEntry* displays a list box which allows the user to select a template from the merged one-off table. When an entry is selected,

NewEntry retrieves the one-off's entry ID and passes it to a call to *OpenEntry* on the address book container supplying the template. The *OpenEntry* call returns an interface on which *NewEntry* then calls *OpenProperty(PR_DETAILS, …)*. This call displays a property sheet that the user can fill with the one-off recipient's addressing information (and whatever else the page supports). When the user dismisses the details dialog, *IAddrBook* creates an in-memory entry containing properties set by the user and returns its entry ID.

This entry is like any other address book provider entry *except* that it exists only in memory and doesn't belong to any address book provider. One consequence of its "in-limbo" status is that it can't be saved anywhere. But it can be opened and its properties retrieved and set. *GetProps* on the in-memory entry returns the properties as entered by the user, which can be merged into an *ADRLIST* and passed to *IMessage::ModifyRecipients*, as illustrated in the following client code fragment:

```
    ⋮
LPMAILUSER      pUser = NULL;
ULONG           cbNewEntry,
                ulObjType,
                cProps;
LPSPropValue    pProps = NULL;
LPENTRYID       pEIDNewEntry;
SizedADRLIST(1, AL);

hRes = pAddrBook -> NewEntry((ULONG)hDlg,
                             0,
                             0,
                             NULL,
                             0,
                             NULL,
                             &cbNewEntry,
                             &pEIDNewEntry);

    ⋮

hRes = pAddrBook -> OpenEntry(cbNewEntry,
                             pEIDNewEntry,
                             NULL,
                             MAPI_BEST_ACCESS,
                             &ulObjType,
                             (LPUNKNOWN *)&pUser);

    ⋮
```

(continued)

413

```
hRes = pUser -> GetProps((LPSPropTagArray)&g_sptRecips,
                         0,
                         &cProps,
                         &pProps);

pProps[RECIP_TYPE].Value.l = MAPI_TO;
pProps[RECIP_TYPE].ulPropTag = PR_RECIPIENT_TYPE;

AL.cEntries = 1;
AL.aEntries[0].cValues = cProps;
AL.aEntries[0].rgPropVals = pProps;

hRes = pMsg -> ModifyRecipients(0, (LPADRLIST)&AL);
  ⋮
```

The code fragment above demonstrates how this is done. Although this example shows client-side code, it's illustrative of how the supercontainer calls on the installed address book providers to service a client's request.

A writable address book provider also provides a table of one-offs that represents the kinds of entries that can be *created* in a container. This table is returned from *IABContainer::OpenProperty* on PR_CREATE_TEMPLATES. The table the provider returns should include the entries it returned to MAPI in *GetOneOffTable*, but it can also include entries from other address book providers if the provider allows the creation of foreign entries (entries based on another address book provider's template) in its containers. The provider gets the merged session table from the *IMAPISupport::GetOneOffTable* method, selects the rows corresponding to entries it wants to support, adds its own templates, and returns the table in the *OpenProperty* call. The code is almost identical to *IABLogon::GetOneOffTable*, except you must call *IMAPISupport::GetOneOffTable* and *HrQueryAllRows* to get the session table rows containing the other providers' templates. (We refer the interested reader to *IABLogon::OpenTemplates* in ABPAB.)

The same columns required for the one-off table returned in *GetOneOffTable* are also mandatory in the one-off table returned from PR_CREATE-_TEMPLATES. A client can select a row from this table and use its entry ID in a call to *IABContainer::CreateEntry*. Calling *SaveChanges* on the newly created entry promotes the one-off entry from the "limbo" state to full membership in an address book container.

Notice that the entry IDs for the templates are hard-coded, that is, the row occupied by the "ABPAB Address" one-off will always have the same value for its entry ID column. Returning a fixed entry ID for each of your templates means that a client can obtain a template's entry ID once and use it to create multiple entries (in a loop, for example). So the client should be able to count on the value remaining the same, instead of having to get the one-off table each time. Using constant values also makes it easier to tell what kind of entry we're being asked to create.

Writable Address Book Providers

In Figure 9-6 on page 356 and Figure 9-7 on page 357, we listed the properties an address book provider exposes. Writable address book providers support the same set of properties as read-only implementations but also include some additional properties. (See Figure 9-17.)

Property Tag	Description
PR_CONTAINER_FLAGS	Any container in which entries can be created must have the AB_MODIFIABLE bit set. AB_RECIPIENTS must also be set if the container can have recipients, not just containers (i.e., it has a contents table). These two bits are required if the container is a personal address book provider.
PR_CREATE_TEMPLATES	Calling *IABContainer::OpenProperty* on this tag returns a one-off table of the entries that can be created in the container. A client can pass the entry ID of a template in this table to *IABContainer::CreateEntry*.
PR_DEF_CREATE_DL	The entry ID of a distribution list one-off. If a container supports creating one or more distribution lists, you choose a template for one type of DL, which will serve as the default. A client can retrieve this property via *GetProps* and pass it to *CreateEntry*.
PR_DEF_CREATE_MAILUSER	This property serves the same function as PR_DEF_CREATE_DL, but the template is for a mail user.

Figure 9-17.
Writable address book provider properties.

IABContainer::CreateEntry

Of course, the whole point of making an address book provider writable is to allow a client to create entries in it. A new entry can be added to a container by calling *IAddrBook::NewEntry*, passing the entry ID of the target container. *NewEntry* allows you to choose a creation template from the session one-off table, or you can pass a template's entry ID obtained from PR_CREATE-_TEMPLATES, PR_DEF_CREATE_DL, or PR_DEF_CREATE_MAILUSER.

A client can also create entries directly in a container using *IABContainer::CreateEntry*. This is what *NewEntry* does, although it also calls *OpenProperty(PR_DETAILS, …)* on the one-off to display UI for gathering the new entry's properties. *CreateEntry* takes an entry ID in the *lpEntryID* parameter. The value in *lpEntryID* can be either the entry ID of a one-off template obtained from PR_CREATE_TEMPLATES or PR_DEF_CREATE_XXX or it can be the entry ID of an existing entry in a foreign address book provider that is to be copied to your database. The following code illustrates *CreateEntry*:

```
STDMETHODIMP CABContainer::CreateEntry(ULONG        cbEntryID,
                                       LPENTRYID    lpEntryID,
                                       ULONG        ulCreateFlags,
                                       LPMAPIPROP * lppMAPIPropEntry)
{
    HRESULT       hRes = S_OK;
    PABPAB_EID    pEID = (PABPAB_EID)lpEntryID,
                  pOOEID = NULL;
    ULONG         ulEntryType;

    *lppMAPIPropEntry = NULL;

    ⋮

    ulEntryType = m_pLogon -> CheckEID(cbEntryID, lpEntryID);

    // Convert fixed one-off entry ID to meaningful database ID.
    // This applies only if it's one of our one-offs.
    if (ulEntryType & ONEOFF_ENTRY)
    {
        if (M_FAIL(hRes = m_pLogon -> CreateEID(ulEntryType, &pOOEID)))
            goto Quit;

        pEID = pOOEID;        // So we can free new EID later
    }

    switch (ulEntryType)
    {
        case MY_ABCONT:
```

416

```
            // Don't support containers other than ROOT, DIR.
            hRes = MAPI_E_NO_SUPPORT;
            break;

    case MY_DISTLIST:
    {
        LPCABCont pCont = new CABContainer(…);

        if (!pCont)
        {
            hRes = MAPI_E_NOT_ENOUGH_MEMORY;
            goto Quit;
        }

        if (M_FAIL(hRes = pCont -> InitContainer()))
        {
            delete pCont;
            goto Quit;
        }
        else
            *lppMAPIPropEntry = pCont;

        break;
    }

    case MY_MAILUSER:
    {
        PMailUser pMailUser = new CMailUser(…);

        if (!pMailUser)
        {
            hRes = MAPI_E_NOT_ENOUGH_MEMORY;
            goto Quit;
        }

        if (M_FAIL(hRes = pMailUser -> Init()))
        {
            delete pMailUser;
            goto Quit;
        }
        else
            *lppMAPIPropEntry =  (LPMAPIPROP)pMailUser;

        break;
    }
```

(continued)

```
case FOREIGN_ENTRY:
{
    LPMAPIPROP pProp = NULL;

    if (M_FAIL(hRes = CreateTemplateEntry(…, &pProp)))
        goto Quit;
    else
        *lppMAPIPropEntry = pProp;
    break;
}

default:
    hRes = MAPI_E_INVALID_ENTRYID;
}
    ⋮
}
```

CreateEntry's main purpose is to recognize a one-off's entry ID and return an interface appropriate to the type of recipient the template represents. In other words, *CreateEntry* should return an *IMailUser* interface if the entry ID belongs to a mail user one-off, an *IDistList* interface if the entry ID is for a distribution list, and so on. ABPAB encodes the type of entry in the entry ID, so this is easily done by a call to *CheckEID*. Remember that the one-off's entry ID stored in PR_CREATE_TEMPLATES or PR_DEF_CREATE_XXX is a constant so that a client can create many entries using the same value. But if we add this new entry to the database, it must have a unique entry ID. MAPI doesn't require the entry ID to be unique (or even to exist at all) as long as the newly created entry is in the "limbo" state (until *SaveChanges* is called), but we find it convenient to give the new entry a unique record ID at this time, so we call *CreateEID* to ask the database to generate a new record number, which we then merge into an entry ID.

We then create a new object based on the entry type—mail user, DL, or foreign entry—and return it in *lppMAPIPropEntry*. Creating a new object entails instantiating it through a call to *new*, incrementing its reference count, creating a database record for the "in-limbo" entry, and putting some default properties in the object's property cache. The caller can make use of the methods on the returned interface as it would for an existing entry. For example, a client can fill in the blank entry by setting its properties, displaying its details, and so on. If the object is released without calling *SaveChanges*, the object is destroyed and the "in-limbo" database record is deleted. *SaveChanges* flushes the entry's property cache to the database, making any changes to the entry permanent.

Creating Foreign Entries

Creating an entry based on a one-off template that is native to the provider is comparatively straightforward. A far more interesting (a euphemism for complicated) situation exists when the new entry is based on a foreign address book provider's template or when it is copied from an existing entry in another provider.

In that case, you get called at *CreateEntry* with an entry ID that doesn't belong to your provider. *CreateTemplateEntry* handles this case for *CreateEntry*:

```
STDMETHODIMP CABContainer::CreateTemplateEntry(ULONG        cbEntryID,
                                               LPENTRYID    lpEntryID,
                                               ULONG        ulCreateFlags,
                                               LPMAPIPROP * lppMAPIPropEntry)
{
    HRESULT          hRes          = S_OK;
    LPMAPIPROP       pForeignObj   = NULL;
    CTemplateDL   *  pHostDL       = NULL;
    CTemplateUser *  pHostUser     = NULL;
    LPSPropValue     pSrcProps     = NULL;
    PABPAB_EID       pEID          = NULL;
    ULONG            ulEntryType   = (ULONG)MAPI_E_NOT_FOUND,
                     ulCnt,
                     i,
                     ulID;
    SPropValue       SIG,
                     spvTID;

    spvTID.ulPropTag = 0;
    spvTID.Value.err = MAPI_E_NOT_FOUND;

    *lppMAPIPropEntry = NULL;
    SIG.ulPropTag = PR_NULL;

    // Open the foreign entry.
    if (FAILED(hRes = m_pLogon  ->
                  m_pSupObj -> OpenEntry(cbEntryID,
                                         lpEntryID,
                                         NULL,
                                         0,
                                         &ulEntryType,
                                         (LPUNKNOWN *)&pForeignObj)))
        goto Quit;
```

(continued)

419

```
// Stash the src props we need; copy the rest to our object.
if (FAILED(hRes = pForeignObj -> GetProps(NULL, …, &pSrcProps)))
    goto Quit;

// Set the ones we don't want to copy to PR_NULL.
for (i = 0; i < ulCnt; i++)
{
    switch (pSrcProps[i].ulPropTag)
    {
        // Save whether this is a foreign mail user, DL.
        case PR_OBJECT_TYPE:
            ulEntryType = ENTRY_TYPE(pSrcProps[i].Value.l) |
                            FOREIGN_ENTRY;
            break;

        case PR_TEMPLATEID:
            spvTID = pSrcProps[i];
            break;

        case PR_MAPPING_SIGNATURE:
            SIG = pSrcProps[i];                // Save data for later.
            pSrcProps[i].ulPropTag = PR_NULL; // So SetProps won't copy
            break;

        case PR_ENTRYID:
            pSrcProps[i].ulPropTag = PR_NULL;
            break;

        default:
        {
            if (PT_OBJECT == PROP_TYPE(pSrcProps[i].ulPropTag))
                pSrcProps[i].ulPropTag = PR_NULL;

            if (PROP_ID(pSrcProps[i].ulPropTag) > 0x7FFF)
            {
                // Copy foreign proptag to array.
                pNamedTags -> aulPropTag[pNamedTags -> cValues] =
                                        pSrcProps[i].ulPropTag;

                // Save index into SPropValue array for replacement.
                Idx[pNamedTags -> cValues++] = i;
            }
        }
    }
}

⋮
```

```
// Save whether the object supports OpenTemplateID.
ulEntryType |= (MAPI_E_NOT_FOUND != spvTID.Value.err &&
                PR_TEMPLATEID   == spvTID.ulPropTag ?
                HAS_TEMPLATEID : 0);

    ⋮

// We need a new ID for our local object.
if (FAILED(hRes = NextID(m_pLogon -> m_pDB, ulID)))
    goto Quit;

if (FAILED(hRes = m_pLogon -> NewEID(…, &pEID)))
    goto Quit;

switch (ulEntryType)
{
    case FOREIGN_DL:
    case TEMPLATE_DL:
        pHostDL = new CTemplateDL(m_pLogon,
                                  &m_MyEID,
                                  pEID,
                                  ulCreateFlags,
                                  this,
                                  TRUE);

        if (!pHostDL)
        {
            hRes = MAPI_E_NOT_ENOUGH_MEMORY;
            goto Quit;
        }

        if (FAILED(hRes = InitTemplateDL(pForeignObj,
                                         pHostDL)))
            goto Quit;

        if (TEMPLATE_DL == ulEntryType)   // Has PR_TEMPLATEID in
                                          // spvTID
        {
            hRes = m_pLogon  ->
                   m_pSupObj -> OpenTemplateID
                                (spvTID.Value.bin.cb,
                                 (LPENTRYID)spvTID.Value.bin.lpb,
                                 FILL_ENTRY,
                                 pHostDL,
                                 NULL,
                                 &(pHostDL -> m_pRemoteIProp),
                                 NULL);
```

(continued)

421

```
                if (FAILED(hRes))
                    goto Quit;

                // If OpenTemplateID returns a wrapped IMAPIProp with
                // our pHostDL embedded, it'll AddRef us, so Release.
                // If it doesn't wrap us, it just returns our pHostDL
                // without AddRef'ing us.
                if (pHostDL != pHostDL -> m_pRemoteIProp)
                    pHostDL -> Release();

                *lppMAPIPropEntry = pHostDL -> m_pRemoteIProp;
            }
            else
                // Server won't delegate; all OpenProperty calls go
                // first to CTemplateUser::, then CMAPIProp::.
                *lppMAPIPropEntry = pHostDL;
            break;

        case FOREIGN_USER:
        case TEMPLATE_USER:
            ⋮
            break;

        default:
            ASSERT(0);
    }

    if (pNamedTags -> cValues)
    {
        if (FAILED(hRes = pForeignObj -> GetNamesFromIDs(…)))
            goto Quit;

        if (FAILED(hRes = GetIDsFromNames(…)))
            goto Quit;

        // Replace foreign ID with ID from our mapping.
        for (i = 0; i < (int)pNamedTags -> cValues; i++)
            SWAP_IDS(pSrcProps[Idx[i]].ulPropTag, pTags -> aulPropTag[i]);
    }
    // Copy some of the foreigner's properties to our object.
    hRes = (*lppMAPIPropEntry) -> SetProps(ulCnt,
                                    pSrcProps,
                                    NULL);
Quit:
    ⋮
    return hRes;
}
```

CreateTemplateEntry essentially copies an entry from the foreign address book provider. First we call *IMAPISupport::OpenEntry* to open the foreign object, then call *GetProps(NULL, ...)* to retrieve all its properties. We scan the *SPropValue* array and save the PR_TEMPLATEID and PR_OBJECT_TYPE properties. We overwrite PR_ENTRYID and PR_MAPPING_SIGNATURE with PR_NULL because we intend to replace the foreign entry ID with our own. Next we instantiate an object of the appropriate type, which we'll call the *host* object to differentiate it from the remote object we are copying.

OpenTemplateID   The remote object supports *OpenTemplateID* if it has the PR_TEMPLATEID property. *OpenTemplateID* is a way for the remote object to intercept *IMAPIProp* method calls made on the host object. MAPI routes a call on the host object's *IMAPIProp* interface to the remote object's *IMAPIProp* implementation and returns the result through the host interface.

OpenTemplateID is useful for entries with large PT_OBJECT properties, where copying actual data from the foreign entry to the host's database would be impractical. An example would be the contents table of a container or distribution list (PR_CONTAINER_CONTENTS). For a distribution list with 1000 members, it would be better *not* to copy each member's data to the host provider and, instead, to simply get the remote object's contents table whenever *OpenProperty(PR_CONTAINER_CONTENTS, ...)* is requested on the host object.

OpenTemplateID makes this remote *IMAPIProp* available to the host provider by returning an *IMAPIProp* interface that wraps the remote interface. Now any *IMAPIProp* call passes first to the remote interface, which decides whether or not to handle the call. If the remote interface does handle the call, it services the request and returns the result; otherwise, the remote interface passes the call through to the local object's method.

To make this scenario work, you pass your host object in the fourth parameter (*pHostDL*, in our example), which contains a pointer to the remote object. What you get back in the pointer is an *IMAPIProp* that the foreign address book provider wraps around your host *IMAPIProp*. The wrapper has a pointer back to the host *IMAPIProp*, as Figure 9-18 on the following page illustrates.

When an *IMAPIProp* method call is made, the remote object has first crack at it. If the remote object wants to service the call, it does—otherwise it calls the host *IMAPIProp* method. If the remote object doesn't support remoting the *IMAPIProp* interface, it sets the remote pointer equal to the host pointer, which means *IMAPIProp* calls are *always* delegated back to the host interface. You test for this host pointer/remote pointer equality to determine which *IMAPIProp* to return from *CreateEntry*; if the host pointer is not equal to the remote interface pointer, return the remote interface—the remote object will decide which calls to delegate. Notice that if the remote interface delegates, it will call *AddRef* on the host object, making a call to *Release* necessary:

```
m_pSupObj -> OpenTemplateID(…, pHostDL, …, &(pHostDL -> m_pRemoteIProp),
                            …);
⋮
if (pHostDL != pHostDL -> m_pRemoteIProp)
    pHostDL -> Release();

*lppMAPIPropEntry = pHostDL -> m_pRemoteIProp;
⋮
```

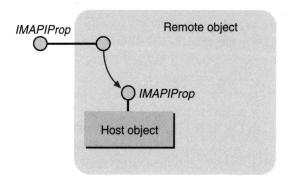

Figure 9-18.
The relationship between the host IMAPIProp *and the remote* IMAPIProp *interfaces for an object copied from a foreign address book provider that supports* OpenTemplateID.

The details table for a foreign entry   Your address book provider should also copy the foreign entry's details table so that when the foreign entry is displayed from your provider it looks the same as when opened in the foreign address book provider.

We accomplish this subterfuge by calling *OpenProperty(PR_DETAILS, …)* on the foreign object to get back the PR_DETAILS display table. We then call *HrQueryAllRows* and copy each row to the local object. We save the table rows in a separate stream belonging to the entry's database record so that we can reconstruct the display table when we service the *OpenProperty* call.

This scheme has the advantage of being simple and easy to implement, but it also has several drawbacks. The first drawback is that it's wasteful of memory and storage space. If you copy 1000 foreign mail users from the foreign provider into your address book provider, you'll end up with 1000 copies of the same table in your database (assuming, of course, that each entry uses the same details page).

The second drawback is that the table rows can be large (over 2 KB for one provider we know of), which makes copying the foreign entry slow, especially if the foreign address book provider is server-based and the data must be passed over the wire (via RPCs, for example).

A better approach is to cache the foreign table when the first entry that uses it is copied. Every time you copy a foreign entry, you first consult the cache. If the details table has already been cached, you mark the entry as using the cached table; otherwise, you download the details table and add it to the cache. This scheme requires you to calculate a unique "key" value that differentiates multiple tables from different providers. PR_PROVIDER_UID, which is a UID that is unique for a given provider (but the same for all instances of that provider), can be used to advantage here.

Note that the DTBLXXX controls from which the display table was built might link a control to a named property, so when we save the foreign entry's display table, we have to remap the foreigner's named properties to our own ID mapping. (See *SaveForeignDetails* in BASEPROP.CPP on the companion CD-ROM for implementation details.)

Named properties   A named property is a custom property that is known by name instead of by a hard-coded ID. Although MAPI defines a property tag for almost every imaginable purpose, it also allows vendors to extend the predefined property set by creating their own properties and publishing the property type and a string or numeric name. We discuss named properties in detail in Appendix A, and you might want to read that material before proceeding.

ABPAB supports named properties because objects copied from foreign address book providers are likely to contain them. When an entry is copied from the foreign provider, as in *CreateTemplateEntry* above, we get its properties from the source object and set them on our newly created entry. The named properties pose a problem, though, because they have IDs originating from the foreign provider's mapping. The foreign address book's IDs are probably meaningless in our mapping, so before we save the newly copied entry into our address book provider, we must remap all the named properties into our own name space. The following lines of code check each property ID to see whether it's in the named ID range:

```
if (PROP_ID(pSrcProps[i].ulPropTag) > 0x7FFF)
{
    // Copy foreign proptag to array.
    pNamedTags -> aulPropTag[pNamedTags -> cValues] =
        pSrcProps[i].ulPropTag;

    // Save index into SPropValue array for replacement.
    Idx[pNamedTags -> cValues++] = i;
}
```

If the ID belongs to a named property, we remember its position in the *SPropValue* array so that we can easily find the property tag and replace the foreign ID with one from our own mapping. Later, before we call *SetProps* on the new entry, we call *GetNamesFromIDs* on the source object to get the fixed names for each of the foreigner's IDs and then call *GetIDsFromNames* on our new entry to look up (or possibly create) the ID in our mapping:

```
if (pNamedTags -> cValues)
{
    if (FAILED(hRes = pForeignObj -> GetNamesFromIDs(…)))
        goto Quit;

    if (FAILED(hRes = GetIDsFromNames(…)))
        goto Quit;

    // Replace foreign ID with ID from our mapping.
    for (i = 0; i < (int)pNamedTags -> cValues; i++)
        SWAP_IDS(pSrcProps[Idx[i]].ulPropTag, pTags -> aulPropTag[i]);
}
```

GetNamesFromIDs We use an *ITableData* object to save the name-to-ID mapping. The first row in this table contains a counter that tells us the next available ID in our 0x8000 through 0xFFFE name space. Each remaining row in the table corresponds to a named property for which we have an ID in our mapping. The table columns include the ID, the property set GUID, the property's Unicode string name (if the name *is* a string), the property's numeric name (if it has a numeric name instead of a string), and the kind of name (string or numeric).

We create a view of the table by calling *GetMapTable* and cache the view the first time *GetNamesFromIDs* or *GetIDsFromNames* is called. We then set up a restriction to use in finding rows matching the desired IDs. If the *ppPropTags* parameter is NULL, the caller is requesting names for all known properties in our mapping. If *lpPropSetGuid* points to PS_MAPI, we return all known names belonging to the PS_MAPI property set. *GetAllNames* does the work by calling *HrQueryAllRows*.

```
STDMETHODIMP CBaseProp::GetNamesFromIDs(LPSPropTagArray * ppPropTags,
                                        LPGUID            lpPropSetGuid,
                                        ULONG             ulFlags,
                                        ULONG           * lpcPropNames,
                                        LPMAPINAMEID  * * lpppPropNames)
{
    SPropValue    spv;
    HRESULT       hRes,
                  hr = S_OK;
```

```
SRestriction    sr,
                * pRes = NULL;
LPSRowSet       psr = NULL;
LPMAPINAMEID    * ppNames = NULL;

if (!m_pLogon -> m_pMapView)
    if (M_FAIL(hRes = m_pLogon -> GetMapTable()))
        return hRes;

sr.rt = RES_PROPERTY;
sr.res.resProperty.relop = RELOP_EQ;
sr.res.resProperty.lpProp = &spv;

if (!*ppPropTags)
{
    if (lpPropSetGuid && PS_MAPI == *lpPropSetGuid)
    {
        spv.ulPropTag = PR_MAP_UID;
        spv.Value.lpguid = (LPGUID)&PS_MAPI;

        sr.res.resProperty.ulPropTag = PR_MAP_UID;
        pRes = &sr;
    }

    M_FAIL(hRes = GetAllNames(pRes, ppPropTags, lpppPropNames));
    *lpcPropNames = (*ppPropTags) -> cValues;
    return hRes;
}

int cNames = (int)(*ppPropTags) -> cValues;

for (int i = 0; i < cNames; i++)
{
    if (FAILED(hRes = gAllocBuff(sizeof(LPMAPINAMEID) * cNames,
                                 (LPVOID *)&ppNames)))
        goto Quit;

    sr.res.resProperty.ulPropTag = PR_MAP_ID;

    spv.ulPropTag = PR_MAP_ID;
    spv.Value.l   = PROP_ID((*ppPropTags) -> aulPropTag[i]);
    TraceString1("    %08x\n", spv.Value.l);

    EnterCriticalSection(&m_pLogon -> m_MapCS);
```

(continued)

```
if (SUCCEEDED(hRes = m_pLogon -> m_pMapView ->
    FindRow(&sr, BOOKMARK_BEGINNING, 0)))
    hRes = m_pLogon -> m_pMapView -> QueryRows(1, 0, &psr);

LeaveCriticalSection(&m_pLogon -> m_MapCS);

if (MAPI_E_NOT_FOUND == hRes)
{
    ppNames[i] = NULL;
    hr = MAPI_W_ERRORS_RETURNED;
}
else
{
    if (M_FAIL(hRes))
        goto Quit;

    if (M_FAIL(hRes =
        CopyNamedID((LPVOID)ppNames, &psr -> aRow[0],
                    &ppNames[i])))
        goto Quit;

    FreeProws(psr);
    psr = NULL;
}
}

*lpppPropNames = ppNames;
    :

}
```

If the property set GUID isn't PS_MAPI, we loop through the property tag array, set up a restriction on the ID, and call *FindRow* to see if the ID is in our table. If it is, we copy the name to a newly created *MAPINAMEID* structure and set a pointer in the *ppNames* array to point at it. If the ID isn't in our table, we set the pointer in the array to NULL and the error code to MAPI_W-_ERRORS_RETURNED. *GetIDsFromNames* works exactly the same way but in reverse: We loop through the array of *LPMAPINAMEID* structures passed in *lppPropNames* and, for each element in the array, set up a restriction based on the property set's UID (*MAPINAMEID::lpguid*) and the property name. We again use *FindRow* to search the table, but if the name isn't known to us (i.e., *FindRow* returns MAPI_E_NOT_FOUND), and MAPI_CREATE is passed in the *ulFlags* parameter, we create a new mapping for the name.

Creating the new mapping is a two-step process:

1. Retrieving the next available ID from the first row of our table, incrementing it, and saving the row back to the table

2. Creating a new row, using the next ID and the name information passed in the *LPMAPINAMEID* array

The new rows are added to the table with *HrModifyRows*, and the table is flushed to persistent storage.

Notifications

A client can register for notifications on an object in an address book provider by calling *IAddrBook::Advise*. *IAddrBook* passes this call through to the appropriate provider's *IABLogon::Advise* method.

```
STDMETHODIMP CABLogon::Advise(ULONG            cbEntryID,
                              LPENTRYID        lpEntryID,
                              ULONG            ulEventMask,
                              LPMAPIADVISESINK lpAdviseSink,
                              ULONG *          lpulConnection)
{
    HRESULT    hRes = S_OK;
    PABPAB_EID pEID = (PABPAB_EID)lpEntryID;
    ULONG      ulCnx;
    SizedNOTIFKEY(sizeof(ABPAB_EID), Key);

        ⋮

    // Make sure it's an event we can support.
    if (ulEventMask & ~SUPPORTED_EVENTS)
    {
        M_FAIL(hRes = MAPI_E_NO_SUPPORT);
        goto Quit;
    }

    Key.cb = cbEntryID;
    memcpy((LPVOID)Key.ab, (LPVOID)lpEntryID, Key.cb);

    // Let MAPI do the work.
    if (M_FAIL(hRes = m_pSupObj -> Subscribe((LPNOTIFKEY)&Key,
                                    ulEventMask,
                                    0,
                                    lpAdviseSink,
                                    &ulCnx)))

        goto Quit;

    // Save the connection number.
    if (!m_pAdviseList -> Queue(ulCnx))
```

(continued)

```
        {
            M_FAIL(hRes = MAPI_E_NOT_ENOUGH_MEMORY);
            goto Quit;
        }

        *lpulConnection = ulCnx;
Quit:
        ⋮
        return hRes;
}
```

First we check *ulEventMask* and make sure the requested event is one we're prepared to support. If it is, we construct a notification key based on the entry ID of the object for which notifications are being requested and pass the key and the requested events to *IMAPISupport::Subscribe.* We save the returned connection number in a list so we can call *Unsubscribe* when we are logged off. Whenever an object is created, deleted, or modified, we call *IMAPISupport-::Notify* to broadcast notifications to any interested parties. MAPI handles the problem of figuring out who, if anybody, has requested notifications on this object and then delivers them.

IABLogon::Advise handles external notification requests, but a far more important use of the MAPI notification engine (at least for our implementation) is generating notifications that are used internally. These notifications are generated when an entry is added to, deleted from, or modified in a container, and are used to update the container's contents or hierarchy table.

Using the MAPI notification engine greatly simplifies your life, since most of the messy implementation details are handled for you. When a container object is opened or created, it calls *Subscribe* to register for notifications on the fixed set of events specified by the constant fnevChildEvent:

```
STDMETHODIMP CABContainer::Subscribe()
{
    SizedNOTIFKEY(sizeof(ABPAB_EID, Key));
    PABPAB_EID    pEID = (PABPAB_EID)Key.ab;

    Key.cb = sizeof(ABPAB_EID);
    memcpy((LPVOID)pEID, (LPVOID)&m_MyEID, sizeof(ABPAB_EID));

    // Later when our child does a notify, it'll construct
    // the entry ID on the fly knowing only the ID number. We won't
    // know or care what the object type is.
    pEID -> ID.Type = DONT_CARE;
```

```
        return m_pLogon -> m_pSupObj -> Subscribe((LPNOTIFKEY)&Key,
                                            fnevChildEvent,
                                            0,
                                            m_pAdviseSink,
                                            &m_ulCnx);

}
```

Notice that this use of *Subscribe* is slightly backwards from how we use notifications in *IABLogon::Advise*. Instead of the container requesting notifications on its children by passing *their* entry IDs, it creates a key using *its own* entry ID. This way, the container doesn't have to figure out who its children are and construct keys for each of them. Instead, whenever the child changes, it figures out who its parents are, constructs keys based on their entry IDs, and calls *IMAPISupport::Notify* using these keys. This scheme is more efficient and easier to maintain since a child typically has only one or two parents, while a container (or DL) can potentially have thousands of children. *CBaseProp::NotifyParents* implements the logic for passing notifications from a child object to its parent:

```
STDMETHODIMP CBaseProp::NotifyParents(RECORD_NUMBER & MyRecNum,
                                      ULONG          ulEvent,
                                      PCFlatPropList pFlatPropList)
{
    HRESULT            hRes = S_OK;
    CList<ABPAB_ID>    ParentIDList;
    ABPAB_ID         * pID;
    SizedNOTIFKEY(sizeof(ABPAB_EID, Key));
    PABPAB_EID         pEID = (PABPAB_EID)Key.ab;
    NOTIFICATION       Notif;
    ULONG              ulFlags;
    LPSPropValue       pCTblRow = NULL;
    SRow               srChanged;

    // Convert my cached flat props into a contents table row
    // that we can pass to parent in the notification.
    if (FAILED(hRes = m_pLogon -> GetCTblRow(pFlatPropList,
                                      &pCTblRow)))

        goto Quit;

    srChanged.cValues = NUM_CTBL_COLS;
    srChanged.lpProps = pCTblRow;

    ZeroMemory(&Notif, sizeof(Notif));
    Notif.ulEventType          = fnevChildEvent;
```

(continued)

431

```
Notif.info.tab.ulTableEvent = ulEvent;
Notif.info.tab.propIndex    = pCTblRow[CT_INST_KEY];
Notif.info.tab.row          = srChanged;

if (FAILED(hRes = Fetch(MyRecNum,
                        fldPARENTS,
                        &ParentIDList)))
    goto Quit;

if (ParentIDList.Size())
{
    for (pID = ParentIDList.Scan(0);
         pID;
         pID = ParentIDList.Scan())
    {
        Key.cb = sizeof(ABPAB_EID);
        // Create the parent object's EID on the fly.
        // The only unique fields per object are
        // the object type (we don't care) and the ID.
        // The MUID is the same for all objects in this instance,
        // so copy our MUID, get the ID from the parent list,
        // and DONT_CARE the object type.
        memcpy((LPVOID)Key.ab, &m_MyEID, sizeof(ABPAB_EID));
        pEID -> ID.Type = DONT_CARE;
        pEID -> ID.Num  = pID -> Num;

        ulFlags = 0;
        hRes = m_pLogon -> m_pSupObj -> Notify((LPNOTIFKEY)&Key,
                                               1,
                                               &Notif,
                                               &ulFlags);

        if (FAILED(hRes))
            goto Quit;
    }
}

Quit:
    :
}
```

Notice that we create the entry's contents table row and pass it to *IMAPISupport::Notify* in the *Notif* structure. Because fnevChildEvent contains only table events (fnevTableModified, to be precise), we can pass the table row that is affected by the change to the *AdviseSink* handling the notification. When the parent container receives the notification, it calls *HrModifyRow* on the *ITableData* backing the contents or hierarchy table. *HrModifyRow* updates the

table with the new data and automatically triggers table notifications in any
open views. If the parent container isn't open, MAPI ignores the notification:

```
STDMETHODIMP_ (ULONG) CContAdviseSink::OnNotify(ULONG cNotif,
                                                LPNOTIFICATION pNotifs)
{
    HRESULT     hRes = S_OK;

    for (ULONG i = 0; i < cNotif; i++)
        switch (pNotifs[i].ulEventType)
        {
            case fnevChildEvent:
                switch (pNotifs[i].info.tab.ulTableEvent)
                {
                    ⋮

                    case ABPAB_CHILD_CHANGED:
                    case ABPAB_CHILD_MODIFIED:
                        // Update contents table on any change in my
                        // children.
                        SRow    sr = pNotifs[i].info.tab.row;

                        if (m_pCont -> m_pCntsTblData)
                            hRes = m_pCont ->
                                        m_pCntsTblData ->
                                        HrModifyRow(&sr);
                        break;

                    default:
                        hRes = MAPI_E_NO_SUPPORT;
                        break;
                }
                break;

            ⋮

            default:
                hRes = MAPI_E_NO_SUPPORT;
        }

    return hRes;
}
```

DeleteEntries

This method removes one or more children from a container. It takes a list of
the entry IDs identifying the children to delete and removes each one from the

parent's list of children. It also opens each child's entry and removes the parent from the child's list of parents. If deleting the parent container from the child's list of parents leaves the list empty, the child is an orphan and its record is purged from the database:

```
STDMETHODIMP CABContainer::DeleteEntries(LPENTRYLIST  lpEntries,
                                         ULONG        ulFlags)
{
    HRESULT             hRes = S_OK,
                        hr   = S_OK;
    ULONG               i;
    CList<ABPAB_ID>     DeleteList;
    SPropValue          Prop;
    SizedSPropTagArray(1, sptTag) = {1, PR_CONTAINER_CONTENTS};

        ⋮

    for (i = 0; i < lpEntries -> cValues; i++)
    {

        PABPAB_EID  pEID = (PABPAB_EID)lpEntries -> lpbin[i].lpb;
        ⋮

        Prop.ulPropTag = PR_INSTANCE_KEY;
        Prop.Value.bin.cb = sizeof(pEID -> ID.Num);
        Prop.Value.bin.lpb = (LPBYTE)&(pEID -> ID.Num);

        // Make a list of the deletions.
        DeleteList.Insert(pEID -> ID);

        if (m_pCntsTblData)
            if (M_FAIL(m_pCntsTblData -> HrDeleteRow(&Prop)))
                hr = MAPI_W_PARTIAL_COMPLETION;
    }

    // This does the work recursively.
    hRes = DeleteChildren(m_MyEID.ID, &DeleteList);
    m_pLogon -> Notify(fnevObjectModified,
                       NULL,
                       &m_MyEID,
                       (LPSPropTagArray)&sptTag);

        ⋮

}
```

We first construct a list of entry IDs of the children to delete and remove each one's row in the *ITableData* backing the contents table. Next we call

DeleteChildren, passing the list of entry IDs. *DeleteChildren* removes the child-parent relationship by recursively traversing the container's tree. Notice that a child can be a container (a DL), so deleting a child can sometimes mean deleting an entire subtree. The condition that stops the recursive descent is reaching a leaf node in the tree, i.e., a childless entry (a mail user or an empty DL).

We open the current tree node, fetch a list of its children and remove the current list of "deletees" from this list, then update the container's *fldCHILDREN* field. Next we walk the list of deletees and call *DeleteChildren* on each one. When we get to a leaf node in the tree, we end the recursion and remove the parent container from the leaf node's list of parents. If the parent list is empty as a consequence, the child is an orphan and we can purge it from the database by calling *DeleteRec*; otherwise, we simply update the child's modified parent list and notify that it's been removed from the parent container.

```
STDMETHODIMP CABContainer::DeleteChildren(ABPAB_ID          &MyID,
                                          CList<ABPAB_ID> * pDeletions)
{
    HRESULT              hRes         = S_OK;
    PABPAB_ID            pID          = NULL;
    CList<ABPAB_ID>    * pDeleteList = NULL,
                         Parents,
                         Children;

    DECLARE_REC_NUM(RecNum);

    if (FAILED(hRes = Open(…, MyID, RecNum)))
        return hRes;

    if (SUCCEEDED(hRes = Fetch(RecNum, fldCHILDREN, &Children)))
    {
        if (pDeletions)          // Only some of my children will be
                                 // deleted.
        {
            Children -= *pDeletions;
            pDeleteList = pDeletions;
        }
        else
        {
            pDeleteList = &Children;  // I.e., delete all my children.
            Children.Destroy();      // Write back an empty list of
                                     // children.
        }
```

(continued)

435

```
        hRes = Update(RecNum, fldCHILDREN, Children);
}

Close(RecNum);

// E_NOT_FOUND isn't an error; we've reached an empty DL.
if (FAILED(hRes))
    return (MAPI_E_NOT_FOUND == hRes ? S_OK : hRes);

// pDeleteList depends on the container's critical section.
for (pID = pDeleteList -> Scan(0);
     pID;
     pID = pDeleteList -> Scan())
{
    PABPAB_ID    pDel = NULL;

    if (FAILED(hRes = DeleteChildren(*pID, NULL)))
        break;

    // Remove me from my children's lists of parents, i.e.,
    // make this child "no child o' mine."
    if (FAILED(hRes = Open(…, *pID, RecNum)))
        break;

    if (SUCCEEDED(hRes = Fetch(RecNum, fldPARENTS, &Parents)))
    {
        Parents.Delete(MyID, …);

        if (Parents.Size())
            hRes = Update(RecNum, fldPARENTS, Parents);
        else
        {
            // If child is an orphan, delete it from DB
            // and notify listeners that it's gone.
            if (SUCCEEDED(hRes = DeleteRec(m_pLogon -> m_pDB,
                                            RecNum)))
            {
                ABPAB_EID eidMe,
                          eidChild;

                    ⋮

                m_pLogon -> Notify(fnevObjectDeleted,
                                   &eidMe,
                                   &eidChild,
                                   NULL);
            }
        }
```

```
        }

        Close(RecNum);

        ⋮
    }
    return hRes;
}
```

SaveChanges

SaveChanges implements the transaction model that *IDistList* and *IMailUser* objects must adhere to. This model requires an explicit call to *SaveChanges* to make permanent any modifications to an existing entry or to add a new entry to the database. In the case of a newly created object, *SaveChanges* has the effect of changing the "in-limbo" status of a one-off to that of a full-fledged entry.

Recall that we assigned the one-off entry a unique database ID in *CreateEntry*, even though the MAPI specification doesn't require a new entry to possess an entry ID until *after* the first *SaveChanges* call. A one-off object that is returned from *OpenEntry* retains the fixed one-off entry ID. We can now easily differentiate between a one-off object hailing from a *CreateEntry* call and one coming from *OpenEntry*. The distinction is important because the object returned in *CreateEntry* can be saved, whereas calling *SaveChanges* on a one-off object returned from *OpenEntry* does nothing.

The first step in our implementation of *SaveChanges* is to open the entry's database record. Both existing entries and "in-limbo" entries will have a record, although in the second case the record will have no data in it. Remember that we create a blank record in the call to *CreateEntry* and add the new entry's entry ID to the orphan list in case the object is never saved. (We walk the orphan list on logoff and delete any entries therein from the database—a kind of database garbage collection.)

If the entry is newly created, we need to know the ID of the container in which it was created. This information is recorded by the *CreateEntry* call but is unknown (and irrelevant) if we're opening an existing record. The reason why we need this information in the *CreateEntry* case is to create a parent-child relationship between the new child object and the parent container in which it was created. We create this relationship by opening both entries' database records and calling the *InsertRec* method to update the relationship fields in both records. This relationship is already present between existing entries and their parents.

A rather peculiar situation can occur when a DL is created and members are added to it before the *SaveChanges* on the DL. The members added to this new DL can themselves be newly created entries, and it's possible that *SaveChanges* is called on the new children *before* it's called on the parent. If we didn't create the database record in *CreateEntry*, we would have the odd situation of having to create the parent's record when we save the child, just so we could add the relationship to the child's record.

Newly created entries also must respect the CREATE_CHECK_DUP-_STRICT and CREATE_CHECK_DUP_LOOSE flags in *CreateEntry*. These flags tell the implementation how to handle adding entries to a container that might already have similar or identical entries within it. We interpret CREATE-_CHECK_DUP_LOOSE to mean "replace any existing entries that have the same display name as the new entry" and CREATE_CHECK_DUP_STRICT to mean "replace any existing entries that have the same display name *and* search key as the new entry." The *DeleteDups* method handles this processing by setting up a contents table restriction based on PR_DISPLAY_NAME or PR_DISPLAY-_NAME *and* PR_SEARCH_KEY, as appropriate. Any rows in the contents table that match the restriction are removed. Of course, we exclude the new entry from the restriction so that we don't delete the entry we just added!

We check the entry's dirty flags and flush the property cache if any properties have been changed. Finally, we notify external objects and call *Notify-Parents* to update any open parent containers' contents tables:

```
STDMETHODIMP CBaseProp::SaveChanges(ULONG ulFlags)
{
    HRESULT         hRes = S_OK;
    PABPAB_ID       pID = NULL;

    DECLARE_REC_NUM(ParentRecNum);
    DECLARE_REC_NUM(RecNum);

    // We're a one-off; we can't be saved. This can happen only if a
    // client gets the one-off EID from one-off table and does an
    // OpenEntry and then a SaveChanges. CreateEntry changes the EID to a
    // new one.

    if (m_MyEID.ID.Type & ONEOFF_ENTRY)
        return S_OK;

    if (FAILED(hRes = Open(…, m_MyEID.ID, RecNum)))
        goto Quit;

    if (m_CreateContainerEID.ID.Num)            // 0 if OpenEntry existing
                                                // record
    {
        if (M_FAIL(hRes = Open(m_pLogon -> m_pDB,
```

```
                                OPEN_ONLY,
                                m_CreateContainerEID.ID,
                                ParentRecNum)))
    {
            goto Quit;
    }

    // Insert me in my parent.
    if (M_FAIL(hRes = InsertRec(m_pLogon -> m_pDB,
                                ParentRecNum,
                                RecNum)))
        goto Quit;

    Close(ParentRecNum);
    DeleteDups(m_pParentCont);  // Do last, in case insert fails.
}

m_pLogon -> m_OrphanRecs.Delete(m_MyEID.ID, &pID);

:
// Write all the new properties to the DB.
if (m_fDirtyFlags & PROPS)
{
    LPSPropTagArray psptTags = NULL;

    if (M_FAIL(hRes = m_pPropCache -> Flush(RecNum)))
        goto Quit;

    if (SUCCEEDED(GetPropList(0, &psptTags)))
    {
        m_pLogon  -> Notify(fnevObjectModified,
                            NULL,
                            &m_MyEID,
                            psptTags);
        gFreeBuff((LPVOID)psptTags);
    }
}

hRes = NotifyParents(RecNum,
                    m_bNewEntry ? ABPAB_CHILD_ADDED :
                                    ABPAB_CHILD_MODIFIED,
                    m_pPropCache -> m_pProps);
m_bNewEntry = FALSE;

Quit:

    :
}
```

CopyEntries

The last method we will cover is *CopyEntries*, which is used to place one or more entries in a container. The destination container is the container object on which the call is made, and the source entries are specified in the *lpEntries* parameter. If an entry in the list is native to our database, we simply call *InsertRec* to update the parent-child relationships, call *UpdateCTbl* to update the parent's contents table, and then notify any listening objects. If the entry is being copied from another address book provider, we call *CreateEntry* and let it copy the foreign entry to our provider, and then we call *SaveChanges* on the new object to commit the new record. Notice that *CopyEntries* returns a warning if some of the entries couldn't be successfully copied.

```
STDMETHODIMP CABContainer::CopyEntries(LPENTRYLIST        lpEntries,
                                       ULONG              ulUIParam,
                                       LPMAPIPROGRESS     lpProgress,
                                       ULONG              ulFlags)
{
    LPMAPIPROP          pNewEntry  = NULL;
    ULONG               ulFailures = 0;
    int                 i;

    DECLARE_REC_NUM(ParentRecNum);

    ⋮

    for (i = 0; i < (int)lpEntries -> cValues; i++)
    {
        PABPAB_EID pEID         = (PABPAB_EID)lpEntries -> lpbin[i].lpb;
        ULONG      ulEntryType = m_pLogon -> CheckEID(…);

        DECLARE_REC_NUM(ChildRecNum);

        switch (ulEntryType)
        {
            case MAPI_E_INVALID_ENTRYID:
                ulFailures++;
                break;

            case PSS_DISTLIST:
            case PSS_MAILUSER:
            case PSS_ABCONT:
            case TEMPLATE_USER:
            case TEMPLATE_DL:
            case FOREIGN_USER:
            case FOREIGN_DL:
                if (SUCCEEDED(Open(…, m_MyEID.ID, ParentRecNum)))
```

```
        {
            if (SUCCEEDED(Open(…, pEID -> ID, ChildRecNum)))
            {
                if (SUCCEEDED(InsertRec(…, ParentRecNum,
                                            ChildRecNum)))
                {
                    if (SUCCEEDED(UpdateCTbl(ChildRecNum, NULL)))
                        m_pLogon  -> Notify(fnevObjectCopied,
                                            &m_MyEID,
                                            pEID,
                                            NULL);
                    else
                        ulFailures++;
                }
                else
                    ulFailures++;
                Close(ChildRecNum);
                Close(ParentRecNum);
                break;
            }
            else
            {
                Close(ParentRecNum);
                ulFailures++;
                break;
            }
        }
        else
        {
            ulFailures++;
            break;
        }   // Fall through.

case PSS_ONEOFF_USER:
case PSS_ONEOFF_DL:
case FOREIGN_ENTRY:     // Another AB's entry ID, not in DB
                        // yet
    if (SUCCEEDED(CreateEntry(lpEntries -> lpbin[i].cb,
                                (LPENTRYID)lpEntries ->
                                    lpbin[i].lpb,
                                ulFlags,
                                &pNewEntry)))
    {
        if (M_FAIL(pNewEntry -> SaveChanges(0)))
            ulFailures++;
```

(continued)

```
                    pNewEntry -> Release();
                }
                else
                    ulFailures++;

                break;
        }
    }
    return (0 == ulFailures                 ? S_OK :
            ulFailures == lpEntries -> cValues ? MAPI_E_INVALID_ENTRYID :
            MAPI_W_PARTIAL_COMPLETION);
}
```

Server-Based Address Book Providers

We now turn our attention from local-based address book providers to server-based implementations. You should consider implementing a server-based address book provider when you want to provide multiuser access to the database. A common example is a corporatewide address book provider, or *global address list*. Your decision to implement a server-based provider might also be dictated by a requirement to access an existing centralized database (a database of employee records, for example).

Server-based providers have some different requirements from their local-based cousins. For example, the provider is a DLL that is installed locally on the user's machine but the database resides on a remote server. Service requests are passed from the client to the MAPI subsystem through the client interface, MAPI sends the request to the provider DLL (through the service provider interface), and the provider connects to the server to query the remote database. The results of a query are passed from the remote server back to the local provider, which returns them through an interface. The protocol the provider uses to talk to the server is determined by the implementation; the MAPI subsystem and the client making service requests are blissfully ignorant of this detail.

Another difference is that the back-end server is likely to require the provider to supply security credentials before honoring connection requests. The provider can use whatever scheme is convenient to gather the necessary credentials, for example, by obtaining them from the user or the operating system.

The Design of ABWDS

ABWDS is a read-only server-based provider that implements a typical multiuser address book. The hierarchy of containers is shown in Figure 9-19:

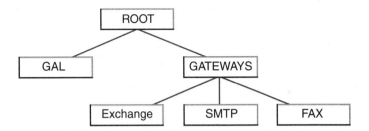

Figure 9-19.
The ABWDS container hierarchy.

The global address list (GAL) contains all recipients known by the provider, including any found in the subcontainers. The GATEWAYS container has no recipients—only subcontainers that contain recipients reachable through one of three "gateways": an Exchange server, an SMTP gateway, or a FAX server.

Although the database resides on the server, the user can access the GAL when a network connection is unavailable because a copy of the GAL is downloaded to a local file for use in offline operations. The user can choose offline operation or full network connection at logon time. The provider automatically switches from online to offline operation if the network connection fails.

Online operations mean that the provider queries the remote database for data to service client requests. Examples include getting properties of an entry or retrieving contents or hierarchy tables.

In offline operations, the provider accesses the local file for this data. The local file is a copy of the GAL container's contents table in which the column set includes all the properties of each DL and mail user. Like ABPAB, ABWDS creates this file when the service is added to a profile and updates it when the user clicks the "Download User List" button in the configuration dialog box. Downloading the GAL causes an RPC to the server, which creates a named pipe whose name is returned in the RPC. APWDS uses this name to open the pipe and read the GAL contents table into the local file. The local file doesn't allow access to PR_OBJECT properties such as PR_CONTAINER_CONTENTS, so you can't see the members of a DL, for instance.

The *CBackEnd* Object

ABWDS declares the *CBackEnd* class for accessing the remote database. *CBackEnd* manages the provider-to-server connection and handles switching from online operations to offline operations in the event of a network error or timeout. *CBackEnd* also implements a set of database access primitives that make requests from the back-end server and return the results in MAPI tables or objects. Here are some of the important methods:

■ *OpenObject.* This method makes an RPC to the server or accesses the local file to retrieve an object's properties from the database. The properties are returned in a linked list. Each object (*IMailUser, IDistList*, etc.) caches its properties internally. DLs and containers also cache the *ITableData* interfaces backing their contents and/or hierarchy tables.

■ *GetTable.* For offline operation, this method returns the cached *ITableData* backing the object's contents or hierarchy table. For online operation, the *ITableData* is created in the *GetTable* call. *GetTable* is called the first time *GetContentsTable/GetHierarchyTable* is called to create the cached *ITableData*; subsequent calls simply return a view on the cached *ITableData*. The *ITableData* is updated by the server when the database changes.

■ *FillHierarchyTable.* This method adds rows to an *ITableData* using hard-coded values for the containers.

■ *FillContentsTable.* This method adds rows to an *ITableData* using data read from the local file (for offline operation) or from a named pipe connected to the server (for online operation).

■ *GoOffLine.* This method changes the connection status from online to offline operation.

■ *GoOnLine.* This method changes the connection status to online operation.

Entry IDs

ABWDS uses an entry ID scheme similar to the scheme implemented by ABPAB. The entry ID maps to a record number in the database and also specifies the type of object that the entry ID represents.

IABProvider::Logon

Since the purpose of each method has been explained in our treatment of ABPAB, we'll cover only those methods that are significantly different in the server-based implementation. The first of these is the *IABProvider::Logon* method. The *Logon* method opens the profile section and retrieves the stored configuration settings. These properties include the server name and location, the user's name and password, the name of the local file used in offline operation, and whether the user wants online or offline operation.

If online operation is requested, the provider makes an RPC to the server (which is the user's post office), validates the user's password, and confirms that the user has a mailbox on the server. *DoServerLogon* handles this processing.

This function creates a mailslot on the client side through which the provider can receive notifications from the server when the database changes. The notifications are *not* MAPI notifications but an implementation-defined protocol. The provider creates a separate thread that blocks on the mailslot, waiting for activity.

Next we create a *CNamePropMgr* object for managing our mapping of named properties to IDs. This object provides support for our implementation of *IMAPIProp::GetNamesFromIDs* and *IMAPIProp::GetIDsFromNames.*

We then open the remote database in the call to *OpenRemoteDataBase,* which returns the name of a pipe that the server created to pass data between the two processes. The pipe is used to stream large sets of data (the members of a distribution list, for example) to and from the server because it's more efficient to pass data as a byte stream than as data structures in an RPC. If the user requests offline operation, *OpenRemoteDataBase* opens the local file containing the downloaded GAL contents table.

OpenRemoteDataBase also creates the *CBackEnd* object, which is cached in the new *CABLogon* object that we create next. The *CABLogon* object is passed back in **ppABLogon,* and we return:

```
STDMETHODIMP CABProvider::Logon(LPMAPISUP        pSupObj,
                                ULONG            ulUIParam,
                                LPTSTR           pszProfileName,
                                ULONG            ulFlags,
                                ULONG *          pcbSecurity,
                                LPBYTE *         ppbSecurity,
                                LPMAPIERROR *    ppMAPIError,
                                LPABLOGON *      ppABLogon)
{
    ⋮
    CGeneric obj;
    *ppMAPIError = NULL;
    *ppbSecurity = NULL;
    *pcbSecurity = 0;

    LPSPropValue pProps = NULL;
    CBackEnd *   pBEobj = NULL;
    CABLogon *   pABLogonObj = NULL;

    CFGDLG           CfgDialog = { 0 };
    MAILBOX_INFO     UserMBInfo = { 0 };
    ULONG            ulPropCount;
    DWORD            dwConnectionID;
    LPPROFSECT       pProfileObj;
```

(continued)

```
CNamePropMgr * pNPList = NULL;

HRESULT hResult = OpenServiceProfileSection(pSupObj,
                                            &pProfileObj,
                                            GetMAPIFreeBuffer());
⋮

hResult = pProfileObj -> GetProps((LPSPropTagArray)&sptLogonArray,
                                  fMapiUnicode,
                                  &ulPropCount,
                                  &pProps);

// Fill in the logon UI structure.
CfgDialog.hInst    = m_hInstance;
CfgDialog.hWnd     = (HWND)ulUIParam;
CfgDialog.ppProps  = &pProps;
CfgDialog.pSupObj  = pSupObj;
CfgDialog.hUIMutex = hUIMutex;

// In case we get MAPI_W_ERRORS_RETURNED, ignore it and reset
// to S_OK. Now display the logon configuration dialog.
if (MAPI_W_ERRORS_RETURNED == hResult)
{
    if (PR_SMP_MAILBOX_ID        != pProps[MAILBOX_ID].ulPropTag      ||
        PR_SMP_CONNECTION_TYPE != pProps[NET_CON].ulPropTag           ||
        PR_SMP_LUL_LAST_UPDATE != pProps[LUL_LASTUPDATE].ulPropTag ||
        PR_SMP_LUL_FILENAME    != pProps[LUL_FILENAME].ulPropTag)
    {
        hResult = MAPI_E_UNCONFIGURED;
        if (!(LOGON_NO_DIALOG & ulFlags))
        {
            PrivInitialize3DCtl(m_hInstance);
            PrivateMessageBox(IDS_MSG_SERVICE_NOT_PROPERLY_CFG,
                          (HWND)ulUIParam);
        }
        goto ErrorExit;
    }

    hResult = S_OK;
    if (PR_SMP_REMOTE_SERVER != pProps[SERVER_NAME].ulPropTag ||
        PR_SMP_MAILBOX_NAME != pProps[MAILBOX_NAME].ulPropTag ||
        PR_SMP_USER_NAME != pProps[USER_NAME].ulPropTag ||
        PR_SMP_MAILBOX_PASSWORD != pProps[PASSWORD].ulPropTag)
```

```
    {
        if (AB_NO_DIALOG & ulFlags)
        {
            hResult = MAPI_E_UNCONFIGURED;
            goto ErrorExit;
        }
        PrivInitialize3DCtl(m_hInstance);
ReStartLogonDlg:
        hResult = DoLogonDlg(&CfgDialog);
        if (hResult)
        {
            goto ErrorExit;
        }
        hResult = pProfileObj -> SetProps(ulPropCount, pProps, NULL);
        if (hResult)
            goto ErrorExit;
    }
}

if (LAN_CONNECT == pProps[NET_CON].Value.l)
{
    hResult = DoServerLogon(&UserMBInfo,
                            pProps,
                            pProfileObj,
                            !(AB_NO_DIALOG & ulFlags),
                            (HWND)ulUIParam,
                            TRUE,
                            WINDS_NOTIF_ON_AB | WINDS_NOTIF_ON_USER,
                            &dwConnectionID,
                            FALSE);
    if (S_FALSE == hResult)
        goto ReStartLogonDlg;
}

// DoServerLogon returns MAPI_W_NO_SERVICE in client context
// and MAPI_E_NETWORK_ERROR in spooler context.
if (OFFLINE_CONNECT == pProps[NET_CON].Value.l ||
    MAPI_W_NO_SERVICE == hResult               ||
    MAPI_E_NETWORK_ERROR == hResult)
{
    hResult = S_OK;
    pProps[NET_CON].Value.l = OFFLINE_CONNECT;
    dwConnectionID = 0;
}
```

(continued)

447

```
if (!hResult)
{
    pNPList = new CNamePropMgr(GetMAPIAllocBuffer(),
                              GetMAPIAllocMore(),
                              GetMAPIFreeBuffer());
    if (!pNPList)
    {
        hResult = E_OUTOFMEMORY;
    }
    else
    {
        pNPList -> InitializeForInMemoryUse();
    }
}
if (hResult)
{
    goto ErrorExit;
}

// Since we are going to allocate a new object and manipulate the
// list of sessions, lock the provider until we are finished.
EnterCriticalSection(&m_csObj);
hResult = OpenRemoteDataBase(pProps[SERVER_NAME].Value.LPSZ,
                            &guidProvider,
                            (OFFLINE_CONNECT ==
                                pProps[NET_CON].Value.l),
                            pProps[LUL_FILENAME].Value.LPSZ,
                            &pBEobj);
if (!hResult)
{
    try
    {
        pABLogonObj =
            new CABLogon(m_hInstance,
                        pBEobj,
                        pNPList,
                        pSupObj,
                        dwConnectionID,
                        &UserMBInfo,
                        pProps[MAILBOX_ID].Value.l,
                        pProps[SERVER_NAME].Value.LPSZ,
                        (CONNECTION_TYPE)pProps[NET_CON].Value.l,
                        pProps[LUL_FILENAME].Value.LPSZ,
                        pProps[LUL_LASTUPDATE].Value.LPSZ,
                        hUIMutex);
```

448

```
            if (!pABLogonObj)
                hResult = E_OUTOFMEMORY;
        }
        catch (CException & Exception)
        {
            hResult = Exception.GetError();
        }
        if (!hResult)
        {
            AddWindsABNamedPropsToList(pNPList);
            // To avoid closing it below. If we fail, the destructor
            // in CABLogon will take care of this.
            pNPList = NULL;
            hUIMutex = NULL;

            // The guidProvider is used in the entry ID of this provider.
            // The UID is hard-coded because only ONE instance of the provider
            // is allowed to be in the profile at any time. If multiple
            // instances of the same address book provider are allowed, then
            // a new UID provider must be generated for each session (i.e.,
            // IMAPISupport::NewUID()) and saved in the
            // profile section of your provider.
            hResult = pSupObj -> SetProviderUID(&guidProvider, 0);
            if (!hResult)
            {
                // Also register support for this UID in entry IDs, which WINDS
                // transports set to open entries in this address book provider.
                hResult = pSupObj -> SetProviderUID(&guidXPEntries, 0);
                if (!hResult)
                {
                    pABLogonObj -> InitializeStatusRow();
                }
            }
        }
    }
    // Unlock the critical section.
    LeaveCriticalSection(&m_csObj);

ErrorExit:
// If we failed, clean up before leaving.
    if (hResult)
    {
        ⋮
    }
    else
```

(continued)

```
    {
        // We were successful, copy objects into the return parameters.
        ASSERT(pABLogonObj);
        *ppABLogon = (LPABLOGON)pABLogonObj;
    }
    return hResult;
}
```

IABLogon::OpenEntry

The ABWDS implementation of *OpenEntry* is essentially the same as ABPAB's except that the newly instantiated object is initialized either by reading data from the local file or by querying the remote database:

```
STDMETHODIMP CABLogon::OpenEntry(ULONG            cbEntryID,
                                 LPENTRYID        pEntryID,
                                 LPCIID           pInterface,
                                 ULONG            ulFlags,
                                 ULONG *          pulObjType,
                                 LPUNKNOWN *      ppUnk)
{
    ⋮
    //In out implementation we support only read-only access to objects.
    if (ulFlags & MAPI_MODIFY)
        return E_ACCESSDENIED;

    HRESULT hResult = S_OK;
    PRIVATE_ENTRYID  eidXPEntry = { 0 },
                     * pEID = cbEntryID ? (PRIVATE_ENTRYID *)pEntryID : NULL;

    if (CB_PRIVATE_XP_EID == cbEntryID)
    {
        PRIVATE_XP_ENTRYID * pXPEID = (PRIVATE_XP_ENTRYID *)pEntryID;
        if (!IsValidXPEntryID(pXPEID))
            return MAPI_E_INVALID_ENTRYID;

        hResult = GetABEntryIDFromXPEntryID(*pXPEID, &eidXPEntry);

        pEID = &eidXPEntry;
        cbEntryID = CB_PRIVATE_EID;
    }

    if (pEID)
    {
        if (CB_PRIVATE_EID != cbEntryID ||
            !m_pBEobj -> IsValidEntryID(pEID))
            return MAPI_E_INVALID_ENTRYID;
```

```
    if (pInterface)
    {
        BOOL fBadInterface = FALSE;
        switch (pEID -> bObject)
        {
            case MAPI_DISTLIST:
            case MAPI_ABCONT:
                if (IID_IABContainer    != *pInterface &&
                        IID_IDistList        != *pInterface &&
                        IID_IMAPIContainer != *pInterface &&
                        IID_IMAPIProp        != *pInterface &&
                        IID_IUnknown         != *pInterface)
                {
                    fBadInterface = TRUE;
                }
                break;
            case MAPI_MAILUSER:
                if (IID_IMailUser != *pInterface &&
                        IID_IMAPIProp != *pInterface &&
                        IID_IUnknown  != *pInterface)
                {
                    fBadInterface = TRUE;
                }
                break;
        }
        if (fBadInterface)
            return E_NOINTERFACE;
    }
}


// Create an entry ID of the root and have it readily available to
// supply it as the parent of the entries.
PRIVATE_ENTRYID eidRoot = { 0 };
eidRoot.uidGlobal = m_pBEobj -> GetBackEndUID();
eidRoot.bVersion = ENTRYID_VERSION;
eidRoot.bObject = MAPI_ABCONT;
eidRoot.dwObjID = ROOT_CONTAINER_ID;
// This is the entry ID of the ROOT container, { 0, NULL }.
if (!pEID || MAPI_ABCONT == pEID -> bObject)
{
    if (NULL == pInterface ||
        IID_IABContainer   == *pInterface ||
        IID_IDistList      == *pInterface ||
        IID_IMAPIContainer == *pInterface ||
        IID_IMAPIProp      == *pInterface ||
        IID_IUnknown       == *pInterface)
```

(continued)

```
        {
            if (!pEID || ROOT_CONTAINER_ID == pEID -> dwObjID)
                pEID = &eidRoot;
        }
    else
            return E_NOINTERFACE;
    }


CABContainer * pContObj;
CMailUser * pUserObj;
CPropList * pList = NULL;
BOOL fIsOneOff = FALSE;


EnterCriticalSection(&m_csObj);


// If entry ID is for a MAILUSER object, check if ID is for a ONE-OFF.
if ((MAPI_MAILUSER == pEID -> bObject) &&
    (0xFFFFFFFF    == pEID -> dwObjID))
{
    // Bingo, this is a special case for us. Get properties for one-off.
    fIsOneOff = TRUE;
    hResult = GetOneOffProperties(&pList);
}
if (!hResult && !fIsOneOff)
    // Object is a regular one. Ask the back end to supply
    // its properties.
    hResult = m_pBEobj -> OpenObject(*pEID, &pList);


PRIVATE_ENTRYID * pParentEID = &eidRoot;
if (!hResult && (MAPI_ABCONT   == pEID -> bObject ||
                 MAPI_DISTLIST == pEID -> bObject))
{
    // Allocate new container. Since DLs and address book containers
    // have the same interfaces, they were implemented in the sample
    // class. When behavior needs to be different between the two, we
    // check object's flags and the entry ID's object type field.
    pContObj = new CABContainer(this,
                                pParentEID,
                                pEID,
                                (MAPI_ABCONT == pEID -> bObject ?
                                    MAPI_ABCONT : MAPI_DISTLIST),
                                pList,
                                m_pNPList,
                                MAPI_ACCESS_READ);
    if (pContObj)
    {
        // These types of containers have only containers.
        if (ROOT_CONTAINER_ID       == pEID -> dwObjID ||
            GATEWAY_CONTAINERS_ID == pEID -> dwObjID)
```

```
            {
                pContObj -> m_ulObjFlags |= OBJECT_MAY_HAVE_CONTAINERS;
            }
            else
            {
                // These types of containers have only recipients.
                pContObj -> m_ulObjFlags |= OBJECT_MAY_HAVE_RECIPIENTS;
            }
        }
        else
        {
            hResult = E_OUTOFMEMORY;
        }
    }
    if (!hResult && (MAPI_MAILUSER == pEID -> bObject))
    {
        pUserObj = new CMailUser(this,
                                 pEID,
                                 pList,
                                 m_pNPList,
                                 MAPI_ACCESS_READ);
        if (pUserObj)
        {
            if (fIsOneOff)
            {
                pUserObj -> m_ulObjFlags |= OBJECT_IS_ONE_OFF;
            }
        }
        else
        {
            hResult = E_OUTOFMEMORY;
        }
    }
    LeaveCriticalSection(&m_csObj);
    if (hResult)
        :
    else
    {
        // Return the object to the caller with the appropriate object
        // type set. Note that the constructor of the object placed the
        // reference count of the object to 1, meaning that the object
        // has been AddRef'ed and the caller is responsible for
        // releasing it.
        if (!pEID || MAPI_ABCONT == pEID -> bObject)
```

(continued)

453

```
        {
            *pulObjType = MAPI_ABCONT;
            *ppUnk = (LPUNKNOWN)pContObj;
        }
        else
        {
            if (MAPI_DISTLIST == pEID -> bObject)
            {
                *pulObjType = MAPI_DISTLIST;
                *ppUnk = (LPUNKNOWN)pContObj;
            }
            else
            {
                ASSERT(MAPI_MAILUSER == pEID -> bObject);
                *pulObjType = MAPI_MAILUSER;
                *ppUnk = (LPUNKNOWN)pUserObj;
            }
        }
    }
    }
    return hResult;
}
```

OpenEntry calls *CBackEnd::OpenObject* to get the entry's property list from the remote database or the local file. The entry ID passed in the call identifies the database record backing this entry. We then create a new object (a *CABContainer* or *CMailUser*, as appropriate). The list of properties in **pList* is passed to the object's constructor and cached in the object.

Because ABWDS is read-only, we don't have to worry about copying foreign entries into its database, storing a foreign entry's details table, or calling *OpenTemplateID* as we did for ABPAB.

IABContainer::ResolveNames

ABWDS's implementation of *ResolveNames* is very similar to ABPAB, except the criteria for finding a match is based on the entry's PR_DISPLAY_NAME *and* PR_ACCOUNT properties:

```
STDMETHODIMP CABContainer::ResolveNames(LPSPropTagArray    pPropTagArray,
                                        ULONG              ulFlags,
                                        LPADRLIST          pAdrList,
                                        LPFlagList         pFlagList)
{
    ⋮

    LPSPropValue    pProps,
                    pOneProp;
```

```
LPSRowSet       pRows;
LPSRow          pOneRow;
LPTSTR          pszName;
ULONG           k, j,
                ulReqPropTag,
                ulPropCount;
BOOL            fNameResolved;
DWORD           dwInstID;
HRESULT         hPropError,
                hOpError,
                hSearchResult,
                hResult = S_OK;
SPropValue spvString = { 0 }, spvInstKey = { 0 };

spvInstKey.ulPropTag = PR_INSTANCE_KEY;
spvInstKey.Value.bin.cb = sizeof(DWORD);
spvInstKey.Value.bin.lpb = (LPBYTE)&dwInstID;

SRestriction SRes = { 0 };
SRes.rt = RES_CONTENT;
SRes.res.resContent.lpProp = &spvString;
EnterCriticalSection(&m_csObj);

// Get view on contents table of this container.
LPMAPITABLE pTable;
hResult = GetGALTable();

if (!hResult)
{
    hResult = m_pContTable -> HrGetView(NULL, NULL, 0, &pTable);
    if (!hResult)
    {
        hResult = pTable ->
                    SetColumns((LPSPropTagArray)&sptResolveNamesCols,
                               TBL_BATCH);
        if (!hResult)
            // Sort table so we can use it for resolving name
            // with FindRow.
            hResult = pTable -> SortTable(&sosDefaultSort, TBL_BATCH);
    }
}
if (!hResult)
{
    for (k = 0; k < pAdrList -> cEntries; k++)
```

(continued)

```
{
    // Skip entries with 0 properties or resolved by other ABs.
    if (0 == pAdrList -> aEntries[k].cValues ||
        MAPI_UNRESOLVED != pFlagList -> ulFlag[k])
        continue;

    fNameResolved = FALSE;
    dwInstID = 0;
    // Get the display name we are resolving.
    pOneProp = PpropFindProp(pAdrList -> aEntries[k].rgPropVals,
                             pAdrList -> aEntries[k].cValues,
                             PR_DISPLAY_NAME);

    SRes.res.resContent.ulFuzzyLevel = FL_FULLSTRING | FL_IGNORECASE;
    SRes.res.resContent.ulPropTag = spvString.ulPropTag = PR_ACCOUNT;
    pszName = pOneProp -> Value.LPSZ;

    // Skip any beginning blanks or tabs in the name to resolve.
    while (*pszName == ' ' || *pszName == '\t')
        pszName++;

    spvString.Value.LPSZ = pszName;
    // Try a full hit or PR_ACCOUNT.
    hSearchResult = pTable -> FindRow(&SRes, BOOKMARK_BEGINNING, 0);

    if (S_OK == hSearchResult)
        // Hit on PR_ACCOUNT. I don't need to do anything else here.
        fNameResolved = TRUE;
    else
    {
        // The display name does not match any account name.
        if (MAPI_E_NOT_FOUND == hSearchResult)
        {
            // Search on ALL names in table that meet this criteria.
            // Use substring search.
            SRes.res.resContent.ulFuzzyLevel = FL_SUBSTRING |
                                                FL_IGNORECASE;
            SRes.res.resContent.ulPropTag = spvString.ulPropTag =
                                            PR_DISPLAY_NAME;
            hSearchResult = pTable -> FindRow(&SRes,
                                              BOOKMARK_BEGINNING,
                                              0);

            // If we found at least ONE name matching subrestriction,
            // process table rows.
            if (S_OK == hSearchResult)
```

```
        {
            // Use the helper function.
            ResolveOneName(pszName,
                        pTable,
                        pFlagList -> ulFlag[k],
                        dwInstID);

            if (dwInstID)
                fNameResolved = TRUE;
        }
    }
}

// Got a full hit, and name can be resolved in this
// address book provider.
if (fNameResolved)
{
    hOpError = S_OK;
    // If instance is 0, it's because hit was on the ACCOUNT name.
    // We need to get the current row in the table.
    if (0 == dwInstID)
    {
        hOpError = pTable -> QueryRows(1, 0, &pRows);

        if (!hOpError)
            CopyMemory(&dwInstID,
                        pRows -> aRow[0].lpProps[2].Value.bin.lpb,
                        sizeof(DWORD));
    }
    else
        pRows = NULL;

    if (!hOpError)
    {
        // svpInstKey has instance key of row where hit
        // occurred. Use it to get all properties of row
        // on ITableData object.
        hOpError = m_pContTable -> HrQueryRow(&spvInstKey,
                                            &pOneRow,
                                            NULL);
        if (!hOpError)
        {
            // Was this property in an entry of this ADRLIST?
            ulPropCount = pPropTagArray -> cValues;
```

(continued)

457

```
        if (PpropFindProp(pAdrList -> aEntries[k].rgPropVals,
                          pAdrList -> aEntries[k].cValues,
                          PR_RECIPIENT_TYPE))
            ulPropCount++;

        // Allocate the array for the new entry properties.
        hOpError =
            PrivMAPIAllocate(ulPropCount*sizeof(SPropValue),
                            (LPVOID *)&pProps);
        if (!hOpError)
        {
            for (j = 0; j < pPropTagArray -> cValues; j++)
            {
                ulReqPropTag = pPropTagArray -> aulPropTag[j];

                // Display & transmittable name are same
                // for us.
                if (PR_TRANSMITABLE_DISPLAY_NAME ==
                    ulReqPropTag)
                    ulReqPropTag = PR_DISPLAY_NAME;

                pOneProp = PpropFindProp(pOneRow -> lpProps,
                                        pOneRow -> cValues,
                                        ulReqPropTag);

                if (pOneProp)
                    hPropError =
                        PropCopyMore(&pProps[j],
                                    pOneProp,
                                    GetMAPIAllocMore(),
                                    pProps);
                else
                    hPropError = MAPI_E_NOT_FOUND;

                if (hPropError)
                {
                    pProps[j].ulPropTag =
                        PROP_TAG(PT_ERROR,
                                PROP_ID(pPropTagArray ->
                                        aulPropTag[j]));
                    pProps[j].Value.err = hPropError;
                }
                else
                    pProps[j].ulPropTag = pPropTagArray ->
                                            aulPropTag[j];
            }
        }
```

```
                        PrivMAPIFree((LPVOID *)&pOneRow);
                    }
                    if (pRows)
                        FreeProws(pRows);
                }

                if (!hOpError)
                {
                    pOneProp =
                        PpropFindProp(pAdrList -> aEntries[k].rgPropVals,
                                      pAdrList -> aEntries[k].cValues,
                                      PR_RECIPIENT_TYPE);
                    if (pOneProp)
                    {
                        pProps[ulPropCount-1].ulPropTag =
                            pOneProp -> ulPropTag;
                        pProps[ulPropCount-1].Value = pOneProp -> Value;
                    }
                    // Now replace entry with new property array and set
                    // flag to fully resolve (MAPI_RESOLVED).
                    PrivMAPIFree((LPVOID *)&(pAdrList ->
                                                aEntries[k].rgPropVals));
                    pAdrList -> aEntries[k].rgPropVals = pProps;
                    pAdrList -> aEntries[k].cValues = ulPropCount;
                    pFlagList -> ulFlag[k] = MAPI_RESOLVED;
                }
            }
        }
    }
    LeaveCriticalSection(&m_csObj);
    return S_OK;
}
```

We first get a view of the container's contents table, call *SetColumns* on it, and then sort the table in ascending order. These steps are necessary because the cached view might have been changed (by a client calling *SetColumns* or *SortTable*, for example). If we resolve the name, we will return its properties from a row in the table, so we need to ensure that each row has the full set of properties. We need to sort the table because we use the *FindRow* method to search for matches, and *FindRow* only returns meaningful results when the table is sorted in the same order as the search direction.

We call *FindRow* to search for an entry having the target string in the entry's PR_ACCOUNT_NAME value. The account name is unique within the ABWDS database, so if there is a hit, the name is unambiguously resolved. If there is no hit, we move the table cursor back to the beginning of the table and try *FindRow* again, this time using PR_DISPLAY_NAME.

If the target name is a substring of a display name in the table, *FindRow* positions the cursor on that row and returns S_OK. We then call the *ResolveOne-Name* helper function to determine the quality (and quantity) of the match. We call *QueryRows* to retrieve the current row. We then compare the target string to the display name, set a flag if the two match, and get the next row. We again compare the target string to the display name in the new row, and if they match, we flag the entry as ambiguous. If they don't match, a single matching entry in the contents table exists and the name can be resolved. We pass back the instance key of the matching row, which *ResolveNames* passes to *HrQueryRow* in order to return the row containing the hit. We allocate an *SPropValue* array for the resolved name's properties and copy them from the "hit" row into the array. The order in which the properties appear in the *ADRENTRY* must match that given in *pPropTagArray*, so we walk the *pPropTagArray* and search the row for each property to copy.

Table Notifications

ABWDS doesn't support notifications on individual objects, so *IABLogon::Advise* is just a stub that returns MAPI_E_NO_SUPPORT. We do support table notifications on a container's contents or hierarchy table, however.

Since ABWDS is read-only, a table view can change only when the WINDS post-office administrator adds, deletes, or modifies an entry in ABWDS, rather than as a result of any action on the user's part. We rely on *ITableData* to generate notifications from the client-side provider to any open views. Notifications from the WINDS server to the ABWDS provider are handled by our own notification broadcasting, which uses Win32 mailslots:

```
CABLogon::CABLogon(…, DWORD dwConnectionID, …) : CGeneric()
{
    DWORD dwThreadID;
    HRESULT hResult;
    TCHAR szMailslotName[64];

    // If connection ID is 0, server couldn't set a notification link
    // to us. Don't bother creating a mailslot and listening thread.
    if (dwConnectionID)
    {
        wsprintf(szMailslotName,
                CLIENT_MAILSLOT_SINK_NAME_FORMAT,
                AB_WINDS_NOTIFICATION_MAILSLOT,
                dwConnectionID);
        m_hMailslot = CreateMailslot(szMailslotName, …,
                                    MAILSLOT_WAIT_FOREVER, …);
        if (INVALID_HANDLE_VALUE == m_hMailslot)
```

```
            {
                ⋮
            }
            else
            {
                HANDLE hThread = CreateThread
                                    (NULL,
                                     0,
                                    (LPTHREAD_START_ROUTINE)ABMailslotListenThreadProc,
                                     (LPVOID)this,
                                     CREATE_SUSPENDED,
                                     &dwThreadID);
                if (hThread)
                {
                    SetThreadPriority(hThread, THREAD_PRIORITY_LOWEST);
                    ResumeThread(hThread);
                    CloseHandle(hThread);
                }
                else
                {
                    ⋮
                }
            }
        }
        ⋮
    }
```

We start by creating a mailslot at logon time when the provider creates the new *CABLogon* object. The mailslot's name is decided by the server, which creates a unique ID number that identifies the connection. This ID is returned in *IABProvider::Logon* via *DoServerLogon*, which makes an RPC to the server to obtain this number. The mailslot's ID number is passed to *CABLogon* in the *dwConnectionID* parameter and is used to compose a string name for the mailslot.

CABLogon starts a worker thread that blocks waiting for activity on the mailslot. The server calls *CreateFile* to create the broadcasting end of the mailslot (in this case, the WINDS server is the mailslot client and ABWDS is the mailslot server) and writes to it whenever an entry is changed in the database.

```
DWORD WINAPI ABMailslotListenThreadProc(CABLogon * pLogon)
{
    HANDLE hMailslot = pLogon -> GetListenMailslot();
    DWORD dwRead;
    FILETIME ftLastNotifTime = { 0 };
    WINDS_NOTIF_EVENT LastEvent;
```

(continued)

```
WINDS_NOTIFICATION Notif;
HRESULT hReadError;
LPTABLEDATA pTable;
while (TRUE)
{
    pTable = NULL;
    if (!ReadFile(hMailslot, &Notif, sizeof(WINDS_NOTIFICATION),
                  &dwRead, NULL))
    {
        ⋮
        continue;
    }
    // Mailslot msgs are received in each installed network protocol stack.
    // Check the time stamp and event of the last notification received. If it
    // is the same, drop it and continue to listen for new and different
    // incoming data on the mailslot.
    if (ftLastNotifTime.dwLowDateTime  == Notif.ftEventTime.dwLowDateTime &&
        ftLastNotifTime.dwHighDateTime == Notif.ftEventTime.dwHighDateTime &&
        LastEvent                      == Notif.Event)
    {
        continue;
    }
    // Save the last event information.
    ftLastNotifTime = Notif.ftEventTime;
    LastEvent = Notif.Event;
    ⋮
    pLogon -> GetCachedGAL(&pTable);
    ⋮
    switch (Notif.Event)
    {
        case AB_USER_DELETED:
        case AB_DL_DELETED:
            {
                DWORD dwInstKey;
                if (AB_USER_DELETED == Notif.Event)
                {
                    dwInstKey = Notif.Info.MB.dwObjID;
                }
                else
                {
                    if (AB_DL_DELETED == Notif.Event)
                    {
                        dwInstKey = Notif.Info.DL.dwObjID;
                    }
                }

                SPropValue spvInstKey = { 0 };
                spvInstKey.ulPropTag = PR_INSTANCE_KEY;
```

```
            spvInstKey.Value.bin.cb = sizeof(DWORD);
            spvInstKey.Value.bin.lpb = (LPBYTE)&dwInstKey;
            pTable -> HrDeleteRow(&spvInstKey);
        }
        break;
    case AB_USER_ADDED:
    case AB_USER_MODIFIED:
    case AB_DL_ADDED:
    case AB_DL_MODIFIED:
        {
            SPropValue spvProps[CONTENTS_TABLE_PROPS] = { 0 };
            SRow row = { 0 };
            row.cValues = CONTENTS_TABLE_PROPS;
            row.lpProps = spvProps;
            PRIVATE_ENTRYID eidObject = { 0 };
            eidObject.uidGlobal = pLogon -> GetBackEndUID();
            eidObject.bVersion = ENTRYID_VERSION;

            DWORD dwInstKey;
            for (ULONG i = 0; i < CONTENTS_TABLE_PROPS; i++)
            {
                spvProps[i].ulPropTag =
                    sptContainerContProps.aulPropTag[i];
            }

            TCHAR szEmailAddress[64];
            LPTSTR pszServer = pLogon -> GetServerName();
            BOOL fBadEntry;

            spvProps[CONT_INST_KEY].Value.bin.cb = sizeof(DWORD);
            spvProps[CONT_INST_KEY].Value.bin.lpb = (LPBYTE)&dwInstKey;
            spvProps[CONT_ADDRTYPE].Value.LPSZ = WINDS_ADDRESS_TYPE;
            spvProps[CONT_ENTRYID].Value.bin.cb = CB_PRIVATE_EID;
            spvProps[CONT_ENTRYID].Value.bin.lpb = (LPBYTE)&eidObject;
            spvProps[CONT_RTF].Value.b = TRUE;
            spvProps[CONT_EMAILADDR].Value.LPSZ = szEmailAddress;

            fBadEntry = FALSE;
            switch (Notif.Event)
            {
                case AB_USER_ADDED:
                case AB_USER_MODIFIED:
                    spvProps[CONT_OBJTYPE].Value.l = MAPI_MAILUSER;
                    spvProps[CONT_DISPTYPE].Value.l = DT_MAILUSER;
                    spvProps[CONT_ACCOUNT].Value.LPSZ =
                        Notif.Info.MB.szMailboxName;
```

(continued)

463

```
                    wsprintf(szEmailAddress,
                            TEXT("%s\\%s"),
                            pszServer,
                            Notif.Info.MB.szMailboxName);
                    spvProps[CONT_DISPNAME].Value.LPSZ =
                        Notif.Info.MB.szFullName;
                    spvProps[CONT_TITLE].Value.LPSZ =
                        Notif.Info.MB.szJobTitle;
                    spvProps[CONT_OFFICE_LOC].Value.LPSZ =
                        Notif.Info.MB.szOffice;
                    spvProps[CONT_OFFICE_PHONE].Value.LPSZ =
                        Notif.Info.MB.szPhone;
                    spvProps[CONT_OTHER_PHONE].Value.LPSZ =
                        Notif.Info.MB.szAltPhone;
                    spvProps[CONT_FAX].Value.LPSZ =
                        Notif.Info.MB.szFax;
                    spvProps[CONT_COMMENT].Value.LPSZ =
                        Notif.Info.MB.szComments;
                    eidObject.dwObjID = Notif.Info.MB.dwObjID;
                    break;

                case AB_DL_ADDED:
                case AB_DL_MODIFIED:
                    spvProps[CONT_DISPTYPE].Value.l = DT_DISTLIST;
                    spvProps[CONT_OBJTYPE].Value.l =
                        MAPI_DISTLIST;
                    spvProps[CONT_ACCOUNT].Value.LPSZ =
                        Notif.Info.DL.szDLAlias;
                    wsprintf(szEmailAddress,
                            TEXT("%s\\%s"),
                            pszServer,
                            Notif.Info.DL.szDLAlias);
                    spvProps[CONT_DISPNAME].Value.LPSZ =
                        Notif.Info.DL.szDLFullName;
                    spvProps[CONT_TITLE].Value.LPSZ = szBlank;
                    spvProps[CONT_OFFICE_LOC].Value.LPSZ =
                        szBlank;
                    spvProps[CONT_OFFICE_PHONE].Value.LPSZ =
                        szBlank;
                    spvProps[CONT_OTHER_PHONE].Value.LPSZ =
                        szBlank;
                    spvProps[CONT_FAX].Value.LPSZ = szBlank;
                    spvProps[CONT_COMMENT].Value.LPSZ = szBlank;
                    eidObject.dwObjID = Notif.Info.DL.dwObjID;
                    break;
            }
```

```
                        dwInstKey = eidObject.dwObjID;
                        eidObject.bObject = (BYTE)spvProps[CONT_OBJTYPE].Value.l;
                        pTable -> HrModifyRow(&row);
                    }
                    break;

                case SERVER_IS_SHUTTING_DOWN:
                    ⋮
                    break;

                case SERVER_HAS_RESTARTED:
                    ⋮
                    break;

                case RESET_LINKS_WITH_SERVER:
                    ⋮
                    break;

                case AB_GET_LOCAL_ABDATA_NOW:
                    ⋮
                    break;

            }
            ⋮
        }
    return S_OK;
}
```

The server writes a message to the mailslot that tells the listening thread what happened. The relevant information is contained in a *WINDS_NOTIFICA-TION* structure which includes fields that specify the affected entry's database record number, its display name, and so on. (Other notifications not related to tables are also broadcast to the same mailslot, but we won't discuss those right now.) The entry's complete property set can be calculated from all the information in the *Notif* structure, and an *SRow* is created on the fly from these properties. The *SRow* is passed to *HrModifyRow,* which creates a new row (or replaces the old one) in the *ITableData* that backs the contents table. *HrModifyRow* causes a table notification to occur on any open view.

It's important to reiterate that our implementations rely on *ITableData,* which is implemented by MAPI. We use the *ITableData* methods to return views and update the table rows. Our implementation is greatly simplified because *ITableData* automatically generates table notifications on any open views whenever *HrModifyRow* is called. But our implementation is just one implementation, and you might find it convenient or necessary to implement *IMAPITable* directly, especially if your provider must talk to an existing database back end, such as an SQL server.

In that case, you might want to eliminate the *ITableData* middleman and query the database directly whenever you service an *IMAPITable* method. If you do, you'll have to supply your own table notification logic such that changes to the data source trigger a call to *OnNotify* on any *AdviseSink* objects passed to the table's *Advise* method. The server must communicate these changes to the provider by some form of IPC; we use mailslots because they let you broadcast the event to any interested listeners.

Once the event is received on the provider side, the provider must then figure out a way to notify (i.e., call *OnNotify*) anyone holding a view that is affected by the change. Notice that not all changes to the database will affect all views: Adding an entry in container X shouldn't trigger a notification in container Y's contents table, for example. Once you figure out a scheme that meets these requirements, you can use the MAPI notification engine to manage calling the correct *OnNotify*s.[5]

The Status Table

ABWDS supports the following columns in the status table:

- *PR_IDENTITY_DISPLAY.*

- *PR_IDENTITY_SEARCH_KEY.*

- *PR_IDENTITY_ENTRYID.* The user's identity is given by these three properties. It's convenient for the address book provider to provide identity since these properties are easily calculated from information that is already in the address book for every user on the WINDS post office.

- *PR_RESOURCE_METHODS.* We support the *SettingsDialog* and *ChangePassword* methods, so this property value is STATUS_CHANGE_PASSWORD ¦ STATUS_SETTINGS_DIALOG.

- *PR_STATUS_CODE.* The value represents the status of ABWDS's connection with the WINDS server: STATUS_OFFLINE or STATUS_AVAILABLE.

---

5. For example, you might want to have a member in your *IMAPITable* object that associates the table with the container whose data it represents. This information can be encapsulated in the *NOTIFKEY* structure you pass to *IMAPISupport::Subscribe* when you handle *IMAPITable::Advise*.

The *CMAPIStatus* Object

A client gains access to a provider's *IMAPIStatus* object by calling *IMAPISession-::GetStatusTable* and searching (or restricting) for the provider's row. The entry ID column in the table is computed by MAPI and identifies the *IMAPIStatus* object of the provider in that row, not the provider supplying the status object. When a client calls *IMAPISession::OpenEntry* using the status object's entry ID, MAPI delegates the call to the provider's *OpenStatusEntry* method. *OpenStatusEntry* creates an *IMAPIStatus* object, which *OpenEntry* returns to the caller.

Our implementation creates the status object the first time *OpenStatusEntry* is called and caches it to service future calls. Notice that we also open the provider's profile section to handle *GetProps* on PR_RESOURCE_FLAGS, whose value is copied from the INF file to the profile section by MAPI:

```
STDMETHODIMP CABLogon::OpenStatusEntry(LPCIID          pInterface,
                                       ULONG           ulFlags,
                                       ULONG *         pulObjType,
                                       LPMAPISTATUS *  ppEntry)
{
    HRESULT hResult = S_OK;

    ⋮

    if (pInterface)
        if (IID_IMAPIStatus != *pInterface &&
            IID_IMAPIProp != *pInterface)
            return E_NOINTERFACE;

    // If we don't have an object, create it, and save copy in the logon
    // object.
    if (!m_pStatusObj)
    {
        LPPROFSECT pProfileObj = NULL;

        m_pSupObj -> OpenProfileSection(NULL, 0, &pProfileObj);
        m_pStatusObj = new CMAPIStatus(this, pProfileObj);

        if (!m_pStatusObj)
            hResult = E_OUTOFMEMORY;

        // The constructor of CMAPIStatus called AddRef on this object.
        if (pProfileObj)
            pProfileObj -> Release();
    }
```

(continued)

```
    // If we do have an object, AddRef and return it.
    if (!hResult)
    {
        m_pStatusObj -> AddRef();
        *pulObjType = MAPI_STATUS;
        *ppEntry = m_pStatusObj;
    }
    ⋮

}
```

IMAPIStatus::SettingsDialog lets a client display and/or modify a provider's configuration settings. We open the message service's profile section and retrieve the configuration settings, which are used to populate the configuration property sheet in the call to *DoLogonDlg*. This is the same *DoLogonDlg* we called in *ServiceEntry* to configure the provider.

```
STDMETHODIMP CMAPIStatus::SettingsDialog(ULONG ulUIParam, ULONG ulFlags)
{
    // Open the profile for our provider, and get whatever is set there.
    LPPROFSECT    pProfileObj = NULL;
    LPSPropValue  pProps = NULL;
    CFGDLG        CfgDialog = { 0 };
    HRESULT       hResult = S_OK;

    ⋮

    hResult = OpenServiceProfileSection(…,
                                        &pProfileObj,
                                        GetMAPIFreeBuffer());

    if (hResult)
        goto ErrorExit;

    hResult = pProfileObj -> GetProps((LPSPropTagArray)&sptLogonArray,
                                      …, &pProps);

    if (FAILED(hResult))
        goto ErrorExit;

    // Fill in the logon UI structure.
    CfgDialog.hInst    = m_pLogon -> m_hInstance;
    CfgDialog.hWnd     = (HWND)ulUIParam;
    CfgDialog.ppProps  = &pProps;
    CfgDialog…

    ⋮
```

```
ShowPropsAgain:
     hResult = DoLogonDlg(&CfgDialog);

     // If the dialog was displayed read-only, we don't need to verify
     // anything because the user didn't change anything, and we are
     // still running with the logon setting of the session.
     if (hResult || (ulFlags & UI_READONLY))
         goto ErrorExit;

     if (!PingRemoteServer((HWND)ulUIParam, pProps))
         goto ShowPropsAgain;

     lstrcpy(m_pLogon -> m_szServer, pProps[SERVER_NAME].Value.LPSZ);
     lstrcpy(m_pLogon -> m_UserInfo.szMailboxName,
             pProps[MAILBOX_NAME].Value.LPSZ);
     lstrcpy(m_pLogon -> m_UserInfo.szFullName,
             pProps[USER_NAME].Value.LPSZ);
     lstrcpy(m_pLogon -> m_UserInfo.szPassword,
             pProps[PASSWORD].Value.LPSZ);
     m_pLogon -> m_UserEID.dwObjID = pProps[MAILBOX_ID].Value.l;

     hResult = pProfileObj -> SetProps(NUM_LOGON_PROPERTIES, pProps, NULL);

     // Set the new/changed identity in the status row of the provider.
     hResult = m_pLogon -> InitializeStatusRow(STATUSROW_UPDATE);

ErrorExit:
     ⋮

}
```

ChangePassword just makes an RPC to the server to change the user's password:

```
STDMETHODIMP CMAPIStatus::ChangePassword(LPTSTR    pszOldPass,
                                         LPTSTR    pszNewPass,
                                         ULONG     ulFlags)
{
    HRESULT hResult =
            ChangeMBServerPassword(m_pLogon -> m_szServer,
                                   m_pLogon -> m_UserInfo.szMailboxName,
                                   pszOldPass,
                                   pszNewPass);
    ⋮
    return hResult;
}
```

Template ID

We saw in ABPAB how one provider can call *IMAPISupport::OpenTemplateID* on a foreign entry ID to obtain a remote *IMAPIProp* interface from the foreign provider. Now we'll discuss how the foreign provider provides the remote interface by supporting *IABLogon::OpenTemplateID*. The prototype for *IMAPISupport-::OpenTemplateID* looks like this:

```
HRESULT OpenTemplateID(ULONG            cbTemplateID,
                       LPENTRYID        lpTemplateID,
                       ULONG            ulTemplateFlags,
                       LPMAPIPROP       lpMAPIPropData,
                       LPCIID           lpInterface,
                       LPMAPIPROP FAR * lppMAPIPropNew,
                       LPMAPIPROP       lpMAPIPropSibling);
```

The caller passes the provider's PR_TEMPLATEID property in *lpTemplateID*, and the support object uses this value to decide to which provider's *IABLogon-::OpenTemplateID* method the call should be delegated.

ABWDS supports only a remote *IMAPIProp* interface on distribution lists, and the remoted interface intercepts and handles calls only to *IMAPIProp-::OpenProperty(PR_CONTAINER_CONTENTS, …)*; all other calls are passed through to the host *IMAPIProp* interface. We don't support template IDs for *IMailUser* objects because there's no particular advantage to doing so. Distribution lists, on the other hand, can have many members and can consequently have large contents tables. We remote calls to *OpenProperty(PR_CONTAINER-_CONTENTS, …)* to save the performance hit of maintaining a local copy of a DL's contents table when the DL is copied to a local-based address book provider like ABPAB:

```
STDMETHODIMP CABLogon::OpenTemplateID(ULONG          cbTemplateID,
                                      LPENTRYID      pTemplateID,
                                      ULONG          ulTemplateFlags,
                                      LPMAPIPROP     pMAPIPropData,
                                      LPCIID         pInterface,
                                      LPMAPIPROP *   ppMAPIPropNew,
                                      LPMAPIPROP     pMAPIPropSibling)
{
    HRESULT hResult = S_OK;

    // Make sure the entry ID is for a DL object in our address book
    // provider.
    PRIVATE_ENTRYID * pTempID = (PRIVATE_ENTRYID *)pTemplateID;
```

```
if (CB_PRIVATE_EID           != cbTemplateID         ||
    NULL                     == pTempID              ||
    EID_OBJTYPE_DL_TEMPLATE  != pTempID -> bObject   ||
    ENTRYID_VERSION          != pTempID -> bVersion)
{
    ⋮
}


// If called to FILL the entry ID, just return the passed IMAPIProp,
// because we don't implement this (we don't need to).
if (FILL_ENTRY & ulTemplateFlags)
{
    hResult = SetDefDLProps(pMAPIPropData);
    *ppMAPIPropNew = pMAPIPropData;
    return hResult;
}


// Allocate wrapper IDistList, which will delegate all the methods to
// the contained IMAPIProp except OpenProperty(PR_CONTAINER_CONTENTS).

PRIVATE_ENTRYID ObjectEID = *pTempID;
ObjectEID.bObject = MAPI_DISTLIST;
CDLTemplate * pDLTempID = new CDLTemplate(pMAPIPropData,
                                         this,
                                         m_pBEobj,
                                         ObjectEID);

if (pDLTempID)
{
    // This is the object the foreign address book provider returns to
    // the client doing an open entry on it.
    *ppMAPIPropNew = (LPMAPIPROP)pDLTempID;
}
else
{
    ⋮
}
⋮
}
```

If the FILL_ENTRY bit in *ulTemplateFlags* is set, the implementation should initialize the host *IMAPIProp* in *pMAPIPropData* by calling *OpenEntry*

471

on the foreign object and copying properties to the new object. If FILL-
_ENTRY is clear, the *OpenTemplateID* method should return the wrapped
IMAPIProp object in **ppMAPIPropNew*. The caller will set the FILL_ENTRY
bit on the first call to *OpenTemplateID* (when the host copy is first created) or
when it intends to update the host copy, and clear it at all other times.

FILL_ENTRY

The semantics of *OpenTemplateID* with the FILL_ENTRY flag aren't
clearly defined in the MAPI specification. Passing this flag is supposed
to let the caller force the implementation to initialize the host *IMAPI-
Prop* with data from the foreign entry, i.e., to *fill* a new host entry with
properties from the foreign entry. Unfortunately, MAPI doesn't say
exactly which properties, if any, the implementation is required to copy.
A commonsense approach would be to copy all properties from the
foreign entry to the host object *except* for PT_OBJECT properties or
those properties that are intrinsic to the foreign provider, such as
PR_ENTRYID and PR_MAPPING_SIGNATURE.

The way things stand now, the FILL_ENTRY flag's meaning is
implementation-defined. Some implementations don't set any properties at all; some call *CopyTo*. Since MAPI doesn't specify which properties
(if any) will exist on the object when *OpenTemplateID* returns, the caller
has to open the foreign entry and manually copy its properties anyway
if it wants to work properly with all implementations.

We first validate the entry ID passed in **pTemplateID* to make sure it is
indeed our PR_TEMPLATE_ID property. We then create a *CDLTemplate* object
which implements the remote *IMAPIProp* interface. This object is a wrapper
for the caller's *IMAPIProp* interface, which is passed to us in *pMAPIPropData*.
The wrapper contains a pointer to the caller's *IMAPIProp*; we delegate all
method calls except *OpenProperty(PR_CONTAINER_CONTENTS, ...)* to the
pMAPIPropData interface. *OpenProperty(PR_CONTAINER_CONTENTS, ...)* is
handled by the wrapper's *OpenProperty* method.

We return the wrapper to the caller in **ppMAPIPropNew*. Now when any
IMAPIProp methods are called, the wrapper (the remote interface) has first
crack at them. In effect, the foreign interface (ABWDS, in this case) is in the
driver's seat: It decides which methods and properties it wants to handle and
which to delegate to the wrapped interface. It's really not as confusing as it
sounds, and, of course, a picture helps. Take a look at Figure 9-20.

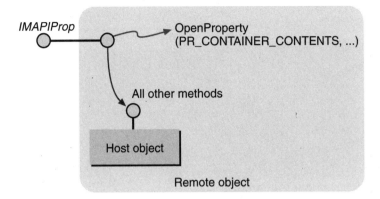

Figure 9-20.
The remoted IMAPIProp *interface is a wrapper for the caller's* IMAPIProp. *The wrapper decides which methods it will handle itself and which to delegate to the caller's* IMAPIProp.

The object of this exercise, at least in our implementation, is to let the server supply the contents table of a DL when one is copied from ABWDS to another address book provider. Doing so relieves the destination provider of the time and expense of copying the DL's members to its local database.

Developing Message Store Providers

Message store providers are the most complex MAPI components and the most difficult to implement. Because they supply most of the functionality clients depend on for handling messages, the performance of the store provider frequently dictates the performance of client applications and the responsiveness of the entire system. In this chapter we examine message store providers in detail. We'll take a look at the store provider's role in the MAPI architecture, how it does its job, and how it interacts with the MAPI subsystem. We'll also list some general requirements that apply to all message store providers and give some pointers on how to begin writing one. Finally, we present the case studies of the Local Message Store (MSLMS), a store provider for accessing and manipulating a database of email messages and folders, and the WINDS Public Folders Store (MSWDS), which allows multiple users to simultaneously view and manipulate public folders in which users can post messages viewable by all users of the WINDS systems.

What Is a Message Store Provider?

Message store providers manipulate the contents of a database. The database can contain almost any type of record. The most common use of a MAPI message store provider is to access databases of electronic mail messages. These messages are grouped in containers called folders. Store providers can also be developed to access other data sources, such as voicemail systems, document libraries, SQL databases, and so on. The MAPI specification allows a great deal of flexibility to implementers, so that almost any data source can potentially back a store provider. The features we describe in this chapter represent the most general implementations; keep in mind that many of the features we discuss are tied to our particular implementations and that your requirements will most likely differ from ours.

Message store providers present the contents of their databases in the form of message objects, each of which represents a single logical database record. The properties in a message object correspond to the data fields in one of these logical records. Collections of messages are presented to the client application as a hierarchy of folders; each folder can contain subfolders, messages, or both. Although MAPI allows arbitrarily complex hierarchies to be constructed, a store provider is *required* to expose only a single root folder. And even though the view of the store provider's contents is arranged hierarchically, the database backing the store provider doesn't have to be organized that way at all: It can be based on tables (RDBMS), a tree structure, a flat file, and so forth.

The cases we made in Chapters 8 and 9 about how providers allow MAPI systems to be highly interoperable and easily extensible apply to message store providers as well. The idea of accessing different data sources is also part of the scheme of the Universal Inbox, where a single MAPI-based mail client can access different message store providers, each representing messages stored in distinct messaging systems or databases.

How Message Store Providers Interact with the MAPI Subsystem

Message store providers execute in two process contexts: the client's context and the MAPI spooler context. So a store provider will have two instances running, one in each process, where both instances access a single database. (See Figure 10-1.) When a client submits a message, that message object lives in the store provider. The store provider's responsibility is to hand it off to the MAPI spooler. To do so, the provider instance in the client process notifies the spooler instance (through some form of interprocess communication) that a new message has been submitted. The message is then picked up by the spooler and handed to a message transport for delivery.

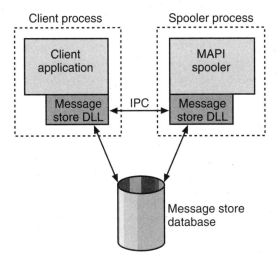

Figure 10-1.
Message store provider DLLs are loaded in two processes simultaneously to access a single database source in which the message and folder reside. They communicate through some IPC mechanism.

Logging On to a Message Store Provider

The MAPI subsystem on the client side logs on to the message store provider and obtains an *IMSLogon* interface by calling the *IMSProvider::Logon* method. This interface is used exclusively by the MAPI subsystem to manipulate the store provider, its folders, its messages, and the status object. Through the same logon method call, the subsystem gets back an *IMsgStore* interface, which is handed back to client applications requesting access to the store provider. On the spooler side things happen a little differently: The spooler logs on to the store provider through the *IMSProvider::SpoolerLogon* method, but it also obtains *IMsgStore* and *IMSLogon* interfaces.

Once the spooler has logged on to the message store provider, it requests a table that lists the messages pending delivery by calling *IMsgStore::GetOutgoing-Queue*. When a message is submitted, the store provider adds a new row to this table and then the spooler, which has a notification link set on it, receives a notification of the new addition. Store providers are required to support notifications on this table.

How Message Store Providers Interact with Address Book Providers and Message Transport Providers

A client calls *IMessage::SubmitMessage* to submit a message for delivery. This call executes in code implemented by the message store provider. At this point the store provider must process the outgoing message before handing it to the MAPI spooler. Its main task is to ask MAPI to expand any personal distribution lists (see Chapter 9) that might exist in the message's recipient table. Expanding a distribution list means replacing the DL with its members, i.e., explicitly adding each member to the message's recipient table. This expansion must occur on the client machine before a message is delivered. Message submission occurs in the store provider, but delivery is actually handled by a message transport provider. Store providers don't usually call transports directly to deliver a message. Instead, the message is given to the spooler, which chooses a transport and passes a copy of the message to it. A *tightly-coupled* store/transport provider is the exception—it can be thought of as a store provider that also has the ability to deliver messages. A tightly-coupled store/transport provider can bypass the MAPI spooler entirely in the submission and delivery process so that the message can be submitted and delivered by the same module. (Tightly-coupled store/transport providers are beyond the scope of this book, but we'll talk some more about them in our discussion of the *IMessage::Submit-Message* method.)

Client Access to Message Store Providers

A MAPI client application accesses a message store provider by first calling the *IMAPISession::OpenMsgStore* method, which calls *IMSProvider::Logon* and returns the resulting *IMsgStore* object. Through this object, clients can open individual folder and message objects if the entry ID of the desired object is known. The call to *IMAPISession::OpenMsgStore* is what causes the MAPI subsystem to log on to the service provider, so for every *OpenMsgStore* call, MAPI calls a store provider's *IMSProvider::Logon* method. A client can log on to the same message store provider several times in a single session (e.g., from multiple threads). It is up to the client-side instance of the provider to satisfy these requests. Typically a store provider maintains a list of opened store provider objects (*IMsgStore* and *IMSLogon* interfaces), and if a client logs on to the same store provider for the second time, the store provider simply returns the same interface. This technique is called *piggybacking* onto an open store provider, and we discuss how this is accomplished later in the chapter.

Requirements of All Message Store Providers

All message store providers must satisfy certain requirements in order to achieve minimal interoperability with MAPI clients and the MAPI subsystem. In general, store providers are expected to adhere to the same requirements, which MAPI imposes on all providers:

- They are implemented in DLLs.

- They can return MAPI_E_NO_SUPPORT for unsupported methods.

- They export an *XXXProviderInit* function—*MSProviderInit*, in this case.

- They are configured through a message service's *ServiceEntry* routine.

Other functionality that all store providers must support is described in the following sections.

Store Providers Must Support Opening a Root Folder and Getting a Hierarchy and Contents Table on It

The root folder of a message store provider has a NULL entry ID; to open it, a client application calls *IMsgStore::OpenEntry(0, NULL, ...)* and gets an *IMAPIFolder* object back. The root folder must support hierarchy and contents tables, therefore the *IMAPIFolder::GetHierarchyTable* and *IMAPIFolder::GetContentsTable* methods must be implemented.

Store Providers Must Register at Least One UID

Store providers typically assign a different UID to each database in which objects are stored or created. This assignment allows a single message store provider to simultaneously open multiple databases and quickly discern which database to access when a client calls *XXX::OpenEntry*. The UID for each database is embedded in the store provider's entry ID or in the store provider's objects. When a store provider logs on, the UID for each data source is registered with MAPI through the call to *IMAPISupport::SetProviderUID*. MAPI uses this information to determine which provider's *OpenEntry* method to invoke when *IMAPISession::OpenEntry* is called with a particular entry ID.

Store Providers Must Support the Interfaces Required to Interact with Client Applications and the MAPI Subsystem

Message store providers are required to implement the following interfaces for minimal functionality:

- *IMSProvider.* This is used to log on to the provider, initialize it, and return *IMSLogon* and *IMsgStore* objects.

- *IMSLogon.* This is used exclusively by the MAPI subsystem to interact with the current store provider object. A single instance of this interface exists per logon. When a store provider uses the piggybacking technique discussed earlier, it should not return a new or existing *IMSLogon* object in the *IMSLogon* method call. Instead, it should return NULL for this parameter so that MAPI can detect the piggybacking and adjust itself accordingly. MAPI also detects piggybacking by looking at the UID set during the *IMSProvider::Logon* call.

- *IMsgStore.* This object is the basic entity through which clients access the message store provider and its contents. Clients use this interface to open folders and messages, get information about the options supported by the store provider, and so on. The spooler also obtains an *IMsgStore* object through which it accesses the table of outgoing messages.

- *IMAPIFolder.* This is the store provider–specific implementation of *IMAPIContainer.* Folder objects manipulate messages through operations such as create, move, delete, and copy. *IMAPIFolder* also allows manipulation of subfolders and includes methods for creating, deleting, moving, and copying entire folders and their hierarchies.

- *IMessage.* Messages are the entities that store the actual data abstracted from a database record. The data is represented in the form of properties. For store providers that support message submission, a message will have properties that enable delivery of the message, such as recipient and sender information.

- *IMAPITable.* This interface is required on a message store provider. Client applications use tables to browse the list of messages in a container, the list of recipients in a message, the list of attachments in a message, and so on. Clients shouldn't assume that all table operations are available on every table. The functionality in each table might be slightly different depending on how the store provider chooses to implement it for a particular type of object. For instance,

IMAPITable::FindRow is supported on contents and hierarchy tables of folders but might not be supported in the *IMAPITable* interface returned from *IMessage::GetAttachmentTable*. Providers are afforded a great deal of discretion in determining which table operations are and are not supported, so they can tailor an implementation to best fit a particular circumstance. Client applications must be prepared to handle unsupported *IMAPITable* methods.

- *IAttach.* This interface is required only for store providers that support attachments to their message objects. *IAttach* has no unique methods of its own; basically, it is just an *IMAPIProp* implementation.

- *IMAPIStatus.* This interface is optional. Client applications use *IMAPIStatus* to access and manage the provider's connection with the data source and to programmatically control the configuration settings of the current session. Developers of store providers are not required to implement this interface; however, a message store provider is still required to register a status row even if it doesn't implement the *IMAPIStatus* interface.

Store Providers Must Support the Opening of Their Objects Through *IMsgStore::OpenEntry* and *IMSLogon::OpenEntry*

A client must obtain an object's entry ID to open the object. This entry ID is passed to the store provider to obtain an interface pointer for the object in question. All objects in a store provider live in a specific folder, be it the root folder or any other subfolder underneath it. A consumer of message store provider objects doesn't have to access the desired object's parent folder to open the object. Instead, MAPI puts this burden on the service provider, allowing client applications to open any object directly on the *IMsgStore* or *IMSLogon* objects without regard to which container the object lives in. The provider is responsible for mapping the call internally to the actual container where the object is stored and for making this behavior transparent to the caller. If a client has only the short-term entry ID, it should make the *OpenEntry* call as close to the object's container as it can. The implementation must decide whether it can honor opening an object from the top level (*IMsgStore*) with a short-term entry ID.

All Store Provider Interfaces Must Be Thread-Safe

Most of the MAPI interfaces allow an object obtained in one thread to be used in another or in many threads at the same time. Clients should be able to access interfaces from multiple threads without having to worry about the consequences to the provider's internal data. Message store provider interfaces must be reentrant and should therefore protect shared information from being manipulated by several threads simultaneously. To achieve this, operating system primitives such as critical sections should be used to guard the interface's data.

Store Providers Must Expose Their Capabilities in PR_STORE_SUPPORT_MASK

Since the MAPI specification allows so much flexibility in what is and isn't supported in a store provider implementation, a store provider must expose its capabilities through the PR_STORE_SUPPORT_MASK property. Clients can use this property to find out what capabilities are supported by a store provider. If a store provider does not support a needed feature, a client should emulate the missing functionality as best it can or disable menu items or other UI to prohibit end users from triggering requests for unsupported functionality in the message store provider. Message store providers are required to provide PR_STORE_SUPPORT_MASK *in all objects*. The value of PR_STORE_SUP-PORT_MASK is a bitmap that indicates the specific functionality available in a store provider implementation or in the current configuration state. The table in Figure 10-2 describes what each bit, when set, indicates.

Capability Bit	Description/Indication
STORE_ENTRYID_UNIQUE	The store provider promises never to *reuse* an entry ID, even if the object for which the entry ID was created has been destroyed.
STORE_READONLY	The store provider is read-only. It does not support creating objects such as folders or messages. It also indicates that existing objects cannot be opened with the MAPI_MODIFY flags for read/write access.

Figure 10-2. *(continued)*
List of possible bits that might be present in the PR_STORE_SUPPORT_MASK property of message store provider objects. Each bit indicates a different capability of the store provider implementation. A client should check this information before attempting to call methods on store provider objects.

Figure 10-2. *continued*

Capability Bit	Description/Indication
STORE_SEARCH_OK	The store provider implementation allows the client to create a search folder and start a search for specific messages based on a search criterion. (In other words, the store supports creating folders of type FOLDER_SEARCH and implements the associated search methods in the *IMAPIContainer* interface.)
STORE_MODIFY_OK	The store provider allows existing objects to be opened with the MAPI_MODIFY flag so that an object's properties can be modified. This flag alone does not indicate the capability for creating new objects.
STORE_CREATE_OK	Clients can create new objects such as folders or messages. This flag alone does not indicate the capability for modifying existing objects.
STORE_ATTACH_OK	The store provider implements the *IAttach* interface and supports creating, opening, and/or deleting attachments on message objects.
STORE_OLE_OK	The store provider supports opening properties and requesting the *IStorage* interface to be opened on them. This is used mainly to discern whether OLE attachments can be added to message objects via the *IStorage* interface on the PR_ATTACH_DATA_OBJ property of an attachment.
STORE_SUBMIT_OK	The message store provider implements the *IMessage::SubmitMessage* method and the MAPI spooler-logon related methods.
STORE_NOTIFY_OK	The store provider implements notifications—at least on its table interfaces—so that clients will be advised of changes to the rows in particular tables.

(continued)

Figure 10-2. *continued*

Capability Bit	Description/Indication
STORE_MV_PROPS_OK	The *IMAPIProp*-derived objects in the store provider implementation allow the storage and/or retrieval of multivalue properties. (See Appendix B for details.)
STORE_CATEGORIZE_OK	The implementation supports the categorization methods in the *IMAPITable* interface returned in the contents tables of its *IMAPIFolder* objects.
STORE_RTF_OK	Tells the client that the store provider understands Rich Text Format (RTF) so the provider can convert plaintext to RTF and RTF to plaintext. Advanced clients implementing sophisticated user interfaces are especially interested in this bit because without it, storing formatted text for mail messages is more difficult. If the bit is present, the client assumes the store provider will do the conversion internally.
STORE_RESTRICTION_OK	The store provider supports the restriction methods in the *IMAPITable* interface it returns in its contents tables of *IMAPIFolder* objects.
STORE_SORT_OK	The store provider supports the *IMAPITable::SortTable* method in the *IMAPITable* interface it returns in the contents tables of its *IMAPIFolder* objects.
STORE_PUBLIC_FOLDERS	A bit that indicates that the provider is a public folders store provider implementation. Based on this information, clients can adjust their UI.
STORE_UNCOMPRESSED_RTF	A store provider that supports RTF will, by default, store it in a compressed format. If for some reason the store provider does not or cannot store this information in compressed RTF format, it indicates so and clients adjust properly to avoid attempting to decompress RTF information that has not been compressed.

Support for Notifications

Notifications are set on store providers by clients that want to be advised of changes to individual objects or events such as new mail arrival, search completion, and so on. This is done through the *IMsgStore::Advise* and *IMSLogon::Advise* methods. The *IMAPITable::Advise* method notifies the caller of changes, additions, or deletions to the current table data.

Although notifications are not required for a minimal implementation, they are essential for good interaction between the message store provider and client applications. Clients depend on notifications to maintain the contents of a store provider container and to keep the user interface up to date. Many commercial MAPI clients do not work correctly with message store providers that do not support, at the least, notifications of changes on the hierarchy and contents table. Fortunately, the MAPI notification engine implements most of the functionality for adding notifications to a provider implementation. Store providers can quickly support notifications by using the notification engine methods *IMAPISupport::Subscribe*, *IMAPISupport::Notify*, and *IMAPISupport::Unsubscribe*.

Store Providers with Unique Requirements

Thus far we have discussed the requirements that are common to all kinds of message store provider implementations. However, certain types of message store providers have additional requirements.

Default Message Store Providers

A default message store provider is a store provider implementation that contains the Inbox folder in mail applications. This store provider receives inbound messages from all transports and is the hub from which all outgoing messages are sent. These requirements imply support for the following functionality:

- *Message submission.* A client application assumes that a message can be submitted through the default store provider. Consequently, a store provider's *IMessage* interface must support the *SubmitMessage* and the *IMsgStore::GetOutgoingQueue* methods if the store is to be the default. The default store provider must also set the STORE_SUB-MIT_OK bit in PR_STORE_SUPPORT_MASK. The table returned by the *IMsgStore::GetOutgoingQueue* must support notifications.

- *Read/Write access.* When a message is submitted, some of its properties are modified and the changes are propagated to the underlying message storage. A writable store provider clears the STORE_READ-ONLY bit and sets the STORE_MODIFY_OK and STORE_CREATE-_OK bits in PR_STORE_SUPPORT_MASK.

- *Named properties in its* IMessage *and* IAttach *interfaces. GetNamesFrom-IDs* and *GetIDsFromNames* must be implemented in these interfaces. This is especially important for MAPI forms,[1] which depend heavily on named properties. It is not necessary for either the folder or store provider objects to support named properties.

- *Multivalue properties in the* IMAPIProp *implementation of* IMessage *and* IAttach. This functionality is required mostly for forms that store multivalue attributes. The folder or message store provider objects do not have to support multivalue properties, even if the multivalue bit is set in the PR_STORE_SUPPORT_MASK property.

- *Notifications on hierarchy and contents tables and notifications of new mail arrival.* A client's user interface is typically dynamic—it changes when new mail arrives or when a message is added, modified, or deleted from the current opened folder. To manage the list of current folders and its contents, clients can get the hierarchy table and contents table of a given folder. The client constructs a view of the message in the store provider using these tables. A client registers for notifications on these two tables so that it can update its UI when something changes the messages in a folder. Store providers that don't support table notifications won't work properly with most clients, since a client usually won't poll the store provider for changes if the provider doesn't support notifications. Support for this feature implies adding the STORE_NOTIFY_OK bit to the PR_STORE-SUPPORT_MASK property. Also note that a client's performance

---

1. MAPI form objects implement *IMAPIForm*, among other interfaces. A discussion of these objects is outside the scope of this book. We suggest you consult the *MAPI Programmer's Guide* and both volumes of the *MAPI Programmer's Reference* for further information about these objects.

will be much enhanced if the TABLE_ROW_ADDED/MODIFIED/-DELETED notifications are supported, since these events include the row of modified properties.

- *Associated messages and the associated contents tables in its folders.* The call to *IMAPIFolder::CreateMessage* needs to support the MAPI-_ASSOCIATED flag. Associated message objects are identical to standard messages except that they are listed in a different contents table. Some clients rely on the default message store provider to support this functionality in order to operate correctly (e.g., the Microsoft Exchange client.)

- *Support for creating new messages.* Client applications create new messages in the default store provider prior to message submission. The store provider must set the STORE_CREATE_OK bit on the PR_STORE_SUPPORT_MASK property.

- *Setting the receive folder and its associated table.* The default store provider must support the mapping of message classes to receive folders so that messages of a specific message class are moved to the indicated folder and not the default Inbox folder in the IPM subtree. This avoids cluttering the user's Inbox with messages that might not be viewable by the IPM form. To support receive folders, store providers implement the *IMsgStore::GetReceiveFolder, IMsgStore::Set-_ReceiveFolder,* and *IMsgStore::GetReceiveFolderTable* methods.

- *Creating messages outside the IPM hierarchy.* This is a side effect of supporting receive folders. Some automated applications create messages and folders outside the normally viewable mail message hierarchy. Default store provider implementations must support this capability.

- *Support the IPM folder hierarchy.* After a message store provider is added to a profile and the first call to *IMSProvider::Logon* has been made, MAPI will create several special folders that clients are guaranteed will always exist. The folders are described in the table in Figure 10-3 on the following page. After these folders are created, MAPI will get the PR_IPM_XXX_ENTRYID properties and copy them into the *IMsgStore* object. An implementation can pre-create the IPM subtree if it wants to do the extra work, but it must then set the properties documented in *HrValidateIPMSubtree.*

IPM Folder Name	Description
IPM Root	The root folder of which other IPM folders are subfolders.
Deleted Items	The folder where deleted items are stored. When an item is deleted, it is first moved to the Deleted Items folder. When the folder is emptied, its contents are destroyed.
Inbox	The folder where normal viewable messages are placed after having been received by a transport.
Outbox	A view of the store provider's outgoing queue. Messages that have been submitted are typically moved to this folder and are pending delivery by one or more of the transports installed in the profile.
Sent Items	After a message has been submitted, the MAPI spooler moves the message to this folder.

Figure 10-3.
IPM folders in the default message store provider.

Public Folder Store Providers

Public folder store providers exhibit slightly different behavior from standard store providers. The most important characteristic of a public folder store provider is that it does not support message submission (the STORE_SUBMIT_OK bit is clear in PR_STORE_SUPPORT_MASK). Thus it does not implement an outgoing queue or a receive folder and does not support setting the receive folder or implementing the receive folder table. Consequently, a public folder store provider can never be the default store provider.

Except for the submission requirements, public folder store providers have requirements similar to those of the default store provider. Namely, public folder store providers must support associated contents tables and messages, named properties, and multivalue properties. The rest of a public folder store provider's feature set is greatly dependent on the system it is designed to interface with. For example, public folder store providers might or might not support attachments. A store provider sets the STORE_PUBLIC_FOLDERS bit in PR_STORE_SUPPORT_MASK to advertise to clients that it's a public folder store.

Read-Only Store Providers

Read-only store providers are implemented when it's not necessary or desirable to let users create or modify records in the underlying database. For example, a read-only store provider might be developed to let users browse files in a document library. This kind of store provider implementation falls into the *information sharing* store provider category. You could have a read-only message store provider that looks at messages in a user's machine or a read-only public folder store provider to control access to the contents of a bulletin board system. A developer might implement a read-only store provider as the initial release of a message store provider that accesses an existing system. The vendor can bring the provider to market quickly, deferring the complexities of a writable implementation for a second version.

Implementing a read-only message store provider is quite straightforward because it doesn't allow changes to any of its contained objects. Read-only store providers should exhibit the following behavior:

- The call to *IMSProvider::Logon* and *IMSProvider::SpoolerLogon* should not accept the MDB_WRITE flag. It should reject the call with MAPI_E_NO_ACCESS.

- *XXX::OpenEntry* should return MAPI_E_NO_ACCESS when a client passes the MAPI_MODIFY flag.

- All the objects returned are read-only, and their PR_ACCESS and PR_ACCESS_LEVEL properties are set accordingly.

- Calls to *DeleteProps* and *SetProps* should not allow properties to be deleted, added, or modified. The calls themselves might return S_OK, but the problem array is returned filled with the MAPI_E_NO-_ACCESS error code for each property.

- Calls to *XXX::SaveChanges* do nothing, even though they might return S_OK.

- Calls to *XXX::GetIDsFromNames* with the MAPI_CREATE flags return MAPI_E_NO_ACCESS.

- Any method used to create or delete contained objects, such as *IMAPIFolder::CreateFolder, IMessage::CreateAttach*, or *IAttach::OpenProperty(…, MAPI_CREATE, …)*, fails with the error code MAPI-_E_NO_ACCESS.

Read-only store providers can have other subtle requirements, such as how the store provider records a message's read/unread state, how it stores indexes for sorting operations, and so forth. These operations might require writable storage of some kind even though the entries' data is not user-modifiable. These considerations become important if the developer intends to distribute the database on read-only media, such as CD-ROM.

489

Developing a Message Store Provider

In this section we describe the techniques we used to develop the sample Local Message Store (MSLMS) and the WINDS Public Folder Store (MSWDS). Again we must stress that there is no single "right" way to develop a message store provider, so consider the following to be our recommendations only. Here are the steps we recommend you follow:

1. Start by implementing stub interfaces with methods that return MAPI_E_NO_SUPPORT.

2. Add the entries to the system's MAPISVC.INF for the message service that configures your message store provider so that you can add the provider to a profile.

3. Implement *ServiceEntry* so that you can configure the service containing your provider.

4. Add the service containing the message store provider to a profile, and then configure it.

5. Implement *MSProviderInit*.

6. Implement *IMSProvider*.

7. Implement *IMsgStore*.

8. Implement *IMSLogon*.

9. Implement *IMAPIFolder*. This implies implementing *IMAPITable* for the hierarchy and contents tables of the folder.

10. Implement *IMessage*.

11. Implement *IAttach*.

12. Implement the *OpenProperty* interfaces: *IStream* and *IStorage*.

13. Implement *IMAPIStatus*.

Implementing Stub Interfaces

As we discussed in Chapter 8, we recommend that you implement stub interfaces that have no code in them other than trace information and parameter validation. You create these skeleton classes for the interfaces you return so that you can compile the provider and load it.

The following fragment gives an example of how the *IMsgStore* interface would be implemented in your skeleton:

```
STDMETHODIMP CMsgStore::GetOutgoingQueue(ULONG            ulFlags,
                                         LPMAPITABLE * ppTable)
{
    InfoTrace("CMsgStore::GetOutgoingQueue method called");
    Validate_IMsgStore_GetOutgoingQueue(this,
                                        ulFlags,
                                        ppTable);
    return MAPI_E_NO_SUPPORT;
}

STDMETHODIMP CMsgStore::SetLockState(LPMESSAGE pMessageObj,
                                     ULONG       ulLockState)
{
    InfoTrace("CMsgStore::SetLockState method called");
    Validate_IMsgStore_SetLockState(this,
                                    pMessageObj,
                                    ulLockState);
    return MAPI_E_NO_SUPPORT;
}
```

Adding the Entries of Your Store Provider to MAPISVC.INF

You'll need to add entries that are specific to your message store provider and the service that configures it to MAPISVC.INF before you can configure and use the provider in a MAPI session. You can do this manually, or you can write a short INF file and use the MERGEINI utility to copy it into MAPISVC.INF. This is the INF section for MSLMS:

```
[Services]
MSLMS=Sample Local Message Store

[MSLMS]
Providers=MS_LMS
PR_SERVICE_DLL_NAME=MSLMS.DLL
PR_SERVICE_ENTRY_NAME=ServiceEntry
PR_SERVICE_SUPPORT_FILES=MSLMS.DLL
PR_SERVICE_DELETE_FILES=MSLMS.DLL
PR_RESOURCE_FLAGS=SERVICE_NO_PRIMARY_IDENTITY
WIZARD_ENTRY_NAME=WizardEntry

[MS_LMS]
PR_PROVIDER_DLL_NAME=MSLMS.DLL
PR_RESOURCE_TYPE=MAPI_STORE_PROVIDER
PR_RESOURCE_FLAGS=STATUS_DEFAULT_STORE
PR_PROVIDER_DISPLAY=Sample Local Message Store
PR_DISPLAY_NAME=Sample Mailbox
```

These are the entries for the MSWDS:

```
[Services]
MSWDS=WINDS Public Folders

[MSWDS]
Providers=MS_WDS
PR_SERVICE_DLL_NAME=MSWDS.DLL
PR_SERVICE_ENTRY_NAME=ServiceEntry
PR_SERVICE_SUPPORT_FILES=MSWDS.DLL
PR_SERVICE_DELETE_FILES=MSWDS.DLL
PR_RESOURCE_FLAGS=STATUS_NO_PRIMARY_IDENTITY | SERVICE_SINGLE_COPY
PR_DISPLAY_NAME=WINDS Public Folders
WIZARD_ENTRY_NAME=WizardEntry

[MS_WDS]
PR_PROVIDER_DLL_NAME=MSWDS.DLL
PR_RESOURCE_TYPE=MAPI_STORE_PROVIDER
PR_RESOURCE_FLAGS=STATUS_NO_DEFAULT_STORE
PR_PROVIDER_DISPLAY=WINDS Public Folders
```

We want to point out certain key differences between an INF for an implementation that *can* be set as a default store provider and an INF for an implementation that cannot. The main distinction is the PR_RESOURCE_FLAGS entry under the provider section. Default store provider implementations must set the STATUS_DEFAULT_STORE bit (and clear STATUS_NO_DEFAULT_STORE), and nondefault store provider implementations (such as read-only store providers or public folder store providers) must set the STATUS_NO_DEFAULT_STORE bit (and clear STATUS_DEFAULT_STORE). These bits allow the MAPI subsystem to treat each implementation appropriately—for example, the Control Panel applet will not allow a public folder store provider to be selected as the default store provider for a profile.

Another important difference between default and nondefault store provider implementations is the capability to add several instances of a provider to a profile. For example, the MSWDS service sets the SERVICE_SINGLE_COPY flag, which means that a user can add the provider only once to a profile. This makes sense in this implementation because we allow users access to only one WINDS post office at a time. The MSLMS implementation, on the other hand, doesn't have this restriction, so users can access several message databases concurrently.

Implementing *ServiceEntry*

The service entry implementation of a message store provider is similar to the service entry implementation for the transport and address book providers discussed in Chapters 8 and 9. We won't bore you with the details here, except to note the differences between the implementations. Here is a fragment of the *ServiceEntry* implementation in MSWDS:

```
HRESULT STDAPICALLTYPE ServiceEntry
                        (HINSTANCE      hInstance,
                         LPMALLOC       pMallocObj,
                         LPMAPISUP      pSupObj,
                         ULONG          ulUIParam,
                         ULONG          ulFlags,
                         ULONG          ulContext,
                         ULONG          ulCfgPropCount,
                         LPSPropValue   pCfgProps,
                         LPPROVIDERADMIN pAdminProvObj,
                         LPMAPIERROR *  ppMAPIError)
{
    HRESULT hResult = S_OK;
    ⋮
    // Open the Profile Section for this message store provider.
    LPPROFSECT pProfileObj;
    hResult = OpenProviderProfileSection(pAdminProvObj,
                                         &pProfileObj);
    ⋮
    if (MSG_SERVICE_CREATE == ulContext ||
       (MSG_SERVICE_CONFIGURE == ulContext &&
        pCfgProps &&
        ulCfgPropCount))
    {
        hResult = InitStoreProps(pProfileObj);
        ⋮
    }
    ⋮
    // Clean up.
    ⋮
    return hResult;
}


HRESULT WINAPI CreateStoreEntryID(MAPIUID * pStoreUID,
                                  LPSBinary pStoreEID)
{
    PRIVATE_ENTRYID eid = { 0 }; // Initialize the contents to 0.
    eid.uidGlobal = *pStoreUID;
    eid.bVersion = ENTRYID_VERSION;
    eid.bObject = MAPI_STORE;
```

(continued)

```
        HRESULT hResult = WrapStoreEntryID
                                (0,
                                 MS_DLL_NAME_STRING,
                                 CB_PRIVATE_EID,
                                 (LPENTRYID)&eid,
                                 &pStoreEID -> cb,
                                 (LPENTRYID *)&pStoreEID -> lpb);
        ⋮
        return hResult;
    }


HRESULT WINAPI InitStoreProps(LPPROFSECT pProfObj)
{
    ULONG i = 0;
    SPropValue rgProps[6] = { 0 };

    // The name of the provider is hard-coded.
    rgProps[i].ulPropTag = PR_PROVIDER_DISPLAY;
    rgProps[i++].Value.lpszA = PROVIDER_DISPLAY_NAME_STRING;

    // The name of the public folder store provider is hard-coded.
    rgProps[i].ulPropTag = PR_DISPLAY_NAME;
    rgProps[i++].Value.lpszA = WINDS_STORE_NAME;

    // WINDS_PF_MSG_ENTRIES is a hard-coded UID for
    // the ENTRYID in our public folder store provider.
    MAPIUID uidResource = WINDS_PF_MSG_ENTRIES;
    SBinary StoreEID;
    HRESULT hResult = CreateStoreEntryID(&uidResource,
                                         &StoreEID);
    if (!hResult)
    {
        // Entry ID of the store provider for the store provider's
        // table in the IMAPISession
        rgProps[i].ulPropTag = PR_ENTRYID;
        rgProps[i].Value.bin.cb = StoreEID.cb;
        rgProps[i++].Value.bin.lpb = (LPBYTE)StoreEID.lpb;

        rgProps[i].ulPropTag = PR_STORE_ENTRYID;
        rgProps[i].Value.bin.cb = StoreEID.cb;
        rgProps[i++].Value.bin.lpb = (LPBYTE)StoreEID.lpb;

        rgProps[i].ulPropTag = PR_MDB_PROVIDER;
        rgProps[i].Value.bin.cb = sizeof(MAPIUID);
        rgProps[i++].Value.bin.lpb = (LPBYTE)&guidProvider;

        rgProps[i].ulPropTag = PR_RECORD_KEY;
        rgProps[i].Value.bin.cb = sizeof(MAPIUID);
```

```
        rgProps[i++].Value.bin.lpb = (LPBYTE)&uidResource;
        hResult = pProfObj -> SetProps(i, rgProps, NULL);
        // Call the provider's MAPIFreeBuffer function.
        PrivMAPIFree((LPVOID *)&StoreEID.lpb);
    }
    return hResult;
}
```

Message store providers have an extra responsibility when a service is installed. During the call to *ServiceEntry,* when the context is MSG_SERVICE-_CREATE (or MSG_SERVICE_CONFIGURE if the provider is created and configured through the Profile Wizard), a store provider is responsible for adding certain special properties to its profile section. These properties are used by the MAPI subsystem to properly construct a row for the provider in the session message store table. The table in Figure 10-4 lists the properties needed in the store provider profile section. After these properties have been added to the profile section, the rest of *ServiceEntry* is exactly the same as discussed in Chapters 8 and 9.

Property	Description
PR_PROVIDER_DISPLAY	The name of the provider. This is an ANSI string which should not be localized to a foreign language, e.g., "WINDS Public Folders." This string is not displayed by email clients but can be used by applications to identify your provider when searching the message store table or status table.
PR_DISPLAY_NAME	The name of the store provider in the current profile. This could be hard-coded or configurable. In the MSWDS sample, this is hard-coded to "WINDS Public Folders."
PR_ENTRYID	The entry ID of the store provider. This is the entry ID exposed in the *IMAPISession::GetMsgStoreTable.* This entry ID is constructed by creating an implementation-defined entry ID structure and calling the MAPI API *WrapStoreEntryID,* which adds information MAPI uses to find the store provider in question.

Figure 10-4.   *(continued)*

Minimal set of properties needed in the profile section of a store provider.

Figure 10-4. *continued*

Property	Description
PR_STORE_ENTRYID	This property has the same value as the PR_ENTRYID property discussed above.
PR_MDB_PROVIDER	This property is a hard-coded GUID generated only once during the development of the message store provider. This uniquely identifies a particular implementation. It is similar to PR_PROVIDER_DISPLAY_NAME except that a GUID guarantees uniqueness under all circumstances. The PR_MDB_PROVIDER property is available in all store provider objects.
	The value of this property is identical in all instances of a message store provider in a profile.
PR_RECORD_KEY	This is a unique ID that represents the database backing the message store provider.

Implementing *MSProviderInit*

To log on to a message store provider, MAPI loads the store provider's DLL and calls the *MSProviderInit* entry point function. *MSProviderInit* instantiates and returns an *IMSProvider* object that the MAPI subsystem uses to log on to the provider. *MSProviderInit* does the same version handshaking as *XPProviderInit* and *ABProviderInit*. (See Chapters 8 and 9 for more details.) Here is an abridged version of the *MSProviderInit* function in the MSLMS sample:

```
STDINITMETHODIMP MSProviderInit
                (HINSTANCE        hInstance,
                 LPMALLOC         pMallocObj,
                 LPALLOCATEBUFFER pfnAllocateBuffer,
                 LPALLOCATEMORE   pfnAllocateMore,
                 LPFREEBUFFER     pfnFreeBuffer,
                 ULONG            ulFlags,
                 ULONG            ulMAPIVer,
                 ULONG *          pulProviderVer,
                 LPMSPROVIDER *   ppMSProviderObj)
{
    *pulProviderVer = CURRENT_SPI_VERSION;
    if (ulMAPIVer < CURRENT_SPI_VERSION)
```

```
{
    return MAPI_E_VERSION;
}
// Allocate space for the MSProvider object. The constructor
// will be called to initialize member variables.
CMSProvider * pMSProvider = new CMSProvider(hInstance);
if (NULL == pMSProvider)
{
    hResult = E_OUTOFMEMORY;
}
// Copy pointer to the allocated object back into the
// returned IMSProvider object pointer.
*ppMSProviderObj = (LPMSPROVIDER)pMSProvider;
return hResult;
}
```

Debugging Message Store Providers

Most store provider code is called from the client process, so whichever client application you are using should be set as the "executable for the debug session" under VC++. To debug interaction between the client-side store provider DLL and the spooler-side store provider DLL, you might also want to start another instance of the debugger using the MAPI spooler (MAPISP32.EXE) as the debugging executable. Having two debugger sessions running in parallel lets you set breakpoints in each instance of the provider, so you can see the effect of an action like submitting a message, which triggers events in both contexts. Some of the methods called only on the spooler side are *IMSProvider::SpoolerLogon, IMsgStore::GetOutogingQueue, IMsgStore::SetLockState,* and *IMsgStore::NotifyNewMail.*

Implementing MSLMS and MSWDS

The remainder of this chapter is devoted to a case study of two message store providers, MSLMS and MSWDS. The complete source code is included on the companion CD-ROM, so the code fragments you see in this chapter might be excerpted from the full source to save space. In particular, we might omit showing some details like error handling and parameter validation even though it's important to have this code in your provider. We'll start by describing the functionality common to both implementations, then dive into the details of the

MSLMS implementation. Finally, we'll discuss some details of the MSWDS implementation and explain how it differs from MSLMS.

The source code for these two components, like all the code in this book, is targeted at Microsoft Windows 95 and Microsoft Windows NT platforms exclusively. We don't target 16-bit platforms at all. If you're writing a 16-bit message store provider, you will still find the accompanying samples useful but you will have to modify portions of the code, especially where we rely on WIN32 APIs. The principles we demonstrate and the MAPI interfaces themselves, however, remain the same across platforms.

Our principle objective in these samples is to demonstrate how to write MAPI message store providers. Clarity and readability were higher priorities than performance, so in some cases we have chosen less-than-optimal solutions over optimal solutions for the sake of clarity.

Common Design Features

Before diving into our discussion of MSLMS and MSWDS, we present some of the design elements common to both implementations. We've tried to create some generic base classes that could be used by both implementations. If you understand how these pieces work, you might be able to adapt them for use in your own projects.

The Root Class *CGeneric*

This class implements only two methods: *SetLastError* and *GetLastError*. *SetLastError* stores the last error code and the context where the error occurred so that a call to *GetLastError* returns the appropriate message. It also contains data members that are common to all interfaces we implement. Two of these data members are the critical section structure and the reference count of the object.

Implementing *IMAPIProp:CGenericProp*

IMAPIProp contains the bulk of the code in most implementations.[2] In Chapters 6 and 9, we discussed the benefits of implementing a single *IMAPIProp* base class. Here's another example of how doing so can save you some work: *CGenericProp* gets reused by most interfaces in our message store provider (including *IMsgStore*, *IMAPIFolder*, and *IAttach*) because most message store provider interfaces derive from *IMAPIProp*.

---

2. This might be a philosophical issue. Some say *IMAPITable* is the real ogre; others say *IMAPIProp*.

Rather than reimplement the same code for each interface, we implement a single base class that handles all the generic property manipulations. The core of this class is a singly linked list that stores nodes of data. Each data node contains a property tag and value for one of the properties in a MAPI object. An object's properties are loaded into memory when the object is initialized—it effectively becomes an in-memory image of the object's permanently stored properties. This makes it simpler to support transacted *IMAPIProp* interfaces such as *IMessage* and *IAttach*, since all we have to do to commit any changes is flush the list's contents to persistent storage.

CGenericProp has methods for getting a list of all available property tags (*IMAPIProp::GetPropList*) and for opening interfaces on properties (*IMAPIProp::OpenProperty*). This implementation also supports storing multivalue properties and named properties.

We implemented some helper classes to handle specific tasks. The *CGenericProp* class instantiates these objects and accesses them through pointer data members. The helper classes are the following:

- *CPropList*. This is the class that implements the list of properties. It has methods for finding and deleting properties, copying itself to a new list, and so on.

- *COpenPropertyList*. This class keeps track of which properties have opened interfaces (e.g., *OpenProperty* for *IStream*, *IStorage*, and *IMessage*) and checks whether the property has been modified and needs to be committed to the underlying data storage.

- *CNamePropMgr.* Named properties are handled transparently in this class. This class maintains a private mapping of named properties to numeric IDs. Our message store provider implementations have a single named property mapping at the store provider level, so only one of these objects exists. *CNamePropMgr* is used only within the *CGenericProp* class, and the mapping is global to all objects that derive from *CGenericProp.*

Accessing the Underlying Storage: *CBackEnd*

We haven't mentioned how *CGenericProp* stores the data for an object's properties. We deliberately avoided tying our *IMAPIProp* implementation to a specific storage mechanism because we wanted to be able to reuse the code for several different projects. To accomplish this goal, we designed a base class that abstracts the data storage and retrieval functionality and separates it from the *IMAPIProp* implementation. (See the discussion of the ABWDS provider beginning on page 442 in Chapter 9.)

CBackEnd provides a layer between the MAPI-specific code in the provider interfaces and whatever storage mechanism a particular implementation uses. Most *CBackEnd* methods are declared *pure virtual* with the expectation that implementations will override them with the specific code for getting data out of whatever storage medium the provider implementation is using. The class's methods return MAPI objects in many cases, making it easy for the user to support many MAPI interfaces. For example, some *CBackEnd* methods return *ITableData* objects containing data already stored in *ITableData* rows. *ITableData* can be used directly by an *IMAPIFolder* implementation to return *IMAPITable* interfaces without any additional work on the part of the *IMAPIFolder* interface.

For our message store provider implementation, we derive two classes from *CBackEnd*:

- *CFileBackEnd.* This is the implementation used in the MSLMS store provider. It overrides *CBackEnd* with methods that interface with the *CDataBase* class presented in Chapter 7.

- *CPFServerBackEnd.* This is the implementation used in the MSWDS provider. It encapsulates the details and housekeeping chores for the remote procedure calls (RPCs) that retrieve and store objects in the public folder server of the WINDS post office.

The *IMAPITable* Implementation

IMAPITable can also be fairly complex to implement, so Microsoft provides a generic implementation for developers who don't want to "roll their own." To obtain one of MAPI's table objects, a provider calls *CreateTable*, which returns an *ITableData* interface. The provider can add, delete, and modify rows in the underlying data set by calling *ITableData* methods. To return a view of the data, the provider calls the *ITableData::HrGetView* method, which returns an *IMAPITable* interface that can be passed back to the client. Figure 10-5 illustrates the *ITableData* interface.

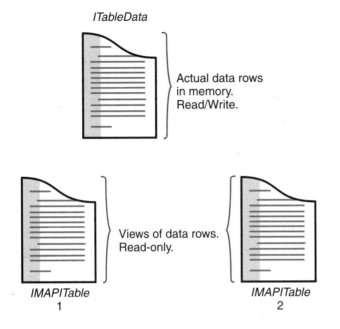

ITableData

Actual data rows
in memory.
Read/Write.

Views of data rows.
Read-only.

IMAPITable
1

IMAPITable
2

Figure 10-5.
The ITableData *interface is used to manage the data rows in a table. It provides an implementation of* IMAPITable *for viewing the rows in the data set.*

The MAPI table implementation has some particular characteristics you should be aware of before you decide to use it in your project.

- *It supports notifications.* This *IMAPITable* implementation already implements *IMAPITable::Advise* and *IMAPITable::Unadvise,* thus satisfying the requirements of *IMAPIFolder* contents and hierarchy tables in a store provider.

- *The data are in memory at all times.* MAPI's *IMAPITable* implementation limits the number of rows a table can have to 32,768 rows. If you foresee your folders' contents tables having more than 32K items in them, you won't be able to use MAPI's table implementation.

- *The MAPI table implementation doesn't support categorization. IMAPITable::SortTable* doesn't support categories in the sort criteria. Sophisticated clients (such as the Microsoft Exchange client) can create *views* that group messages in a contents table by *categories* such as subject, conversation thread, and so on. The client relies on the store provider's categorization capability to provide this functionality.

■ *Collapsing and expanding table rows isn't supported.* When tables are sorted by categories, they get *collapsed* so that the only rows listed in the tables are the titles of the various categories. Some of the methods that expose collapsing functionality in tables are *IMAPITable::CollapseRow* and *IMAPITable::ExpandRow.*

The Entry ID Scheme

Both MSLMS and MSWDS use the same scheme for their entry IDs. Their entry IDs are defined as follows:

```
typedef struct _PRIVATE_ENTRYID
{
    // MAPI-required fields
    // MAPI Flags
    BYTE        abFlags[4];     // 4 bytes
    // UID Unique for the back end
    // (i.e., at the database file level)
    MAPIUID     uidGlobal;      // 16 bytes

    // Provider-defined fields
    // Version of the entry ID schema
    BYTE        bVersion;       // 1 byte
    // Object type
    BYTE        bObject;        // 1 byte
    // Pad to align the structure to 4-byte boundaries.
    BYTE        bPad[2];        // 2 bytes
    // Object ID (container or object)
    DWORD       dwObjID;        // 4 bytes
                                // 28 bytes total
} PRIVATE_ENTRYID;
```

The UID contained in *uidGlobal* is required in all entry IDs. This UID is registered by the store provider during *IMSProvider::Logon* and *IMSProvider::SpoolerLogon* with the call to *IMAPISupport::SetProviderUID.* For MSLMS, the UID is unique to each database file backing the store provider. MSLMS can tell if an entry exists in the store provider by simply comparing the *uidGlobal* field with the UID of the open database file. For MSWDS, the UID is hard-coded because the database exists only on the server, and MSWDS can talk to only one server at a time.

The *bObject* member tells us what type of object the entry represents, which makes it easier to narrow the criteria we use to search for the entry in our database.

Finally, *dwObjID* is a number that maps to a key in the database that uniquely identifies each object. In the MSLMS implementation, the object ID is a record number in the underlying database file.

For both MSLMS and MSWDS, all entry IDs are long-term entry IDs; we don't supply short-term entry IDs in any of our tables.

How Notifications Are Implemented

MSLMS and MSWDS both support notifications on all tables and on individual objects. Our implementation uses the MAPI notification engine. Here is an excerpt from the MSLMS implementation of *IMsgStore::Advise*:

```
STDMETHODIMP CMsgStore::Advise(ULONG            cbEntryID,
                               LPENTRYID        pEntryID,
                               ULONG            ulEventMask,
                               LPMAPIADVISESINK pAdviseSink,
                               ULONG *          pulConnection)
{
    PRIVATE_ENTRYID * pEID = (PRIVATE_ENTRYID *)pEntryID;
    HRESULT hResult = S_OK;
    *pulConnection = 0;
    DWORD cbSize;
    LPBYTE pKeyData;
    // If an entry ID was supplied and the size of it matches
    // our internal entry ID structure size, we assume the caller is
    // trying to set a notification with a particular object
    // in the store provider. We must check the size so as not to
    // be confused by clients that passed the entry ID of the store
    // provider to set an advise with the store provider object. We
    // handle that possibility in the ELSE case below.
    if ((cbEntryID == CB_PRIVATE_EID) && pEID)
    {
        if (!m_pBEobj -> IsValidEntryID(pEID))
        {
            hResult = MAPI_E_INVALID_ENTRYID;
            goto ErrorExit;
        }
        cbSize = CB_PRIVATE_EID;
        pKeyData = (LPBYTE)pEID;
    }
    else
```

(continued)

```
    {
        // If the entry ID size is nonzero, it better be
        // the entry ID of the store provider object. Otherwise,
        // we assume the client is giving us a bogus (to us)
        // entry ID.
        if (cbEntryID)
        {
            if (cbEntryID != m_StoreEID.cb ||
                memcmp(pEntryID, m_StoreEID.lpb, cbEntryID))
            {
                hResult = MAPI_E_INVALID_ENTRYID;
                goto ErrorExit;
            }
        }
        cbSize = sizeof(MAPIUID);
        pKeyData = (LPBYTE)&m_StoreUID;
        pEID = NULL;
    }
    LPNOTIFKEY pKey;
    hResult = AllocateNotifKey(cbSize, pKeyData, &pKey);
    if (hResult)
    {
        goto ErrorExit;
    }

    EnterCriticalSection(&m_csObj);
    // In our implementation of notifications in this
    // store provider, we utilize the MAPI notification
    // engine. When we set an advise link on an object we
    // must supply MAPI with a unique key (an SBinary
    // structure) that identifies that object. Since
    // the entry IDs in our store provider are unique for
    // all the objects, the entry ID of the object will be
    // enough to satisfy MAPI. For the store provider object,
    // we pass the provider UID as the key.
    hResult = m_pSupObj -> Subscribe(pKey,
                                     ulEventMask,
                                     0,
                                     pAdviseSink,
                                     pulConnection);
    PrivFree((LPVOID *)&pKey);
    if (!hResult)
    {
        if (pEID)
        {
            hResult = UpdateSubscriptionList(pEID,
                                             *pulConnection,
                                             TRUE);
```

```
            if (hResult)
            {
                m_pSupObj -> Unsubscribe(*pulConnection);
            }
        }
        else
        {
            m_ulNotifAllObjects++;
        }
    }
    LeaveCriticalSection(&m_csObj);
ErrorExit:
    if (hResult)
    {
        *pulConnection = 0;
        SetLastError(hResult);
    }
    return hResult;
}

STDMETHODIMP CMsgStore::Unadvise(ULONG ulConnection)
{
    Validate_IMsgStore_Unadvise(this, ulConnection);
    HRESULT hResult = m_pSupObj -> Unsubscribe(ulConnection);
    if (!hResult)
    {
        EnterCriticalSection(&m_csObj);

        UpdateSubscriptionList(NULL, ulConnection, FALSE);

        LeaveCriticalSection(&m_csObj);
    }
    SetLastError(hResult);
    return hResult;
}
```

Advise first checks the entry ID to be sure the object is one of ours. A NULL entry ID means the caller is setting up a notification link on the store provider itself, as opposed to setting up a notification link on an object owned by the provider.

To use the MAPI notification engine, each advise link must be identified with a unique binary key. Since our entry IDs are unique, we can use the entry ID of the object being notified on as the key. *AllocateNotifKey* is a private method that turns an entry ID structure into a *NOTIFKEY* structure.

We register the notification with the notification engine by calling *Subscribe* and get back a token value that identifies the connection just made. We

505

return this token to the caller so that it can terminate a notification link to us. For efficiency, we store this token number along with the entry ID of the object in a list we maintain internally in the *IMsgStore* object. Each time one of our objects (e.g., a folder or a message) is modified, we tell the *IMsgStore* object and *IMsgStore* walks the list of connections. If it finds at least one node in which the entry ID matches that of the modified object, a notification is triggered by calling *IMAPISupport::Notify*. We can easily reconstruct the key because we know the entry ID of the object that was modified. Note that if an object is not transacted, the object changes as soon as properties are set on it, so the notification should occur immediately (e.g., in *SetProps*). For transacted objects such as *IMessage*, the object should notify in the *SaveChanges* method. Here is a code fragment from the MSLMS implementation:

```
STDMETHODIMP CMAPIFolder::SetProps
                    (ULONG                  cValues,
                     LPSPropValue           pPropArray,
                     LPSPropProblemArray * ppProblems)
{
    ⋮

    BOOL fObjectModified = FALSE;
    HRESULT hTagError, hResult = S_OK;
    EnterCriticalSection(&m_csObj);
    for (ULONG i = 0; i < cValues; i++)
    {
        ⋮
        hTagError = S_OK;
        switch (pPropArray[i].ulPropTag)
        {
            ⋮
        }
        if (!hTagError)
        {
            hTagError = AddPropToList(&pPropArray[i]);
            if (!hTagError)
            {
                fObjectModified = TRUE;
            }
        }
        ⋮
    }
    if (!hResult && fObjectModified)
    {
        ⋮
```

```
            NOTIFICATION notif = { 0 };
            notif.ulEventType        = fnevObjectModified;
            notif.info.obj.cbEntryID  = CB_PRIVATE_EID;
            notif.info.obj.lpEntryID  = (LPENTRYID)&m_ObjectEID;
            notif.info.obj.cbParentID = CB_PRIVATE_EID;
            notif.info.obj.lpParentID = (LPENTRYID)&m_ParentEID;
            notif.info.obj.ulObjType  = MAPI_FOLDER;
            m_pStore -> NotifyClients(&m_ObjectEID, 1, &notif);
            :
        }
    LeaveCriticalSection(&m_csObj);
    :
    return hResult;
}


STDMETHODIMP CMsgStore::NotifyClients
                        (PRIVATE_ENTRYID * pEID,
                         ULONG             ulNotifsCount,
                         LPNOTIFICATION    pNotifs)
{
    LPNOTIFKEY pKey;
    HRESULT hResult = S_OK;
    ULONG ulFlags = fMapiUnicode;
    // First, check if there are notifications
    // set at the store provider level.
    if (m_ulNotifAllObjects)
    {
        hResult = AllocateNotifKey(sizeof(MAPIUID),
                                   (LPBYTE)&m_StoreUID,
                                   &pKey);
        if (!hResult)
        {
            hResult = m_pSupObj -> Notify(pKey,
                                          ulNotifsCount,
                                          pNotifs,
                                          &ulFlags);
            PrivFree((LPVOID *)&pKey);
        }
    }
    // If an entry ID was passed in, see if that
    // specific entry ID is in the list of objects with
    // notification links.
    if (pEID && !hResult)
    {
        if (IsObjectInNotifList(pEID))
```

(continued)

507

```
        {
            hResult = AllocateNotifKey(CB_PRIVATE_EID,
                                       (LPBYTE)pEID,
                                       &pKey);
            if (!hResult)
            {
                hResult = m_pSupObj -> Notify(pKey,
                                              ulNotifsCount,
                                              pNotifs,
                                              &ulFlags);
                PrivFree((LPVOID *)&pKey);
            }
        }
    }
    return hResult;
}
```

We don't need to worry about triggering notifications on our table objects, because we are using MAPI's built-in *IMAPITable* implementation, which provides native support for notifications. When the *ITableData* interface is used to modify the rows in the table, it automatically sends notifications to all subscribers.

Implementing *IMSProvider*

The implementation of *IMSProvider* is quite straightforward. The MAPI subsystem logs on to our store provider every time a client calls *IMAPISession::OpenMsgStore*. Here's a trimmed-down version of the *IMSProvider::Logon* implementation:

```
STDMETHODIMP CMSProvider::Logon(LPMAPISUP       pSupObj,
                                ULONG           ulUIParam,
                                LPTSTR          pszProfileName,
                                ULONG           cbEntryID,
                                LPENTRYID       pEntryID,
                                ULONG           ulFlags,
                                LPCIID          pInterface,
                                ULONG *         pcbSpoolSecurity,
                                LPBYTE *        ppbSpoolSecurity,
                                LPMAPIERROR *   ppMAPIError,
                                LPMSLOGON *     ppMSLogon,
                                LPMDB *         ppMDB)
    {
        :
```

```
// This wrapper of IMAPISupport is here for
// debugging purposes. This is not required when
// implementing a message store provider.
CMAPISupport * pPrivSupObj = new CMAPISupport(pSupObj);
if (NULL == pPrivSupObj)
{
    return E_OUTOFMEMORY;
}


// This is used to return a valid MAPIERROR
// structure in case of a failure.
CGeneric obj;

// NULL these parameters.
*ppMAPIError = NULL;
*ppbSpoolSecurity = NULL;
*pcbSpoolSecurity = 0;

LPSPropValue pProps = NULL;
CBackEnd * pBEobj         = NULL;
CMsgStore * pMsgStoreObj = NULL;
CMSLogon * pMSLogonObj   = NULL;
SBinary StoreEID         = { 0 };
MAPIUID uidResource      = { 0 };
long lAccess = (MDB_WRITE ? MAPI_ACCESS_MODIFY : 0) |
               (MDB_WRITE ? MAPI_ACCESS_DELETE : 0) |
                MAPI_ACCESS_READ |
                MAPI_ACCESS_CREATE_HIERARCHY |
                MAPI_ACCESS_CREATE_CONTENTS |
                MAPI_ACCESS_CREATE_ASSOCIATED;

// Since we are going to allocate a new object and
// manipulate the list of sessions, lock the
// provider until we are finished.
EnterCriticalSection(&m_csObj);

// The configuration options from the profile section
HRESULT hResult = GetProfileProps(pPrivSupObj,
                                  &pProps,
                                  (HWND)ulUIParam);
if (hResult)
{
    goto LogonFinished;
}
```

(continued)

509

```
// If we can piggyback on an existing open message store
// on this session, then do so. If we piggyback, then don't
// return a logon object or AddRef the support object.
if (IsStoreAlreadyOpen(pProps[STORE_PATH].Value.lpszA,
                       &pMsgStoreObj))
{
    goto LogonFinished;
}


char szStoreName[32+1], szStoreComment[32+1];
// Copy the name of the store provider and its comment.
lstrcpy(szStoreName,
        pProps[STORE_NAME].Value.lpszA);
lstrcpy(szStoreComment,
        pProps[STORE_COMMENT].Value.lpszA);
CopyMemory(&uidResource,
           pProps[STORE_FILE_UID].Value.bin.lpb,
           sizeof(MAPIUID));

// Open the database file, and get back CBackEnd
// object for uniform access to data sources.
hResult = OpenMsgStoreDataBase
            (pPrivSupObj,
             pProps[STORE_PATH].Value.lpszA,
             szStoreName,
             szStoreComment,
             &uidResource,
             TRUE,
             &pBEobj);
if (!hResult)
{
    // Create a MAPI-wrapped store provider entry ID with
    // this instance information.
    hResult = CreateStoreEntryID(&uidResource, &StoreEID);
}
if (hResult)
{
    goto LogonFinished;
}
// Copy the name again since it might have changed
// during the call to OpenMsgStoreDataBase.
lstrcpy(szStoreName, pProps[STORE_NAME].Value.lpszA);
lstrcpy(szStoreComment, pProps[STORE_COMMENT].Value.lpszA);

try
```

```
    {
        // Allocate an instance of an IMsgStore object.
        pMsgStoreObj = new CMsgStore
                    (this,
                     pPrivSupObj,
                     pProps[STORE_PATH].Value.lpszA,
                     szStoreName,
                     szStoreComment,
                     StoreEID,
                     pBEobj,
                     !!(ulFlags & MAPI_DEFERRED_ERRORS),
                     lAccess,
                     uidResource,
                     FALSE);
        if (!pMsgStoreObj)
        {
            hResult = E_OUTOFMEMORY;
        }
    }
    catch (CException & Exception)
    {
        hResult = Exception.GetError();
    }
    if (hResult)
    {
        goto LogonFinished;
    }
    // This is the UID of the entry IDs in our message
    // store provider objects (IMAPIFolder, IMessage, etc.).
    hResult = pPrivSupObj -> SetProviderUID(&uidResource, 0);
    if (!hResult)
    {
        // Now set up the IPC notification for the
        // spooler-context reciprocate of this message
        // store provider. This notification mechanism is used to
        // notify the other context of message submissions
        // and new mail arrival.
        char szNotifKey[64] = { 0 };
        CopyMemory(szNotifKey, &uidResource, sizeof(MAPIUID));
        lstrcat(&szNotifKey[sizeof(MAPIUID)],
                MSLMS_INTERNAL_KEY);
        LPNOTIFKEY pKey;
        LPMAPIADVISESINK pAdviseSink;
        hResult = AllocateNotifKey(sizeof(szNotifKey),
                                   (LPBYTE)szNotifKey,
                                   &pKey);
```

(continued)

511

```
    if (!hResult)
    {
        hResult = HrAllocAdviseSink(ContextNotify,
                                    pMsgStoreObj,
                                    &pAdviseSink);
        if (!hResult)
        {
            hResult = pPrivSupObj -> Subscribe
                (pKey,
                 fnevNewMail | fnevExtended,
                 0,
                 pAdviseSink,
                 &(pMsgStoreObj -> m_ulIntConnection));
            pAdviseSink -> Release();
        }
        PrivFree((LPVOID *)&pKey);
    }
    CopyMemory(pMsgStoreObj -> m_szIPCNotifKey,
               szNotifKey,
               sizeof(szNotifKey));
}
if (!hResult)
{
    // Allocate a new instance of an IMSLogon object
    pMSLogonObj = new CMSLogon(pMsgStoreObj);
    if (NULL == pMSLogonObj)
    {
        hResult = E_OUTOFMEMORY;
    }
    else
    {
        // Modify our profile section so that we
        // appear in the session store provider table.
        pPrivSupObj -> ModifyProfile(0);
        // Add this object to the list of
        // opened message store providers.
        AddStoreObjectToList(pMsgStoreObj);
    }
}

LogonFinished :
    // Unlock the critical section.
    LeaveCriticalSection(&m_csObj);
    if (pBEobj)
    {
        pBEobj -> Release();
    }
```

```
        PrivMAPIFree((LPVOID *)&pProps);

        // If we failed, clean up before leaving.
        if (hResult)
        {
            if (pMsgStoreObj)
            {
                pMsgStoreObj -> Release();
            }
            if (pMSLogonObj)
            {
                pMSLogonObj -> Release();
            }
            PrivMAPIFree((LPVOID *)&StoreEID.lpb);
            obj.SetLastError(hResult);
            obj.GetLastError(hResult,
                            fMapiUnicode,
                            ppMAPIError,
                            m_hInstance,
                            PROVIDER_DISPLAY_NAME_STRING);
            delete pPrivSupObj;
        }
        else
        {
            // If the logon object that we are supposed to
            // return is still NULL, then it means that we are
            // piggybacking on an open message store provider, so
            // the private support object that we use
            // must be deleted.
            if (NULL == pMSLogonObj)
            {
                delete pPrivSupObj;
            }
            else
            {
                // This call has opened a brand new message
                // store provider. AddRef the support object now
                // that we are successful.
                pPrivSupObj -> AddRef();
                pMSLogonObj -> InitializeStatusRow();
            }
            *ppMSLogon = (LPMSLOGON)pMSLogonObj;
            *ppMDB = (LPMDB)pMsgStoreObj;
        }
        return hResult;
    }
```

Here is the list of things we do in this method:

1. Get the profile properties from the profile. The configuration properties can be stored in either the provider section or the message service profile section in the call to *ServiceEntry*. In the MSLMS sample, the properties are stored in the *provider* profile section. We call the private helper function *GetProfileProps* to retrieve the properties for us.

2. Check to see if we have an open *IMsgStore* interface that is already using the message database indicated in the configuration properties. We maintain a list of opened *IMsgStore* objects inside the *IMSProvider* object and walk this list searching for a match on the database filename and path. If a match is found, we can *AddRef* the *IMsgStore* object and return it plus a NULL *IMSLogon* object. If a store provider is not currently open on the target data file, we open one. The function *IsStoreAlreadyOpen* checks the list for us.

3. Open the message store provider database file with the *OpenMsgStoreDataBase*. This function returns a *CBackEnd* object we can use to access the database file. It also returns the store provider's UID that is associated with this database file and the name and a comment. The name of the database and the comment are the string values for the PR_DISPLAY_NAME and PR_COMMENT properties in the *IMsgStore* object.

4. Call *CreateStoreEntryID*, which creates the entry ID of the store provider. This is the PR_ENTRYID property of the *IMsgStore* object and the PR_STORE_ENTRYID property of all objects returned by our store provider.

5. We create a new *IMsgStore* instance. The *CMsgStore* constructor takes some parameters that are used to initialize the contents of the *IMsgStore*. In particular, we pass a pointer to a *CMAPISupport* object, which is the *IMAPISupport* object given to us in *IMSProvider::Logon* wrapped in some debug code. The constructor saves the support object in a member variable. We also pass other configuration values that become properties of the object during its lifetime.

6. The UID we obtained from the database in Step 3 is the UID we put in the entry ID of every object returned by this store provider implementation. We register the UID by passing it in a call to the *IMAPISupport::SetProviderUID* method. We support only a single UID, but

other implementations might support several UIDs by calling *SetProviderUID* repeatedly with different values. See Chapter 6 for a discussion of why it might be desirable to do this.

7. As Figure 10-1 on page 477 illustrated, message store providers are loaded in two process contexts simultaneously. The store provider implementation must communicate between the two contexts with some kind of IPC mechanism so that one context can inform the other of events that might be of interest to it. In our store provider implementation, we use the built-in MAPI notification engine as the IPC mechanism because of its simplicity and the flexibility it allows in passing data between two processes. We implement a callback function that is invoked whenever a notification arrives. This callback has a pointer to the *IMsgStore* object, which invokes the actual method that responds to the event.

8. Create a new instance of *IMSLogon*, which is returned to the MAPI subsystem. Note that if we are returning an existing *IMsgStore* (as we did in Step 2) because the store provider is already open (i.e., we're piggybacking) then we don't allocate a new *IMSLogon* object and we return NULL instead.

9. Call *IMAPISupport::ModifyProfile* so that MAPI adds our store provider to the session message store table. We also add the current *IMsgStore* object to the list of open databases.

The implementation of *IMSProvider::SpoolerLogon* is almost identical to *IMSProvider::Logon* except for a few details and the fact that internally we tell our *IMsgStore* and *IMSLogon* objects that they are running in the spooler context.

The other *IMSProvider* methods (*IMSProvider::Shutdown* and *Compare-StoreIDs*) are fairly straightforward, so the source code on the companion CD-ROM should be self-explanatory.

Implementing *IMsgStore*

IMsgStore is one of the core interfaces in our implementation. This interface represents the database entity we are abstracting. It derives from the *IMAPIProp* interface, so you can set and get its properties, which represent attributes of the database. Figure 10-6 on the following page enumerates the properties a message store provider is expected to support.

Property Supported by a Store Provider	Description
PR_RECEIVE_FOLDER_SETTINGS	A placeholder property. If present, the store provider has a receive folder settings table. This property is present only on providers that can be set as the default store provider or on tightly-coupled store/transport providers.
PR_ACCESS	A bitmap with the accessing and creating capabilities of the store provider.
PR_ACCESS_LEVEL	Set to MAPI_MODIFY if the store provider allows read/write access. Set to 0 if it allows only read-only access.
PR_OBJECT_TYPE	The type of object. This is set to MAPI_STORE.
PR_STORE_SUPPORT_MASK	A bitmap with the capabilities of the store provider.
PR_VALID_FOLDER_MASK	A bitmap with the special folders that exist in the store provider.
PR_FOLDER_TYPE	This property is set to FOLDER_ROOT because the *IMsgStore* represents the root of the database hierarchy (if any). This is an optional property.
PR_CONTENT_UNREAD	The number of unread messages in the root folder. This is an optional property.
PR_STORE_STATE	This is a bitmap indicating an ongoing action on the message store provider. Currently only one bit is defined for this: STORE_HAS_SEARCHES. It indicates a search has been triggered and is running in the background.
	Store providers that don't support searches don't have to supply this property. Optionally they might supply this property but set it to 0 (recommended).
PR_SUBFOLDERS	Indicates the root folder has subfolders. Optional.
PR_CURRENT_VERSION	Current version of the implementation. Optional.

Figure 10-6.
Properties of the IMsgStore *object.*

(continued)

Figure 10-6. *continued*

Property Supported by a Store Provider	Description
PR_COMMENT	Comment about the database.
PR_DISPLAY_NAME	Readable name of the database.
PR_MAPPING_SIGNATURE	Mapping signature used in named property support. In our implementation, the value is the same in all our objects because we implement a global named property mapping.
PR_STORE_RECORD_KEY	The record key of the store providers. This is the same in all the objects.
PR_RECORD_KEY	The record key of this object.
PR_IPM_SUBTREE_ENTRYID	The entry ID of the IPM root folder. The IPM root folder is the parent of the familiar Inbox, Sent Items, Deleted Items, and Outbox folders. The IPM root folder is a direct descendant of the message store provider root folder. This property is found only in message store providers with an IPM subtree, such as a default store provider.
PR_IPM_SENTMAIL_ENTRYID	The entry ID of the Sent Items folder in the IPM hierarchy. This property is found only in store providers with an IPM subtree, such as a default store provider.
PR_IPM_WASTEBASKET_ENTRYID	The entry ID of the Deleted Items folder in the IPM hierarchy. This property is found only in message store providers with an IPM subtree, such as a default store provider.
PR_IPM_OUTBOX_ENTRYID	The entry ID of the Outbox folder in the IPM hierarchy. This property is found only in message store providers with an IPM subtree, such as a default store provider.

(continued)

Figure 10-6. *continued*

Property Supported by a Store Provider	Description
PR_VIEWS_ENTRYID	The entry ID of the folder where clients store view settings and categorization criteria associated with particular folders. This folder is located outside the IPM hierarchy. Clients don't show the contents of this folder to end users.
PR_COMMON_VIEWS_ENTRYID	The entry ID of the common views folder. The common views folder stores general view settings about any folder. This folder is not in the IPM hierarchy, and end users can't look at its contents from a normal client application.
PR_FINDER_ENTRYID	The finder folder is where a client creates search results folders, which are used to present the results of searches in a store provider. The entry ID of the finder folder is stored in this property.
PR_PARENT_ENTRYID	The entry ID of the parent of the store provider object. Its value is the same as the PR_ENTRYID property.
PR_ENTRYID	The entry ID of the store provider object.
PR_STORE_ENTRYID	Same as PR_ENTRYID.
PR_MDB_PROVIDER	A hard-coded UID for the current implementation of the message store provider.

IMsgStore::SaveChanges

The *IMsgStore* object is not transacted, so this method does nothing but return S_OK.

IMsgStore::SetProps

Implementations typically allow only a limited number of properties to be set on the *IMsgStore* object. In our implementation, only PR_DISPLAY_NAME and PR_COMMENT can be set. Attempting to set anything else returns MAPI_E_NO_ACCESS (or MAPI_E_COMPUTED) in the problem array. Note that calls to *SetProps* take effect immediately without the need for *SaveChanges*.

Unsupported Methods

Typically the *IMsgStore* implementation does not support the following methods: *OpenProperty, CopyTo, CopyProps, DeleteProps, GetNamesFromIDs,* and *GetIDs-FromNames*. In our implementation, we support only the named property methods, *GetNamesFromIDs* and *GetIDsFromNames*, because it is easy for us to do so—not because it is required.

Opening Objects in the Store Provider

Store providers are required to support opening any *IMAPIFolder* or *IMessage* object through the *IMsgStore::OpenEntry* method. Here is the code for our implementation of *IMsgStore::OpenEntry*:

```
STDMETHODIMP CMsgStore::OpenEntry(ULONG          cbEntryID,
                                  LPENTRYID      pEntryID,
                                  LPCIID         pInterface,
                                  ULONG          ulFlags,
                                  ULONG *        pulObjType,
                                  LPUNKNOWN *    ppUnk)
{
    ⋮
    if (!(m_lAccess & MAPI_ACCESS_MODIFY) &&
        (ulFlags & MAPI_MODIFY))
    {
        SetLastError(E_ACCESSDENIED);
        return E_ACCESSDENIED;
    }
    // If the user requested MAPI_BEST_ACCESS, a provider
    // should give the client the maximum access level it
    // can. In our object, if we are writable, give the
    // user WRITE access. It is the easiest for us to handle.
    if (ulFlags & MAPI_BEST_ACCESS)
    {
        if (m_lAccess & MAPI_ACCESS_MODIFY)
        {
            ulFlags != MAPI_MODIFY;
        }
    }
    PRIVATE_ENTRYID eidRoot = { 0 };
    eidRoot.uidGlobal = m_StoreUID;
    eidRoot.bVersion = ENTRYID_VERSION;
    eidRoot.bObject = MAPI_FOLDER;
    eidRoot.dwObjID = ROOT_FOLDER_ID;
```

(continued)

```
PRIVATE_ENTRYID * pEID = cbEntryID ?
                    (PRIVATE_ENTRYID *)pEntryID : NULL;
CMAPIFolder * pFldObj;
CMessage * pMsgObj;
CPropList * pList = NULL;
HRESULT hResult = S_OK;
if (cbEntryID)
{
    if (!m_pBEobj -> IsValidEntryID(pEID))
    {
        return MAPI_E_INVALID_ENTRYID;
    }
}
EnterCriticalSection(&m_csObj);
long lAccess, lType = FOLDER_GENERIC;
// This is the entry ID of the ROOT FOLDER { 0, NULL }.
if (!pEID !! pEID -> bObject == MAPI_FOLDER)
{
    if (!pEID !! ROOT_FOLDER_ID == pEID -> dwObjID)
    {
        lType = FOLDER_ROOT;
        // Note that for the ROOT folder only,
        // its parent entry ID is reflexive to
        // its own entry ID.
        pEID = &eidRoot;
    }
}
if (pEID -> bObject == MAPI_FOLDER !!
    pEID -> bObject == MAPI_MESSAGE)
{
    hResult = m_pBEobj -> OpenObject(*pEID, &pList);
}
else
{
    hResult = MAPI_E_NOT_FOUND;
}
PRIVATE_ENTRYID * pParentEID = NULL;
if (!hResult)
{
    SPropValue spvOne = { 0 };
    pParentEID = (PRIVATE_ENTRYID *)spvOne.Value.bin.lpb;
}
if (!hResult && (pEID -> bObject == MAPI_FOLDER))
{
    // Grant access rights to the object
    // according to what the user requested,
```

```
            // provided the store provider object can
            // grant these.
            lAccess =
                (ulFlags & MAPI_MODIFY ? MAPI_ACCESS_MODIFY : 0) |
                (ulFlags & MAPI_MODIFY ? MAPI_ACCESS_DELETE : 0) |
                MAPI_ACCESS_READ |
                MAPI_ACCESS_CREATE_HIERARCHY |
                MAPI_ACCESS_CREATE_CONTENTS |
                MAPI_ACCESS_CREATE_ASSOCIATED;
            pFldObj = new CMAPIFolder
                            (this,
                             pParentEID,
                             pEID,
                             lType,
                             pList,
                             !!(ulFlags & MAPI_DEFERRED_ERRORS),
                             lAccess,
                             m_pNPList);
        if (pFldObj)
        {
            pFldObj -> m_ulObjFlags |=
                ((m_ulObjFlags & OBJECT_RUNNING_IN_SPOOLER) ?
                OBJECT_RUNNING_IN_SPOOLER : 0);
        }
        else
        {
            hResult = E_OUTOFMEMORY;
        }
    }
    if (!hResult && (pEID -> bObject == MAPI_MESSAGE))
    {
        lAccess =
            (ulFlags & MAPI_MODIFY ? MAPI_ACCESS_MODIFY : 0) |
            (ulFlags & MAPI_MODIFY ? MAPI_ACCESS_DELETE : 0) |
            MAPI_ACCESS_READ;
        pMsgObj = new CMessage
                        (this,
                         pParentEID,
                         pEID,
                         pList,
                         !!(ulFlags & MAPI_DEFERRED_ERRORS),
                         lAccess,
                         NULL,
                         m_pNPList);
```

(continued)

521

```
            if (pMsgObj)
            {
                pMsgObj -> m_ulObjFlags |=
                    ((m_ulObjFlags & OBJECT_RUNNING_IN_SPOOLER) ?
                        OBJECT_RUNNING_IN_SPOOLER : 0);
            }
            else
            {
                hResult = E_OUTOFMEMORY;
            }
        }
        LeaveCriticalSection(&m_csObj);

        if (hResult)
        {
            if (pList)
            {
                delete pList;
            }
            SetLastError(hResult);
        }
        else
        {
            if (!pEID || MAPI_FOLDER == pEID -> bObject)
            {
                *pulObjType = MAPI_FOLDER;
                *ppUnk = (LPUNKNOWN)pFldObj;
            }
            else
            {
                if (MAPI_MESSAGE == pEID -> bObject)
                {
                    *pulObjType = MAPI_MESSAGE;
                    *ppUnk = (LPUNKNOWN)pMsgObj;
                }
            }
        }
        return hResult;
    }
```

Here are the things we do in *OpenEntry*:

1. We check the access rights of the *IMsgStore* object. *OpenEntry* should not allow the caller to open a read/write object through a read-only object. If the client requested MAPI_BEST_ACCESS, we try to grant them read/write access, but if we can't, we'll return a read-only instance of the requested object.

2. After the access has been verified, we validate the entry ID of the object to make sure it is one of ours. To do this, we cast the entry ID to one of our PRIVATE_ENTRYID structures and let the *CBackEnd-::IsValidEntryID* method look at its components. If the entry ID is NULL, then the client is trying to open the root folder.

3. From the entry ID, we can tell what type of object the caller wants to open. We validate that the requested object is either a folder or a message. Next we get the stored properties from the back-end storage through the *CBackEnd::OpenObject*. This method returns a *CPropList* object initialized with the object's properties.

4. If the requested entry is a folder, we create a new *CMAPIFolder* object (our implementation of the *IMAPIFolder* interface). Note that we save a bitmap (in m_ulObjFlags) of the permissions in the object's constructor. The value becomes the PR_ACCESS property. (See Figure 10-7.)

5. If the entry ID is for a message object, we create an instance of *CMessage*, which is our implementation of the *IMessage* interface.

6. When the appropriate interface has been created, we set the object type, call *AddRef* on the object, and return the object's interface pointer in **ppUnk*.

Access Mask	Description
MAPI_ACCESS_MODIFY	The object's properties can be modified.
MAPI_ACCESS_DELETE	The object's properties can be deleted.
MAPI_ACCESS_READ	The object's properties can be read.
MAPI_ACCESS_CREATE_HIERARCHY	The object supports creating sub-containers (e.g., *IMAPIFolder* objects) in it.
MAPI_ACCESS_CREATE_CONTENTS	The object supports creating sub-objects (e.g., *IMessage* objects) in it.
MAPI_ACCESS_CREATE_ASSOCIATED	The object supports creating associated subobjects (e.g., associated *IMessage* objects) in it.

Figure 10-7.
Bits and their meanings for the PR_ACCESS property in IMAPIFolder *and* IMessage *objects.*

Support for Setting the Receive Folder

A store provider supports receive folders by implementing the *IMsgStore::SetReceiveFolder*, *IMsgStore::GetReceiveFolder*, and *IMsgStore::GetReceiveFolderTable* methods and exposing a stub property, PR_RECEIVE_FOLDER_SETTINGS, in the *IMsgStore* object's property list.

The columns that must be present in the receive folder table are the following:

- *PR_INSTANCE_KEY*: The instance key for a particular row in the table. This is unique for each row.

- *PR_ENTRYID*: The entry ID of the receive folder for messages of the specified class.

- *PR_RECORD_KEY*: The record key of the folder indicated by the PR_ENTRYID column.

- *PR_MESSAGE_CLASS*: The message class of messages that will be placed in the receive folder given by a particular row in the table.

Store providers that support receive folders must have default settings for messages of the "IPM" and "IPM.Notc" message classes and for messages with no message class property (NULL message class). By default, incoming messages of these classes must be routed to the Inbox folder in the IPM folder hierarchy.

Clients create new receive folder entries by calling *IMsgStore::SetReceiveFolder* and passing both the entry ID of a folder in our store provider and a properly constructed message class. To validate the message class, we call the helper function *IsValidMsgClass*. A valid message class is defined as a series of one or more period-delimited tokens, with each token being a series of one or more ASCII characters in the range 32 through 126 (inclusive) excluding the period ('.') character. This definition excludes message classes with a leading or trailing period or two or more consecutive periods, because this would imply the existence of a zero-length token. Store provider developers must validate the message class string using these rules.

The Message Store Provider Outgoing Queue Table

The outgoing queue table is simply an *IMAPITable* with five columns. The columns are described in Figure 10-8.

Column	Description
PR_INSTANCE_KEY	The instance key of the row. This is unique for every row.
PR_ENTRYID	The entry ID of the submitted message.
PR_SUBMIT_FLAGS	The submission flags for the message. The SUBMITFLAG_PREPROCESS bit is set if the message needs to be preprocessed.
PR_SPOOLER_STATUS	This is set to 0 by the message store provider.
PR_CLIENT_SUBMIT_TIME	The time when the message was submitted. This is in UTC time format.

Figure 10-8.
Columns of the outgoing queue table.

In our implementation, the outgoing queue is created using the MAPI's *IMAPITable* implementation (through *CreateTable* and *ITableData*). Rows are added to the outgoing queue table in two different scenarios:

- The spooler asks us for the outgoing queue table after *IMSProvider::SpoolerLogon* is called. We look at the contents table of the Outbox folder and add any pending messages to the outgoing queue table.

- When a message is submitted through the *IMessage::SubmitMessage* call, the store provider instance in the client process communicates with the spooler instance through the IPC channel to let it know of a newly submitted message. The spooler-side instance updates the outgoing queue table, the spooler receives a table notification indicating there's a new outbound message, and the spooler picks up the message for delivery.

The spooler will request the outgoing queue table only if the STORE_SUBMIT_OK bit is set in *IMsgStore*'s PR_STORE_SUPPORT_MASK property.

Methods Called Only by the MAPI Spooler

IMsgStore has several methods which are for use only by the MAPI spooler. If a client calls them, the store provider is free to return an error code (e.g., MAPI_E_NO_SUPPORT). These methods are the following:

- *IMsgStore::SetLockState.* This method is used to lock a message while it is being submitted. While a message is locked, it can't be opened by any other process.

- *IMsgStore::FinishedMsg.* This method is called just before the spooler removes the outbound message from the queue table. The store provider should do any last minute processing on the message such as changing the message flags to reflect the message's new state (i.e., clear the MSGFLAG_SUBMIT and MSGFLAG_UNSENT bits in PR_MESSAGE_FLAGS).

- *IMsgStore::NotifyNewMail.* When a new message arrives through one of the transports running in the session, a new message is created in the default store provider. When the transport has finished setting all the inbound message's properties, the MAPI spooler notifies the spooler instance of the store provider that new mail was delivered by the message transport. The spooler-side store provider will then notify the client-side store provider of the new message, and the client-side store provider will send out new mail notifications to any parties that subscribed for new mail notifications.

- *IMsgStore::GetOutgoingQueue.*

Aborting Submitted Messages

In our store provider implementation, we don't support aborting messages that have been submitted, so *IMsgStore::AbortSubmit* always returns MAPI_E-_UNABLE_TO_ABORT.

Logging Off from a Store Provider

When clients terminate a session with a message store provider, they log off from it by calling *IMsgStore::StoreLogoff* with certain flags. The store provider might do some preliminary logoff chores and return success to the client, but the actual logoff does not occur until the *IMsgStore* object is destroyed. Here is our implementation:

```
STDMETHODIMP CMsgStore::StoreLogoff(ULONG * pulFlags)
{
    ⋮
    EnterCriticalSection(&m_csObj);
    m_ulCachedStoreLogOffFlags = *pulFlags;
    LeaveCriticalSection(&m_csObj);
    *pulFlags = LOGOFF_COMPLETE;
    return S_OK;
}
```

The store provider must save the flags obtained from the client. In the *CMsgStore* class destructor, we call *IMAPISupport::StoreLogoffTransports* with the flags the client gave us. This call to the support object tells the MAPI spooler to log off all transports from our store provider because we are shutting down.

Implementing *IMSLogon*

Our implementation of *IMSLogon* is the easiest one you can choose for any message store provider. We simply defer all method calls to the contained *IMsgStore* object, so we have to maintain only the *IMsgStore* implementation discussed in the previous section.

The only extra capability in *CMSLogon* is adding our status row to the status table when the provider is initialized for the current session (*IMSProvider-::SpoolerLogon*). The code is straightforward:

```
STDMETHODIMP CMSLogon::InitializeStatusRow()
{
    SPropValue spvStatusRow[5] = { 0 };

    //////////////////////////////////////////////////////////
    // Set the PR_PROVIDER_DISPLAY property: the
    // message store provider readable name.
    ULONG i = 0;
    spvStatusRow[i].ulPropTag = PR_PROVIDER_DISPLAY;
    spvStatusRow[i++].Value.lpszA =
        PROVIDER_DISPLAY_NAME_STRING;

    //////////////////////////////////////////////////////////
    // Set the PR_RESOURCE_METHODS property. We don't
    // support the IMAPIStatus interface.
    spvStatusRow[i].ulPropTag = PR_RESOURCE_METHODS;
    spvStatusRow[i++].Value.l = 0;

    //////////////////////////////////////////////////////////
    // Set the PR_STATUS_CODE property.
    spvStatusRow[i].ulPropTag = PR_STATUS_CODE;
    spvStatusRow[i++].Value.l = STATUS_AVAILABLE;

    //////////////////////////////////////////////////////////
    // Set the PR_STATUS_STRING property.
    spvStatusRow[i].ulPropTag = PR_STATUS_STRING;
    spvStatusRow[i++].Value.lpszA = "Available";
```

(continued)

527

```
///////////////////////////////////////////////////////
// Set the PR_DISPLAY_NAME property.
spvStatusRow[i].ulPropTag = PR_DISPLAY_NAME;
spvStatusRow[i++].Value.lpszA = "Sample Mailbox";

ASSERT(NUM_STATUS_ROW_PROPS == i);

// Write the entries on the provider's session
// status row.
HRESULT hResult =
    m_pStore -> m_pSupObj -> ModifyStatusRow
                            (i,
                             spvStatusRow,
                             0);
    return hResult;
}
```

Implementing *IMAPIFolder*

Our implementation of *IMAPIFolder* is based on the *CGenericProp* class discussed earlier. We restrict the client access to some properties on our *IMAPIFolder* objects. Most message store providers will restrict access and not let the client arbitrarily modify any folder property. Most implementations will also not allow any of these properties to be deleted. Folder implementations usually expose the properties described in Figure 10-9.

Property	Description
PR_ACCESS	The access mask of the folder instance.
PR_ACCESS_LEVEL	Indicates whether or not this instance of a folder and its contents can be modified.
PR_ENTRYID	The folder's long-term entry ID.
PR_PARENT_ENTRYID	The long-term entry ID of this folder's parent folder.
PR_STORE_ENTRYID	The entry ID of the store provider (i.e., the same value as in *IMsgStore*'s entry ID property).
PR_STORE_RECORD_KEY	The record key of the store provider. (The same value as in *IMsgStore*.)

Figure 10-9.
Properties in folder objects.

(continued)

Figure 10-9. *continued*

Property	Description
PR_RECORD_KEY	A unique identifier that distinguishes the data of a folder. In our implementation, we use the same value for both the object's entry ID and the record key.
PR_MAPPING_SIGNATURE	A binary UID for the named property mapping. Because our named properties are mapped at the store provider level, all objects share the same mapping signature value.
PR_CONTENT_COUNT	The number of messages in the folder. This includes read and unread messages but not associated messages.
PR_CONTENT_UNREAD	The number of unread messages only.
PR_ASSOC_CONTENT_COUNT	The number of associated messages in the folder. Note that there is no such thing as a read or unread associated message.
PR_CONTAINER_HIERARCHY	This property is used to indicate that the folder has a hierarchy table. It is used to either exclude or include a folder's subfolders when the folder is copied to another folder.
PR_CONTAINER_CONTENTS	This property is used to indicate that the folder has a contents table. It is used to either exclude or include a folder's messages when the folder is copied to another folder.
PR_FOLDER_ASSOCIATED-_CONTENTS	This property is used to indicate that the folder has an associated messages contents table. It is used to either exclude or include the folder's associated messages when the folder is copied to another folder.
PR_FOLDER_TYPE	The type of folder. Normal folders are of type FOLDER_GENERIC. The root folder of a store provider should be of type FOLDER-_ROOT. If a folder is a search results folder, the type will be FOLDER_SEARCH.
PR_OBJECT_TYPE	This is always set to MAPI_FOLDER.
PR_STORE_SUPPORT_MASK	The same value as in the *IMsgStore* object.

(continued)

Figure 10-9. *continued*

Property	Description
PR_SUBFOLDERS	A Boolean value that indicates whether a folder has subfolders in it.
PR_CREATION_TIME	The date and time the folder was created. In our implementation, this is a computed value that clients cannot set. The format is UTC.
PR_LAST_MODIFICATION_TIME	The date and time the folder was last modified in any way. Modifications that cause this property to be updated include creating subfolders, creating messages, altering any of its properties, and so on. In our implementation, this is a computed value that clients cannot set. The format is UTC.
PR_CREATION_VERSION	The version of the implementation.
PR_DISPLAY_TYPE	On normal folders, this is set to DT_FOLDER. Public folders or other sophisticated store provider implementations can create *link* folders, which are actually mirror images of a real folder. For those folders, the property value is set to DT_FOLDER_LINK. Client applications use this value to display the UI (e.g., which icon is associated with the folder) indicating the kind of folder a user is looking at.
PR_DISPLAY_NAME	The name of the folder.
PR_COMMENT	A comment describing a folder.
PR_STATUS	The folder's status. Clients can set whatever value they want in this property. The store provider implementation does not enforce any rule regarding acceptable values but simply saves whatever value a client sets.

We would like to mention several characteristics about our *IMAPIProp* implementation as it applies to folder objects. Most of these will be standard behavior for any store provider implementation.

■ The *IMAPIFolder::SaveChanges* method does nothing because folder objects are not transacted. However, it should return S_OK for read/write folders and MAPI_E_NO_ACCESS if the folder is read-only.

■ *IMAPIFolder::OpenProperty* is not implemented in our objects because clients should not open interfaces (e.g., *IStream* and *IStorage*) on any folder property. However, a store provider implementation might choose to allow clients to open an *IMAPITable* interface on PR_CONTAINER_HIERARCHY, PR_CONTAINER_CONTENTS, and PR_FOLDER_ASSOCIATED_CONTENTS in order to get at the respective tables in the folder. *OpenProperty* on PR_CONTAINER_CONTENTS, for example, is exactly equivalent to *GetContentsTable* on the folder object. Most clients will use the *GetContentsTable* method, so supporting the *OpenProperty* method on these properties is completely optional.

■ Our *IMAPIFolder::SetProps* implementation allows only three properties to be set: PR_DISPLAY_NAME, PR_COMMENT, and PR_STATUS. Setting any other property is not allowed, and the MAPI_E_NO_ACCESS error is returned in the problem array. The provider should immediately write any set properties to persistent storage and not expect clients to call *SaveChanges*. Remember, folders are not transacted. Also note that we notify interested subscribers that the object has been modified (i.e., an fnevObjectModified notification) and update the hierarchy table of our parent folder to reflect our new name, comment, status, and last modification time.

■ We don't let clients delete any properties in *IMAPIFolder::DeleteProps*. Instead we return a problem array filled with MAPI_E_NO_ACCESS for every property a client tries to delete. We recommend that even if you don't allow properties to be deleted in your folders, you return S_OK from the call and the proper problem array. This will ensure smooth interaction with client applications that don't (*gasp*) handle errors from this method.

■ The *IMAPIFolder::CopyTo* implementation simply defers the operation to MAPI's *IMAPISupport::CopyTo*. This lets MAPI take care of the details of copying and moving messages and subfolders from the source to the destination, even when the source and destination objects are in different store providers. We do the same for the *IMAPIFolder::CopyProps* method.

■ Named properties are supported in our *IMAPIFolder* objects because it was trivial for us to do so—not because it is required on *IMAPIFolder* implementations. You can return MAPI_E_NO_SUPPORT for the *IMAPIFolder::GetNamesFromIDs* and *IMAPIFolder::GetIDsFromNames* methods without breaking the MAPI specification rules.

Folder Tables

Our *IMAPIFolder* implementation supports hierarchy tables, normal contents tables, and associated contents tables. When our folder implementation needs a table, it asks the *CBackEnd* object to supply one. The storage class, *CFileBack-End*, takes care of reading the database record of each message in the specified folder and loading its data into the requested table.

The available columns in a contents or hierarchy table vary from implementation to implementation. They are usually the properties that the store provider can easily and rapidly compute and add to the rows of a table. Also, recall that implementations can limit to 255 the number of bytes they load into a table's column. For example, a contents table is only required to supply the first 255 bytes of the PR_BODY property in all its messages. Because store providers truncate the data obtained from a table to 255 bytes, clients must check the size of binary and string data; if the size is exactly 255 bytes, the client should assume that the data has been truncated and open the object and obtain the property through *GetProps*.

In our implementation, we use the utility method *CFileBackEnd::IsContentTableProp* to determine whether a field in the message's database record belongs in the contents table. For hierarchy tables, the back-end class has a fixed list of properties that are added to rows in this table. Each property in this list is guaranteed always to exist for every folder object in the database.

We don't support arbitrary column sets in our tables because the available columns are a predefined subset of properties on each object. Providers are not required to support adding arbitrary columns to their hierarchy or contents tables. A client request to include any properties not in the set of available columns (through *IMAPITable::SetColumns*) will not be honored.

Opening Objects in a Folder

The behavior of *IMAPIFolder::OpenEntry* is identical to *IMsgStore::OpenEntry*. (See the discussion beginning on page 519.)

Managing Folder Messages

The *CreateMessage, CopyMessages, DeleteMessages, SetReadFlags, GetMessageStatus,* and *SetMessageStatus* methods are used to manipulate messages within a folder. *IMAPIFolder::CreateMessage* creates new messages in our store provider. The logic is as follows:

1. We call *IMAPISupport::NewUID* to get a new UID. This UID is the search key of the message object.

2. We let the *CBackEnd* object create and initialize the properties of the new message by calling *CBackEnd::CreateObject*. The new message does not yet have a physical record in the database and won't until the client calls the *SaveChanges* method. The *CreateObject* call lets the message store provider create an entry ID for the message by asking the *CDataBase* object for the next available record ID number. Note that the entry ID of a message is not guaranteed to be available until the first *SaveChanges* call, so this step is for the convenience of our implementation, not a MAPI requirement.

3. When *CreateObject* returns, the initialized properties of the *IMessage* object have been added to the *CPropList* object. We then modify the message flags and create a new *CMessage* object, which is our implementation of *IMessage*. This object is returned to the client. To support associated messages, we simply tell the *CBackEnd* store provider that the object is associated. This information is used when the object is saved so that its entry ID information is added to the associated contents table of the parent folder.

Here is our implementation of *IMAPIFolder::CreateMessage*:

```
STDMETHODIMP CMAPIFolder::CreateMessage
                          (LPCIID      pInterface,
                           ULONG       ulFlags,
                           LPMESSAGE * ppMessage)
{
    :
    PRIVATE_ENTRYID eidNewMessage = { 0 };
    long lAccess;
    CPropList * pList;
    CMessage * pMsgObj;
    MAPIUID uidSearchKey;
    HRESULT hResult =
                m_pStore -> m_pSupObj -> NewUID(&uidSearchKey);
    if (!hResult)
    {
        hResult = m_pBEobj -> CreateObject
                (m_ObjectEID,
                 &eidNewMessage,
                 &pList,
                 MAPI_MESSAGE,
                 (LPVOID)&uidSearchKey,
                 (LPVOID)!!(ulFlags & MAPI_ASSOCIATED));
```

(continued)

```
if (!hResult)
{
    if (OBJECT_RUNNING_IN_SPOOLER & m_ulObjFlags)
    {
        SPropValue spvMsgFlags = { 0 };
        if (S_OK ==
            pList -> Find(PR_MESSAGE_FLAGS,
                          &spvMsgFlags))
        {
            spvMsgFlags.Value.l &=
                ~(MSGFLAG_READ |
                  MSGFLAG_UNSENT);
            pList -> Insert(&spvMsgFlags);
        }
    }
    // Inherit the parent's access rights.
    lAccess = MAPI_ACCESS_READ |
              MAPI_ACCESS_MODIFY |
              MAPI_ACCESS_DELETE;
    pMsgObj = new CMessage
                  (m_pStore,
                   &m_ObjectEID,
                   &eidNewMessage,
                   pList,
                   !!(ulFlags & MAPI_DEFERRED_ERRORS),
                   lAccess,
                   NULL,
                   m_pNPList);
    if (pMsgObj)
    {
        *ppMessage = (LPMESSAGE)pMsgObj;
        pMsgObj -> m_ulObjFlags |=
            OBJECT_JUST_CREATED |
            OBJECT_NEVER_SAVED |
            ((ulFlags & MAPI_ASSOCIATED) ?
             OBJECT_ASSOCIATED : 0) |
            ((m_ulObjFlags & OBJECT_RUNNING_IN_SPOOLER)
             ? OBJECT_RUNNING_IN_SPOOLER : 0);
        pMsgObj -> LoadObjectTables();
    }
    else
    {
        hResult = E_OUTOFMEMORY;
        delete pList;
    }
}
}
```

534

```
        SetLastError(hResult);
        return hResult;
}
```

CMAPIFolder::CopyMessages

To copy messages from one folder to another, the *IMAPIFolder::CopyMessages* implementation calls *IMAPISupport::CopyMessages*. The support object's *Copy-Messages* method copies the message to the destination folder and also handles the details of copying message attachments and named properties.

CMAPIFolder::DeleteMessages

The *IMAPIFolder::DeleteMessages* implementation delegates the work of deleting one or more messages to the *CBackEnd* object. *DeleteMessages* copies the list of entry IDs specified in the *pMsgList* parameter, and it passes the list to *CBackEnd::DeleteObjects*, which deletes the storage records of the corresponding messages from the database. After the objects have been deleted, the folder sends notifications about the messages that were successfully deleted and updates the folder's properties (PR_CONTENT_COUNT, PR_UNREAD_COUNT, and so on).

CMAPIFolder::SetReadFlags

Messages in a folder are either read or unread. A client is responsible for setting the message to the read state by calling *IMessage::SetReadFlags* when it opens the message. If the client wants to toggle the read or unread status of more than one message, it can call *IMAPIFolder::SetReadFlags*. Our implementation changes the read status of messages by opening each message indicated in the entry ID list and calling a method in the *CMessage* class to set the read flag. After a message's read state has been altered, a notification is sent to inform clients that an object (the message) has been modified.

CMAPIFolder::Get/SetMessageStatus

The PR_MSG_STATUS property exists only in a folder's contents table. Its value is 32 bits, and it holds a bitmap of flags. Some of its bits are reserved by MAPI, and only the eight high-order bits are usable by a client application for whatever purpose it sees fit. To manage getting and setting the status of a message in the contents table, clients call the *IMAPIFolder::GetMessageStatus* and *IMAPIFolder::SetMessageStatus* methods. Our implementation of these methods simply opens the object and either gets the PR_MSG_STATUS property and returns it (for *GetMessageStatus*) or sets the property (*SetMessageStatus*).

535

Managing Subfolders

Subfolders are created, copied, or deleted within a folder by the *IMAPIFolder- ::CreateFolder, IMAPIFolder::CopyFolder,* and *IMAPIFolder::DeleteFolder* methods, respectively.

CMAPIFolder::CreateFolder

To create a folder, we do the following:

1. Attempt to create the folder with the given name. If another folder exists with that name, open it if the client passed the OPEN_IF-_EXISTS flag. Otherwise, return MAPI_E_COLLISION.

2. Create a new *CMAPIFolder* object, and set properties on it.

3. If a new folder object was created, modify the parent folder and send out notifications about the new object that was created and about the parent folder where the new object was created.

Here is our implementation of *IMAPIFolder::CreateFolder*:

```
STDMETHODIMP CMAPIFolder::CreateFolder
                        (ULONG          ulFolderType,
                         LPTSTR         pszFolderName,
                         LPTSTR         pszFolderComment,
                         LPCIID         pInterface,
                         ULONG          ulFlags,
                         LPMAPIFOLDER * ppFolder)
{
    ⋮
    // Allocate an empty entry ID structure
    // for the new folder.
    PRIVATE_ENTRYID eidNewFolder = { 0 };
    BOOL fFolderCreated = TRUE;
    CMAPIFolder * pFldObj;
    CPropList * pList;

    // Lock for exclusive access to the
    // data on this object.
    EnterCriticalSection(&m_csObj);
    // Let the back-end storage create the
    // space for the new object.
    HRESULT hResult = m_pBEobj -> CreateObject
                            (m_ObjectEID,
                             &eidNewFolder,
                             &pList,
                             MAPI_FOLDER,
                             pszFolderName,
```

```
                                        pszFolderComment);
if ((MAPI_E_COLLISION == hResult) &&
    (ulFlags & OPEN_IF_EXISTS))
{
    // If there is a folder with that name already,
    // and the user said so, open it.
    hResult = m_pBEobj -> OpenObject(eidNewFolder,
                                     &pList);
    fFolderCreated = FALSE;
}
long lAccess;
if (!hResult)
{
    // Inherit the parent's access rights.
    lAccess =
        (m_lAccess & MAPI_MODIFY ? MAPI_ACCESS_MODIFY : 0) |
        (m_lAccess & MAPI_MODIFY ? MAPI_ACCESS_DELETE : 0) |
         MAPI_ACCESS_READ |
         MAPI_ACCESS_CREATE_HIERARCHY |
         MAPI_ACCESS_CREATE_CONTENTS |
         MAPI_ACCESS_CREATE_ASSOCIATED;
    pFldObj = new CMAPIFolder
                     (m_pStore,
                      &m_ObjectEID,
                      &eidNewFolder,
                      ulFolderType,
                      pList,
                      !!(ulFlags & MAPI_DEFERRED_ERRORS),
                      lAccess,
                      m_pNPList);
    if (pFldObj)
    {
        // Set the returning object, and
        // set some internal flags.
        *ppFolder = (LPMAPIFOLDER)pFldObj;
        pFldObj -> m_ulObjFlags |=
                ((m_ulObjFlags & OBJECT_RUNNING_IN_SPOOLER) ?
                OBJECT_RUNNING_IN_SPOOLER : 0);
    }
    else
    {
        // Darn..., we must get more RAM!!!
        hResult = E_OUTOFMEMORY;
        delete pList;
    }
}
```

(continued)

537

```
// If we are successful at creating a new folder on the folder,
// get ready to send the client notifications....
if (!hResult && fFolderCreated)
{
    NOTIFICATION notif = { 0 };
    BOOL fObjectChanged = FALSE;

    // When a new folder is created, if it is the
    // same on the folder, we must update the
    // PR_SUBFOLDERS property, and, if modified,
    // send the appropriate notification to the
    // client subscribers. If this property is
    // modified, we must also update any
    // in-memory hierarchy table of the parent of
    // this folder object.
    SPropValue spvSubFolders = { 0 }, spvLastModTime = { 0 };
    m_pList -> Find(PR_SUBFOLDERS, &spvSubFolders);
    if (!spvSubFolders.Value.b)
    {
        fObjectChanged = TRUE;
        spvSubFolders.ulPropTag = PR_SUBFOLDERS;
        spvSubFolders.Value.b = TRUE;
        // The properties must be updated in our list
        // BEFORE we send out notifications so that
        // clients can get the proper value after
        // receiving the notification from our store provider.
        m_pList -> Insert(&spvSubFolders);

        // Commit the properties changed on this object.
        // This updates the last modification time
        // of the object.
        CGenericProp::SaveChanges(KEEP_OPEN_READWRITE, NULL);

        m_pList -> Find(PR_LAST_MODIFICATION_TIME,
                        &spvLastModTime);

        // Send a notification that the parent folder
        // has been modified if this is the first
        // folder created in it.
        notif.ulEventType       = fnevObjectModified;
        notif.info.obj.cbEntryID  = CB_PRIVATE_EID;
        notif.info.obj.lpEntryID  = (LPENTRYID)&m_ObjectEID;
        notif.info.obj.cbParentID = CB_PRIVATE_EID;
        notif.info.obj.lpParentID = (LPENTRYID)&m_ParentEID;
        notif.info.obj.ulObjType  = MAPI_FOLDER;
        m_pStore -> NotifyClients(&m_ObjectEID, 1, &notif);
```

```
        // Update the in-memory hierarchy table for
        // the parents of this folder.
        UpdateParentTable();
    }


    // Send a notification that a new object has
    // been created. This is at the store provider level.
    notif.ulEventType        = fnevObjectCreated;
    notif.info.obj.cbEntryID = CB_PRIVATE_EID;
    notif.info.obj.lpEntryID = (LPENTRYID)&eidNewFolder;
    notif.info.obj.cbParentID = CB_PRIVATE_EID;
    notif.info.obj.lpParentID = (LPENTRYID)&m_ObjectEID;
    notif.info.obj.ulObjType = MAPI_FOLDER;
    m_pStore -> NotifyClients(NULL, 1, &notif);


    // We must update the hierarchy table of
    // any instance of this folder that
    // may be open on the store provider.
    LPSPropValue pProps = NULL;
    DWORD dwLastAllocated = 0;
    CMAPIFolder * pFldObj =
            (CMAPIFolder *)m_pStore -> m_OpenObjList.Walk
                                        (m_ObjectEID,
                                         WALK_START,
                                         NULL);
    while (pFldObj)
    {
        if (fObjectChanged && (pFldObj != this))
        {
            pFldObj -> m_pList -> Insert(&spvSubFolders);
            pFldObj -> m_pList -> Insert(&spvLastModTime);
        }
        if (pFldObj -> m_pHierTable)
        {
            hResult = m_pBEobj -> GetTableProps
                        (TABLE_HIERARCHY,
                         m_lAccess,
                         &m_ObjectEID,
                         &eidNewFolder,
                         pList,
                         &pProps,
                         dwLastAllocated,
                         pFldObj -> m_pHierTable,
                         (LPVOID)&m_pStore -> m_StoreEID,
                         (LPVOID)ulFolderType);
        }
```

(continued)

```
                    pFldObj -> Release();
                    pFldObj =
                        (CMAPIFolder *)m_pStore -> m_OpenObjList.Walk
                                                    (m_ObjectEID,
                                                    WALK_CONTINUE,
                                                    pFldObj);
                }
                PrivFree((LPVOID *)&pProps);
                // We don't care if we couldn't add the
                // folder to the in-memory hierarchy table.
                hResult = S_OK;
            }
            LeaveCriticalSection(&m_csObj);
            SetLastError(hResult);
            return hResult;
        }
```

CMAPIFolder::CopyFolder

Our implementation delegates the work of copying a folder to the *IMAPI-Support::CopyFolder* method.

CMAPIFolder::DeleteFolder

To delete a subfolder, the client calls *IMAPIFolder::DeleteFolder*, passing the entry ID of the subfolder to be deleted. Our implementation calls the *CBackEnd-::DeleteOneObject* method to purge the subfolder's database record. Before the subfolder is deleted, its children must be deleted. When both the subfolder and its children are deleted, we send fnevObjectDeleted notifications for each child and for the subfolder itself as well as an fnevObjectModified notification on the parent of the deleted subfolder.

Deleting a Folder's Children

To delete the contents of a folder, a client calls *IMAPIFolder::EmptyFolder*. This method deletes all messages and subfolders contained in the folder through which the call is made. The implementation has several responsibilities:

- It must delete the appropriate objects based on the flags passed in the *ulFlags* parameter. Subfolders and normal messages are deleted without regard for the value of *ulFlags*, but associated messages are deleted only if the DEL_ASSOCIATED bit is set by the caller.

- It must send out notifications for every object deleted and for the folder object itself to indicate that its properties (e.g., PR_CONTENT-_COUNT and PR_LAST_MODIFICATION_TIME) have changed.

■ It must adjust any properties of the folder object that depend on the contents of the folder and update the contents table and hierarchy table to reflect the state of the folder. Properties that get updated after the folder contents have been deleted are PR_SUBFOLDERS, PR_CONTENT_COUNT, PR_CONTENT_UNREAD, PR_ASSOC-_CONTENT_COUNT, and PR_LAST_MODIFICATION_TIME.

An implementation can return an error after a call to *IMAPIFolder-::EmptyFolder*, but client applications shouldn't assume that failure means that nothing was deleted. The error might have occurred at any point during the delete process, and some objects might have been deleted before the error occurred. The store provider should send the appropriate notifications for each deleted object.

Unsupported Methods in Our *IMAPIFolder* Implementation

The following methods are not supported in the current implementation of our sample message store providers.

■ *IMAPIFolder::SetSearchCriteria.* We don't support searches.

■ *IMAPIFolder::GetSearchCriteria.*

■ *IMAPIFolder::SaveContentsSort.* This is used by clients to store specific sort criteria for a contents table. If a store provider implementation supports this method, a client can save the sort order to persistent storage and the message store provider would be responsible for applying the sort criteria every time the client requests the contents table of the specific folder where the sort order is saved. Not many implementations support this method.

Implementing *IMessage*

The basis of the *IMessage* implementation is its underlying *CMAPIProp* implementation. As with all our other *IMAPIProp*-derived objects, the *CMessage* class derives from the *CGenericProp* class. The properties you will initially find in a message object vary depending on the implementation. However, the minimal set you will almost always find is described in Figure 10-10 on the following page.

Property	Description
PR_ACCESS	Access mask of the message instance.
PR_ACCESS_LEVEL	Indicates whether or not a message and its contents can be modified through that instance.
PR_ENTRYID	The long-term entry ID of the message. This property is not guaranteed to be available until after the first *SaveChanges*.
PR_PARENT_ENTRYID	The long-term entry ID of the parent folder of this message. This property is not guaranteed to be available until after the first *SaveChanges*.
PR_STORE_ENTRYID	The entry ID of the store provider in which this message resides (the same value as in *IMsgStore*).
PR_STORE_RECORD_KEY	The record key of the store provider (the same value as in *IMsgStore*).
PR_RECORD_KEY	A unique identifier that distinguishes a message. Similar to an entry ID but this is a property that client applications can do a binary comparison against to determine whether the two record keys refer to the same object.
PR_SEARCH_KEY	A unique identifier that distinguishes the data of a message. Two messages can have the same PR_SEARCH_KEY value if they are backed by the data set—for example, when a message is copied to another, the second message will have the same search key as the original because they have the same data.
PR_MAPPING_SIGNATURE	A UID for the named property mapping. Because our named properties are mapped at the store provider level, all objects share the same mapping signature value.
PR_HASATTACH	A Boolean value that indicates whether a message has attachments in it.
PR_OBJECT_TYPE	This is always set to MAPI_MESSAGE.

Figure 10-10.　　　　　　　　　　　　　　　　　　*(continued)*

Minimal set of properties found in an IMessage *object.*

542

Figure 10-10. *continued*

Property	Description
PR_STORE_SUPPORT_MASK	The same as in the *IMsgStore*.
PR_CREATION_TIME	The date and time the message was created. In our implementation, this is a computed value that clients cannot set. The format is UTC.
PR_CREATION_VERSION	The version of the implementation.
PR_LAST_MODIFICATION_TIME	The date and time the message was last modified in any way. Modifications include creating attachments, modifying the message's recipients, altering any of its properties, and so on. In our implementation, this is a computed value that clients cannot set. The format is UTC.
PR_MESSAGE_ATTACHMENTS	Indicates that the message has an attachment table. This is used when the message is copied to another message in order to either exclude or include the attachments in the copy operation.
PR_MESSAGE_RECIPIENTS	This property is a placeholder for the recipient table. It is used when the message is copied to another message to either exclude or include the recipient table in the copy operation. A client can use *OpenProperty* on PR_MESSAGE_RECIPIENTS to obtain the recipient table.
PR_MESSAGE_SIZE	The size, in bytes, that the message object's contents occupy in the database.
PR_MESSAGE_CLASS	A string with the class name of the message. By default this is set to "IPM."
PR_MESSAGE_FLAGS	A bitmap of flags that indicate the state or attributes of the message. The flags might change dynamically after clients perform some tasks in the message store provider (e.g., submit a message).
PR_PRIORITY	The delivery priority of the message. Possible values are PRIO_NONURGENT, PRIO_NORMAL, and PRIO_URGENT.

Getting Properties

Our processing of *CMessage::GetProps* is broken up into two stages. First, we call the base class's *CGenericProp::GetProps* method, passing the property tag array specified by the caller. This function creates and allocates the property value array and sets the property tags in each entry. It also replaces any PT_UN-KNOWN property types with the property's correct type. At this point we have an empty array of *SPropValue* structures. The second part of our implementation walks this array and searches our set of predefined properties or the property list (*CPropList*) for each desired property.

If the target property is found, we copy it into the proper array element. If it is not found, we change the array element's property type to PT_ERROR and set the *Value.err* member of the *SPropValue* structure to MAPI_E_NOT-_FOUND.

Our implementation, like all implementations, limits the number of bytes a call to *GetProps* can return for a single property. We allow only up to 16 KB of data per property. This is to avoid running out of memory for large properties. However, there is no restriction on the *number* of properties returned, which is limited only by the amount of memory available.

Setting Properties

Setting properties on our *IMessage* objects is accomplished in two stages:

1. First we look at the property tag to see whether it is one of the properties that requires special processing.

2. If the property can be set, we call the base class *CGenericProp* and add it to the object's property list.

Properties Requiring Special Processing

For *IMessage* objects, the properties which require special processing include the following:

■ *PR_DISPLAY_BCC, PR_DISPLAY_CC, PR_DISPLAY_TO.* Clients cannot set these properties on message objects because they are computed by the implementation. The implementation looks at the recipient table and, based on the PR_RECIPIENT_TYPE column of each recipient, a concatenated string of all the display names is created in the form: "<Name 1>; <Name 2>; ...; <Name n>." The *IMessage* implementation is responsible for computing these properties if the message objects don't have any recipients. If there are no recipients

of a given PR_RECIPIENT_TYPE, the corresponding PR_DISPLAY-
_XXX property value is assigned an empty string ("").

■ *PR_NORMALIZED_SUBJECT.* This is the normalized version of the
PR_SUBJECT property. We must point out that the PR_DISPLAY-
_XXX and PR_NORMALIZED_SUBJECT properties are not guaranteed to be synchronized with the current list of recipients and the
current message subject until *SaveChanges* is called. However, implementations (like ours) can compute them dynamically after a client
modifies the recipient table or changes the message subject.

■ *PR_SEARCH_KEY.* This property can be set by clients as many
times as they want prior to the first call to *SaveChanges* on the new
message object. After the first *SaveChanges* call, the implementation
sets the access level of this property to read-only and its value cannot change.

■ *PR_MESSAGE_FLAGS.* The same rule applies to this property as
with PR_SEARCH_KEY: Its bits can be altered by client applications up until the first *SaveChanges*. After that, the message store
provider computes the bits dynamically. In our implementation,
we make sure the client is not trying to set bogus bits, such as
MSGFLAG_HASATTACH.

In addition to the properties listed above (and apart from the intrinsic
properties of the message), a client can pretty much set any message property
it wants to. As in *GetProps*, we have a limit of 16 KB of data per property that
can be set through the *SetProps* call. For large data values, the client should call
OpenProperty and request an *IStream* interface on the specified property tag.

Opening Interfaces on Properties

Our implementation allows clients to open three interfaces on properties. The
first, *IMAPITable*, is available on only the PR_MESSAGE_ATTACHMENTS
and PR_MESSAGE_RECIPIENTS property tags. MAPI doesn't require a store
provider to support *IMAPITable* on these properties.

The other two interfaces we support are *IStorage* and *IStream*. The *IStorage*
interface can be opened on any PT_OBJECT property, and the *IStream* interface can be opened on any PT_BINARY or any string-type (e.g., PT_STRING8
and PT_UNICODE) property. We don't allow clients to open interfaces on
multivalue properties, and we return E_INVALIDARG on the call to
IMessage::OpenProperty if this is requested.

Deleting Properties

The call to *DeleteProps* delegates to the *CGenericProp* interface, which actually deletes the property from the property list (*CPropList* or *COpenPropList*). When a property is deleted in a message, it is deleted only from the in-memory image of the property list. Later, when the client calls *CMessage::SaveChanges*, the property is permanently deleted from storage.

Copying the Object and Its Properties

One message is copied onto another using either *CMessage::CopyTo* or *CMessage::CopyProps*. Both of these methods delegate to the *IMAPISupport* object and call *IMAPISupport::DoCopyTo* and *IMAPISupport::DoCopyProps*. The support object takes care of the details of copying the recipient table, copying any contained attachments, remapping named properties, and so on.

Named Property Support

Our *IMessage* objects support named properties, and the scope of the name-to-ID mapping is the entire store provider—thus a given named property will have the same ID in all the messages in any folder of our provider.

The main benefit of this scheme is that the named IDs can be copied normally without computing a new ID in the destination object. (Another way of saying the same thing is that all objects in the store provider have the same mapping signature.) Thus, the performance of copying objects is greatly improved.

Managing Recipients

Recipients in a message are stored in a table within the message object. This table might contain information from the address book provider that the transport uses to send the message to the appropriate user on the destination system. To view and modify this table, clients call *IMessage::GetRecipientTable* and *IMessage::ModifyRecipients*, respectively.

In our implementation, the recipient table is based on MAPI's built-in *IMAPITable*. To fill the rows in the table, we call the *CBackEnd* object which takes care of reading the properties for each recipient and loading the rows into the table. The typical columns you'll find in the recipient table of a message are listed in Figure 10-11:

Column	Description
PR_ROWID	This property is computed by the message store provider and is unique for every row in the recipient table. Clients use this value when they need to modify a particular row in the table.
PR_SEARCH_KEY	The search key of the recipient indicated in a row. This is the search key of the address book provider's object. In address book providers, the search key is a normalized string of the form "<AddrType>:<Email-Address>."
PR_INSTANCE_KEY	The instance key of the current row. This is an optional column, but, to be consistent, all our tables have instance key columns.
PR_ENTRYID	The recipient's address book provider entry ID. When a recipient has the long-term entry ID, the entry is considered resolved and the message can be delivered to this recipient.
PR_DISPLAY_NAME	The display name of the message recipient.
PR_RECIPIENT_TYPE	The type of recipient, e.g., the value can be MAPI_TO, MAPI_CC, or MAPI_BCC.
PR_ADDRTYPE	The recipient's address type string.
PR_EMAIL_ADDRESS	The recipient's email address.
PR_OBJECT_TYPE	The type of object that the recipient is. Possible values include MAPI_MAILUSER and MAPI_DISTLIST.
PR_DISPLAY_TYPE	This is set to either DT_MAILUSER or DT_DISTLIST.

Figure 10-11.
Columns in a message's recipient table.

Our implementation of *IMessage::ModifyRecipients* does the following:

1. If a message recipient is being modified or added, *ModifyRecipients* opens the address book provider and makes sure it has the necessary recipient properties for the row the client is adding.

2. If a recipient is being modified or deleted, it makes sure the caller has the PR_ROWID property in each row of the set passed in.

3. *ModifyRecipients* adds or modifies the recipient in the existing message recipient table. If the table is empty or nonexistent and recipients are added, it creates a new table and adds rows to it.

4. It generates the appropriate PR_DISPLAY_XXX strings.

Any recipient information modified in the table or added during a call to *CMessage::ModifyRecipients* is not saved permanently in the message database until the client calls the *CMessage::SaveChanges* method.

Managing Attachments

Attachments in a message are handled with the following methods:

■ *CMessage::GetAttachmentTable*. This method returns a table with the list of attachments in a message. The typical columns that you'll find in the attachment table are listed in Figure 10-12. Our implementation bases its attachment table on MAPI's built-in *IMAPITable* implementation. To construct the attachment table, we simply delegate the task to the *CBackEnd* object, which walks the available attachment records of the message and adds the rows to the attachment table. To decide if a property should be added to the attachment table, the storage class uses the *CBackEnd::IsAttachmentTableProp* helper method.

■ *CMessage::OpenAttach*. This method opens an existing attachment in the message given its attachment identifier (PR_ATTACH_NUM). The implementation of this method is similar to the *OpenEntry* methods on the *IMsgStore* and *IMAPIFolder* interfaces. First we request the list of properties from the attachment table. After we have the *CPropList* object loaded with the attachment's properties, we create a new instance of the *CAttach* class (the implementation of *IAttach*), which is returned to the caller.

■ *CMessage::CreateAttach*. This method creates an attachment in a message. As with the *IMAPIFolder::CreateMessage* and *IMAPIFolder-::CreateFolder* methods, the *CBackEnd* object allocates the storage and attachment number for the new object. The initial properties of the attachment object are set in the returned *CPropList* class, and with this, a new *CAttach* instance is created and returned to the client. The required behavior is that the new attachment is not permanently stored in the provider's database until the client calls *SaveChanges* on the attachment *and* on the message object.

■ *CMessage::DeleteAttach.* This method deletes an existing attachment from the current message. If the message does not have an attachment, the call does nothing and returns MAPI_E_NOT_FOUND. Our implementation calls the *CBackEnd* object, which deletes the attachment record. However, an attachment isn't permanently deleted until the client calls *SaveChanges* on the message. To defer the deletion, we have a list of transacted actions on an attachment and for each delete action on an attachment we add a node to the list. When *SaveChanges* gets called on the message, we walk the list of transacted action nodes and proceed to delete the attachment at that time.

Column	Description
PR_INSTANCE_KEY	The instance key of the row.
PR_STORE_ENTRYID	The entry ID of the store provider object. (Same value as in *IMsgStore*.)
PR_STORE_RECORD_KEY	The record key of the store provider. (Same value as in *IMsgStore*.)
PR_RECORD_KEY	The record key of the attachment object.
PR_MAPPING_SIGNATURE	A UID for the named property mapping. Because our named properties are mapped at the store provider level, all objects share the same mapping signature value.
PR_OBJECT_TYPE	This is always set to MAPI_ATTACH.
PR_ATTACH_NUM	The number of the attachment. Clients use the attachment number to open a specific object and get back an *IAttach* interface.
PR_ATTACH_METHOD	The method or type of attachment.
PR_CREATION_TIME	The date and time the attachment was created. The format is UTC.
PR_LAST_MODIFICA-TION_TIME	The date and time the attachment was last modified in any way. The format is UTC.
PR_ATTACH_SIZE	The size, in bytes, of the attachment's properties.
PR_DISPLAY_NAME	The name of the attachment object.

Figure 10-12.

Columns in a message's attachment table.

Submitting Messages

Submitting a message is a fairly involved process for the message store provider. The *MAPI Programmer's Guide* details these steps, which we will not repeat here. Instead, we'll discuss our implementation of *IMessage::SubmitMessage*, shown below:

```
SizedSPropTagArray(2, sptSubmitRecipTable) =
{
    2,
    {
        PR_ROWID,
        PR_RESPONSIBILITY
    }
};

STDMETHODIMP CMessage::SubmitMessage(ULONG ulFlags)
{
    :
    SYSTEMTIME st;
    FILETIME ft;
    GetSystemTime(&st);
    SystemTimeToFileTime(&st, &ft);
    SPropValue spvProp = { 0 };
    BOOL fFlagChangedAndSaved = FALSE;
    // Lock the object for exclusive access.
    EnterCriticalSection(&m_csObj);
    HRESULT hResult = PrepareRecipsForSubmission();
    if (hResult)
    {
        goto ErrorExit;
    }
    m_pList -> Find(PR_MESSAGE_FLAGS, &spvProp);
    if (spvProp.Value.l & MSGFLAG_SUBMIT)
    {
        :
        // Resubmit the message.
        :
    }
    spvProp.ulPropTag = PR_MESSAGE_FLAGS;
    spvProp.Value.l |= MSGFLAG_SUBMIT;
    m_pList -> Insert(&spvProp);
    spvProp.ulPropTag = PR_CLIENT_SUBMIT_TIME;
    spvProp.Value.ft = ft;
    m_pList -> Insert(&spvProp);
    hResult = SaveChanges(KEEP_OPEN_READWRITE);
```

```
    if (!hResult)
    {
        fFlagChangedAndSaved = TRUE;
        if (OBJECT_RUNNING_IN_SPOOLER & m_ulObjFlags)
        {
            m_pStore -> AddMsgToOutGoingQueue(ft,
                                              m_ObjectEID);
        }
        else
        {
            m_pStore -> SubmitToSpoolerContextStore
                        (ft,
                         m_ObjectEID);
        }
    }
ErrorExit :
    if (hResult)
    {
        if (fFlagChangedAndSaved)
        {
            // If something failed, remove the submit
            // bit from the message flags.
            m_pList -> Find(PR_MESSAGE_FLAGS, &spvProp);
            spvProp.Value.l &= ~MSGFLAG_SUBMIT;
            m_pList -> Insert(&spvProp);
            SaveChanges(KEEP_OPEN_READWRITE);
        }
        SetLastError(hResult);
    }
    LeaveCriticalSection(&m_csObj);
    return hResult;
}


STDMETHODIMP CMessage::PrepareRecipsForSubmission()
{
    LPMAPITABLE pTableView;
    HRESULT hResult = S_OK;
    ULONG ulRecipCount,
          ulPrepareSubmitFlags = 0,
          ulExpandRecipsFlags = 0;
    if (!m_pRecipTable)
    {
        hResult = GetRecipientTable(0, &pTableView);
        if (!hResult)
```

(continued)

```
            {
                pTableView -> Release();
            }
        }
        if (hResult)
        {
            goto ErrorExit;
        }
        hResult = m_pRecipTable -> HrGetView(NULL,
                                             NULL,
                                             0,
                                             &pTableView);
        if (!hResult)
        {
            hResult = pTableView -> GetRowCount(0,
                                                &ulRecipCount);
            if (!hResult)
            {
                if (0 == ulRecipCount)
                {
                    hResult = MAPI_E_NO_RECIPIENTS;
                }
                else
                {
                    hResult = HrAddColumns
                                (pTableView,
                                (LPSPropTagArray)&sptSubmitRecipTable,
                                GetMAPIAllocBuffer(),
                                GetMAPIFreeBuffer());
                }
                BOOL fContinue = TRUE;
                LPSRowSet pRows;
                ULONG ulRow;
                while (fContinue && !hResult)
                {
                    hResult = pTableView -> QueryRows(15, 0, &pRows);
                    if (!hResult)
                    {
                        if (pRows -> cRows)
                        {
                            for (ulRow = 0; ulRow < pRows -> cRows; ulRow++)
                            {
                                // We don't want responsibility for any
                                // recipient. If this isn't the spooler
                                // calling, then force ALL
                                // responsibilities to FALSE
                                // regardless of what they were.
```

```
                        if (PR_RESPONSIBILITY !=
                            pRows ->
                                aRow[ulRow].lpProps[1].ulPropTag ¦¦
                            !(m_ulObjFlags &
                              OBJECT_RUNNING_IN_SPOOLER))
                        {
                            pRows ->
                                aRow[ulRow].lpProps[1].ulPropTag =
                                    PR_RESPONSIBILITY;
                            pRows -> aRow[ulRow].lpProps[1].Value.b =
                                FALSE;
                            m_pRecipTable -> HrModifyRows(0, pRows);
                        }
                    }
                }
                else
                {
                    fContinue = FALSE;
                }
                FreeProws(pRows);
            }
        }
    }
    pTableView -> Release();
}
if (hResult)
{
    goto ErrorExit;
}
SPropValue spvSubmitFlags;
hResult = m_pStore -> m_pSupObj -> PrepareSubmit
                                    (this,
                                     &ulPrepareSubmitFlags);
if (!hResult)
{
    hResult = m_pStore -> m_pSupObj -> ExpandRecips
                                        (this,
                                         &ulExpandRecipsFlags);
    if (!hResult)
    {
        spvSubmitFlags.ulPropTag = PR_SUBMIT_FLAGS;
        if (NEEDS_PREPROCESSING & ulExpandRecipsFlags)
        {
            spvSubmitFlags.Value.l = SUBMITFLAG_PREPROCESS;
        }
```

(continued)

553

```
                else
                {
                    spvSubmitFlags.Value.1 = 0;
                }
                m_pList -> Insert(&spvSubmitFlags);
            }
        }
        if (!hResult)
        {
            m_fRecipTableDirty = TRUE;
        }
ErrorExit :
    return hResult;
}
```

We perform the following steps to submit a message:

1. We verify that the object has read/write access. Since some of its properties will be modified, a client must have read/write access to the object before it can commit the modifications to disk.

2. If the message is an associated message, we fail the submission process with MAPI_E_NO_SUPPORT. Implementations that support submissions are not required to support sending associated messages.

3. We verify the message has recipients. If it doesn't, we return MAPI_E_NO_RECIPIENTS.

4. We process the recipient table of the message and make sure it has the PR_ROWID and PR_RESPONSIBILITY columns in each of its rows. The PR_RESPONSIBILITY property of each recipient must be set to *FALSE*, so that the MAPI spooler will know whether or not the message has already been delivered to that recipient.

5. Call *IMAPISupport::PrepareSubmit* to check whether the message needs to be preprocessed.

6. Call *IMAPISupport::ExpandRecips* to expand all personal distribution lists and custom recipients and replace all changed display names with their original names. This call also removes duplicate names from the recipient table.

7. Add the MSGFLAG_SUBMIT bit to PR_MESSAGE_FLAGS to indicate the message is being delivered. Get the system time and stamp the current time in PR_CLIENT_SUBMIT_TIME. The submit time is in UTC format.

8. Call *SaveChanges* on the submitted message to commit any client transactions on the message prior to the call to *SubmitMessage* and to save our changes to the properties thus far in the *IMessage::SubmitMessage* call.

9. At this point we call the *CMsgStore::AddMsgToOutGoingQueue* helper method, which uses the IPC mechanism (the MAPI notification engine) to tell the store provider in the spooler context that a new message has been submitted.

10. When the store provider in the spooler context receives the notification about a newly submitted message, it adds a row to the outgoing queue table and the message is then processed by the spooler and delivered through the available transports.

Modifying the Message Read State

We've already mentioned how a client application can set the read state of a message by calling *IMessage::SetReadFlag*. This call causes the store provider to modify some of the bits in the PR_MESSAGE_FLAG property to indicate whether the message has or hasn't been read yet.

Changing the state of a message might trigger some actions if the original sender of the message requested to be notified when the message was read. A client might call the *SetReadFlag* method and indicate that a receipt not be sent out even if one was requested. The store provider implementation decides whether it wants to honor the receipt-suppression request from the client or not. In our implementation, we support all the flags for *IMessage::SetReadFlag*. We even support suppressing read reports on messages.

Follow these steps when implementing *IMessage::SetReadFlag*:

1. Check the flags passed in. If the caller wants to suppress read receipt and the implementation does not support suppressing read notifications, then return MAPI_E_NO_SUPPRESS.

2. Look for PR_READ_RECEIPT_REQUESTED in the properties of the message. If present and the value is *TRUE*, then a receipt must be generated for the originator of the message.

3. To generate the receipt, call *IMAPISupport::ReadReceipt*. Pass in the current message and a new message. MAPI will set the new message's properties for the read receipt. After the properties have been set in the new message, submit it by calling *IMessage::SubmitMessage* on the new message.

4. If setting the read state of a message changes the value of PR_MESSAGE_FLAGS, and the message has been saved at least once, immediately commit the changes.

Saving Changes on a Message

Any changes to the properties or attachments of a message are deferred until the client calls *SaveChanges*. The first *SaveChanges* call on an *IMessage* object might have significant side effects in some implementations. For instance, after the first call to *SaveChanges*, properties such as PR_ENTRYID and PR_PARENT-_ENTRYID will appear. Other properties will change their access rights from read/write to read-only. During the call to *SaveChanges*, implementations are responsible for the following tasks:

1. Saving the property set of the object to permanent storage. This implies removing deleted properties from the storage.

2. Generating or updating the appropriate properties, such as the PR_DISPLAY_XXX properties PR_NORMALIZED_SUBJECT, PR_LAST_MODIFICATION_TIME, etc.

3. If this is the first call to *SaveChanges*, sending out the fnevObject-Created event notification to interested subscribers. If it is not the first call to *SaveChanges*, then an fnevObjectModified event notification is sent out instead.

4. Updating the contents table of the parent folder. On the first call to *SaveChanges*, a new row is added. On subsequent calls, the existing row is modified to reflect any change in the message's properties. The requirement to update the contents table of the parent folder also implies that some folder properties (e.g., PR_CONTENT-_COUNT or PR_ASSOC_CONTENT_COUNT) must be adjusted to reflect the state of the folder's contents.

Implementing *IAttach*

The *IAttach* methods are similar to those in the *IMessage* implementation. *GetProps* and *SetProps* have the same limitation on the amount of data that can be retrieved at once. Figure 10-13 lists the minimum set of properties that an attachment object must support.

Property	Description
PR_ACCESS	The access mask of the attachment instance.
PR_ACCESS_LEVEL	Indicates whether or not an attachment and its contents can be modified through that instance.
PR_ATTACH_NUM	A numeric identifier of the attachment. This number is determined by the message store provider. Two attachments in the same message cannot have the same attachment number, although attachments in two different messages can.
PR_ATTACH_SIZE	The size (in bytes) that the attachment and its properties occupy in the database.
PR_STORE_ENTRYID	The entry ID of the store provider. (Same value as in *IMsgStore*.)
PR_STORE_RECORD_KEY	The record key of the store provider. (Same value as in *IMsgStore*.)
PR_RECORD_KEY	The record key of the attachment object.
PR_MAPPING_SIGNATURE	A UID for the named property mapping. Because our named properties are mapped at the store provider level, all objects share the same mapping signature value.
PR_OBJECT_TYPE	This is always set to MAPI_ATTACH.
PR_STORE_SUPPORT_MASK	The same as in *IMsgStore*.
PR_CREATION_TIME	The date and time the attachment was created. In our implementation, this is a computed value clients cannot set. The format is UTC.
PR_CREATION_VERSION	The version of the implementation.
PR_LAST_MODIFICATION_TIME	The date and time the attachment was last modified in any way. Modifications include adding new properties, modifying existing properties, and so on. In our implementation, this is a computed value clients cannot set. The format is UTC.

Figure 10-13.
Required properties on an attachment object.

Opening Interfaces on Properties

Our implementation supports opening the following interfaces on single valued properties:

- *IStream.* On any property of type PT_BINARY and string-type properties (PT_STRING8 and PT_UNICODE).

- *IStorage.* On properties of type PT_OBJECT, such as PR_ATTACH-_DATA_OBJ. Implementations are required to open this interface on PR_ATTACH_DATA_OBJ if they support OLE objects in their attachments. When an implementation supports *IStorage* in the *OpenProperty* method, it should set the STORE_OLE_OK bit in the PR_STORE_SUPPORT_MASK property of all its objects.

- *IMessage.* We allow this property only on the PR_ATTACH_DATA-_OBJ property tag so that an embedded message can be created.

The *IStream* Interface

The *IStream* interface we return from the *OpenProperty* call in the *IAttach* and *IMessage* interfaces is based on two existing implementations. If the data on which we are opening the stream is less than 65 KB in size, we call the *CreateStreamOnHGlobal* Win32 API, which returns an *IStream* interface that lives in memory at all times. The storage class *CBackEnd* will copy the data from the database to the in-memory stream. If the data is equal to or larger than 65 KB in size, we create a stream using the *OpenStreamOnFile* MAPI API, which returns an *IStream* interface backed by a temporary file. The storage class *CBackEnd* copies the data from the database to the temporary file. Clients are actually dealing with a copy of the attachment property, so changes are easily transacted and rolled into the database when the client calls *SaveChanges* on the attachment and its parent message.

The *IStorage* Interface

For the *IStorage* interface, we use MAPI's implementation through the *HrIStorageFromStream* API, which creates an *IStorage* interface on top of an existing *IStream.* The stream we use for the new *IStorage* object is always the one returned from *OpenStreamOnFile* so that the storage lives in a temporary file while the user interacts with it. When the changes to the attachment are committed to the database, we simply copy the underlying *IStream* of the storage into the native *IStream* interface of the database record.

Implementing Embedded *IMessage* Objects

Our implementation of *IAttach* supports opening the *IMessage* interface on the PR_ATTACH_DATA_OBJ. To do this, we simply create a new message on the database and set the attachment object as the parent of the message. Embedded messages in attachments are not required to support the following properties because they are not regular messages:

- *PR_ENTRYID.* Clients cannot open embedded messages from any container except through the attachment object itself. In our implementation, it is easier for us to supply this property than not to.

- *PR_PARENT_ENTRYID.* The parent of an embedded message is an attachment. Because attachments don't have entry IDs, embedded messages don't have a parent entry ID.

- *PR_SEARCH_KEY and PR_RECORD_KEY.* These properties might or might not be present in an embedded message. The implementation decides whether to supply them.

Committing Changes in Attachments

Saving client transactions on our attachment objects is a two-step process. Because attachments live inside *IMessage* objects, saving changes in the attachments is simply a transaction that must be cached in the parent message until *IMessage::SaveChanges* is called.

First the client calls *IAttach::SaveChanges*, which causes the attachment object to save the request in a transaction node on the parent message. Nothing is saved to the database yet. When the client calls *SaveChanges* on the attachment's parent message, we call a method in the *CAttach* class that actually saves the changes in the attachment to the database.

In the case of embedded messages, the transaction goes one level deeper. When a client calls *SaveChanges* on one of our embedded *IMessage* objects, the request is saved with the *IAttach* object in a transaction node. When the attachment object is saved during a call to the attachment's parent message, the *CAttach* class walks the list of transactions from the embedded messages and performs the request at that time.

Conclusion

The store provider specification is the part of the MAPI specification that is most diverse and open to interpretation. The samples we have presented in this chapter were developed to illustrate a general implementation of the specification and to demonstrate the important concepts. We recommend you design your provider so that its behavior is similar to other standard implementations, such as the Microsoft Personal Folders store provider. Doing so will ensure maximum compatibility with existing client applications.

APPENDIXES

A P P E N D I X   A

Named Properties

A named property is a custom property that is known by name rather than by a hard-coded ID. Although MAPI defines a property tag for almost every imaginable purpose, it also allows vendors to extend the predefined property set by creating their own properties and publishing the property type and a string or numeric name. But access to properties is based on the property ID, not a name, so how do you *Get* or *Set* a named property?

The answer is that a client or service provider that needs to access a named property must ask the object on which the *Get/SetProps* call is made to *create* an ID corresponding to the published name. Only the property name is fixed; the ID is created by the object dynamically. So the ID is produced by the provider, which must maintain its own internal mapping of names to IDs.

The first time the property is added to a MAPI object, the implementation picks a property ID from a range of available IDs, and the full property tag is constructed at run time. A client that wants to obtain an ID for a named property passes the published name to the *IMAPIProp::GetIDsFromNames* method, which returns the ID mapped to that name. If the property name is already known to the object's name-to-property mapping, it returns the current property ID. If it is not known and the caller passed the MAPI_CREATE flag in the method call, a new ID is allocated and the named property is added to the mapping.

The implication is that no two objects will necessarily return the same ID for a given name. The mapping is global to all objects returned by a provider, so typically, no two providers will have the same mapping, and even two instances of the *same* provider will probably not have the same mapping. This is because the mapping is dynamic—the mapping is created for a given name the first time the ID is requested for that name. The IDs for named properties are chosen from the 0x8000 through 0xFFFE range, giving a provider an effective range of 32766 entries from which to allocate and return IDs to clients.

Named properties are grouped into logical domains known as *property sets*. Each property set is identified by a unique GUID, resulting in a virtually limitless number of sets that can be defined. Vendors defining named properties

563

publish the name, type, and the property set GUID for use by any interested party. The name of the property can be either a numeric value or a Unicode string. The string's length is limitless. Because the GUID is unique, including it in the property set precludes the possibility of name collisions between two vendors that happen to choose the same name.

Microsoft has defined GUIDs for two important property sets: PS_MAPI (for the MAPI standard property set) and PS_PUBLIC_STRINGS (for the mapping of document properties to MAPI properties). There are a few others, but they are used most often by developers writing gateways or applications that route workflow documents through gateways.

PR_MAPPING_SIGNATURE

This property is available in MAPI objects that support named properties. It is used to determine whether two objects share the same name-to-ID mapping. If object A has the same mapping signature value as object B, then a client or provider knows that if both objects return the same ID, that ID refers to the same property, and if the IDs are different, each refers to a distinct named property. That is, a property with the name "Document Author" has the same ID on both A and B, but it does not have the same ID as "Number of Paragraphs."

PR_MAPPING_SIGNATURE is used when two objects are being copied. If two objects share the same mapping signature, then the copy can be done more quickly since the caller doesn't have to call *GetIDsFromNames*—it already knows the ID will be the same. If the objects don't have the same mapping signature, then whoever is copying the object must ask the source object for the literal strings of any named properties on the source object and then request that new IDs be assigned to those names in the destination object.

Getting the List of Named Properties in an Object

Let's say a client obtains a list of property tags from a call to the *GetPropList* method. The array comes back with properties that have IDs in the 0x8000 through 0xFFFE range (the named property range). How does the client know what the names of these properties are? The client calls *IMAPIProp::GetNamesFromIDs*, which passes an array of property tags in the named property range and gets back an array of *property names* for all the properties in the mapping. The information about the named properties returns in an array of pointers to *MAPINAMEID* structures. If a property tag for which a name does not exist is passed in, the provider returns a NULL pointer to a *MAPINAMEID* structure in the *LPMAPINAMEID* array element whose index is the same as the requested property's *SPropTagArray* index. The structure where the named property is returned is defined as follows:

```
typedef struct _MAPINAMEID
{
    LPGUID lpguid;
    ULONG ulKind;
    union
    {
        LONG lID;
        LPWSTR lpwstrName;
    } Kind;
} MAPINAMEID, *LPMAPINAMEID;
```

The *ulKind* member indicates which member of the *Kind* union the *IMAPIProp* implementation must look for. The mapping of the property name can be accomplished using a specific numeric identifier instead of a literal string. However, it is more common for vendors to publish named properties with a readable Unicode string name than with a constant numeric identifier.

After a client is finished using the information returned, it must release the allocated array by using the *MAPIFreeBuffer* function. The client code used to perform this operation would look like the following:

```
LPSPropTagArray pTags;
// Call to GetPropList to get list of all properties
⋮
// Now the pTags array is constructed with all the
// named properties above or equal to 0x8000 or less than
// or equal to 0xFFFE.
// These properties are then passed to the GetNamesFromIDs
// function below.
⋮
ULONG ulPropNames;
LPMAPINAMEID * ppPropNames = NULL;
HRESULT hResult = pMessage -> GetNamesFromIDs
                            (&pTags,
                             NULL,
                             0,
                             &ulPropNames,
                             &ppPropNames);
```

(continued)

```
if (SUCCEEDED(hResult)) // Test for warnings.
{
    if (ppPropNames[0])
    {
        // Do something with named properties.
        :
    }
}
MAPIFreeBuffer(ppPropNames);
:
```

Setting Named Properties

When setting named properties on a MAPI object, a client application must first obtain a property ID. This ID is assigned by the provider to the given property name. A client retrieves the provider's version of the ID by using the *IMAPIProp::GetIDsFromNames* method. In this call, the client passes the name of the property as a Unicode string (ANSI strings must be converted), and the provider then looks up the name in its internal table. If the property name already has an ID assigned to it, the implementation returns it; otherwise, the provider picks an unused ID within the named property range. The client application needs to do this only once per service provider for each named property if the scope of the named property mapping is *global* to the entire service provider. The client can tell whether the scope is global by comparing the PR_MAPPING_SIGNATURE of different objects in different containers. If PR_MAPPING_SIGNATURE is the same for two objects, both use the same mapping.

After a call to *IMAPIProp::GetIDsFromNames*, the service provider returns an array of property tags (an *SPropTagArray*) in the same order as the list of names. Each of the property tags contains the new property ID assigned by the implementation, but with the type set to PT_UNSPECIFIED. The client application must change the property tag type to the appropriate type (using the *CHANGE_PROP_TYPE* macro) when it creates an *SPropValue* containing the property's value. When the client is finished using the property tag array returned in the *GetIDsFromNames* call, it should free it using the *MAPIFreeBuffer* function. The client-side code looks something like this:

```
LPMESSAGE pMessage;
// Code to get an IMessage object
:
LPMAPINAMEID ppNames[3] = { 0 };
MAPINAMEID NamedProp1 = { 0 };
MAPINAMEID NamedProp2 = { 0 };
MAPINAMEID NamedProp3 = { 0 };
```

```
NamedProp1.lpguid = (LPGUID)&PS_PUBLIC_STRINGS;
NamedProp2.lpguid = (LPGUID)&PS_PUBLIC_STRINGS;
NamedProp3.lpguid = (LPGUID)&PS_PUBLIC_STRINGS;

NamedProp1.ulKind = MNID_STRING;
NamedProp2.ulKind = MNID_STRING;
NamedProp3.ulKind = MNID_STRING;

NamedProp1.Kind.lpwstrName = L"Sample - Document Author";
NamedProp2.Kind.lpwstrName = L"Sample - Document Title";
NamedProp3.Kind.lpwstrName = L"Sample - Document Version";

ppNames[0] = &NamedProp1;
ppNames[1] = &NamedProp2;
ppNames[2] = &NamedProp3;

LPSPropTagArray pPropTags = NULL;
HRESULT hResult = pMessage -> GetIDsFromNames
                              (3,
                               ppNames,
                               MAPI_CREATE,
                               &pPropTags);
if (FAILED(hResult)) // There might be warnings.
{
    // Clean up the code here.
    ⋮
    return hResult;
}
// If one of the property tags came back 0, then we can't
// set them on the object.
if (0 == pPropTags -> aulPropTag[0] ||
    0 == pPropTags -> aulPropTag[1] ||
    0 == pPropTags -> aulPropTag[2])
{
    // Clean up the code here.
    ⋮
    return hResult;
}
// Now change the property tag types and their values.
SPropValue spvProps[3] = { 0 };
spvProps[0].ulPropTag =
        CHANGE_PROP_TYPE(pPropTags -> aulPropTag[0], PT_STRING8);
spvProps[0].Value.lpszA = "Microsoft Corporation";
```

(continued)

```
spvProps[1].ulPropTag =
        CHANGE_PROP_TYPE(pPropTags -> aulPropTag[1], PT_STRING8);
spvProps[1].Value.lpszA = "MAPI Specification";

spvProps[2].ulPropTag =
        CHANGE_PROP_TYPE(pPropTags -> aulPropTag[2], PT_LONGLONG);
spvProps[2].Value.li.LowPart = 1;
spvProps[2].Value.li.HighPart = 0;
hResult = pMessage -> SetProps(3, spvProps, NULL);
MAPIFreeBuffer(pPropTags);
    ⋮
```

Some Idiosyncrasies of *IMAPIProp::GetIDsFromNames*

The names of the properties passed to this function are case-sensitive. For example, the property name L"Document Title" would receive a different identifier than L"document title." The name of the property is not normalized, so the provider takes the name of the property *as is* without further processing.

Changes to the mapping of property names to IDs occur immediately in the underlying data storage. Because the changes are permanent as soon as the *GetIDsFromNames* call returns, we don't need to commit the object we are working on before the named property can be seen in other objects that share the same named property table.

APPENDIX B

Multivalue Properties

The properties described so far are single-valued, that is, there is a one-to-one correspondence between their property tags and their data. This is adequate for most situations but can be cumbersome in others, so MAPI lets a single property tag refer to a set of similar data elements. Properties of this type are called *multivalue* properties. A multivalue property tag has an extra bit set in the property type field. This bit is called the multivalue flag, and its constant is MV_FLAG.

In the *SPropValue* structure that MAPI defines to hold a property, the *Value* member union has multivalued equivalents for all the single-value data members. They are listed in Figure B-1.

Single-Value Member	Multivalue Member	Multivalue Type
i	MVi	*SShortArray*
l	MVl	*SLongArray*
flt	MVflt	*SRealArray*
dbl	MVdbl	*SDoubleArray*
cur	MVcur	*SCurrencyArray*
at	MVat	*SAppTimeArray*
ft	MVft	*SDateTimeArray*
bin	MVbin	*SBinaryArray*
lpszA	MVszA	*SLPSTRArray*
lpszW	MVszW	*SWStringArray*
lpguid	MVguid	*SGuidArray*
li	MVli	*SLargeIntegerArray*

Figure B-1.
Single-value data members and their multivalue counterparts.

An example illustrates the benefits of a multivalue property tag. Suppose we are setting the home phone numbers of the users in the address book provider by using the *IMailUser* interface, which derives from the *IMAPIProp* interface. MAPI has defined a standard property tag for this attribute called PR_HOME_TELEPHONE_NUMBER. A single-value property would only allow one home telephone number per user, but there might be users who have more than one home phone number. Rather than define some arbitrary number of home telephone properties (PR_HOME_NUMBER_2, PR_HOME-_NUMBER_3, and so on), we would simply change the property type of PR_HOME_TELEPHONE_NUMBER to multivalue so that more than one phone number could be stored in the same slot of the PR_HOME-_TELEPHONE_NUMBER property. To use a multivalue property, the code could look something like the following:

```
LPSPropValue pProp;
// Code to get the data from the object
  ⋮
if (MVI_PROP(PR_HOME_TELEPHONE_NUMBER) == pProp -> ulPropTag)
{
    for (int j = 0; j < pProp -> Value.MVszA.cValues; j++)
    {
        LPSTR szPhone = pProp -> Value.MVszA.lppszA[j];
        // Code to use the telephone numbers
          ⋮
    }
      ⋮
}
```

In the previous code fragment, we use the MAPI-defined *MVI_PROP* macro, which adds the MV_FLAG bit to the property tag before comparing it to the property tag returned by the *IMAPIProp* object. Again, be aware that not all implementations of *IMAPIProp* support setting and retrieving multivalue properties, so consumers of the *IMAPIProp* interface must be ready to handle the implementations that don't.

MAPI client applications can find out whether a message store provider supports multivalue properties before attempting to get or set multivalue properties in its objects. To do this, the client application should request the PR_STORE_SUPPORT_MASK property from any of the store provider's objects (e.g., *IMsgStore*, *IMessage*) and use the AND bitwise operator to compare it to the constant STORE_MV_PROPS_OK.

INDEX

Note: An *italic* page-number reference indicates a
figure, a table, or a program listing.

A

Abort method, 106

ABPAB address book service provider. *See also*
   ABWDS address book service provider

   ABPAB.INF file, 354, *354–55*

   caching object properties in memory, 344

   configuration property sheet, 348, *350*

   features, 244, 344–45

   introduced, 243–44, 343–45

   logging on

      address book provider properties, 355, *355,
         356*, 357, *357, 358–59*

      database primitives, 360–70, *362*

      editing the MAPISVC.INF file, 354, *354–55*

      introduced, 345–46

      provider logon, 350–54

      returning the root hierarchy, 359

      service configuration, 346–50, *350*

   resolving names

      IABLogon::PrepareRecips method, 405–8

      introduced, 398–403

      one-offs and the session one-off table,
         408–15, *410*

      PR_ANR property, 404–5

   returning recipient entries

      derived classes, 381–83, *382*

      IABLogon::OpenEntry, revisited, *383*, 383–90,
         384

      implementing *IMAPIProp*, 370–81, *371, 372*

      introduced, 370

   table implementation, 345

   viewing entries

      display tables, 391–97, *394*

      introduced, 391

ABPAB address book service provider, *continued*

   writable address book providers and

      CopyEntries method, 440–42

      creating foreign entries, 419–29, *424*

      DeleteEntries method, 433–37

      IABContainer::CreateEntry method, 416–29,
         424

      introduced, 340–41, 415, *415*

      notifications, 429–33

      SaveChanges method, 437–39

ABProviderInit function, *200, 202*, 351–52

abstract base classes, 27

ABWDS address book service provider. *See also*
   ABPAB address book service provider

   caching object properties in memory, 344

   design

      CBackEnd object, 443–44

      CMAPIStatus object, 467–69

      entry IDs, 444

      IABContainer::ResolveNames method, 454–60

      IABLogon::OpenEntry method, 450–54

      IABProvider::Logon method, 444–50

      introduced, 343–45, 442–43, *443*

      status table, 466

      table notifications, 460–66

      template ID, 470–73, *473*

   features, 344–45

   introduced, 239–40, *240*, 343–45, 442–43, *443*

   table implementation, 345

acknowledgement (ACK), 331

AddRecips method, *167–68*, 187–88

AddRef method, 28

address book service providers
   ABPAB (*see* ABPAB address book service
      provider)
   ABWDS (*see* ABWDS address book service
      provider)
   containers, 20
   database implementation, 342–43
   defined, 20
   details pages, 125
   entry point function, 200–201, *202*
   interfaces implemented, 200–201, *202*, 203–5
   introduced, 15, *15*, 20, *21*, *24*, 335
   logging on
      address book provider properties, 355, *355,*
         356, 357, *357, 358–59*
      database primitives, 360–70, *362*
      editing the MAPISVC.INF file, 354, *354–55*
      introduced, 345–46
      provider logon, 350–54
      returning the root hierarchy, 359
      service configuration, 346–50, *350*
   message store interactions with, 478
   requirements
      entry IDs, 341–43, *342*
      interfaces, 337–38
      introduced, 336
      provider-to-database interface, 338–39, *339*
      writable address book providers (*see* writable
         address book providers)
   resolving names
      IABLogon::PrepareRecips method, 405–8
      introduced, 125, 126–27, *128*, 398–403
      one-offs and the session one-off table, 408–15,
         410
      PR_ANR property, 404–5
   returning recipient entries
      derived classes, 381–83, *382*
      IABLogon::OpenEntry, revisited, *383*, 383–90,
         384
      implementing *IMAPIProp*, 370–81, *371, 372*
      introduced, 370
   transport interactions with, 249

address book service providers, *continued*
   viewing entries
      display tables, 391–97, *394*
      introduced, 391
   writable
      CopyEntries method, 440–42
      creating foreign entries, 419–29, *424*
      DeleteEntries method, 433–37
      IABContainer::CreateEntry method, 416–29,
         424
      introduced, 340–41, 415, *415*
      notifications, 429–33
      SaveChanges method, 437–39
AddressTypes method, 226, 247, 281–82
Admin (administrator) program, *235*, 235–36,
   236, 237
ADRLIST structure, 126–27, *128*
Advise method, 89, 106–7, 110, 211, 231, 485
ANSI strings, 53
associated contents tables, 72–74, *73*, 487, 532
AttachFile method, *169–72*, 189
attachments
   defined, 79
   introduced, 79
   WINMAIL.DAT, 255
attributes of clients, 116
automated mailbox agents, messaging-based
   clients and, 115

B

back-end messaging system. *See* WINDS mail
   system
base classes
   abstract, 27
   IUnknown, 28
binary-comparable properties, 41
BOOKMARK_BEGINNING bookmark, 102
BOOKMARK_CURRENT bookmark, 102
BOOKMARK_END bookmark, 102
BOOKMARK structure, 102
Boolean expressions, 90–91, *91*

BuildDisplayTable API, 88

bulletin boards, 7

C

CABContainer class, 203–5, 381–83, *382*, 387–90

CBackEnd class, 499–500

CBackEnd object, 443–44

CContext class, 136–37

CDataBase object, *242*, 242–43, *243*, 244

CGeneric class, 498

ChangePassword method, 206, 314

CHANGE_PROP_TYPE macro, 566

CheckParameters_XXX_YYY functions, 207–8

classes

  base

    abstract, 27

    IUnknown, 28

  CABContainer, 203–5, 381–83, *382*, 387–90

  CBackEnd, 499–500

  CContext, 136–37

  CGeneric, 498

  CMailUser, 381

  CNamePropMgr, 499

  COpenPropertyList, 499

  CPropList, 499

  CSession, 136

  IMAPIProp:CGenericProp, 498–99

  IPM, 7, 37, 487, *488*

  message, 7, 37, 115

clients. *See also* HelloMAPI (a minimal MAPI mail client)

  access to the messaging system, 116–17

  attributes, 116

  basic operations, 118–19

  defined, 10, 16, 113–15, *114*

  interactions with providers, 120–21, *122–24*, 125, 129

  introduced, 10, *11*, 12, 14, *15*, *16*, 16–17, 113–15, *114*

  MAPI sessions and, 116, *117*, 117–18

  message store provider access, 478

  transport access, 255–56

CMailUser class, 381

CMAPIFolder object, 535–40

CMAPIStatus object, 467–69

CNamePropMgr class, 499

Component Object Model (COM)

  MAPI error handling and, 42–45

  MAPI interfaces introduced, 4, 13–14, 27–28

ComposeNote dialog procedure, 141–44, *160–63*, 186

compound files, 59

computed properties, 56, 62

ConcatRecips method, *180–81*, 193

containers

  address book providers, 20

  arrangement of data in, *69*

  data tables of, 70–74, *73*

  introduced, 67–69, *68*, *69*

  logical relationship between containers and objects, 67, *68*

  opening objects in, 74–76

  search, 76–78

  standard container interface, 69–70

  supercontainers, 125

  tables available in, 70–74, *73*

contents tables, 72–73, *73*, 532

CONVENIENT_DEPTH flag, 121, 369

COpenPropertyList class, 499

CopyEntries method, 440–42

CopyFolder method, 540

copying computed properties, 62

copying object contents, 61–64

copying properties, 30, 31, 61–63

CopyMessages method, 535

CopyProps method, 30, 31, 61–63, 378

CopyTo method, 30, 31, 63–64

CPropCache object, 370–73, *371*, *372*

CPropList class, 499

CreateAttach method, 489

CreateBookmark method, *87*, 102

CREATE_CHECK_DUP_LOOSE flag, 438

CREATE_CHECK_DUP_STRICT flag, 438

CreateEmptyRecord method, 243

CreateEntry method, 70, 416–29, *424*

CreateFolder method, 70, 489, 536–40

CreateMessage method, 70, 121

CreateRecord method, 243

CreateReplyNote method, *174–76*, 191

CSession class, 136

CURRENT_SPI_VERSION macro, 268

custom properties, 37–39, *38*

CXPLogon object, 269–70

D

data tables of containers, 70–74, *73*

debugging message store providers, 497

deferred delivery, 248

DeleteEntries method, 433–37

DeleteFolder method, 540

DeleteMessages method, 535

DeleteMsg method, *159–60*, 186

DeleteProps method, 30, 31, 59–61, 377–78, 489

deleting properties, 30, 31, 59–61

Details method, 33, 121, 125, 126, 184, 205, 336

details pages, 125

display tables, 391–97, *394*

distribution lists, 20, 79

DLLs. *See* dynamic-link libraries (DLLs)

DONE lists, 331

DTBLPAGE structure, 396–97

DTBLXXX structures, 394, 396

DTCTL structure, 394–95, 397

DTPAGE structure, 265, 394

dynamic-link libraries (DLLs)

    MAPI32.DLL, 184

    MAPI run time as, xxi

    service providers as, 200–201, *202–3*

    WINDS message service as, 237

E

E_ACCESSDENIED error, 58, 65

E_INVALIDARG error, 545

EndMessage method, 229, 248, 303–4

E_NOINTERFACE error, 55

entry identifiers (entry IDs), 39–41, 74, 211, 221–24, 341–43, *342*, 444, 502–3

ENTRYID structure, 40, 74

envelope properties, 125

E_OUTOFMEMORY error, 54

error handling, 42–45. *See also specific errors (E_ and MAPI_E_ entries)*

ExpandRecips method, 227

F

FILL_ENTRY flag, 472

filtering primitive for tables, *87*, 90–91, *91, 91–93*, 93–94, *94–96*, 96–98, *98*

FindRow method, *87*, 102–4, *103–4, 104–5*, 481

FIsTransmittable macro, 254

flushing state, 225

FlushQueues method, 129, *159*, 185, 206, 256, 282–85, 314

folders

    defined, 78

    introduced, 78

    public

        defined, 7, 78

        introduced, 7, 78

        messaging-based clients and, 115

    search results, 78

FORCE_SAVE flag, 65

foreign entries for address book providers, 419–29, *424*

form objects, 486

forms

    defined, 6

    introduced, 6–7

    messaging-based clients and, 115

form servers, 7

form viewers, 7

FreeBookmark method, 102

FreePadrlist function, 127

FreeProws API, 86

G

GAL (global address list), 442, 443, *443*

GetAttachmentTable method, 481

GetContents method, 69, 72–73

GetContentsTable method, 88, 90, 323–25, 387–90, 479

GetHierarchyTable method, 70–72, 121, 479

GetIDsFromNames method, 31, 486, 489, 563–68

GetLastError method, 29, 31, 44–45, 135

GetMessageStatus method, 535

GetMsgStoresTable method, 120

GetNamesFromIDs method, 30, 486, 564

GetOutgoingQueue method, 477, 485–86

GetProcAddress function, 200

GetPropList method, 30, 31, 49–50, 376–77, 564

GetProps method, 30, 31, 48–49, 50–53, 54, 74, 121, 208, 373–75, 563

GetProviderTable method, 223

GetReceiveFolder method, 230, 487

GetReceiveFolderTable method, 487

GetRowCount method, 101, 106

GetSearchCriteria method, 70, 77–78

GetSpoolerStatus function, *152–53*, 185

GetStatus method, 89, 106

GetStatusTable method, 205

global address list (GAL), 442, 443, *443*

globally unique identifiers (GUIDs), 182, 247, 563–64

H

HeapAlloc API function, 209, 210

HeapFree API function, 209, 210

HelloMAPI (a minimal MAPI mail client)

  classes and data structures, 136–37

  ComposeNote dialog procedure, 141–44, *160–63*, 186

  features not supported, 119

  implementation

    AddRecips method, *167–68*, 187–88

    AttachFile method, *169–72*, 189

    ComposeNote dialog procedure, 141–44, *160–63*, 186

HelloMAPI (a minimal MAPI mail client), implementation, *continued*

    ConcatRecips method, *180–81*, 193

    CreateReplyNote method, *174–76*, 191

    define directives, *144*

    DeleteMsg method, *159–60*, 186

    FlushQs function, *159*

    FlushQueues method, *159*, 185

    GetSpoolerStatus function, *152–53*, 185

    include directives, *144*

    Init function, *148–49*

    InitSession function, *147–48*, 183–85

    introduced, 144, 182–83

    LoadListBox function, *156–59*

    OpenDefStore function, *149–50*, 183

    OpenIPMSubtree function, *150–52*, 184

    PopulateNote function, *165–67*, 186–87

    PopulateReadNote method, *163–65*, 186–87

    PrefixSzProp function, *181–82*

    Save method, *169*, 189

    SenderDetails method, *168–69*, 188

    SendNote method, *172–73*, 190

    SetOutgoingProps method, *173–74*, 190

    SetReplyRecips method, *177–79*, 191–93

    ShowDialog method, *154*, 185

    SizedSPropTagArray macro, *144–45*, 183

    ViewInbox method, *154–56*, 185–86

    WndProc procedure, *145–47*, 183

  introduced, 135, 144, 182–83

  program description, 135–36

  properties, 129, *130–34*

  requirements, 118–19

  user interface

    dialog boxes and dialog processing, *137*, 139–44, *140*

    introduced, *137*, 137–39

  WM_COMMAND message handling, 142–44

  WM_CREATE message handling, 135

  WM_INITDIALOG message handling, 141–42

hierarchy tables, 70–72, *73*, 532

HRESULT information, 42–45

HrQueryAllRows method, *87*, 101, 135, 185–86

HrThisThreadAdviseSink API, 107, 108

I

IABContainer interface, 33, 72, 74, 203–5, 244, 337, 338, 416–29, *424*, 454–60

IABLogon interface, 337, *362*, 362–70, *383*, 383–90, *384*, 405–8, 450–54

IABProvider interface, *200, 202*, 337, 352–54, 444–50

IAddrBook interface, 33, 121, 125, 126, 184, 205, 336

IAttach interface, 32, 39, 79, 481, 556, *557*, 558–59

identity properties, 41–42

IDisplayTable notifications, 395–96

IDistList interface, 32, 41, 70, 72, 74, 79, 337, 338

Idle method, 308–9

IIDs (interface identifiers), 54, 63, 182

IMailUser interface, 32, 41, 79, 337, 338, 570

IMAPIAdviseSink interface, 106–7, 110

IMAPIContainer interface

  distribution lists and, 79

  folders and, 78

  IMAPIFolder interface and, 480

  IMAPIProp interface and, 70, 204

  IMessage interface and, 67

  introduced, 67, 69–70

  method overview, 69–70

  opening objects, 74–76

  search containers and, 76–78

  tables available, 70–74, *73*

IMAPIFolder interface

  associated objects and, 74

  child object methods and, 70

  clients and, 120, 121

  folders and, 78, 479

  message store provider implementation, 528, *528–30*, 530–41

  multiview objects and, 33

  store provider–specific implementation, 480

  transports and, 207

  XPWDSR implementation, 322–27

IMAPIProp:CGenericProp class, 498–99

IMAPIProp interface

  address book provider implementation, 370–81, *371, 372*

  attachments and, 79

  available properties, 49–50

  copying object contents, 61–64

  deleting properties, 59–61

  distribution lists and, 79

  folders and, 78

  generic design, 211–12, *212*

  GetLastError method, 44–45

  IAttach interface and, 481

  IMAPIContainer interface and, 70, 204

  introduced, 28–31, *29*

  mail user objects and, 79

  MAPI error handling in, 42–45

  memory management model for MAPI, 46–49, *47*

  messages and, 79

  method overview, 29–31

  multivalue properties and, 570

  named properties and, 563–68

  nontransacted objects, 31, 32–33, *33*

  Profile Wizard and, 219

  requesting properties, 50–55

  saving object changes permanently, 64–65

  setting properties, 55–59

  transacted objects, 31–32, *32*

IMAPISession interface, 28, 120, 121, 205, 206, 256, 478, 479

IMAPISession object, 116

IMAPIStatus interface

  client interactions and, 481

  introduced, 33, 129, 185, 205–6, 207, 251, 256

  XPWDS implementation, 311, *312–13*, 313–14

  XPWDSR implementation, 327–33

IMAPISupport interface, 107–8, 205, 210–11, 227, 229, 248, 251, 255, 479, 485

IMAPITable interface

  address book providers and, 337, 339

  basics

    introduced, 83, *84*

IMAPITable interface, basics, *continued*
    SRowSet structure, 84–86, *85*, 88
    SRow structure, 84–86
  client interactions and, 480
  defining queries, 88
  introduced, 68, 81–83
  message store provider implementation,
    500–502, *501*
  method overview, 86–87, *86–87*, 105–6
  notifications and, 485
  obtaining, 88
  primitives
    filtering, *87*, 90–91, *91*, *91–93*, 93–94, *94–96*,
     96–98, *98*
    positioning, *87*, 101–4, *103*, *104*, *104–5*
    querying, *87*, 100–101
    selecting, *86*, *89*, 89–90
    sorting, *87*, 99–100, *100*
IMessage interface
  client interactions and, 480
  clients and, 120
  embedded objects and, 559
  IMAPIContainer interface and, 67
  messages and, 79, 121, 125
  message store interactions and, 478
  message store provider implementation, 541,
    542–43, 544–56, *547*, *549*
  message submission (outbound processing)
    and, 227, 246, 249, 485–86
  parameter validation and, 208
  snapshot objects and, 32
IMsgServiceAdmin interface, 221
IMsgStore interface
  client interactions and, 120, 121, 480, 481
  logging on and, 477
  message reception (inbound processing) and,
    230–31, 248, 249
  message store provider implementation, 515,
    516–18, 518–27, *523*, *525*
  message submission (outbound processing)
    and, 227, 485–86

IMsgStore interface, *continued*
  multiview objects and, 33
  notifications and, 485
  object opening and, 481
  receive folders and, 487
  root folders and, 479
  store provider DLL and, 184
IMSLogon interface, 477, 480, 481, 485, 527–28
IMSProvider interface, *200*, *203*, 477, 478, 480,
    487, 489, 508–15
inboxes, universal, 12–13, 245–46
information sharing store providers, 488–89
InitSession function, *147–48*, 183–85
interface identifiers (IIDs), 54, 63, 182
interprocess communications (IPC) mechanism,
    235, *235*
IPM class, 7, 37, 487, *488*
IProfSect interface, 219–20, *220*, 221, 223–24
IProviderAdmin interface, 223
IStorage interface, 54, 59, 558
IStream interface, 54, 59, 135, 242, *242*, 243, *243*,
    558
ITableData interface, 500, *501*
IUnknown base class, 28
IUnknown interface
  attachments and, 79
  distribution lists and, 79
  folders and, 78
  mail user objects and, 79
  messages and, 79
  service provider interfaces and, 203–5
IXPLogon interface
  implementation
    AddressTypes method, 281–82
    EndMessage method, 303–4
    FlushQueues method, 282–85
    Idle method, 308–9
    IMAPIStatus interface, 311, *312–13*, 313–14
    introduced, 278–79
    OpenStatusEntry method, 310–11

IXPLogon interface, implementation, *continued*
  Poll method, 308–9
  RegisterOptions method, 279–81
  SendMailMessage method, 292–303
  StartMessage method, 304–8
  SubmitMessage method, 288–92
  TransportLogoff method, 308
  TransportNotify method, 285–88
  ValidateState method, 309–10
  inbound logic and, 248
  introduced, 207, 225, 226, 229, 251, 278–79
  outbound logic and, 247–48, 249
  XPWDS implementation, 258
IXPProvider interface, *200, 202*, 225, 248, 269–70, *270–74, 274–75, 275–76, 276–77, 278*
IXXXProvider interfaces, *200*, 200–201, *202–3*

K

KEEP_OPEN_READONLY flag, 65, 76
KEEP_OPEN_READWRITE flag, 65
Kind union, 565

L

learning curve for MAPI, xxi–xxii
lightweight remote procedure calls (LRPCs), 256
linked memory blocks, 46–49
LoadLibrary function, 200
LoadListBox function, *156–59*
local-based service providers, 442. *See also* ABPAB address book service provider; MSLMS message store service provider
Local Message Store service provider for WINDS. *See* MSLMS message store service provider
logging on
  address book providers
    address book provider properties, 355, *355, 356*, 357, *357, 358–59*
    database primitives, 360–70, *362*
    editing the MAPISVC.INF file, 354, *354–55*
    introduced, 345–46
    provider logon, 350–54

logging on, address book providers, *continued*
    returning the root hierarchy, 359
    service configuration, 346–50, *350*
  introduced, 116, *117*, 117–18, 345–46
  message store providers, 477
Logon method, 208, 210, 352–54, 444–50, 477, 478, 480, 487, 489
long-term entry IDs, 74
LRPCs (lightweight remote procedure calls), 256

M

mail-aware applications, 114–15
mailbox agents, automated, messaging-based clients and, 115
MAILBOX_INFO structure, 269
mail systems. *See* HelloMAPI (a minimal MAPI mail client); WINDS mail system
mail user objects, 79
MAPI (Messaging Application Programming Interface)
  architectural overview, xx, 10–13, *11, 12*
  COM and
    error handling, 42–45
    interfaces introduced, 4, 13–14, 27–28
  component overview, 13–18, *15, 16, 19*, 20, *21, 22–23, 24, 25* (*see also* clients; MAPI subsystem; service providers)
  defined, 3–5
  error handling, 42–45 (*see also specific errors (E_ and MAPI_E_ entries)*)
  historical motivation, 5–6
  introduced, xx–xxi, 3–5
  learning curve, xxi–xxii
  memory management, 46–49, *47*, 209–10
  messaging and, ii, 6–9, *9*
  Microsoft's contribution to, xx–xxi
  run-time component
    defined, 17–18
    introduced, xxi, 14, *15*, 17–18
  simple, 4
MAPI32.DLL, 184
MAPI_ACCESS_MODIFY flag, 59

MAPIAllocateBuffer function, 46, 47, 48, 85–86, 127

MAPIAllocateMore function, 46, 47, 48, 85–86

MAPI_ASSOCIATED flag, 72–73, 487

MAPICODE.H header file, 44, 54

MAPI_CREATE flag, 58, 489, 563

MAPI_DEFERRED_ERRORS flag, 43

MAPIDEFS.H header file, 39

MAPI_E_BAD_CHARWIDTH error, 53

MAPI_E_BUSY error, 329

MAPI_E_COLLISION error, 536

MAPI_E_COMPUTED error, 62, 64, 518

MAPI_E_INTERFACE_NOT_SUPPORTED error, 55

MAPI_E_NO_ACCESS error, 31, 58, 340, 489, 518, 530, 531

MAPI_E_NO_RECIPIENTS error, 554

MAPI_E_NO_SUPPORT error, 31, 199, 210, 257, 345, 460, 479, 490, 525, 531, 554

MAPI_E_NO_SUPPRESS error, 555

MAPI_E_NOT_ENOUGH_MEMORY error, 54

MAPI_E_NOT_FOUND error, 89, 103, *104*, 389, 428, 544, 549

MAPI_E_NOT_ME error, 290

MAPI_E_OBJECT_CHANGED error, 65

MAPI_E_OBJECT_DELETED error, 65

MAPIERROR structure, 45

MAPI_E_TOO_COMPLEX error, 97, 99

MAPI_E_UNABLE_TO_ABORT error, 526

MAPI_E_UNCONFIGURED error, 217

MAPI_E_VERSION error, 268

MAPI_E_XXX errors, 44

MAPIFreeBuffer function, 46, 48, 49, 50, 51–52, 57, 127, 565–66

MAPIInitialize function, 108, 117, 183

MAPILogonEx API, 28, 117, 118, 183–84

MAPI_MODIFY flag, 59, 75, 489

MAPI_MOVE flag, 63

MAPI_MULTITHREAD_NOTIFICATIONS, 108

MAPINameID structure, 564–65

MAPI_NO_MAIL flag, 225

MAPI run-time component
    defined, 17–18
    introduced, xxi, 14, *15*, 17–18

MAPI sessions, 116, *117*, 117–18

MAPI spooler
    defined, 22, 225
    introduced, 14, *15*, 22–23, *24*, *25*
    overview, 225–26

MAPI subsystem
    defined, 10
    introduced, 10–11, *11*, *12*
    message store provider interactions with, 476–78
    transport interactions with
        inbound logic, 248
        introduced, 246–47
        outbound logic, 247–48

MAPISVC.INF file, 214, *215*, 220, *220*, 258–59, *259*, 354, *354–55*, 491–92

MAPI unique identifiers (MUIDs), 341, *342*

MAPI_W_ERRORS_RETURNED warning, 51, 428

MAPI_W_XXX warnings, 44

MAP_XXX_METHODS(IMPL) macros, 203–5

MDB_WRITE flag, 489

memory management, 46–49, *47*, 209–10

MERGEINI utility, 214, 258

message-based applications, 115

message classes, 7, 37, 115

messages
    accessing, 120–21, *122–24*, 125
    data encapsulation using TNEF, 254–55
    defined, 79
    introduced, 79
    nondelivery report (NDR), 226
    paths during sending and receiving
        introduced, 226
        message reception (inbound processing), 229–31, *230*
        message submission (outbound processing), 227, *228*, 229

message service for WINDS, introduced, 237–38,
239. *See also* ABWDS address book service
provider; MSWDS message store service
provider; XPWDSR transport service provider; XPWDS transport service provider

message services, 16, 17

message store service providers

associated contents table support, 73

client access to, 478

client interactions with, 120–21, *122–24*, 125,
129

debugging, 497

default, 485–87, *488*

defined, 18, 475–76, *477*

development

adding entries to MAPISVC.INF, 491–92

implementing *MSProviderInit*, 496–97

implementing *ServiceEntry*, 492–95, *495–96*

implementing stub interfaces, 490–91

introduced, 490

entry point function, 200–201, *203*

information sharing, 488–89

interactions

with address book and message transport
providers, 249, 478

with the MAPI subsystem, 476–78

interfaces implemented, 200–201, *203*, 203–5

introduced, 15, *15*, 18, *19*, *24*, *25*, 475–76, *477*,
490

logging on, 477

MSLMS (*see* MSLMS message store service
provider)

MSWDS (*see* MSWDS message store service
provider)

properties, *495–96*, *516–18*

public folder, 488

read-only, 488–89

requirements

general, 479–82, *482–84*, 485

special, 485–89, *488*

summarized, 560

messaging and MAPI, xx, 6–9, *9*

Messaging Application Programming Interface.
See MAPI (Messaging Application
Programming Interface)

messaging system, back-end. *See* WINDS mail
system

methods

Abort, 106

AddRecips, *167–68*, 187–88

AddRef, 28

AddressTypes, 226, 247, 281–82

Advise, 89, 106–7, 110, 211, 231, 485

AttachFile, *169–72*, 189

ChangePassword, 206, 314

ConcatRecips, *180–81*, 193

CopyEntries, 440–42

CopyFolder, 540

CopyMessages, 535

CopyProps, 30, 31, 61–63, 378

CopyTo, 30, 31, 63–64

CreateAttach, 489

CreateBookmark, *87*, 102

CreateEmptyRecord, 243

CreateEntry, 70, 416–29, *424*

CreateFolder, 70, 489, 536–40

CreateMessage, 70, 121

CreateRecord, 243

CreateReplyNote, *174–76*, 191

DeleteEntries, 433–37

DeleteFolder, 540

DeleteMessages, 535

DeleteMsg, *159–60*, 186

DeleteProps, 30, 31, 59–61, 377–78, 489

Details, 33, 121, 125, 126, 184, 205, 336

EndMessage, 229, 248, 303–4

ExpandRecips, 227

FindRow, *87*, 102–4, *103–4*, *104–5*, 481

FlushQueues, 129, *159*, 185, 206, 256, 282–85,
314

FreeBookmark, 102

GetAttachmentTable, 481

GetContents, 69, 72–73

GetContentsTable, 88, 90, 323–25, 387–90, 479

methods, *continued*

GetHierarchyTable, 70–72, 121, 479

GetIDsFromNames, 31, 486, 489, 563–68

GetLastError, 29, 31, 44–45, 135

GetMessageStatus, 535

GetMsgStoresTable, 120

GetNamesFromIDs, 30, 486, 564

GetOutgoingQueue, 477, 485–86

GetPropList, 30, 31, 49–50, 376–77, 564

GetProps, 30, 31, 48–49, 50–53, 54, 74, 121, 208, 373–75, 563

GetProviderTable, 223

GetReceiveFolder, 230, 487

GetReceiveFolderTable, 487

GetRowCount, 101, 106

GetSearchCriteria, 70, 77–78

GetStatus, 89, 106

GetStatusTable, 205

HrQueryAllRows, 87, 101, 135, 185–86

Idle, 308–9

IMAPIContainer overview, 69–70

IMAPIProp overview, 29–31

IMAPITable overview, 86–87, *86–87,* 105–6

Logon, 208, 210, 352–54, 444–50, 477, 478, 480, 487, 489

ModifyRecipients, 125, 126

ModifyStatusRow, 205, 251, 255

NewEntry, 210

Notify, 107–8, 211, 485

NotifyNewMail, 231, 248, 249

OnNotify, 106–7, 108, *108–10,* 110

OpenEntry

  discussed, 70, 74–76, 120, 121, 206, 210, 227, 230

  implementation of, 256, 337, 341, *362,* 362–70, *383,* 383–90, *384,* 450–54, 479, 481

OpenMsgStore, 120, 478

OpenProfileSection, 219, 221, 223

OpenProperty, 30, 50, 53–55, 57–59, 61, 96–97, 379–81, 489

OpenRecord, 243

OpenRecordField, 243

methods, *continued*

OpenStatusEntry, 310–11

OpenTemplateID, 423–24, *424,* 472

Poll, 248, 308–9

PopulateReadNote, 163–65, 186–87

PrepareRecips, 405–8

PrepareSubmit, 227

pure virtual, 204

QueryColumns, 90, 105

QueryInterface, 28, 203

QueryPosition, 105

QueryRows, 85, *87,* 100–101, 102, 185–86

QuerySortOrder, 106

RegisterOptions, 279–81

Release, 28

ResolveName, 126–27, *128*

ResolveNames, 244, 454–60

Restrict, 87, 90–91, *91, 91–93,* 93–94, *94–96,* 96–98, *98,* 101

RowApprox, 185–86

Save, 169, 189

SaveChanges, 30, 31, 32, 64–65, 76, 121, 229, 248, 340–41, 437–39, 489, 518

SeekRow, 87, 102

SeekRowApprox, 87

SenderDetails, 168–69, 188

SendMailMessage, 292–303

SendNote, 172–73, 190

SetColumns, 86, 89, 89–90, 93, 101

SetLockState, 227

SetMessageStatus, 325–27, 535

SetOutgoingProps, 173–74, 190

SetProps, 30, 31, 55–57, 59, 60, 121, 219, 375–76, 489, 518, 563

SetProviderUID, 211, 341, 479

SetReadFlags, 535

SetReceiveFolder, 487

SetReplyRecips, 177–79, 191–93

SetSearchCriteria, 70, 76–77

SettingsDialog, 206, 313

ShowDialog, 154, 185

Shutdown, 278

methods, *continued*

  SortTable, 87, 99–100, *100,* 101

  SpoolerLogon, 477, 489

  SpoolerNotify, 229, 248, 251

  SpoolerYield, 251

  StartMessage, 229, 248, 249, 304–8

  SubmitMessage, 121, 227, 229, 246, 247–48, 249, 288–92, 478, 485

  Subscribe, 107–8, 211, 485

  TransportLogoff, 308

  TransportLogon, 248

  TransportNotify, 207, 285–88

  Unadvise, 106–7, 110, 211

  Unsubscribe, 211, 485

  ValidateState, 206, 309–10, 328–33

  ViewInbox, 154–56, 185–86

Microsoft Exchange Server, 74

Microsoft Personal Folders store provider, 560

middleware, 11

ModifyRecipients method, 125, 126

ModifyStatusRow method, 205, 251, 255

MSGSERVICEENTRY function, 215–16, 259, 346

MSLMS message store service provider

  CDataBase object, *242,* 242–43, *243,* 244

  development

    adding entries to MAPISVC.INF, 491–92

    implementing *MSProviderInit,* 496–97

    implementing stub interfaces, 490–91

    introduced, 490

  features, 241–42, 498–508

  implementation

    CBackEnd class, 499–500

    CGeneric class, 498

    entry IDs, 502–3

    IAttach interface, 556, *557,* 558–59

    IMAPIFolder interface, 528, *528–30,* 530–41

    IMAPIProp::CGenericProp class, 498–99

    IMAPITable interface, 500–502, *501*

    IMessage interface, 541, *542–43,* 544–56, *547, 549*

MSLMS message store service provider, implementation, *continued*

    IMsgStore interface, 515, *516–18,* 518–27, *523, 525*

    IMSLogon interface, 527–28

    IMSProvider interface, 508–15

    introduced, 497–98

    notifications, 503–8

  introduced, 241–42, 497–98

  MSLMS.INF file, 491

MSProviderInit function, *200, 203,* 479, 496–97

MSWDS message store service provider

  development

    adding entries to MAPISVC.INF, 491–92

    implementing *ServiceEntry,* 492–95, *495–96*

    implementing stub interfaces, 490–91

    introduced, 490

  features, 498–508

  implementation

    CBackEnd class, 499–500

    CGeneric class, 498

    entry IDs, 502–3

    IAttach interface, 556, *557,* 558–59

    IMAPIFolder interface, 528, *528–30,* 530–41

    IMAPIProp::CGenericProp class, 498–99

    IMAPITable interface, 500–502, *501*

    IMessage interface, 541, *542–43,* 544–56, *547, 549*

    IMsgStore interface, 515, *516–18,* 518–27, *523, 525*

    IMSLogon interface, 527–28

    IMSProvider interface, 508–15

    introduced, 497–98

    notifications, 503

  introduced, 240, 497–98

  MSWDS.INF file, 492

MUIDs (MAPI unique identifiers), 341, *342*

multivalue properties, 35, 486, *569,* 569–70

multiview objects, 31, 32–33, *33*

MVI_PROP macro, 570

N

named properties, 37, 425–26, 486, 563–68

NDR (nondelivery report) messages, 226

NewEntry method, 210

new operator, 209–10

news services, 7

nondelivery report (NDR) messages, 226

nontransacted objects, 31, 32–33, *33*

nontransmittable properties, 254

notification engine, 107–8, *108–10,* 110–11

notifications

    IDisplayTable, 395–96

    introduced, 106–7

    message store provider, 485, 503–8

    notification engine, 107–8, *108–10,* 110–11

    table, 460–66

    writable address book provider, 429–33

Notification structure, 110–11

Notify method, 107–8, 211, 485

NotifyNewMail method, 231, 248, 249

O

object containment, 212

objects

    CBackEnd, 443–44

    CDataBase, 242, 242–43, *243,* 244

    CMAPIFolder, 535–40

    CMAPIStatus, 467–69

    copying contents, 61–64

    CPropCache, 370–73, *371, 372*

    CXPLogon, 269–70

    form, 486

    IMAPIAdviseSink, 106

    IMAPISession, 116

    introduced, 28–29, *29*

    logical relationship between containers and, 67, *68*

    mail user, 79

    multiview, 31, 32–33, *33*

    nontransacted, 31, 32–33, *33*

    object containment, 212

objects, *continued*

    overview of common MAPI objects, 78–79

    saving changes permanently, 64–65

    snapshot, 31–32, *32*

    transacted, 31–32, *32*

OLE technology, 212

one-off entry IDs, 412–13

one-offs, 274, 359, 408–15, *410*

one-off templates, 409–10

OnNotify method, 106–7, 108, *108–10,* 110

OpenDefStore function, *149–50,* 183

OpenEntry method

    discussed, 70, 74–76, 120, 121, 206, 210, 227, 230

    implementation of, 256, 337, 341, *362,* 362–70, *383,* 383–90, *384,* 450–54, 479, 481

OPEN_IF_EXISTS flag, 536

OpenIPMSubtree function, *150–52,* 184

OpenMsgStore method, 120, 478

OpenProfileSection method, 219, 221, 223

OpenProperty method, 30, 50, 53–55, 57–59, 61, 96–97, 379–81, 489

OpenRecordField method, 243

OpenRecord method, 243

OpenStatusEntry method, 310–11

OpenTemplateID method, 423–24, *424,* 472

OPTIONDATA structure, 279–80

order forms, 7

P

parameter validation, 207–8

Personal Address Book service provider for WINDS. *See* ABPAB address book service provider

piggybacking onto open store providers, 478

Poll method, 248, 308–9

PopulateNote function, *165–67,* 186–87

PopulateReadNote method, *163–65,* 186–87

positioning primitive for tables, *87,* 101–4, *103, 104,* 104–5

post office. *See* WINDS mail system

PR_7BIT_DISPLAY_NAME property, *359*

PR_AB_PROVIDER_ID property, *357*

PR_ACCESS_LEVEL property, 58–59, 489, *516, 528, 542, 557*

PR_ACCESS property, 59, 489, *516, 523, 528, 542, 557*

PR_ADDRTYPE property, 83, 90, 126, *133,* 225–26, 227, 247, *358, 410, 547*

PR_ANR property, 404–5

PR_ASSOC_CONTENT_COUNT property, *529*

PR_ATTACH_DATA_BIN property, *134,* 241

PR_ATTACH_DATA_OBJ property, 241

PR_ATTACH_FILENAME property, *134*

PR_ATTACH_METHOD property, *134, 549*

PR_ATTACH_NUM property, *134, 549, 557*

PR_ATTACH_SIZE property, *549, 557*

PR_BODY property, 37, 53–54, *131,* 135

PR_CLIENT_SUBMIT_TIME property, 227, *525*

PR_COMMENT property, *355, 517, 530*

PR_COMMON_VIEWS_ENTRYID property, *518*

PR_CONTAINER_CONTENTS property, 63, *356, 529*

PR_CONTAINER_FLAGS property, 340, *356, 415*

PR_CONTAINER_HIERARCHY property, *529*

PR_CONTENT_COUNT property, 63, *529*

PR_CONTENT_UNREAD property, *516, 529*

PR_CREATE_TEMPLATES property, *357, 415*

PR_CREATION_TIME property, 35, 62, 65, *530, 543, 549, 557*

PR_CREATION_VERSION property, *530, 543, 557*

PR_CURRENT_VERSION property, *313, 516*

PR_DEFAULT_STORE property, *129*

PR_DEF_CREATE_DL property, *357, 415*

PR_DEF_CREATE_MAILUSER property, *357, 415*

PR_DELETE_AFTER_SUBMIT property, 229, 248

PR_DELIVER_TIME property, 125

PR_DEPTH property, *356, 410*

PR_DETAILS_TABLE property, *356, 358*

PR_DISPLAY_NAME property, 37, 53, 83, 90, 126–27, *133, 312, 355, 356, 410, 495, 530, 547*

PR_DISPLAY_NAME_W property, 53

PR_DISPLAY_TIME property, *517, 549*

PR_DISPLAY_TO property, 46, 48

PR_DISPLAY_TYPE property, *356, 358, 410, 530, 547*

PrefixSzProp function, *181–82*

PR_EMAIL_ADDRESS property, 37, 83, 90, *134, 358, 547*

PR_ENTRYID property

  discussed, 37, 39, 56, 62, 65, 90, 126, *133,* 225–26, 227

  implementation of, 247, *312, 356, 358, 410, 495, 525, 528, 542, 547*

PrepareRecips method, 405–8

PrepareSubmit method, 227

PR_FINDER_ENTRYID property, *518*

PR_FOLDER_ASSOCIATED_CONTENTS property, *529*

PR_FOLDER_TYPE property, *516, 529*

PR_HASATTACH property, *132, 542*

PR_HEADER_FOLDER_ENTRYID property, *316*

PR_HOME_TELEPHONE_NUMBER property, 570

PR_IDENTITY_DISPLAY property, *313*

PR_IDENTITY_ENTRYID property, *313*

PR_IDENTITY_SEARCH_KEY property, *313*

PR_INSTANCE_KEY property, 111, 227, *312, 410, 525, 547, 549*

PR_IPM_OUTBOX_ENTRYID property, *130, 517*

PR_IPM_SENTMAIL_ENTRYID property, *130,* 229, *517*

PR_IPM_SUBTREE_ENTRYID property, *130, 517*

PR_IPM_WASTEBASKET_ENTRYID property, *130, 517*

private message classes, 115

PR_LAST_MODIFICATION_TIME property, 62, *530, 543, 549, 557*

PR_MAPPING_SIGNATURE property, 62, *517, 529, 542, 549, 557,* 564, 566

PR_MDB_PROVIDER property, 496, *518*

PR_MESSAGE_ATTACHMENTS property, 60–61, 96, *131, 543*

PR_MESSAGE_CLASS property, 115, *131,* 229, *543*

PR_MESSAGE_DELIVERY_TIME property, *132, 253*

PR_MESSAGE_FLAGS property, *131, 543*

PR_MESSAGE_RECIPIENTS property, 60, 96, 98, 125, *131, 543*

PR_MESSAGE_SIZE property, 62, 93, *543*

PR_NORMALIZED_SUBJECT property, *131*

PR_OBJECT_TYPE property, *312, 356, 358, 516, 529, 542, 547, 549, 557*

profile provider, 219–20

profiles

  adding and configuring message services, 216–18

  adding services using the Profile Wizard, *218,* 218–19

  creation of, 213

  defined, 17

  introduced, 213

  profile sections

    accessing multiple profile sections, 222

    defined, 219

    introduced, 219

    obtaining the *IProfSect* interface, 223–24

    provider, 219

    service, 219

    setting profile properties, 219–20, *220*

    storing custom properties, 221–22

    storing sensitive properties, 222–23

profile session, 118

Profile Wizard, *218,* 218–19

properties. *See also IMAPIProp* interface; *specific properties (PR_ entries)*

  address book provider, 355, *355, 356,* 357, *357, 358–59*

  attachment object, *557*

  available, 49–50

  binary-comparable, 41

  computed, 56, 62

  custom, 37–39, *38*

  defined, 34

  deleting, 59–61

  entry identifiers (entry IDs), 39–41, 74, 211, 221–24, 341–43, *342,* 444, 502–3

properties, *continued*

  envelope, 125

  folder object, *528–30*

  HelloMAPI, 129, *130–34*

  identity, 41–42

  IMessage object, *542–43*

  IMsgStore object, *516–18*

  introduced, 34

  message attachment table, *549*

  message recipient table, *547*

  message store provider, *495–96, 516–18*

  multivalue, 35, 486, *569,* 569–70

  named, 37, 425–26, 486, 563–68

  nontransmittable, 254

  remote transport, 315, *316*

  requesting, 50–55

  setting, 55–59

  standard, 37–39, *38*

  transport, *252–54*

  writable address book provider, 415, *415*

property IDs

  defined, 35

  ranges, 35, 37–39, *38*

property names, 564

property sets, 563–64

property tags

  array of, 50, 51

  defined, 35

  introduced, 35, 37

property types, 35. *See also specific property types (PT_ entries)*

PROP_TAG macro, 39

provider profile sections, 219

PR_PARENT_ENTRYID property, 62, *518, 528, 542*

PR_PRIORITY property, *543*

PR_PROVIDER_DISPLAY property, 205, 206, 216, *495*

PR_PROVIDER_DLL_NAME property, 206, 216, *312*

PR_PROVIDER_SUBMIT_TIME property, *253*

PR_PROVIDER_UID property, 223

PR_RCVD_REPRESENTING_ADDRTYPE property, *254*

PR_RCVD_REPRESENTING_EMAIL_ADDRESS property, *254*

PR_RCVD_REPRESENTING_ENTRYID property, *253*

PR_RCVD_REPRESENTING_NAME property, *254*

PR_RCVD_REPRESENTING_SEARCH_KEY property, *254*

PR_RECEIVED_BY_ADDRTYPE property, *253*

PR_RECEIVED_BY_EMAIL_ADDRESS property, *253*

PR_RECEIVED_BY_ENTRYID property, *253*

PR_RECEIVED_BY_NAME property, *253*

PR_RECEIVED_BY_SEARCH_KEY property, *133, 253*

PR_RECEIVE_FOLDER_SETTINGS property, *516*

PR_RECIPIENT_TYPE property, 126–27, *133, 547*

PR_RECORD_KEY property, 41–42, 56, 62, *496, 517, 529, 542, 549, 557*

PR_REMOTE_PROGRESS property, *316*

PR_REMOTE_PROGRESS_TEXT property, *316*

PR_REMOTE_VALIDATE_OK property, *316*

PR_RENDERING_POSITION property, *134*

PR_RESOURCE_FLAGS property, 216, 222, *312*

PR_RESOURCE_METHODS property, 205, *312*

PR_RESOURCE_TYPE property, 206, 216, *312*

PR_RESPONSIBILITY property, 226, 247–48

PR_ROWID property, *312, 547*

PR_RTF_COMPRESSED property, 54, 135

PR_SEARCH_KEY property, 41, *134, 358, 542, 547*

PR_SELECTABLE property, *410*

PR_SENDER_ADDRTYPE property, *252*

PR_SENDER_EMAIL_ADDRESS, *252*

PR_SENDER_ENTRYID property, *252*

PR_SENDER_NAME property, 46, 48, *132, 252*

PR_SENDER_SEARCH_KEY property, *252*

PR_SENDER_XXX properties, 125, 249

PR_SEND_RICH_INFO property, *359*

PR_SENTMAIL_ENTRYID property, 248, 254

PR_SENT_REPRESENTING_ADDRTYPE property, *132, 252*

PR_SENT_REPRESENTING_EMAIL_ADDRESS property, *132, 252*

PR_SENT_REPRESENTING_ENTRYID property, *132*

PR_SENT_REPRESENTING_NAME property, *132, 252*

PR_SENT_REPRESENTING_RECIP_TYPE property, *134*

PR_SENT_REPRESENTING_SEARCH_KEY property, *133, 252*

PR_SENT_REPRESENTING_XXX properties, 249

PR_SERVICE_DLL_NAME property, 216

PR_SERVICE_ENTRY_NAME property, 216

PR_SERVICE_UID property, 223–24

PR_SMP_AB_PATH property, *355*

PR_SMP_CONNECT_TYPE property, 260

PR_SPOOLER_STATUS property, *525*

PR_STATUS_CODE property, 205, 251, 256, *312*

PR_STATUS property, *530*

PR_STATUS_STRING property, 206, 251, *313*

PR_STORE_ENTRYID property, *496, 518, 528, 542, 549, 557*

PR_STORE_RECORD_KEY property, 42, *517, 528, 542, 549, 557*

PR_STORE_STATE property, *516*

PR_STORE_SUPPORT_MASK property, 62, *130, 482, 482–84, 486, 487, 488, 516, 529, 543, 557, 570*

PR_SUBFOLDERS property, *516, 530*

PR_SUBJECT property, 46, 48, 93, *131*

PR_SUBMIT_FLAGS property, 227, *525*

PR_TRANSMITTABLE_DISPLAY_NAME property, *359*

PR_VALID_FOLDER_MASK property, *130, 516*

PR_VIEWS_ENTRYID property, *518*

PR_XXX_A properties, 53

PS_MAPI property set, 564

PS_PUBLIC_STRINGS property set, 564

PT_APPTIME property type, *36*

PT_BINARY property type, *36,* 46, 55

PT_BOOLEAN property type, *36*

PT_CLSID property type, *36*

PT_CURRENCY property type, *36*

PT_DOUBLE property type, *36*

PT_ERROR property type, *36,* 89

PT_FLOAT property type, *36*

PT_I2 property type, *36*

PT_I4 property type, *36*

PT_I8 property type, *36*

PT_LONGLONG property type, *36*

PT_LONG property type, *36*

PT_MV_XXX property types, 35

PT_NULL property type, *36*

PT_OBJECT property type, *36,* 55, 61, 88, 96–97, 125

PT_R4 property type, *36*

PT_R8 property type, *36*

PT_SHORT property type, *36*

PT_STRING8 property type, *36,* 38, 46, 55

PT_SYSTIME property type, 35, *36*

PT_UNICODE property type, *36,* 46, 55

PT_UNSPECIFIED property type, *36,* 566

PT_XXX_W property types, 53

public folders

   defined, 7, 78

   introduced, 78

   messaging-based clients and, 115

public folder store providers, 488

Public Folder Store service provider for WINDS.
    See MSWDS message store service provider

pure virtual methods, 204

Q

queries, 88

QueryColumns method, 90, 105

querying primitive for tables, *87,* 100–101

QueryInterface method, 28, 203

QueryPosition method, 105

QueryRows method, 85, *87,* 100–101, 102, 185–86

QuerySortOrder method, 106

R

read-only store providers, 488–89

RECORD_NUMBER structure, 360, 361

reentrancy issues, 206–7

RegisterOptions method, 279–81

Release method, 28

remote procedure call (RPC) functions, 235, 256

remote transports. *See also* XPWDSR transport
    service provider

   introduced, 314–15, *315*

   properties, 315, *316*

   requirements, 315, *316*

remote viewers, 315, *315*

RES_AND operator, *94*

RES_BITMASK operator, *94*

RES_COMMENT operator, *94*

RES_COMPAREPROPS operator, *94*

RES_CONTENT operator, *95,* 98

RES_EXIST operator, *95*

RES_NOT operator, *95*

ResolveName method, 126–27, *128*

ResolveNames method, 244, 454–60

resolving names

   IABLogon::PrepareRecips method, 405–8

   introduced, 125, 126–27, *128,* 398–403

   one-offs and the session one-off table, 408–15,
      410

   PR_ANR property, 404–5

RES_OR operator, *95*

RES_PROPERTY operator, *96*

RES_SIZE operator, *96*

RES_SUBRESTRICTION operator, *96,* 98

Restrict method, *87,* 90–91, *91, 91–93,* 93–94,
    94–96, 96–98, *98,* 101

Rich Text Format (RTF), 54

RowApprox method, 185–86

row sets, 82, 88

RPC (remote procedure call) functions, 235, 256

RTF (Rich Text Format), 54

run-time component. *See* MAPI run-time
    component

S

SaveChanges method, 30, 31, 32, 64–65, 76, 121, 229, 248, 340–41, 437–39, 489, 518

Save method, *169*, 189

saving object changes permanently, 64–65

SCODE information, 42

search containers, 76–78

search results folders, 78

SeekRowApprox method, *87*

SeekRow method, *87*, 102

selecting primitive for tables, *86, 89,* 89–90

SenderDetails method, *168–69,* 188

SendMailMessage method, 292–303

SendNote method, *172–73,* 190

server-based service providers, 442. *See also* ABWDS address book service provider; MSWDS message store service provider; XPWDSR transport service provider; XPWDS transport service provider

ServiceEntry function, 200, 259–61, *261–64,* 264–65, *265–67, 267,* 268, 479, 492–95, *495–96*

service profile sections, 219

service provider interface (SPI), 200–201

service providers. *See also* profiles; WINDS mail system

  address book (*see* address book service providers)

  defined, 10

  design considerations, 198–99

  implementation

    IMAPIProp interface generic design, 211–12, *212*

    IMAPIStatus interface, 205–6

    IMAPISupport interface, 210–11

    interfaces, 203–5

    introduced, 197–98, 200–201, *202–3*

    memory management, 209–10

    parameter validation, 207–8

    reentrancy issues, 206–7

    status tables, 205–6

    thread-safe issues, 206–7, 251

service providers, *continued*

  installation, registration, and configuration (*see also* profiles)

    adding new services, 214–16, *215*

    introduced, 213–14

    MAPISVC.INF file, 214, *215,* 220, *220*

  introduced, 10, *11,* 11–12, *12,* 14, 15, *15,* 197–98, 200–201, *202–3*

  local-based, 442 (*see also* ABPAB address book service provider; MSLMS message store service provider)

  message paths during sending and receiving

    introduced, 226

    message reception (inbound processing), 229–31, *230*

    message submission (outbound processing), 227, *228,* 229

  message store (*see* message store service providers)

  server-based, 442 (*see also* ABWDS address book service provider; MSWDS message store service provider; XPWDSR transport service provider; XPWDS transport service provider)

  spooler and (*see* MAPI spooler)

  spooler hook providers, 201, 226

  transport (*see* transport service providers)

SERVICE_SINGLE_COPY flag, 222, 258

sessions, 17

SetColumns method, *86, 89,* 89–90, 93, 101

SetLockState method, 227

SetMessageStatus method, 325–27, 535

SetOutgoingProps method, *173–74,* 190

SetProps method, 30, 31, 55–57, 59, 60, 121, 219, 375–76, 489, 518, 563

SetProviderUID method, 211, 341, 479

SetReadFlags method, 535

SetReceiveFolder method, 487

SetReplyRecips method, *177–79,* 191–93

SetSearchCriteria method, 70, 76–77

SettingsDialog method, 206, 313

short-term entry IDs, 74

ShowDialog method, *154,* 185

Shutdown method, 278

simple MAPI, 4

SizedSPropTagArray macro, 53, 90, *144–45,* 183

SizedSSortOrderSet macro, 100

snapshot objects, 31–32, *32*

sorting primitive for tables, *87,* 99–100, *100*

SortTable method, *87,* 99–100, *100,* 101

SPI (service provider interface), 200–201

spooler. *See* MAPI spooler

spooler hook providers, 201, 226

SpoolerLogon method, 477, 489

SpoolerNotify method, 229, 248, 251

SpoolerYield method, 251

SPropProblemArray structure, 56–57, 59, 61, 62, 64

SPropProblems structure, 56–57

SPropTagArray structure, 50, 51, 59, 63, 90, 566

SPropValue structure, 34–36, *36,* 46, 51, 55, 57, 219, 566, 569

SPropValue.Value union, 35, *36*

SRestriction, 90–91, *91–93*

SRowSet structure, 84–86, *85,* 88, 90, 97

SRow structure, 84–86

SSortOrder structure, 99–100

standard properties, 37–39, *38*

StartMessage method, 229, 248, 249, 304–8

status tables, 185, 205–6, 466

StgCreateDocfile OLE API, 59

StgOpenStorage OLE API, 59

SubmitMessage method, 121, 227, 229, 246, 247–48, 249, 288–92, 478, 485

Subscribe method, 107–8, 211, 485

subsystem. *See* MAPI subsystem

suggestion boxes, 7

supercontainers, 125

surveys, 7

T

TABLE_CHANGED notification, 111

table notifications, 460–66

TABLE_RELOAD notification, 111

TABLE_ROW_DELETED notification, 111

tables

  abstract operations, 86–87, *86–87, 87*

  associated contents, 72–74, *73,* 487, 532

  basics

    introduced, 83, *84*

    SRowSet structure, 84–86, *85,* 88

    SRow structure, 84–86

  in containers, 70–74, *73*

  contents, 72–73, *73,* 532

  defining queries, 88

  display, 391–97, *394*

  hierarchy, 70–72, *73,* 532

  introduced, 81

  primitives

    filtering, *87,* 90–91, *91, 91–93,* 93–94, *94–96,* 96–98, *98*

    positioning, *87,* 101–4, *103, 104, 104–5*

    querying, *87,* 100–101

    selecting, *86, 89,* 89–90

    sorting, *87,* 99–100, *100*

  rationale for, 81–83

  row sets, 82, 88

  status, 185, 205–6, 466

  views of, 82, 83, *84,* 88

TBL_ALL_COLUMNS flag, 90

TBL_ASYNC flag, 89, 90

TBL_BATCH flag, 89, 90

TBL_NOADVANCE flag, 101

template IDs, 470–73, *473*

thread-safe issues, 206–7, 251, 481–82

tightly-coupled stores, 18, 478

tightly-coupled transports, 245, 478

time cards, 6

TNEF (Transport Neutral Encapsulation Format), 254–55

TO-DO lists, 331

transacted objects, 31–32, *32*

TransportLogoff method, 308

TransportLogon method, 248

Transport Neutral Encapsulation Format (TNEF), 254–55

TransportNotify method, 207, 285–88

transport service providers
  client access to, 255–56
  defined, 20, 22
  entry point function, 200–201, *202*
  interactions with message store and address book providers, 249
  interactions with the MAPI subsystem
    inbound logic, 248
    introduced, 246–47
    outbound logic, 247–48
  interfaces implemented, 200–201, *202*, 203–5
  introduced, 15, *15*, 20, 22, *24, 25*, 245
  message store interactions with, 478
  properties, *252–54*
  remote (*see also* XPWDSR transport service provider)
    introduced, 314–15, *315*
    properties, 315, *316*
    requirements, 315, *316*
  requirements, 249–51, *252–54*, 254
  tightly-coupled, 245, 478
  using TNEF for message data encapsulation, 254–55
  XPWDS (*see* XPWDS transport service provider)
  XPWDSR (*see* XPWDSR transport service provider)

U

UIDs (unique identifiers), 211, 221–24, 479, 502, 514–15

Unadvise method, 106–7, 110, 211

Unicode strings, 53

unique identifiers (UIDs), 211, 221–24, 479, 502, 514–15

Universal Inbox, 12–13, 245–46

Unsubscribe method, 211, 485

User Account property sheet for WINDS, components, 238

V

ValidateState method, 206, 309–10, 328–33

Validate_XXX_YYY functions, 207–8

Value member union, 569

Value union, 35, *36*

ViewInbox method, *154–56*, 185–86

views of tables, 82, 83, *84*, 88

W

Windows Open Systems Architecture (WOSA) standard, 27

WINDS mail system. *See also* ABPAB address book service provider; MSLMS message store service provider
  Admin (administrator) program, *235*, 235–36, *236, 237*
  components, 233, *234*
  introduced, 233, *234*
  Local Message Store service provider (*see* MSLMS message store service provider)
  message service, introduced, 237–38, 239 (*see also* ABWDS address book service provider; MSWDS message store service provider; XPWDSR transport service provider; XPWDS transport service provider)
  Personal Address Book service provider (*see* ABPAB address book service provider)
  server, 234–35
  User Account property sheet components, 238

WINDS_NOTIFICATION structure, 465

WINMAIL.DAT attachment, 255

WizardEntry function, 200

WIZARD_ENTRY_NAME key, 218

wizards, Profile Wizard, *218*, 218–19

WM_COMMAND message, HelloMAPI handling, 142–44

WM_CREATE message, HelloMAPI handling, 135

WM_INITDIALOG message, HelloMAPI handling, 141–42

WndProc procedure, HelloMAPI, *145–47*, 183

WOSA (Windows Open Systems Architecture) standard, 27

writable address book providers
    CopyEntries method, 440–42
    creating foreign entries, 419–29, *424*
    DeleteEntries method, 433–37
    IABContainer::CreateEntry method, 416–29, *424*
    introduced, 340–41, 415, *415*
    notifications, 429–33
    SaveChanges method, 437–39

X

XPProviderInit function, *200, 202,* 207, 251, 268–69
XPWDSR transport service provider. *See also*
    XPWDS transport service provider
  implementation
    IMAPIFolder interface, 322–27
    IMAPIStatus interface, 327–33
    introduced, 316–22
  introduced, 240–41, 316–22

XPWDS transport service provider. *See also*
    XPWDSR transport service provider
configuration property sheet, 264–65, *267*
editing the MAPISVC.INF file, 258–59, *259*
implementation
    IXPLogon (*see IXPLogon* interface)
    IXPProvider interface, 269–70, *270–74,*
      274–75, 275–76, 276–77, 278
    ServiceEntry function, 259–61, *261–64,*
      264–65, *265–67, 267,* 268
    stub interfaces, 257–58
    XPProviderInit function, 268–69
  introduced, 240–41, 256–57
  XPWDS.INF file, 258, *259*
XXXProviderInit functions, *200,* 200–201, *202–3,*
    479

The manuscript for this book was prepared and submitted to Microsoft Press in electronic form. Text files were prepared using Microsoft Word for Windows 95. Pages were composed by Microsoft Press using Aldus PageMaker 6.01 for Windows, with text in New Baskerville and display type in Helvetica bold. Composed pages were delivered to the printer as electronic prepress files.

Greg Erickson, Greg Hickman

Cover Illustrator
Glenn Mitsui

Interior Graphic Designers
Kim Eggleston, Pam Hidaka

Interior Graphic Artist
Travis Beaven

Principal Compositor
Barb Runyan

Principal Proofreader/Copy Editor
Richard Carey

Indexer
Foxon-Maddocks Associates

Irving De la Cruz

Growing up in the Caribbean (Puerto Rico and the Dominican Republic) presented Irving De la Cruz with a difficult choice: spend the sunny afternoons in front of a computer or go enjoy better things like surfing and diving. Luckily, Irving did not become a beach bum or a computer freak. Instead he moved to the Pacific Northwest.

Irving first joined Microsoft in 1991 as an intern working in the FORTRAN and C/C++ compiler support group. In 1993, he moved to the Windows Developer Support Group where he worked with independent software vendors to develop MAPI client and service providers. Currently Irving is a software design engineer in the Exchange Product Unit at Microsoft Corporation. Irving holds a B.S. in electrical engineering and is working toward a master's degree in software engineering. He can be reached on the Internet at irvingd@microsoft.com.

Les Thaler

Les Thaler joined Microsoft Corporation as a software engineer in 1994 and has been involved with MAPI ever since. Before coming to Microsoft, he spent five years at the Jet Propulsion Laboratory in Pasadena, California, where he designed and implemented real-time systems for NASA's Deep Space Network.

Originally a musician by trade, he lived for a time in Los Angeles playing trumpet for artists as diverse as Barry White and Iris Chacon. He was also active in the L.A. salsa scene until an acute case of cumbia poisoning cut short his career. His involvement with computers started in the late 1980s when he became interested in electronic music and MIDI instruments.

After leaving the music business, Les attended California State Polytechnic University, graduating magna cum laude in 1992 with a degree in computer science. He is a single parent (one son, Greg), an avid jazz enthusiast (*ESP* by Miles Davis is his favorite album), and a mediocre tennis player. His definition of wealth is "any restaurant, any time." Les can be reached on the Internet at lest@microsoft.com or lest@sprynet.com.

ISBN 1-55615-891-2
860 pages with one CD-ROM
$45.00 ($59.95 Canada)

The Microsoft®
Visual C++® development
system combines the power of object-
oriented programming with the efficiency of the
C language. And the application framework approach
in Visual C++—centering on the Microsoft Foundation Class
Library—enables programmers to simplify and streamline the process of
creating robust, professional applications for Windows.

INSIDE VISUAL C++ takes you one step at a time through the process of creating
real-world applications for Windows—the Visual C++ way. Using ample source
code examples, this book explores MFC, App Studio, and the product's nifty
"wizards"—AppWizard and ClassWizard—in action. The book also provides a
good explanation of application framework theory, along with tips for exploiting
hidden features of the MFC library.

Enhance your
communications
capabilities today—
with

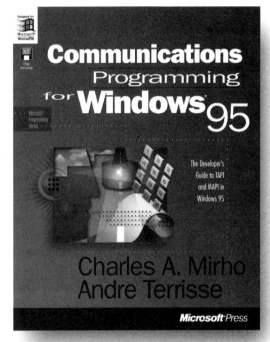

Communications and the computer have become inseparable. Programmers for Windows® face the challenge of building software that interfaces with telephone, fax, voice mail, video, and other messaging services—applications that provide the "on-ramp" to the information superhighway. COMMUNICATIONS PROGRAMMING FOR WINDOWS 95 explains from the ground up the two most important communications components in Windows: the Telephony API (TAPI) and the Messaging API (MAPI). The book also includes valuable advice for adding communications capabilities to existing software applications.

Got the message? The most effective way to learn communications programming for Windows 95 is with COMMUNICATIONS PROGRAMMING FOR WINDOWS 95.

U.S.A.	**$39.95**
U.K.	£37.49
Canada	$53.95
ISBN 1-55615-668-5	

Microsoft Press

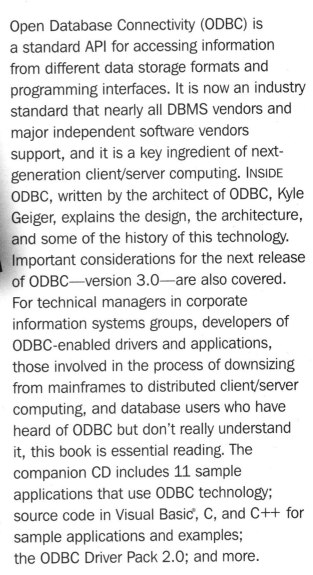

Register Today!

Return this
Inside MAPI
registration card for a Microsoft Press® catalog

U.S. and Canada addresses only. Fill in information below and mail postage-free. Please mail only the bottom half of this page.

| 1-57231-312-9A | *INSIDE MAPI* | *Owner Registration Card* |

NAME

INSTITUTION OR COMPANY NAME

ADDRESS

CITY STATE ZIP

Microsoft®Press
Quality Computer Books

**For a free catalog of
Microsoft Press® products, call
1-800-MSPRESS**

BUSINESS REPLY MAIL
FIRST-CLASS MAIL   PERMIT NO. 108   REDMOND, WA

POSTAGE WILL BE PAID BY ADDRESSEE

MICROSOFT PRESS REGISTRATION
INSIDE MAPI
PO BOX 3019
BOTHELL WA   98041-9946

NO POSTAGE
NECESSARY
IF MAILED
IN THE
UNITED STATES